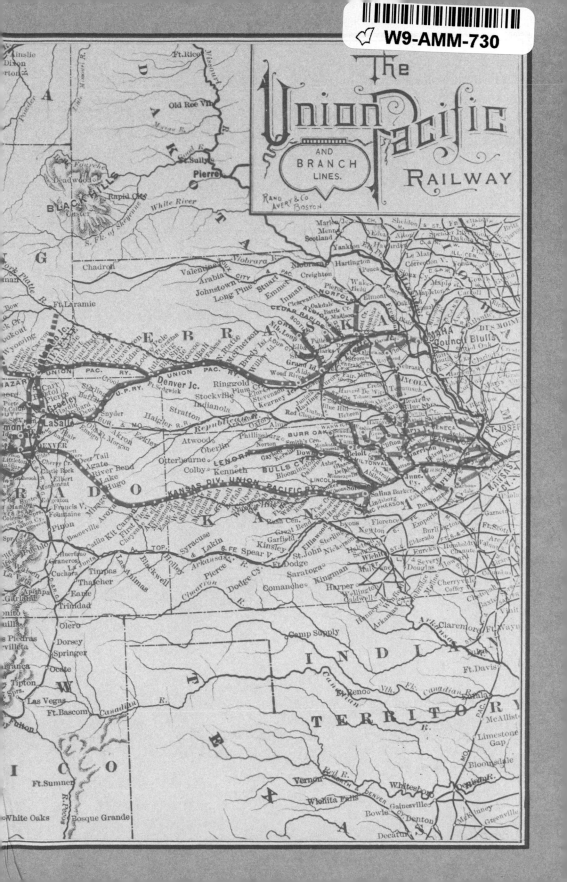

The Union Pacific AND BRANCH LINES. RAILWAY

Rand Avery & Co Boston

UNION PACIFIC
Birth of a Railroad: 1862–1893

UNION PACIFIC

Birth of a Railroad
1862–1893

by

MAURY KLEIN

Doubleday

NEW YORK   LONDON   TORONTO   SYDNEY   AUCKLAND

All photographs contained herein, except those so noted, are the property of the Union Pacific Railroad Museum.

Published by Doubleday, a division of
Bantam Doubleday Dell Publishing Group, Inc.,
666 Fifth Avenue, New York, New York 10103

Doubleday and the portrayal of an anchor with a dolphin
are trademarks of Doubleday, a division of
Bantam Doubleday Dell Publishing Group, Inc.

Library of Congress Cataloging-in-Publication Data

Klein, Maury, 1939–
Union Pacific.

Bibliography: v. 1, p. 663
Includes index.
Contents: v. 1. The birth of a railroad.
1. Union Pacific Railroad Company.   I. Title.
TF25.U5K53   1987   385'.065'78   86-16732
ISBN 0-385-17728-3 (v. 1)

2 4 6 8 9 7 5 3

BG

For STEPHANIE
My favorite first edition
and
ROBIN and STEPHEN
My favorite reprints
and
ANDREW, GREGORY, and CRISTINA
My favorite works in progress

ACKNOWLEDGMENTS

The research and writing of this book was funded by the Union Pacific Corporation, which not only provided generous support but agreed to allow the author free access to the company's files (except for certain records involved in pending litigation) and complete editorial freedom. The interpretations expressed in this volume, therefore, are mine and in no way represent those of the corporation.

The support of the Union Pacific Corporation and the Union Pacific System went far beyond its financial commitment. Without exception its officers and employees have cheerfully heeded my requests for material or information and gone the extra mile to expedite my work. Their cooperation helped transform a chore into a pleasure, and their keen interest and encouragement has given me a host of new associations for which I shall always be grateful. To a large extent they are responsible for the virtues of the book and I for whatever errors and weaknesses remain.

While it is impossible to name every individual who rendered assistance, a few merit special attention. In the corporate office in New York, Marvin H. Zim handled my every need with dispatch and sympathy. James P. Coughlin, the office manager, was invaluable for his knowledge of the older records and diligence in providing me access to them. I am also grateful to Richard W. Anthony, Irene J. Colgan, Nancy R. Connors, and Harvey Turner. At the Union Pacific System's offices in Omaha, my efforts were greatly smoothed by Joe McCartney. Thomas E. LaHood, Ken Longe, Eileen M. Wirth, and William R. Ulrich handled a variety of requests for information or services. In the law department Michael P. Flanagan, Mark B. Goodwin, and Peter W. Hohenhaus were especially helpful. Donald D. Snoddy, now curator of the Union Pacific Museum, has been indefatigable in his help both in Omaha and in his former position at the Nebraska State Museum and Archives in Lincoln, where the early Union Pacific papers are housed. In Portland, George J. Skorney and Randall B. Kester, the former general solicitor, kindly lent me assistance. At the Missouri Pacific Railroad headquarters in St. Louis, Tim

Hogan and Robert L. Sponsler answered my requests with their usual good cheer and competence.

Librarians and archivists extended to me their usual courtesy and professional expertise. I wish especially to thank Mary Chatfield, librarian at the Baker Library of the Harvard Graduate School of Business Administration, who not only expedited my research in several ways but also tracked down and procured for me access to the original diaries of Oliver Ames. Florence Lathrop and Mary Daniels of Baker's Manuscripts and Archives section expertly fielded a host of inquiries and requests. Robert A. McCown of the University of Iowa library did me innumerable favors in obtaining copies of key material, especially from the Leonard collection. Louise M. Kenneally, archivist of Stonehill College, granted me access to some important correspondence of Oliver Ames. At the Nebraska State Museum and Archives Andrea Paul, Patricia M. Churray, and Mary Pazderka were uniformly helpful, as were Phyllis E. McLaughlin of the Iowa State Department of Archives and History, John Aubrey of the Newberry Library, W. Thomas White of the James J. Hill Reference Library in St. Paul, Richard Crawford, William Creech, and Ed Schmel of the National Archives, and Margaret N. Haines of the Oregon Historical Society.

At home Mimi Keefe and the staff of the University of Rhode Island library did everything within their power to assist the project. I am especially grateful for the help of Marie Rudd, Vicki Burnett, Lucille W. Cameron, Roberta E. Doran, Martha Hills, Sylvia C. Krausse, and Judith MacDonald, all of whom rendered aid far beyond the line of duty.

Special thanks go to my research assistant, Martha A. Parker, for her dedication to a difficult job and willingness to put in more hours than anyone had a right to ask. Arthur D. Hyde kindly provided me with copies of letters of Samuel B. Reed. My editor at Doubleday, Harold W. Kuebler, lent his expertise and encouragement in guiding the manuscript over its final hurdles. Finally, I wish to thank two people whose support was essential if indirect. John C. Kenefick, president of the Union Pacific System, has been the mainspring of this project from its inception, and I hope the final product justifies his determination to see it done. My wife, Diana C. Klein, has once again sustained me through a long and difficult project with consideration that I can never hope to repay.

CONTENTS

INTRODUCTION

The importance of the railroad to nineteenth-century America is well known. It played a primary role in transforming the country from an agricultural to a complex industrial society. Transportation has always been a catalyst of change in every corner of life. Within a century the modern world has been revolutionized by its progress from horse to rail to highway to airplane. In this process the railroad was present at the creation. It swept away all rival forms of land transportation by routinizing the shipment of goods and people. On regular schedules trains hauled larger volumes of more kinds of items at greater speeds than any other method of transport. Unlike boats, trains could go virtually anywhere in any weather, and unlike wagons they could carry immense loads. By lowering the cost of inland transportation they opened the continent to settlement. A once empty hinterland filled with people and blossomed into a vast marketplace.

Railroads did more than provide reliable transportation. They became a major customer for other nurturing industries, notably iron and steel, coal, lumber, and heavy machinery. A significant part of American industry owed its early growth to a symbiotic relationship with the railroad. As the nation's first big business, railroad corporations pioneered in new methods of finance and new forms of organization. Their far-flung operations required elaborate administrative structures, professional managers, and more sophisticated accounting techniques. As the first employer of a large labor force they set the pattern for modern labor relations. The railroads were the first major industry to be unionized and the first to be regulated by government. As the first big businesses they became the model on which giant corporate enterprise was fashioned. In effect they introduced Americans to the whole Pandora's box of industrialization.

The impact of the railroad on American life can hardly be exaggerated. It rearranged the nation's economic geography, trained several generations of businessmen and financiers, and laid the foundation for many of the era's great fortunes. Everyone got a piece of the action. The railroad opened new land for settlers, new markets for merchants, new sources of profit for financiers, new resources for industrialists to exploit, new jobs for everyone from managers to itinerant laborers, and new enterprises for the ambitious. Cities and towns regarded the presence of the railroad as a barometer of their commercial destiny. The passion to convert wilderness into wealth led bankers, merchants, promoters, and civic groups into the belief that rails could transform the sleepiest hamlet into a thriving entrepôt.

All these things can be measured to some degree, but there is no way to measure the impact of the railroad on the American imagination. The locomotive was the dominant symbol of the age for Americans from every walk of life. Nothing else fired such lofty visions of their private and national destinies. Other mechanical wonders impressed or even inspired them, but none touched them more deeply or passionately. The steam engine revolutionized manufacturing, but its presence in the factory lacked the dramatic thrust of its appearance on bands of steel spanning a vast continent. To a people overwhelmed by the sheer spaciousness of their realm, the railroad opened vistas of possibility which even dreamers of an earlier age could not conceive. The steamboat had conquered the waters of America but could not penetrate its vast interior. The telegraph bridged enormous distances but could move only information.

Nothing rivaled the awe in which Americans held the locomotive. For rural folk the clang of its bell evoked images of distant places to which the train might someday carry them. It was not only the excitement of strange cities that stirred them but the urge for new prospects, better lives than could be found at home. To many an ambitious farmboy the locomotive whistle wailing across the endless prairie or plains was a call of destiny, promising freedom, adventure, and new possibilities for the future.

Within a remarkably short time the railroad became part of American folklore, its tales an important chapter in the saga of our national development. No tale occupies a more prominent place than that of the first transcontinental road and its climax, the driving of the golden spike. For that reason the Union Pacific occupies a unique niche in American history. As part of the first line to bridge the continent it became a central chapter in the national mythology. Four years after the golden spike the Union Pacific was caught up in a scandal that enshrined it within another and less savory chapter, that of Crédit Mobilier. Together these myths have dominated the road's image for a century.

The result has been to perpetuate confusion about the road's past. Although much has been written about the Union Pacific, there has never been a full history of the company. There are plenty of books on the building of the first transcontinental road, but none of them put the event in any perspective other than the saga of the national myth. Like so much popular writing on the tall tales of our past, these accounts are often riddled with errors handed down from one generation of writers to the next. No one has even attempted a history of Crédit Mobilier or tried to explain what it was all about. There are a number of studies by scholars dealing with the Union Pacific. Although many of them are informative and useful, all are confined to some specialized aspect of the company's past. No history of the company from the inside has been written except in a general or cursory fashion.

For that reason the story of the Union Pacific still lies buried beneath successive layers of myth and mystery. In this book I have tried to excavate it from the rubble of misperception and reveal its complexities in a new light. Like so many chapters of our history, the actual story is far more interesting than the myth. Few roads boast a more intriguing or contrasting cast of characters. During these years the company suffered greatly from internal bickering and lack of strong leadership. I have made these conflicts my central theme because their imprint on the road's destiny proved decisive in the end. The character of any company is drawn from the officers and men who dominate it, just as its performance reflects their abilities or weaknesses. That is why corporations sometimes change personalities for better or worse, and why their managers set the tone for how they are perceived by others.

Maury Klein
Narragansett, R.I.

RAILROAD REFERENCE KEY

A & N	Atchison & Nebraska
Alton	Chicago & Alton
Atchison	Atchison, Topeka & Santa Fe
B & M	Burlington & Missouri River in Nebraska
Burlington	Chicago, Burlington & Quincy
Burlington & Northern	Chicago, Burlington & Northern
Cedar Rapids	Cedar Rapids & Missouri
Central	Colorado Central
Central Branch	Central Branch Union Pacific
Chillicothe	St. Louis, Council Bluffs & Omaha
Council Bluffs	Kansas City, St. Joseph & Council Bluffs
Frisco	St. Louis & San Francisco
Grand Island	St. Joseph & Grand Island
Hannibal	Hannibal & St. Joseph
Katy	Missouri, Kansas & Texas
Lake Shore	Lake Shore & Michigan Southern
M & M	Mississippi & Missouri
Manitoba	St. Paul, Minneapolis & Manitoba
Navigation	Oregon Railway & Navigation Company
Northwestern	Chicago & Northwestern
O & C	Oregon & California
Panhandle	Denver, Texas & Fort Worth
Rio Grande	Denver & Rio Grande
Rio Grande Western	Denver & Rio Grande Western
Rock Island	Chicago, Rock Island & Pacific
Short Line	Oregon Short Line
Sioux City	Sioux City & Pacific
South Park	Denver, South Park & Pacific
St. Joseph	St. Joseph & Denver City (Western)
St. Paul	Chicago, Milwaukee & St. Paul
Transcontinental	Oregon & Transcontinental
W & I	Washington & Idaho
Wabash	Toledo, Wabash & Western
Wabash	Wabash, St. Louis & Pacific
Wyandotte	Kansas City, Wyandotte & Northwestern

UNION PACIFIC
Birth of a Railroad: 1862–1893

PROLOGUE

The Monument
1965

The monument sits like an ancient ruin atop a desolate corner of wilderness in Wyoming, its granite blocks weathered and smoothed by a century of fierce storms and raging winds. On every side of the sixty-five-foot pyramid the view is spectacular. To the south the broad tableland of Sherman Pass rolls gradually toward the distant Front Range of the Colorado Rockies, their gleaming crests topped by Long's Peak. The Medicine Bow Range with its thick stands of forest form a barrier to the west and the Black Hills, tumbled, lumpish mounds of pinkish rock and gray sagebrush, to the north. Between them, barely visible, lies the Laramie Basin through which the railroad snakes its way around the mountains. There is no obstacle to the southeast, where the open plains stretch unbroken toward the South Platte River a hundred miles away.

Nothing stirs the landscape except the shadows of clouds hurried along by the prod of a chilly west wind. On a still day the silence is as awesome as the scenery. The solitude is overwhelming, inescapable, the language of ghosts belonging to an age when the place was not so quiet or remote. When the directors of the Union Pacific Railroad decided in 1875 to honor two of its founders, Oakes and Oliver Ames, with a monument, they chose to locate it at the highest elevation on their main line, in a town called Sherman. In those days a few hundred people lived in Sherman, with its two hotels, two saloons, general store, post office, and schoolhouse. The railroad had a station house, water tank, and a pair of section houses. At the summit all trains were inspected before descending the severe grades in both directions.

The monument was impressive. No less an architect than H. H. Richardson designed it, and Augustus Saint-Gaudens contributed square granite plaques of each brother in half-relief. Completed in 1882, it seemed destined to honor the memory of Oakes and Oliver for as long as trains crossed the Rockies. But twenty years later the line was relocated southward and a new station house erected three and a half miles southeast of the monument. The old Sherman station was abandoned, and the town vanished with it. For that matter the passengers who once glimpsed the monument from passing trains have gone elsewhere as well. Only the monument remains, a rugged, brooding presence set against the grandeur of distant mountains.

Time has smoothed its controversies no less than its surfaces, but not yet enough to remove the blemishes. It is only fitting that a tribute to Oakes and Oliver stand neglected and unnoticed, for that is also the place consigned them by history. They risked their fortunes and their reputations on the grandest enterprise yet undertaken by Americans. In return they received not praise but censure as participants in the major scandal of an age busy with scandals. Thanks to the uproar over Crédit Mobilier, the Ames brothers have enjoyed about the same image in the public mind as the notorious James brothers. The comparison is hardly fair, but the facts of history push slowly and often helplessly against the weight of popular myth.

In reality the Ames brothers were neither heroes nor villains but merely figures in a complex drama filled with intrigue, fascinating characters, and unexpected twists of plot. The history of the Union Pacific has been burdened with more than its share of myth and misunderstanding. Its story has been told many times, but never fully and never from the vantage point of its inner workings. From that perspective the epic of the first transcontinental railroad takes on quite another flavor, one rooted not in folklore but in the clash of visions, interests, and ambitions among the men who shaped its destiny. Their struggles were ceaseless and often petty or sordid, yet their achievement was immense in its significance. They built a railroad that endured and opened a vast part of the continent to settlement and development. They spearheaded the process by which an agricultural society was transformed into an industrial one within the lifetime of their own generation. They were harbingers of that most prized of commodities to Americans, progress.

Of all their hopes and aspirations, their visions and venalities, their strivings and struggles, little remains except the vague association with a scandal bearing an exotic name. History has abandoned them much as the railroad abandoned the monument, leaving their memory and their achievement in the care of descendants and antiquarians.

In 1965 Charles E. Ames, who would later publish a book vindicating his forebears, made a pilgrimage to the Ames monument. Driving west of Cheyenne on the Lincoln Highway, he turned onto an unmarked, unpaved road that led to the pyramid. There he found a recent but already broken state marker dangling between two posts. The noses on both of St. Gaudens's plaques were missing, the victims of weather or possibly the whim of a passing sharpshooter. This alteration at least fit the Ames brothers, whose noses were often out of joint in their Union Pacific days. In a sheltered crevice between the blocks Ames found a fat badger comfortably installed, an appreciative if not informed audience.

The experience was a forlorn and depressing one for Ames, but his gloom did not last. He understood that the true monument for the Ames brothers and their colleagues was not a forgotten pyramid standing vigil on a remote elevation in Wyoming. It was rather the enduring presence of the railroad they built and of the West itself, which they did so much to develop.

PART ONE

The Challenge
1862–69

1

THE VISION

The vision was not new. It was as old as the railroad itself in America, where people had always trafficked heavily in dreams. In 1832, only four years after ground was broken for the nation's first railroad, a Michigan editor called boldly for the building of a line from New York to Oregon on a route between the 41st and 42nd parallels from the Mississippi to the Rocky Mountains and to the coast along the valley "of that stream, called the southern branch of Lewis' river." Half a century later the line projected by this unknown dreamer would be occupied by the Union Pacific Railroad and its Oregon Short Line.

Years later a fierce dispute would arise among those claiming to have first suggested the notion of a Pacific railroad, but none could establish earlier credentials. For another decade the idea was tossed about in speeches and articles, usually as prophecy but sometimes with estimates of the cost or proposals for government aid. The Michigan editor presumed that the federal government would undertake the project or at least grant a private company three million acres of land to finance the work. Details on how so enormous an enterprise would be organized or carried out were not forthcoming, but then detail is never the strong suit of visionaries.

The public dismissed these schemes as nothing more than the reveries of overheated imaginations. Who could take seriously a plan to build 3,000 miles of railroad at a time (1832) when the country possessed exactly 229 miles of track? The government's *total* expenditures that year were about $17.3 million, far less than it would cost to construct such a road. Existing technology was nowhere near equal to the challenge of a transcontinental line. Most of the land to be crossed did not even belong to the United States but to Mexico and Great Britain.

Even if the land had been ours, few saw any use for it. The region between the Mississippi River and the Pacific coast was considered not only barren but hostile to white settlement. Nothing lived there except Indians, some trappers, immense herds of buffalo, and assorted creatures of the desert and mountains. The first Americans to explore the region—Meriwether Lewis and George Rogers Clark, Zebulon Pike, Major Stephen H. Long—all came to the conclusion that the flatlands were a vast desert lacking timber and water. By 1832 their reports and the drawings of cartographers had firmly imprinted the notion of the Great American Desert on the national consciousness. For decades the conviction lingered that the plains were unfit for white men to inhabit. Senator George Duffie of South Carolina expressed the prevailing sentiment in 1843 when he called the entire region "a desert . . . which no American citizen should be compelled to inhabit unless as a punishment for crime." The senator saw no potential for agriculture in the land acquired by Jefferson. "I would not for that purpose give a pinch of snuff for the whole territory," he thundered. "I wish to God we did not own it."

To Americans in the age of Jackson the dimensions and obstacles of the project were as awesome as those of landing on the moon would be to a later generation. Yet the vision persisted, nursed along by lonely voices crying in the wilderness of public indifference. In 1840 it acquired a crucial convert in Asa Whitney, a merchant who made it his personal crusade for a dozen years. A ride on an English railroad in 1830 had impressed Whitney with the railway's future in shortening the avenues of commerce. Later experience in China fired his imagination with the possibilities of Far Eastern commerce if some way could be found to deliver goods to the Pacific coast. For Whitney the project became not merely a business enterprise but a great national work. "My desire and object," he averred, "have been . . . to give my country this great thoroughfare for all nations without the cost of one dollar. . . . If they will but allow me to be their instrument to accomplish this great work, it is enough; I ask no more."

After his return from China in 1844, Whitney presented Congress with his first petition for a Pacific railroad. For the rest of the decade he lobbied incessantly, following each failed petition with another, buttonholing public men in person or bombarding them with letters, flooding newspapers and journals with articles, touring the country to hold meetings in major cities, pleading his case with anyone in Washington who showed an interest in his project. His plan in simple terms was to build a road from Lake Michigan to Oregon and to finance it by the sale of public land to settlers. He estimated the cost at about $65 million and thought the road should charge only enough to cover expenses of maintenance and management. Whitney would own and manage the completed road until it could earn expenses, at which point he would turn it over to the federal government. His profit would come from any lands still unsold after all construction expenses had been paid.

Despite growing interest in his proposal, Whitney never got the land grant he sought from Congress. Having squandered his personal fortune in the attempt, he was reduced in later years to keeping a dairy and selling milk in Washington for a livelihood. Yet he succeeded in that way visionaries have of influencing events without sharing in the outcome of their efforts. He kept the issue alive for a decade in forums that changed its image from a crackpot scheme to a serious public question. His enthusiasm as well as his persistence sparked a response in enough men of standing to give the matter a legitimacy it had never before possessed. By 1850 the Pacific railroad seemed an idea whose time was about to come, even though the first rails into Chicago from the East would not be laid for another two years.

Whitney's crusade took place during an era of tumultuous events that helped reshape attitudes toward a Pacific railway. Expansionist fever sent a tidal wave of settlers rolling westward to the Mississippi and beyond. An expedition to the Oregon country in 1842 by John C. Frémont had stirred the popular imagination with its reports of fertile land and abundant forests and water. A growing stream of pioneers undertook the long trek across the plains and through the mountains to reach this new paradise. Most of them followed a route familiar only to explorers and fur traders until the flood of emigrants popularized it as the Oregon Trail. Still gripped by the myth of the Great American Desert, they endured the hardships of the journey to find conditions resembling those they had left behind.

What those bound for Oregon sought to avoid, the Mormons embraced willingly. Hounded out of the Midwest by religious persecution, they migrated not to the fertile coast but to the wasteland of the Salt Lake Valley. In that barren region, surrounded by mountains, they founded the state of Deseret in 1847 and hoped to dwell forever without interference from the outside world. It was a reasonable hope, yet their isolation lasted scarcely a decade. In 1846 the United States acquired by treaty all of Oregon below the 49th parallel, and plunged into war with Mexico. Two years later it emerged victorious with a vast stretch of territory including present-day California, Arizona, Nevada, and Utah, and parts of Colorado, Wyoming, and New Mexico as the spoils of victory. The discovery of gold in California triggered a mad rush of fortune hunters into that region.

Suddenly, unexpectedly, the nation found itself possessed of a continent without a means of transportation or communication to connect its opposite ends. Two thousand miles of hostile wasteland and mountains separated the frontier town of Chicago from the burgeoning population of the Pacific coast. The trip by sea from New York required thirty-five days to cover 5,250 miles if one sailed to Panama and crossed the malaria-infested isthmus to catch another ship. An alternative route via Cape Horn was 13,300 miles and took four times as long. The overland stage route from St. Louis to San Francisco cut the mileage to 2,800 and the time to thirty days for travelers who could endure the discomfort and the danger.

By 1850 the westward movement had wrought a dramatic change in attitude toward the vision of a Pacific railway. What had once been dismissed as a pipedream now seemed a national necessity. The obstacles to constructing a road were as formidable as ever, but for the first time practical men began to consider the project seriously. Whitney's dogged efforts had helped inject the question into the political mainstream. Although Congress rejected his proposal, even skeptical members now viewed the matter as a major issue. During one session of the Thirty-second Congress the Senate gave the Pacific railway more time and attention than any other subject. Several attempts were made to push a bill through Congress but without success. Finally, in March 1853, both houses agreed to appropriate $150,000 for a survey to find "the most practical and economic route" from the Mississippi to the Pacific Ocean."

The appropriation was a compromise, the debate preceding it a harbinger of the struggle to come. Once thrust into the political arena, the Pacific railway ran afoul of certain harsh realities. State rights hardliners objected on principle to federal aid for internal improvement or other projects; two earlier experiences, the Bank of the United States and the Cumberland Road, still clanked in their memories like the Ghost of Christmas Past. Difficult as this opposition was, it paled before the growing bitterness of sectional politics. It was one thing to agree on the need for a Pacific road, quite another to decide *where* the road should be built. If, as everyone assumed, only one transcontinental line would be built, northerners and southerners alike wanted it for their section. Unable to resolve the question of location, yet aware of the public clamor for some action on the matter, Congress temporized with the survey appropriation.

For nearly a decade these two obstacles frustrated all efforts to pass a Pacific railway bill. One debate raged over whether the road should be a private, government, or mixed enterprise, another over the choice of route. Predictably, the two issues got entangled with each other as the dispute dragged on. Advocates of a government road pressed three arguments: they feared that in private hands the road would become a dangerous monopoly, that it would become the plaything of speculators, and that the impact of railroads on the regions they traversed gave them a public character unique among business enterprises. These were not only powerful but far-sighted arguments; all three questions would haunt American politics long after the Pacific road was built. Nevertheless, as one bill after another went down to defeat, Congressional opinion gradually tilted in the opposite direction. By 1859 there emerged a growing consensus that the proper role of government was to offer financial assistance to private interests willing to undertake the project.

But even those who agreed that government aid was essential split violently over the choice of routes. Here was yet another instance of a national need caught in the coils of sectional conflict. Two speeches by Senator Alfred Iverson of Georgia illustrated the dilemma shared by many others. In one he vigorously defended government aid on the ground that without it "no Pacific railroad can or will be built for half a century." Later he repeated this belief but declared himself unwilling to vote "so much land and so much money" for a road built outside the South which would bring the North alone "the countless millions of commercial benefits." Senator Stephen A. Douglas, who had already fanned the flames of sectional controversy by introducing the Kansas-Nebraska Act, tried to defuse the location issue with a proposal to construct three Pacific roads. His bill passed the Senate but died aborning in the House.

The survey ordered by Congress did nothing to resolve the dispute. Secretary of War Jefferson Davis dispatched five corps of engineers, surveyors, and scientists to explore each of the routes considered feasible: the Northern route (47th–48th parallels), the Overland route (41st–42nd parallels), the Buffalo Trail (38th–39th parallels), the 35th parallel, and the Southern route (32nd parallel). The exploring parties did a magnificent job. Their reports filled eleven huge volumes with text, maps, engravings, profiles, and tables describing not only the topography of what was still *terra incognita* to Americans but also its geology, flora, fauna, and anthropology. Valuable as this mass of information was, it served only to confirm the general belief that several practical routes existed for a Pacific road. Davis recommended the southern route as the shortest and easiest to build, but his views were drowned in a sea of sectional acrimony.

By 1859 the Pacific railway had advanced from the visionary to the practical stage. The country possessed nearly 29,000 miles of track, and the technology of railroading had improved considerably. The need for what boosters liked to call "the great national highway" had never been more urgent. Settlers continued to stream westward, and a mining boom had begun to lure prospectors to Colorado. The brief threat of war with the Mormons in 1858 put a military expedition on the trail to Utah. Although a clash was avoided, the episode demonstrated again the vulnerability of supply lines across the plains. And always the China trade beckoned invitingly to commercial men convinced that fortunes could be made if efficient transportation to the coast could be had.

During the 1850s an overland freight business sprang into existence to supply the military posts, mining camps, Mormon trade, and sparse but growing settlements in the mountains and along the Trail. Stage lines carried passengers and mail between the Missouri River and Salt Lake City. In 1860 the service was extended to California and the exciting but short-lived experiment of the Pony Express was tried. For two decades overland freighting flourished on the plains, but its shortcomings underscored the need for a railroad. Long trains of mule or oxen-drawn wagons simply could not match the iron horse in hauling large quantities of goods over a long distance at a reasonable speed for a decent price. From the river towns wagon trains took more than a month to reach Denver and nearly twice as long to cross the mountains into Utah. Winter weather shut down the Utah trade entirely and reduced the Colorado business to a trickle of wagons willing to risk the cold and blizzards of the plains.

The Mormon conflict and worsening tensions with the Indians emphasized the military necessity for reliable supply lines. The public demanded faster mail and passenger service, merchants craved faster, cheaper shipment of goods, and businessmen drooled at the commercial possibilities of a rail connection to the Rockies and the Pacific coast. Statesmen deemed it vital to the national interest that the isolated coastal states be linked to the rest of the country. Congress was alive to the importance of the project but could find no way to remove it from the cockpits of sectional conflict and local self-interests. The wrangle over local interests grew so intense as to provoke a delegate from New Mexico into complaining that no one would vote for a Pacific railroad bill "unless it starts in the corner of every man's farm and runs through all his neighbors' plantations."

President James Buchanan had consistently urged Congress to act since taking office. In his annual message of 1859 he tactfully avoided the dispute over choice of routes and concentrated instead on that other sticky issue, the method of construction. Buchanan opposed letting the government build and control the road, arguing that it would "increase the patronage of the executive to a dangerous extent, and would foster a system of jobbing and corruption which no vigilance on the part of federal officials could prevent." He recommended that the work be done by private companies or agencies.

That notion still produced arched eyebrows. In January 1859 the New York *Evening Post* argued confidently that the Pacific road was not a commercial venture but "a political scheme altogether—a work for the government to undertake" simply because "the road, as a carrier of passengers or freight, would be worthless." Others harbored fears in quite another direction. In April 1860 the newly created House Committee on the Pacific Railway, headed by Samuel R. Curtis of Iowa, reported out a new bill providing for construction by a "company" composed of forty-five persons named in the bill. The Curtis bill marked a decisive shift in emphasis from previous efforts. It offered even more government aid than earlier bills but took the government out of the construction business. In effect the bill invited private interests to build the road using a government loan of $60 million in the form of bonds and a land grant.

The report came from a divided committee and drew fire at once. Apart from the predictable quarrel over choice of route, opponents denounced the idea of leaving construction to the "lynx eye of capital." Representative John H. Reagan of Texas, who a quarter century later would ride the Interstate Commerce bill to passage, implied that lobbyists and promoters were behind the Curtis bill. Such men, he charged, would never touch the enterprise if they were "limited to just and honest profits on the capital invested." No evidence of any influence was produced, but Reagan's suspicions were correct in at least one sense. The Curtis bill reflected an important transition that soon became obvious to anyone with eyes and ears in Washington: The visionaries had given way to the promoters, who, like predators sniffing prey from afar, had picked up the first faint scent of profits.

They did not find it at once. The bill did not pass the House until the following December. An amended version passed the Senate in January 1861, but by that time Congress was preoccupied with the secession crisis. At first the outbreak of war seemed to doom the project by diverting the Union's attention and resources to the military effort. In fact it had the opposite effect. Secession removed from Congress the advocates of a southern route and many who opposed giving federal aid to the project. It also strengthened the argument of military necessity. The Pacific coast states were loyal but isolated, and more Indian trouble loomed on the plains at a time when troops were needed elsewhere. A railroad would help bind California to the Union and enable the army to supply the frontier outposts with greater efficiency.

Friends of the project sensed that their hour had come and reintroduced the Curtis bill at the special session called by President Lincoln in July 1861. Other bills followed, indicating that important differences remained. The southern route had been abandoned, but three others still competed: the northern Pacific route, one from the border of Iowa, and a third from the border of Missouri. Nor had the questions of how to finance and construct the road been resolved. After years of debate the opposing camps shared only the common ground of suspicion. One side pleaded for a strong role by the government because it feared the depredations of speculators and private contractors; the other wanted the work done by private interests to avoid the corruption of public men and agencies. Apparently the belief prevailed that constructing the transcontinental road would taint someone's hands, and public policy therefore amounted to choosing the lesser of two evils.

In this sense the project bore the scarlet letter of suspicion from the beginning. Since the way of public policy is not to make choices but to effect compromises, the stage was set to obtain the worst of both worlds. Moreover, Congress was on unfamiliar ground. The federal government had not chartered a corporation since the ill-starred Second Bank of the United States in 1816. Beset by the distractions of war and delayed by inept handling in both houses, the bill made slow progress through the thicket of conflicting interests. After much wrangling the Senate finally passed the bill on June 20 and the House on June 24, 1862. A week later, while the desperate Seven Days' Battle still raged on the outskirts of Richmond, Lincoln signed into law "An Act to aid in the Construction of a Railroad and Telegraph Line from the Missouri River to the Pacific Ocean, and to secure to the Government the Use of the same for Postal, Military and Other Purposes."

The provisions of the act were even more cumbersome than its title. The squabble over choice of route was resolved by offering concessions to all sides. The road would be not one line but a four-pronged system between the Missouri River and the California border. A new corporation, to be known as the Union Pacific Railroad Company, was chartered to build from California to the 100th meridian (near Fort Kearney, Nebraska). From this "initial point" four branches would be constructed to cities on the Missouri River. The Union Pacific was authorized to build the "Iowa Branch" to Omaha as part of its line. Other companies with state charters were authorized to complete roads between the initial point and Kansas City, Atchison, and Sioux City.

The original house bill had designated the 102nd meridian as the initial point, but Senator James Harlan of Iowa succeeded in forcing a change. His shrewd maneuver insured that the trunk line would connect with Chicago, leaving St. Louis only the branch via Kansas City. The road between the California border and San Francisco was to be constructed by a company already chartered in that state, the Central Pacific, on the same terms and conditions granted the Union Pacific. Whichever of the two roads first reached the California border could continue building until it joined the other; no meeting point was stipulated. In fact the Central Pacific was authorized to construct as much of the main line and branches as needed to complete the system.

The new corporation was to be organized within three months by a board of 163 commissioners named in the act. They were to open subscription books in several cities offering a total of ten thousand shares at one thousand dollars each. The act required investors to pay par for the shares and 10 percent at time of subscription. When two thousand shares had been subscribed, the commissioners were to call a meeting to elect officers and at least thirteen directors. The President would then appoint two more directors who were not stockholders to represent the government. Once the new board organized, the commissioners were to retire from the organization.

Financial help was tendered in two forms. The Union Pacific received its right-of-way through the public domain and an outright grant of half the land on a strip ten miles wide on both sides of the track for each mile of road built. This amounted to ten square miles or 6,400 acres per mile of track. The government gave the Union Pacific the odd-numbered sections and kept the even-numbered sections for itself. Patents on the land would be issued to the company only after each forty miles of road was certified by three government commissioners as being completed and equipped as a "first class railroad." The government retained all mineral rights but granted any timber on the land to the company.

Some form of land grant had been part of the Pacific railway project since Whitney's first memorial, but the Act of 1862 added a new wrinkle in the form of bond subsidies. For each forty-mile section of track certified by the government inspectors the company would receive United States bonds amounting to $16,000 per mile on the plains, $32,000 per mile on the plateau between the Rockies and the Sierras, and $48,000 per mile in the mountain regions. The amounts were scaled to differences in the anticipated cost of construction caused by the rugged terrain west of the plains. These bonds were to be issued at 6 percent for thirty years and comprised a first mortgage on the road. They were *not* an outright subsidy but a loan which the government expected to be repaid in full at maturity. Any bonds issued by the company would therefore stand as a second mortgage. The total issue of government bonds for all eligible roads was limited to $50,000,000.

In return for this aid the companies were obliged to keep their roads in good repair and to transport mails, troops, supplies, or perform other services required by the government. All earnings from government business were to be applied to the payment of the government bonds and accumulated interest. In addition, the companies were required to pay on this same account 5 percent of their net earnings. The Union Pacific was to complete its road by July 1, 1874, or forfeit the franchise. To guarantee performance, the government withheld from 15 to 25 percent of the bonds due until the company had complied with all provisions of the act. A stipulation that all rails and other iron used had to be of American manufacture did much to increase the ultimate cost of construction. Congress could reduce rates on the road under certain conditions and reserved its right to amend the act in any way it deemed fit. Grades and curves were not to exceed the maximum on the Baltimore & Ohio Railroad, and the completed road was to be operated as "one connected continuous line."

At first glance the Act of 1862 in all its twenty sections seems impressively full and detailed. In fact it proved a cornucopia of ambiguities. The language of nearly every section was vague and loosely drawn, in some cases deliberately so, to sidestep controversial points. Three generations of lawyers and lobbyists owe their prosperity to its shortcomings. It is unnecessary to itemize the act's weaknesses here, for they will surface like leitmotifs throughout this narrative. The framers of the act and its subsequent amendments did something far more than charter the first transcontinental railroad; they unwittingly shaped (some would say warped) the next thirty-five years of its history.

But all this lay in the future. By 1862 the vision of a transcontinental road had been transformed into legislation, which is not to be confused with reality. The idea had at last been accepted and enacted into law offering federal aid to those who would take up the challenge. The dispute over whether the project should be built by the government or private interests had resulted in the compromise of a mixed enterprise. Private parties would do the work with Uncle Sam peering over their shoulders to make sure it was done properly. Neither side had any experience with such an arrangement; it was an experiment born in the hothouse of expediency. To some extent that was inevitable, if only because the dimensions of the project were unprecedented.

In 1862 the country possessed 32,120 miles of railway, but its longest road, the Illinois Central, had only about 700 miles of track. No line had been constructed through terrain as awesome as the western mountains and desert.

More important, the experiment was sown in an age where precedent was fast losing its relevance as a guidepost. The war knocked the usual order of things out of joint. Even before its impact was felt, the onrushing forces of industrialization were fast changing the ground rules of economic and political relationships. Ultimately the war would accelerate these forces, leaving in its wake an environment primed for rapid business and industrial expansion. Wartime opportunities offered to a generation of ambitious young men the chance to earn a fortune and invaluable business experience while others marched off to battle. The war swept away the bitter controversies of antebellum politics and entrenched the Republican Party firmly in power for half a century. In the aftermath of victory the business of America was business on a scale never before witnessed.

Inevitably these forces left their imprint on the origins of the Union Pacific. The wonder was not that promoters took hold of the project but that they were so slow to step forward. Congress and the public assumed that the Act of 1862 would lure the capitalists and contractors needed to build the road. They were wrong. The act offered too little too late to entice investment. Wartime offered businessmen too many other opportunities to make large profits at low risk. No one cared to hazard large sums on a dubious enterprise for uncertain returns. The cost of materials was soaring and the supply of labor dwindling. The sharpest of speculators could not yet find a way to turn a dollar from the business, and honest men conceded that the timing could not have been worse for launching so ambitious a construction project.

On September 2 the commissioners dutifully opened the subscription books and published notices in the papers of twenty-four cities, but only twenty shares of Union Pacific stock were sold. Earnest discussion among the commissioners and "prominent railroad men" at their first meeting led to the conclusion that the terms offered by the act were insufficient. Patriots could not afford the project, and promoters saw nothing in it unless Congress offered some "further inducements." The lynx eye of capital scrutinized the prey and dismissed it as not worth the chase. But the scent had been caught and might in time be worth following.

2

THE PROMOTERS

The birth of the Union Pacific as a mixed enterprise insured that for decades to come it would remain a creature of politics. All railroads had to deal in politics at the state and local level, but only the Union Pacific (and, to a lesser extent, the Central Pacific) was at the mercy of Congress. This dependence subjected the road to all the whims and passions, the vagaries and shifts in mood of public opinion, the pressures and venality, that gave national politics so distinctive a flavor. It forced the company into the lobbying business, not simply to get what it wanted but to protect itself from those who used Congress to attack the road for their own purposes.

To make matters worse, the Union Pacific was still an idea struggling to be born in the midst of the most terrible war ever fought on the continent. Congress was needed as midwife, but Congress was distracted by the tug and haul of a thousand demands. Washington was a madhouse of confusion and clashing ambitions. The city itself resembled a work in progress, a set of unfulfilled pretensions. Nothing had changed since 1800, sneered young Henry Adams; it was "the same rude colony . . . in the same forest, with the same unfinished Greek temples for workrooms, and sloughs for roads." The mood within the capital was volatile, swinging wildly with each shift in the war effort. The scramble for decent rooms was as savage as the scramble for jobs, for favors or contracts or bills, for largess in all its infinite forms.

In this frenzied atmosphere congressional friends of the Pacific railroad made slow progress. The indifferent response to the call for subscribers led them to seek amendments sweetening the government's offer. A modest attempt passed the Senate in February 1863 but died in the House. In March

Congress managed with difficulty to agree on a bill stipulating that the Pacific road and its branches be of standard gauge, but little enthusiasm could be mustered for what Horace Greeley called the "grandest and noblest enterprise of our age." The war was going badly for the North. Costs and casualties were mounting, and there was growing disillusionment with the waste and corruption of army contractors, jobbers, speculators, and other parasites who fed on the government. It was only natural to suspect that the Pacific road would fall into the same unclean hands as other government work. The election results of 1862 left the Republicans shaken and Congress timid.

The day of mere visionaries had passed. To breathe life into the project, promoters were needed, tough, practical, persistent men capable of lobbying for what they required, organizing a vast enterprise, and pushing it in the face of every obstacle. They would hardly be disinterested patriots, though certainly they would trumpet their effort as a service to the country. A few would be men simply looking for profit in places where others failed to see it. The majority, however, would come to the Pacific railroad as an extension of other interests that would benefit from its construction.

One such group had been charting the project for nearly a decade, searching for ways to utilize it on behalf of their construction activities east of the Missouri River. Henry Farnam, a noted engineer, had looked westward even while struggling to complete the Chicago & Rock Island. In May 1853, nine months before the Rock Island reached the Mississippi River, Farnam organized the Mississippi & Missouri Railroad (M & M) to build across Iowa. His partner wanted no part of the Iowa venture, but another contractor was eager to take his place. In this modest way Thomas C. Durant first thrust himself onto the stage of western railway construction.

A native of Massachusetts, Durant graduated from Albany Medical College in 1840 but never practiced medicine. His degree served only to bestow on him the nickname of "the Doctor." Instead, he joined the New York export house of his uncle. While expanding the firm's business he also developed a taste for speculating in stocks. It is not known when railroads seized Durant's imagination, but in 1851 he joined Farnam in constructing the Michigan Southern Railroad and then part of the Rock Island. This work elevated him to a full partner in the Iowa project. Tall, lean, slightly stooped, with sharp features and penetrating eyes, his mouth covered by a drooping mustache and straggly goatee, Durant looked the part of the riverboat gambler some thought he was. In 1852 he was only thirty-two years old, bristling with nervous energy and filled with grandiose and often contradictory ambitions. A close associate noted perceptively that "his mainspring seems to be not love of money for itself, or of notoriety in any sense, but a love for large operations—a restless desire to be swinging great enterprises and doing everything on a magnificent scale."

Besides Farnam and Durant, the M & M directors included William B. Ogden, the dynamic mayor of Chicago, and Ebenezer Cook, mayor of Davenport. As president the board chose John A. Dix, a cultivated New Yorker with distinguished credentials as a soldier and politician. Dix had just withdrawn from public life and was glad to have what amounted to a sinecure. In June 1855 the M & M laid the first rail put down in the state of Iowa. The track reached Iowa City by the year's end but then languished for want of funds. The Panic of 1857 threw the road into receivership amid rumors that Durant had pledged the paper of Farnam & Durant to some of his own speculative ventures. Although details of this episode remain obscure, it resulted ultimately in a bitter quarrel that separated the partners. Farnam was the first associate to find the Doctor too fast for his blood; he would by no means be the last.

Prior to its financial woes, the M & M had taken steps to survey not only the route across Iowa but also the region west of the Missouri. Farnam appointed as chief engineer Peter A. Dey, who at twenty-seven had already made his mark on the Rock Island, and sent him to find a line across Iowa. Dey took with him as assistant a young engineer who had impressed him during his short time with the Rock Island, Grenville M. Dodge. In May 1853 they started work and found themselves in a race west with survey crews from another road eager to reach the Missouri River, the Chicago & Northwestern. By September both parties had finished running lines to Iowa City and headed into the wilderness. Dey and Dodge won the race by a week, tramping the entire length of the state via Fort Des Moines to reach the village of Council Bluffs on November 22. The inhabitants welcomed both parties as harbingers of the railroad that would lift them out of isolation. Their jubilation was premature; the rails would not appear for another fourteen years.

Dodge was not yet finished. A few days later Dey sent him across the river at the head of a party to survey the ground west of Omaha. Dodge got as far as the Platte Valley before turning back, enough to give him a feel for where a line west from the Missouri should run. Only twenty-two years old, he could not know that he had just glimpsed a preview of his life's work. No other man would be more important to or more closely identified with the history of the Union Pacific than Grenville M. Dodge. He would influence its destiny from the first survey to its reorganization thirty years later. This first cursory survey in the waning autumn of 1853 set in motion the forces that would tie Dodge inextricably to the region and to the vision of a transcontinental railroad.

After marrying in May 1854, Dodge took his bride to homestead on the Elkhorn River, twenty-five miles west of Omaha. The M & M had shut down work for lack of funds and a dispute over whether Council Bluffs or Florence should be the western terminus. Dodge was among the first to grasp that the terminus of any road building across Iowa hinged on the decision of where to locate the Pacific road. The project soon grew into an obsession with him. It fascinated him as an engineer, beckoned to him as the rainbow leading to where his fortune would be found. He read everything he could find on the subject, absorbed the survey reports with the zeal of a convert studying scripture, collected information from the immigrants moving along the overland trail. When Indian trouble drove him from his land in August 1855, he settled in Council Bluffs, where he would remain for the rest of his life. He would dwell beside the river he loved and in the town which, he was already convinced, should be the terminus of the Iowa roads and the starting point for the Pacific road.

Dodge backed this conviction with words and deeds. When work on the M & M resumed in 1856, its directors remained divided over the choice of terminus. Cook and the Davenport interests owned a bank in Florence; Farnam's group had invested heavily in land along the Council Bluffs route surveyed by Dey and Dodge. After months of indecision Dodge settled the matter by filing on his own initiative a map committing the road to the Council Bluffs route. Cook was furious and blistered Dodge's ear, but the damage was done.

The episode revealed an important aspect of Dodge's character. He believed strongly that the Council Bluffs route was far superior and acted on that belief even if it meant resorting to highhanded tactics. It was a matter of principle that happened to coincide with his self-interest. Dodge too had invested heavily in land along the route and faced ruin if it were abandoned. All his life he would demonstrate this gift for weaving principle and self-interest inextricably together in policies for which he could argue with frankness and sincerity. Few men accused Dodge of being anything but earnest. He may have been guilty of self-deception but not of deceit.

The M & M barely started work when the Panic of 1857 throttled it again. Farnam and Durant paused in their squabbling long enough to summon Dodge to the company's headquarters in New York. At their insistence the directors of the Rock Island and M & M assembled to hear Dodge's report on routes west of the Missouri. They were not a receptive audience. As the secretary read the report aloud, the directors fidgeted in their seats and began leaving the room. In the outer chamber one director asked why they had been summoned to hear such nonsense. When the secretary finished, only Farnam, Durant, and Dodge remained in the room. Durant had heard every word and understood their importance. Already he and Farnam sensed that renewed public interest in the Pacific road would enable them to raise money easily for the M & M. For Durant the report may have been the experience that fired his imagination with the possibilities of a transcontinental railroad.

Nothing came of the report beyond the impression it made on Durant. No one suspected even remotely the extent to which the destiny of the Pacific railroad was tied to the difficulties of a half-finished line in Iowa.

Dodge went home dejected but unshaken in his convictions. In the spring of 1859 Farnam sent him to the Platte Valley again to reconnoiter. Shortly after returning to Council Bluffs, Dodge encountered a prominent Illinois lawyer who shared his interest in the transcontinental project. Abraham Lincoln was no stranger to western railroads, having been counsel for the M & M in a celebrated Mississippi River bridge case. Dodge heard Lincoln give a political speech and was later introduced to him on the porch of the Pacific Hotel. The meeting was no accident; Lincoln had been told that Dodge knew more about railroads than any two men in the country.

Lincoln squeezed into a chair, crossed his legs, and swung his foot idly before asking, "Dodge, what's the best route for a Pacific railroad to the West?"

"From this town out the Platte Valley," came the immediate reply.

Lincoln pondered that a bit. "Why do you think so?" he asked finally.

For two hours Lincoln in his inimitable way coaxed from Dodge every particle of information he had gathered for Farnam. As Dodge put it years later, "He completely 'shelled my woods.' " If Dodge felt annoyed at having been picked dry, he would come to be grateful for the impression it made on Lincoln. By 1859 Dodge had converted to the Republican Party. The next year he took charge of the M & M lobby seeking state aid in Des Moines. Although unsuccessful, he showed considerable skill as a lobbyist and joined a circle of political friends who would prove invaluable to him in the coming years. Iowa produced a remarkable crop of young, ambitious politicians during these years, most of whom played some role in the Union Pacific's history. They included John A. Kasson, a shrewd lawyer; Herbert M. Hoxie, a politician who became a capable railroad man; William B. Allison, soon to enter Congress; James Harlan, a senator since 1855; James W. Grimes, the other senator; James F. Wilson, who would enter the House in December 1861; Hiram Price, a prominent lawyer and later congressman; and Samuel R. Curtis, representative and author of the Pacific railroad bill bearing his name.

The Iowa Connection did not all agree or work together, but they exerted a formidable influence on behalf of their state. Most believed the Pacific railroad vital to the state's (and their own) interest and supported Lincoln because of his known advocacy of the project. In 1860 Dodge was persuaded to join the Iowans working for Lincoln's nomination in Chicago. Their efforts were rewarded and Kasson helped write a plank demanding a Pacific road into the Republican platform. Doggedly the M & M once again resumed work on a limited basis. In August the line crawled toward Marengo, thirty miles west of Iowa City. Beyond that, Dey reported, all looked bleak. "Farnam smells magnificently well," he added wryly, "verily believes himself the great Rail Road man of the North west. The Dr. blows hot and cold as the spirit moves him." Dey doubted Durant's ability "ever to carry the thing beyond Grinnell," thirty-five miles west of Marengo.

The election of Lincoln opened a new door of opportunity. Having helped carry the state for the new President, Dodge joined the Iowa contingent that descended on Washington seeking jobs, favors, contracts, and a Pacific railroad bill. Kasson was made assistant postmaster and Hoxie a United States marshal. Then came the secession crisis, which threw the capital into confusion and also forced the M & M to suspend work again. After Fort Sumter the collision between personal ambition and national catastrophe affected men in different ways. Dodge felt obliged to enlist despite the pleas of his friends to stay home. Allison and Hoxie reminded him of the profits to be made from the crisis. "There must be money in this war some place & we ought to have our share," Hoxie said bluntly. "How shall we go to work to get it? That is the question." Charles Durant, the Doctor's brother, regretted that Dodge did not remain in New York where "we could have made something out of war contracts. There has undoubtedly been and will still be good pickings."

Military service claimed not only Dodge but Samuel Curtis, sponsor of the House bill for a Pacific road. Dodge was on duty rebuilding the Mobile & Ohio Railroad when the Pacific Railway Act of 1862 passed Congress, but his friends were at their posts in the capital lobbying for the bill. Farnam and Mayor Ogden were among the commissioners who assembled at the first meeting in September, and Ogden was elected president of the yet unborn organization. Dey attended the sessions and was sent west to run preliminary surveys as far as Salt Lake City if possible. "Mr. Farnham [sic] seems to take hold of the project with a great deal of energy," he wrote Dodge, "and acts more as he used to than any time for the last four years. I wish he was ten years younger."

Appearances proved deceiving. By the spring of 1863 no progress had been made. Farnam felt his age and losses, the M & M still languished, and he was tired of jousting with Durant. In June he surrendered the presidency of the Rock Island to Charles Durant and retired from railroading. His departure served as a cue for the Doctor, who had for months been scheming not merely to revive the M & M but also to thrust himself prominently into the muddled Pacific road picture. By mid-1863 he had come to the realization that the Pacific road was the greater prize, the proper stage on which to play out his grandiose visions. Having lingered in the background for so long, the Doctor suddenly burst forth in an explosion of energy that continued undiminished for six years.

The challenge facing Durant was formidable. He had to enlist enough subscribers to enable the company to organize while keeping control of its board in his own hands. He had to persuade Congress to modify the Act of 1862 in ways that would provide adequate means to construct the road. If he succeeded in these efforts, he could then turn to the gigantic task of organizing and building the line. Men of ambition and good sense shrank from any one of these undertakings; Durant embraced them all with the willingness of a zealot who had found his cause.

Drawing on his considerable powers of persuasion, the Doctor made the rounds of his acquaintances in Wall Street, alternately charming and badgering them to subscribe. Later he claimed to have influenced a dozen or so parties to subscribe by putting up cash for the first 10 percent installment himself and guaranteeing them against loss. John A. Dix, the M & M's president, agreed to come in on this basis. The Doctor himself took fifty shares and his two brothers twenty each. Another twenty went to the quixotic George Francis Train, a brilliant but erratic promoter and self-styled "Champion Crank" who had earned a fortune in shipping and devoted himself to seeking political office and tilting at the windmill of sensational causes. Already Durant and Train had drawn together in a number of speculations, including one in contraband cotton.

Confident that he could peddle enough shares to launch the company, Durant took Dey off the M & M and sent him west again with orders to examine four different routes to the north bend of the Platte. Dey found some men to help with those surveys and went on to look over Bridger and Cheyenne passes. At his request Durant asked Brigham Young to take care of the survey between Fort Bridger and Provo. Young belonged to that group of subscribers whose installment had been paid by the Doctor and was happy to oblige. Durant also hired a geologist and dispatched him to search for coal and iron deposits in the Black Hills. By mid-October Dey had the surveys well enough in hand to offer suggestions for bridging the Missouri River.

On October 29, 1863, the moribund Union Pacific sprang abruptly to life, at least on paper. The commissioners were discharged and a nominal board of thirty directors elected. When the new board assembled the next day, Dix was made president and Durant vice president. This was precisely the sort of arrangement the Doctor wanted. Here as on the M & M the dignified, genteel Dix served as a figurehead, leaving Durant free to exercise power as vice president. The board was too unwieldly to interfere and unlikely to challenge his leadership, if only because he was so far ahead of everyone else. Scarcely had the directors warmed their chairs and elected officers when Durant presented them with reports of the earlier surveys by Dey and Dodge on the Platte Valley route and blandly informed them that "fearing that it would be impossible to accomplish much this season . . . if nothing was done until after the company was organized," he had taken the liberty of sending Dey west again two months earlier. Four parties of engineers and a geologist were busy surveying the entire route under Dey's supervision, all at the Doctor's expense.

Durant had been busier than anyone knew. He needed from Washington not only amendments to the Act of 1862 but a decision on the road's eastern terminus. The act required the President to designate the terminus, and several towns were still vying for the honor. Two in particular occupied the Doctor's attention. In Iowa the Northwestern's attempt to beat the M & M across Iowa had revived under the leadership of John I. Blair, a New Jersey financier. Blair had organized a new company, the Cedar Rapids & Missouri, and was building toward the river on a line that could terminate above Council Bluffs and connect with the Pacific road via Fremont. To the south certain St. Louis promoters were anxious to locate the terminus at Kansas City, where it would connect with the projected Missouri Pacific road from St. Louis.

Both challenges were real and had friends in Washington. Blair had subscribed to the Union Pacific and was on the board; so was Samuel C. Pomeroy, a Kansas senator interested in the branch from Kansas City. Durant understood the threat. If the Union Pacific dawdled and the St. Louis parties built rapidly to the 100th meridian, they might annul the charter of the Omaha line and make the Kansas branch the main stem. There was no time to lose in getting the surveys completed or a terminus decision.

Dodge appeared to hold the key to the latter problem. In June he had been summoned to Washington by Lincoln, who wanted his advice on the terminus question. Dodge reiterated his belief in the Platte Valley route and Omaha as the best terminus. In his blunt way he also posted Lincoln on certain deficiencies in the Act of 1862 that made it difficult to raise capital. Lincoln hinted that he might ask Congress to remedy the problem. Elated, Dodge hurried to New York to inform Durant and his circle about the interview. From that moment Dodge loomed large in the Doctor's plans. Although Dodge could not be induced to leave the army, he let Durant know of his desire "to identify myself with the project in some active capacity." At present, he added, "I probably can do you more good in my present position while matters are being settled by Congress and others."

Above all, Dodge needed money. His finances were in disarray and he could do little for them in the field. Once the terminus was decided, he urged Durant, "telegraph or write my Brother at Bluffs, so that he can invest a little money for me or else give me a chance with you if you make any . . . *bear this in mind.*" In return Dodge would take care of the Iowa delegation to Congress. "Hoxie will go to Washington," he noted, "and it will not cost very much."

Durant appreciated that Dodge was useful as both engineer and lobbyist, but at the moment he had Dey, who was merely a good engineer. "Want preliminary surveys at once to make location of starting point," he telegraphed Dey in a style he would soon make notorious. "Delay is ruinous. Everything depends on you." Dey gathered up his maps and hurried to New York on November 5. The Doctor was pressing Lincoln for a decision and needed all the ammunition he could muster. On November 17, two days before he was to make some remarks at Gettysburg, a distracted Lincoln scribbled off an executive order defining the terminus as "so much of the western boundary of the State of Iowa as lies between the north and south boundaries of . . . the city of Omaha." It was not the clearest language that ever flowed from Lincoln's pen. Durant scrutinized it, shrewdly construed it to mean Omaha rather than a point across the river, and stuffed it in his pocket.

The scramble for real estate in Omaha was on. At the suggestion of both Dodge and Dey the Doctor recruited banker Augustus Kountze to acquire land for right-of-way and depot grounds. Kountze was a Union Pacific director and eager to run with the hounds. While he searched the land market and buttonholed politicians, the Doctor decided to stage a groundbreaking ceremony in Omaha. Besides confirming the road's presence in Omaha, the event would garner some publicity and perhaps impress Congress, which was about to convene. Dey was ordered to rush preparations along to be ready on December 1. "You are behind time for so important an enterprise," Durant snapped on Monday, November 30. "Break ground on Wednesday."

Omaha treated itself to a holiday for the occasion. No matter that the Central Pacific had broken ground in California eleven months earlier, the Pacific road had come to town at last and folks were in a jubilant mood. They flocked to the bottom land near the old ferry landing at Seventh and Davenport streets to watch the governor turn the first shovel of dirt. Bands played, whistles blared, cannon roared, flags waved, and fireworks flashed in the falling dusk. The orator of the day was Train, who read notes of congratulations from Lincoln and other dignitaries before rousing the crowd with a speech of his own. Afterward the mayor hosted a banquet and ball at the Herndon House and presided over another fervent exchange of vows between the politicians and real estate promoters. Train was content with the day's work. "Five (5) oclock the child is born," he wired Durant.

In New York the Doctor was unimpressed. "May as well have had no celebration as to have sent such meagre accounts," he fired back. "Send full particulars."

The ceremony touched off an orgy of land speculation in Omaha. Nathan Dodge crossed the river to watch the proceedings and wrote his brother that he had never seen people so wild. "Every man, woman and child who owned enough ground to bury themselves upon was a millionaire, prospectively," he laughed. "They have got corner lots up to '57 prices." The cheers for Durant's name, however, soon turned to curses. Having moved with vigor and decisiveness for months, the Doctor hesitated over the precise location of the line. Two possibilities had already been explored. One ran north of Omaha through Florence; the other began at the village of Bellevue, south of Omaha. On December 1 Durant chose the Florence line, but trouble arose with the land company holding title to much of the route. "If they want to black mail you make application to get hold of the Charter on south side of Platte and they will come to terms," Dodge advised from distant Tennessee. "I would not pay them *one cent for it.* If you commence in that you will have to buy your way clear through to the Pacific."

Dey asked Durant to leave the final decision in his hands but was refused with a curt order to say nothing about the location to anyone, including other directors. Aware that speculators were snatching up land in the Platte Valley, Dey wired frantically for the Doctor to get the land office closed up but got no response. He surveyed the Florence line and, finding it more expensive than expected, decided to run a third line from the south end of Omaha but over different ground. It would, he promised Durant, reduce his earlier estimates by eight thousand dollars per mile. By mid-December Dey had run the line as far as Fremont. He had also secured about six thousand acres of land from the county and the entire river front and two thirds of the bottom land from the city. The Doctor rewarded his efforts with an outburst of complaints that drove Dey to resign on December 24. A week later Durant notified him of his official appointment as chief engineer and brushed the resignation aside with the comment, "Better regard letters as friendly advice and act accordingly."

While Dey puzzled over this turn of events, the Doctor hurried to Washington. He was playing a deeper game than anyone yet knew. In his mind the line controversy had already gone beyond the choice of the best route out of Omaha to whether the terminus should even be located at Omaha. On one side John Blair insisted that the best line from the Missouri to the Platte began at De Soto, some twenty-two miles north of Omaha. If Durant started his road there, Blair would push his Cedar Rapids road across Iowa to a point north of Council Bluffs for direct connection. The M & M might then be merged with the Cedar Rapids, thereby leaving Council Bluffs and Omaha in the cold. On the other side, Durant was beguiled by overtures from promoters of the Kansas branch, who wanted a terminus south of Omaha.

From this web of intrigue emerged the first demonstration of Durant's peculiar business style. His manner of dealing with a complex situation was not to thread his way through the maze of possibilities but rather to sweep along with him everyone and everything that might be useful, leaving conflicts and choices to be sorted out later. Action and not direction was his forte. He longed to be at the center of events, barking orders to and demanding absolute obedience from subordinates whom he kept in ignorance of his true design. Often he did not know himself what his ultimate design was. Like an inept monarch, he was more certain of his authority than of his policy, and had a tendency to heed the last voice that advised him. The result was a pattern of frenzied activity riddled with false starts, wasted motion, confusion, and contradiction followed by hesitation, uncertainty, and delay. Fueled by nervous energy, Durant was a whirlwind blowing furiously, wreaking havoc in its wake before dying away.

Dey was slow to grasp the Doctor's purpose. Asked to survey the De Soto line, he replied that it was even worse than the Florence line and complained that it was "difficult to make surveys without forming some idea of what you are doing and what it is for." When the light dawned, Dey was furious. Durant was "managing it as he has everything else that is in his hands," he grumbled to Dodge. "A good deal spread and a good deal do nothing. He considers it a big thing, the Big Thing of the age, and himself the father of it." Blair was a systematic, persevering man, he added, capable of using Durant as he pleased. The logical connecting point for the Cedar Rapids or any road was Council Bluffs, and the best line for the Union Pacific was through Fremont by the shortest route. "I cannot make him see it, however," Dey lamented, "and if I attempt to put a little common sense in his head, he flies off in a fit of excitement."

Instead of deciding on a line, Durant bombarded Dey with new possibilities. "If the geography was a little larger," Dey snapped, "I think he would order a survey round by the moon and a few of the fixed stars, to see if he could not get some more depot grounds or wild lands [or] something else, that he don't want, and he does not know what to do with it when he gets it." Time was pressing. Contracts had to be let for ties and grading if work was to commence when the weather turned. Dey had pushed on these matters, but the Doctor would not move or decide on the line. A few days later Hoxie complained to Dodge that considerable work had to be done with the legislature, but he could get no instructions from Durant. Early in February 1864, Kountze alerted Dodge to the scheme of a single line across Iowa "which if effected and carried out fully will completely ruin Omaha and Council Bluffs." He warned that Durant had turned against them.

Dodge scribbled off two letters urging Durant to reconsider. On the rumored shift of the M & M's terminus to De Soto, he said bluntly, "I did not believe you had any such idea . . . But if you have, let me advise you to drop it . . . it is not the route, but far from it, one of the worst you could accept. No *present benefit* that Mr Blair or anybody else can promise you will repay the future detriment it will be to you." Logic and nature dictated that the route run through Council Bluffs-Omaha and the Platte Valley. That this argument coincided with Dodge's self-interest did not deter from its force. The change was ruinous from both an engineering and political standpoint. Apart from giving a worse line, it aggravated the bridging problem; the Missouri was three miles wide at Council Bluffs, eight miles at De Soto. Furthermore, if Durant insisted on the change, he would antagonize both the Iowa and Nebraska legislatures.

While this controversy raged, the Doctor was busy opening a new front. In Washington the lobbyists and railroad chieftains gathered for a concerted run at amending the Act of 1862. Collis P. Huntington of the Central Pacific was there along with the promoters of what would become the Kansas Pacific.* The Kansas project was riddled with internal dissension. Its charter had been acquired by John C. Frémont and a brash plunger named Samuel Hallett, who then awarded himself a construction contract and proceeded to lay forty miles of road in such shoddy fashion that his own engineer urged Lincoln not to award bonds for the work. Frémont wanted none of Hallett's tactics and

* This road was originally known as the Leavenworth, Pawnee & Western. The name was changed to Union Pacific, Eastern Division, and then to Kansas Pacific. To avoid confusion the latter name is used throughout this book.

tried to oust him from the company. The result was a fight that created opposing boards of directors and led to a crossfire of injunctions.

Durant wasted little time injecting himself into this fracas. The Kansas promoters had antagonized key members of Congress with their squabbling and could expect nothing unless their claims and disputes were settled. However, they still hoped to beat the Union Pacific and could do much to prevent any amendments to the Act of 1862. The Doctor saw that, as he later testified, "we could not get along unless we headed them off at their quarters." He decided to side with Hallett and his partner by taking a one-third interest in Hallett's construction contract. This gave him leverage in the enemy camp and allowed him to copper his bets if things went badly for the Union Pacific. Perhaps Durant also toyed with the idea of a southern connection, for Dey had just informed him that the Bellevue route was the cheapest of all the lines west.

This investment bought Durant the possible help of the Kansas Pacific promoters in getting amendments. The House bill contained a section denying all aid to the Kansas project until the disputes among its promoters were resolved; everything depended on persuading them to close ranks. To that end Durant hired a lobbyist named Joseph B. Stewart and, together with Hallett, armed him with about $250,000 in bonds to use in reconciling the warring factions. For this service Stewart received $38,000 from Durant/Hallett and another $2,000 from Huntington. Later it would be charged that Durant spent the better part of a "suspense account" totaling $435,754 to obtain the legislation he wanted that session. Stewart adamantly refused to tell a congressional committee who got the bonds he dispensed, stating only that none went to any member of Congress. There was "no necessity for it at that time," Durant added blandly, "it was not a measure that there was any opposition to in Congress. It was the local interests that made the fight." St. Louis, Chicago, even the eastern roads wanted to control the terminus, "and that was what made all the trouble."

Durant was not the only Union Pacific man in Washington that winter. He had come to town with another director and large stockholder, Cornelius S. Bushnell. A merchant and shipbuilder from New Haven, Bushnell was already known in Washington as the man who had helped build the *Monitor* and urged its acceptance by the government. Large, dynamic, full of the promoter's enthusiasm, Bushnell had accumulated some political chits of his own, including Senator Pomeroy, who had interests in both the Union Pacific and Kansas Pacific. As a lobbyist the affable Bushnell was more effective than Durant, who had too many irons heating to keep his eye on any one for very long.

Aware that the terminus question remained a stumbling block with some congressmen, Durant and Bushnell pressed Lincoln to clarify his original order, which for some reason had not been entered on any official record. Early in March Lincoln sent a new order to the Senate fixing the terminus on the western boundary of Iowa opposite Omaha. That ought to have settled the matter, but Durant still refused to be pinned down. Nathan Dodge figured the Doctor's line relocation scheme was "a stock operation entirely," but others weren't so sure. Durant neither embraced an Omaha line nor disavowed his interest in connecting with Blair's road. He advanced funds for the Kansas Pacific to resume work under Hallett's contract and sent the M & M's superintendent, Joseph E. Henry, to take charge. Henry looked the work over and reported with a straight face that the first forty miles were in fair shape "when you consider that it has been built without engineers. They have no profile of the road as graded, or estimate of the quantities of work done or to be done." Durant and his new friends controlled the board, and Stewart was hard at the task of buying harmony among the aggrieved. The Doctor was keeping his options open, north and south. His running about left Bushnell to shoulder much of the hard work buttonholing congressmen in Washington. "Were you here today," an annoyed Bushnell telegraphed on one occasion, "I think you could secure all you wish."

In Omaha, Dey was at his wit's end. Durant was badgering him and Kountze to secure land for right-of-way on a line yet to be finalized. Dey had recruited two fine engineers, Samuel B. Reed and James A. Evans, to head parties surveying the line from the Black Hills to Salt Lake. They needed to start at once to complete the work before autumn, but Durant dragged his feet in approving expenditures to outfit the parties. Neither would he commit himself to the contracts needed to begin work on the road's first hundred miles. Dey did not even know his compensation as chief engineer and begged the Doctor to have the board set a figure.

"Durant is vacillating and changeable," he grumbled to Dodge in April, "and to my mind utterly unfit to head such an enterprise." All Dey wanted was to build the road as cheaply and efficiently as possible, "but it is like dancing with a whirlwind to have anything to do with him. To-day matters run smoothly and tomorrow they don't. . . . If there were parties managing in New York that would be governed by what I write them and furnish the money without desiring to meddle with the details I could build the work for less money and more rapidly than can be done the way they propose to do it."

Thus was the Union Pacific charged with mismanagement before it had laid a single rail. Durant neglected matters in Omaha partly because he was absorbed with maneuvers in Congress. Washington was a city of ambulances and hearses that spring as casualties poured in from the Battle of the Wilderness. While citizens waited apprehensively for the outcome of the bloodbath to the south, lobbyists swarmed the halls of the capitol seeking a final push on the railroad and other bills. The cross-currents of intrigue among vested interests were merely one set of pressures on congressmen keenly aware that issues of war and peace still hung in the balance and elections were but a few months away. Small wonder, then, that a chaplain opened one April session with the prayer, "O Lord, give us that Thou wilt in thine infinite wisdom vouchsafe to our rulers and legislators in this Congress assembled more brains—more brains, Lord."

It is unclear from the evidence whether this appeal was heeded. The railroad bill was approaching the moment of decision. In December 1863 the Senate had discarded its select committee in favor of a standing committee on the Pacific railroad, which reported a bill on May 18 embodying important changes in the status and amount of bonds. Instead of lending its own bonds, the government would allow the company to issue its own bonds at the enlarged rate of $24,000 per mile on the plains, $48,000 per mile on the plateau, and $96,000 per mile for the mountain region. The government would also pay the first year's interest and guarantee interest for another nineteen years.

The Senate bill was an improvement, but in Durant's view it didn't go nearly far enough. In the House a bill introduced by Hiram Price of Iowa on March 16 was referred to the usual select committee of thirteen. Chaired by the redoubtable Thaddeus Stevens of Pennsylvania, the committee included two new representatives of more than passing interest. One was Ignatius Donnelly of Minnesota, who would offer a bill for a People's Pacific Railroad; the other was a well-known Massachusetts shovel manufacturer, Oakes Ames. The presence of members from Kansas, Missouri, California, and Oregon, together with Price, insured that every faction would have a voice in the committee.

The Union Pacific lobby concentrated its effort to get desirable amendments on this select committee. In this work Bushnell, Train, and Hoxie did yeoman service along with Stewart. Huntington of the Central Pacific and the Kansas Pacific people also hounded the committee, as did certain Oregon and Minnesota interests seeking a rail connection for their states. Although Durant was often absent in New York, it is possible that his contact with the committee brought him together with Oakes Ames for the first time. Through the long hours of horse trading the Union Pacific lobbyists kept the inside track, taking care also to enlist the support of representatives outside the committee such as S. S. "Sunset" Cox of Ohio. Early in May the committee reported out a bill containing much of what Durant wanted, but the House did not take it up until the evening of June 16. By that time the backstage maneuvering had brought (or bought) harmony among the Kansas Pacific and some California interests, who threw their support behind the bill.

Opposition to the bill was small but vociferous. John Pruyn of New York reiterated his belief that the government itself should build the road, but his amendment was quashed. William Holman of Indiana distrusted railroads in general and the motives of the promoters in particular, but his amendments too were rejected by large majorities. E. B. Washburne of Illinois called one section of the bill "the most monstrous and flagrant attempt to overreach the government and the people that can be found in all the legislative annals of the country." He charged angrily that the project had fallen into the hands of

"Wall Street stock jobbers who are using this great engine for their own private means." It was all to no avail. After brushing aside motions to postpone consideration and to adjourn, the House passed the bill on June 21 in a tumultuous evening session before packed galleries. Washburne later called the scene a "tempest of wildest disorder" in which "lobbyists, male and female," crowded and jostled through the corridors, forced their way onto the floor, and even occupied the seats of members.

The House and Senate promptly refused to accept each other's bill, and the matter was referred to a joint committee that included Stevens, Senator Harlan of Iowa, and a member of each house from California. In short order the committee reported a bill virtually embodying the House version with two amendments as concessions to the Senate. There was no time to print or read the committee's report; both Houses accepted a scant verbal description of it on the last day of the session. On July 2 Lincoln signed the bill into law.

The Pacific Railway Act of 1864 contained some very important changes from its predecessor. Under its provisions the Union Pacific could issue its own first mortgage bonds in an amount equal to the government bonds, thereby relegating the latter to a second mortgage. It was this subordinating of the government bonds that so outraged Washburne; later Stewart would proclaim himself the author of it. The bonds could be issued upon completion of twenty-mile sections instead of every forty miles. In addition, the land grant was doubled to provide ten alternate sections on each side of every mile or about 12,800 acres per mile. This grant was made unconditional by deleting earlier restrictions on its sale, and the company was given rights to coal and iron lands. Durant regarded these rights as vital because his geologist had already found evidence of coal and iron in the Black Hills, and Dodge had stressed the urgency of not losing what he considered "a mine of wealth to the Co in the future." Dodge thought the Doctor should be able to "slip a clause in that will not draw attention that will fix the matter."

Both the subsidy (government) bonds and land patents were to be issued on completion of twenty-mile sections. In mountain regions the company could collect two thirds of its subsidy once the roadbed of a twenty-mile section was prepared, with the rest being paid after rails were laid. The new act repealed the provision whereby the government retained a portion of the bonds until the road was completed and also allowed the company to collect from time to time one half the sum due on government business instead of applying the entire amount to repayment of the subsidy. To attract investors, the par value of Union Pacific stock was reduced from $1,000 to $100, and the limit on the amount held by any one person was removed. The board was increased from fifteen to twenty and the number of government directors from two to five, with the stipulation that one of the government appointees should serve on every standing or special committee. Once again Congress reserved the right to alter, amend, or repeal the act.

Some curious vagaries could be found tucked among the act's provisions.

The Central Pacific could build only 150 miles east of California and the Union Pacific no more than 300 miles west of Salt Lake City, but no meeting point was designated. The clause authorizing two thirds payment for grading sections in mountain country allowed the companies to put crews at work in the region long before the railhead approached it. No clear language on the method and timetable for repaying the subsidy was included, and several key provisions proved to be monuments to ambiguity.

Time would reveal the Act of 1864 to be a vague, hasty, ill-drawn piece of legislation. That is hardly surprising, given the welter of forces and interests that had a hand in its shaping. Congress had ventured into virgin territory. In the past it had offered railroads land grants but never a subsidy of bonds or a federal charter. Under the best of circumstances it would have been fiendishly difficult to grasp the ramifications or anticipate the problems spawned by so complex an act; amid the distractions of war it was impossible. One might demand of congressmen more brains, but one could not expect them to be prophets. The object, after all, was to induce private parties to build the road that everyone agreed must be built. Yet somehow the outcome left a sour taste in the mouths of those who were advocates in principle. Two years earlier Holman of Indiana, the harsh critic of 1864, had made one of the most eloquent appeals for the project:

> This road could never be constructed on terms applicable to ordinary roads. Every member of the committee knows that it is to be constructed through almost impassible mountains, deep ravines, canons, gorges, and over arid and sandy plains. The Government must come forward with a liberal hand, or the enterprise must be abandoned forever. The necessity is upon us. The question is whether we shall hold our Pacific possessions, and connect the nations on the Pacific with those on the Atlantic Coast, or whether we shall abandon our Pacific possessions.

For better or worse, Congress had at last responded to this appeal, with results no one could predict. For the moment Durant and his allies had what they wanted. No one ever found out exactly what it cost them, but a few glimmers survived. Of the $250,000 in bonds distributed by Stewart, $20,000 went to Charles T. Sherman, eldest brother of the senator and the general, for "professional services" rendered the Kansas Pacific on June 9. According to Hoxie, Sherman wanted a seat on the Union Pacific board to satisfy his brother John, who was "not willing that he shall take a fee as a lawyer without being interested in the company otherwise." Instead Sherman settled for an appointment as one of the first government directors. Another $10,000 went to Alexander Hay for helping Stewart distribute bonds to the proper hands.

Durant and Train had also recruited the services of Congressman S. S. "Sunset" Cox of Ohio, who lent his influence to the cause in return for considerations that apparently included "expenses" and stock in the Kansas road. That autumn he did not hesitate to ask Durant for a contribution to his reelection campaign. The Doctor spread his largess wherever it would do some good. Clark Bell, a young New York lawyer who drafted much of what went into the Act of 1864 and lobbied persuasively for it, eventually received more than $20,000 for his effort. Hoxie was content with $1,000 plus expenses, and Train claimed his share as well. After the bill passed, the flamboyant Train went wheeling off to what he grandly called "the seat of Empire." That summer he would charge the Union Pacific $4,000 for "expenses and services" involved in three trips to Omaha.

Lobbyists and legislators alike found Durant a genial paymaster. An associate later called him "the most extravagant man I ever knew in my life." He was, noted Sidney Dillon ruefully, "a fast man. He started fast, and I tried to hold him back awhile; but he got me to going pretty fast before we got through. . . . he was a man who when he undertook to help to build a railroad didn't stop at trifles in accomplishing his end."

For the moment, however, the Doctor still lived on promises. He had an improved act but not yet the wherewithal to build the road. Something more was needed to lure capital to the project. Months before the bill passed, he had been busy on that front as well.

3

THE COMPANY

The Act of 1864 dangled the prospect of improved federal aid for the Union Pacific but did not solve the problem of generating funds to get construction underway. Two obstacles discouraged investors from subscribing to the enterprise. The charter still required that stock be purchased at par with cash, and stockholders had to accept unlimited liability for the company's obligations. These handicaps were enough to give prudent investors pause in a known enterprise; they were insuperable for a venture of such unprecedented scale and risk as the Pacific railroad. The costs of construction would be enormous and difficult to estimate. No one knew how long it would take to build the road or even whether trains could actually be run through the mountains in winter. Much would have to be learned by trial and error, a school with high tuition costs. Since no railroad yet reached Council Bluffs, supplies would have to be floated down the Missouri or hauled overland by wagon.

Small wonder that conservative capitalists shrank from risking their fortune or reputation on the project. They understood clearly that, stripped of patriotic rhetoric, the Pacific road amounted to a reckless gamble for high stakes at long odds. Respectable men of means did not care to gamble and had better ways to invest their money. They might endorse the venture, perhaps even buy a few shares, but they would not assume leadership of it. The government offered financial assistance but declined to build the road itself. Who then was left to take charge of the enterprise except promoters and plungers, men willing to wager on long shots? Durant, Bushnell, and Hallett, although very different from one another, were all men of this stripe. They were willing to take large risks in hopes of large returns, but they were not fools. Their first task was not merely to raise capital but to find ways to minimize the risk involved.

Congress expected the necessary funds to be raised from three sources: sale of stock, the government subsidy, and sale of first mortgage bonds. However, promoters knew from experience that a road could not be built from the proceeds of stock sales. Investors realized that on railroad stocks the risks were great and dividends (if any) long in coming. Bonds were more attractive because they promised a regular return provided the road earned enough to pay its interest. The Union Pacific was rich in potential assets, but these could be tapped only after the road was built. Construction required an enormous amount of working capital on which little or no return could be expected until the road opened for business. To minimize risk, therefore, some way had to be found not only to raise money but to earn short-term profits as well.

Shrewd promoters had already discovered a neat solution to this dilemma. By organizing themselves into a construction company, they could earn immediate profits from building the road. If the completed road proved successful, they could also make money from its operation; if not, they would still come away with something. The construction company also enabled promoters to limit their liability. If the road was built by a corporation rather than by individual stockholders, they would be liable only to the extent of their investment in that corporation. All profits on construction would accrue to them and could be easily divided according to their share in the construction company. As stockholders in both the railroad and the construction company they would in effect make a contract with themselves, which allowed them to put the work at figures guaranteeing a profit. They would have little difficulty selling stock if they wished to do so, for investors who would not touch railroad securities would gladly buy into a construction company. Along the way they would also have contracts, jobs, and other benefits to distribute to "friends" of the road.

Durant was not slow to grasp these advantages, and he had before him the example of John Blair, an adept practitioner of the device. In March 1864, while the railroad bill was still making its way through Congress, Durant and Train bought control of an obscure Pennsylvania corporation called the Pennsylvania Fiscal Agency. Chartered in 1859 with generous and elastic powers including "the purchase and sale of railroad bonds and other securities, and to make advances of money and credit to railroads," the company had not organized until May 1863 and even then transacted no business until a special meeting on March 3, 1864, at which Durant and Train were made directors and the Doctor became president. In May the number of directors was increased from six to seven and Bushnell joined the board. An executive committee consisting of Durant, Bushnell, and Train was appointed, and Durant as president was authorized to make any contracts he deemed suitable for the company's interest.

One other piece of business was transacted at the May meeting. Train had spent some time in France and come home impressed with the work of a company called *Crédit Mobilier de France.* Founded in 1852, it built the Paris Gas Works, organized the Paris Omnibus Company and the Grand Hôtel du Louvre, and carried on large railway operations. At Train's urging the company's name was changed to Crédit Mobilier of America. This seeming bit of trivia turned out later to be a disastrous mistake. In overlooking the tendency of Americans to distrust anything they could not pronounce, Train and Durant swapped a homespun name for one that smacked of foreign exotica to which any suspicion of villainy or fraud could be easily attached.

Durant now had a suitable vehicle for his purposes, but he let it lie dormant for several months. Perhaps he was still uncertain of how best to utilize it. He could employ the company to construct the Union Pacific or the Kansas Pacific or even the M & M or any combination of these projects. Given his penchant for keeping his options open, he may have delayed action until the proper course suggested itself to him. If he was waiting for a sign, fate was quick to oblige.

The Kansas Pacific lacked a chief engineer because Hallett had fired the incumbent, O. A. Talcott, apparently for refusing to falsify a report certifying the first twenty miles of road as finished and ready for subsidy. Indignant at this treatment, Talcott wrote Lincoln alerting him to "the Bigest [sic] swindle yet." Lincoln referred the letter to his Secretary of the Interior, John P. Usher, a Kansan who had sided with Hallett in the fight against Frémont. Usher knew Hallett was then in Washington seeking the subsidy and passed a copy of the letter along to him. Furious at being thwarted, Hallett wired his brother Thomas to find Talcott and whip him. None of the Hallett brothers were known as genteel souls, and Thomas beat the engineer senseless. When Sam Hallett returned to Wyandotte on the morning of July 27, Talcott was waiting for him. His wrath bypassed Thomas and went directly to the source. As Sam started down the street from the depot, Talcott shot him dead.

Suddenly the Kansas project was in shambles. While the overworked Joseph Henry struggled to keep work going, Durant sent out a new engineer who had insinuated himself into his confidence. Silas Seymour met Durant through John F. Tracy of the Rock Island. As chief engineer of the Washington Aqueduct he had a wide circle of acquaintances in the capital and was an ardent if not always adept lobbyist. The Doctor liked men who could be useful in more than one capacity and in July appointed Seymour as consulting engineer for the Union Pacific. From first to last he remained Durant's man; the bond between them extended beyond their years together on the Union Pacific.

Before Henry and Seymour could get much done, John D. Perry, Hallett's partner in the Kansas Pacific, arrived from St. Louis and found everything to be "confusion and clamour." Informing Durant that "the waste has been terrible and apparant [sic] now to all," Perry did what he could to sort matters out. The remaining Hallett brothers were sent packing, and an attempt was made to reduce the mountain of unpaid bills. One problem, the status of the Hallett contract, defied easy solution and soon gave rise to a bitter dispute. Durant declared himself ready and willing to carry out its terms, but Perry had come to doubt his motives or at least his mixed allegiance. The Kansas Pacific had elected some new directors who were unhappy with the contract. In August Henry warned Durant that the new board would use Hallett's death as an excuse to take the contract into its own hands. Three months later the board repudiated the contract and opened negotiations with other contractors.

Durant had no intention of surrendering without a fight. He ordered Henry to continue work while the legal sparring went on and dispatched Seymour to plead his case with Usher. The Secretary, who had helped draft the Act of 1862, had personal interests in Kansas and was anxious to mediate the dispute that blocked the road's progress, but he was helpless against Durant's peculiar genius for intransigence. In many respects the battle with Perry presaged the Doctor's career with Union Pacific. For months he befuddled his opponents, bellowing righteous indignation one moment and cooing overtures of peace the next, content to wear them down without budging an inch on his claims or rights under the Hallett contract. He was always eager to settle and about to settle, but somehow settlement was never reached for reasons beyond his control. Meanwhile, progress on the Kansas Pacific slowed to a crawl.

The squabble in Kansas complicated Durant's attempt to breathe life into the Union Pacific. Apart from the funds tied up in the Hallett contract, he could not decide how or where to use the Crédit Mobilier or even what terminus would best suit his interest. The Union Pacific needed money to build enough mileage to begin collecting the subsidy and to give it credibility in Congress and on Wall Street. In May 1864 the company appointed a special committee to let a construction contract, but nothing was done that summer. While grappling with the difficulties caused by Hallett's death, Durant arranged for a contract to construct the first hundred miles of the Union Pacific. For this purpose he called once again on the services of the obliging "Hub" Hoxie.

Historians have echoed Oliver Ames's dismissal of Hoxie as "a man of no means." In fact he was much more than the front man for what became a notorious contract. A native New Yorker, Hoxie had moved to Iowa as a child and settled eventually in Des Moines. He took up politics at an early age and showed considerable talent for it. After joining the Republican Party, he and his wife ran a station on the Underground Railroad for runaway slaves. Restless and ambitious, he followed the rush to Colorado to pan for gold in 1858 but came home without a fortune. For a time he tried farming and then the hotel business, but neither satisfied his urge for a career that paid handsomely. His association with Dodge helped convince him that the mixture of railroading and politics offered a promising avenue to wealth, but in 1864 he was still at loose ends over his future. When Durant beckoned, therefore, he leaped eagerly at the opportunity.

In August 1864 Hoxie submitted a proposal to build and equip the first hundred miles of road west of Omaha for $50,000 a mile. He had neither the means nor the experience for such an undertaking, yet on September 23 the special committee accepted his offer and drew up a contract. Eleven days later the contract was extended another 147 miles to the 100th meridian on the same terms, making 247 miles at a total cost of $12.35 million.

Hoxie never intended to do the work himself. He was merely an agent whose function was to obtain the contract on behalf of certain Union Pacific directors who did not wish to let it to themselves. For this service he was promised $5,000 in cash, $10,000 in Union Pacific stock, and a position with the company. On September 30 he assigned the contract to Durant, who in turn shared it with Bushnell, H. W. Gray, Charles A. Lambard, and H. S. McComb on October 7. Only McComb was a Union Pacific director; the others were stockholders. Together they subscribed $1.6 million to carry out the contract, of which 25 percent was paid in at once. Hoxie also gave his power of attorney and proxy for all stocks in his name to Durant's confidential secretary, Henry C. Crane.

Durant and his friends later insisted that they took the contract on this basis because it was the only way to raise money for construction. Bushnell asserted that every director and stockholder knew about the arrangement with Hoxie. "Participation in said contract was offered to the stockholders," he testified. "Nearly every stockholder was invited and urged by myself personally to become interested in the contract." A different version was offered by banker George Opdyke, a Union Pacific director, who denied knowing that the contract "belonged in any way to Mr. T. C. Durant, or that Mr. Hoxie was in any way an agent of Mr. Durant's." Opdyke also believed that Durant had made the contract without any instruction or authority from the board but rejected the idea that the Doctor or anyone else had done so for his own personal profit.

On one point all parties agreed: something had to be done to raise money because subscriptions were not coming in. The Hoxie contract at least offered the prospect of getting the work started and earning a decent profit for someone. All Durant needed was a set of estimates on the cost of construction that fit the generous figures of the contract. On October 20 he sent Dey a copy of the contract with instructions to do just that.

* * *

The year had gone badly for Peter Dey. Months had been consumed in trying to fix a line and get the Doctor to stick to it, ordering equipment, arranging tie contracts, recruiting survey parties and wheedling funds from Durant to outfit them. Wartime inflation made supplies expensive, and labor was so scarce that Durant asked the government to provide him with black contraband workers for the road. In Washington Clark Bell worked out an arrangement with Usher for use of the contrabands only to have it fall through at the eleventh hour. Crews were needed for grading and excavating, to say nothing of tie cutting, but no contractor would take a contract without a reliable labor force. Dey tried some workers imported from Canada but found them "the hardest set to manage that I have encountered."

Early in July, while others celebrated Lincoln's signing of the Act of 1864, Dey was mourning the death of his youngest son from scarlet fever. A few weeks later Durant ordered him to submit estimates for work on the first hundred miles. Dey sifted through the reports of his engineers and returned a figure of $30,000 a mile. To his surprise Joseph Henry appeared at his office shortly afterward with orders from Durant to supply a higher figure. He muttered something about embankments that could be widened and a grade just west of Omaha that might be reduced. Dey arched an eyebrow at the request but supposed the Doctor wanted the higher estimate as leverage to persuade the board to let a contract. He gave Henry a revised estimate of $50,000 a mile and thought no more about it until Durant's letter arrived with the Hoxie contract.

Dey received the letter on November 1 from Henry, who arrived in Omaha to take charge of all construction on behalf of the contractor, leaving Dey as chief engineer. For five weeks Dey brooded over the Hoxie contract, and always it came out the same to him. The extended version covered 247 miles at $50,000 a mile; Dey's own estimates, which he considered liberal, put the cost per mile at $30,000 for the first hundred miles and $27,000 for the remainder. His own figures had been used to justify a contract that would cost the company about $60,000 a mile by his reckoning, an amount he believed "would so cripple the road that it would be impossible, with that load upon it, to ever build the road." He saw other objectionable provisions in the contract that reinforced this conviction.

He knew Hoxie well, knew that he had neither capital, credit, nor experience for such a contract. Dey guessed it was another of Durant's schemes. The Doctor had made his life miserable for the past year and now had used him in a way Dey found unconscionable. On December 7 he tendered Dix his resignation. "My reasons for this step," he explained, "are, simply, that I do not approve of the contract made with Mr. Hoxie . . . and I do not care to have my name so connected with the railroad that I shall appear to endorse this contract." In the same envelope Dey enclosed a second letter amplifying his views. The contract had been made against his known views, and he did not see how in good conscience he could execute it. "You know the history of the M. and M.," he reminded Dix, "a road that to-day could be running to this point if its stock and bonds only represented the amount of cash that actually went into it." He wanted no part of repeating that mistake and so, with reluctance, "resigned the best position in my profession this country has ever offered to any man."

Dix did not reply for three months and then explained only that the contract price was a measure of expediency. In April 1865 Jesse L. Williams, a government director, told Dey that the government directors knew nothing of the contract until it was presented to them at the October meeting. "From the first, the contract price appeared to me high," he admitted; "at present, with the probable decline, it seems extravagant. When made, however, there were considerations justifying a liberal price." The war was going badly, inflation was rampant, and national finances were in disarray. Gold was at a premium, which made currency-paying bonds a poor investment. Work on the road had to be pushed forward, but no subsidy could be obtained until some mileage was built and no one would advance funds for that purpose.

In retrospect the contract was portrayed as a burden imposed by necessity, regrettable but unavoidable if progress was to be made. At the time it succeeded only in driving the chief engineer from the company. Dey stayed on long enough to receive the reports of his surveyors in the mountain region. When he departed on December 31, 1864, the Union Pacific had yet to lay a rail and had graded less than twenty miles of roadbed. A month later the Central Pacific would complete its first thirty-one miles of track to Newcastle.

* * *

For Durant and his associates the Hoxie contract was a halfway house. They did not want to carry the entire financial load themselves, especially on a basis of unlimited liability. To protect themselves, and to attract other investors, the obvious next step was to assign the contract to a construction company. Bushnell offered to furnish a charter acquired from the Connecticut legislature, but Durant preferred the Crédit Mobilier with its broader grant of powers. Early in 1865 Durant's lawyers worked out the details for transferring the contract to Crédit Mobilier.

By March Durant had the new arrangement in shape. Crédit (Mobilier) had already opened a New York office under the charge of Henry Crane as assistant treasurer. Although the company was obliged by charter to retain a Philadelphia office, its real business was transacted in a room adjoining the Union Pacific office in New York. The Hoxie contract was reassigned to Crédit Mobilier, which created a "Railway Bureau" of five managers to oversee work done under the contract. Capital stock was put at $1.6 million and could not be increased beyond $2 million without the consent of three fourths of the outstanding stock. The $1.6 million subscribed earlier by Durant and his associates was applied toward subscriptions to Crédit Mobilier stock. A few days after this was done, Crane issued Durant a check for $302,700, presumably to reimburse him for outlays already made by him.

The protection of a corporate charter proved decisive in the campaign to attract new investors. Men who shrank from exposing themselves to unlimited liability now agreed to take stock in the new company. Bushnell and Lambard canvassed vigorously among their wide circle of acquaintances in

New England. Their appeal brought in Sidney Dillon of Connecticut, Rowland G. Hazard and his brother Isaac of Rhode Island, and a coterie of Bostonians: John Duff, John M. S. Williams, William T. Glidden, Benjamin E. Bates, Samuel Hooper, Oliver S. Chapman, and the Ames brothers, Oakes and Oliver. The only new investor from outside New England was Ben Holladay, the young "Stagecoach King," who saw in the venture a bonanza for his overland freight line.

Of this group only Dillon and Duff, both railroad contractors, were directly involved in the industry. Williams and Glidden operated clipper ships, Bates was a banker, Hazard owned a textile mill, and the Ames brothers manufactured shovels. Most of them expected to play a passive role in the enterprise; Hazard told Lambard he would subscribe only if he did not have to devote an hour's thought or work to the business. Events would later cloak the remark in savage irony, but at the time this attitude suited the Doctor just fine. Desperate as he was for fresh capital, he did not want to surrender control or even share it with new partners. For a time it appeared as if he could have everything his way.

From the first it was apparent that the Ames brothers would be key figures among the newcomers. They were men of means and reputation whose influence could attract other investors. As a member of the House committee on the Pacific railroad Oakes was in a position to help win political support in Congress. The brothers subscribed jointly for two thousand shares of Crédit Mobilier, all of which stood in Oliver's name on the company books. Only three days after the subscriptions were made, Bushnell asked Oakes for a loan of fifty thousand dollars and offered half of his own two thousand shares as collateral. It was but the first of a flood of requests for money that would draw the Ameses ever deeper into the Pacific railroad.

Much has been written about the motives of the Ames brothers in connecting themselves with this enterprise. Oakes alluded to the familiar bedfellows of profit and patriotism as his reasons for going in, but his accounts are too vague and conflicting to be helpful. Over the years the rhetoric inspired by scandal and the tortuous speculations of historians have done little more than cloud the issue. A satisfactory explanation is not difficult to find if one bears in mind an obvious but curiously ignored point: the Ames brothers did not know in the beginning how things would turn out in the end. In making their initial investment, they could not have had the slightest inkling of the extraordinary chain of events that would follow. As one complication piled atop another, they were compelled at each stage to decide anew whether to extend or curtail their commitment. Their involvement was not a plunge but a process of accretion, subtle but inexorable, which drew them ever deeper into the venture until their interest was so large they had no choice but to see the project to completion.

Far from being unique to the Ames brothers, this pattern of involvement was typical of investment in western railroads. Their securities had no market until the road was built, and no profits could be expected until it began operating. The only immediate return lay in profits from construction, but these were paid largely in securities of the road. In short, everything depended on getting the road open for business, which required an enormous outlay of capital at great risk. If the project was a success, profits would flow from operations, from an increase in the value of securities, and from investments in such related sources as land, minerals, and business enterprises along the line. The promise of long-term profits and growth was glowing, but only if the investors could carry the financial load during the period of construction. For the Union Pacific the load was extraordinary in amount and in the length of time it had to be carried.

A large commitment in western railroads was no game for the faint of heart to play. In 1865, however, it seemed a logical arena for the Ames brothers to enter. The westward movement and the war had earned for the shovel works an impressive surplus that needed investing. Already Oakes had made loans to the Central Pacific, and the brothers had put money into Blair's Cedar Rapids road. The venture into the Union Pacific, therefore, was but a logical extension of their Iowa interest. The two projects had a symbiotic relationship that promised large profits if all turned out well. Blair was a tough-minded businessman capable of looking after the Cedar Rapids with little help. The brothers had not yet taken Durant's measure, but they knew Bushnell and Lambard and probably assumed those two worthies could manage the work well enough.

For Crédit Mobilier to succeed, there had to be a generous spread between the contract price and the actual costs of construction. Part of the difference was of course profit to the contractors for the work, but that was only the beginning. A second part covered all the outlays not conveniently lumped under construction, including promotion, lobbying and legal fees, office overhead expenses, travel and other expenses for the government commissioners, advertising, land department expenses, interest on loans, and interest, discount, and commissions on bonds issued. Finally, the spread had to absorb the difference between the face value of the securities received for the work and their actual market value. Stock had by law to be accepted at par even though it could not be sold at anything near that price, and both classes of bonds could be peddled only at heavy discounts. For these reasons the spread must be taken as a measure not merely of profits but of the risks involved. As Bushnell declared, "All admitted that the securities would be worthless if the enterprise fell through before completion."

Approval of the spread required a harmony of interests between the boards of Crédit Mobilier and Union Pacific. In 1865 the same group of men dominated both companies, which insured acceptance of the contract. On April 6 the Union Pacific directors accepted the transfer of Hoxie's contract to Crédit Mobilier. Seven of the fifteen regular directors, including Durant, Dix, and Lambard, and all five government directors were present. Later Charles Sherman testified that the government directors protested the contract but let it go because they considered it binding on the company. He neglected to mention that the government directors could have blocked transfer of the contract simply by voting against it at the April 6 meeting, or that he personally made the motion for its acceptance. It was not the first or the last time that Sherman's memory proved discreetly selective.

Three days after the meeting, Lee surrendered at Appomattox. The war was over, and with it passed the argument that the Pacific road was urgently required for national defense. On April 14 the assassination of Lincoln plunged the nation into gloom and turmoil. The slain President, a staunch friend of the project for so long, did not live to see it completed. In fact he did not live to see it even begun, for in April 1865 the first rail had yet to be laid. The new president, Andrew Johnson, was not known to be a friend of the Pacific railroad. In the aftermath of war and the turbulence of Reconstruction, Congress and the people alike would view the project in a changed light.

With these lightning strokes the march of events overtook the Union Pacific. No one knew what effect the new circumstances would have, but all agreed that to stand still invited disaster. Dodge, now stationed in St. Louis, warned Durant that he would surely have trouble in the next Congress if he did not open forty miles of road by December 1. He suggested a "pleasure party" for Congressmen across the plains, where the wonders of the land and work on the Union Pacific could be shown them. It would, he promised, "do more good than all the money you can spend in Washington." The Iowa roads had to be pushed as well and a federal subsidy got for construction between Des Moines and Council Bluffs. Blair had managed to get aid from his eastern connections; why should the M & M not do the same? Above all, work had to be pressed on the Union Pacific. Dodge put the case to Durant with his usual mixture of savvy and candor. "The war is about to close and the great project before the people will be the Union Pacific," he noted. "You should have this in view and allow no outside projects to attract your attention. It is big enough for the biggest man in America."

Durant was far from the biggest man in America. Having thrust himself onto center stage at last, he proved unequal to the role. His craving for the limelight was matched by an inability to keep his focus on the business at hand. For months he had scattered his energies among a variety of projects while the Union Pacific languished. During the autumn of 1864 he was trying to smuggle cotton out of the South with help from Seymour and Usher in Washington and Lambard in Boston. The Kansas Pacific imbroglio still occupied his attention, and he continued to dicker with Blair over a union of interests in Iowa. Attempts to obtain a land grant for the M & M had been swallowed by events in Washington where, as Seymour reported, "the Presidents death seems to paralyze everything."

During these months the Doctor had arranged the Hoxie contract and transferred it to the Crédit Mobilier, but his preoccupation with larger affairs left in its wake a host of unattended details and unmade decisions. For a year Dey had pressed Durant to buy timberland and contract for ties in advance of construction; in December 1864 Seymour found himself pleading the case anew. Henry needed authorization to contract for truss bridges west of Omaha and dared not put men to work without funds to pay them. "If I knew how much work you would like to have done each month," he wrote tactfully, "we would try to have it done." The force in Omaha cried for a strong hand to take charge. Henry was capable but had too many responsibilities to look after all of them, and his agent refused to take action without direct orders from Durant. Dey had urged the Doctor to appoint a permanent supervisor of work, but to no avail. His departure left the company without a chief engineer and therefore at the mercy of its newly appointed consulting engineer, the ubiquitous Seymour.

The one constant in Omaha was the cry for money to carry on the work. It began during the winter of 1864–65 and would swell over the years to a banshee wail. Contrary to expectations, the new investors in Crédit Mobilier did not provide immediate relief. Several of the subscribers were slow to pay their first assessment. Lambard's friends in Boston paid up promptly and began to wonder why the others were not doing their share. The first clue came in May when Lambard complained to Durant of being "annoyed by some enemies of *yours* in New York who are doing all they can to embarrass & weaken confidence in the Crédit Mobilier, & Pacific RR affairs generally." Lambard did not know who was behind the attacks, but he warned that "their assertions & innuendos in regard to *extravagances, foolish expenditures, & 'probable failures'* help render abortive my efforts for the good of the concern."

Durant brushed the complaint aside and accused Lambard of prying into his affairs and questioning his integrity. Caught off balance, Lambard admitted that months earlier he had inquired into Durant's record in railroad management to satisfy not only himself but those friends he asked to invest in the enterprise. He confessed to being "somewhat staggered by what seems to me a very free use of money," and his friends worried that lagging assessments would jeopardize the work. Oakes Ames for one was uneasy about the situation, but Lambard assured the Doctor that "I have been *always* able to induce Mr. Ames to do anything of the kind I want him to."

The great enterprise was barely underway, and already the first signs of dissension had appeared. It was not an auspicious beginning. The situation demanded that construction be pushed as vigorously as possible. Instead Durant plunged headlong into yet another round of controversy.

The Doctor, Thomas C. Durant *(left, above)*, pulls some figures out of his hat, to the dismay of his detractors: *(clockwise)* Oliver Ames, Oakes Ames, and Rowland G. Hazard. *(Photograph of Oakes Ames courtesy of the National Archives, Rowland G. Hazard courtesy of The Rhode Island Historical Society)*

Grenville M. Dodge *(above)* and four field officers who served with distinction: *(counterclockwise from top left)* Samuel Reed, "Hub" Hoxie, James Evans, and Jack Casement. *(H. M. Hoxie photograph courtesy of the Iowa State Historical Department)*

A meeting of mismatched minds: H. M. Hoxie *(left)* and Sam
Reed watch as *(seated from left)* Silas Seymour, Dillon, Durant,
and Duff transact some business around the table.

And a good time was had by all: *(Right)* On the grand excursion of October 1866 a group of Union Pacific directors pose happily beneath the arch marking the 100th meridian. Note the flag and antlers on the locomotive. *(Courtesy of the National Archives)*

(Below) The party of excursionists pose for one of several group pictures intended as much for publicity as memorabilia. Those sitting in front include Dillon *(far left)*, Dodge *(third from left)*, and Durant *(center)*.

In camp the Doctor (gray hat) chats with some of the guests while, at his feet, the eloquent George Francis Train enjoys a rare moment of silent repose.

The gaggle of reporters invited to join the excursion pause long enough to have their own group picture taken.

The Pawnee soldiers, who first frightened the wits out of the excursionists and then entertained them, pose in front of two of the passenger cars.

4

THE SURVEYS

In 1864 the question of what route the Union Pacific should follow had yet to be answered. The Platte Valley offered an obvious and easy trail from the Missouri to the Rockies. Over the years it had been tramped by buffalo, Indians, fur traders, Mormons, and emigrants bound for Oregon and California. But Dey's surveys of the previous year did not convince skeptics that a feasible line could be found through the rugged, largely unknown terrain of the Rockies. Several crucial questions demanded answers that only more complete surveys could provide.

The first difficulty arose at the fork of the Platte River. The line could follow the Oregon Trail along the North Platte and Sweetwater rivers, crossing the mountains through South Pass to the Green River. Or it could take the South Platte, using either Lodgepole Creek or the Cache la Poudre branches to reach the Black Hills (Laramie Mountains)* and cross the Wyoming Basin to Green River. From Green River a route had to be found across or around the Wasatch Mountains to the Great Salt Lake. At that point the line could be run either south of the lake via Salt Lake City or north of the lake. Once past the lake, a suitable route had to be located across Nevada to the California border. Other factors besides the requirements of engineering were involved in selecting the best line. The company had also to consider probable sources of traffic and trade. Every settlement in the region saw that its destiny hinged on the decision and tried to influence the location in its

---

* During the construction era the Laramie Mountains were usually referred to as the Black Hills. To avoid confusion the latter name will be used here.

favor. The Mormons, whose assistance was vitally needed, were adamant that the road pass through their capital, and Denver pressed its claims vigorously.

No one knew better than Peter Dey the importance of finding a suitable line through the mountains and beyond. During the winter of 1863–64 he organized the road's engineering department and went hunting for capable men to do the surveys that could make or break the company's future. Turning again to the best of those he had known on the Rock Island and M & M, he brought Jacob E. House to Omaha as resident engineer and put James A. Evans and Samuel B. Reed in charge of survey parties. Dey wanted to put two more parties in the field but had trouble finding men to head them. After his first choices declined to serve, he settled on Francis M. Case and Ogden Edwards.

By strenuous efforts Dey managed to wheedle funds from Durant to outfit the parties. Evans was ordered to explore the region from the Black Hills to Green River and Reed from Green River to Salt Lake. Case was assigned the area between the Cache la Poudre and Arkansas rivers, while Edwards confined his work to the Platte and Republican valleys. Each party included two assistant engineers, rodmen, chainmen, axemen, teamsters, herders, and sometimes a hunter to provide meat. Those venturing into Indian country went armed and prepared to fight. Most were veterans of the war and needed little drill. They had no illusions about what lay ahead. It was hard, dangerous work in a wilderness filled with hostile Indians. For hardy men it was also one of the grandest adventures of the age.

* * *

Although Sam Reed did not realize it, his journey westward offered a unique glimpse at the West as it was before the coming of the railroad. In 1864 the train took him only as far as Grinnell, Iowa, where he boarded a stagecoach for Omaha. Tired and cramped, he reached Omaha on a Sunday morning in April and was surprised to find it so crowded and busy. He waited there three weeks for orders, using the time to find out all he could about Utah. Brigham Young took a keen interest in the road and had been one of its original subscribers. He had assisted Dey the previous summer and agreed to outfit Reed's party. One of his sons was in Omaha preparing to lead an emigrant train across the plains. Reed found him helpful and full of valuable information, as were all the Utah men he met in Omaha. All assured him that the Indians posed no danger in the region he was to survey.

When his orders finally arrived on April 28, Reed found it impossible to book passage on a stage. The discovery of gold in Montana had created a stampede of fortune seekers. "Hundreds pass through here every day," Reed observed wryly, "old men, young men, the lame and the blind with women and children all going westward seeking the promised land." He took a boat downriver to Atchison and managed to get seats on a stage for himself and an assistant named Mathewson. Atchison was crowded not only with gold seekers but with runaway slaves from Missouri as well. Dozens of newcomers arrived daily, hoping to get passage west only to be told they must wait. The stage line raised the fare to $200 and charged a dollar a pound for luggage above twenty-five pounds, which cost Reed another $150 for his instruments.

On May 7 the two engineers squeezed into the coach with seven other passengers and started west. For thirteen days and nights the stage rattled monotonously onward except when storms or mud forced the driver to lay up. During one downpour the passengers were grateful to find refuge on beds of hay in a stable; another night was spent jostling for space on a rancher's floor. The hills of southern Nebraska looked dreary and desolate to Reed, broken only by an occasional cabin or stage station, where teams were changed and a meal of bacon and hard bread could be gulped down. At one stop the passengers all got sick from drinking alkali water. On the road the hours passed like days in the cramped, jouncing coach.

A week after leaving Atchison the stage pulled into Latham Station, where the Denver passengers changed coaches. Reed and Mathewson alone continued through the mountains, crossing the divide at Bridger's Pass. Reed had his first glimpse at the Rockies, the barrier through which he was expected to find an opening. At journey's end Salt Lake City came as no less a revelation to the tired and dirty Reed than the towering ranges that shielded it from the outside world. Reed did not share the prejudice of most Americans against the Mormons, but he was astounded to discover that their Zion in the Wilderness was something more than myth. "I have never been in a town of this size in the United States where everything is kept in such perfect order," he marveled. "No hogs or cattle [are] allowed to run at large in the streets and every available nook of ground is made to bring forth fruit, vegetables or flowers for man's use."

Brigham Young greeted the engineers warmly and provided them with three teams, tents, camp equipment, and fifteen men, all able and willing but green. Reed gave them a week of training and headed north to where the Weber River emerged from the mountains into Salt Lake Valley. By pure coincidence he commenced his survey not far from the spot that five years later would become the western terminus of the Union Pacific Railroad. Entering the canyon, Reed was awed by the sight of the deep narrow gorge through which the river snaked between towering walls of mountains rising several thousand feet. It was, he enthused, "the wildest place you can imagine." He had found Devil's Gate.

For nearly four months the party hacked its way through thick brush and clambered along canyon walls. Occasionally they stumbled onto a valley tucked behind the ridges and were grateful for the relief from their exertions. At night they slept on the ground beneath buffalo robes. Food was plentiful while they lingered near the Mormon settlements scattered through the valleys. On Young's orders the faithful furnished the surveyors with fresh mutton, butter, eggs, and milk. Reed's men caught trout and shot an occasional antelope to vary their diet of bacon, bread, beans, and dried fruit. "I can eat more at a meal than ever before in my life," Reed wrote happily, "and don't care how often the meals occur."

Fieldwork had a bewitching effect on engineers, and already its magic had begun to affect Reed. The harder he worked, the better he felt. The challenge of finding a good line through the wilderness drove him joyously onward. He came to love the country itself—its spectacular beauty, the hard, clean brilliance of the air, the warm days, and cold nights when ice as thick as window panes formed on the dishes even in summer. Life was elemental and palpable, stripped of all cant, transparent in its excitement as well as its dangers. Reed had made in fact what would become in fiction a central theme of the American experience: the pilgrimage from civilization back to nature. He would not be the only engineer to treasure that journey as a time when, for a few brief months, his life seemed to transcend the mundane level of ordinary affairs. Nor was he alone in failing to see the irony in his mission. He had come as agent of those forces eager to transform the wilderness by harnessing it to the blessings of civilization and progress.

It was not the same for all the men. Mathewson lacked the stamina to endure the rigors of field life and had to be sent back to Salt Lake City for a time to recuperate. The Mormon volunteers saw no magic in the wilderness, but they were sturdy, dutiful, and intelligent. Only once did they cause trouble, by striking over wages. Brigham Young showed no sympathy for the protests. He responded with a stern letter admonishing the men to complete all work before showing their faces again in Salt Lake City. The men complied meekly and Reed heard nothing more on the subject. It was the only intrusion from the outside world on his work that summer.

The first line Reed roughed out ran from Salt Lake City to the mouth of Weber River Canyon, up the river to Echo Creek, then followed that stream across the mountains to Sulphur Creek, a tributary of Bear River. It proved a better line than he dared hope. He tried another line eastward across the range to Bear River via Chalk Creek and found it inferior. With the help of an old explorer who knew the country, Reed extended his survey from Bear River over the summit eastward, following Muddy Creek and Black's Fork to Green River, where he was to connect with Evans's line. He tried to explore the region between the Green River and Bitter Creek, but reports of hostile Indians limited his movements. Much of the country was desert unrelieved by vegetation except for scattered patches of greasewood or sagebrush. The slate gray mountain walls were also barren of growth, and the water in some creeks was so black with alkali that it reminded Reed of strong lye. For several days the surveyors could find no drinking water beyond what they carried with them in kegs.

Reed returned to the capital in mid-August and pitched his tent in Brigham Young's yard. The next day a telegram arrived with orders to run a second line south of the city down the Timpanogas River. Wearily he took a reduced party out for another two months of surveying. The results were disappointing. For a time Reed prowled through the Wasatch, Uinta, and Bear River mountains, searching in vain for an opening through which the road might pass. The results satisfied him that the original Weber River–Echo Creek line was the best route available. His argument was convincing, for the railroad was built along that line.

Reed finished this work on October 21 and hurried back to settle his accounts with Young. It was late in the season, and the weather had begun to turn. He was exhausted and eager to get home, but no sooner had he arranged his departure than a telegram arrived with orders to explore on horseback the desert country west of the city. Unable to get a horse and someone to accompany him, he decided to put it off until the following summer. It was a wise choice, for he had already lingered too long. The journey back to Omaha was a nightmare, twenty bone-rattling days and nights of riding through blizzards and fierce winds that, he moaned, "almost froze the life blood out of me."

* * *

Like Reed, the other surveyors ran out of time. Delays in orders from New York caused them to start late, and Indian uprisings that summer hampered their movements. Although tales of the raids filtered into Utah, Reed managed to avoid trouble. His only encounter came with a band of Utes who welcomed him after learning he was with Mormons. "All the Indians in this part of the country," he discovered, "fear and respect the head of the church in Utah." Sandpitz, the chief, begged some supplies but assured Reed solemnly that "Wino (goog) chief go anywhere, Indians no hurt and no steal from Wino chief, Indians steal from bad men only."

Evans was not so fortunate. A detachment of cavalry escorted his party to the place where his survey was to commence, an abandoned camp at the eastern base of the Black Hills, and stayed with them through the summer. On the march from Fort Kearney to the valley of Lodgepole Creek, Evans found what he deemed an excellent line except for its lack of timber. From the campsite he crossed Cheyenne Pass and trekked across the Laramie Plains through Rattlesnake Pass to the North Platte River, which curled along the Medicine Bow Range. Evans ran his line along the river to Bridger's Pass, then crossed to a branch of Muddy Creek and followed it to the broad tableland at the head of Bitter Creek. From there the valley along the creek offered a good line to the junction with Green River.

West of Rattlesnake Pass, Evans found the country progressively more barren. Once at Bitter Creek he was obliged to run his line with unseemly haste, sometimes covering twelve miles a day because he could find no forage for his animals. All along the route he inventoried the available timber and searched for evidence of coal. Dey had urged Durant to send a geologist with

Evans, but his requests were ignored. Nevertheless Evans concluded from his own observations that coal could be found in abundance.

Although Evans had found a promising line, he was not satisfied with the results. The most glaring defect was the lack of a good line across the Black Hills. Evans reached the Green River on July 26 and started back at once to explore the country south of his line through the Black Hills and the canyon of the Laramie River. He did not have time to do all he wished, and what he found disappointed him. Laramie canyon was unsuitable for a railroad, and elevations at the crest on the west side of the Black Hills range were too great. Orders reached Evans at Fort Halleck asking him to examine South Pass on his way home, but the Indian uprising had alarmed the entire region from Fort Laramie to the South Pass. Without an escort or transportation, Evans reluctantly gave up the idea. Instead he discussed the route with Jim Bridger, who offered some useful advice on the difficulties of a line up the North Platte.

Evans returned to Omaha without having found a line through the Black Hills. To the south Case fared little better. His party investigated six passes through the southern Rockies on the upper reaches of the South Platte and surveyed two of them. All of them had the same defects: high elevations, heavy snowfall, and steep slopes that would require tunneling. An old trapper told Case he could find a line through either Rabbit Ear or Georgia Pass, but Case was skeptical. Instead he surveyed the Cache la Poudre route through Antelope Pass onto the Laramie Plains, where he reached Evans's line. One possibility struck his eye in the form of a line across the Black Hills through some pass at the head of Crow Creek or Box Elder Creek. Since the foot of the mountains was much higher than the point where Evans began his survey, a uniform grade to the summit might be found. Case did not discover any such pass, but he knew one had been mentioned in the report by Captain Howard Stansbury, who had done the Pacific survey in 1853. He urged the company to search for it next season.

The survey parties of 1864 did splendid work under difficult circumstances. Their findings confirmed the feasibility of a continuous line across the mountains provided certain problems could be solved. The most critical need was a suitable passage through the Black Hills. The engineers hoped also to discover a better route to the Green River via the North Platte, and they had yet to determine whether the road should run to the north or south of Great Salt Lake. Finally, a favorable line had to be found from the lake to the California border. These questions would comprise their agenda for the coming season.

* * *

On the plains, where the work should have been easy, everything went wrong. The party under Ogden Edwards had only to locate the line across the Platte Valley, but it managed to get only as far as the 100th meridian. Indian raids terrorized the entire region west of Fort Kearney, disrupting wagon trains and driving out settlers. Three times Edwards tried to approach the area between the Platte and Republican rivers only to find Indians concentrated there in large numbers. The military was anxious to help, but all its troops were needed to protect the overland stage route. As late as November Dey informed Durant that "the part of the Republican Valley that you want explored is the camping ground of several Indian tribes very hostile." Nothing could be done without an escort of at least a hundred men, which the army could not spare.

As if there were not problems enough on the lines yet unsurveyed, a crisis boiled up on that portion already approved and under construction. It happened that the worst grades encountered across Nebraska lay in the first twenty-one mile stretch between Omaha and the Elkhorn River. Dey located his line straight across this plateau of rolling hills, arguing that its directness compensated for maximum grades that could be reduced later. Durant accepted his argument and so did Lincoln, who approved Dey's map on November 4, 1864. Considerable excavating and grading had already been done on the section when Silas Seymour unexpectedly reopened the question by suggesting a change in Dey's original line.

During his tenure with the Union Pacific, Seymour perfected the art of finding fault with lines surveyed by others. Whether he took this mission upon himself or was charged with it by Durant remains unclear, but Dey was the first to feel its effects. In December Seymour recommended a change that would reduce grades by adding nine miles of track in the form of an arc or "ox-bow." To do this meant abandoning work already done, incurring the expense of extra construction, and getting the President's approval for the new line. Dey protested vehemently any alteration based on what he called the "undigested views of Mr. Seymour, who cannot know the relative advantages of one route over another, because he has not been over the country, and, from the tenor of his letter, not even examined the profiles in the New York office."

But Dey had no influence with Durant and had already resigned his position. Seymour managed to enlist the support of government director Jesse L. Williams and five prominent engineers. In January 1865 the Union Pacific board approved the change and Durant ordered work begun on the ox-bow line. He could not have overlooked the fact that nine extra miles of road would fetch the company another $144,000 in government bonds and 115,200 acres of land besides allowing it to issue another $144,000 of its own bonds for construction that Seymour insisted would be cheaper than Dey's original line. However, the Doctor soon discovered that his action inflamed another controversy of his own making.

Although Lincoln's order of March 1864 appeared to settle the terminus question, some Omaha citizens remained unconvinced. Rumors still floated that Durant intended to move the terminus if it served his connections with the Iowa roads or the Kansas Pacific. Despite generous donations of land, the company still had not secured all it needed for a right-of-way. A few holders wanted to see work started on buildings or track layed before parting with their land. The resignation of Dey, followed closely by the ox-bow incident, rekindled fears about Durant's intentions. Asked for reassurance, the Doctor replied blandly, "The line has been changed to avoid heavy grades, not with intention of interfering with terminus. See engineer's report."

In fact the ox-bow could also be used as part of a line from Bellevue, nine miles downriver from Omaha. Dey had earlier termed the Bellevue route an excellent one, and in March 1865 Henry called it "in point of grades, and expense of building, all that could be asked for." To complicate matters, work on the ox-bow proceeded even though the President's approval for the change had not yet been secured. The company was short of money, expenses were piling up, and its credit was shaky in Omaha. On May 12 Dix finally sought President Johnson's permission for the change only to encounter delays which Durant attributed to opposition from Omaha. The Doctor responded by instructing House to "make no permanent investments at Omaha" and ordering a survey made from Bellevue to the ox-bow. A few days later he wired House to arrange for temporary track from Bellevue and facilities for a sawmill there. "Do no work north of Junction," he added. "We have no time to loose [sic] and must commence at Bellevue as our only alternative to save enterprise." Boats carrying iron from St. Louis were ordered to land at Bellevue.

These dispatches raised a storm of protest in both Omaha and Council Bluffs. Public meetings were held, citizens' committees appointed, and protests voiced in print. Dodge, who had been sent to Leavenworth to campaign against the Indians, found himself deluged with letters and telegrams sounding the alarm. He thought Durant had acted "simply to threaten and scare Omaha," but as usual the Doctor's motives were more complex. He may have hoped to frighten the landowners trying to extract high prices into more reasonable settlements. The line change might also force opponents of the ox-bow route to reconsider and help Durant obtain quick approval from Washington.

Whatever his reasons, Durant found himself embroiled in battle at a time when he could least afford it. His name had already been tarnished that spring by a congressional investigation into cotton speculations with Confederate agents. Some newspapers were calling the Union Pacific a "rotten" enterprise in the hands of manipulators. The Omaha citizens' committee accused Durant of a "covert design to change the terminus for speculative purposes." The uproar prompted Dodge to intervene by pacifying the citizens' committee and warning Durant that he could not fight the entire western contingent in Congress and hope to win. The important thing, he stressed anew, was to get forty miles of road built.

Durant gestured weakly at pacifying the Omaha interests but continued work on the ox-bow. He did not intend building from Omaha to the junction this year, regardless of whether the government approved the line or forced him to keep the old one. "Bridges and iron are laying at Bellevue," he wired Dodge. "It is this or nothing done this year."

"The Doctor is pursuing a suicidal course," Hoxie cried, and Dodge agreed. "Your plan won't work," he told Durant bluntly. The government would not permit a change of terminus and would reject the ox-bow unless it connected with Omaha. Any other tactic would "lose the ablest support the road has in the West." Still Durant would not listen. "The plan will be carried out or the works abandoned," he thundered. ". . . This is too important an enterprise to be controlled by a local interest. The road can be built by the Kansas line if in no other way. No road through Iowa will terminate at Omaha. If line with heavy grades is adopted the M. & M. will be abandoned for the present."

In this one telegram the Doctor revealed the conflicting tangle of his interests. No one yet knew that his threats were a game of bluff. He was being shoved out of both the Kansas Pacific and the M & M, but the weaker his hand the more he played as if he held all the cards. When the citizens' committee offered to aid the ox-bow line if Durant would assure them that Omaha would remain the terminus, the Doctor dismissed the compromise with imperious scorn. "We will consult the interests of the road," he snapped, "whether citizens of Omaha aid us or not; we have had enough of interference. You will destroy your last chance for a connection. [The] Cedar Rapids road will cross above you, and you can have no eastern connection. The line west will do you no good. I can connect the Mississippi and Missouri with the Cedar Rapids road and run to De Soto, for a million dollars less than go to Omaha."

While demonstrating again his gift for antagonizing those whose help he needed most, Durant also played the one good card he held. Usher had been replaced as Secretary of the Interior by none other than James Harlan of Iowa, who was closer to Durant than anyone suspected. Their relationship went back to the campaign to secure the Act of 1862, during which Harlan urged the Doctor to "go into the new corporation and in this way control its destiny." Having received financial help from Durant in the past, Harlan now returned the favor by appointing Lieutenant Colonel James H. Simpson of the Engineer Corps to make an independent survey of the disputed line. The Doctor was elated. "All we want is to act in concert with the Gov't and have the road built as rapidly as possible," he cooed to Harlan. "Tell us what you want us to do and we will either do it or give you a good reason why it is not done."

At last Durant saw the gravity of the crisis he had spawned. The ox-bow incident had cost the company dearly in time lost and money wasted on duplicate lines. Dodge was right: Durant had to lay track as fast as possible, not only to get the funds he desperately needed but also to convince Congress

and investors that the enterprise was legitimate. He could not lay much track
while the location of the line remained uncertain, and he found it hard to
raise money to keep the work going. The cotton investigation damaged his
reputation; rumors asserted that he would be prosecuted for blockade running and that losses in gold and cotton speculations made his notes dangerous. In Omaha the Doctor had lost both his credit and his credibility.

After months of delay, controversy, and indecision, Durant burst into a
frenzy of activity. He had hoped to lay a hundred miles of track that summer;
now he would be lucky to complete sixty. He fired waspish directives in all
directions and tried to impress Harlan that "every day now is worth a week
to us two months hence." But Simpson and government director Springer
Harbaugh did not reach Omaha until July 4, and their work went slowly.
They heard testimony from the citizens' committee, solicited the views of
Dey, and studied the findings of D. H. Ainsworth, who was acting as chief
engineer. With Seymour at his elbow, Simpson made his own survey of the
disputed lines. Seymour was confident of influencing Simpson's decision if
only he could figure out what Durant really wanted. "I feel anxious to serve
you," he wrote, "but in order to do so intelligently & effectively, you must
keep me posted fully." Lest Durant miss the point, he added, "A great deal of
money can be made at Bellevue if some *things* can be known in advance."

Simpson's labors consumed six weeks. During that time the Omaha interests worked doggedly to strike a compromise with Durant. Dr. George L.
Miller, editor of the Omaha *Herald,* tried with Dodge's help to ease the
tension, but Durant would not relent. In a long letter to Dodge he insisted
that "neither yourself nor the citizens of Omaha seem fully to comprehend
this matter of change of line." He blamed the delays largely on Harlan, who
had "certainly misunderstood the whole thing," and blithely declared it "unfortunate that Mr. Harlan should have interfered in this matter at all." On
the terminus question Durant gave Omaha cold comfort. He warned Dodge
of "a stronger influence over the country in favor of a terminus south of that
place than you are aware of. My motto is, first the road—local interest,
afterwards."

A dejected Miller grumbled that "Durant gives his friends no ground to
stand on." In Omaha the Doctor had few friends left. Henry found it difficult
to get credit or currency for his crews, and a landowner along the ox-bow
applied for an injunction to stop work there. When Dey submitted his views
to Simpson as requested, Durant countered with a bitter tirade against his
former engineer, protesting that he should never have been consulted. Beset
from all sides, Simpson finished his surveys late in August and submitted his
report to Harlan on September 18. Far from dousing the fires of controversy,
it succeeded only in fanning the flames.

In effect Simpson recommended a line different from that surveyed by Dey
or proposed by Seymour. Known as the Child's Mill line, it also differed from
the route on which the company had already done work. To complicate

matters, Simpson declared the Bellevue line 30 percent better than any other route and predicted that the roads building through Iowa would force the terminus to be relocated there. He advocated the Child's Mill line on the assumption that the road had to commence at Omaha; even then he approved it only when the company agreed to amend the line according to a survey made by Ainsworth. Harlan endorsed the report and President Johnson approved it on the express condition that the proposed amendments be incorporated into the line.

Durant had his line but the cost was high. At a time when money was scarce and time precious, the fight wasted ten months and about $500,000 spent on work abandoned and new work to replace it. The loss in credibility and good will was incalculable. The Chicago *Tribune* called the change an "outrage" perpetrated by "a set of unprincipled swindlers" intent on "building the road at the largest possible expense to the Government and the least possible expense to themselves." In Omaha the Doctor had in effect fouled the company's own nest. So deeply did the bitterness run that forty-five years later an oldtimer called it a "seismic subject" still rankling "in the minds of the surviving few."

The change may have been good engineering, but it was bad politics. As matters turned out, it was not even good engineering. Time proved Simpson wrong in all his conclusions. No Iowa road terminated at Bellevue or tried to bridge the river there. The estimates of improvements in Dey's line made by Simpson and Ainsworth never panned out. In building the ox-bow Durant completely ignored the proviso for an amended line, and the government examiners accepted the finished road even though it violated the conditions imposed by the government. After reading Simpson's report, Dey said of his own line, "I contend I am right in that location if Omaha was to be the starting point." He lived long enough to witness his vindication. When E. H. Harriman straightened the main line in 1908, he constructed the "Lane Cut-Off" directly across the route laid out by Dey.

* * *

Long before spring the engineers were itching to go out again. Case admitted to being "a little tired of city life" and hoped for another appointment. Young Fred Hodges, who had served the previous summer as rodman for Case, was eager for promotion to transit man. Both got their wishes. Seymour organized the parties into two divisions working opposite sides of the continental divide. Reed took charge of the Pacific division and Evans the Atlantic, with Case as his assistant. All three men went back for another look at the regions they had explored the year before. In the Platte Valley, Edwards tried again to locate a hundred miles of line west of the Loup River. The Indian menace had grown worse since the infamous Chivington Massacre in November 1864 and would hamper the surveyors' movements throughout the summer.

Reed started west from Omaha with two assistants on May 14. At Fort Kearney the stage picked up a military escort for the ride to Denver. Along the route the settlers had long since fled and most of the buildings had been burned by Indians. In Salt Lake City Brigham Young again outfitted the engineers with men and supplies. Reed tried first to find a line from Weber Canyon to the Green River by crossing the Wasatch Mountains south of the towering Uinta Mountains. The search convinced him that no practical route could be located there. After picking up an escort at Fort Bridger, he explored a line through South Pass but ruled it out as well. The route was much longer, and oldtimers in the region warned him that storms clogged the pass with snow every winter. Nothing looked promising along the Wind River Range.

Discouraged, Reed returned to Salt Lake City to await instructions from Durant about surveys west of the lake. To his dismay the Indians had cut all communication by telegraph and mail. Durant telegraphed orders on August 17, but the message did not reach the Mormon capital until September 7. By that time Reed had taken Brigham Young's advice to run the line across the desert south of Great Salt Lake that he had been unable to survey the previous year. With great difficulty he located some 285 miles of line through the mountains and valleys of the desert to the Humboldt River. Water was scarce and the men were blinded by the glare from the salt-alkali crust. Reed had to leave the last seventy-five miles of desert unsurveyed because he could not find water, but he came home satisfied that a line could be run into the Humboldt Valley with grades not exceeding seventy-five feet. He advised building eastward from California with the help of camels.

On the other side of the divide Evans was instructed to search for a better route across the Black Hills than either Cheyenne or Antelope Pass. He was also to explore the region west of the North Platte and south of Bridger's Pass. If nothing turned up there, he was to examine the country between the Cache la Poudre and Lodgepole valleys. Convinced by his previous surveys that he had found the best line from the Laramie River to Green River, Evans concentrated this time on the Black Hills conundrum. He thought the best hope lay along the South Platte and Cache la Poudre rivers, but he could find no better crossing to the Laramie Plains than Antelope Pass. Despite its shortcomings this line met the requirements imposed by the government and seemed the best of a bad lot. Evans tried a new line from Lodgepole via Crow Creek to a new pass later named in his honor. It was longer and lower at the summit than the Cheyenne Pass route, shorter and higher than that through Antelope Pass. To the north Case found the Laramie River canyon impossible for a railroad and saw little value in following the North Platte around the Laramie Mountains. The hope Evans held for South Pass would later be dashed by Reed's work.

On the plains Edwards pushed his surveys despite constant threat of attack. At Fort Kearney a few of his men deserted rather than head into Indian country. His escort of Missouri cavalry was surly to the point of insubordination, complaining that they had enlisted to fight the rebels, not wander about the wilderness chasing Indians. At night every man in the party emptied his cartridges into his hat and slept with loaded carbine in his blanket and a pistol next to his head. Early in November Edwards reached the 100th meridian, wrapped up his survey, and started the return march. Two days later Evans galloped into camp and announced that he had orders to extend the survey past the 100th meridian. The men grumbled, none more loudly than the troopers. Evans ordered the survey party into line and asked those unwilling to go back to step forward three paces. There was some shuffling about, but no one stepped forward.

Sullenly the troopers followed the party back across the chilly Platte into the teeth of an oncoming storm. The weather had turned cold, and as snow began to fall they marched past the graves of a dozen men killed recently in an Indian raid. Undaunted, Evans led them into an area where some of the worst fighting had occurred, the region between the Platte and Republican rivers. "This is a terrible country," wrote an uneasy engineer, "the stillness, wildness & desolation of which is awful. Not a hill to be seen, nothing but a sucession of hill & valley." They were startled by herds of buffalo and wild horses, but the Indians left them alone long enough for Evans to complete his work.

In all, the engineers ran an impressive 1,254 miles of line that season. They collected much valuable information that confirmed the viability of the route in some areas and narrowed the possibilities elsewhere. Two major problems remained unsolved. Evans's line through the Black Hills barrier was marginal at best, and the route west of Great Salt Lake was still undecided. No one expected the next year's work to be any easier. "The hostility of the Indians (everywhere) made explorations extremely difficult and dangerous," Evans reported. "Until they are exterminated, or so far reduced in numbers as to make their power contemptible, no safety will be found in that vast district extending from Fort Kearney to the mountains, and beyond."

Ironically, the same Indians who had done so much to hamper the surveys inadvertently provided the most important discovery of the year. The recipient of this stroke of luck was Dodge, who had been put in charge of the Indian campaign and had gone west to take command personally. In September Dodge decided to reconnoiter the Black Hills, a region dear to the Indians and the Union Pacific alike. Both were very much on Dodge's mind. The Indian uprising complicated the railroad's work and Dodge's own future. Durant still wanted him as chief engineer once he could get free of the army, which depended in part on the outcome of the plains campaign. An expedition to the Black Hills enabled Dodge to survey the terrain for signs of Indians and a good line for the road at the same time. He understood the problem that stymied Evans; the engineers had kept him fully informed of their work all summer. Dodge knew they could get onto the Laramie Plains with a decent grade but had found no way to penetrate the eastern slope with a grade of less than 116 feet.

From Fort Laramie Dodge led his small command as far north as the divide between the North Platte and Powder rivers. This was country little known to white men. To the northwest lay the Big Horn Mountains, the sacred enclave of the Sioux, Crow, and Arapahoes. Satisfied that only a bloody war could claim the region for a railroad or anyone else, Dodge turned back and followed Chugwater Creek to the eastern slope of the Laramie Mountains. From there he headed south to Lodgepole Creek, scanning the mountains constantly for a suitable pass. Nothing turned up. Leaving his wagon train to follow the base of the mountains, Dodge took two scouts and a dozen troopers with him to explore Cheyenne Pass. A few hours later, as they neared the summit, one of the scouts looked back and saw a large band of Crow Indians between the detachment and the distant wagons. "I saw in a moment that we were likely to get into trouble," Dodge recalled. "They had discovered us about the same time we discovered them."

Quickly Dodge dismounted his men, put the horses under cover to protect them, and started his men down the summit. He set a fire on the ridge to attract the attention of his other troopers. This was a prearranged signal for trouble, but somehow the cavalry did not see the smoke. For a time Dodge's men played cat and mouse with the hostiles, slowing their progress with a few well-aimed shots. A small body of Crow worked through the rocks trying to cut the troopers off, but before they succeeded the cavalry noticed the smoke and galloped toward the ridge. At their approach the Indians fled down a branch of Crow Creek.

Once out of danger, Dodge's eye was drawn to the ridge along which the Indians had escaped. He followed it down to the plains and discovered that he was on the divide between a branch of Crow Creek and another stream. Carefully he marked the spot by the lone tree near what would later be called Lone Tree Creek. Gazing back at the unexpectedly gentle slope he had scrambled down, he knew at once what he had found. In a calm voice that concealed his excitement, Dodge told the men that if they got out with their scalps he thought he had discovered a line through the Black Hills.

5

THE ORGANIZATION

The first rail went down in Omaha July 10, 1865, on the bottomland near the ferry. Unlike the groundbreaking ceremony eighteen months earlier, the mood was anything but festive. The townspeople were furious with Durant over the ox-bow incident and unimpressed by the laying of a few measly strips of iron. There were no crowds to cheer, no bands to play, and only a small force of workmen to watch because most had been laid off for want of money to pay them. The first locomotive had arrived two days earlier and sat forlornly like a beached whale. For several weeks it would have little over a mile of track on which to roam. Government director Springer Harbaugh tried to lift the gloom by telegraphing Dix his hope that the "locomotive power of this government will vigorously prosecute this great national work to the Pacific."

The event was buried in obscurity because at that moment the first forty miles of track seemed as remote as the Rocky Mountains. Durant blamed the lack of progress on the government's delay in approving the line, but the fault lay closer to home. The ox-bow incident was a crisis of his own making, and it compounded a more fundamental error of neglect on the Doctor's part. The building of a railroad in so remote a place was a logistical nightmare, especially with regard to the transporting of supplies. No Iowa railroad yet extended past Grinnell. The nearest rail link was the Hannibal & St. Joseph, which reached the Missouri 175 winding miles downstream from Omaha. The river was navigable by steamboat only for three or four months during the spring rise; even then, sandbars and snags made passage treacherous.

Otherwise goods had to be hauled by wagon to Council Bluffs and ferried across to Omaha.

Under these conditions procurement became a herculean task. Heavy, cumbersome loads of iron rails, chairs, fish plates, spikes, bolts, locomotives, rolling stock, shop equipment, tools, and countless other items had to be conveyed to Omaha in huge quantities. Stockpiling goods was expensive, but if the right materials were not on hand when needed, the crews sat idle. Nothing bedeviled the company more than the lack of good lumber. Immense amounts were needed for ties, trestles, buildings, and other purposes. Every mile of track used about 2,500 ties, which made them a costly investment. Cottonwood, the only native wood available in quantity, was too soft and perishable for most uses. Railroad men knew that cottonwood would not do for ties, but the cost of importing good hardwood was prohibitive.

Solving these problems required above all else an efficient organization to coordinate the engineering, construction, and supply efforts. In the end Durant's fatal flaw was his inability to create such an organization. He was by nature and temperament wholly unsuited for the task. Perhaps the job was too big for any man, but certainly he was not a big enough man for it. Distracted by problems of finance and his own muddled interests, he could not give close attention to matters in the field. Yet he refused to delegate authority to subordinates on the scene who were better versed than himself. He insisted on making all important decisions personally but had no time to consider them. The result was inevitably delay and confusion compounded by the Doctor's habit of changing his mind frequently.

Instead of building an organization, Durant improvised as he went along, taking care to keep ultimate authority firmly in his own hands. Railroad men accustomed to orderly methods of procedure found this lack of system exasperating. Durant aggravated their discomfort with his talent for antagonizing everyone who worked for him. Ever the man on horseback, he issued orders in a tone that was imperious if not insulting. The Doctor's peculiar methods and his insensitivity had the effect of demoralizing the most loyal of subordinates. Already he had driven off his best engineer and was content to leave the position open until Dodge got free of the army, relying meanwhile on the supervision of Henry and the advice of Seymour. After some fumbling, Hoxie was made transfer agent to oversee the transporting of supplies.

This was hardly a staff or an organization equal to the enormity of the task. Laborers were still in short supply. Henry brought men over from Iowa but had trouble keeping them because Durant was slow meeting the payrolls. Dodge went so far as to offer captive Indians for the grading. The war's end ultimately released thousands of men eager for work, but by that time Henry had contracted to import a force of Irishmen. The Irish worked hard but they were volatile and turned surly when their pay was not forthcoming, which was more often than not. "What a happy time we have been having here for the last four weeks," a weary Henry reported in July, "with drunken Irishmen after their pay, I can assure you it is enough to make men crazy."

Journalists following the progress of the Great National Highway found in California a refreshing contrast to the delays and disorder in Omaha. There Charles Crocker persuaded his reluctant associates to fill the construction gangs with docile, hard-working Chinese. Some 1,800 men were reported at work on the Central Pacific, and efforts to raise money were beginning to show results. Although it was much too early to talk of a race between the two roads, there was little doubt as to which one was making the most progress.

* * *

The cry for money was incessant. Durant's hope that the funds raised from new subscribers to Crédit Mobilier would see the work through the summer was dashed by his extravagance and the imbroglio over the ox-bow. With great fanfare the Union Pacific attempted a public stock subscription that spring, but, according to Charles Sherman, the offering flopped so badly that "not a dollar was subscribed." Gloomily the company abandoned all effort to finance the work by sale of stock and in May negotiated the first of many loans. "For a year or two we . . . paid 19 percent for money in New York," Oliver Ames recalled. "We were deeply in debt and very much embarrassed, and we were using our credit to the utmost extent in driving the work along."

During these bleak days the Union Pacific needed nothing more than good credit. Durant's antics had done little to help and much to hurt its standing. "You do spend an *awful* pile of money," Charles Lambard told the Doctor only half in jest, "& I doubt if we can raise en[ou]gh to keep you going." For his part Lambard was annoyed at the constant demands placed on him. "I shall charge *roundly* for such services," he promised, "as I am a small stockholder & am working very hard for others benefit." Grudgingly Durant realized that more capital was required than he or his friends could procure. Help was needed from someone with the influence and prestige to inspire confidence among investors. One obvious choice was Oakes Ames.

In 1865 the Union Pacific had no more prominent or prosperous friend than Oakes Ames. For two decades the family shovel works had done a spectacular business thanks to the westward movement, the California gold rush, railroad building, and the Civil War. The brothers had a large fortune to invest and had already put money into Iowa railroads. They had gone into Crédit Mobilier as an extension of that interest. Through his work in Congress, Oakes was intimately acquainted with the Pacific road and one of its staunchest political supporters. He was popular and respected in Washington as a hard-working committeeman who wasted little time on speeches.

That spring Oakes got wind of a complaint by a government director that the company was "not doing anything towards building the Road, and that the Act would be repealed next winter." In June he went to Chicago, heard a progress report from Henry, and came home satisfied that the most pressing need was money. He took more Crédit Mobilier stock for himself and persuaded John B. Alley, Samuel Hooper, and other friends to subscribe. On one occasion he negotiated a loan from the Bank of Commerce in Boston and also induced its president, Benjamin E. Bates, to buy Crédit Mobilier. Other directors recruited new investors, including Oliver S. Chapman and Cyrus H. McCormick, but none worked as hard at it as Ames. When Lambard could not cover Durant's drafts or new subscribers were slow to pay, Oakes raised the money. By summer's end he had become the driving force behind the quest for new sources of capital.

Still it was not enough. Durant ran through money faster than his associates could collect it until even Oakes complained that "I dont see how I am to pay these drafts." More investors were needed, which meant that Crédit Mobilier had to issue more stock. "You better have the capital increased to 2½ or even three millions than to be so cramped for money," Oakes advised. Durant agreed reluctantly. As president of Crédit Mobilier and vice president of Union Pacific, the Doctor still had control of the enterprise in his own hands. Already the newcomers diluted his unilateral authority over its affairs; the issue of more stock might bring more new faces aboard. But the shortage of funds left Durant no choice. In September steps were taken to increase Crédit Mobilier's stock to $2.5 million. Earlier its Railway Bureau, which had authority to approve all contracts, payments, and appointments, had been expanded from five to seven members.

A subtle turning point had been reached. To relieve the money cramp Durant could not avoid having his style cramped. He would find it more difficult to pack committees or the enlarged bureau with his friends, and the Bostonians showed no inclination to give him free rein with their money. John M. S. Williams was the first to let the Doctor know of their uneasiness over his secretive ways. In doing so he put his finger on the organizational duality that would haunt them all through years of bitter dispute:

> We are associated with you in the management of the Credit Mobilier & thus become in fact (with you) the actual managing Builders of the U Pac R Road *(& will be held responsible as such)* —We have an Organization ahead of us—the *Rail Road Company* —in whose management *you* lead—but in which we are not recognized, thus you have power and authority which we do not.
>
> But, for the purposes of the Credit Mobilier, it is necessary that we should know *all* that is going on, & that I should have free access to all Books and papers. . . .

* * *

Progress on the Union Pacific would always be measured in twenty-mile sections, the yardstick that fetched bonds and land from the government and allowed the company to issue its own bonds. The law required completion of the first hundred miles by June 27, 1866. Durant had talked confidently of building that amount during 1865, but the ox-bow incident destroyed that possibility. In September he conceded privately that the company would be lucky to complete sixty miles that year. Using the new funds raised by Ames, the Doctor mounted a desperate campaign to reach that goal.

Throughout the spring Hoxie grappled with procuring transportation for iron and other supplies at the cheapest price. By early July he managed to deliver enough material to Omaha for the tracklaying to begin in earnest. On the roadbed crews had graded about fifty miles, every foot of it tough, back-breaking labor. Crude scrapers drawn by animals smoothed the bed after the excess dirt had been hauled away by men with wheelbarrows or dump carts pulled by a single horse. On heavy cuts two different models of excavators were tried with success, but the tools available were primitive at best. Every mile of the Union Pacific would rely less on machines than on the sweat, stamina, and muscle of the men who built it. Nothing came easy for them. Even the timber for their tents and shanties had been hauled three hundred miles across Iowa from the Mississippi River. As the road moved westward, the crews picked up their housing and lugged it along with them.

Shortages plagued the work constantly. The terrain yielded nothing except some limestone for masonry work, not even gravel for ballast. Bridge trusses were shipped to Omaha framed and ready for raising. As lumber arrived, it was fed into a large sawmill at Omaha or two portable sawmills upriver to be cut into ties. Forced by necessity to use cottonwood for most of the ties, the company resorted to burnettizing, a chemical process to preserve the wood. The machine installed at Omaha could burnettize five hundred ties a day, but the process was costly and never lived up to expectations. Durant's inability to solve the tie dilemma did not go unnoticed in the East. "I am sorry to hear that you are coming short of ties," Oakes Ames scolded, "it is bad for us and will be against us in congress next winter." In September Oakes went out to inspect the work for himself.

The Doctor paid less heed to fire from the rear than to advice from the front. The problem, Henry explained, was not lack of ties—he had 300,000 under contract—but lack of means to transport them. Scows were ineffective in low water, and the steamboats ignored contracts if a better offer turned up. "Unless we own the Boats," Henry concluded, "we cannot depend on them." Despite vigorous efforts by Hoxie, the track gangs ran through ties faster than they could be supplied. Nor was that the only obstacle. "You have no idea," Henry echoed wearily, "how much our work is delayed by our not being able to pay promptly."

Unmoved, Durant drove the work in the style that would make him the scourge of all who felt his lash. Bristling with nervous energy, he pelted Omaha with demands like hailstones: "How much track now laid how much do you lay per day. Run the Burnetizing machine night and day." "Increase your force on ties. Important the track should be laid faster, cant you lay one mile per day." "Do you or do you not want more men to lay sixty miles this fall, if so what kind." "What is the matter that you cant lay track faster." When that did not suffice, Durant went personally to Omaha to goad Henry onward. Hoxie was impressed with the results, but the Doctor remained dissatisfied. He wanted Henry to push the gangs harder and also to keep him informed of all developments. Henry protested that he could not be at end of track and in the office at the same time. "I insist upon being fully advised," Durant replied adamantly. "If you have those in your employ who can attend to work on line as well as yourself have no objection to your staying in office."

If nothing else, the visit brought Durant his first glimmer of a defect in organization. He responded by sending his brother Frank to take charge of the fieldwork. The move served only to divide responsibility and spread the Doctor's wrath around. Frank learned quickly that ties of blood did not render him immune to criticism. "If men are not fed well and made comfortable they will not stay—see to this," the Doctor demanded. "You represent me and have full authority and I hold you responsible. . . . If you dare not take the responsibility I have no use for you at Omaha." When Frank ventured to assert himself, he was promptly reminded that "my orders must be followed let the consequences be what they may."

This muddled situation was further complicated by the presence of Seymour, who functioned outside the regular chain of command. In June 1865 Seymour, at Durant's urging, quit his post in Washington to devote full time to the Union Pacific. He longed to be chief engineer, but Durant preferred Dodge for that position and found Seymour more useful as ambassador without portfolio. The consulting engineer became not only Durant's advisor but his agent in the field, an instrument loyal to him personally. More than friendship bound Seymour to the Doctor, for like Dey he made the mistake of signing on without knowing what his salary was to be and soon found himself utterly dependent on Durant's good will.

By November 18 the first hundred miles had been graded but only twenty-eight miles of track had been laid. Seymour presented Durant with a detailed report on what must be done to finish the first sixty miles before the ground froze and prepare for work in the spring. His advice was ruthlessly practical, designed to meet the inspection required for government approval. If the government commission did not insist on burnettized ties, for example, he recommended abandoning the process to eliminate the "expense, annoyance, delay and uncertain results." Untreated cottonwood ties would last three or four years, he thought. By that time one of the Iowa roads would have reached the Missouri and replacement lumber could be obtained cheaply. Above all, someone had to push the work forward during the next six weeks. The task was neither desirable nor properly that of a consulting engineer, Seymour noted coyly, but he was willing to do it "provided that the position assigned me there can be such that I will feel enabled to accomplish all that may be expected of me."

Durant ignored this hint but not the advice. Working at a furious pace, the crews managed to finish forty miles of road with all the required sidings, station houses, and water stations before the weather closed them out. Once the government accepted the sections in January 1866, Durant turned his attention to the glaring problem of organization. The past year's experience had finally convinced him that changes were needed. Henry had been only a stopgap and was ready to go back to Iowa. So too with Frank Durant, whose stay in Omaha was mercifully brief. In quick succession the Doctor made several moves that would ultimately transform past embarrassments into a model of efficiency. He took Reed off the surveys and put him in charge of construction, turned the task of tracklaying over to the Casement brothers, and appointed Dodge chief engineer of the road.

A Vermonter by birth, Reed had migrated to Illinois and made his home in Joliet before going to work on the M & M. He was forty-seven when Durant made him Superintendent of Construction and Operations. Quiet, likeable, methodical in his habits, Reed was a conscientious man who disliked controversy and avoided a fight whenever he could. He supervised all grading, tracklaying, bridging, and tunneling, which obliged him to keep meticulous records on quantities of material handled and estimates of payments due contractors. It was a tough, demanding position, the lightning rod for any hint of scandal involving contracts or inferior performance by contractors. No area was more politically sensitive or more visible to critics of the road.

Reed's task was made easier when the Casement brothers signed on in February 1866. John Stephen Casement was a New Yorker transplanted to Ohio, where he had already earned an impressive reputation as a tracklayer before the war. Turning the business over to his younger brother Daniel, he enlisted in an Ohio regiment and served with distinction until the war's end. As a division commander he showed the same qualities of leadership and reliability that had made him successful in railroading. His gallantry at the Battle of Franklin helped earn him a promotion to brigadier general. Always popular with his men, he was known thereafter as "General Jack."

After the war he and his brother became partners in the firm of J. S. & D. T. Casement. The Union Pacific contract was their first major venture together. Jack became the field leader and disciplinarian, Dan the organizer and bookkeeper. They were not impressive specimens physically. Jack stood only five feet four, Dan "five feet nothing" according to one wag. But Jack was not a man to be crossed. Just turned thirty-seven, stocky, muscular, hardbitten, and fearless, he could handle the roughest of crews. He married in 1857 and settled in Painesville, but between the war and the railroad work his wife Frank (Frances) saw precious little of him. During the war she lost their first child to a fever and was disconsolate for years. Jack never grew comfortable being away from home for such long periods. Like Grant, he had a tendency to find solace for his loneliness in a bottle. Frank implored him to resist the habit even after Jack had sworn a vow for temperance.

Jack served the Union Pacific as he had the Union, enlisting early and staying to the end. So too with Dodge, who had been present at the creation but only now was free to enter the company's employ. He resigned from the army on March 10, but a conference with the Indians prevented him from going to Omaha until May 1866. Early in March Durant sent him a vague telegram suggesting that he wanted Dodge to take the field as a surveyor. Dodge promptly declined and offered the Doctor some shrewd advice. He suspected from all he had heard that the situation at Omaha was disorganized and demoralized. This was the problem to be addressed before all others:

> Let me impress upon you the importance of commencing the years work by placing at Omaha a chief in whom you have confidence who in all things you will support and who you can hold responsible that your orders are carried out—and who all connected with the road will know they must obey. . . . These *divided interested independent commands*—with the master in New York—makes [sic] each chief jealous of his power and rights and it is not condusive [sic] to *harmony, energy, economy* or *celerity.*

Late in April Dodge met Durant in St. Joseph and refused flatly to accept the position unless he received absolute control. His military experience had shown him the disastrous effects of a divided command. In rough country without law, discipline counted for everything. As chief engineer he would "obey orders and insist on everyone under me doing the same." Durant agreed to his demand. He had long believed Dodge was the best man for the post. In addition, he realized that military protection from the Indians was essential, and no one commanded more respect from Grant and Sherman than Dodge.

Nothing Durant ever did served the Union Pacific better. Short and slight of build, Dodge was an ordinary-looking man with some extraordinary qualities. He listened well and had a quick, analytical mind that leaped to sound conclusions before most men understood the question. To others he seemed always in motion, talking and moving rapidly, driving himself so hard that friends thought he would surely work himself to death. The most remarkable thing about Dodge, however, was not his intelligence and good sense but his way with other men. A man of strong convictions, he did not hesitate to express his views even when they were unpopular or unwanted. Yet such was Dodge's sincerity that his candor did not provoke resentment or antagonism in others. His manner was forceful, earnest, and utterly lacking in wit or humor. He took life seriously and expected others to do the same. His loyalty was legendary. Dodge seldom remembered a slight and never forgot a friend. He was always too busy for pettiness and never too busy to help a comrade in need. He was that rare sort of individual in whom all parties of a dispute confided, believing him to be sympathetic and certain that he would not betray their trust. This ability to act as the eye of a storm was to prove crucial in the rough weather that lay ahead.

When Dodge arrived in Omaha on May 6, he saw firsthand the fruits of Durant's neglect. No one was in charge. The engineering, construction, and operating departments reported separately to New York and got their instructions from Durant with little attempt at coordination. Reed had taken hold of construction and Jack Casement the tracklaying gangs. Dodge left House in charge of his headquarters in Omaha and persuaded an unhappy Hoxie to stay on as transfer agent. "I would rather be at Omaha under you than to be here with a much larger salary," Hoxie admitted. "I am heartily sick of this living at hotels, without my wife, and both ends pushing me for freight. I can't make the river higher."

These men became the nucleus of an organization built along strict military lines. The engineers and track gangs venturing into Indian country had to be armed and trained to defend themselves. Many were veterans from both armies and already familiar with drill. Dodge discovered that a number of his former soldiers on the plains had left the army and found jobs on the railroad. Before his arrival, each survey party had been left to arrange its own escort. Dodge obtained from Grant and Sherman full authority to request troops from local commanders whenever needed, but there were barely enough soldiers on the plains to protect the outposts. Every request for more men was countered by demands that military expenditures be cut. No one wanted to prolong a costly war, yet there could be no chance of peace so long as settlers and miners kept streaming into Indian country in defiance of treaties. A tragedy of epic proportions was unfolding, as General John Pope observed with startling foresight:

> All the tribes of Indians east of the mountains are in open hostility. . . . The Indian, in truth, no longer has a country. He is reduced to starvation or to warring to the death. . . . The U. S. Troops, small in number and utterly incapable of affording security to the whites or protection to the Indians, have been strictly on the defensive. . . . The Indians' first demand is that the white man shall not drive off his game and dispossess him of his lands. How can we promise this unless we prohibit emigration and settlement? . . . It is idle to talk of treaties of peace when no promise can be fulfilled. . . . Whatever may be the abstract right or wrong, the result must inevitably be the dispossession of all his lands and their occupation by civilized men. The only practical question is how this can be done with the least inhumanity.
>
> My duties as a military commander require me to protect the emigration, the mails, and the settlements against hostile acts of the Indians. This necessity demands a large military force on the

plains, which will have to be increased as the Indians are driven to desperation. The end is sure and dreadful to contemplate. . . .

Dodge wasted no sympathy on the plight of the Indians, believing that "There were really no friendly Indians." He saw only that the conflict would hamper everything the Union Pacific did and therefore bent his energies to preparing his men for the struggle. By summer he had instilled a new mood of discipline and confidence in Omaha, but his authority was far from absolute. Durant retained the title of "Vice President and General Manager," which meant that Reed and Hoxie still reported to him. Dodge was given charge of engineering but even there he had to reckon with Seymour, who took orders only from Durant. Although the consulting engineer had no authority, he did have access to his master's ear. As Dodge would discover, the anomaly of Seymour's position gave him a great capacity for mischief.

The season's work was well underway before Dodge arrived. In March Jack Casement rounded up crews and had boarding cars built for the men, but the cars were delayed and the river was too low for iron to be shipped. "It is a slow country to drive business in," he grumbled impatiently. Brother Dan was sent to bid on a contract to lay track on Blair's Cedar Rapids road, the completion of which would solve the transportation problem. Earlier Durant, in one of his grand gestures, had offered Blair a $500,000 bonus if his road reached Council Bluffs within eighteen months, but the connection would not be made that season.

Despite valiant efforts by Hoxie, the first iron did not start upriver until late March. Frustrated by the shipping bottleneck, Durant decided on a bold experiment. Experienced navigators had long dismissed barges as unsuitable in the treacherous waters of the Missouri. No slave to conventional wisdom, Durant ordered two barges built along with a steamboat to haul them. The new Union Pacific fleet made its first run in July, when the *Elk Horn* towed the barges safely to Omaha from St. Louis in less than ten days. Delighted observers showered Durant with praise for opening a new era by proving the worth of barges on the Missouri River.

Once supplies began pouring into Omaha, the long-awaited surge westward began in earnest. In mid-April 1866 the government commissioners found only sixty-three miles of road completed, but Casement was driving his crews at a steady pace. He reached the hundred-mile post on June 4 with the help of a temporary pile trestle thrown across the Loup Fork until the 1,700-foot bridge was finished. The second hundred miles was a tracklayer's dream —flat and straight with light grading. Late in July the gangs passed Grand Island (153 miles) and swung toward Fort Kearney. Casement was moving so fast he outran his own contract, which called for no more than a mile of track a day at $750 per mile. Durant pushed him to keep a pace of two or three miles a day but made no provision for the expense of the extra men required. When Casement complained, Sidney Dillon intervened with a promise to do right by him. If the board "should not be disposed to be half white," he sympathized, "let them take the track & lay it themselves."

As the perceptive Dodge had long argued, nothing gave the company more credibility than the presence of track with trains running on it. Editors who had criticized Durant now heaped praise on him for the road's progress. Although Durant drove the work hard, he caused delays in the flow of supplies by demanding that all shipping contracts be approved by him personally. It was a reasonable request, but he was often slow to respond. Nevertheless, Hoxie and Harbaugh, who were busy procuring rails, kept enough material moving toward Omaha for Casement to maintain his pace. Through stifling heat and country scorched by drought the gangs sweated onward until they reached the 100th meridian, 247 miles from Omaha, on October 6.

In one frantic summer the company had built the mileage covered by the Hoxie contract. Crews were already grading the third hundred miles, and Reed only needed Durant's approval to let contracts for the fourth. The men had ventured into the worst of Indian country and looked nervously for raids. Dodge had scrounged more arms from the government, but the crews impressed Reed as "very timid and at the first appearance of Indians would all leave the work." Meanwhile, Dodge found himself with an Indian problem of quite another kind. The man who believed there were no friendly Indians had been asked by Durant to find some to perform at an excursion he was planning. The Doctor was not about to let the reaching of the 100th meridian pass without a gala promotion to garner some publicity.

Dodge took charge of the arrangements, drawing again on his influence with the military to procure what he needed. Late in October two trains chugged out of Omaha with antlers crowning the locomotives and bunting streaming alongside the shiny new Pullman Palace Sleeping Cars. The first carried an army of employees, provisions, bedding, tents, buffalo robes, wood for bonfires, and cases of champagne. Behind it came the sightseeing special crowded with dignitaries, their wives and servants, three government commissioners, reporters, a photographer, a phalanx of Union Pacific directors, caterers, barbers, and a band sent over from St. Joseph by Hoxie. The guest list was heavy with senators, congressmen, capitalists, and others who could be useful to the company. An outbreak of cholera scared off a few invitees, but 140 brave souls came along for the fun.

For three days Durant introduced them to the wilds and wonders of the prairie, carefully orchestrated. The guests camped first at Columbus, where Dodge lit a huge bonfire in the center of a great circle. Some were taken to watch Casement's men lay track; others visited a prairie dog colony or went to hunt buffalo and antelope. In the evening there was a grand feast of game washed down with champagne. Early one morning they were roused suddenly by the fierce war cries of Indians in war paint racing through the camp. Ladies shrieked and men peeped timidly out of their tents until Dodge assured them that the invaders were friendly Pawnees. When everyone had dressed, the Pawnees did a few war dances and a mock battle complete with scalping. Impressed, the guests tossed the Indians coins and chatted with those who spoke English.

The Pawnees were scouts and soldiers who had served under Dodge, borrowed from a unit camped nearby. Durant was delighted with their performance. On the last night he treated his guests to the spectacle of a staged prairie fire set at a safe distance. Reporters scribbled notes furiously on everything they saw. Dodge obliged them by spicing his information with "a great deal of romance" of the sort on which eastern papers doted. He knew the extravaganza had cost a lot of money but concluded that "from a sight-seeing point of view, it may be considered as very successful." Everyone went home to tell their friends about the Real West. An ecstatic Durant resolved to stage excursions whenever the Union Pacific had something to celebrate. The selling of the West had begun in earnest, and even at this early stage the market value of self-parody had been discovered. Sam Reed, who was laid up with typhoid fever, was grateful to have missed the whole affair.

The tourists departed, but Jack Casement stayed on, laying track through North Platte to the 305-mile post before quitting late in December. When the ground froze, he lingered awhile longer, building a blacksmith shop, ice house, slaughterhouse, wash house, and stock pens for the coming season. His anxious wife reminded him again to "beware of *the tempter* in the form of strong drink." Not to worry, Jack reassured her; there was "no *wine or liquor,* we have the only temperance house in this country."

* * *

The most urgent business for Dodge that season was to solve the Black Hills riddle and connect previous surveys into a continuous line (or two) from the Missouri to the California border. Evans was sent to compare his earlier findings with the Lone Tree Creek line Dodge had found. "What we want," Dodge stressed, "is a direct practicable line through the Black Hills as soon as possible." Evans's assistant, Percy T. Browne, followed the Republican and South Platte rivers to Denver and looked again for a suitable pass through the mountains. L. L. Hills took charge of surveying the region from the Platte Valley to Lodgepole Valley. With Reed busy elsewhere, the surveys west of the divide were given to Thomas H. Bates. Evans and Bates were also ordered to collect mineral specimens along the route. A geologist, David Van Lennep, went along with Evans to explore the Black Hills region.

Durant's interest in minerals went beyond the need for coal as fuel in timber-scarce country or even the iron specimens Evans had found earlier. The Doctor had a case of gold fever and instructed Dodge to put some prospectors at work in the mountains. It was the mining boom that made the Cache la Poudre route so attractive to the Union Pacific. Dodge recognized that the company would need a line to Denver, which made it desirable to penetrate the mountains as far south as possible. The problem was finding a suitable pass. Former Governor John Evans, who would become Colorado's most indefatigable railroad promoter, insisted that the mining district could be reached through Berthoud Pass, but Case's survey showed the grade line at the summit of Berthoud to be 2,233 feet higher than the Cache la Poudre route. The line also required a tunnel three miles long through solid granite and promised a rugged meander to the Green River on the other side.

Browne's explorations confirmed these findings, but the lure of Colorado continued to exert its influence on the route question. If Denver had to be reached by a branch road, the distance would be much shorter from Cache la Poudre than from the Lone Tree line. The more Evans examined the Lone Tree line, however, the better he liked it. In mid-August he telegraphed Dodge that it was "far ahead of anything yet found." Pleased at having his chance discovery verified, Dodge passed the news along to Durant. "Throwing aside the commercial importance of Cache la Poudre," he emphasized, "the new line is decidedly the best." Before Dodge left to look over the line for himself, Durant telegraphed that Seymour and government director Jesse Williams would join him. No decision would be made, the Doctor added, until Dodge submitted his report.

After reaching Denver on September 15, Dodge went to meet Evans while Seymour and Williams inspected Berthoud with Browne. A hired carriage pulled by mules took them within two miles of the summit, where they switched to horses for the steep climb. Gazing westward toward the splendor of the Middle Park, Seymour thought the view exceeded anything he had ever witnessed. They examined Clear Creek Valley, pushed on to Empire City and Central City, and tried to explore Boulder Valley before a blizzard drove them back to Denver. When the snow eased, they joined Dodge and Evans at Laporte for the trek into the Black Hills.

Dodge and Seymour differ on what happened next. Much later Dodge declared that Seymour and Williams "did not go to examine the Black Hills line," but at the time Seymour wrote Durant two letters describing their tour of the route. The two versions agree on details of movements. Perhaps Dodge meant that Seymour looked but did not see; more likely he rearranged his memories in light of the controversy that later erupted. Seymour's letters give no sign that he was attentive or grasped the significance of what he saw. On the trip he amused himself chiefly by shooting small game. He regaled Durant with tales of his marksmanship but remained noncommittal about the Lone Tree line, saying only that Dodge's report would enable the Doctor to "form an intelligent opinion as to the proper route for the road." Dodge came away convinced that Seymour and Williams were wedded to the Cache la Poudre line and would use their influence in its favor.

After their departure on October 1, Dodge had Evans and Hills run connecting lines toward each other between Crow and Lodgepole creeks. He was looking not only for a connection but also for the best route to Denver from the Lone Tree line. To nail down his argument for that line, he joined Browne for a look at Boulder Canyon, where a fierce snowstorm drove them into the Middle Park for shelter. There Dodge sat shivering on October 10, oblivious to the fact that at home in Iowa his friends were voting him into Congress. Later he figured himself to be the only man "elected to Congress who forgot the day of election." When the storm cleared, he sent Browne to run a line from Denver to connect with Evans's line at Lodgepole Creek.

Dodge incorporated all the findings of Evans, Browne, and Hills in a report submitted to the Union Pacific board on November 22. From it emerged the first clear picture of a feasible route through the region east of the continental divide. Browne's surveys had dismissed all hope of a line west of Denver. In all, Evans had run five lines between Cache la Poudre and Laramie Canyon, none of which compared favorably with the Lone Tree line. It was shorter, had gentler grades, less curvature, no canyons, required little bridging, was relatively free of snowdrifts, and could be reached easily from the mouth of Lodgepole Creek, the best of four different approach routes surveyed. A branch to Denver, running due south from Crow Creek, would extend only 112 miles over easy terrain rich in coal and iron. As a precaution Dodge had some of Evans's men stay the winter at Evans's (later Sherman's) pass in the Black Hills to observe the weather, wind, and snow drifting.

West of the divide, Bates and his men had to march a thousand miles to run 371 miles of line. Bates concluded that a decent line could be run to California north or south of Salt Lake along the Humboldt and Truckee river valleys. His surveys gave the company, in Dodge's words, "practically a connected line from the Missouri River to the California State line." Several problems remained unsolved, notably determining the best routes across the Wyoming Basin and passage through the Wasatch Mountains into Salt Lake valley. These would occupy the engineers during the coming season.

The engineers under Dodge had done splendid service. "Often threatened by Indian attacks, sometimes without escorts," he acknowledged, ". . . they have all had narrow escapes, have had stock stolen, camps attacked, and been caught in heavy snowstorms, in extreme cold without fires, but, as yet, we have not lost any lives or any stock of great value." None had worked harder than Dodge himself. Much of his time went to arranging military escorts, dealing with the government commissioners who inspected finished sections of the road, ordering supplies, and handling land matters. When Hills, who had replaced Ainsworth, botched his survey of the fourth hundred miles, Dodge and Reed examined it themselves and ordered changes. As Casement's gangs bore down on North Platte, Dodge had already concluded that the river was tame enough for a trestle bridge 2,300 feet long built on cedar piles. The difficult Loup Fork bridge was also completed by the year's end.

Everywhere Dodge looked out for the company's land and mineral interests. He arranged for selection of the first lands received along the completed road and had the regions adjacent to the surveys examined carefully for coal, iron, and other minerals. As track snaked across the plains, Dodge had towns laid out and lots recorded. At crucial points such as Kearney and North Platte, he took care to reserve a large acreage for depots, shops, sidings, and other needs for future use on the premise that it was best to "take all the property needed or that ever would be needed while the land was vacant." To assist in this work he hired a young lawyer, Andrew J. Poppleton, to handle the company's growing legal business. The choice proved a wise one. Poppleton not only started the Union Pacific's legal department but remained its bulwark for two decades. His presence marked another important step toward the creation of an efficient organization. Every railroad required skilled lawyers, and none would keep them busier than the Union Pacific.

* * *

Oakes Ames saw nothing untoward in pressing Crédit Mobilier stock on Congressmen. He merely solicited subscriptions from all his friends, several of whom happened to be in government. Two fellow representatives from Massachusetts, John B. Alley and Samuel Hooper, bought 500 shares each, and Senator Grimes of Iowa took 250, but many more refused than accepted. No question of ethics was involved; most simply did not consider Crédit Mobilier a good investment. So too with the businessmen Oakes approached. Elisha Atkins and Thomas Nickerson took some shares, but the majority declined. Only with great difficulty was the increased capital of $2.5 million subscribed in full. By May 1866 the Ames brothers and their friends held slightly more than half of Crédit Mobilier's 25,000 shares. Oakes and Oliver more than doubled their personal holdings to 4,025 shares or 16 percent of the total. Durant remained the largest holder with 6,041 shares and was reelected president on May 19.

As the pace of construction quickened, the demand for money grew voracious. The government bonds received for completed sections could be sold, but Union Pacific bonds had no market value and could be used only as collateral for loans at heavy discount. As John Duff quipped, the stock was so worthless it could be sold only "to people who would take a risk as they would at a faro-bank." Since Crédit Mobilier had by law to accept Union Pacific stock at par, it devised an arrangement for selling the stock to its own stockholders for $4.50 a share. Ultimately the loss in this transaction would be added to construction costs, but at the moment Union Pacific stock was useless for raising money. Those trying to borrow for the company found the going rough. Conservative financiers doubted that the road would ever be built or that it would pay even if completed. A man who risked his credit on such a venture was apt to have his loans called by prudent bankers.

While the associates were busy scrounging funds, Congress delivered them an unexpected blow. The Act of 1864 authorized the Kansas Pacific to connect with the Union Pacific main line at the 100th meridian. In mid-May a friendly senator warned Durant of a bill extending the point of connection fifty miles beyond Denver. The danger of allowing the Kansas Pacific to parallel the Union Pacific all the way to Denver was obvious, yet Durant was slow to respond. While the senators wandered down a labyrinth of debate over the difference between the Union Pacific *main* line west of the 100th meridian and the *branch* lines to that point, advocates of the Central Pacific slyly inserted a provision of their own. The Act of 1864 restricted the Central Pacific from extending more than 150 miles into Nevada; the amendment would allow it to build until it met the Union Pacific. The 150-mile limit was never intended in the original act, Senator John Conness of California assured his colleagues. "It was stolen in through the corruption of some parties and the clerk who eventually made the report." The statement was a barefaced lie, but no one called Conness on it.

The new provision invited a race between the two companies in which the Union Pacific had nothing to win and everything to lose. Every additional mile built by the Central Pacific meant more subsidy bonds and lands at the expense of the Union Pacific. Charles Sherman did what he could against the bill and urged Durant to come lobby in person. Harbaugh happened to be in Washington on other business when the bill passed the Senate and was astonished to learn of its existence. "I cannot find any body . . . sent here for the purpose of bringing up influence to arrest it," he wrote to Dix. A week later the bill sailed through the House despite the efforts of Oakes and Alley. Belatedly Dix and Seymour hurried to Washington in hopes of persuading Johnson to veto the bill. The President listened courteously and then signed the bill into law on July 3.

The Central Pacific crowd celebrated the victory with a grand excursion that did not go unnoticed by Durant. Collis Huntington later boasted that he got the bill passed "without the use of a dollar." The Union Pacific matched Huntington in virtue if not in achievement: Dix severely rebuked a lobbyist promised bonds by a third party if he could secure the veto. But the damage had been done and would cost the Union Pacific dearly. The Kansas Pacific was free to build to Denver and the Central Pacific to lay rails as far east as it could manage. The stage had been set for a race as extravagant as it was desperate.

*   *   *

Three months later the Union Pacific reached the 100th meridian, where the Hoxie contract terminated. Since no provision had been made to carry on the work, the question arose within days of the annual election in which Dillon, Duff, and Oliver Ames joined the Union Pacific board for the first time. Dillon and Duff had already been appointed to Crédit Mobilier's enlarged Railway Bureau, which included Durant, Bushnell, Lambard, John Williams, and G. Griswold Gray. The newcomers were now entrenched in both companies, but Durant still ruled the roost. On his motion a committee headed by Bushnell was appointed to arrange with Crédit Mobilier for work west of the 100th meridian. It was assumed that the new contract would in essence be an extension of the old one. No one suspected even remotely that the Hoxie contract would be the only one Crédit Mobilier would ever have.

At the next Union Pacific board meeting in November, Bushnell's committee reported a new contract offered by J. M. S. Williams on behalf of Crédit Mobilier. Williams proposed extending the Hoxie contract to cover fifty-three miles already built and constructing another 650 miles at prices ranging from $50,000 a mile on the plains to $85,000 a mile in the mountains. Since Dodge was on his way to New York, the board deferred action until his report on the Black Hills line could be heard. Williams was asked to withdraw his proposal so that it could be modified in light of Dodge's estimates.

No one knew that a few days earlier Durant had on his own initiative signed a contract with L. B. Boomer to construct 150 miles of road west of the 100th meridian at the extraordinarily low price of $19,500 per mile to the North Platte River and $20,000 per mile thereafter. Why the Doctor let the work at such threadbare figures remains a mystery. Perhaps he hoped that by assuming personal responsibility for the contract he would be in a position to determine its assignment. Oliver Ames later characterized it as a "secret arrangement" with a man "of no responsibility." He was wrong on at least one count. Boomer was a well-known bridge contractor who had done work for the M & M and would build most of the spans for the Union Pacific.

On November 22 and 23, the Union Pacific board met to consider Dodge's report on the Lone Tree line. The issue went beyond one of engineering. What excited the directors was the prospect of an unexpectedly cheap route through the region where the government subsidy jumped from $16,000 per mile to $48,000. For the hard-pressed company this amounted to a windfall that overrode even the desire for a line nearer Denver. That it happened also to be the best and shortest route only made the choice easier. The Committee on Location and Construction unanimously recommended its adoption. It also endorsed Dodge's proposal for a branch to Denver from which lateral lines could be run into the mining areas. Impressed by the geologist's report on finds of coal and iron, the committee stressed the need to "bring the ores and the fuel together when the scanty supply of mountain pine shall have been exhausted."

During the Crédit Mobilier investigation in 1873, controversy erupted over whether the directors knew of this cheaper route when a new construction contract was made in August 1867. Both Ames brothers testified that they did not, Oakes in passing and Oliver at some length when pressed on the subject. There can be no doubt they were lying. Dodge's report to the board was detailed and explicit. He had sent profiles of the line to Durant in August 1866, just after Evans completed his work. Durant too hedged on the question when in fact he had full knowledge of the route. There is reason to believe he grasped its importance at once, for on September 4 he issued an order forbidding engineers and department heads from giving out information, data, maps, or profiles to anyone, including other directors and government officials. The penalty for violation was immediate dismissal.

The evidence is conclusive that not only the directors but the government itself knew about the route in detail. The government directors were at the meeting when Dodge presented his report; indeed Charles Sherman moved the resolution to adopt the line. Their report of January 7, 1867, noted that the new line had been adopted. Jesse Williams described the route in his report after returning from the Black Hills, and Dodge did the same in a letter to General Sherman. On December 10 Oliver Ames asked the new Secretary of the Interior, Orville H. Browning, to fix the point at which the $48,000 subsidy would begin. He informed Browning that the company had adopted the new line, enclosed a copy of Dodge's map, and suggested that the higher subsidy "commence on the crossing of Crow Creek." A railroad journal described the new route for its readers in January 1867.

The timing of the discovery assumed importance only in retrospect, when the hot breath of scandal blew the issue out of proportion. In December 1866 the Lone Tree route was a matter of public knowledge, but no one outside the company grasped its importance. Browning showed more interest in technicalities over the measurement of completed sections and fixing the point for increase of subsidy. When he brought Ames's request before the cabinet, there was unanimous agreement to delay decision until a government engineer looked over the ground. Browning was anxious too that all documents bear the signature of the proper officer, for the Union Pacific had just changed presidents.

Dix had been appointed minister to France and did not resign the presidency but merely took leave of it. His departure awakened the board to the realization that it could no longer afford a figurehead president. It was no longer willing to let the irrepressible Doctor have his way, as Dix had so amiably done. On November 24 it met for the third consecutive day, this time to elect a temporary president. Durant coveted the office for himself, but to his chagrin he received only one vote against thirteen for Oliver Ames and two for Treasurer John J. Cisco. Belatedly the directors had learned about the Boomer contract, for which Durant drew a pointed rebuke. Immediately after the election Lambard offered a resolution denying the authority of any individual to act for the board or make contracts without its consent. Together the election and the resolution delivered a blunt message: the Union Pacific was no longer the Doctor's to run as a personal fiefdom.

Burning with resentment, Durant was in no condition to fight. Since spring he had driven himself past exhaustion, and his nerves were tapped out. A concerned Train urged him to see a specialist. "Do it or you will have a stroke of paralysis," he warned. "You cant strike the Almighty in the face as you do without getting a lick back. If you get sick the Road will go to the devil." In December the Doctor fell ill again, postponing his clash with the Bostonians for another few weeks.

Nevertheless, a showdown loomed. The election of Oliver Ames brought to a head differences that could not be reconciled. Where Durant acted on his own counsel, the Bostonians preferred rule by committee. Appalled by the Doctor's careless and secretive way with records, they insisted that proper books be kept, audited, and made available to the entire board. The office staff had to be reorganized and its practices made to conform with sound business principles. Since most of the officers and clerks in the New York office were loyal to Durant, the Bostonians had to find some way of compelling them to serve the entire board rather than their accustomed master. The Doctor's private secretary, H. C. Crane, had charge of the office and, as one Bostonian observed sourly, "No one seems to be able to do anything without consulting him."

In trying to harness Durant the Bostonians had to overcome two major obstacles. They controlled Crédit Mobilier but not Union Pacific, where the Doctor remained strong. This division of authority was compounded by the fact that the Ameses and their friends were based in Massachusetts, while both Union Pacific and Crédit Mobilier transacted business in New York. Among Oliver's friends only Sidney Dillon had his office in New York, where Durant held sway. In the months ahead the distance between Boston and New York would become much more than a matter of miles.

Durant was quick to see the advantages offered him by these divisions and slow to reveal his hand. He complained that the Bostonians did not fully appreciate the difference between the railroad company and the construction company. If Oliver would give him an hour or two, the Doctor would inform him fully on matters that were best not discussed at meetings in the presence of the government directors. But Oliver seemed never to have the time. The Bostonians were more interested in settling accounts for construction already done before letting more contracts. That meant closing up the Hoxie contract, which in turn required a close look at Durant's notorious suspense account. The Doctor wanted those expenses charged to construction without being examined too closely; the Bostonians were pressing to have everything audited carefully by their own man.

Like those interludes during the Civil War when the battered armies paused to lick their wounds and regroup, the period of Durant's illness was but a calm between storms. Already the promoters of Union Pacific had been well tested by adversity, but the worst was yet to come. At a time when unity of purpose was essential, they were never again to know a moment's peace.

Rails West: Despite the constant bickering and infighting, the ribbon of track marched steadily across the barren countryside of the West.

(Left) A copy of Durant's letter accepting the terms of the Casement brothers for laying track. Note the endorsement by John M. S. Williams.

(Below) An endless stream of supplies arrived by steamboat at Omaha, where they were transferred to rail cars and hauled to end of track.

Master of all he surveys: The Doctor inspects the roadbed stretching toward the western horizon in August 1866. The bar lying in the foreground is a track gauge used to measure and align the distance between rails. The implements left of the ties are certain to be Ames shovels.

Jack Casement, looking more like a Cossack than a Westerner, inspects his construction train. Note the penthouse accommodations atop the cars.

One by one, the cumbersome rails are laid in place and spiked down by Casement's crews. Note the wide variety in the cut of the ties.

The Reception Committee: Somehow the remarkable photographer A. J. Russell induced this band of Ute Indians to pose for his camera.

The excursion party that crossed the continent with Dodge in 1867 sat for its portrait. Seated from left are David Van Lennep, the geologist; John R. Duff, the director's son; General Dodge; General John A. Rawlins, who would soon die of consumption; and Major W. M. Dunn of Rawlins's staff. Standing from left are Lieutenant J. W. Wheelan; Lieutenant Colonel J. K. Minzer, commanding the cavalry and infantry escort; Dr. Henry C. Terry, the army surgeon; and John E. Corwith of Galena, Illinois. Dodge honored Rawlins by naming a town on the Union Pacific line in Wyoming after him.

The showdown at Fort Sanders. During the confrontation, the dignitaries paused long enough to have several pictures taken. In this one General Grant stands with his hands on the fence. Dodge is framed in the doorway while his antagonist, the Doctor, perches casually atop the gate behind the imposing figure of General W. S. Harney. The others include *(from left)* Sidney Dillon, General Phil Sheridan *(front),* Mrs. J. H. Potter, Frederick Dent, Mrs. John Gibbon, General John Gibbon, the Gibbon children, General William T. Sherman, and General Joseph H. Potter *(far right).*

A trio out of tune: Cornelius S. Bushnell, John B. Alley, and John Duff. *(Photograph of Bushnell courtesy of Gus Johnson and the Connecticut State Library; Alley photograph courtesy of the National Archives)*

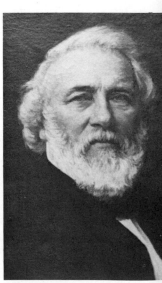

6

THE FALLING OUT

More than the usual number of Union Pacific men crossed paths in January 1867 on the sloshy streets of New York. Jack Casement came to see Dillon but tarried no longer than he had to, grumbling to his wife that "this town has no charms for me." He ran into Reed who, barely recovered from typhoid fever, was just as eager to leave but found himself detained the entire month. Hoxie was there, too, seeking a promotion to superintendent or land commissioner but convinced that Reed opposed him because he was a Republican and "to [sic] much of a politician for a railroad man." Dodge had gone to Washington for a brief fling at being a congressman, but Seymour was on hand, watching the clash with a wary eye and clutching anxiously at the Doctor's coattail lest his place be lost in an upheaval.

Rumors were flying in every direction. Reed heard tales of "very stormy" meetings that promised a radical change in management. Hoxie learned that Durant was attempting a corner in Northwestern and had been burned by a market slump that dropped the stock from 84 to 61. "He is attending to that now," Hoxie observed, "& dont do anything about RR matters except to badger his men." Reed was afraid the squabbling would delay progress on the road. Preparations for the coming season could not be made until the board decided several important questions, but weeks passed without definite action.

The directors themselves were tense and uneasy, aware that much had to be done but hesitant to do anything. Contracts had to be let and decisions made on a bridge across the Missouri River. A new construction contract had to be arranged and money raised. More organizational changes were needed;

an operating department had to be created now that trains were running. The usual line of supplicants had been forming for months. Charles Sherman desired a grading contract for a friend, from which he personally could "make an honest penny." Dr. George Miller of the Omaha *Herald* wanted to put a warehouse at end of track but could get no answer from Durant.

He was not alone in that problem. The Doctor seemed inert, unresponsive. Was it concern over market reverses or illness or the growing sentiment to oust him that distracted his attention? Reed thought the latter. "The Doctor will not do anything towards starting the work," he surmised, "until all questions are settled." For his part Reed preferred Durant with all his caprices to rule by committee. Moreover, the Doctor's vengeance would be terrible to behold. Like Samson he would not hesitate to pull down the temple even if it meant burying himself along with his enemies. But Reed thought it would not come to that. "Mr. Durant is full of suggestions," he observed, "and, if I mistake not, he will set some trap into which they will all fall and allow the work to go on as heretofore."

* * *

When the board met early in January 1867, wrangling broke out at once over the administrative reforms pressed by the Bostonians. The Auditing Committee's report was first accepted, then sent back to committee. Resolutions were passed to appoint a full-time auditor and to open a cash book for recording all disbursements. These were not abstract matters of policy but shafts aimed at Durant and his profligate spending habits. Oliver Ames brought in as auditor Benjamin F. Ham, who was also assistant secretary and treasurer of Crédit Mobilier. No one doubted where Ham's loyalty lay; Reed called him "the tool of Ames & Co."

The committee to settle the Hoxie contract felt obliged to submit a majority and minority report. Their efforts had run afoul of two items in particular, the extra cost of the ox-bow and the Doctor's suspense account, which included the funds dispensed in Washington to secure the Act of 1864. Dodge was ordered to examine the ox-bow accounts while Oliver Ames and John J. Cisco were made a committee to audit all claims on the suspense account, which was fast emerging as a major bone of contention between the opposing factions. On the surface it involved the accounting problem of how to spread the $435,754 item across the entire road rather than charge the whole to one contract. For some directors, however, the real issue was Durant's refusal to account for the expenditures. Suspicion lingered that some or all of the money had gone into the Doctor's own pocket.

Having snatched the purse strings from Durant's hands, the board brushed aside the Boomer contract as if it didn't exist by extending the Hoxie contract to cover the fifty-eight extra miles already built at fifty thousand dollars per mile instead of the low figure in Boomer's contract. Durant later testified that the board passed this resolution in his absence, but the minutes record him as one of four directors who were present but did not vote on the question. Eight others supported the motion while four government directors opposed it. Possibly Durant left before the vote was taken, but it is unlikely that his adversaries would have passed such a measure behind his back. They knew his talent for mischief and rarely even met in his absence. The Doctor's response was swift and unexpected. When the board met again on January 23, he greeted it with a written protest backed by an injunction against extending the Hoxie contract.

This blow came at a time when the Union Pacific was starved for funds to pay for past work and new construction. Lambard pleaded that "the hard work is over when we have built 200 miles more road—we *must not* therefore allow our credit to be impaired." But Durant's injunction prevented payment on the fifty-eight miles and hamstrung negotiations on another contract. Although the company had agreed to pay Crédit Mobilier about $2 million on account, the Hoxie contract still dangled in limbo. To meet the crisis the Bostonians resolved to increase the stock of Crédit Mobilier by $1.25 million. As inducement they offered stockholders a $1,000 Union Pacific first mortgage bond as bonus for each thousand dollars subscribed.

Weeks earlier Charles Sherman had urged Durant to "neutralize certain influences now existing" by spreading Crédit Mobilier stock among new investors, but the suggestion came too late. The Doctor saw that the Ameses and their friends had gained the upper hand in Crédit Mobilier and seemed bent on snatching Union Pacific from him as well. Having lost the one, he was determined to keep his place in the other. If he could not rule, then he would ruin his enemies or at least force them to terms through obstruction and delay. If he could not have Crédit Mobilier, then he would see to it that Crédit Mobilier had no contract without him. For this purpose he resorted to an unwonted display of virtue, the trading value of which he had discovered long before.

Originally Crédit Mobilier had been created as a vehicle by which those interested in Union Pacific could make a contract with themselves for constructing the road. This arrangement worked splendidly as long as the interests in both companies remained identical. To insure unity of interests, Crédit Mobilier in 1866 offered all Union Pacific stockholders the choice of selling out at cost or exchanging their shares for stock in the construction company. But the clash between Durant and the Bostonians ruptured this union. Donning his mask of virtue, the Doctor roared indignation at his discovery that extension of the Hoxie contract amounted to certain parties making a contract with themselves. The injunction, he proclaimed, had been brought to protect the government and the company from being overcharged for mileage already completed at a cost well below fifty thousand dollars per mile. He would not suffer allowing Union Pacific stockholders interested in Crédit Mobilier to reap huge profits at the expense of those with holdings only in Union Pacific.

The effrontery of this tactic stymied the Bostonians. In another round of heated sessions the Union Pacific board rescinded the extension of the Hoxie contract and approved a revised version of the Williams proposal. This time Oliver joined the four government directors in opposition. Durant approved the resolution only to switch his vote the next day, claiming he had misunderstood the question. On his motion a committee of directors not interested in Crédit Mobilier was appointed to negotiate a new contract with that company. The result was a stalemate. Durant knew nothing could be done unless Crédit Mobilier raised enough money through its new subscription for work to proceed, and he had only to withhold his support to stall that effort. As a disgusted Hoxie put it, "the Dr wont subscribe a cent yet . . . & Boston dont know what to do."

By February the need for funds had grown desperate. Dodge scrambled about, covering overdue bills for his survey parties, and warned that he was "about to end of my ability to carry." Frantic efforts by the assistant treasurer to raise money for maturing notes proved futile. The only hope for relief lay with the Bostonians themselves. "The [Company] *are in urgent need of money,*" Williams wrote Hazard, "so Loans better be made while other matters are being fixed." He implored Hazard to help keep the company "out of the Jews hands." Oliver persuaded other Crédit Mobilier stockholders to make loans while a plan was being worked out. In all, the Bostonians held notes for $1.2 million of the nearly $3.5 million in loans owed by the Union Pacific.

Meanwhile Lambard devised a plan to accommodate all sides. Crédit Mobilier offered to buy nearly $6 million in Union Pacific bonds and loan the company the $1.25 million raised by Crédit Mobilier's new subscription. In return Union Pacific would agree to settle the Hoxie contract and extend it another hundred miles at a rate of $42,000 per mile. Payment of the suspense account would be spread across the entire line as a concession to Durant, who endorsed the plan. The executive committee approved the proposal only to have the board reject it after heated debate. The mood was tense and strained. Before considering the proposal, the directors showed their temper by ordering Durant's earlier protest of the Hoxie extension expunged from the minutes. After a short recess to clear the air, the board proceeded to scold the executive committee for exceeding its authority and declared frostily that it would consider "various parts of the Report . . . as reccommendations [sic] only."

In fact the board rejected only those terms favorable to Durant. The next day it approved the bond sale and loan tendered by Crédit Mobilier. Instead of the Hoxie extension, however, it accepted a new proposal from Williams to build 100 miles at $42,000 per mile and 168 miles at $45,000 per mile. Nothing was said about the suspense account or settlement of the Hoxie contract. The directors were counting on a $1 million bank loan to tide them over until the new Crédit Mobilier subscription bore fruit. The terms negotiated by

Durant for the money appalled the Bostonians, however, as did the slipshod methods of doing business in the New York office, where Ham complained that he "never saw so much unaccomplished work as there is here."

In March 1867 the Ames group concluded that it was no longer possible to work with Durant. The division between them, Alley later claimed, was that the Bostonians believed the road once built could be operated at a profit, while Durant was intent on getting everything he could out of its construction. Anyone who expected a return on investment from operations, sneered the Doctor, was "a damned fool." This belief prevailed widely among financiers, and even the Ames group showed no reluctance to profit from construction contracts. Their differences had less to do with policy than with personality and style. Oakes argued that "Durant should not be allowed to control everything" because if he did, "there will not be much profit in it." Where the Bostonians insisted on conducting business according to proper procedures, Durant was a lone wolf unwilling to share authority and incapable of doing things by the book. His erratic, unpredictable ways had become intolerable to men of regular habits, and his flamboyant style grated on their sense of propriety. He could not be relied on, an unpardonable sin in an age where a man's reliability was his reputation.

While the Bostonians brooded over how to rid themselves of Durant, the financial situation deteriorated. Crédit Mobilier stockholders were slow to take the new offering and the $1 million loan still had not materialized. Late in March the Ames group showed its hand at a Crédit Mobilier stockholders meeting. One resolution guaranteed the new Williams contract and approved subletting the work to contractors at $25,000 per mile, which insured a decent spread for profits and other expenses. Another authorized a probe into Durant's stock account to see, as Oliver noted privately, "if stock has all been pd for properly." Oliver suspected that Durant had not paid the required subscription on all the stock held in his name. Later Dillon would discover 650 shares of Crédit Mobilier issued to the Doctor but never paid for. This block of stock would loom large in later negotiations.

As was their custom, the Bostonians scheduled meetings of both Crédit Mobilier and the Union Pacific board on the same day. Durant did not even bother to attend the Crédit Mobilier session, but scarcely had the Union Pacific directors settled in their chairs than he protested the new Williams contract on the same grounds that he had objected to the Hoxie extension. The board gave him scant notice and proceeded to approve a recommendation that the Hoxie contract be settled in full by paying Crédit Mobilier slightly less than $2 million. Lacking funds to pay this obligation, the Union Pacific later gave Crédit Mobilier a note for the amount. For nearly a decade this note would become the source of bitter controversy.

The most pressing need was money to keep the work going. With the bank loan still uncertain, the Union Pacific board authorized Rowland G. Hazard to negotiate the sale of $10 million in first mortgage bonds. No one was more surprised at this action than Hazard. At sixty-six he had recently retired from business, leaving his mill operations in the hands of his son Rowland while he indulged his fondness for travel, study, and the writing of philosophical treatises. A tough, grizzled Rhode Islander with features as granitic as his sense of integrity, Hazard was a curious mixture of shrewd practicality and fierce idealism. His reputation was widespread as a reformer on such diverse issues as national finance, education, temperance, and political corruption. During the 1850s he earned a national reputation as an outspoken critic of railroad monopolies and advocate of rate regulation. Hazard was known as a man who, once he took hold of a matter, pursued it relentlessly to a conclusion. This quality was what attracted the Bostonians to him; later it would come back to haunt them.

Hazard wanted nothing more to do with active business but relented when Lambard insisted that no one else could raise the money needed. For two weeks Hazard pounded the streets in search of loans. The more bankers he saw, the less he liked what he found. Most were willing to deal with him but confided that they would not lend a dollar to any company in Durant's charge. From them Hazard heard tales of what he later called "Durant's spoilations," although the details still eluded him. The Union Pacific's finances were in shambles and some of its notes on the verge of protest. Never one to mince words, Hazard told Oliver bluntly that "some radical change must be made" in the financial affairs of both Union Pacific and Crédit Mobilier. The message was clear: Durant had to go.

The Ames brothers and their friends were willing but hesitant. The problem was not only how to get rid of Durant but who should replace him. Oliver was tired of bickering with the Doctor and, with the shovel works to run, was reluctant to take full charge of the road. Oakes was tied up in Congress, and none of the other Bostonians showed any appetite for command. In desperation Oliver and Hazard tried to persuade John Blair to take hold of the Union Pacific. Blair's Cedar Rapids road had just won its race with the M & M to Council Bluffs, giving the Union Pacific its long-awaited rail connection with Chicago. Oakes and Lambard had long been associated with Blair in the road and were impressed by his ability, but Blair could not be tempted.

While Oliver and Hazard were courting Blair, the Doctor gave the financial snarl another awkward twist. On April 4 he and Cornelius Bushnell endorsed Hazard's proposition to market the $10 million in bonds and procure a $1 million loan. The agreement was put in writing but did not yet have formal approval from the board. A few days later Durant blithely closed a deal with Clark, Dodge & Company for the same bonds and loan. A large part of the money for the loan was to be furnished by Bushnell and other insiders. Oliver approved the arrangement and then told Hazard the board had no choice but to accept it. A disgruntled Hazard acquiesced on condition that he receive the next $5 million of bonds to sell on the terms of his original contract. Later he would discover that the terms of the Clark, Dodge deal had been misrepresented to him.

In mid-April Oliver, Durant, Duff, Dillon, and Harbaugh journeyed west to formally receive the 305 miles of completed road from the contractors. It took them nearly two weeks to reach Omaha. The worst storms and flooding in years had torn up lines on both sides of the Missouri River. Reed was disconsolate that his track "which was in such good shape should be at this season of the year so badly cut up," but the directors were pleased with what they saw. Oliver noted that the road "where not washed runs very well." He and the others inspected the line, poked around the shops, and examined possible locations for a bridge across the Missouri. In January the board had authorized a new position of General Superintendent for Operations, thereby enabling Reed to devote full time to overseeing construction. During the visit Oliver appointed Webster Snyder, the freight agent at Omaha and a close friend of Hoxie, to the post. He took care also to approve personally Snyder's choice of subordinates and to draw up instructions for the new position.

In these decisions Oliver pointedly ignored Durant. Throughout the trip an undercurrent of tension had been building between the Doctor and the others. The officers in Omaha felt it and trod delicately to avoid taking sides, but they were also anxious to know something definite about plans for the coming season. A host of contractors eager for work were on hand as well, but no decisions could be made until Durant and the Bostonians resolved their differences over a contract. On May 4 the storm burst when Oliver bluntly warned Durant "about his lawless way of doing work taking the whole thing into his hands—& forbid his doing it without consultation." The meeting broke up in a row. Two days later Oliver and the others left Omaha, declaring that no decisions would be made until the conflict was settled.

Durant lingered in Omaha a few days, stewing with rage, suspicious of all about him but powerless to act. Dillon notified Dan Casement that any contract let by the Doctor would not be binding on the company. Reed and the other officers found themselves in an impossible position. Long accustomed to taking orders from Durant, they no longer knew who was in charge and hesitated to do anything that might draw fire. Like clerks caught in the coils of a palace intrigue, they were fearful of choosing sides prematurely. The stalemate in New York had cast its pall on Omaha as well.

Something had to be done, and fast. Hazard boldly suggested a coup. While the others were on tour, he continued his rounds of bankers in New York and Providence with the same discouraging results: few were willing to lend while Durant remained in charge. To restore credibility, Hazard argued, Durant had to be ousted from Crédit Mobilier at its annual meeting on May 18. The Bostonians agreed to a surprise attack. On his way to Philadelphia, Oliver stopped at New York, where he saw Durant and Bushnell. Since neither planned to attend the meeting, a tight-lipped Oliver collected their proxies and hurried to Philadelphia. Still the largest individual stockholder in

Crédit Mobilier, the unsuspecting Doctor had turned his 5,558 votes over to men ready to use them against him.

The Bostonians moved with ruthless efficiency. Durant was dumped as president and director of Crédit Mobilier along with one of his allies. Dillon, Alley, and Hazard were elected to the board. Dillon assumed the presidency when Hazard declined the office, and Hazard and Alley were put on the executive committee. Ham replaced Crane as assistant secretary and treasurer in the New York office. When the smoke cleared, Durant had been stripped of all influence in Crédit Mobilier. Even this did not satisfy Hazard, who demanded a full judicial investigation into the sums for which Durant had not made account.

On May 21 Crédit Mobilier's new officers returned to New York and confronted Durant with their coup. In blunt language they told the Doctor that his practices would no longer be tolerated. Train tried to intercede with Hazard later that day but was rebuffed with a vow to push an investigation into "Durants defalcations." But Durant was not easily cowed. Far from chastened, the Doctor left his dressing down by Dillon and Alley agitated and bent on vengeance. While Train pleaded his case, Durant worked feverishly to secure another injunction against the Williams contract. When the Union Pacific board met the next day, he waited until some routine business had been transacted before signaling Clark Bell to serve the papers. The meeting broke up in turmoil. Seymour watched the proceedings uneasily. "This of course is a declaration of war on the part of the Doctor," he informed Dodge, "and what the result may be God only knows."

Now it was the Bostonians' turn to rage. The normally mild-mannered Oliver was beside himself. Durant's ouster from Crédit Mobilier, he sputtered to Dodge,

> has raised the very devil in that amiable Gent and he has come down upon us with injunctions and proposes to visit us with every form of Legal Document to keep us honest. Such a lover of honesty and fair open dealing cant bear to see the money of the UPR wasted on such scoundrels as make up the balance of the Board of Directors. I cannot understand such a change as has come over the Dr. The man of all others who has from the beginning stole wherever he had a chance & who is to-day we think holding stock and a large portion of his stock on fictitious claims and trumped-up a/cs [accounts]. He is now in open hostility to the Road and . . . is now seeking to favor other roads and other interests.

Dillon urged Hazard to press his investigation of Durant's account. "Unless he does what is right dont let up on him," he exhorted. "He will be very smooth to your face but will stab you in the back if he gets the chance." Bushnell talked hopefully of buying the Doctor out.

At the board meeting the next day Durant slouched in his chair, smiling nervously while the directors upbraided him for his conduct. He knew he had put them in a tight place. Two or three company notes had gone briefly to protest. Nobody knew about it, thanks to Hazard, who avoided publicity by hastily arranging loans to cover them. However, the injunction had squelched the Williams contract and threatened to shut work down entirely. Some other arrangement had to be made until this latest tangle was resolved. Hazard wanted the pious Doctor eliminated from any share in a contract and suggested forming a new construction company. In the long run this may have proved the wisest course, but none of the others favored it.

Instead the Bostonians chose to meet the challenge head on. Durant watched placidly while the board appointed a committee of five to contract for building the road to the base of the Rocky Mountains. It also created a new committee to settle the Hoxie contract and engaged as attorney Samuel J. Tilden, who managed to get the injunction lifted by the month's end. Oliver telegraphed Omaha that Durant had no authority for making contracts or anything else. Alley, Bushnell, and Hazard were put in charge of raising money. Alley proclaimed grandly that he could create a market for Union Pacific bonds. To encourage his efforts, Oliver rashly promised him a share of his own future profits from Crédit Mobilier if Alley would devote half his time to the task.

Late in May Dillon and Dodge headed west to oversee the work and prepare for another junket of dignitaries across the road. Durant followed close behind, and Oliver feared his ability to curry favor with the excursionists. He warned Dodge to notify banks, contractors, and other parties that Durant was "now hostile to the Road" and would "do every thing possible to injure its Progress. . . . You will be able to meet him at all points and with Dillon checkmate him." Oliver also authorized Dodge to let contracts for construction to the base of the mountains. Whatever new trick Durant might have up his sleeve, the work would go forward.

The falling out between Durant and the Bostonians marked a fateful turning point in the history of the Union Pacific. Had the break not occurred, the saga of the road's construction would have turned out quite differently. Instead the conflict blighted not only the company's immediate future but its destiny for decades to come. From its machinations flowed years of strife and litigation that kept the company in constant turmoil and spawned the scandal that would forever taint the Union Pacific. The genesis of the Crédit Mobilier investigation, which probably did more to blacken the public image of railroads than any other event of the nineteenth century, lay in this rupture. Just as the Golden Spike came to signify the achievement of American railroads, so did Crédit Mobilier become the symbol of their disgrace.

* * *

For weeks they watched the river anxiously, straining to catch some sign that the break was coming. Fierce storms and frigid cold had frozen every river in the Platte Valley with ice nearly four feet thick. The feeder streams too were solid, and the plains lay buried in snow. A last blizzard roared across Nebraska late in March, crippling trains on both sides of the Missouri. "We are out of luck in this country," wired one of Reed's men from Grand Island, "wind blowing and snow drifting worse than ever, half [of the] men either blind or frozen, looks bad." Then the weather turned mild, and Reed braced for the worst.

The ice broke first in Loup Fork, punching vainly at the bridge before separating into two packs that roared with irresistible force through the embankments on both sides and piled up in immense heaps along four miles of track. To Reed's relief all the bridges withstood the surging ice except one at Prairie Creek, which was swept downstream. Everywhere water poured across the roadbed. East of Grand Island a stream half a mile wide washed away the track, rushed twenty miles inland, and crossed the track again, wiping out ties, rails, and embankments. In some places track and ties dangled without embankments; elsewhere the reverse was true. The Missouri stayed frozen until April, then spilled wrathfully over its banks as meltwater and heavy rains fed it for weeks. No one could recall ever seeing the rivers this high. "Hereafter," Reed observed glumly, "I shall have no faith in the saying of the oldest inhabitant."

Jack Casement eyed the rain and rising waters impatiently. He had a new contract for $850 per mile and was anxious to get started. Enough rails and ties had been stored up over the winter to lay 150 miles, and Jack's call for men had fetched responses from as far east as Cleveland. The Cedar Rapids road had laid track to the river on February 11, giving the Union Pacific its long-awaited rail connection to the east. But high water blocked the passage of goods, and work crews could not get to end of track until the flood damage was repaired.

Once the waters receded, Reed pushed his men hard to get the road in shape before the committee of directors arrived from New York. Dodge had wired him early in March to start work on the fourth hundred miles so as to have it ready for the visitors, but the weather destroyed that hope. It was all Reed could do to get the road passable for the inspection tour. "I do not feel any trembling in my boots," he wrote as Durant and the others reached Omaha. "I . . . know I have done my whole duty for him and the company he represents." The directors found no fault with his efforts, but Reed took little comfort. He had survived the storms of the west only to find himself paralyzed again by the storm of dissension that blew in from the east. Until the contract muddle was resolved, he could not even be sure of his job. For days he stepped gingerly about the combatants. When Oliver and Durant parted in anger, Reed talked gloomily of resigning.

In May the clouds finally lifted. Although Durant's injunction locked the management in combat, the board at least ordered contracts let. The appointment of Snyder allowed Reed to move his headquarters to North Platte to oversee construction. Casement's men hurried forward to lay rails behind an army of graders working furiously to keep ahead of them. Contractor Lewis Carmichael led a party of fifty men to commence work on the eastern slope of the Black Hills. All supplies were hauled by rail to end of track and from there to crews in the field by an endless shuttle of wagons. It took forty cars to carry the material, equipment, fuel, and supplies to lay one mile of track. The overland freighters, aware that the Union Pacific would soon put them out of business, hustled to get one last season of cargoes from the military and the railroad. Dodge later estimated that the company employed ten thousand men and the same number of animals when construction was in full swing.

On the plains the grading crews could cover a hundred miles a month under ideal conditions, but that summer Indians made their lives miserable. After December 1866, when they ambushed and massacred eighty-one soldiers, the Indians grew bolder in their raids. Aware that the railroad crews and surveyors were venturing into country where the Indians were most active, Dodge spent the winter pleading with Grant and Sherman for more protection. "It is hard to make a lot of Irishmen believe," he reminded them. "They want to see occasionally a soldier to give them confidence." The generals were sympathetic but lacked enough troops to fill all the demands on them. Reconstruction policy siphoned off part of Grant's command for occupation duty in the South, and enlistments were down. On the vast reaches of the plains the army was trying to protect the railroad, the stage routes, and settlements as well as mount active campaigns against the Indians.

"I regard this road of yours as the solution of the Indian affairs and the Mormon question," Sherman assured Dodge, "and, therefore, give you all the aid I possibly can." Both Sherman and General C. C. Augur, commander of the Department of the Platte, thought the best tactic was not to defend the road but to pursue the Sioux relentlessly in the field. The railroad crews, Sherman explained, should be told "they are more safe along the Lodge Pole with our soldiers two or three hundred miles north, than if those same soldiers were close at hand." Dodge knew the army was stretched thin, but it made his task no easier. An abortive campaign south of the Platte did little more than give the Cheyenne new confidence to roam farther northward. "The Arapahoes will soon be heard from," Dodge warned Sherman. "They are working towards Laramie Plains, and when they get to work we will have fun."

In May, while Augur prepared an expedition to the Powder River, the Indians struck the road with lightning raids. They stole the supplies of two subcontractors in northeastern Colorado and, in Dodge's words, "scared the workmen out of their boots, so they abandoned the work and we can not get them back." At Ogallala they chased a survey party and ripped out their stakes. Tie cutters in the Black Hills were routed and their equipment burned. The worst attack hit Percy Browne's survey party near Rock Creek, killing his assistant and a trooper. Three stagecoach stations were burned and livestock stolen. Railroad men, stage agents, telegraphers, ranchers, and settlers all clamored for more protection.

Dodge did what he could to suppress news of the raids from the papers, fearing that "should our men get at the real truth, they will stampede." Fresh from the sickbed, he urged Sherman to keep Augur on the line instead of sending him to Powder River. Durant warned Grant that "the entire work will be suspended" if protection could not be furnished. Within days the Sioux struck again, killing and scalping five of six men in a section gang only 220 miles west of Omaha. Another party hit a train at end of track, slaying three men and driving off livestock; a third surprised a survey camp, killing one man and taking thirty head of stock.

One delegation of Washington's own got the message firsthand. On May 27 Dodge accompanied three government commissioners to examine forty miles of track for acceptance. Afterward the party pushed on to end of track in Lodgepole Valley. When they arrived at noon, the crews were eating lunch under the eye of a military guard. Suddenly a large band of Indians swooped down on a grading crew and made off with their horses and mules before the men could scramble for their rifles. The commissioners watched incredulously and went home to argue the need for more troops. Reed despaired of holding his men unless more soldiers were provided, but Dodge countered that "the men defending themselves were of far more benefit than the troops that could be gotten there." He reminded the grading party chiefs that their men outnumbered the Indians and were ex-soldiers who knew how to defend themselves. The chiefs went away determined to rely on their own ranks in the future. When Augur finally received more cavalry to protect the line, Dodge asked that it be used for scouting instead of guard duty.

* * *

Despite the turmoil in the boardroom and the Indian raids, Reed doggedly urged his crews onward. Contracts for the last of the fourth hundred had been let in April, and Dodge pressed Dillon to let the fifth hundred before the Indians burned the ties already distributed along that ground. On June 24 Casement's men laid rails into Julesburg, 374 miles from Omaha. By then graders were pitching into the fifth hundred, which would bring the road into Wyoming. As the tracklaying proceeded, the supply bases at end of track sprang magically into bustling, brawling boomtowns that presented Reed and Casement with problems of quite another kind. Traders, gamblers, saloon keepers, and prostitutes poured in to feed on the railroad men, teamsters, miners, soldiers, stagecoach travelers, and adventurers who gathered in these stop points immortalized by some unknown wag with the apt name of "Hell on Wheels."

A year earlier Durant had ordered Reed to open a second supply base west of Loup Fork because it would "not answer to have men so near whiskey shops as Columbus." But Columbus paled in comparison with the spectacle of North Platte. A young medical officer passing through in May found fifteen buildings, of which nine were saloons and one a billiard room. Traders and miners driven in by the Indians helped swell the population to five thousand restless souls who were "having a good time, gambling, drinking, and shooting each other." The only law in town was provided by a hastily organized vigilante committee. Within six weeks the town shriveled to a few hundred residents as tents and shacks were knocked down and packed up to follow the rails westward. "Hell on Wheels" had moved to Julesburg.

In June the population of Julesburg was forty men and one woman; by the end of July it swelled to four thousand. The old stage station had become the "Wickedest City in America," its dusty streets choked with stores, saloons, warehouses, gambling dives, and a theater. Reed called it a place where "vice and crime stalk unblushingly in the mid-day sun." When General Augur and his staff came to town eager to see the sights "by the gas light," the prudish Reed enlisted as guide Dan Casement, who knew his way around town. Dan took them first to a dance hall graced by a fresh supply of whores, where an incredulous Reed witnessed profanity and indecency that "would disgust a more hardened person than I." At a gambling house he saw drunken men squandering their bankrolls on the turn of a card or throw of the dice. Women clung to their reeling companions, egging them on or picking the pockets of those who managed to remain sober. When they tired of the sport, Dan led them on to other establishments where the same scenes were repeated. At last they came to the theater and, as special guests, were invited behind the curtain to peek at the girls.

Dodge called Julesburg "a much harder place than North Platte." As land agent for the Union Pacific he laid out the town and left an agent in charge of selling lots. In his absence the gamblers joined forces and decided to take their lots without paying for them. The helpless agent telegraphed the news to Dodge, who was furious. Vice was one thing, the seizing of company lands quite another. Dodge wired Jack Casement to have his men clean up the town and hold it until the gamblers paid for their lots. He knew Jack would enjoy the cleanup as much as Dan relished the nightlife. Jack marched into town with two hundred men and held a parley with the gamblers, who spat contempt at him. With icy calm Jack ordered his men to open fire, "not caring whom he hit." The gamblers fled in terror and afterward paid willingly for their lots. When Dodge came to town and asked what had happened, Jack led him to a nearby hill humped with fresh graves. "General," he told Dodge solemnly, "they all died in their boots and Julesburg has been quiet since."

* * *

For the surveyors, 1867 was the year of decision. If all went well, Dodge predicted to Sherman, the road would reach the Laramie River by season's end. To keep ahead of Casement's crews, Dodge sent L. L. Hills to complete the 140 miles from Crow Creek to the base of the mountains. Evans took charge of finishing the line over the Black Hills to the Laramie River. From there Percy Browne would work the 275 miles to the Green River, a dangerous stretch through the worst of Indian country. At the far end Dodge ordered T. H. Bates to explore some alternative routes through the rugged Wasatch Mountains to Green River, especially one leading up the Bear River that might connect with Reed's survey in the valley of the Black Fork.

Dodge himself was in a quandary that dismal winter. The chief engineer wanted to go west, but as a congressman and lobbyist he dared not leave Washington for a while. He tried without success to get a subsidy for a branch line to Denver. The March blizzards on the plains inspired Senator Conness of California to fresh mischief by promoting rumors that the Union Pacific had stopped work entirely. Above all, the company needed a decision on the point at which mountain work began. Dogged lobbying by Dodge and the government directors finally moved Secretary of the Interior Browning to appoint Jacob Blickensderfer of Ohio as the engineer to determine the base of the mountains. Dodge didn't know Blickensderfer personally but found he had a reputation for being competent and reliable.

Unfortunately, Blickensderfer could not go west until late June. Disgusted with Washington and bothered by an old war wound, Dodge went home to Council Bluffs. The survey parties were making good progress despite the Indians. Evans had gone out early to join the men who had wintered over in the Black Hills. Because the line would have a crucial bearing on Blickensderfer's work, the company ordered it completed in two months. Evans not only finished in May but produced a line that satisfied Dodge in every respect. On the plains Hills was approaching the end of his survey. Dodge notified him of the recent attack on Browne's party and warned him to be cautious. Browne's slain assistant, he added, "was away from camp and picked off; therefore, be careful, vigilant and make your men the same."

It was good advice. The Indians grew more brazen in their surprise attacks. On June 2, just before sunrise, they hit every survey camp along a twenty-mile stretch of Lodgepole Valley. In one camp young Arthur Ferguson was awakened by the cry, "Here they come, here they come, boys!" Surveyors and soldiers tumbled half-naked from their tents, rifles in hand, to see the Indians charging down from a bluff. After a hot exchange of fire the Indians retreated, carrying off their wounded and most of the camp's animals. The soldiers gave chase and managed to retrieve some of the stock. One of the engineers brought back a grisly trophy captured from the Indians: the scalp of a white woman, so fresh that it was still green. A week later fifty Cheyennes struck Julesburg, killing two men before reinforcements drove them off. A medical officer arrived to find the bodies scalped and mutilated horribly, one of the victims "pinned to the earth by an arrow through his neck. He must have been shot after he had been scalped."

All along the vast stretch of plains the survey parties huddled together, forlorn and anxious in their isolation, waiting for the next blow. Yet, as

Dodge himself admitted, something in the nature of the engineers made them careless of danger. On June 14 Hills wandered a short distance from his party when a band of Arapahoes attacked. Paralyzed with fright, Hills tried to reach his men but was riddled with arrows. A young axman named J. M. Eddy outraced the others to camp and rallied the confused men. After fighting off the Indians, Eddy led the party to the outpost at Fort Collins. Later Dodge learned that Eddy had served in his own corps during the war at the age of sixteen. He would remain in the service of Dodge and the railroads for the rest of his life.

Eddy's valiant effort saved the party but could not help Hills. The men reclaimed his body and buried it alongside the Cache la Poudre where, young Arthur Ferguson mourned, "he now sleeps in his lonely grave . . . amid the awful silence of this wild and boundless region, his solitary resting place uncared for, with no kind friend to strew a flower or to shed a sympathetic tear over him." At the year's end the company sent Ferguson and some others to exhume Hills's body and bring it home for burial. Ferguson never forgot this ghastly experience, and Dodge saw to it that Hills was not forgotten. When the railroad came through later that summer, Dodge named the town nearest where his engineer was slain Hillsdale.

The loss of Hills came at the worst possible time for Dodge. Hills had not quite finished his survey between Pine Bluffs and Crow Creek crossing, a difficult section where Dodge wanted a grade not exceeding thirty-five feet per mile. Blickensderfer was about to come west with Seymour at his elbow. Already Dodge had a letter from Seymour requesting maps and profiles of Evans's Black Hills line to enable him to "judge of the effect which any slight change" might have on the cost of the work. Knowing Seymour's knack for meddling in the work of others, Dodge sniffed trouble coming. To make matters worse, Dodge's constituents wanted him back in Washington just when he was anxious to examine the entire route still under survey. Without hesitation Dodge chose to go west instead of east. Ill health still plagued him, he announced blandly, and the doctors had ordered him to recuperate in the mountains.

By the time Dodge left Julesburg on June 28, his party had grown into an excursion. Evans, Reed, and Jack Casement accompanied him, as did Blickensderfer and Seymour. Grant had asked Dodge to take along his close friend and chief of staff, General John A. Rawlins, already ill with the consumption that would kill him two years later. Rawlins brought along his aide and two friends from Galena, one of them a reporter. Young John R. Duff was there at his father's request, the rich young man sent west to learn the ropes. David Van Lennep, the geologist, General Augur and his staff, and some officers heading west rounded out the party. For protection Sherman provided two companies of cavalry and two of infantry. With this mixed bag of companions Dodge set forth on one of the most critical missions he would ever undertake for the Union Pacific.

The first task was to get Hills's party back in the field. A hard march brought the party to a bend on Crow Creek where Dodge pitched camp. Finding that no work had been done since Hills's death, he combined two survey parties under Evans and sent them to finish the work between Pine Bluff and Crow Creek Crossing. While Evans went to work, Dodge looked over the ground about his camp. As land agent he had been authorized to lay out town sites along the road at points of his own choosing. His sharp eye concluded that the railroad's division point at the base of the mountains belonged precisely where his tents now stood. Hastily he laid out a town, setting aside 320 acres for the railroad's use. For all his hatred of Indians, Dodge honored the dominant tribe in the region by naming the new town Cheyenne.

The country about them was in full bloom. Across vast expanses to the horizon thick plains grass flowed in the wind like a heaving green sea tinted with flowers. In the bottomlands delicate white lilies sprouted through the grass like winding streams of milk. Even the cacti were awash with red and golden blossoms. Beyond the green sea to the west loomed the snow-capped peaks of the Rockies shimmering in the sunlight. At 6,100 feet the sun burned by day and everyone crawled under blankets to escape the chill at night. A young officer reveled in the small pleasures of camp life, "the pipe of tobacco as you lie in the warmth of the camp-fire digesting your hearty meal, smoking and either engaged with your own thoughts or listening to some legend that is always told among a party of officers."

On the fourth of July the party got up a celebration featuring an eloquent speech by Rawlins. Their festive mood was blasted the next day, when a Mormon grading outfit coming in from Utah approached the camp on their descent from the Black Hills. As they drew within sight, a band of Indians sprang from cover and rushed the wagon train. The cavalry mounted hastily and galloped to their rescue, but the Indians killed two or three men and drove off some stock before vanishing back into the hills. Rawlins and the others were astounded at seeing them attack in the face of so large a force of troops camped nearby. Because they had seen no Indians on the march to Cheyenne, some of the easterners thought the menace was all humbug— though Reed noticed they were careful not to stray far from the train. They were all believers now. Dodge ordered the dead buried on the site of his new town. Cheyenne had its first inhabitants.

* * *

The continental divide was not at all what Percy Browne expected to find. To his surprise the Rockies dropped from thirteen thousand feet down to six thousand feet onto an open plain. The divide itself turned out to be a great basin five hundred feet lower than the surrounding country. Browne thought a stream must lead across part of this basin to the Pacific. Leaving his party camped along the last creek where they knew good water could be had, Browne headed toward the south rim of the basin in search of water and a possible line. He took along an assistant and five troopers for protection. In three days they covered sixty miles across the arid flats of the Red Desert, where the sand shifted color in the changing light. On the night of July 22 they camped in a dry creek bed that ran into Bitter Creek near the stage station at Laclede.

Next morning Browne started down the valley of the creek bed. At about ten o'clock he noticed a large party of Sioux in the distance. The corporal in charge of the escort had spotted their ponies half an hour earlier but inexplicably said nothing about it. Browne and his men galloped toward one of the ridges along the valley, but the Indians gained too much ground on them. The engineers and three soldiers dismounted and formed a line while the other two troopers led the horses toward the ridge. Those Indians with rifles also dismounted and crept through the sagebrush behind a running fire while the rest swept forward on horseback, yelling and blowing their whistles to unnerve the whites. The cavalrymen stayed calm, keeping up a steady fire while they edged toward the ridge with the engineers behind them.

The fight raged for half an hour. Suddenly Browne shrieked in pain, wounded by a ball that passed through his abdomen. He managed to stagger a few hundred feet before slumping to the ground. Shoot me first if you must leave me, he begged his assistant, but the men would not abandon him. Instead they let the horses go, hoping the Sioux would go after them. When they did, the troopers helped Browne make it to the ridge, where they waited the rest of the day. The Sioux returned after capturing the horses, but seemed hesitant to attack and finally left. The men improvised a litter by lashing their carbines together. At nightfall, carrying Browne with them, they trudged down the ridge toward the road leading to the stage station. Once on the road they were lucky enough to meet a wagon train, which took the wounded engineer to Laclede.

Throughout this long ordeal Browne never groaned or complained, though his agony was great. Shortly after being hit, he had murmured to his assistant that he did not expect to live, for he had known only one man to survive such a wound. The stubborn loyalty of his comrades had been in vain. To their sorrow Browne died half an hour after reaching the station.

* * *

Dodge lingered in Cheyenne until July 21, when Evans completed his work. Settlers were already pouring in, fired by assurances that the railroad was coming. The next Hell on Wheels was underway. To protect the newcomers, General Augur established a post just north of town and named it Fort A. D. Russell. Once Dodge selected the railroad grounds, Reed, Casement, and some others returned to Julesburg. Reed's assistant stayed behind to supervise the crews already toiling in the Black Hills. Blickensderfer was already at work west of Cheyenne. Dodge wanted Seymour to accompany Blickensderfer on his inspection of the Cheyenne Pass and Cache la Poudre routes to Denver, but Seymour replied loftily that it was "none of his business to show him that country." He preferred instead to examine Evans's line across the summit of the Black Hills. Already shorthanded, Dodge had to send another engineer with Blickensderfer.

The consulting engineer, with his airs and pomposity, was getting on Dodge's nerves. "Seymour does nothing but complain of work done, lines &c. takes his ease and wants to be waited on," he grumbled to Dillon. "Everybody along notices it and makes him a standing joke." On the trail the sight of him kept the Pawnee scouts in stitches. Settled astride a derelict horse (for which he had paid a handsome sum), his poncho, bedding, and other gear wound about a barrel wedged behind him, his carbine tightly strapped and buckled in its case "to be convenient in case of a sudden Indian attack," Seymour would hoist his umbrella and placidly follow the escort or lead them forward.

Seymour might be the butt of many a joke, but Dodge knew better than to underestimate him. His tongue was sharp enough that its victims called him the "Insulting Engineer." No one was spared its lash, not even the Doctor. Above all, Seymour was a master of insinuation. He talked a good game and wrote with a glibness convincing to those without close knowledge of the subject. His manner was as disarming as it was devious. Dodge could not abide a man who was not a worker, and no one accused Seymour of overexertion. Seymour was more than a nuisance; he was a dangerous enemy.

And he was up to something, Dodge was sure of it. His first inkling of trouble came when Seymour, after several days of poking about the line across the Black Hills, reported that he had found a better one down from the summit with an eighty-foot grade "at about the same expense" as Evans's line with its ninety-foot grade. Even more, he thought his line could avoid the necessity for a high bridge through the treacherous gorge at Dale Creek. Since the improved grade would in his opinion be worth "a quarter million dollars" to the company, Seymour asked for a survey party to help confirm his findings.

Dodge replied at once that he considered Evans's line superior to any other and would recommend no change, but he agreed to furnish the survey party. Seymour let it be known that he did not regard the supervision of survey parties as part of his duties, but he deemed the matter of grades important enough for him to undertake the work. There must be no delay, "as contractors are now at work upon some portions of the line involved in the change of grade, and others will soon be upon the ground." Meanwhile, he added ominously, he would send word of his findings to the board in New York for their views.

Was this the ox-bow all over again? Seething inwardly, Dodge left Cheyenne early on July 21 and led his party across the summit to Dale Creek on the edge of the Laramie Plains. While his men fished for trout, Dodge studied the creek itself. Here was the obstacle that defied him: a puny stream trickling through a gorge 130 feet deep and 713 feet wide. To cross it would require a trestle bridge 125 feet high and 1,400 feet long. For several days he prowled over the ground descending from the summit, searching for alternative routes. The results merely confirmed what he already believed: Evans's grade could be improved only by putting in too much curvature, and the high bridge could be avoided only by long tunnels that would delay the road's progress interminably. On the eastern slope Dodge found he could reduce the grade to eighty feet by spending another $200,000. He wrote Oliver Ames urging that it be done.

Having satisfied himself, Dodge gathered up his party and went on to Fort Sanders. He paused long enough to lay out a town nearby that would become Laramie. For days he had been trying to learn the whereabouts of Browne's party; at the fort he heard for the first time that Browne was dead. The news shriveled even Dodge's stout heart. Except for Evans he considered Browne the best and brightest of his engineers. Now he was gone, and with him the notes and information collected on the region west of Fort Sanders. Much of it would have to be done over again. Two of his survey chiefs were dead, and Dodge himself still felt weak. On the long trek west he had suffered "everything but death from my rides—how long I can stand it God only knows."

Dodge was not a man to wallow in despair or self-pity, but he was tired, sick, overworked, and shorthanded. For two weeks the Indians had been "attacking everything and everybody," and all the parties were skittish even with escorts. The burden of finishing Browne's work now fell on him and Evans. Seymour wanted no part of leading a survey party except to pick at the Black Hills line. Asked to lend a hand, he responded that it was poor policy to send parties out during Indian uprisings. There would be plenty of time next year, he assured Dodge.

That tore it for Dodge. Enraged and maddened with grief, he poured out his bitterness in a letter to Dillon. Seymour was no help to him at all, he snarled, and "seems not to care a damn whether the Indians get the road or not so long as he can play gentleman and have a big company to foot his bills. He will . . . sell any or all of us if he can better Seymour." To his wife Dodge was even more blunt, calling Seymour "the worst sneak I think I ever met; [he] means mischief to our company—professionally dishonest and corrupt—and the quicker the company gets rid of him the better."

Dodge had made an enemy of Seymour, but something else worried him more. He was convinced that Seymour intended to cause trouble over the Black Hills line even though it was obvious that any delay would be disastrous for the company. What was he up to? Had the Doctor put him up to it? Dodge had no way of knowing, but he fretted over Seymour's ability to sway Oliver or at least stir fresh fires of dissension within the board. For that reason he pressed both Oliver and Dillon to decide the question at once and let him know before he moved on. When no reply came, he wired Dillon again. "I must push West," he stressed. "The Indians hold the country from here to Green River and unless I get out there, we will fail in all our plans for 1868."

He would not like the answer that came.

7

THE STANDOFF

The most striking fact about the early history of the Union Pacific was its lack of strong leadership. This shortcoming has gone virtually unnoticed in all that has been written about the company, yet it was decisive in shaping the road's destiny. During these difficult years a parade of personalities tugged at its management, many of them forceful and capable men. Whatever else they achieved, none provided the sense of direction or unity of purpose essential for a successful enterprise. Some, like the Doctor, left their imprint in the form of scar tissue; others left no mark at all. The result was a legacy of drift and dissension that burdened the road for decades. Ultimately the Union Pacific endured not because of its managers but in spite of them.

Fate did not treat the Union Pacific kindly in this respect. On the Central Pacific, the Big Four bickered constantly over policy but managed to submerge their differences in quest of their goals. But the Central Pacific had Collis P. Huntington, a man of indomitable spirit and relentless energy who could move mountains and was not overly particular about how he did it. No figure comparable to Huntington emerged within the divided councils of the Union Pacific. Durant longed desperately to play the role but had already shown himself unfit for it. Blair might have succeeded but declined the opportunity. Among the Bostonians could be found men of many talents but none suited for taking command of so vast an enterprise except possibly Oakes Ames. Unfortunately, Oakes was not available for the task and his brother was.

True to his name, Oakes was a tower of strength. His tall, brawny, barrel-chested frame radiated the vitality of a man weaned on outdoor life and hard work. A smile came easily to his strong, square face with its gray-blue eyes and massive jaw. Born in 1807, the eldest of eight children, Oakes learned early to bear responsibility. Never much of a student, he left school early to enter his father's shovel works. By nature he was what men liked to call a "doer"; he knew how to get things done, how to drive work forward. He tended to be impetuous and careless of details. His plain-spoken, simple manner caused some to regard him as naive in his dealings, but Oakes was no fool. He took care of his own without earning a reputation for being sharp or cunning. Men admired his lack of pretension and his willingness to take on difficult tasks. Lincoln liked to call him "the broad shouldered Ames."

Oliver was of quite another temperament. Four years younger than his favorite brother, he was more studious and reflective. For a time he contemplated a career in law before joining Oakes in the shovel works. A tall, handsome man of slighter build than his brother, Oliver had a quiet, gentle disposition that shrank from conflict. Brighter than Oakes but more timid, his mind grasped subtleties that utterly escaped Oakes and was more alert to the proprieties. He typified that breed of New England businessman who would not knowingly touch a dishonest transaction and therefore believed that any transaction he touched must be honest; who would not knowingly commit an unscrupulous act and therefore assumed that any act he committed on behalf of his properties must be scrupulous.

The contrast between the brothers was striking. Oakes was the man of action, Oliver the punctilious bookkeeper who clucked disapprovingly at his brother's recklessness. Where Oakes was disarming in his frankness, Oliver was tactful and cautious. Once decided on a plan, Oakes plunged ahead with little regard for consequences; Oliver calculated and agonized himself into fits of indecision. Oakes was a man who saw forests and was careless about trees, Oliver one who best understood forests through an inventory of trees. They complemented each other well so long as Oakes steered and Oliver served as brake. Unfortunately, it was Oliver who found himself president of the Union Pacific at a critical time. He did not want the office and would gladly have surrendered it to the right man. The duties required of him made the most of his weaknesses and the least of his virtues. He was not the man to harness disparate personalities into an efficient team.

Above all, Oliver lacked the temperament or the backbone to handle the Doctor. Without that ability no one could impose harmony on the Union Pacific. Oakes might have done it, but he was not available. The hapless Oliver became the wrong man in the wrong job at the wrong time. Fate had doomed him to a role he despised, that of playing hedgehog to Durant's fox.

* * *

In June 1867 Durant hosted another of his junkets for politicians and reporters. After long silence the press had begun to praise the road's progress, and the Doctor was happy to furnish them with fresh adventures. Since the public knew nothing of the company's inner turmoil, the excursion also allowed him to bask in the limelight while promoting the road. Once again the Doctor treated his 140 guests to a good show, including a reprise by the Pawnee soldiers, who muddied the effect by performing the war dance in their military uniforms. Nevertheless, Durant garnered some lavish rhetoric from the senators and favorable publicity in several major papers. Train went along to amuse and enlighten during the long hours of travel. As one reporter quipped, "With GEORGE FRANCIS TRAIN to deliver impromptu orations upon all conceivable subjects, from the great empire of the West to the wrongs of the poor Indian, the time could not fail to pass pleasantly."

The Doctor's absence made Oliver expansive about future prospects. "I and all in connection with the road here," he wrote Dodge, "have never been so sanguine of the success and great merit of this Road as we are since Durant has been put out of its management." Durant might remain a source of trouble, but how much bite could he have left? Bankers now smiled on the company and offered money at better rates. Alley and Hazard were hard at work trying to raise funds. Once the financial house was put in order and a new general contract was arranged, nothing could stop the road's progress.

No sooner did he utter these sentiments than an ugly quarrel broke out among his friends over that botched transaction, the loan from Clark, Dodge & Company. Had Oliver recognized the danger at once, he might have avoided or at least minimized the damage, but he was slow to grasp the issue or its potential for shattering the unity within his own ranks. His failure would cost the company dearly.

The Clark, Dodge arrangement had been made when the Union Pacific was hungry for cash and desperate to sell its mortgage bonds. In February 1867 Durant and Bushnell proposed that the bankers lend the company $1 million at 7 percent plus 2½ percent commission and a bonus of 2 percent. In addition, Clark, Dodge was to sell $10 million of the company's first mortgage bonds for a commission of 5 percent. Nor was that all. Ever alert to opportunity, Durant and Bushnell offered Clark, Dodge an extra bonus of $40,000 provided that half the money was repaid them once the deal was approved. For some reason the negotiations hung fire until April, when the offer was tendered without the extra bonus.

Even this version amounted to an inside deal. Most of the loan came not from Clark, Dodge but from Bushnell and other directors who used the banking firm as an agent to conceal their involvement. Although Oliver had no share in the loan, he knew of this arrangement and approved it in writing. He did not bother telling Alley and Hazard about it when they took charge of the road's finances; they were informed only that the company had tendered the offer and that they must work around it. Alley and Hazard agreed that this "onerous contract" was a bad bargain for the company and a "most formidable difficulty" in trying to raise money. For weeks they buttonholed bankers in New York, Boston, Hartford, Providence, and New Bedford, seeking loans at better rates and a market for the company's bonds.

In May the situation changed abruptly. A few days after the turnover in Crédit Mobilier, Clark, Dodge refused to advance funds under the loan agreement. One of the bankers told Hazard and Alley that his firm had never intended to accept the proposal and would not provide money because, in Hazard's words, "they wanted to see if we were going to break up." After all, the banker added, Clark, Dodge was a "mere figurehead" in the deal. Hazard and Alley eyed him blankly; this bit of intelligence was their first clue that others were involved in the loan. Hazard promptly advised withdrawing the offer to Clark, Dodge. Under his earlier agreement with Oliver, both the loan and sale of bonds now reverted to him. In his methodical way Hazard took pains to inform Oliver and several directors of this change, assuring them that he and Alley could get much better terms for the company. Twice he discussed the matter with Oliver, who joined the others in giving his consent.

Or so Hazard thought.

The board took no formal action on the agreement. In June the company's finances improved markedly, thanks to swelling receipts from the road and a small but steady sale of first mortgage bonds at a price of 90. This was the first time the Union Pacific had managed to peddle its own bonds. Although the company advertised the offering heavily, the response surprised everyone. Hazard and Alley attributed it to their intensive efforts to restore confidence among the bankers. Oliver chose to see it as the fruit of replacing Durant's erratic influence with sound management. Whatever the reason, this unexpected showing threw the Clark, Dodge agreement into an entirely new light. The wily Bushnell now saw he had a good thing if the deal could be revived on its original terms.

While Hazard and Alley were busy wooing bankers, Bushnell persuaded Oliver that the company was obliged to stand by its offer to Clark, Dodge. He also tried to disarm Hazard by offering him a tenth interest in the loan; the old gentleman promptly spurned it as improper. McComb, who had been rebuffed in his earlier attempt to lend two hundred thousand dollars under the Clark, Dodge arrangement, complained to Oliver that Hazard's efforts to raise money had "injured rather than benefited" the company's finances. For his part Oliver already regretted his private arrangement with Alley, whose style of "producing a great grand impression" had begun to grate on him. Oakes added to his disenchantment by passing along the opinion of a friend who called Alley "the most selfish grasping man he ever knew."

A leather dealer by profession, Alley was a sharp trader and an emotional character with strong opinions that he did not hesitate to express. Politics had only partly sated his appetite for the large gesture; he had just closed his career in Congress after four terms and was eager to leave his mark on the Pacific railroad. Like Hazard he made no bones about his dislike of Durant, and this issue may well have been at the heart of Oliver's dilemma over the

Clark, Dodge muddle. The board had put Union Pacific finances in charge of two men (Hazard and Alley) who were Durant's most implacable foes, while the two key figures behind the Clark, Dodge deal (Bushnell and McComb) were the Doctor's friends and served as his intermediaries with Oliver. To Oliver's dismay the Doctor, still belligerent and unreconciled, continued to haunt him. On June 21 Durant made it clear to Oliver that he wanted back into the management. That same day Oliver decided to accept the Clark, Dodge proposition.

Were the two matters connected? The evidence suggests that they were. For Oliver the paramount issue was getting a contract that would enable them to complete the road. Williams stood ready to renew his proposal, which the Doctor could trump with another injunction. Like it or not, the Bostonians could do nothing without Durant's cooperation. Reluctantly they entered into a tortuous round of negotiations to hammer out some sort of agreement. In this context Oliver's acceptance of the Clark, Dodge deal emerges as a gesture toward placating the Doctor and his friends. Bushnell was present the day the decision was made. A large, bubbly man full of enthusiasms, he had grown adept at playing on the hopes and fears of his staid president. If anyone could persuade Oliver that good would flow from the Clark, Dodge agreement, it was Bushnell.

Whatever hopes Oliver entertained were quickly dashed. In effect he had gone back on his friends to appease his enemies. Hazard was outraged at having the profits of his labor snatched away by "a clique of active directors, an inside ring as it is techinally [sic] called." He lost, and the company lost by paying more for money than it should. Oliver offered a lame defense which Hazard demolished in his rejoinder. The same vigor Hazard had shown in raising money now went into a relentless campaign to have the terms of his agreement honored and in pressing the suit against Durant. Although he still worked for the Union Pacific, the dispute left him an embittered seeker after justice. Too late Oliver realized how right Hazard had been. In February 1868, when the Clark, Dodge account was settled, he noted in disgust that profits on the $1 million loan amounted to $165,000 or 16½ percent, and that Bushnell got another $15,000 from the company "with no right." By then Oliver too was referring to the "CD & Co Ring."

During July 1867 feverish efforts were made to reach a settlement. Durant still had the Williams proposal tied up in court and showed no inclination to relent until the dispute over the suspense account was resolved and his place in the management restored. The government directors tried to intervene as mediators without success. At a board meeting on July 10 Bushnell moved to revoke the agreement with Hazard and ratify the "informal engagement" made earlier with Clark, Dodge. The motion was tabled. That night Oakes came up from Washington to bargain with Durant in hopes of persuading him, in Oliver's words, "to disgorge ill got gains, withdraw his injunction and go on again smoothly." Since March, Oakes had been struggling to get the suspense account settled. "I don't exactly know where the block is," he confessed, and Durant did not enlighten him that evening. The board met again next day but accomplished nothing.

That night Durant took some of the government directors to Newport for what Oliver termed "corrupt purposes." When they returned a few days later, the Doctor sprang his ambush. On July 16 the board received a proposal to build 667 miles of road from Alley and H. C. Crane, Durant's confidential secretary. Alley did not follow Hazard into moral exile over the Clark, Dodge controversy but in his shrewd, politic way straddled the issue. Now he lent himself to a compromise plan hatched by Durant which, if approved, would put the Doctor in a strong position to dominate the new contract. Oliver saw the danger at once. All Durant needed was a majority vote, and the Bostonians were short-handed at the meeting. Lambard and Cyrus McCormick were in France; others had scattered to the resorts. With most of Durant's allies present, the government directors held the balance of power. The Doctor had thought of that too.

The new proposal was sent to a committee composed of Oliver, McComb, and Charles Sherman. The Clark, Dodge resolution was then recalled, but before it was discussed the board recessed for half an hour. When it reassembled, McComb immediately moved to compensate the government directors for their services. Harbaugh was tendered five thousand dollars, the other four three thousand dollars each. The motion passed and the board adjourned until the next day, giving everyone time to do some dealing. A stunned Oliver had no doubts about what had happened. "Govt directors evidently bought to support Durant's schemes," he noted sourly. A thankless evening of bargaining left them "Unable to agree on the mode of and parties to carry out [the] contract."

Next day the proceedings took some bizarre twists. Oliver could not prevent McComb and Sherman from reporting favorably on the Alley-Crane proposal; it was promptly approved with only Oliver and Duff dissenting. The motion to compensate the government directors was then brought back and handed to a committee for reconsideration. Apparently Ebenezer Cook objected to his services going unrewarded, for his name was added to the list. The Clark, Dodge resolution was dredged up again and finally approved. After a motion to adjourn failed, Sherman abruptly moved to reconsider the Alley-Crane proposal. For reasons that are unclear, he succeeded in getting the proposal tabled. The board then reversed itself yet again on the compensation matter by rescinding the action to create a committee and passing anew the original motion with Cook included among those receiving three thousand dollars.

Victory barely eluded the Doctor's grasp. He had caught the Bostonians divided among themselves and napping at their posts. Oliver hurried home and, together with Dillon, drew up a new contract proposal in the name of Oliver Chapman. Durant sent Bushnell after him to parley for a compromise.

The Doctor's terms were simple: he wanted "his old position in the Road." Oliver understood what that meant: control over construction and the letting of contracts, which he would handle in the same profligate style that had alarmed the Bostonians in the first place. He would ride the work like a whirlwind, sowing antagonisms and chaos in his wake, then walk away with his pockets stuffed full of illicit profits from subcontracts or other secret deals. There could be no harmony on those terms.

While Bushnell dickered, the Doctor surprised the board with a new contract proposal in his own name at lower figures than the Alley-Crane offer. He tried to get a meeting to consider the proposal but could not muster a quorum. When Dillon and Bushnell left with several of the government directors to inspect the road, the Bostonians blocked a quorum until their return by staying home. Durant countered by having his allies call for a special meeting on August 15, at which he expected to ram through his proposal. He also asked the court to delay hearings on his injunction, leaving it poised to wield against any plan offered by the Bostonians.

Oliver eyed his prospects bleakly. By one count Durant had ten directors in tow; the Bostonians could muster only six. Duff was bedridden with typhoid fever, depriving Oliver of a staunch ally at a critical time. Lambard and McCormick were still in Paris, where Lambard's wife had fallen seriously ill. Furious at Durant's maneuvers, Lambard advised securing an injunction if the Doctor's proposal carried. Alley suggested combining this action with the suit Hazard was preparing against Durant. Since the Crédit Mobilier election, the Bostonians had spurred Hazard on in his determination to sue Durant for recovery of the unaccounted funds. Although not sharing Hazard's zest for battle, Oliver and Dillon agreed to hire Samuel J. Tilden and his associate, Judge W. F. Allen, as counsel in the suit.

Hazard took their encouragement at face value. With the zeal of a crusader he advised against bargaining with Durant until the Doctor lifted his injunction, but Oliver had no stomach for so hard a stand. He preferred diplomacy to war, even with Durant. The July meetings gave Hazard his first hint that efforts were underway to negotiate a settlement, and he was quick to protest. The Ames brothers, finding it ever more difficult to please all sides, resorted again to mixed signals. They urged the suit along and also sounded Hazard on a compromise proposal to create a sort of railway bureau that would include both himself and Durant. Hazard spurned it wrathfully as "disgracing myself and destructive to the Co." On one point he was implacable: he would tolerate no arrangement that let Durant back into the management.

John Williams urged him to reconsider. "Our great opponent is alive to all kind [sic] of expedients," he pleaded, "& springs them suddenly after wearying us out talking about matters he means to yield to, in an unguarded moment, get [sic] in *something important, as a trifle*—wish we could get clear of him." But they could not. Time was running out. If the August 15 meeting could not be avoided, some plan was needed to counter Durant's proposal. Oakes came up from Washington to handle that matter. Hazard was in New York, too, getting papers ready to serve against Durant. Alley, Dillon, and the Ames brothers examined the complaint and suggested improvements.

On that steamy August day the board did not manage a quorum until four in the afternoon. Bushnell and Dillon had come back from the West weak with fever. Bushnell never appeared and Dillon staggered in late, but all five government directors were present. After some perfunctory remarks the directors adjourned to their favorite haunt, the Fifth Avenue Hotel, for an evening of hard bargaining. What transpired in room 90 that night has never been revealed. Hazard, who spent the time wrangling with Durant's counsel, doubted the Doctor would "agree to any thing that will not give him control (virtually)." Oliver noted in his diary that "nothing was done." But something happened, and the force behind it was Oakes Ames.

When the board reassembled next morning a startling reversal occurred. The Alley-Crane proposal was withdrawn and replaced by one from Oakes covering 667 miles of road at the same prices offered earlier by John Williams. In effect Oakes assumed personal liability for a contract totaling $47.9 million, leaving the details to be arranged between himself and a committee of the board. One "detail" in particular had to be determined: to whom would Oakes ultimately assign the contract? Evidently Durant was confident he would be included in any assignment. No righteous injunction was forthcoming this time even though the same figures had drawn his wrath earlier. The Doctor and his cohorts voted in favor of the proposal, as did everyone else except two government directors, who objected to high prices for work that stopped short of the Wasatch Mountains. One of them, Jesse Williams, tried to limit the contract to the Laramie River but was voted down. After approval the proposal was sent to the executive committee to thrash out the details.

That would not be easy. Oakes's contract avoided a crisis but solved nothing. Oliver had predicted that the Doctor would "soon find that he is not Genl Manager," but Durant could still block approval in the executive committee unless he got what he wanted. Nothing had been done about the suspense account, and Hazard's suit still loomed. The result was not a compromise but a standoff. Oliver tried to put a brave face on it, telling Dodge that the contract had "no provision to favor Durant or any other individual." Hazard feared the showdown might come at the September meeting and implored Lambard and McCormick to come home in time. The last word belonged to Charles Sherman, who thought the contract would finally be settled in September, giving everyone "a 'big thing.'" Sherman had arranged to get a twenty-thousand dollar slice of the pie for himself, but he was dubious. "Such a selfish, grasping set I never met before," he sighed, "and therefore I do not rely on them."

* * *

Two thousand miles from New York the repercussions of this clash hounded Dodge's journey across the forbidding terrain west of Fort Sanders. All summer long Oliver had stressed the urgency of pushing the work as fast and cheaply as possible. That impulse dictated his response to Dodge's report that he could obtain an eighty-foot grade on the eastern slope of the Black Hills for an additional cost of two hundred thousand dollars. "The great desire of the Country is a rapid completion of this Road," he asserted. For now he was content with a line that conformed to the government's maximum specifications "even if we had to reduce them after we get in opperation [sic]." Jesse Williams objected to this policy as "a great cheat" because many roads did not improve their lines for years afterward. Dodge too entered his protest but in vain.

Oliver had another compelling reason for this policy. He thought Durant was poisoning the minds of the government directors with the notion that the work was lagging. "I do not wish the Dr to make any Capital out of this," Oliver wrote Dodge, and any delay would play directly into his hands. The letter reached Dodge after he had left Fort Sanders. Ignorant of the machinations in the East, he knew only that trouble was brewing and he was helpless to do much about it.

From Fort Sanders Dodge's party followed Browne's line to Cooper's Lake and then west to Rock Creek. It was wild, forbidding country, bordered on the south by the snow-capped Medicine Bow range, "mountain piled on mountain with immense cañons . . . broken by perpendicular walls." As Dodge plodded on, his imagination was fired by what a spectacle the scenery would make from the window of a railroad car. In the Rattlesnake Hills (now Saddleback Hills), he found a pass striking the head of Mary's Creek, which cut through steep ridges on a zigzag course to the North Platte. Dodge named the pass in Browne's honor and later gave the name Percy to a station at the head of Mary's Creek. Near the top of Browne's Pass, Van Lennep found immense coal deposits at a place Dodge called Carbon. The company's first coal mine would be located there.

The North Platte was broad, cold, and high with meltwater, a welcome relief from tramping over ground thick with alkali. The party was forty or fifty miles north of the stage road to Bridger's Pass. Aware that the place was a favorite rendezvous point for Indians, General Gibbon established another post, this one called Fort Steele. Dodge paused a few days to examine the country, then crossed the river and headed toward the continental divide. After a day's march through barren country, he ordered everyone to fan out in search of water. Wandering southward, Dodge and Rawlins struck a spring gushing from some solid rock. Rawlins tasted the water and declared it "the most gracious thing" he had ever found. Then, Dodge smiled, we will call it Rawlins Spring. Already he had grown fond of Rawlins. "He is one of the purest, highest minded men I ever saw," Dodge wrote his wife, "and that he must die with that dread consumption seems too bad." At night, beneath the black sky, Rawlins entertained the soldiers and engineers around the campfire by reading poetry to them from books he had brought along.

Dodge discovered that water from the spring had cut its way through the ridge beyond, making passage easy for a railroad. Browne had run his preliminary line this way, and so far it had been remarkably good. But where was his party? Dodge found them at the stage station, without horses or water and still mourning the loss of Browne. After refitting they were sent to run a line back to the North Platte while Dodge pushed west, taking with him Browne's assistant, Francis Appleton. Blickensderfer and Seymour also parted company with Dodge, declaring they had seen enough parched wilderness to satisfy them that no railroad could run through it. A better line, they agreed, must lie farther north along the Sweetwater River to South Pass, and they wanted to search it out.

Dodge knew better. He remembered the country from his Indian campaigns, but he gave Blickensderfer and Seymour an escort and sent them on their way. Nothing came of their explorations, although Seymour continued to argue that a good route could be had north of Browne's line. While they wandered northward, Dodge led his party across the continental divide. The terrain beyond astounded him as it had Browne. The mountains gave way to a series of basins, each with its own drainage. At the center of the main divide lay a giant basin some three hundred feet below the surrounding country. A vast plain running two hundred miles east-west and nearly one hundred miles north-south stretched before him, with little vegetation and no living streams. It would make an easy line if water could be found.

All this Dodge learned the hard way. He assumed that the ground beyond the divide descended toward Green River. Instead his party found themselves plodding into the giant basin and through the alkali wastes of the Red Desert. On the third day the water ran out and scouts found only dry creek beds, the "shallow graves of deceased rivers." Burned and blinded by the sun, their tongues swollen with thirst, the men and animals endured two days' march without water before stumbling across an alkali lake. The water was not palatable, but they swarmed gratefully to it. Dodge and Rawlins went up a rise to scan the basin with their glasses. In the distance Dodge spotted what he thought to be Indians until he saw teams with them. Hurrying forward, he discovered it to be Bates's survey party working east from Green River. The men had been without water for three days and were in terrible shape. A few were violently ill from stagnant or poisonous water they had found in the Red Desert.

Comparing notes with Bates brought Dodge to the realization that the divide had not one but two summits, at opposite ends of the basin. He replenished Bates's supplies and sent his party to test the country north of Browne's line. Dodge's party followed an old trail in search of an outlet over the western rim of the basin to Bitter Creek. He saw clearly now that "it was all-important to cross these plains on the shortest possible route that would carry our line from running water to running water." After some rugged going they struck Bitter Creek Valley at Point of Rocks, the sandstone cliffs carved into bizarre shapes by the wind. Dodge guessed that an excellent line with low grades could be had across the divide by leaving the basin earlier and finding a gentler approach to Bitter Creek. Appleton was dispatched with an escort to find a smoother line to the south, which he managed to do only after months of difficult work and great hardship.

From Bitter Creek Dodge followed the splendid line run by Evans in 1864 through the winding valley to Green River. There he met the survey party headed by young Fred Hodges. In May Dodge had ordered Bates to create a second party to explore a route east from Salt Lake to the Green River via the Bear River. Hodges had run this line as far north as Soda Springs and briefed Dodge on his findings. The results left Dodge uncertain as to the best route from Green River to Salt Lake. Reed's survey had established that the line must run between the north rim of the basin and the rugged Uinta Mountains that walled its southern edge. Two major obstacles barred the way: the steep western rim of the divide and the Wasatch Mountains, described by Dodge as "rugged, bold, and narrow."

Dodge decided to follow Reed's old line from Green River along Black's Fork to Fort Bridger, up Muddy Creek, and across the divide to Bear River Valley, which led into Echo Canyon. Close inspection showed it to be a good line, and some changes could make it better. From Echo his train wound its way into Weber Canyon and through the narrows to Salt Lake Valley on August 30. The trip convinced Dodge that the true line lay north of Salt Lake and probably along a refined version of Reed's original survey. Several obstacles had to be overcome, notably the need for a long tunnel at the head of Echo, severe grades, and another tunnel with heavy work in the Weber Narrows. Hodges tackled these problems for the rest of the season with impressive results.

Something more was at stake in the tortuous ravines of Weber and Echo. Central Pacific engineers appeared in the canyons to do preliminary surveys. Huntington told Jesse Williams that the Californians had decided to run north of Salt Lake. Oliver thought the Central Pacific would try to reach the lake first and warned Dodge that it was "of the utmost importance to us to have the Salt Lake business for our Road." In fact Huntington had a far more ambitious plan: he wanted to beat the Union Pacific not merely to Salt Lake but to the Green River. The engineers prowling about the canyons offered the first hint of this larger scheme.

Dodge had a grand notion of his own about a route all the way to Puget Sound via the Snake River. On the return trip he followed Hodges's line north to Soda Springs and beyond to Gray's Lake, where he reached the waters of the Snake. What he saw convinced him that a route along the Snake

River Valley "would be by far the best line from the Atlantic to the Pacific, would avoid the high elevation of the Wahsatch and Sierra Nevadas with their heavy grades and troublesome snows." From atop a ridge he peered across a magnificent wilderness through which the Union Pacific would later build its Oregon Short Line.

The journey homeward also gave Dodge a chance to explore the route along the Sweetwater River. His findings confirmed that no feasible line lay farther north in the Red Desert than the one Browne had located. At Lumbard's Spring he found Bates, who had examined the route suggested by Seymour and Blickensderfer and discarded it as impractical. Satisfied that he had the best line, Dodge put Bates and Appleton to the task of perfecting Browne's work. He lingered awhile, checking work he had ordered done earlier, searching in his restless, urgent way for improvements. Then, grudgingly, he pushed on toward the Black Hills.

During the season Dodge's engineers traveled 5,193 miles and reconnoitered 3,310 miles to stake 1,675 miles of line. The result of this effort was 665 miles of continuous if tentative line from Julesburg to the Salt Lake. But Dodge had done more than survey a railroad route. Along the way he had mapped a part of the West, filling it with names and places that would grow into legend. Despite his earnest swipes at self-promotion, Dodge has never received honor or recognition worthy of his immense achievements. Whatever pride or satisfaction he felt at the time got shortchanged by the controversy over the Black Hills line that had boiled up in his absence.

At every stop along his journey the mail pouch brought Dodge the latest chapter in a farce he was helpless to prevent. Seymour's report of a change that might lessen the grade on the western slope and avoid the high bridge at Dale Creek impaled Oliver on a nasty dilemma. Any delay in the work could be used by Durant to cast the Bostonians in a bad light, and who was in a better position to delay work than Seymour, the Doctor's own tool? Oliver did not trust Seymour's judgment anyway, but he dared not ignore it. Jesse Williams thought him a good engineer, and Seymour could be convincing to the uninitiated. He had been retained, Oliver noted contemptuously, "more for the purpose of . . . whitewashing his (the Dr) rascalities than for any real Engr service he has done or will do the Co." If his findings were accurate, however, he and the Doctor could make a potent case against the Bostonians for ignoring them. To avoid that trap Oliver gave Seymour permission to make his survey even though it meant still more delay.

Dodge counted on Evans keeping an eye on Seymour, but Evans was called suddenly back to Omaha, where his wife died of fever before he could get home. "The shock to my oldest boy, a very sensitive nervous subject makes me tremble for his safety," he wrote Dodge. "He is very low and I cannot leave him." Alarmed by Seymour's pawing over his line, he implored Dodge to return at once "to watch change in location," but Dodge could not leave his expedition. The distraught Evans put aside his grief long enough to write Dillon a powerful defense of his line. His argument was persuasive but in vain. In his innocence Evans did not yet realize that the dispute involved far more than matters of engineering.

Using the survey party provided him by Dodge, Seymour attacked not only the western slope but the eastern approach as well. Within days his puttering brought chaos out of order. James Maxwell, head of the survey party, admitted that some of Seymour's changes improved Evans's line on the western slope but declared an eighty-foot grade on the eastern slope impractical. His assistant, John O'Neill, ran another line combining Seymour's changes with the eighty-foot grade on the eastern approach. Reed didn't like any of the changes and decided to look the situation over in person. The graders were already at work and wanted to know which line to grade. A bewildered Dodge tried to clear the air by approving some changes and wiring Reed to choose the best line. Seymour was wasting time and tying up Maxwell's party. "I need that party badly west of us," he complained to Oliver. "Wish you would telegraph Seymour that work cannot be delayed for any more surveys."

On August 21 Seymour informed Oliver that too much grading had already been done on the eastern approach to make a change feasible. A week later he announced that he and Blickensderfer could reduce the eastern approach to an eighty-foot grade and save $120,000 in the bargain. The change would also move the fixed base of the mountains three miles east, giving the company an additional $48,000 in subsidy bonds.

Oliver hesitated. This extraordinary find by one he had privately denounced as a "lazy inefficient man prone to criticize others & do nothing himself" ought to have made him suspicious, but Seymour dangled bait too tempting to refuse: more bonds, cheaper construction, and a better grade. Oliver's demand for haste was tempered by the fear that "if we make the Road cost too much It will never pay dividends." The Oakes Ames contract did not yet have final approval, and a struggle loomed for control of the company at the annual election on October 2. Nothing must be done that Durant could use to advantage in the contest. Seymour was "an extremely plausible man with excellent ability as a writer" who "if he can make a point against us and in the interest of Durant will do it." And he was, after all, the consulting engineer, which meant he could not be ignored.

Or so Oliver explained his decision to Dodge. Seymour's new line was "certainly the most desirable route, and *if so* should be adopted." Cutting through Oliver's platitudes, Dodge saw that the board had chosen to believe Seymour instead of him. Maxwell's party was held captive awhile longer in the Black Hills as Seymour plied his art on both sides of the summit. The grading bogged down in hopeless confusion. The man in charge of the crews wired Dodge that he couldn't "get any grades here from the summit west; parties at Dale Creek waiting for work." No one could fathom O'Neill's version of Seymour's line or keep up with Seymour's constant alterations.

The bewildered graders trudged from one line to another. "The folks are still sweating in the Black Hills," Evans reported on his return late in September. "As I came along three separate lines of grading could be distinctly traced in places showing that some of the changes had been changed." The last weeks of good summer weather slipped away in these futile exercises.

Government director T. J. Carter hurried west to inspect the work, but Reed feared Seymour could "wind Carter around his fingers at will." Was Seymour trying to delay the work on purpose, Reed wondered. "The object apparently is to injure somebody's reputation," he suggested darkly, with Dodge the likely scapegoat. Dodge was convinced that "all delays were going to be laid on me if possible." But it was Reed that Oliver castigated for "want of System and Application to duty . . . he prefers doing any thing but his duty." This was a curious outburst at an improbable target. Although Reed had opposed Seymour's changes from the first, he submitted meekly to the decision of his superiors. Privately he talked again of resigning.

When Dodge returned at last from his expedition, he was appalled by the time and money wasted in grading three separate lines to the summit. A quick survey convinced him that Seymour's changes on the western slope would not work. On his own initiative he ordered all surveys stopped and grading resumed on Evans's original line. Seymour challenged the order and informed Oliver he had found a route across Dale Creek that would save $200,000 and three months' work. Oliver clung to this hope long enough to drag the controversy out another two months, but in the end even he had to concede glumly that all of Seymour's "wonderful improvements" amounted to nothing. Carter, not so malleable as Reed thought, told him as much after returning from the West. Fortunately Reed had managed to postpone grading on the western slope until Dodge could arrive. On the eastern approach the best Dodge could do was patch together a line incorporating some of Seymour's changes but still using a ninety-foot grade to connect with Evans's original line descending from the summit. Later it was found that an engine could haul more cars up Evans's approach than on Seymour's proposed eighty-foot grade with its excessive curvature.

If Seymour's intent was to delay the work, he could claim a brilliant success. More time and money had been squandered at the height of the season with nothing to show for it except hard feelings all around. The major responsibility for this fiasco belonged to Oliver, who again showed a tendency to vacillate at critical moments. Foolishly he ignored the advice of a man he respected in favor of one whose judgment he held in contempt. He had demanded speed as a way to avoid Durant's traps only to allow Seymour to create the worst bottleneck of the year. But the fault did not lie with Oliver alone. The control of events never lay firmly in his grasp; he could do nothing without looking over his shoulder. As a result decisions had less to do with the situation in the West than with the ongoing struggle for power in the East, where Durant sprang yet another surprise.

* * *

In the glare of an investigation, Oakes insisted that he "took that contract without any regard to anybody else," and Oliver, Alley, even Durant swore this was so. The statement may be literally correct, but there is not an ounce of truth in it. Oakes never intended to assume personal liability for a $48 million contract. The problem was how to assign it to his friends without having to include his foes as well. Durant had vowed never to let Crédit Mobilier have another contract and stood ready to block any such attempt. Hazard and John Williams bitterly opposed any arrangement that allowed Durant back into the management. For the Ames brothers the alternatives looked bleak. They must either crush the Doctor entirely or embrace him in a compromise that would split their own ranks.

The obvious solution was to dump the Doctor from Union Pacific at the annual election. "I dont feel that we should do right to put Durant in as director unless he withdraws his injunction suits and submits to the will of the majority," Oakes told McComb in what proved to be prophetic words; "he cannot hurt us half as badly out of the direction as he can in." Oliver was confident his friends would have enough votes to fill the board with reliable men, especially if they could lure Bushnell and McComb to their side. Both were practical men who never let personal loyalty stand in the way of self-interest. To woo their support a scheme was devised for handling Oakes's contract in a way that allowed them to defect gracefully.

The plan was designed to get around the objection of assigning the contract outright to Crédit Mobilier. Instead it would be given to seven trustees empowered to supervise construction and distribute the profits *only* to those Crédit Mobilier stockholders who also owned Union Pacific stock and signed irrevocable proxies allowing the trustees to vote 60 percent of their Union Pacific shares. As a third party to the agreement, Crédit Mobilier would provide the trustees with funds for construction in the form of loans at 7 percent interest and 2½ percent commission. The trustees would decide all matters by majority vote and replace any of their number who interfered with execution of the contract.

This unwieldy arrangement had several advantages. If enacted, it would restore harmony among the warring factions of the two companies. At the very least it created a third body with full authority to push work forward even if the bickering continued. Through the irrevocable proxies the trustees could control enough Union Pacific stock to insure a friendly board at elections. Since profits from the contract would be in the form of Union Pacific securities, all Crédit Mobilier stockholders who signed the proxy agreement would own shares in Union Pacific. Any construction contract was merely a vehicle for transferring these securities as payment for work done; the real profits came when the securities acquired a market value. By thwarting attempts to get a contract, Durant had succeeded in blocking distribution of these securities. The trustee arrangement would eliminate that obstacle and hopefully prevent others from arising.

By mid-September the papers were drawn, but two problems loomed. The most obvious had to do with naming the trustees. The Ames brothers preferred to avoid Durant but reasoned that he could be included as long as his friends did not comprise a majority. Hazard objected even to his presence and refused to surrender his proxies to any such arrangement. Differences also arose over the idea of pledging votes to a board to be named by the present board, which would give Durant and his allies a large voice in the selection. In the bargaining that followed, the Doctor continued to resist any proposal that left him a powerless figurehead. Privately Oliver dared hope that no deal be made with Durant "unless he comes to our terms."

He should have known the Doctor better than that. On September 19 Judge Allen, the Bostonians' lawyer, warned Oliver that Durant was busy with some project "by which he expects to succeed or else to foil & defeat the election. I dont know what it is. He is hard at work & is unscrupulous & reckless." The answer came two days later when Oliver learned that someone friendly to Durant had subscribed for 20,000 shares of Union Pacific. The "someone" turned out to be that clown prince of finance, Jim Fisk, whose outlandish antics concealed a shrewd and cunning mind. Somehow Durant had induced Fisk to help him corral enough shares to control the election. In all the Durant forces tendered offers for 49,000 shares in New York and 20,000 more in Chicago.

Caught by surprise, the Bostonians realized they were in a dogfight. Durant and his cohorts offered 55 for the stock on the grounds that current holders had been assessed only that amount so far. Cisco, the treasurer, declined the offer, insisting that he could only accept par by law. This was the opening Oliver and his friends needed. Frantically they scurried about the city scrounging all the cash they could muster. Blair agreed to pledge $1 million, and Hazard secured funds from several parties including his friend Charles Gould. On September 25 they stunned Durant by offering to buy an astounding $50 million of Union Pacific stock at the same price of 55. Oliver thought this clever ploy ensured victory. If all offers for 55 were accepted, the Bostonians would have enough stock to carry the election; if Cisco held firm in refusing offers at that price, Durant and his friends would still be thwarted.

Well before the election both sides flocked to New York where, grim and apprehensive, they traded, cajoled, threatened, and conspired with the urgency of diplomats on the eve of war, hoping for a compromise to end hostilities or a weakness capable of crushing the enemy. Neither turned up. Two years of bickering had driven them all into a maze of conflicting interests and personal animosities so tangled that not even the lawyers could find exits. The line between peace and war had grown too opaque even for the statesmen among them. Never did the lack of leadership seem more glaring than during these desperate, futile intrigues before the election. No one emerged with the force or authority to command support from all sides. Tragically, the strongest personality among them happened also to be the chief source of controversy and division. Once again the Bostonians were to learn that the Doctor could not be subdued by committee.

Through these dreary days Oliver struggled to unite his ranks around the trustees agreement. A frenzied round of meetings brought the wavering Alley into line, but Hazard and John Williams would not relent. Hazard urged Oakes to start work under his contract and not assign it until assured of a friendly board in Union Pacific. As a precaution he also persuaded Williams and Charles Gould to prepare injunctions in case the election went against them. Oliver clung to the notion that McComb held the key to success if somehow he could be induced to desert Durant. To gain his support Oliver resorted to drastic action. He agreed to surrender the presidency to McComb if he would join in "electing [a] new board of directors & such other things as an honest administration of Pac RR interests required." The offer was no sacrifice for Oliver, who longed to be rid of the job. His concern was whether McComb could be trusted to live up to the bargain. Harmony could be achieved, he noted, "if our own man will follow our counsel." But McComb proved more slippery than he suspected.

Oliver had reason to fret. The absence of Dix, Lambard, and Duff reduced the executive committee to a quartet of Oliver, Durant, Bushnell, and Harbaugh. The key vote belonged to Harbaugh, who had thrown in with Durant along with two other government directors, Sherman and George Ashmun. Harbaugh wished to be reappointed; Oakes preferred another man and rashly asked McComb's help in getting him the post. When the executive committee met on October 1, Durant made his first move. He and Harbaugh blocked action on the Oakes Ames contract until they got an amendment requiring written approval by Union Pacific stockholders. Later that day the board rewarded Harbaugh with a resolution urging his reappointment.

The board convened to appoint the election inspectors. Samuel Tilden had stressed to Oliver the importance of getting friendly inspectors. Early that morning the Bostonians agreed on Oliver, Cisco, and Carter as their inspectors, but Bushnell talked Oliver into including him instead. "Don't do that," Alley barked when Oliver told him just before the meeting, but it was too late. Ashmun got the jump on Bushnell and nominated a ticket slanted in the Doctor's favor. Bushnell tried lamely to amend but was voted down. The Doctor promptly moved that the board adjourn to meet again that evening at the Fifth Avenue Hotel, where he expected some trading to take place. Oliver seemed unfazed by the setback. A puzzled Hazard watched him emerge from the boardroom "smiling & joking as if well satisfied with the result."

While the directors closeted in one room of the Fifth Avenue Hotel, Hazard met in another with Alley, Tilden, Allen, and General Ben Butler, a tough, savvy politico who had been summoned as counsel by the Bostonians. Working furiously, they readied two injunctions on behalf of Charles Gould and John Williams as front men to keep Hazard's name out of the case. Meanwhile the directors thrashed over the trustees agreement late into the night until a potential slate of names emerged: Oliver, Alley, and Dillon on one side and Durant, Bushnell, and McComb on the other. After much haggling it was agreed that the seventh trustee would be Benjamin E. Bates, president of the Bank of Commerce in Boston and an ally of the Ameses. It is possible that Oliver agreed to accept Durant if the Doctor would accept Bates as the swing member. A motion to endorse the assignment was tabled pending receipt of the guarantee from Crédit Mobilier. Bushnell went to fetch the trustees contract from Allen, who refused to surrender it. Tempers flared, hot words followed, and Bushnell left empty-handed. Spent and peevish, the directors filed wearily out to catch a few hours of sleep before the showdown next day. Alley and Hazard lingered until one in the morning with the lawyers, who had returned from procuring the injunction. They were certain Durant had done the same.

When the Bostonians assembled at eight the next morning, Hazard again demanded a new committee to investigate Durant's suspense account. For months the Ames brothers and Dillon had encouraged Hazard in his pursuit of Durant. Unlike Hazard, however, they cared less about redressing wrongs than pressuring the Doctor into a compromise. Hazard was useful to them for that purpose even if his views on justice were too unyielding for practical men, and so they gave him rein once more. Hazard scribbled off a suitable resolution and handed it to Butler, who grunted that he would use it as circumstances dictated. The sly general had a plan for the election superior to anything he had ever managed on the battlefield.

Promptly at ten the combatants, tense and expectant, crowded into the outer office of the Union Pacific rooms at 20 Nassau Street. The fireworks started at once. Oliver succeeded in getting Alley named chairman and then recognized Butler, who moved to rescind that part of the bylaw authorizing the board to appoint election inspectors. Clark Bell, one of Durant's lawyers, was on his feet at once with a motion to table but lost by a stock vote of 25,924–220. Over Bell's persistent objections Charles Gould rammed through a motion for the chairman to appoint new inspectors. Bell tried for adjournment but was beaten down again. Both sides then hauled out their injunctions, forcing a recess to sort out the legal snarls. Butler and Allen hurried to see the judge, who had issued the injunctions for both sides, and persuaded him to modify theirs, enabling the Bostonians to proceed with the election on their own terms. Gould disposed of the disputed 55 percent stock with his injunction, leaving the Ames group with a decisive majority.

When the meeting resumed, the Bostonians felt confident enough to appoint new inspectors and recess again for "refreshments." An hour later they trooped back in and quickly elected a new board with Alley, Hazard, Blair, and other friends in place of the Doctor and his cronies. Still Durant refused to concede defeat. Instead his forces defiantly held their own election under the original inspectors and produced a board minus Oliver and his cohorts. Only seven names appeared on both boards: Bardwell, Bates, Bushnell, Cisco, Dillon, Duff, and McComb. In counting their tallies the Ames inspectors threw out 9,621 "illegal" shares, the Durant inspectors a whopping 44,000. Both sides milled about in confusion, helpless to find a way out of the morass. The election that was supposed to settle the dispute had only encrusted it with another layer of bitterness and complexity.

That evening the Ames board gathered at the Fifth Avenue to choose officers. An unhappy Oliver kept his position, with Hazard as vice president and Cisco as treasurer. McComb reneged on the deal and delivered his votes to Durant in exchange for the presidency of his board. Next day Oliver called the old board together to announce the election results and dissolve the board in favor of his new one. Durant glowered, then stalked out with the old directors. As Williams called the new board together, the Doctor stormed back in, his face scarlet with rage. Before anyone could react, he seized Williams by the collar and began dragging him toward the door. Oakes rushed in and thrust his burly frame between them until the overwrought Doctor released his grip and left the room. When his temper had cooled, he returned with an apology for Williams while his lawyers used the more prosaic weapon of an injunction to break up the meeting.

Well might the Ames brothers have preferred to throttle the Doctor. Once again, in his inimitable way, he had brought matters to a stalemate from which negotiation offered the only obvious escape. All day long and late into the night the leaders on both sides slipped from one group to another like rug merchants bartering for wares. Through all the talk Hazard and Blair staunchly refused any compromise that put them in bed with Durant. Another consideration now influenced Hazard's stance. Having persuaded Gould and Williams to lead the charge by procuring injunctions in their own names, he would oppose any plan that dropped them from the board without their consent. The issue, he told Oliver pointedly, was not money but loyalty.

Oliver thought otherwise. Durant had them over a barrel, he argued. The company's bonds were selling at last, and the track had passed the 435-mile post, which meant nearly 200 miles of road on which profits could be divided if only agreement could be reached on a contract. Surely that was worth some concessions, even to the Doctor. Hazard was unmoved. He would not abandon his friends to make what he considered a pact with the devil for any sum of money. Oliver shrugged wearily. The whole business was distasteful to him. The campaign to get rid of Durant had failed miserably. Oliver had wavered between the policies of war and accommodation without succeeding in either. Months of strife had brought his friends to the same impasse from which they had started, but with one important difference. In the beginning they had been united against Durant; now they were divided among themselves, and the Doctor was the source of their division.

The hard line proffered by Hazard had never appealed to Oliver, and it did not tempt him now. At bottom he and Oakes did not regard principle worth the sacrifice of their interest. On October 4 they struck a bargain with Durant. Both elections were declared void and the new boards wiped out. Since Dix, Lambard, and McCormick were still in Europe, the old board declared their seats vacant. Another resignation gave the Ames group four places to fill with their friends. Hazard, Blair, and Williams held firm in their refusal to associate with Durant. Alley was less squeamish and accepted a seat; the others went to Bates, F. Gordon Dexter, and William Glidden, the partner of John Williams.

This arrangement put the seven trustees and all but one member (Hazard) of Crédit Mobilier's executive committee on the Union Pacific board. Oliver remained president and Durant vice president, with the executive committee evenly divided between the two camps. The path was now smoothed for approval of the trustees agreement, which Oakes, the seven trustees, and Dillon as president of Crédit Mobilier signed on October 15. Through this convoluted arrangement Crédit Mobilier did not get the contract, but its stockholders got the profits. Moreover, its guarantee of the contract freed everyone from personal liability. McComb expressed the hope that everyone would now get along well and profitably. With fine impartiality he praised Hazard for his "manly" stand on behalf of Gould. Oliver noted with obvious relief that "Durant seems disposed to do right now." In explaining events to Dodge he admitted that "we had a stormy time of it but are now all harmony and the Doctor agrees to go along in harmony and for the best interests of the Road."

All was in fact not harmony, but Oliver simply closed his ears to the clang of discord. Gould was outraged at being unceremoniously dumped from the board by the very men who had asked for his help. They had promised him unwavering support, he observed acidly, but were now "quite willing to succeed in their own plans and take care of themselves." Williams felt the same humiliation, magnified in his case by Durant's assault. He especially resented "the idea of *my friends* allowing *my (& our) enemy* to say whether I shall or no. If Mr Alley had consulted *us,* I would willingly have retired to harmonise matters." Oakes and Butler tried to soothe their feelings but did little to relieve their discomfort. "Of course," Williams conceded mournfully, "I shall have to do whatever Mr Oakes Ames wants me to—*finally.*"

Hazard leaped to their defense with a spirited protest, but his influence too had waned. From that day forward his erstwhile allies lost interest in the suit against Durant's "ill-got gains" from the suspense account. Some cringed at the idea of a quarrel with the Doctor now that a settlement had been reached; others declared solemnly that they were "bound by the compromise not to stir up old strifes." Duff grumbled privately that the Ameses had conceded more to Durant than he liked but did nothing about it. In one stroke Hazard found himself transformed from partner to nuisance because he would not let go of the suit. Seeds of bitterness were sown that would be harvested for years to come.

And somewhere in the shadows still lurked the Falstaffian figure of Jim Fisk.

None of these dangers worried the Ames brothers at the moment. For them the sense of relief was overwhelming. The long struggle with Durant was over at last, and the time had come to pluck some reward for their labors. With the agreement in place, Oliver and Dillon prepared to go west with the Doctor on an inspection tour. There would be no more bickering, or so they thought. "The Board of Direction is made up of nice Gentlemen," Oliver warbled happily to Dodge, "who will Look only to the True interest of the Road in their action."

An early stop: the Nebraska House at Grand Island.

Crossing the plains into western Nebraska brought one to the village of Sidney, **named after Sidney Dillon. The railroad shop was obviously the dominant sight.**

The first major stop in Wyoming Territory was Cheyenne, which in 1868 had already mushroomed into a town. This view looks down Sixteenth Street, at the end of which the plains start anew. Note the "Theatre Comique" on the left and the Rollins House on the right.

West of Cheyenne the trains chugged slowly up to the town of Sherman at the highest point on the Union Pacific line. When the line was later relocated, the town of Sherman vanished like so many western settlements that lived only off the railroad. This picture shows the depot and the somewhat less than elegant hotels and restaurants.

This view of Laramie, taken in 1868, shows how western towns often resembled lumps sticking to a plate or outgrowths on some bleak surface.

The Laramie hotel and eating house was somewhat more inviting than others along the line.

The water tank and giant windmill at Laramie. Behind them can be seen the machine shops and part of the twenty-stall roundhouse, both constructed from stone brought from Rock Creek.

West of Laramie lay the wretched town of Benton, where nothing escaped the alkaline dust.

A street scene in Green River, where conditions were a scant improvement over Benton.

The "Hell-on-wheels" town of Bear River. Situated on White Sulphur Creek, 965 miles west of Omaha, it boasted a population of two hundred when this picture was taken but quickly vanished when the crews moved farther west.

Utah brought little improvement in the urban scenery. In this picture the shack city of Corinne squats on a slab of plains north of Ogden.

At the road's end the traveler came to Promontory, another overnight town where transfer was made to the Central Pacific. The buildings on the left are made of canvas, some with board façades. When the transfer point was moved to Odgen, the town of Promontory quickly withered away.

= 8 =

THE PAYOFF

For twenty miles along the track construction trains piled with material sit waiting like the reserve of an army. The eighty-foot boarding cars, fitted with berths, dining hall, kitchen, storeroom, and office, go in first, shoved to end of track. Behind them the first construction train noses into place, ready for unloading. Alongside the track a fleet of wagons, each one drawn by two horses, pulls up to take on a load of forty rails with all the necessary spikes and chairs. Five men spring forward on each side of the wagon to grab the rails, which are thirty feet long and weigh 560 pounds. One man guides the end onto a series of rollers attached to both sides of the wagons; three of his mates pull the rail along the rollers into place; the fifth man seats a chair under the rail and, with a single swing, forces the rail into its chair. "Down!" bellows the crew chief, and the men scurry back for another rail. Every thirty seconds the cry of "Down!" pierces the air like a drumbeat until forty rails are loaded. The teamsters bark and the horses jerk forward, hauling their load to the tracklayers up ahead. When the train is emptied, another will take its place, then another. . . .

When each wagon pulls up at end of track, two men grab the rail on each side and run it forward until others shoulder the rear, then dash forward and on command drop it in place, right side up. Once the rail is down, the gaugers, spikers, and bolters swarm to it in rapid succession, squaring and pounding it into place. Three blows to a spike, ten spikes to a rail, four hundred rails to a mile, sturdy, sweating arms swinging sledges twelve thousand times a mile in a monotonous drumbeat that will echo across a thousand miles of prairie and mountain.

Beneath the boiling sun the tracklayers heave at their work with the steady rhythm of a clock, pausing only to mop their brows or slake their thirst from the water bucket. Inexorably the ribbon of rail marches across the prairie in pursuit of the graders toiling furiously with their shovels and scrapers far ahead. Alongside the crews their chiefs pace restlessly, barking orders, exhorting, pleading, cursing, their eyes glancing constantly in every direction for any sign of Indians. The grading parties are scattered across the countryside in isolated pockets linked together only by the thin tentacle of telegraph wire strung far in advance of the work. Amid the choking dust and sweating bodies only the experienced eye plucks purpose from the swirl of confusion. What unites them all is a fierce determination not to let down those coming on behind. The engineers must have the final line staked for the graders, who in turn must have the roadbed prepared before the track gangs arrive.

Their determination is born of pride, the satisfaction of a day's work well done, spiced with the zest of competition. They will not be outstripped by those pushing on ahead or chasing from behind. Every party is bent on holding up its end. The crew chiefs know this and wring every advantage from it. When it is over, others will claim the glory for furnishing the money or brains. No one will know the names of those thousands who provided the brawn, but the greatest accomplishment of all will be theirs: they built the railroad.

*   *   *

The first payoff from the latest accord was supposed to be harmony, but Reed had his doubts. Seymour was still skulking about the line, getting in everyone's way and promoting a "big row in which no one but himself is likely to get hurt." As for the trustees arrangement, it would in Reed's opinion only make his work "seven times more complicated than heretofore." He was not in the best of moods while waiting for the officers to arrive, having just hosted another junket of editors to end of track. They were delighted with what they saw and gave the road more good ink, but Reed was unimpressed. "Such a set of *ninnies,*" he wrote contemptuously, "I never saw on the plains."

Nor did the presence of the eastern triumvirate reassure him. The Doctor was his usual animated self, a mask of geniality behind which lurked unknown schemes. Reed could not help but feel Oliver's coldness, though little was said to his face. Dillon was friendly but of no help. During a buffalo hunt he fell off his horse and was laid up for the rest of his stay. While he recovered, the others went on to end of track and then, switching to wagons, over the Black Hills line to Dale Creek. Oliver examined firsthand the summit route that six years later he would deny having known anything about when the Oakes Ames contract was signed. He viewed the remains of Seymour's vaunted improvements in the form of abandoned grading. All the talk of avoiding a high trestle bridge at Dale Creek had come to nothing. Convinced at last that Dodge was right, Oliver decided on the spot to go ahead with a high bridge over the gorge.

When the easterners left for home on November 6, the track was but a week shy of reaching Cheyenne, 516 miles from Omaha. That achievement pleased the newspapers but not Jack Casement, who had hoped to be there a month earlier. Indians and short supplies, especially ties, slowed his progress all summer. To Reed's dismay most of the tie contractors failed to deliver. The only wood near the line lay in some canyons below the North Platte where Indians chased the cutters out. In desperation Reed finally bought ties from the Missouri River Valley and had them shipped west. At one point he was compelled to get a supply from Chicago. The shortage of wood for ties, bridge timbers, and fuel not only hindered progress but also set Reed and Snyder to feuding with each other.

After a slow start (only 17 miles put down by May) Casement's gangs laid better than a mile of track a day through the summer of 1867. By the year's end they completed 247 miles to Granite Canyon on the heavy grade toward the summit. Some directors boasted that the road would be finished by 1870, enabling traffic to move from coast to coast in less than a week. "It is hard to realise that so great a distance may be accomplished in so short a time," marveled the New York *Times*.

Casual observers would have been even more impressed by the road's progress had they known about all the obstacles overcome along the way. The new year promised an even more difficult grind. So far track had been laid across prairie land, but now the crews were penetrating mountain and desert country where the going would be rougher. The supply line grew longer and the flow of material more tricky to coordinate. Dodge tried to ease the strain by stockpiling vital supplies at Cheyenne and by throwing a pile bridge across the frozen Missouri River. As the line pushed beyond the Black Hills, it would encounter a severe shortage of water. Dodge anticipated the problem by devising a plan utilizing wells, storage tanks adjacent to sidetracks, and even windmills to assure a constant supply, but the trustees were slow to act on it.

As always the most crucial materials were rails and lumber for ties, bridges, buildings, and telegraph poles. The Casements stopped laying track in December for lack of iron and shut down operations while Jack went east to get a new contract for the coming season. Hoxie's agent in Chicago had trouble learning from New York how much iron had been purchased, and then could not secure enough cars to move it. More delays ensued when a strike shut down the Cambria Rolling Mill briefly. Lumber too was slow to arrive for want of cars. The tie contractors tried again to get wood from the Black Hills but were thwarted this time by deep snow. An attempt was made to buy provisions from the Mormons in Utah, but crops were short and the stage companies had secured most of what was available. What little flour and beef Brigham Young could offer would have to be driven over the mountains to the crews in Wyoming.

An unfinished bridge shut track gangs down as fast as a lack of iron. Despite a squabble with Durant's foes during the summer, L. B. Boomer managed to procure a contract for the remaining bridges on the line. As with earlier spans, he had to buy lumber in Chicago, frame the trusses at Omaha, ship them to end of track, and haul them by teams to the site. This logistical nightmare drove Hoxie to complain that the bridges west of Julesburg were "giving us more trouble than all other things combined & will until we have stone in place of wood."

Casement's crews halted work that winter just ten miles east of the summit. Ahead loomed the gorge at Dale Creek, which threatened to stop the tracklayers cold if Boomer did not have the bridge ready early in the spring. To cross the gorge required thirteen spans, each forty feet long, resting on an elaborate network of double-framed trestles set in a foundation of granite masonry. The bents were spaced forty feet apart, with the track placed on timber trusses supported on the trestle bents. When completed it would be a scary, spidery thing buoyed by guy wires, by far the most spectacular bridge on the road. One exasperated engineer called it "a big bridge for a small brook that one could easily step over."

Apart from the bridges, Reed still had grading and rock work to finish west of the summit. Not all the contractors cared to hack away at frozen ground through the numbing Wyoming winter. Those who stayed scattered their crews along the line as far west as Fort Sanders, braving not only blizzards but the omnipresent danger of attack. The Indians had hit upon a new and deadly tactic during the past summer when some Cheyenne warriors derailed two trains near Plum Creek, killing seven men. After looting the cargo and scalping the victims, the braves torched the cars and circled the flames in a frenzied victory dance. One hardy trainman was shot, clubbed, stabbed in the neck, and scalped but managed to survive and even retrieved his scalp. In distant Massachusetts a shocked Oliver lamented that the government was "not giving sufficient protection."

· Dodge did what he could to arrange protection for the grading crews, for the men struggling to get out ties in the snow-packed timberlands, and for his survey parties. The general had more than his share of worries that winter. When Congress convened, he felt obliged to establish headquarters in Washington and run his operations from there. His absence from the West left him vulnerable to Seymour's machinations and helpless to quell the growing friction in Omaha.

The fiasco over the Black Hills line did not deter Seymour from meddling in the surveys west of that point. He assured Dodge that Browne's line to the North Platte could be improved by one farther north through Medicine Bow Valley, and talked of lending his expertise to the Wasatch survey. Jesse Williams warned Oliver not to allow Seymour into Utah because of "the state of feeling existing between him and the Chief Engineer." Dodge suspected that Seymour was trying to redeem his bruised reputation by getting up a "paper controversy" over the Black Hills line. He wanted no part of it, and neither did Oliver, who talked wistfully of getting rid of Seymour "as soon as a good opportunity presents. His Salary is Larger than his Services."

Dodge was especially anxious to keep Seymour's blighting hand away from the surveys this season because his engineers were under pressure to get the line ready ahead of the grading crews. In December 1867 Evans braved some rugged weather to settle the issue of a line from Fort Sanders to the North Platte. His findings confirmed what Dodge already believed—that Browne's line was fifteen miles shorter with easier grades and fewer undulations than any route through Medicine Bow Valley. In an obvious swipe at Seymour, Dodge described the line to Oliver as "so far superior to all others that no argument is needed to recommend its adoption." He ordered Evans to locate the final line and then get busy on the route west of the North Platte.

For the Utah survey Dodge secured the services of Jake Blickensderfer, whose report on fixing the eastern base of the mountains for subsidy purposes had finally been approved by President Johnson. Blickensderfer was the quintessential Dutchman: stolid, cautious, methodical, fussy over details, and hard-headed. Jesse Williams considered him the best locating engineer around and Dodge was grateful to have an experienced replacement for his slain engineers, but Fred Hodges got a different impression on the long stage ride to Utah. Dodge asked him to accompany Blickensderfer and answer any questions about the country or previous surveys. But no questions were asked, and Hodges discovered to his astonishment that Blickensderfer was not even familiar with earlier reports on the region. When at length Hodges tried to volunteer information, Blickensderfer shrugged, pulled his coat collar about his ears, and muttered that he would look into it later. Hodges came away with the uneasy feeling that his new chief did not realize "how big a thing he had to do."

Elsewhere Dodge's efforts to get all departments ready for the coming season ran afoul of a crisis at Omaha, where long-accumulating tensions exploded into a series of confrontations. For months some directors had voiced dissatisfaction with the construction department. Oliver complained waspishly about Reed's incompetence and talked of replacing him. A suspicious Dodge concluded that Seymour was behind the criticisms reaching the board. Summoned to New York as an advisor, the general stoutly defended Reed and insisted that he remain in charge of construction. Grudgingly the board agreed to leave Reed in command.

"You of course have been blamed when you ought not be," Dodge consoled Reed. To avoid the past season's delays, he suggested that Reed hire assistants, *"good honest* active ones," to shoulder some of his duties. If all went well this year, Dodge thought they could build to Ogden in one grand push. "Keep as harmonious as possible with the Running Department," he urged, ". . . and steer clear of New York complications which we have no direct interest in."

It was good advice but difficult to follow. "New York complications," Reed mused, "will crush any man that stands in the way and it is impossible to steer clear of them all." A man never knew where he stood with Durant, and with Seymour hovering about, no one knew what information reached whose ears in New York. As for the operating department, some friction between Reed and Snyder was inevitable. Reed and the Casements depended on Snyder for a steady flow of materials; Snyder depended on them for a finished product. Supplies never came fast enough to suit the construction people, and Snyder complained that "Reed dont keep up with his work— tanks not enclosed, cuts and embankments not in shape to run trains safely, not a bridge between Sidney and Cheyenne that might pass muster."

Jack Casement had his own bone to pick with Snyder. "As I made him pay us some $33,000 for freight that he expected to get free," Snyder related, "the genl is not one of my warmest friends." The question of what tariff to charge contractors for supplies had never been resolved. Snyder insisted they should pay full freight, not only to provide the road income but for a less obvious reason. Apart from their construction work, the Casements and other contractors ran private stores for their crews and settlers in the region. Free transportation enabled them to ship goods at the railroad's expense, which did wonders for their profits. Merchants complained about this system, and Snyder wanted it stopped. Dodge agreed with him and urged the board to demand full tariff on all supplies except men and teams.

Ironically, Snyder's determination to run a clean operation got him in trouble with New York. As with Reed, every complaint he made somehow reached the board with the emphasis shifted. Dillon did not appreciate the treatment accorded his friend Jack Casement. In November Snyder fired some conductors and trackmen for stealing from the company. Suspicions flew east that Snyder himself was on the take. "If they can find that I have ever made one dime outside of my salary," he retorted indignantly, "I want them to discharge me." Two months later Snyder removed A. A. Bean, the master of transportation, and brought in Hoxie as assistant superintendent. Bean's record was a horror tale of corruption and incompetence, but his compliant attitude made him popular with the contractors. When complaints flooded the New York office, Snyder found himself the eye of another storm.

On one point Snyder was unequivocal. "If held responsible for the management of the road," he insisted, "I must have choice of the men who operate with me." But Oliver rebuked him for making the change and suggested Bean as a very competent man for superintendent of the road west of Cheyenne. Snyder was thunderstruck. He and Hoxie saw Durant's influence behind this response and concluded that the Doctor wanted them out of the way. Both promptly handed Dodge their resignations to be used as he saw fit. The general dutifully went again to New York to clear the air. In outlining his plans for the year to the board, he stressed the importance of having experienced men in charge and warned of disaster if new or incompetent men were put in key positions.

To clinch his argument Dodge showed the directors a letter from Snyder that summarized masterfully the chaotic relationship between Omaha and New York. "In the first place," Snyder wrote, "the Directors know but very little of the affairs of the road here." Letters could not impart the full situation, and Snyder's instructions were always vague at best. The bickering in New York diverted attention from the field and left officers there to hew their own way through difficulties. "The directors ought to know," Snyder warned, "that old R.R. thieves from all parts of the State are flocking here. They look upon this road as a government institution and come here to steal all they can." For months he had urged Oliver in vain to investigate all departments fully. Snyder was willing to clean out the thieves, but an honest policy made enemies. For example, he incurred the wrath of some Omaha interests by refusing to grant them passes or special rates. If the board heeded their complaints, it betrayed not only Snyder but the company's own interest. As for Bean, his removal improved discipline and train service. The loafers were gone, and "whiskey is no longer the principal motive power." In closing, Snyder asserted that no salary or inducement would keep him on the job "if my hands are to be tied and the road plundered under my own eyes."

This powerful statement impressed the board enough to concur in Dodge's plea that Snyder and Hoxie be retained. Oakes thought Bean got what he deserved and urged Oliver not to rush into a change. Dodge wrote Snyder suggesting ways to avoid friction with New York. Benjamin Ham's brother James was sent as accountant to relieve Snyder of the bookkeeping, but Snyder remained doubtful about the future. "If the NY fight is to be transferred to Omaha," he grumbled, "I propose to quit." Bean and his cronies lingered in Omaha, grasping at rumors that the March election would bring another change in the management.

In all these fights Dodge revealed again his unique talent as the one man capable of bridging the gap between field and office. This dubious honor forced him to waste time and energy settling disputes when he had a hundred other things to do. There was trouble with the government in Washington and the threat of another land-grant transcontinental railroad, the Northern Pacific. The board hoped to build a branch to Denver this season, and wanted a survey for a branch to Oregon as well. In Dodge's opinion, the Oregon branch would "give us the *best* and *shortest* route to the Pacific . . . and at same time kill the Northern Pacific." It also thrust new burdens on his already sagging shoulders, as if completion of the main line was not a herculean task in itself.

A railroad stretching unbroken from the Missouri to the Pacific—the vision fired Dodge's imagination as it did others who dreamed on an epic scale. It was all there for the taking; it could be done. With his unquenchable optimism Dodge clung to the belief that everything was possible if all hands concentrated on the work at hand instead of draining their energies with perpetual infighting. How to break out of that vicious cycle remained a far greater challenge than the conquest of an untamed continent.

* * *

Having bought peace with the trustee arrangement, the warring factions hurried to realize the spoils of harmony. For some the profits came in ways that never got discussed before investigating committees in 1873. Bushnell recruited four friends to help peddle $5 million in Union Pacific bonds. In offering Durant a share he predicted that "the Pool will make $250,000 in three months." The Doctor let a contract for ties to a firm in which he had a personal interest, and he was widely suspected of having his thumb in several others as well. Harbaugh got a contract for axles, McComb one for wheels. McComb also saw to it that a contract for machinery went to a shop in Wilmington, Delaware, where he lived. From such sources came large returns that never found their way into the tortuous calculations by later generations of the profits realized from construction of the Union Pacific.

The trustee arrangement also permitted the long-delayed division of profits on construction contracts past and present. On December 12, 1867, the trustees allotted to Crédit Mobilier stockholders 60 percent in bonds and 60 percent in stock of the Union Pacific. Three weeks later the trustees increased the bond allotment to 80 percent. In addition, Crédit Mobilier declared its own dividend of 12 percent covering the years 1866 and 1867, payable in Union Pacific stock at 30. Altogether, Crédit Mobilier holders received 80 percent in bonds and 72 percent in stock as their first direct return on investment.

No cash changed hands in these transactions; the true value of the payment depended on what price the securities could be disposed of in the market. For example, the owner of a hundred shares of Crédit Mobilier stock ($10,000 par value) received $8,000 in bonds and 72 shares of stock. At the prevailing prices of 97 for the bonds and 30 for the stock, the holder selling at once would realize $9,920 or a return of 99.2 percent on his investment. However, prices fluctuated constantly and the stock still attracted few buyers. For most holders the long-term potential was far more important than immediate gains. If the road was completed and operated profitably, the securities would soar in value; if not, they would be worthless. The real payoff, then, depended on the ability of the trustees to push the work along as rapidly as possible.

Alley thought the dividends premature and argued they were eating "the calf up in the cow's belly." As it turned out, his reasons for caution went beyond mere policy. Oakes made no bones about wanting the largest possible dividend. He was overextended and had to promise a worried Oliver that he would take on no new commitments. To those arguing against the bond dividend, Oakes said simply, "if it is paid out we are sure of it, and if the Co want[s] money before we get more bonds we can loan these bonds to them again on the money received for them as we have before."

Even the dividends did not proceed free of controversy, partly because there was a catch to them. The trustees stipulated that payment be made only to stockholders who accepted the terms of the agreement and signed proxies on their Union Pacific shares over to them. Predictably, Hazard bridled at delivering his votes to Durant in any form. When Crane, the trustees' secretary, refused to pay Hazard unless he signed, the impasse dragged on for six weeks until Hazard relented under protest. Settling one dispute left several others still simmering, which the flinty Hazard was determined to press. He would be heard from again.

News of the dividend sent Union Pacific bonds to par and touched off a wild clamor for Crédit Mobilier stock. "There has never been anything like it," young John R. Duff enthused, "and I dont believe there ever will be again." A few shares in Boston changed hands at the incredible price of 350. Only a year earlier the stock had gone begging for buyers; now enough could not be found to satisfy the demand from "friends" who had earlier declined the investment as too risky. This stunning reversal put Oakes in a delicate position. During the spring of 1867, when Crédit Mobilier increased its capital in a desperate attempt to raise money, he had offered shares to several of his fellow congressmen. In December this effort came back to haunt him. As word of the impending dividend spread through the grapevine, the colleagues who had spurned Oakes approached him for the shares they claimed had been promised them.

Oakes was anxious to oblige his friends. Later an entire investigation would revolve around the question of whether his intention was to buy influence for the Union Pacific in Congress. Oakes denied the charge vehemently, but the discovery of new evidence confirms its truth in at least a general sense. The most damning evidence against Oakes in 1873 consisted of three letters written to McComb during the winter of 1868 in which he talked of placing Crédit Mobilier shares "where they will do most good to us. . . . We want more friends in this Congress, & if a man will look into the law, (& it is difficult to get them to do it unless they have an interest to do so,) he can not help being convinced that we should not be interfered with."

The reason for selling shares to congressmen, Oakes explained in his bluff manner, was simple: "We wanted capital and influence. Influence not on legislation alone, but on credit, good, wide, and a general favorable feeling." But legislation mattered more to Oakes than he admitted. The infamous letters to McComb were essentially rewrites of text from letters written to Oliver, which tended to be more candid. In one Oakes spoke of giving Crédit Mobilier stock "to those M.C. [members of Congress] who will pay for it and not over much to any one of them." This would make them "interested to prevent any legislation that will injure us." He was not dealing in abstractions; Representative Cadwalader Washburn of Wisconsin had recently introduced a bill to regulate rates on the Pacific roads. It was quietly buried by the Pacific Railroad committee (of which Oakes was a member) but was sure to reappear later in the session.

There was an even more important reason for needing allies in Congress. "We have all kinds of influences at work here to aid Pacific Railroads," Oakes warned. "They want them in every direction & want lands, Bonds and Guaranteed Stock." The Union Pacific hoped to get a subsidy for a branch to Oregon, which brought it into conflict with another budding project, the Northern Pacific. Oakes wanted not only Crédit Mobilier stock but also fifty thousand dollars worth of Union Pacific which Hiram Price of Iowa, a long-time friend of the road, agreed to place among some colleagues at fifty dollars a share. The combination of these securities, Oakes thought, would "enable us to control the thing so that no wrong shall be done us."

In all of this Oakes saw no impropriety. He was selling stock, not giving it away, touting it as a good investment. His purpose was to build a community of interest in Congress favorable to the Union Pacific. For years the company had courted its good will by supplying certain amenities, such as the Doctor's gala excursions. James F. Wilson of Iowa, chairman of the House Judiciary Committee and a supporter of the road, let Dodge know in August 1867 that he wanted his committee invited on any future excursions, and Dodge was quick to pass the word along to Oliver. Oakes distributed passes liberally to congressmen who wanted them and, in his affable manner, was always there with a favor or a loan or advice on investments.

The renewed interest among his colleagues in Crédit Mobilier delighted Oakes, but where to get stock for them? No one (including Oakes) cared to part with any of their shares on the eve of a huge dividend. All available stock had long since been sold—with one exception. Oakes remembered the block of 650 shares that Durant had put in his name without paying for them. Sometime after the May turnover in Crédit Mobilier the stock had been transferred to Dillon as trustee. These last unowned shares were a prize in another respect: as original stock they still carried the privilege offered in the capital increase of the previous winter. The holder of ten shares, for example, had the right to buy 50 percent more stock (five shares in this case) and receive a one-thousand dollar bond as bonus. The entire fifteen shares would then be eligible for the dividend.

To get the stock Oakes needed the consent of the major stockholders. By assigning it to him, he argued, the shares would go to men who could help the company. Durant countered that he too had prior commitments for the stock, and McComb stepped forward with a claim for 250 shares on the same grounds. After some bargaining a compromise was struck. Nine major stock-holders (including McComb) rejected McComb's claim and agreed in writing to allot Durant 370 of the shares and Oakes 280.

The deal satisfied no one. Duff signed the paper but voiced his indignation, and Hazard filed a written protest. Oakes then discovered that he still did not have enough stock and asked his associates to issue him 93 *new* shares of Crédit Mobilier to fulfill his pledges. When this was done, a disgruntled McComb renewed his demand for 250 shares with full privileges. If new stock could be created for Oakes, why not for him? Oakes tried to appease McComb by lending him 500 of his own shares; McComb took the loan but did not relent in his quest for the shares. This apparently minor dispute dragged on for months with devastating consequences. Ultimately it resulted in a suit that provided material for a sensational newspaper expose, which in turn triggered a congressional investigation of Crédit Mobilier.

In thrashing out these difficulties the astute Alley managed to turn them to his own advantage. Before the dividends were declared, he had rashly sold most of his Crédit Mobilier at what seemed the handsome price of 200. When the trustees met to decide the dividend question, Alley raised objections and counseled delay. Later he insisted that he was only trying to protect the large interests of the Ames brothers, but at the time Durant thought he sniffed another motive. A short recess was called, during which the Doctor offered to sell Alley 250 shares at 160. When the meeting resumed, Alley overcame his hesitancy and voted for the dividend. The transaction with Durant, he explained solemnly to Hazard afterward, had no influence on his change of heart.

Oakes paid the company par for the stock awarded him and sold it at the same price even though transactions were being made at much higher figures. So much controversy arose over who got the shares that one intriguing point has gone entirely unnoticed. In all, Oakes received 373 shares of Crédit Mobilier, not counting the right to a 50 percent increase. Although he wrote Oliver on January 13 that he had "promised all that I was to have," testimony before the Poland Committee revealed that he sold only 160 shares to eleven members of Congress. Others were offered stock but declined to take it, and 30 shares went to a party not connected with Congress. What happened to the other 183 shares and the 50 percent privilege on them? Since Oakes obligingly held all the shares sold to colleagues in his own name as trustee, they could not be traced through the stock ledger. Two possibilities suggest themselves, each one fascinating in a different way. Oakes may have kept the remaining stock for himself, or he may have sold it to congressmen whose involvement escaped the notice of the committee.

The known purchasers were Senators James W. Patterson of New Hampshire and Henry Wilson of Massachusetts, Representatives William B. Allison and James F. Wilson of Iowa, James A. Garfield of Ohio, Henry L. Dawes of Massachusetts, William D. Kelley of Pennsylvania, John A. Logan of Illinois, John A. Bingham of Ohio, Glenni W. Schofield of Pennsylvania, and Schuyler Colfax of Indiana, Speaker of the House, who would become the next Vice President. Each bought ten or twenty shares except for Patterson, who was allotted thirty. In addition, Oakes and three other representatives (Boyer, Grimes, and Hooper) already owned stock in Crédit Mobilier while a fifth, perhaps the most deserving of all, got his stock too late to cash in on the dividends. Dodge had long wanted some Crédit Mobilier, but his friends did not procure him a hundred shares until March.

James Brooks of New York occupied a unique position as both congressman and one of three new government directors appointed in October 1867. An urbane, cultivated man, Brooks had earned renown as a journalist before entering Congress in 1864. He had long been a supporter of the Pacific road and eager to help it as well as himself. That winter he found himself in the awkward position of asking Durant for two hundred shares of Crédit Mobilier he had declined to buy a year earlier. Anxious to recruit allies among the new government directors, Durant agreed to let him have a hundred shares. Since the law did not permit government directors to own stock in the company, Brooks had the shares put in the name of his son-in-law, Charles H. Neilson. As an added precaution he did not formally accept his appointment until March 1868 even though he began to consult with the board and attend meetings much earlier.

The compromise with Durant only whetted Brooks's appetite for gain. No sooner was the bargain struck than he demanded another fifty shares under the privilege of subscribing for 50 percent of his holdings. When the Doctor gave the request a cold reception, the cheeky Brooks tried to play one faction off against the other by going to Oakes with his claim. Oakes did not know whether to laugh or cry. "He says you give it to me at once & show Durant that he Brooks is under more obligation to us than him &c &c," he wrote Oliver. Oakes thought the stock could be better used elsewhere and put Brooks off with a promise to write Dillon on the matter. The persistent Brooks hounded Dillon into getting authorization from the major stockholders for the fifty shares.

The feeding frenzy that winter was not limited to congressmen. McComb tried to enlist Dodge in some stock schemes, including "an operation in Pacific Road whereby we can make a good deal of money." In February the company settled its account with the firm of Clark, Dodge to the disgust of both Oliver and Hazard. Bushnell tried again to resolve the long-standing dispute over the bond sale but could not sway Hazard. The most brazen demand for a payoff, and certainly the most unexpected, came from that eminent statesman, General Dix. Under the October compromise he had been dropped as president and director. To salve his wounded pride (and purse), Dix suggested that the company buy back his five hundred shares of Union Pacific at par, an absurd figure for a stock that had no market. These were the same shares originally put in Dix's name by Durant, who had paid for most or all of them.

Oakes considered it "a kind of black-mailing," but Dix had them in a corner. His lawyer, Samuel Barlow, hinted that the general might say some unkind things in Europe about Union Pacific bonds unless his claim was met, and might even enjoin the forthcoming stockholders' meeting. An exasperated Oliver agreed to pay $32,000 in settlement, but Dix was not placated. Bushnell then offered Dix the full $50,000 and persuaded the others to ratify the agreement. Oliver called it "a complete swindle of the Co." but, unwilling to make a fuss, went along as usual. Oakes suspected the Doctor of being behind Dix's demand. Durant had gone to Europe on January 8 and was known to have met with Dix, but Brooks assured Oakes that no deal had been struck. True to form, Durant's first act after returning home early in March was to denounce the payoff of Dix.

Dix's threat was not the only reason Oliver felt jittery about the forthcoming election. Although Durant was safely tucked away in Europe, a movement was afoot to secure the presidency for McComb. The Ames brothers were unsure of how many votes they could count on. A disgruntled Lambard talked of bringing suit if not put back on the board and seemed willing to support whichever side helped him. Bates too appeared to be wavering. Oakes admonished his brother to line up all the votes he could and be ready for anything. "If we cant go on in peace," he declared fiercely, "I want to take the thing into our own hands and take the consequences. They cant stop the road and they do not dare to have an investigation by Congress."

Soon after Durant's return it became evident that he regarded the McComb boom as a bargaining chip for two purposes: to ensure the vice presidency for himself and to dump Alley from the board. William Glidden resolved one crisis by resigning his seat in favor of Lambard, but it took a whole day of haggling to settle Alley's fate. Finally it was agreed to leave him as a director but replace him as trustee with Duff. These changes enabled the election to proceed without incident. The old board (except for Glidden) was reelected with Oliver as president and Durant as vice president.

The rhetoric of harmony again filled the boardroom. Everyone had reason to feel sanguine about the future. The directors had sated their long pent-up hunger for dividends and, with a new construction season about to begin, looked expectantly for more. Some felt uneasy about how certain transactions might look to the wrong eyes. The payoff to Dix was expunged from the trustees' records; it had never been put into the Union Pacific minute books. Durant objected to entering any account of the October compromise into the record because it would "complicate matters," but the Bostonians insisted that it be done. Doubtless their motive had less to do with conscience or rectitude than with the fear of what the Doctor might attempt if the terms were not listed somewhere in official form. Bushnell raised an even more basic concern. Now that a mechanism for dividing profits was firmly in place, what might a comparison between the size of the dividends and the actual cost of the road reveal to prying eyes? To avoid any embarrassment, he proposed changing the way accounts were kept so that the Union Pacific's books would not disclose the true cost of the road.

Although a fight over the election was averted, the old divisions remained. More than factional intrigue lay behind the movement for McComb. A crisis of leadership still plagued the Union Pacific. The choice between Durant and Oliver was more than ever one between the lesser of two evils. Durant was strong but erratic, Oliver well-meaning but ineffectual. A year of savage infighting had brought the board full circle to the old arrangement of uneasy coexistence between two men who cordially despised one another.

One telling act by the board confirmed its inability to avoid the dilemma it had struggled for so long to escape: it appointed Durant "General Agent" with power to approve changes in grade or location and "do all other things necessary to expedite the construction of the Road" under the Ames contract. In effect the Doctor was again given full throttle to drive the work forward. Everyone knew from bitter experience what he was capable of doing with such license, yet only Alley and Jesse Williams opposed the resolution. Two weeks later, on March 27, the executive committee cloaked Durant with authority to "take such means as may be necessary to ensure early completion of the work West of the Contract."

In these acts Oliver acquiesced meekly. Duff growled at Oakes that he hated both the brothers for being "so damned amiable" and not standing up for their rights, but he too had gone along. The lure of profits had tempted even cautious men into another fling at riding the whirlwind. Oliver offered a lame explanation to Dodge, who saw at once that Durant had somehow inveigled his old powers from the very men sworn to keep him powerless. That meant trouble for all departments, and Dodge was quick to suspect the influence of Seymour. On April 4 the Doctor headed west, eager to wield his new authority. Dodge watched grimly as the whirlwind approached. He had no illusions as to whom it would strike first.

* * *

The tangle of passions and intrigue in Washington reached unprecedented heights that spring as three years of acrimony between Andrew Johnson and Congress over Reconstruction policy marched to an explosive climax. "We are having rather exciting times here," Oakes reported as the House shoved through impeachment charges against Johnson. The President had been no friend of the Union Pacific, and Oakes relished the prospect of his disgrace. It was not Reconstruction that concerned Oakes but a more practical issue. "If we can get Johnson out of the way," he observed, "we can get rid of the present Govt commissioners and directors also if we choose & get in honest men that wont steal."

Amid the excitement a new threat appeared from the Central Pacific. "I have a way," boasted the wily Huntington, "of finding out what is done in the Union Co's office." Apart from the usual spies there was a certain lady to whom the voluble Bushnell confided information that found its way to Huntington's ear. From these sources Huntington learned that his rivals hoped to lay 350 miles of rail during the season regardless of cost. Durant barked that he would be damned if he'd allow the Central Pacific to build more than 200

miles east of California. Huntington blanched at the prospect. Utah was crucial to his plans. He wanted Weber Canyon for its coal deposits, and control
of Salt Lake would enable the Central Pacific to direct through business
westward to San Francisco. However, if the Union Pacific succeeded in shutting him out of Utah altogether, the Central Pacific would terminate somewhere in the barren wastes of Nevada.

The plans of both companies hinged on a clause in the law that allowed
them to grade three hundred miles in advance of a *continuous* line of track
and collect part of the government bonds for each twenty-mile segment
graded. If the Union Pacific could build to within a hundred miles of Ogden,
it could then send grading parties as far west as Humboldt Wells, forcing the
Central Pacific to join rails at that remote Nevada outpost. But there were
obstacles. A good line through Utah had to be located, and the heaviest work
on the entire Union Pacific lay in the Wasatch Mountains. Some tunneling
would be required, notably at the head of Echo Canyon, only about thirty
miles west of the Utah–Wyoming border. The tunneling would slow progress,
but merely reaching Echo would put track little over forty miles from Ogden.

Huntington pored over his maps in dismay. He was anxious to leapfrog
into Utah under the same provision, but a gap at Donner Lake broke his
continuous line and end of track was still several hundred miles from Humboldt Wells, the point at which his crews could legally invade Echo Canyon.
Reality was one thing, however, and a map quite another. On a map holes
could easily be filled with the swipe of a pen by a daring hand. He had no
trouble justifying such an outrageous sham. The Union Pacific was spending
money freely in Washington and was so "very corrupt," he told Edwin
Crocker, that it would not surprise him if Congress "should order a Committee to overhaul all the Cos."

In April Huntington drew a red line across the map of a preliminary
survey and sent it to Secretary Browning along with a letter of explanation.
The line he asked Browning to approve ran north of Salt Lake to Monument
Point, across the Promontory Mountains to Ogden, and from there into the
Wasatch, where it followed the northern fork of Echo Creek. The map was a
fraud, the letter accompanying it a clever fabric of lies. Huntington ignored
the gap in his line, stated that his tracks were at a place they would not reach
for another three months, and misrepresented the distance between that point
and Humboldt Wells. He knew Browning was no student of geography. If the
Secretary could be induced to approve the map, Huntington would occupy
the ground with his crews and argue the fine points while work went forward.
It helped greatly that his chief lobbyist, the shrewd Thomas Ewing, Jr., was
Browning's former associate.

The audacity of this request floored Oakes. He learned of it directly from
Browning, who added that the Central Pacific claimed to be within three
hundred miles of Salt Lake. "Can this be?" Oakes asked Oliver in bewilder-
ment. As a precaution he urged Durant to put men at work a hundred miles

west of Salt Lake "so as to get possession." Dodge knew the country well enough to smell a bluff. Together with Oakes he urged Browning to reject the map, but Huntington and Ewing were pressing the Secretary hard. On May 15 Browning approved the line as far east as Monument Point but withheld decision on the remainder. A fierce battle loomed in Washington for possession of Utah and its traffic. "It is an *important matter,*" Huntington barked, *"and we should be bold and take and hold possession of the line to Echo Canion* [sic]." Oliver reminded Dodge that the stakes also included securing "the point where the Oregon Road will join ours."

Suddenly Durant's mission in the West took on a new urgency. Oakes stressed the need "to build 3 miles a day until next Dec or Jany and get to Salt Lake before the Central." Everything depended on driving the work hard and avoiding delays. Above all it required a unity of purpose. The cynical McComb wondered if that could be done. He could not help admiring Huntington's coup. "I like their vigilance," he wrote Dodge. "They are all of one mind, our people have divers interests, and too many separate axes to grind." In California the crusty Edwin Crocker echoed this sentiment. "Ha! Ha!" he crowed. "What a time the Union Pacific folks have. That is a trouble we do not have. We are all united."

* * *

"Push is the word for this season," Reed proclaimed, and the crews were doing just that. The Casements geared up to lay three miles a day and contracted to do some grading as well. A spring blizzard stalled work for nearly a week, after which the juggernaut rolled relentlessly forward. On April 5 the track climbed the summit at Sherman and started down the slope toward Dale Creek. The last touches were put on the bridge, enabling Casement's men to spike rails across it on April 21. Contracts were let for the 273-mile stretch across the desert to Green River. Before the month's end Carmichael was on his way there with three hundred men to start the heavy work. Everyone was in high spirits, pressed to the limit and glad for it. "I have too much for any mortal man to do," Reed protested half-heartedly. Even Jack Casement admitted that he had "never been hurried up more in my life," but that was what he wanted. "We are now *Sailing,*" he wrote exuberantly on May 2, "& mean to lay over three miles every day." Ten days later the road was open for business to Laramie.

The crews were also high on the wrong kind of spirits. As the men left behind each Hell on Wheels, the whiskey merchants followed like squatters, throwing up instant saloons in tents known as "whiskey ranches." Invariably the binges after payday led to robberies, shootings, and days of lost work. Reed warned that it would "soon be worth a mans life to go over the work. Let us have martial law if necessary to keep off the whiskey." General Gibbon did what he could to shut them down but had no authority. While the Secretary of War tried to get enabling legislation, the contractors did their own enforcing. After two of their mates were shot in a drunken brawl, Carmichael's crews went on a rampage and demolished six whiskey ranches. The indignant proprietors threatened Carmichael with arrest.

Booze was not the only menace that spring. "The Indians are on the Rampage," Jack Casement reported late in April, "Killing and Stealing all along the line." Lightning raids against small parties killed a number of men and so alarmed Snyder that he hesitated to run trains by daylight through Indian country. Oliver was furious at the army's inability to stop the depredations. "I see nothing but extermination to the Indians as the result of their thieving disposition," he raged, "and we shall probably have to come to this before we can run the road safely." Durant took a more practical approach. Convinced that most of the casualties resulted from "the most gross and almost criminal neglect on the part of those in charge of the work," he issued a tough order for contractors and foremen to take all proper precautions against surprise attacks.

Although the raids continued sporadically all summer, the Indian threat was clearly on the wane. Friendly tribes moved their camps to North Platte to avoid the war parties and show their peaceful intentions. Gradually the number of rampaging bucks dwindled into small, isolated bands. Although they derailed another train at Plum Creek in September and burned a bridge near Pine Bluffs in November, these proved to be the last attacks made against the railroad or its crews. After three years of desperate guerrilla warfare, the Indians had failed to halt the advancing rails that would doom their way of life. Young Arthur Ferguson saw what was happening. "The time is coming, and fast too," he observed with mixed feelings, "when in the sense it is now understood, THERE WILL BE NO WEST."

* * *

The engineers did their part to get the final line ready for the oncoming crews. Early in March the gritty Evans did not even bother waiting until his escort was ready before leading his parties into the dangerous country west of Fort Sanders. Slogging through deep snows, bunching his men together for protection, Evans pressed the work vigorously. His perseverance resulted in completion of the final line to Green River on May 6. "We save considerable in distance and altitude both over the preliminary lines," he informed Dodge happily. Case had already finished the preliminary line from Cheyenne to Denver.

Utah posed a thicket of problems besides the presence of the Central Pacific. Dodge wanted a line over the rim of the basin and through the Wasatch with less grade and curvature. He hoped to avoid a long tunnel at the mouth of Echo Canyon and to get through the Narrows with fewer crossings of the Weber River. Hodges was sent north to examine the country between the Cache Valley and Bear River. He tried Box Elder and a half dozen other creeks without success before stumbling on a low pass through Cache Valley from Bear River station. Meanwhile J. O. Hudnutt found a promising route over the rim, and Jake Blickensderfer threaded his way through the treacherous Narrows, clinging to the north side as much as possible to avoid the heaviest snowfall.

In his methodical, painstaking way Blickensderfer extracted the best possible line from a difficult terrain. The younger engineers found him a stern taskmaster, especially the high-spirited Hodges, who was scolded regularly for such high crimes as using too much stationery. The friction between them reached a point where the exasperated Blickensderfer called Hodges "the most insubordinate man I have" and was ready to fire him until Dodge smoothed things over. Both Dodge and Oliver were delighted with the progress in Utah. Oliver held Blickensderfer's judgment in high regard and promised "to do every thing possible to preserve the line as laid out."

Little did he suspect how soon his pledge would be tested, for Seymour was on his way to Utah.

*   *   *

"I think I have never seen the Dr more pliable and anxious to please everybody than now," Oliver chirped late in March. He passed along Dodge's recommendations on water tanks and suggested that Oliver Chapman go west to keep a tight rein on the contractors, but Durant was cool to the idea. The last thing he wanted was a watchdog peering over his shoulder. Dodge himself headed west on April 1 to meet Durant, Dillon, and Seymour in Cheyenne. In his blunt manner Dodge made it clear that the work was progressing smoothly and any interference would be disastrous. Dillon nodded approval. The Doctor brushed these remarks aside with assurances that he was there to help, not to cause trouble. Dillon left Cheyenne on April 26 and Dodge soon followed, summoned back east to fend off the Central Pacific's attempt to gain approval for its fictitious map.

The Doctor's helping hand was extended first to Cheyenne itself. Real estate prices had soared as settlers poured in on the expectation that the Union Pacific would build large shops there and run its branch to Denver from the town. Durant chilled the boom by announcing that the shops should be in Laramie and the Denver branch would not connect with Cheyenne even if it cost him $500,000 personally. This outburst brought sales of company land to an abrupt halt and put Dodge in a bad light. Why Durant raised this ruckus is not clear. He may have been influenced by Seymour, who had sold his own lots in Cheyenne the previous fall for a profit of $1,000 only to have the purchaser realize another $1,400 over that before he had even paid Seymour. As Dodge's agent reported gleefully, "he did not rest well that night I know."

Seymour was not above giving Durant advice based on personal slights, real or imagined. More than once his counsel led the Doctor into rash or foolish acts, and now he did so again even before the Cheyenne uproar had simmered down. With Dodge gone, Seymour argued slyly, who would over-see location of the final line between Fort Sanders and Salt Lake? And who would take charge of construction west of Sanders and push it vigorously? There was no time to waste! Central Pacific engineers were in Echo; a line had to be decided at once and crews thrown across Utah ahead of the enemy.

This reasoning led Durant on May 6 to issue his "General Order No. 1." Seymour and Reed were to examine the entire line west of Sanders and decide all questions of final location. In Dodge's absence Seymour was invested with the full powers of chief engineer. Any orders given earlier by Dodge were rescinded if they conflicted with Seymour's directives. The order appeared in the form of a circular from the "Vice President, and General Agent," but only Evans got a copy signed by Durant. House in Omaha and Oliver received unsigned copies; Dodge was not on the mailing list and only learned of it from Evans.

Signed or not, the order touched off an explosion. Handed his copy by Seymour, Evans immediately resigned his position. He agreed to stay long enough to finish up his paperwork only if exempted from the order. "Why cant you leave Washington and come here," he pleaded to Dodge, who was headed for Chicago to attend the Republican convention that would nomi-nate his old friend Grant. Furious at Durant's betrayal of his promise, Dodge fired off a scorching letter to Oliver. Evans had quit and Blickensderfer would soon follow, he scrawled savagely. "You have allowed such matters to go on for harmony until one after another men leave until no one is left . . . who has one drop of manhood in them." For himself Dodge would quit before allowing his survey parties to be ruled by "a man who has not an honest drop of Blood in his veins, who is connected with the Co for the sole purpose of bleeding it and who the Co say they cannot discharge for fear he will Black Mail it." Already General Sherman had informed Grant of a plot to drive Dodge from his post. The message to Oliver could not have been plainer, but Dodge rammed it home: "It is your duty to *promptly decidedly countermand that order.*"

Even before this protest blistered his ears, Oliver tried to assure Dodge that Durant had authority only over construction, not location. The circular, he said ruefully, was "one of those peculiar exhibitions of character which Durant everywhere exhibits and which shows the impolicy of giving him power which he is sure to abuse always." But Oliver's response lacked enough bite or even bark to suit Dodge. From Washington Oakes prodded his brother to take a firm stand. For weeks he had urged Oliver to "go out once in a while and show them on the line of the road that you are the head of the concern." A break with Durant should be avoided if possible, but Dodge was too in-valuable to lose—not only as an engineer but for his lobbying ability and his contacts with the military. Grant took a personal interest in the matter, and Grant might soon be president. The thing to do, Oakes suggested, was for Dodge to go west and for Oliver to take command of the New York office "nearly all the time say 5 days a week." Above all, Oakes admonished his brother not to let Durant "ride over you as President as he is disposed to do."

Oakes didn't want Seymour out on the road, and the engineers made it clear they would take no orders from him—*"eating dirt,"* House called it. Stunned by this reaction, Durant disclaimed any intention of meddling with location and hastily improvised an arrangement serving several purposes. Reed and Seymour were sent west to help with the Utah surveys. Durant also wished to engage Brigham Young as a subcontractor before the Central Pacific got to him. Reed was the best man for that job, having been on good terms with Young since his first visit to the Mormon capital in 1864. Evans was put in charge of construction from Fort Sanders to Green River. He did not want the position but agreed reluctantly to "take Reeds place during his absence which I hope will be short as it is no sinecure."

But Durant did not retract his obnoxious order, and Oliver merely lectured Seymour on the subject of his power. His letter did not faze Seymour, who assumed that Durant could handle the amiable president. The old and familiar pattern was repeating itself, hatching out another version of what Dodge called the *"Black Hills disgrace."* Seymour was the perfect Warwick, filling Durant's ear with plausible advice, spurring him to rash actions that plunged the company into turmoil from which he hoped to wring advantage. He knew, as Durant did, that Oliver lacked the strength of will to oppose them forcefully. The Doctor had only to sing his lullaby of progress, profits, and harmony to lull Oliver into acquiesence. As Oliver confessed to his diary, "Durant very sanguine of building the road to Salt Lake & dont want any trouble."

But trouble could not be avoided. Dissension rippled through the ranks as if a boil teeming with malignancies had been lanced and its poisons allowed to spread until the body shuddered violently with convulsions. Seymour carried the order west with him to show Bates and Hodges, who had just been sent to locate the final line west from Weber Canyon across Bear River and around the north end of Salt Lake. Brandishing the order at Blickensderfer, Seymour then called in Bates and Maxwell and put them to work elsewhere on the line. Both parties lost a week in shifting around. Meanwhile Seymour and Reed looked over the work at the mouth of Echo. Jake Blickensderfer eyed them impassively and said little while he tried to sort out the conflict between Durant's order and Dodge's instructions. One impression came through indelibly: Seymour wanted the line finished as fast and cheaply as possible. To that end he urged 116-foot grades and more curvature. "This strikes me as singular," Blickensderfer reported to Dodge, "being the very reverse of his views strenuously urged last season in reference to the Black Hills location."

Reed favored holding grades to ninety feet but as usual did not think it worth a row to press his views. Seymour promised Dillon a better, cheaper line and rained telegrams on New York denouncing Blickensderfer's line with its ninety-foot grade as "suicidal policy." Summoned to New York to answer these charges, Dodge convinced the board that a lower grade was worth the extra money. Informed of this decision, Blickensderfer assured Dodge that his instructions would be obeyed but warned that "chips may fly." On the heels of this telegram came one from Durant: "Instruct Blickensderfer by telegraph to obey general order number one." When Dodge objected, Durant began flinging chips. Shaking with rage, he wired Seymour to discharge any division engineer who refused to obey the order. "I do not know as the Board will sustain me," he snarled at Dodge, "but I shall not stay in the Company if they see fit to keep you in their service to run politics to the neglect of your duties as chief engineer."

The vast irony in this charge would surely have staggered less solemn minds than Dodge's, who had neither the time nor the wit to appreciate it. While Seymour pressed Durant to reaffirm his power to fire engineers, an ugly feud was brewing that pitted Reed against Snyder and Evans. For a few golden weeks Reed basked in his Utah mission, far from the scene of battle. "I have not felt so free from care and anxiety since leaving home," he told his wife. Reed appreciated the Mormons and through tactful diplomacy succeeded in contracting with Brigham Young to grade from the head of Echo Canyon to Salt Lake. This coup kept Young and his men out of the hands of the Central Pacific, which also tried to recruit him.

Anxious to get Young's crews at work as early as possible, Reed stayed on in Utah to help Blickensderfer get the final line ready for the graders. He was a good man for the job, having done the original survey in 1864. During these weeks, however, he shared a tent with Seymour, who filled his ear with tales of plots hatching against him. Letters from friends warned Reed of a "reign of personal abuse" against men loyal to him. The Construction Department, he learned, was entirely in the hands of Snyder, "who has found and I say it truly, a *willing tool in the person of J. A. Evans.*" Snyder wanted to discredit Reed, and Evans had "accepted the position merely as a stepping stone to occupying it permanently." By mid-June Reed concluded that Evans "if possible, is a worse enemy than W. Snyder, so say my friends by letter and telegrams."

Suspicion was a two-way street. Reed's habit of avoiding quarrels by remaining silent caused the fiery Evans to dismiss him as "the weakest back'd man I think I ever saw." But this clash of temperaments did not lead Evans into backstabbing. When Seymour tried to meddle in his work, Evans wrote Durant bluntly, "I want either full power here or that Reed should come back soon I dont care which." The prickly Snyder was another matter. Apart from admiring Evans's ability and vigor in comparison with Reed, he harbored dark thoughts about what was going on in Utah. "If the contracting firm west of Green River is not Young, Reed & Seymour," he surmised, "then I dont know the men, or Brigham knows them too well."

Both sides appealed to the hapless Dodge, who had no intention of choosing between friends in a quarrel. He was too far away to get at the root of the misunderstanding, but somehow he had to patch up differences before his entire organization went to pieces. Reed was quick to put his resignation in Dodge's hands, sighing wearily to his wife, "there is so much jealousy and hard feeling . . . both in New York and on the line of the road that there is not much pleasure in trying to advance the work." Dodge was determined not to lose him—or Snyder or Evans for that matter. He had to get out there fast, before more damage was done.

Oliver too was preparing to go west and promised to meet Dodge in Omaha. Durant had gone back to New York and charmed Oliver into hoping that the clash between Seymour and Blickensderfer was blown out of proportion. "I have never seen the Dr so entirely courteous and confiding," Oliver reported to Dodge. Dillon entertained no such illusions. Unable to get away from New York, he warned Dodge to nail the Utah line down so that Seymour could not pick at it. But Dillon had also heard rumors that Reed and Seymour had an interest in the grading contracts, and he wanted Dodge to dig out the dirt. "If you work it right, you can find out all about it," he advised. "Make them all believe that we are all glad. I would give most anything to know if it is so."

A showdown loomed, and no one could predict the results. What then of the harmony promised by the payoff? In only a few months it had brought the company full circle. All the old wounds had been reopened and new ones inflicted. The Doctor had reclaimed his whip as ringmaster, and Seymour had some fresh ideas for him to ponder.

* * *

Money was tight during the spring of 1868, forcing the company to borrow at 13 percent and, on at least one occasion, as high as 18 percent. In June the crunch eased, and bond sales, after a slow start, picked up sharply. First mortgage bonds were offered at 102, a figure they would not again reach until 1874. Dillon took nearly $2 million in government bonds at 103, also a record price. Even the stock began looking good to optimists like Oakes, who rashly bought five hundred shares at 50. He would soon regret the deal, for the stock would not approach that figure again until two years after his death.

Despite their troubles, a rosy glow of enthusiasm pervaded the directors. After years of frantic scrambling to raise money, they indulged the illusion that the worst of their ordeal had passed. The road's progress had at last given it credibility among investors. Buoyed by this confidence, the Trustees agreed upon a payoff of grand proportions. During a three-week period of June and July they declared three dividends (or allotments of profits) totaling altogether 90 percent in cash ($3,375,000), 75 percent in bonds ($2,812,500), and 40 percent in stock ($1.5 million face value). Thus a person owning a hundred shares of Crédit Mobilier stock received $9,000 cash, $7,500 in bonds then selling at par, and forty shares of Union Pacific stock worth maybe $1,600 in cash, for a total return of about $18,100 on an investment of

$10,000. Added to the earlier dividend, the payoff amounted to about $28,020 or a whopping 280 percent.

No one could accuse the Trustees of thinking small. If this largess to themselves stripped the company of working capital, it could be replaced so long as rails went down and bonds continued to sell. In a pinch, bonds or funds could always be lent back to the road at interest. Like most railroads, the Union Pacific's chief source of money had always been its own directors, either directly or as agents on commission. To their eager eyes the summer skies beckoned full steam ahead. The Central Pacific still posed a threat, and Duff Green had filed a mysterious suit against the company in Pennsylvania, but that seemed little more than a nuisance. If the road could be pressed to Salt Lake, another pot of gold waited at the rainbow's end.

9

THE SHOWDOWN

The way Seymour figured it, Durant's courage needed shoring up. The Doctor had let Dodge blunt the effect of General Order No. 1 by reasserting his authority over the survey parties, thereby leaving Seymour in an awkward position. Blickensderfer, obviously relieved, seldom spoke to Seymour and did not even bother answering his letters. The time spent with Reed, however, convinced Seymour that he had won a new ally. Reed seemed to agree with him on the Utah line and appreciated Seymour's support in the fight against Evans and Snyder. Thus encouraged, Seymour scolded the Doctor for discarding his views in favor of Dodge's on the line through Echo. "You are paying at least a million for bad engineering," he warned. Dodge's judgment was "not worth the snap of your fingers. He is trying to recover from the blunder about grades that he made on the Black Hills by going to the other extreme."

Worse still, Dodge wanted the line to run north of Salt Lake. Seymour considered the route around the south end more favorable than anyone realized and urged Durant not to "go it blind" with Dodge's views. Meanwhile, he added, there was more money to be made along the way. Aware that Durant had an interest in the tie contract held by Davis, Sprague & Company, Seymour wanted a subcontract and asked him to arrange it. In return he offered to share his half interest in "the best coal mine in the country." Finally, he urged the Doctor to defend Reed from the attacks by Evans and Snyder. "He is feeling very badly about it," Seymour noted helpfully, "and I think it is wrong."

*   *   *

All Sam Reed wanted was to do his job without interference, but on the Union Pacific that was asking for the moon. He protested to New York and was content to await results, but Jenny Reed was not so philosophical about her husband's battles. She fired off letters warning Dodge of the *"deep* laid plan" against Reed and the "insatiable ambition" of Snyder, who had been laying his snares for the past year. He and Evans wanted control of the Construction Department and were banking on Reed's resignation. "The Dr is either with them or *deceived,"* she added ominously, "I think with them to Let his friends contracts that he know he could not under Mr Reed." She begged Dodge not to let her husband's enemies drive him out.

It was all a misunderstanding, Dodge assured her, but he did not yet have a handle on it. He was as certain that Reed had no interest in any contract as he was that Durant and Seymour did have, but how to convince suspicious directors? And how could Reed manage contractors who were in league with the Doctor? On the long journey to Council Bluffs, Dodge's mind grappled with these problems. Oliver arrived on June 21, several days ahead of Dodge. When they moved on to Laramie, Reed came over from Utah to thrash the issue out. Snyder and Evans were already there.

The meeting between Oliver and Reed was one of mirror images, two amiable, reticent men who loathed quarrels and kept finding themselves caught up in them. On this occasion, however, Reed startled even Dodge by airing his complaints in blunt language. Constant interference and misrepresentation, he emphasized, had not only cost the company dearly but also demoralized its officers. Reed wanted his position reaffirmed or his resignation accepted. A surprised Oliver listened with furrowed brow but was not moved to step out of character. He refused either to take a stand or to allow Reed to quit. Instead he persuaded Reed to return to Salt Lake City while the matter was decided, and came away convinced anew with Reed's inability "to run a very large machine." Reed also had it out with Snyder and Evans, but nothing was settled. Evans insisted earnestly that he meant no harm to anyone. "Actions," snapped Reed tersely, "speak louder than words."

Unable to resolve this dispute, Dodge tried to hurry the Utah line along before Seymour could do more damage there. So far the Insulting Engineer had made little headway against Blickensderfer's polite intransigence. When the telegram reaffirming Dodge's authority arrived, Blickensderfer rode up and down the line showing it to all the party chiefs. In the presence of Reed and Seymour he ordered Maxwell back to his original survey. Seymour blustered that Durant's order had priority over anything Dodge wrote. If you order Maxwell back, Seymour said stiffly, I'll order him to remain. What then? Blickensderfer eyed him coldly. In that case, he replied, I shall dismiss every man refusing to obey my orders, cut off their pay, and organize parties under new chiefs to carry out Dodge's instructions. "I thought this declaration staggered him," he noted wryly to Dodge.

Seymour retreated sullenly and Blickensderfer erased the mischief already done. Hodges had been sent by Seymour to run another line at Echo; he was recalled and put to work on the route west of Promontory Point. Seymour had also dispatched Bates to relocate the entire line at Weber Canyon and raise the grade at Devil's Gate by ten feet. Blickensderfer regarded Bates as the most "totally inefficient" man he knew, but on this occasion his "extreme inertness" saved the day. He had done little before Blickensderfer arrived to recast the line according to Dodge's specifications. By the end of June the Dutchman had most of the line staked for the contractors; none of the grades exceeded the limit of ninety feet imposed by Dodge. East of Echo, Hudnutt had found a promising line over the basin rim with only a sixty-foot grade and lighter work than anyone expected. "All I want," Blickensderfer pleaded, "is a little more time to examine and work out the problem."

Dodge was willing to give the extra time and so was Oliver, who seemed at last to grasp the value of spending more to get the best possible line through such difficult terrain. Oliver fended off a complaint from Seymour that crews were standing idle because the line was not ready for work. He was on the road showing his authority as Oakes had suggested, but during his absence fresh turmoil was brewing in New York.

* * *

Once past Dale Creek, the rail crews headed up the Laramie Basin toward the Medicine Bow River and then westward to the North Platte. Beyond the North Platte lay the forbidding desert of the Great Basin, stretching toward the Green River on the far side of the rim. As the road extended deeper into barren country, the task of supplying the men grew more complicated. By June grading and excavating crews were strung across Wyoming all the way to Green River, while in Utah Brigham Young had put a thousand of the faithful to work. Durant pressed Evans hard to finish the grading to Green River by July 10 so as to free crews for the heavy rock work west of the river. The graders were driving as fast as possible, Evans replied; "it is not a country where people are disposed to linger."

To keep the crews moving required a steady flow of supplies. Contractors cut huge quantities of timber for ties and bridging in the hills along the North Platte and floated them down the river. Two steam-powered sawmills were imported from Chicago and located at strategic points. The luxury of an assured timber supply enabled Reed to increase the number of ties per mile from 2,440 to 2,640 and solved the problem of poles for the telegraph line. In Pittsburgh Harbaugh acted as agent for procuring rails, bolts, spikes, and frogs, but shortages of tools cropped up as the work force increased. The Doctor chafed at delays in providing the Mormons with implements. "Do all in your power to forward what is required," he growled at Evans. "We agreed to furnish Tools and the damage will be heavy. Six thousand men are waiting."

The amount of provisions needed to feed so large a force of men and animals was staggering. Here as elsewhere the wartime experience of supplying an army in the field enabled the company's agents to handle the huge demands thrust upon them. Every day piles of boxes and crates loaded with flour, bacon, coffee, sugar, fruit, vegetables, salt, dried fish, vinegar, beans, rice, molasses, potatoes, butter, corn, and oats rolled toward Wyoming in an endless shuttle. On one day alone ten carloads of corn were dispatched out of Cheyenne. Besides food the boxcars were crammed with tents, shovels, scrapers, candles, brooms, wagon grease, blankets, buckets, pick handles, and other necessities. Like an army the construction crews marched always at the mercy of their supply line, and rarely did it fail them. When shortages occurred, the contractors borrowed from each other until the next train arrived.

"Every body here is crowded with work even to the Cooks," Jack Casement reported. "We have to Bake night & day we use up two Barrells of flour a day." Jack had his hands full between laying track and grading a part of the line; on one day he covered a hundred miles on horseback to check out his crews. Through all the bickering and distractions the track rolled on, passing the six hundred-mile post before the end of May on its way to Rock Creek. Eastern papers praised the road's progress in glowing terms and predicted that the linking of the continent might come as early as the next year. A few carped about the quality of construction and warned that cheap work would cost dearly in the end. What sort of managers, they asked, would skimp and cut corners on what everyone regarded as the great national enterprise? "It is the most unaccountable and anomalous feature of the times," mused the New York *Times,* "that the grandest enterprises are so frequently managed by little men."

* * *

Free at last of Washington, Dodge met Oliver near Rock Creek on June 30. Next day they went on to Carbon, paused to inspect the coal mine, and took stages to the North Platte, then only thirty-five miles from end of track. Crews were at work along the entire route, and the bridge over the river was already going up. On the way they passed the first tunnel on the road; Dodge took one look and pronounced it a bad job. He was more impressed by the timber coming down the river. Oliver did not tarry long. Fatigued by the heat and hard ride through rough, barren country, he hurried back to Laramie. There he learned that in the two days of his absence Jack Casement's crews had laid four and a half miles of track.

Dodge turned his horse west for another long ride over the entire line with Marshall Hurd, the engineer in charge of construction. The route beyond the Laramie River was another thorn in his side. Two locations had been made, one through Rattlesnake Pass by way of Cooper Lake, the other skirting the

Medicine Bow along Rock Creek. The former was the most direct and had sixty-foot grades but considerable heavy work. Dodge preferred it to the Rock Creek route, which was twenty miles longer with lighter work at the price of much more curvature, but the contractors persuaded the company to adopt the longer line on the ground that it could be built in half the time. Forty years later, E. H. Harriman would rebuild the line along the route advocated by Dodge.

The line to Green River convinced Dodge that his engineers had done their job well. He was less happy with how little attention had been given to the critical problem of finding water. At every station he put men to work boring wells and scolded Oliver by letter that "we ought to [have] been at it long ago." The bridge work also displeased him. He urged Oliver not to waste money on temporary trestle bridges; there was still time enough to put in trusses before the track arrived, and stone drains as well. All along the line Dodge found the grading contractors making good progress despite the heat and choking alkali of the desert. Some of Carmichael's men struck for higher wages, demanding four dollars a day instead of three, but Reed paid them off, closed the boarding houses, and got troops to protect the work until the strikers relented.

By the time Dodge reached Fort Bridger on July 16, he was satisfied that prospects for laying track into Utah that season were splendid if all went well. Already the track had crossed the North Platte to Benton, 676 miles from Omaha. The field officers had not let the bickering interfere with their work— at least not yet. A large packet of mail awaited Dodge at Fort Bridger. Among the letters was one that made his heart sink. He learned, two weeks after the fact, that the Doctor had made another move.

* * *

Duff Green's threatened injunction proved to be something more than a nuisance. The company's lawyers obtained a postponement until August 8— or so they thought. Dillon and Durant went west only to be summoned to testify on July 21. When they did not appear, a nasty article in the New York *Herald* suggested that they had fled to avoid the hearing. All this served as a stalking horse for Jim Fisk, who had come away from the election fight of 1867 empty-handed. He had subscribed for stock on behalf of Durant and his friend Josiah Bardwell, who had promised to pay his expenses. The bills amounted to $3,200, but no payment was forthcoming. Fisk accused them of welching and declared angrily that he would get what he could. On July 2, 1868, he filed suit to enjoin the Union Pacific from transacting any business with Crédit Mobilier until his complaint was satisfied. Privately Fisk put a price tag of $75,000 on a settlement, although Bushnell thought he could be bought off for $50,000.

Fisk was no stranger to Oliver. As rivals in the rail and steamship competition on Long Island Sound, they were busy that summer trying to reach agreement on a pool for dividing business. Oliver assumed the suit was black-mail, but he knew Fisk to be both clever and dangerous. A suit in New York meant serious trouble because Fisk and his partner, Jay Gould, had two friendly judges, George Barnard and Albert Cardozo, on the State Supreme Court. Fisk procured an injunction against treasurer John J. Cisco, but Oliver was still in Wyoming when the suit was brought. His absence during these critical days gave Durant a golden opportunity to wring advantage from Fisk's attack.

The threat posed by Fisk was real. He told Bushnell that papers ap-pointing a receiver for the Union Pacific were already signed by a judge and would be served at once unless he was paid off. At the very least Fisk could tie up the company enough to stop work on the road. On July 3, Bushnell, Dillon, Duff, and Durant hastily drew up an agreement releasing Crédit Mobilier from the tripartite contract as a device for getting around Fisk's suit. That same day the executive committee met and approved a resolution giving Durant full power over *all* work on the road including preliminary and final surveys. Ironically, the motion was offered by Duff, the man who had so often chastised Oliver for giving in to the Doctor.

In Washington, Oakes figured that the best way to rid the company of Fisk permanently was to get the suit out of the clutches of his friendly judges. He therefore introduced a bill allowing all suits brought against corporations with federal charters to be removed to federal courts. Exhausted by the im-peachment fight and scorching summer heat, Congress did not dawdle on the measure but passed it with little debate on July 27. In time the so-called "removal act" would have enormous repercussions on American corporate law. For the moment it triggered a dogfight among the lawyers. Fisk coun-tered with an injunction from Cardozo preventing the Union Pacific or Crédit Mobilier from removing any of its "books, papers, money or other property" from the state. Dillon, Durant, and auditor Benjamin Ham fled into exile to avoid contempt citations; the board did not meet again until September. For the rest of the year the company's lawyers tried in vain to get a decision from Barnard on the removal motion. The suit dangled in legal limbo, ready to spring to life again once Barnard ruled on it.

Fisk was content to play the waiting game while his lawyers searched for a way around the removal act. He had other fish to fry, and possibly he wanted the suit as leverage in his steamship negotiations with Oliver. Not so the Doctor. Resolution in hand, he hurried west with jaw set and eyes gleaming, a firebrand bent on igniting his forces for the great push to Utah. Along the line the order flashed that Durant was coming, that officers and men were "subject to his directions and will act accordingly."

*   *   *

The showdown had been a long time coming, was so long overdue that some feared its outcome. "Durant is really down on Genl Dodge," Oakes warned his brother, "and he means to remove him." Alley declared that nothing done by the Durant clique had alarmed him more, and offered Oliver some harsh words. "You have acquiesced in and submitted to wrong," he wrote, "and to the view of outsiders even appeared to countenance and encourage it, until there is great danger, I think, of compromising your character." In return the executive committee had ignored the board, insulted the chief engineer "because he is fearless and honest," and ridden roughshod over the president. The time had come to take a stand, he said sternly, "to resist, by all the power which you possess, these encroachments upon your rights and ours." If Oliver would lead, Alley would willingly fight and so would others. But if "such a state of things must continue, then let me retire from the contest."

How this man of "excessive amiability," as Alley called him, must have agonized over such a rebuke. He too fled New York to avoid being enjoined, but no distance was great enough to spare him the miseries of conflict so repugnant to his nature. Not even Alley's plea could move him to oppose the Doctor. Too much was at stake to risk a confrontation that might plunge them all into a desperate battle. Instead he wrote Dodge a limp explanation of the resolution. "As our great object is to complete the Road," he exhorted, "we must as far as possible set aside all these annoyances and let no ordinary thing turn us from the object." He instructed Dodge to meet Durant at end of track and expressed the wistful hope that the interview would be "all harmonious."

These ineffectual statements reached Dodge after the showdown had already occurred. A stroke of luck enabled Dodge to summon more powerful support than Oliver could offer. It happened that Grant was in the West to attend a treaty council and do some campaigning for the presidency. He agreed to meet with Dodge, Durant, Dillon, Seymour, and Reed at Fort Sanders on July 26. Grant brought with him one of the most impressive gatherings of Union generals since the war. Sherman was there along with Phil Sheridan, Gibbon, Augur, W. C. Harney, and several more. Dodge greeted his old comrades on the twenty-fifth at Benton and doubtless used the opportunity to plead his case in advance. Durant had his resolution, but Dodge had the friendship of the generals, one of whom was about to be elected President.

Next day the distinguished guests crowded into the crude log bungalow used as an officers' club at Fort Sanders. The presence of so notable an array of brass must have shaken Durant; nevertheless, he launched into his charges against Dodge, most of them drawn from Seymour. One by one Dodge refuted them in detail and threatened to quit before tolerating any more changes in his line. Grant listened in his inscrutable manner, puffing absently on the inevitable cigar. When Dodge had finished, he and Sherman made it clear that they expected him to remain as chief engineer and would brook no interference with his line. Afterward Dodge took Grant, Sherman, and Sheridan to his house in Council Bluffs where he took great pains to post Grant thoroughly on Union Pacific affairs.

The impression has lingered that this showdown settled the matter once and for all. In fact it settled nothing but only clarified everyone's position. Durant and Seymour now understood that Dodge could not be driven out because he had too many powerful friends. Dodge was confident of his position but realized that his enemies would continue their intrigues because there was no one to stop them. All sides grasped that Oliver lacked the strength to stop the infighting or the will to force a decision. The lines among the combatants had been drawn and would remain unchanged until the end.

Five days after the meeting Durant issued another general order which, among other things, gave Seymour free rein to alter the Utah line. Seymour promptly resurrected his argument that a 116-foot grade would save not only time but at least $1 million between Echo and the mouth of Weber. To confuse matters, Reed came up with a line requiring only 90-foot grades but a 3,000-foot tunnel. Dodge retorted that both lines were far inferior to the one run by Blickensderfer and would save less than $200,000. Jesse Williams, himself an engineer and the most conscientious of the government directors, registered a strong protest against any change in Blickensderfer's line. Privately he told Dodge that the higher grade was not worth so small a savings. "How much do you suppose the B. & O. R.R. would expend to reduce their 116 to 90 feet?" he mused. "Probably a million or two."

Williams's stand alarmed Oliver. He had been told by Seymour that the line run by Reed would save more than $600,000 but didn't believe a word of it. Then came another steaming letter from Dodge charging bitterly that Seymour was in command of the line and Durant controlled New York:

> If the country knew it to-day more than one injunction would be served on you. Nothing is being *done on repairs* and the order of the Vice President is to skin and skip everything for the purpose of getting track down, & your temporary Bridges will now hardly stand to get trains over them, and winter will close in on you with nothing done. Your immense subsidy will be spent in dividends, and what few men you have among you who have a *name* or reputation will be, in the eyes of the country, disgraced.

Seymour was trying to ruin "the finest location *that was ever made*" with excessive grades and curvature. Oliver had promised to protect the engineers to avoid another Black Hills fiasco; instead he had allowed it to happen again. If left alone, Dodge promised the best line over some of the most difficult terrain in the country. But if Seymour had his way, he added ominously, "somebody will have to answer for the *swindle* . . . I doubt whether a mile of Road will be accepted, with such a location."

These words sent a chill down Oliver's spine. The efficiency and economy of future operations depended on the right line—not only grade and curvature but the best location to avoid snow, minimize tunneling, access to fuel and water supplies. The final choice always boiled down to a compromise between these factors and cost, but in this case something else entered the equation. Williams had the ear of Secretary Browning, and both Dodge and Blickensderfer had powerful friends in Washington. If all three agreed on the line, who could hope to persuade Browning that another was preferable? Oliver passed these anxieties along to Durant and urged him to make no change without "the best Evidence that a change is required for the best interest of the Co."

After months of changes made and unmade, alternative lines run and discarded, wasted motion and hard feelings, the company adopted Blickensderfer's original line. The decision pleased but did not satisfy Williams, who had for months been uneasy over the workmanship on the road. In June he had suggested to the board and to Browning the idea of putting some bonds into a reserve fund to upgrade deficiencies in construction after the road was completed. After an inspection tour he reported to Browning that about $3 million would be needed for such work and urged withholding that amount in government bonds.

"Cisco says I'm entirely right in urging a reserve fund," Williams wrote Dodge, but the notion of withholding so large a portion of their most marketable securities horrified Oliver and most of the directors. Aware that Browning was no friend of the road, they argued that the law gave the government no right to withhold bonds once commissioners had approved the sections on which they were issued. It was a losing battle, especially after the newspapers took up the cry. At a board meeting on September 2 Williams moved to create the fund. Grudgingly the directors approved the idea but substituted first mortgage bonds for the government bonds.

The issue became one more bone of contention between the board and Browning, who still had not decided finally on the Central Pacific's bogus map. A showdown loomed between the rival roads over where they would meet, and the government would play a decisive role in the outcome. Browning seemed to favor the Central Pacific, and President Johnson was, in the opinion of one Union Pacific lobbyist, "as crooked as he can be, and as stubborn as a mule." Grant was a friend of the road, but even if elected he would not take office until March. Meanwhile, the company braced for another struggle with a hostile administration.

*   *   *

All these developments Hazard watched with a jaundiced eye. Through the long summer he kept doggedly at Durant, trying to force his hand on the suspense account. In July the Doctor made a statement before Crédit Mobilier's auditing committee. The money, he explained airily, had been paid him by the Union Pacific and afterward charged to Crédit Mobilier under the Hoxie account. At the time no one wanted it to appear in the railroad's accounts, but now it ought to be charged back to Union Pacific. He would not say to whom the money was paid or for what purpose, only that it was for the company's benefit. This was the story he had used before to slip away from inquiries, and it worked again.

He would not slip away again, Hazard thought grimly. The old man also suspected that Durant, and perhaps others, had an interest in Fisk's suit. For months his lawyers had been preparing to go after Durant if the company refused to act; now it was clear that Oliver would do nothing. Since his suit would be brought in a Rhode Island court, Hazard waited until late August, when Durant turned up in Newport for some pleasuring, to have him arrested on a complaint charging "intent to defraud" the Union Pacific and procuring funds fraudulently "for his own wrongful use." Oakes willingly furnished Hazard an affidavit, but the others shied away, arguing that the move against Durant was "premature." Even John Williams refused to testify unless compelled because so many directors had criticized Oakes.

Like it or not, the other directors were made parties to the suit. When they closed ranks against him, Hazard wrote Dodge asking for help. "Mr Durant," he said dryly, "does not seem so grateful for the opportunity of exculpating himself from suspicion as might be expected from injured innocence." The Doctor made light of his arrest, telling Oliver how eager the police were to accept a bribe for letting him go. An uneasy Oliver followed Durant to the office "via his Malt Shop" for some tough talk. Hazard's suit caught Oliver at a bad time. The reserve fund issue still hung fire, as did his steamboat negotiations with Fisk. Oakes was anxious to get his contract extended to cover the last stretch of road through Utah. The Trustees wanted on account $6.5 million in securities from the Union Pacific for work done.

Aware that Durant could throw a wrench into all these matters, Oliver dared not do anything that might antagonize him. The Doctor was preparing to go west and wanted the deck cleared of certain old business. To emphasize the point, he had the executive committee on September 9 rescind the $6.5 payment to the Trustees authorized five days earlier. That night Oakes came up from Washington to wrap up the extension of his contract but went back empty-handed. The executive committee also voted to employ counsel for the Hazard suit, but the Doctor wanted more, much more. He wanted full power from the executive committee, and he wanted its official absolution on the suspense account question.

Each step taken by Oliver on behalf of his interests had put him one level deeper in league with his foes against his friends. Now he was in too deep to back out and utterly unable to resist the Doctor. In January 1867 Oliver and Cisco had been appointed a committee to examine and report on the suspense account. Nothing was heard from them for eighteen months, but suddenly on September 11 they presented a report to the executive committee. Having examined the account in detail, they concluded that all of Durant's alleged payments had been made "upon proper authority of the Board and proper vouchers and that the facts in the premises are satisfactory to us." For nearly two years Hazard had tried in vain to get Durant to produce vouchers and give names. Only twelve days earlier Oakes had sworn to his failure in the same endeavor. Yet Oliver and Cisco declared themselves satisfied with evidence and explanations produced within a few days if at all.

The executive committee accepted the report and ordered the suspense account closed and charged to construction. That done, it appointed a committee to fix prices for the extension of Oakes's contract. A list of appointments requested by Snyder was referred to Durant with full power to "remove and appoint" all officers, including Snyder himself, while out on the line. Dillon and Duff were already a special committee to oversee such matters, but they now delegated their full authority to Durant as well. "It is one of the miseries of our Road," Oliver had written Dodge two weeks earlier, "that we have a man in it who is so desirous of Power and so jealous of every act that does not coincide with his notions." Evidently the company loved misery, for once again it dealt with the problem by cloaking Durant with the power he sought so avidly.

In fact Oliver spent most of that same September day trying to resolve another nagging problem. All summer long McComb had obstinately pressed his claim for additional shares of Crédit Mobilier stock. Since June he had threatened a suit of his own if not appeased, but repeated attempts at a compromise failed. McComb clung to the issue with a tenacity worthy of Hazard, and no one doubted he would go to court if necessary. Well might the board wonder how many suits were required before all its dirty laundry got aired.

* * *

When summer's heat came on, the track crews pitched tents atop their bunk cars in hopes of catching a cool night breeze. The gangs had found their rhythm and were putting track down at a record pace, sometimes as much as four miles a day. "With the exception of a few Mules that insist on Dieing [sic] on short notice," Jack Casement chortled, "all is going well." Evans kept the flow of material moving steadily, enabling the Irishmen to set a blistering pacc. During seventy-eight working days between July 21 and October 20 they averaged 2.3 miles of track a day or 181 miles in all. There was reason to keep moving. The desert was hot, the water brackish, and the fine alkali dust so choking that in time it drew blood from the lungs. "This is an awfull place," Jack grumbled, "alkali dust knee deep and certainly the meanest place I have ever been in." As Evans had said, it was not country where men were disposed to linger.

The chief obstacle that summer was a flood of excursions to end of track. Everyone wanted to see the work in progress on the great national highway and the Doctor was eager to accommodate regardless of the burden it thrust on busy officers. In July Durant hosted an expedition of journalists headed by

Charles Dana of the New York *Sun.* It was a rousing success; the self-styled "Rocky Mountain Press Club" gave the Union Pacific good ink for two months. A few weeks later Schuyler Colfax, Grant's running mate, toured the road, and behind him came a band of professors from Yale. The visitors went home impressed by what they saw, but Snyder complained that they "have interfered with our work very much & have worn me out." Jack Casement agreed the excursionists were "a great nuisance to the work," but his men laid four miles of track while the professors watched in awe.

By August 1868 the track was already thirty miles past the North Platte, nearly 700 miles from Omaha. On September 21 it reached mile post 815, only a few miles shy of Green River. "The day will soon come, we dare say," rhapsodized the New York *Tribune,* "when it will be nothing unusual for a railroad to measure its length by thousands of miles, instead of by scores and fifties; but an unbroken line of rails so long as this is now almost unprecedented." Along its path new stations sprang up with names reflecting the harsh, exotic beauty of the country: Separation, Creston, Red Desert, Table Rock, Bitter Creek, Black Buttes, Point of Rock, Salt Wells, Rock Springs.

As the track rolled westward, so did Hell on Wheels. The Big Tent that had served Julesburg, Cheyenne, and Laramie packed up and headed for Benton. A hundred feet long and forty feet wide, it had a floor for dancing and a raised platform for the band. An elegant bar glittering with mirrors and paintings dispensed every kind of liquor in cut-glass goblets and pitchers. Beyond the dance floor could be found tables for faro, monte, roulette—any game of chance the reckless cared to try. Around the Big Tent mushroomed a town of tents, shacks, and portable buildings of thinly painted pine that could be bought in Chicago for $300 and erected in a day with screwdrivers. One man constructed a restaurant in sections and carried it west on a freight wagon. Benton, wrote a Cheyenne editor, "like the camps of the Bedouin Arabs, is of tents, and almost a transitory nature as the elements of a soap bubble."

Those hardy enough to visit Benton came away convinced they had glimpsed a suburb of Hell. Novelist J. H. Beadle tromped through the powdery alkali and, in his dark suit, soon resembled a cockroach scurrying across a flour barrel. He found "not a green tree, shrub or patch of grass. The red hills were scorched as bare as if blasted by lightning." Samuel Bowles, the genteel editor of the Springfield *Republican,* was appalled by "a village of a few variety stores and shops, by day disgusting, by night dangerous, almost everybody dirty, many filthy and with the marks of lowest vice, averaging a murder a day, gambling and drinking, hurdy dancing and the vilest of sexual commerce." The alkali was "so fine and volatile that the slightest breeze loaded the air with it, irritating every sense and poisoning half of them." An editor suggested that enough water would transform the dust into "one immense foaming powder."

People were dirty because water cost a dime a bucket and once ran as high as ten dollars a barrel. But "forty rod" whiskey cost only a quarter a glass, and that was what the railroad men wanted along with some gambling and (if any of their pay survived the tables) a woman. As the country grew rougher, so did life in each succeeding Hell on Wheels. Since Wyoming was not yet an organized territory, soldiers from the nearest fort patrolled the streets. Laramie was dominated by outlaws running the notorious "Bucket of Blood" saloon until October 1868, when a vigilante committee broke their stranglehold after a pitched battle. At Benton the troops tried in vain to stop the constant shootings and brawling. The guardhouse at Fort Steele overflowed with horse thieves, gamblers, and murderers.

No attempt was made to bring law to Benton because the town did not last that long. So wretched was its location that virtually the entire population followed the track gangs westward to Green River. Ten months later Beadle returned and found not a single house or tent, only the rubble of a few chimneys and the inevitable layer of alkali covering even the town's only surviving institution, the cemetery.

Through most of the summer Casement's gangs and the graders had done just fine without help from the Doctor. In September, however, Durant hurried west to whip up his own peculiar brand of lather. Illness held him captive in Chicago a few days but did not stop him from firing orders in all directions. "No doubt you are doing all you can," he snapped at Reed, "but I want particulars." Next day Durant wired him to "Work night and day with Malloys force put on all the men that can work. The tracklaying will be increased to four miles per day." Davis, Sprague were ordered to put more men on cutting ties, and Evans was told to "notify Casement that sixteen thousand feet of track per day wont do." Don't bother laying in supplies for next season's work to Salt Lake, he added, "for that work is to be done this fall."

The great push was on. There would be no pause, no end of season, until the track reached Salt Lake. Durant heard ominous tales that the Central Pacific was invading the Utah canyons and letting contracts at high prices payable in gold. He sped toward end of track, pausing at Omaha only long enough to scoop up Snyder. Jack Casement, home for a brief visit with his family, got word of Durant's approach and hastily left Painesville. The whirlwind was on its way, and storm warnings flashed down the entire line.

* * *

Few engineers possessed Seymour's gift for making wrong choices. To an already impressive collection of blunders he added the push for a line south of Salt Lake. The Mormons wanted it there to put their capital on the main line, but no one could find a decent route. In May Dodge put Hodges to surveying north of the lake. All summer long the engineers searched for the best line around the lake or across it to avoid the climb at Promontory. Soundings of the lake were inconclusive, but by August Dodge was convinced that the northern route was far superior. He dismissed Seymour's objections by assuring Durant that there was no comparable route southward. "The projected Lines of Mr Reed do not work," he added. "They run right over top of mountains." The Central Pacific too had decided to build north of the lake despite Brigham Young's efforts to persuade them otherwise. Salt Lake City, like Denver, would require a branch line.

A more serious battle loomed west of the lake, where both sides were trying to seize control of the ground ahead of the other. During July Hodges surveyed the ground from Promontory to Humboldt Wells. Dodge examined it in August and concluded that a good cheap line could be run to the Wells. Early in September the Central Pacific abandoned its surveys east of Monument Point, the limit approved by Browning. Stanford came out, looked matters over, and let contracts to Mormon contractors for grading the hundred miles west of Monument. Dodge thought it absurd to have both companies grade the same route and wanted to strike a deal with Stanford, but Seymour warned the Doctor of a plot by the Central Pacific to prevent "your commencing work west of mouth of Weber or Salt Lake until they get their track within 300 miles of here—so that they can get legal possession of the line before you."

For once Seymour was right. Huntington had become obsessed with the notion of reaching both Salt Lake and Weber Canyon first despite the appalling logistical difficulties of maintaining a supply line across the desert. Those prizes would give him the coal deposits in Weber and enable the Central Pacific to lure Utah traffic to San Francisco instead of eastward. Aware that Durant was a man of "wonderful energy, in fact reckless in his energy," he determined to beat him by hook or crook. The Doctor responded by ordering grading parties to Humboldt Wells and a hundred miles east of the Wells, working toward each other. Dodge located a splendid line 233 miles long from Weber to Humboldt Wells with no heavy work except for the six miles across Promontory Point. By contrast the Central Pacific was having trouble getting its road built fast enough to reach the legal limit. Nevertheless, the Californians spurned a compromise offer from Durant to avoid the possibility of parallel building. There was another way. If Charles Crocker's army of Chinese coolies couldn't win the battle, Huntington concluded, then it must be won in Washington.

There he had an ally in Browning, whose view of the Union Pacific was jaded by his dislike for Durant. During October Browning dealt the company a series of low blows. He seized first on Jesse Williams's earlier recommendation by arbitrarily withholding $2.56 million in subsidy bonds on eighty miles of road already approved by commissioners. This move came at a time when the money market was tight and the company had already sold certificates for some of the bonds, which could not be retrieved. At the same time Browning demanded from the government directors full details on the road's condition. He also created a special commission to examine the road and appointed to it

General Gouverneur K. Warren, General James Barnes, and Jake Blickensderfer. Until they reported to him, Browning would sit on the bonds.

All this occurred before Huntington stepped foot in Washington to lobby for acceptance of his road's map to the head of Echo. Huntington tried to conceal his presence by running down to Washington six days in a row and returning to New York each night so as to appear at his office next morning. The Central Pacific would be at Salt Lake by the year's end, he assured Browning, and could reach Echo Summit by June 1869 if the line was approved. Browning took the proposal to the entire cabinet, where it provoked a heated discussion. "I think the chances are against us," Huntington warned his associates glumly. But on October 20 the line from Monument Point to Echo Summit was approved. In Browning's words, "the unanimous opinion was that the location should be accepted so that work might progress this winter."

If there was logic in this decision, no one has ever found it. The Union Pacific could also work in winter. A few days earlier Oliver reported to Browning that the road was approaching Green River, grading and masonry would be completed to Salt Lake within a month, and a final line had been located to Humboldt Wells. In effect Browning authorized the Central Pacific to build over line already graded and bridged by the Union Pacific. Even worse, Huntington extracted from him a pledge not to notify the Union Pacific of the decision for as long as possible. The company would not discover the awful truth until December, when it appeared in Browning's annual report.

"I did it," Huntington rejoiced to Crocker. The coup gave him a chance to snatch the whole of Utah for his road *if* Crocker could lay track to within three hundred miles of Echo before the Union Pacific learned of his scheme. Otherwise his rival could get bonds simply by building on the approved line. Fiercely, exultantly, he roused Crocker to battle: "By God, Charley, you must work as man has never worked before. Our salvation is in you. Let out another link. Yes, a couple, and let her run. Don't mind Durant's blowing; *say nothing, lay the iron on the approved line."*

* * *

Durant was blowing but in all the wrong directions, leaving dissension and confusion in his wake. He rushed down the line firing orders with General Daniel McCallum in his baggage. Seymour and his claque boasted that McCallum was the "coming man," soon to be superintendent with himself as chief engineer. "Dont care a d—m as I am heartily sick of the constant fight," Snyder groused to Dodge. As the turmoil worsened, Snyder retreated deeper into a shell of bitterness and self-pity. Hoxie was ill with typhoid fever and unable to console him. Grimly Snyder bent at his task of keeping supplies moving forward despite the voices of his enemies ringing in his ears. McCallum spent a couple of days looking over the Omaha operation and decided the job was not for him. "If he tells the Directors what he promised too [sic]," Snyder laughed cynically, "they will not print his report."

There was in Snyder a strain of idealism that made him intolerant of men less honest or hard-working than himself. What bothered him most that dismal season was the growing stench of corruption emanating from the work being done so rapidly across Wyoming and Utah. Earlier Oliver Chapman had warned Oliver that there was "stealing to a large amt." Snyder agreed. The evidence was scattered and fragmentary, but it kept turning up, always from the construction department—Reed's bailiwick. There was also the Davis contract, which no one could touch because the Doctor had an interest in it, and rumors about town lots and contract scams. Snyder had some men poke around discreetly for evidence, although his own mind had long since fastened on the "Seymour-Reed gang" as the guilty parties.

One piece of knavery hit Snyder right in the face. Late in October a new commissioner named Cornelius Wendell arrived to inspect a section of road for acceptance by the government. Oliver learned that Wendell was an "unscrupulous scamp" who was "on to squeeze us and will do every thing in his power to force us to pay him Smart money." Wendell wasted no time with Snyder. After a perfunctory glance at the track, he demanded $25,000 for his approval. Snyder knew the company was in a bad way for money and, with the bonds held up by Browning, could not afford delays on getting new sections approved. If Wendell turned in a negative report, Browning would listen to no one else on the matter. Durant played coy on the matter. He would not sanction the transaction and preferred not knowing the details until it was done, at which time he protested vigorously. Left to decide the matter himself, Snyder rashly paid the money and took full responsibility for it.

Snyder was not the only one unhappy with Durant that autumn. Reed had his own showdown with the Doctor, who retreated rather than lose a man with two crucial assets: he had great influence with Brigham Young, and he was the only engineer trusted by both Dodge and Seymour. Instead he merely lightened Reed's load by giving Evans responsibility for overseeing bridge masonry. This seemingly minor change would later save Reed from considerable embarrassment; for now he was content to do his job and use his friendship with Seymour to keep the Doctor off his back. More than ever Reed was the silent man who kept what he saw to himself, and he was to see much in the coming months.

Evans too was disgusted with the constant fighting. He obliged dutifully when Durant extended his division to the head of Echo, but as the track approached the Utah border, he told the Doctor he wanted out. The work was being done so fast, he complained, that "we find it in bad shape," and he didn't want another clash with Reed over jurisdiction. Unwilling to lose Evans entirely, Durant offered him a contract for building all the truss bridges west of Green River. It looked like a good deal. Evans could do the work at a cheap price, since he could get all the timber in the mountains and thereby save the cost of transportation. The only difficulty was that Boomer already had a contract for *all* the bridges on the road. Durant simply ignored this fact and did not bother to inform Evans of it.

While Durant sowed discord in the ranks, Dodge prepared to escort the special commission across the road. He had spent six weeks with the engineers locating the line west of Salt Lake, then hurried to join Durant, Reed, and Seymour for the trip east. During the ride Seymour assured them that Congress would rip up whatever report the commission presented, but Dodge was taking no chances. He and the Doctor issued protests against the Union Pacific alone being inspected instead of all the Pacific roads and branches. Oliver reminded Dodge that a favorable report was essential. Apart from being desperate for bonds, he considered it "very important to us to have this line far enough west to take in the Oregon Branch." Dodge needed no prodding on the Oregon question; he had just sent Hudnutt to run a preliminary survey in that direction.

For eight days the commission scrutinized the road with Dodge at their side to answer questions. With grim satisfaction he noted how impressed they were with the location of the line except in a few places where Seymour or someone else had meddled: the Black Hills approach, the stretch west of Medicine Bow, and another west of Rawlins. Dodge was quick to display his original reports showing that his recommendations had been ignored in each case. The final report submitted on November 23 was on the whole favorable to the Union Pacific. It estimated that nearly $6.5 million was required to improve the road, but this figure was misleading. The location was criticized for having too many and too sharp curves, but the commissioners concluded that the road was "well constructed" and its route "exceedingly well selected. . . . Deficiencies exist, but they are almost without exception, those incident to all new roads, or of a character growing out of the peculiar difficulties encountered."

The report relieved anxieties in the Union Pacific office but did not pry any bonds loose from Browning. Durant had managed to antagonize him again by criticizing his choice of Blickensderfer as one of the commissioners and urging the President to replace him. When the Doctor also sneered at Jesse Williams as a "watch-dog" for the government (which by law he was supposed to be), the irony of his epithet escaped him entirely. Williams was entirely sympathetic to the road, but unlike Brooks, Ashmun, Harbaugh, and others, he had never been coopted by the company. Where the venal Brooks pestered Oliver to pay him secretly for his services, Williams was honest and serious about his responsibilities to company and government alike.

When Browning demanded complete financial data on the Union Pacific, Oliver declared piously that the books had always been open to government directors. This was true but disingenuous. The actual cost figures, Williams discovered, existed only in the Trustees' books, which were not available to him or anyone else. Even Dodge could not get at the figures in making up his estimates and therefore could not compute the cost reliably. The data put together by Oliver satisfied all the government directors except Williams, who complained that nothing was included on the profits to the contractors. In his report Williams came up with an estimate of $38,824,821 or about $35,000 per mile for 1,100 miles of road. He realized the figures were crude, often incorrect, and contained some glaring omissions. His effort marked the beginning of what proved an enduring controversy over the actual cost of the road and amount of profit realized by its builders. At the time Williams provided a concrete figure for those eager to make political capital out of the matter.

The commission report and Williams's estimates pleased none of the company's officers, especially when Browning showed no inclination to release the bonds. Already some newspapers had pounced on the reports, and more would soon follow. The situation in Washington was volatile and dangerous. "As the days of Andrew Johnson grow less," cautioned one of the company's lobbyists, "these 'sharks' grow ravenous and desperate." On December 1 Durant and Brooks left for Washington to exert some political muscle, little suspecting the surprise that awaited them there.

* * *

Jack Casement took the Doctor's measure early. "Durant is here trying to hurry things up," he noted, "but he only creates delays. We have held him level . . . Our men Idle more than half of the time but as He claims to love to pay for those things I propose to give him His fill of it." Annoyed at cutting short his visit home, he went back to Painesville when his wife Frank complained on their anniversary of how much time they had been apart during eleven years of marriage. Before leaving, however, he arranged the sort of demonstration he knew would impress the Doctor. On October 26, while Jack was at home, his gangs laid a record seven miles and 1,940 feet of track in one day. A pleased Durant promptly wired the news to Oliver, who chirped that the feat "has the *ring* of work in it" and was "the achievement of the year." The men got triple pay, Durant had spectacular results to parade, and everyone was happy. "Things moving nicely here," Dan telegraphed his brother. "Dont be in any hurry back."

In Utah Brigham Young was not so fortunate. The Doctor accused him of breaking faith on his contract only a few weeks after informing him of the decision to run north of the lake. Dodge too was annoyed at Young, who kept his promise of accepting no contracts from the Central Pacific but sent Stanford to hire some of his bishops. "Perhaps you can see the difference tween tweedle dum an' tweedle dee," Dodge grumbled to Oliver, "but I cannot." Still, Dodge was smart enough to know how badly Young's help was needed, and Durant took care to keep Reed on hand as his ambassador to the Mormons. Young denied the charges and was shrewd enough to realize that if the coming of the railroad could not be avoided, then it ought to be embraced.

"The labor being done by the brethren will have a two-fold benefit," he observed. It would help the faithful pay their debts, and it would exclude a class of undesirables from the territory—not the laborers but the saloon keepers, gamblers, and other parasites of vice who preyed on the railroad gangs. They would find no business in Mormon camps.

Young was less bothered by Durant's charges than by his inability to deliver enough tools to the Mormon crews. Months earlier Oliver had carefully ordered special machinery to attack the long tunnel at Echo only to learn that the rock was soft enough to be moved by picks without blasting. But the shortage of scrapers, picks, and other implements persisted into the fall. While Reed scrounged for tools, Durant ordered him to hire a thousand Mormon teams for hauling ties to the line from Weber to Green River. "You are responsible if that work is delayed," he snapped. From Dillon he demanded two steam excavators to handle the heavy cuts beyond Green River. In his frenzy of haste money ceased to be an object and no one was spared the lash of his tongue. As always he proved better at driving the work than paying for it. Young gamely exhorted his men onward even though they had not been paid for work done months earlier.

Whether because of Durant or in spite of him, the rails pushed steadily through the rough country to Green River and beyond. New townsites sprang into existence: Granger, Bryan (named after Snyder's son), and Evanston (for Evans), which Dodge chose as a division point. By early November the track reached milepost 890. Another Hell on Wheels, Bear River City, exploded into being and horrified the Mormons with its excesses. The hanging of three outlaws by vigilantes touched off a pitched battle that resulted in several deaths and the burning of numerous buildings. Troops rushed from Fort Bridger to stop the carnage by imposing martial law. Young calmed the faithful by reminding them that once the track left Bear River City in its wake, "two or three shanties dedicated to the sale of intoxicating liquor to the passing traveler will be all that is left to mark the site where once stood the most reckless and desperate of railroad towns." He was right; within weeks Bear River City would vanish as quickly as it had arisen.

"Straining every nerve to get into Salt Lake Valley before the heavy Snows fall," Jack Casement reported early in November. "Thirty more days of good weather will let us do it." For the gangs in the field the real showdown was not against Durant or any officer but against the Central Pacific and Mother Nature. Already the supply line had begun to sputter from overextension, leaving crews idle part of the time. It would not be easy grading or laying track on frozen ground or floating ties down rivers choked with ice. There would be no rest that winter, no time to knock off and regroup. The showdown was fast turning into a race.

* * *

That autumn the New York office put out a handsome pamphlet to attract investors, but no sooner did it appear than the money market turned sour.

Bond sales slowed and the cost of money rose just as Browning delivered the blow of withholding bonds. Hastily Bushnell devised a plan whereby the company borrowed $2.5 million from its stockholders for four months. The work would not be delayed by lack of funds, he promised Durant. "It is to [sic] late to fear Huntington," he added, "you are bound to beat him to death. . . . We will borrow or Steal all the money you need."

But money was not the only problem. The Duff Green suit was still alive, and Judge Barnard kept delaying a decision on the removal of Fisk's suit. Hazard took his share of the loan but pressed his suit vigorously despite repeated advice to make haste slowly. He appealed again to Oliver to join him only to receive a curt rebuke. "We have a great work on our hands and during its progress we want harmony among our members," Oliver said loftily. "Your Suit disturbs this harmony and tends to retard its progress." For the first time Hazard learned that Oliver had formally approved the suspense account challenged in the suit. "I happened to be present," he retorted testily, "when you completed an examination of the accts & stated as your full belief that he had got all his stock and 200,000 dolls besides out of the companies and your brother still says Doct D declined to account for the monies received by him."

Oliver and his colleagues had long since grown inured to contradictions in these matters. When Hazard sold four shares of Crédit Mobilier to a friend who agreed to join him in the suit, Dillon blustered and delayed, mumbled a threat to resign as president of Crédit Mobilier, then flatly refused to sign the transfer certificate because it would cause more trouble with Durant. Amid this dispute McComb opened a new front by filing suit for the Crédit Mobilier shares he claimed. Although the suit made little headway at first, it was to drag on for years with devastating results. With lawyers scurrying about busily, the directors found themselves spending more time giving depositions than transacting business.

While the legal snarls thickened, Durant sprang another of his patented surprises. Once the track reached milepost 914, just west of Fort Bridger, the Oakes Ames contract expired. Oakes's efforts to extend it had failed, partly because the board, awaiting a decision on the Fisk suit, did not meet between September 1868 and March 1869. On November 1 Durant filled this vacuum by quietly signing a contract with James W. Davis for all the remaining mileage. The terms were identical to those of the Oakes Ames contract, and Davis promptly assigned the contract to the Trustees. All was as before, except that Crédit Mobilier had no part in the arrangement; the Trustees in this instance were to represent Union Pacific stockholders. In an uncanny parallel to the Boomer contract, the Doctor managed to keep the new document a secret for nearly four months.

By December the company's affairs had reached the crisis stage on several fronts. A controversy raged in the papers over the special commission's report. Durant and Seymour rushed into print with a rebuttal which Jesse Williams dismissed as "all humbug." Privately Oakes blasted Williams for having been "at work against us all he could for the last year or more." The acute shortage of funds sent Durant, Brooks, Dodge, and Oliver scurrying to Washington in an effort to wrest the bonds from Browning. Oliver hoped to get additional bonds for the work done in advance of the track, but before he could act Browning dropped his bomb by revealing that he had already approved the Central Pacific's map all the way to Echo.

Devastated by this news, the Union Pacific forces mounted a furious counterattack. Dodge realized the map was a fraud, knew the Central Pacific had run only a preliminary line through Utah. Together with the Ames brothers he rushed to see Browning, who back-pedaled with a lame explanation that neither road owned the route and both should keep building and would continue to receive bonds. Nothing could be done, he added, until the cabinet met. Already Oliver had gone with Brooks to see President Johnson as had Congressman Benjamin Boyer, who received assurances that there would be no further difficulty. The Doctor careened about town, throwing his weight in every direction, convinced that his maneuvers had turned the tide. All except his admirers thought he did more harm than good. "Money," sniffed Oliver in disgust, "seems to be all the influence he has."

Finally, on December 23, a bargain was struck. Browning agreed to release the bonds and accept first mortgage bonds for improvements on the road. On all future work the government would issue its bonds to the company and receive back half the amount in first mortgage bonds until the required $3 million was accumulated. Oliver breathed a sigh of relief, but the Union Pacific still had trouble in Washington. The new session of Congress was already besieged by lobbyists seeking subsidies for new Pacific branch lines, and members were getting churlish on the subject. James F. Wilson of Iowa alerted Dodge to a new complication. The two roads were fast approaching each other, and both had the right to issue bonds for work done a hundred miles in advance of their track. It would not be long before the claims for advance work overlapped. "This being the case," Wilson concluded, "it looks as though the two companies must agree on the point of junction, otherwise run the risk of having govt bonds withheld until the junction shall have been effected."

The bonds did not come soon enough to relieve the company's financial distress. Bills were piling up fast in the West, and the January interest on bonds was about to come due. On December 28 Ham was obliged to borrow $1 million overnight to cover demand notes. "Money is awful tight and we have large amts to pay," Oliver moaned to Oakes. "We hope to get through but things look Blue." Experienced railroad men told Jesse Williams the Union Pacific would go broke soon after it opened, and Williams agreed. "If the contractors get all the subsidy and 1st mortgage as they want," he argued, "they will be very apt to default within 1st year or 18 mo." Something else bothered Williams. "I have no doubt," he added uneasily, "but Durant expects the Road to default."

Reports from the front looked even more gloomy. Dillon and Duff returned from the West displeased with both the work being done and the management at Omaha. Tales of waste and corruption grew more persistent. Dodge encountered repeated obstacles in laying out towns and suspected not only Durant but even Reed of having an interest in lots contrary to that of the company. An edge of hysteria crept into Oliver's letters. "The demands for money are perfectly frightfull," he wailed to Durant. "Awful Stories come down here from outsiders of the corruption of the contractors Engineers and every one in connection with the Road." Only two months earlier the board expected a handsome surplus on hand after completing the road, but now it looked "as though we should have a large floating Debt. Do Something to Stop the theives [sic] from Stealing our last cent and making the Road suffer." In his anxiety to save money Oliver was willing to concede the Central Pacific everything west of Salt Lake. The work at Promontory Point would cost a hundred thousand dollars a mile for five miles; "if there is danger of their getting up to that point leave it for them to do."

He was begging the wrong man to cut corners. Economy was not Durant's forte, especially when there was a race to be won. The Central Pacific had located their line to Ogden and scattered grading parties on the slopes of Promontory and along the mud flats between there and Ogden. The shrewd James F. Wilson showed his confidence in the outcome by closing out his account with Oakes in Crédit Mobilier shares, but not before he cashed in on one last dividend. Undaunted by this sea of financial troubles, the Trustees on December 29 declared a 200 percent dividend payable in Union Pacific stock. No one questioned the wisdom or propriety of such a payment at a time when the company was scrounging desperately for cash to meet its bills. The stock, after all, had little value unless the road endured. At the year's end Oliver tucked a revealing notation into his diary: "Have recd about 360,000 more than pd in besides stock."

This was the last dividend the Trustees would pay, and it was not enough to lift the pall of anxiety over the future. Lambard for one wrung his hands in despair over how the company could get through the winter. Only Bushnell, the eternal optimist, managed a brave front. The problem of raising money, he told Hazard cheerfully, was merely a matter of cost

On the other side Edwin Crocker complained indignantly that the Central Pacific had honored the three-hundred-mile provision while the Union Pacific had ignored it. Furious that Durant had thrown graders as far west as Humboldt Wells, he growled that it was "aggravating to witness these attempts to grasp these portions of the line to which we are clearly entitled." Stanford, who had arrived belatedly at Salt Lake City to direct operations, predicted early in November that Union Pacific rails would reach the mouth of Weber in six weeks if the weather held. A chastened Mark Hopkins rued that the partners had been so slow to heed Huntington's insistence that they take steps to seize the line east of Salt Lake. Now they saw what the Union Pacific crowd already knew: the race was on.

End of Line: The supplies reach end of track and are loaded onto wagons that carry them ahead to the grading parties.

Across the wide Platte: The first bridge across the broad and shallow North Platte River was long, low, and purely functional.

Once into Wyoming, the road encountered the rugged terrain of the Black Hills. One of the most puny obstacles, little Dale Creek, required the most elaborate bridge on the line. The size and precarious appearance of the bridge is captured in this view from below. Few travelers crossed the bridge without a quickened heartbeat.

The Dale Creek Bridge from above. Note the guy wires in both photographs.

Once across Dale Creek Bridge, the route snaked through rough ridges of granite and the train was obliged to slow to a crawl. This view shows the approach to the bridge from the west side.

The twin curses of the construction crews were cuts and fills, both of which required backbreaking labor. This fill at Granite Canyon west of Cheyenne was fifty feet high and a thousand feet long. The dirt had to be piled up one cartload at a time.

Taking the Long View: This picture of the Great Cut at Bitter Creek, one of the longest on the road, reveals in its sweeping panorama yet another cut ahead and the Green River Mountains in the distance.

This magnificent picture of the contractor Carmichael's camp at North Bitter
Creek Valley shows not only the vastness and barrenness of the region but also
one of the huge cuts required there *(left)*.

Just as fills had to be created one cartload at a time, so cuts had to be emptied one cartload at a time. Here some of Carmichael's men pause briefly in their labors. The carts show the scars of hard wear.

How high is it? This cut at Burning Rock was sixty feet high and a hundred feet deep through shale rock. One night a watchman built a fire and was startled to see the wall catch fire and burn with a brilliant flame. The flames were promptly used to illuminate night work. This site, believed to be about eight miles west of Green River, was probably where, during the early 1870s, the company investigated the potential of extracting shale oil.

The Doctor pays a house call: Durant *(standing right)* visits the construction site at Green River to lend the officers his special brand of encouragement. Silas Seymour, the "Insulting Engineer," is seated left in the buggy directly behind Durant.

Beneath the imposing figure of Citadel Rock, work progresses on the bridge across Green River.

(Left) At Wilhelmina Pass, where the road reached its thousandth mile, the track-laying crews found a lone tree towering above the craggy landscape. It was promptly dubbed the "Thousand Mile Tree" and is shown here being admired by an excursion party. Note the lone observer in the tree.

(Below) Once into the Utah mountains, the going got progressively rougher. Today it is hard to grasp the labor required to hack through mountain country with such primitive tools. Here the crews attack a deep cut west of Wilhelmina Pass by digging on five layers simultaneously.

In the rugged country of Weber Canyon the route hugs the sides of mountains toward the temporary bridge at Devil's Gate. The crews stopped work long enough to pose, but the rushing waters did not oblige the photographer's long exposure time.

A glimpse at the breathtaking scenery of Weber Canyon is offered in this view of the line down the canyon from bridge thirty-two.

10

THE RACE

For one corps of the Union Pacific army the great adventure had drawn to a close. The survey engineers had finished their work all the way to Humboldt Wells. Dodge made them run a dozen lines over Promontory Point until he got one that satisfied him. As 1868 waned the survey parties were disbanded to cut down expenses and their chiefs relegated to the paperwork of maps, profiles, and accounts. Some of them remained with the company to work with the contractors on location or help lay out towns; others drifted off in search of new challenges on one of the many unborn roads hoping to build westward. Case was already at work on the Denver branch, Blickensderfer would find employment with the Atlantic & Pacific, Hodges with the Northern Pacific, and Evans with a Texas road. In later years most would look back on their Union Pacific experience as the most exciting chapter of their careers.

They could take pride in a job well done. No achievement in the early history of the Union Pacific was more impressive or enduring than the final line located through a forbidding, unmapped wilderness bristling with natural obstacles. Allowed grades of 116 feet by law, they included none above 90 feet. Time refuted the charge that the road was made longer than necessary to garner more subsidy bonds. When E. H. Harriman spent millions to improve the line at the century's end, his engineers lopped only 30 miles off the original 1,032 miles to Ogden. The two major reductions came at points where the original survey had been altered over the engineer's protests. Seymour's oxbow was rebuilt along a route nearly identical to that located by Dey in 1864, eliminating 9 miles. West of Laramie the change demanded by contractors to save time was discarded in favor of the line originally selected by Dodge.

Today the line is all that remains of the Union Pacific's remote past. Its history and artifacts reside in museums or archives, but trains running from Omaha to Ogden still travel a route not far removed from that used by the first train to venture across the continent. For Dey, Dodge, and their assistants, there could be no finer or more fitting tribute.

* * *

By December Reed saw it clearly: the Doctor had miscalculated so badly that the disaster wrought by his mistake could not be retrieved.

Everyone knew the race now was not only against the Central Pacific but even more against the weather. The great goal was to get through the mountains before winter stalled their progress. Despite the friction and bitterness, every department head was straining to keep pace. Reed had grading parties strung along the line from Bear River to the mouth of Weber. Jack Casement, his joints aching with rheumatism, grumbled when shortages of material stopped his tracklaying cold for a few days early in November. Brigham Young's men, too, pleaded for supplies of all kinds. Durant was on line, a perpetual motion machine barking orders and firing telegrams for supplies as if nothing could or would move unless he personally demanded it.

Ties especially caught the Doctor's eye. By November Davis's crews had cut enough ties and timber to complete the road. Some had been carted to distribution points; the rest lay in the woods for delivery. Reed thought Davis had teams enough to haul them to the line as fast as needed, but when supplies ran short Durant moved at once to correct the situation. Rashly he ordered Davis's teams out of the forests to distribute ties, timber, and other material along the line. He also pulled half the grading force off its work and put it to the same task. The supplies were soon replenished but not before snow buried the cut timber in the woods and grading fell behind on both sides of Echo. Reed had created what he considered a well-balanced system to keep every aspect of the work coordinated with the others. So far it had run smoothly and kept well ahead of Casement's gangs, but in one reckless stroke the Doctor threw everything out of joint.

Once buried in snow, the ties and timber could not be retrieved until spring, leaving the hapless Davis with a serious grievance against the company. The tracklayers needed ties at once; to keep their work moving Durant hired Mormon cutters and teams, as many as he could find, regardless of price, to push out more ties. The delays in grading proved even more costly, for they had come at the worst possible time. Had Durant left the crews alone, they might have finished the excavation work before the ground froze. When they returned to work, frost was in the ground; by mid-December it was two feet deep. Instead of light, easy grading the men had to attack earth as solid as rock which could be dented only by blasting. In desperation the

Doctor doubled the crews and worked them day and night, but progress slowed to a crawl. As delays mounted and the cost of extra work piled up alarmingly, Reed thought even Durant was "getting frightened at the bills. He costs hundreds of thousands of dollars extra every month he remains here and does not advance, but retards the work."

Reed surveyed this fiasco in grim silence. If left alone, he was convinced he could finish the line in half the time and save enough money to build the road to Ogden. The bills would infuriate New York, and the lost time would cost them dearly in the race with the Central Pacific. To Reed fell the thankless task of sweeping up behind a man forever substituting motion for judgment. In his stoic way he said nothing; it was futile to argue with Durant. "If anything goes wrong the H—l is to pay," he wrote home, "the same if all goes swimmingly."

Down the line Snyder listened with savage glee to the cry for more ties and tales of unfinished grading. Unaware of the details, he readily blamed the mess on Reed. Convinced that Reed was his enemy, unwavering in the belief that he was both incompetent and crooked, Snyder missed no chance to bad-mouth him to Dodge. But he kept supplies coming, if only to prevent Reed from complaining about lack of support. Snyder was finding it difficult to juggle scheduled traffic with the swelling volume of supply trains heading westward. One order of ties alone required hauling six hundred cars a distance of four hundred miles. There was not enough rolling stock to handle both commercial and construction needs, and Durant did not ease Snyder's task by surprising him with orders to "convert one hundred of your flat cars into gondola or coal cars." The failure to ensure a good water supply, as Dodge had wanted, also took its toll. Hoxie reported that "water in Bitter Creek country is destroying our Locomotives." On one January day alone brackish water killed ten engines.

There was trouble too in Echo, where the Mormons demanded higher wages and Brigham Young pleaded for the money owed him to keep his men going. The tunnel at Echo went slowly. Three of the four tunnels on the Union Pacific line lay in the Wasatch Mountains, and the one at Echo was the longest—772 feet with deep approach cuts. Although work had started in July 1868, it would not be completed until the following May. As the railhead neared Echo, there was no choice but to bypass the tunnel with a flimsy, eight-mile temporary track over a ridge so steep that a switchback or "Z-track" had to be used. Farther west, two tunnels less than a mile apart in Weber Canyon required blasting through limestone and quartzite. Both tunnels perched on narrow, curving ledges above steep, rocky gorges.

Despite all obstacles the crews pushed relentlessly forward, laying track on frozen surfaces carved from unyielding ground. In the race against winter speed counted for more than workmanship. During December the rails snaked past Evanston and into Utah, reaching the head of Echo on the twenty-eighth. There Snyder laid out a new town called Wasatch for use as a divisional station. By January 9 the railhead had advanced to milepost 1,000, less than thirty miles from Ogden. Salt Lake Valley lay within reach, if only the weather would hold! The Casements ordered up fresh supplies of over-coats, boots, wool socks, and blankets for their men in preparation for the winter campaign. Satisfied with his progress, Durant put Seymour in charge of the unfinished work and hurried back east to stir the political and financial cauldron boiling there.

*   *   *

The papers would not let go of the Pacific railroad. Where earlier they effervesced about its progress and the savings to the government on the cost of transportation, now they hinted darkly at fraud and corruption, scandal and mismanagement. Much of their wrath was directed at attempts to ram new subsidy bills through Congress, but the existing roads absorbed their share of criticism. Their clashes with one another and with the administration kept them on prominent display. Not only editors but a broad array of gen-teel reformers sniffed suspiciously at the cesspool of rumor emanating from Washington. In January 1869 Charles Francis Adams, Jr., newly launched into a career as railroad authority, wrote with Olympian detachment about something called the "Crédit Mobilier," which seemed "as much shrouded in mystery as is the fate of the missing $180,000,000 of capital stock in these roads." Adams thought he knew what it was:

> It is but another name for the Pacific Railroad ring. The mem-bers of it are in Congress; they are trustees for the bond-holders, they are directors, they are stockholders, they are contractors; in Washington they vote the subsidies, in New York they receive them, upon the Plains they expend them, and in the Credit Mobi-lier they divide them. . . . Under one name or another a ring of some seventy persons is struck, at whatever point the Union Pa-cific is approached. As stockholders they own the road, as mort-gagees they have a lien upon it, as directors they contract for its construction, and as members of the Credit Mobilier they build it. . . . Here, however, is every vicious element of railroad construc-tion and management; here is costly construction, entailing future taxation on trade; here are tens of millions of fictitious capital; . . . here is every element of cost recklessly exaggerated . . . and will surely hereafter constitute a source of corruption in the politics of the land, and a resistless power in its legislature.

Talk of "rings" had already become fashionable among reformers, but this first public airing of Crédit Mobilier marked an ominous development for the Union Pacific. Horace Greeley's *Tribune* was quick to seize the issue. "How much has been paid by the Union Pacific to an organization called the 'Credit Mobilier'?" the *Tribune* demanded. "Who are the stockholders of the Credit

Mobilier? What Members of Congress are directly or indirectly connected with its operation?" No answers were forthcoming, but the growing clamor over railroad subsidies, along with charges of corruption, inflamed the already volatile conflict between the Union Pacific and the administration. Huntington did not help matters by informing the Pacific Railroad Committee that the Union Pacific was not building "what the law requires, a first-class road, but is constructing a road with a view of getting as many bonds as possible!"

Huntington discreetly omitted any mention of his own motives, having come to Washington to snatch as many bonds as Browning would allow. The trip east from California had provided his first glimpse of grading parties from both companies scraping furiously in opposite directions along parallel lines. A second shock awaited him in Washington, where he discovered that Dodge and others had made some headway with Browning. When the Secretary appointed a three-man commission to examine the Central Pacific, Dodge protested that it included none of the men who had inspected the Union Pacific. A fair comparison, he argued, required that the same men look at both roads. Browning then chose Warren and Blickensderfer along with Col. R. S. Williamson, one of the original Central Pacific commissioners, and Lewis M. Clements, a Central Pacific engineer. The new commission was ordered not only to examine the Central Pacific but also to decide the question of a meeting point even if it meant choosing an entirely new location.

Possibly Browning included Blickensderfer to spite Durant. In another of those tactless moves that antagonized government officials no less than his colleagues, the Doctor on January 2 summarily fired Blickensderfer for having left his post to serve on the original commission. Aware of the need for Blickensderfer's help in the fight against the Cental Pacific, Dodge tried frantically to ameliorate the damage. Durant ordered a bewildered Thomas B. Morris to replace Blickensderfer, but Morris hesitated until reassured by Dodge. The Doctor also instructed Morris to find a cheaper line to Ogden until Oliver admonished him that it would be disastrous to tamper with Blickensderfer's work. The Doctor's gift for alienating those whose help the company needed most was fast driving everyone to despair. As Blickensderfer delicately phrased it, "The U.P.R.R. Co. would occupy a much better position at Washington if that same Dr. Durant were a less prominent feature in the concern."

Huntington responded to Browning's action with the cynical observation that "the Union Pacific has outbid me." The commission's work would take time and could only snatch from Huntington what he thought he had already won. He wrote a protesting letter to the President, implored Crocker to push his crews harder, prepared a trespass suit against the Union Pacific, and urged Mark Hopkins to stall the commission as long as possible. Twice Oakes came to his hotel room to bargain. Why not simply split the remaining distance between the railheads, Oakes suggested. "I'll see you damned first,"

Huntington snarled, and suggested the mouth of Weber Canyon instead. Oakes retorted in kind. The two bears butted heads through several meetings until Huntington grudgingly conceded a joining at Ogden. Beyond that point, he growled, he would not budge.

There was more bluff than bite in Huntington's stand. Fearful that his crews might not get into Ogden, he hit upon an ingenious scheme to ensure his entry there. The Mormon graders hired by Stanford had finished most of the grading between Monument Point and Ogden, which entitled Huntington to ask for two thirds of the bonds covering that eighty-mile stretch. If he could get them from Browning, the Union Pacific could not—for the government would not pay duplicate subsidies on the same mileage. He tendered the request and was refused. For days Huntington personally lay siege to Browning's office until the Secretary agreed wearily to take the question to the cabinet. On February 26 the cabinet, down to its last week of life, approved the request. Two days before Grant's inauguration Huntington gleefully stuffed nearly $1.4 million of bonds into his satchel and hurried back to New York. "This was the biggest fight I ever had in Washington," he wrote Hopkins, "and it cost me a considerable sum."

Of this coup the Union Pacific knew nothing. Oakes was jousting with Huntington but also had to defend the company in Congress. The new commission had gone west and little could be done until it reported—or so everyone thought. With Grant about to take office, the directors would at least be rid of Johnson's administration. Some were eager to get new government directors who were, in Duff's words, "first class men of standing and who will give confidence in its management." Hazard reminded Dodge that "we are all suffering in reputation & every body seems to deem us fair subjects for plunder."

There was reason for concern. Another predator was on the line in the form of Chauncey H. Snow, newly appointed government director by President Johnson. Hoxie took his measure early. "He is a big t—f," he sneered. "Would take a spittoon or a Palace. . . . Had his pedigree from Wendell." Snow wasted little time in naming his price. Rebuffed by Snyder, he let J. W. Davis know he wanted a contract for coal in return for a favorable report on the road. To make his point he advised Johnson to spend no more money on the Union Pacific "until it is better constructed and managed here." Davis frantically wired Durant for authority, but the Doctor wanted no part of Snow. Thwarted on all fronts, Snow returned to Washington and showed Dodge two reports—one friendly, the other severely critical. The price, he said blandly, was a thousand dollars. When Dodge sent him packing, Snow turned in the derogatory report on March 5, one day before Grant replaced him.

For the moment Snow's report lay dormant. "The Govt Directors are all right," Dodge assured Hazard. Grant had very decided views on the matter, he added, "and says a change must be had if we want to have the confidence of the public or Government." Dodge's friends had another reason for wanting reliable government directors. "It would embarrass us very much," Hazard stressed, "to have even a single one in whose fidelity & aid in any important vote we could not implicitly rely. We may need *every one.*" Dillon was even more blunt. "Be sure that J. B[lickensderfer] will vote every time right if appointed," he cautioned Dodge. "I fear He would be neutral." The annual election was approaching, and with it loomed another struggle for control.

* * *

An eerie sense of déjà vu settled over most of the directors. It was as if they had been transported back to the gloomy winter of 1867. Money was so scarce no one knew how enough could be scraped together to carry on the work. The Doctor was in charge of construction, piling up bills with reckless abandon and sowing discord in his wake, a secret contract in his pocket ready to spring on his unwary associates. Seymour's meddling hand was busy spreading confusion everywhere. Two years of unremitting effort had brought the promoters full circle with one important difference. Through it all the track had advanced steadily until now it approached a destination that once seemed as remote as the moon. But every mile of rail had brought with it fresh layers of bitterness and strife among men who seemed bent on achieving their grand objective in spite of themselves.

The cry for money from Omaha was incessant. "Our vouchers are being hawked around & will soon be in NY & Chicago," Hoxie cried. "We must have $750,000 & it ought to be twice that." In fact Oliver had calls for $2 million, with neither cash to give nor collateral to get it. Creditors in Omaha and Chicago demanded relief from the load they were already carrying. The president of Omaha National, burdened by $200,000 in Union Pacific paper, sighed that his bank was "mighty well off in everything except money" and "not in good shape or in fact any shape at all to carry overdrafts." The size of the floating debt and cost of money threw Oliver into a panic. "It would be an eternal disgrace to us," he whined to Durant, "and to you in particular as the manager of the construction to be forced to suspend for want of funds to continue the work." He begged the Doctor to economize drastically but must have known it was as futile a gesture as the Persian emperor ordering back the waves.

Reluctant to borrow at what he called "ruinous rates of interest," Oliver and some members of the executive committee agreed to raise the money among themselves. The cost was no less steep but at least the profits remained in the family. An appeal to the stockholders of Crédit Mobilier brought pledges of support that encouraged Oliver to believe the worst had passed. "Every thing depends upon the Economy and vigor with which you press the work on Construction," he urged Durant. "We hear here awful Stories of the cost of the work and the thieving of our Employees."

What Oliver saw as clearing skies proved only a lull in the storm. In

Omaha the floating debt surged anew despite all efforts to reduce it. "We are about played out," Hoxie groaned. "These 90 day drafts are nearly *'Hell.'* " More tales of waste and extravagance poured in. Huntington told Oakes that in Utah teams were hauling ties at a charge of twelve dollars per team per day. "In construction the waste of money is awful," Snyder complained, and Hoxie added that Durant, Seymour, and Reed had "cost the Company *Millions.*" Dillon echoed their sentiments as did Jesse Williams, who declared savagely, "The executive committee deserves to be swindled out of two millions as they will be by Durant."

The Doctor returned to New York on February 1 bubbling with confidence about meeting the Central Pacific west of Monument Point and eager to save money by altering the line. Dodge was already so furious at his meddling that Oliver intervened with a plea to "not let your feelings against Durant lead you into any demonstrations against the road." The Doctor was all over Dodge, threatening to suspend him for botched estimates, for not coming to New York when summoned, and for issuing orders without first submitting them to Durant. The Ames brothers blanched in horror at these tactless efforts to drive off not only their best engineer but also their most valuable lobbyist. "Dodge is a perfect steam engine for Energy," declared an admiring Oakes. "He is at work night and day." Dodge merely gritted his teeth and stayed at his post in Washington while Durant ranted from afar.

Something else was bothering the Ames brothers. Early in February the Doctor let slip to Snyder that he had signed a contract with Davis to build the remainder of the road. Snyder passed the news along to an incredulous Dodge. In New York Durant admitted the contract to Alley, who relayed it to the Ameses. Everyone reacted the same way: the Boomer contract had sprung to life again. Oakes had assumed all along that his contract would simply be extended; indeed, as late as February 17 Oliver told Hazard that his brother's offer had been accepted. Not at all, Durant countered. It was absurd to talk of extending the Ames contract. Only he as general agent had the right to make a new contract and he had done so, to speed the work along.

When the executive committee met on February 25 Durant seized the floor with a barrage of financial inquiries that threw the other members off balance and on the defensive for two days. Only then did Durant present his report on the Davis contract. The committee was given the report, he explained, because the board had not met since the contract was signed. He said nothing about why it had not been tendered the committee at some earlier meeting or why it had been kept secret for months. On McComb's motion Durant's report was accepted and referred to a committee of Duff and Bushnell to put in proper form for submitting to the stockholders. The Doctor countered with more inquiries about bonds still in the hands of brokers as collateral for loans already paid off. After some sparring the committee adjourned until the next morning. More fireworks were expected, but the committee was not to meet the next day. In fact, it would not meet again for three months, by which time some radical changes had taken place.

Oakes knew what was coming; he had seen it all before. The Davis contract ignored Crédit Mobilier stockholders and said nothing about what Davis got or even what the road would cost the company. If Durant could get control of the board, he could do what he pleased with the contract. The annual election was only weeks away and already the Doctor was sweet-talking at least one old enemy, Alley. A fight could not be avoided, and Oakes could ill afford to lose. Despite his promise to Oliver, he had not pulled in his speculative horns and was again overextended. His anxieties brought him again to a conclusion reached two winters earlier: Durant had to go. He too believed the Doctor was "a heavy load to carry here in Washington & we should stand much better if he was out of office." Dodge was even more adamant. Unless Durant was removed, he vowed, the company would never see another government bond if he could help it.

To dump Durant, proxies were needed. Oakes and Oliver could not gather them without arousing suspicion. The one man who could was Hazard, who everyone knew wanted Durant out. With unwitting irony Oakes appealed to the old Rhode Islander to join them in a fight Hazard had been waging for two years. He knew that Hazard's desire for Durant's scalp would override all past differences. "We must remove him from the management," Oakes importuned, "or there is no value to our property. We are all satisfied of that, and I will guarantee that there will be no backing down."

* * *

The money crunch had even the irrepressible Jack Casement worried sick. "I am afraid the Union Pacific is in a bad way," he confided to his wife. Still, he hoped that "if the company dont quarrell too hard amongst them Selves we will all come out right." So far the weather had remained warm enough to lay two miles a day. In the Utah canyons the graders hacked fiercely at endless ledges of rock and frozen ground with picks and blasting powder. Seymour roamed the line urging the work forward in such leisurely fashion as to inspire Jack Casement to remark, "Reed is out on the Road looking after things generally so that Seymour may not have to Rupture Himself by over exertion."

Reed was covering forty to sixty miles a day by horseback to oversee the crews. "Too much business is unfitting me for future usefulness," he observed numbly. "I know it is wearing me out." As the track crawled around the tunnel at Echo and threaded its way through the mountains toward Weber Canyon, the way looked clear to Ogden and beyond. But the supply of ties grew short again, and trains were having trouble getting over the temporary track around the Echo tunnel. A heavy cut west of Weber Canyon caved in, burying the roadbed under tons of debris. Snyder predicted it would take thirty days to get track into Ogden. Seymour tried to explain the delays to

Durant but the Doctor was not appeased. "You were left with instructions and power that it was supposed would prevent delay," he snapped, "delays having occured [sic] that should have been prevented you are now at liberty to return to New York."

While Seymour sulked over this outburst of ingratitude, Snyder pondered what he considered the sink of corruption in the construction department. Hoxie too thought "the whole thing at west end is rotten," but for Snyder it had become an obsession. Eyes glinting with righteous malice, he sent agents to ferret out information and dispatched long reports to Dodge on the Durant-Seymour-Reed-Davis gang. He and Reed should have been the most natural of allies, but Reed's habit of silence allowed Snyder to believe the worst of him and, in his wrath, sweep him indiscriminately under the rug of suspicion with the rest. "Durant was crazy on his last trip & discharging me daily," Snyder added. "Seymour & J W Davis dared not let him get out of reach of their voices fearing somebody might expose their operations." The Doctor also infuriated him by assuming a pose of virtuous indignation over the payoff to Wendell. At his wit's end, Snyder could only sputter repeatedly his willingness to quit and press his investigation with the crusader's zeal. He flooded Dodge with detailed examples of wrongdoing, but Dodge was too preoccupied in Washington to do anything with them.

Amid this winter of discontent disaster struck without warning. The weather held splendidly in Utah, but early in February a blizzard roared across the Black Hills, burying the country in snow and shutting the road down. Even before the storm tracklaying had stalled because Casement's crews overran the graders; now their supply line was cut. Frantic efforts by Snyder kept material moving from Bryan westward, but between Laramie and Rawlins howling winds filled cuts with snow faster than men could shovel them out. Snyder put every snowplow and all hands to work clearing the line and hired every able body he could find to help. Passenger and freight trains alike were stranded in stations along the line as the storm continued to rage for days. Weary crews opened one stretch of track only to find another blockaded just ahead.

"Must have assistance from the East before we can do anything," cried an exhausted superintendent from Laramie. "Men all worked out and frozen. Impossible to get work done. Am afraid passengers will suffer unless they get assistance soon."

The road was paralyzed, with no relief in sight. The snow hit Utah, where Jack Casement was already blocked by the slide at Weber. Dan Casement fought his way eastward to Laramie and saw how desperate things were. The only way to get a train through, he concluded, was to open a cut with a plow and send boarding cars and train right behind it. "Have seen a cut fill up in two hours that took one hundred men ten hours to shovel out," he reported glumly. "Train west is well organized, but can't more than keep engines alive when it blows." Hoxie, working his way west, found the valleys in eastern

Utah filled with snow ten feet deep. For weeks fierce winds kept the track buried and the cuts clogged. Even hands familiar with Wyoming blizzards had never seen one like this. No one in the East could comprehend how a storm could blockade the road for weeks. "New York cant appreciate the situation," Snyder mourned, "or the severity of a mountain snow storm." Durant showed his usual graciousness by wiring Snyder to send eight hundred flatcars to Chicago. "If you can't send the cars," he snarled, "send your resignation and let some one operate the road who can."

In Utah the snow fell east of the track gangs, leaving them free to work as long as their material held out. Fortunately Reed had laid in a good store of supplies just before the storm; on February 27 he figured he had enough food to last another twenty days. Hoxie managed to get some ties and iron cached in western depots through to Casement. WHEN ROAD OPENS, he wired Snyder, WILL WANT SUPPLIES FOR MEN FIRST. Casement's men had laid track beyond Devil's Gate, 1,018 miles from Omaha. Ogden was but 14 miles away, and ahead lay 40 miles of finished grading for them to attack if the tie supply held. Even so, Seymour, comfortably ensconced in Ogden where there was no snow, thought progress was lagging. "Can't you," he appealed to Durant, "induce Casement to strike a three mile gait to Bear River?"

As March came on Snyder still struggled to open the line, hoping each day's work would do it only to be thwarted again by the winds. At the other end of the line Jack Casement peeled off his heavy overcoat and fur hat that gave him the appearance of a Cossack and gazed wistfully toward Salt Lake. "Birds are Singing in the valley like Spring," he wrote home, "and farmers in the valley are plowing." No mail had come through for a month, and he was homesick. In his isolation he would have preferred the company of Dodge, a man he honored jovially "for the good whiskey You never loose [sic] the key of." Instead he had the companionship of the Insulting Engineer. In comparison the blizzard made less noise and more sense.

* * *

Hazard was willing to fight Durant and so was Alley, but others held back despite Alley's assurance that Oliver promised "to be stiff." The Ameses did not deserve power, Duff grumbled; they had yielded it again and again after their allies had won it for them. Since Oakes had ignored his advice in 1868, why should Duff risk being abandoned by his friends in another contest? "I am perfectly independent of all the cliques that are trying to get control," he proclaimed to Dodge. McComb was sulking over the resentment aroused by his suit and kept his intentions to himself. Cisco wanted peace even at the price of the existing arrangement, and Bates was not eager to challenge Durant.

On the other hand, Congressmen Brooks and Boyer were ready to switch sides. Brooks, a Democrat, was anxious to keep his place as government director under the new Republican president. Dodge lost no time enlisting

Grant's help in the battle. Two days after the election Grant appointed three new government directors, keeping only Jesse Williams and the pliant Brooks. "The Govt Directors will be with you," Dodge assured Hazard. Grant wanted a change in the Union Pacific management; in particular he wanted Durant out. If that did not happen, "we are ourselves lost so far as any strength with this administration is concerned."

Dodge and Hazard wanted a board purged of Durant, McComb, and their allies, but there was a problem. The Davis contract had not yet been formally approved. Did that leave the provisions of the Ames contract still operative even though all the mileage under it had been built? If so the Trustees still had the right to elect the board, and everyone expected they would simply keep the present directors. Oliver decided that the power to elect still resided with the Trustees and nothing could be done. "To fight on a violation of contract and get beat is bad," he concluded. Oakes and Hazard disagreed vehemently but could not budge Oliver. Why not another coup, suggested John Williams, but his plan was too bold for Oliver to stomach.

Then a fresh complication jolted the conspirators. On March 4 the Fisk suit, dormant for months, sprang to life again when Judge Barnard abruptly denied the petition for removal to a federal court. No one believed it coincidental that the decision came only days before the annual meeting. Hazard and the Ameses were convinced Durant was in league with Fisk. Lambard revealed that Durant had proposed to him buying Fisk's claim for seventy-five thousand dollars and dividing it between them. The Doctor might not have friends in the administration but he had some in New York, and that meant trouble.

On March 9 the directors assembled for their first meeting in months. At once Jesse Williams recorded his objection to the earlier resolutions giving Durant power, the Davis contract, and some other points. In a move reminiscent of 1867, the Doctor countered by protesting all payments made in his absence for work done under the Ames contract because they had not been approved by the stockholders. He then pressed his demand for details about the fifty thousand dollars paid in July 1868 for "legal expenses." The meeting broke up without taking action on the Davis contract or anything else except the naming of election inspectors. That night four of the Trustees met in Bushnell's room at the Fifth Avenue Hotel and decided to cast their proxies for the existing board. At ten the next morning everyone gathered for the stockholders' meeting. Everything went smoothly at first. Bates put in the Trustees' proxies while the others stood about in small groups chatting. Then, shortly after eleven, the porcine figure of Jim Fisk arrived to cast his disputed votes. Rebuffed by the tellers, Fisk departed amiably, leaving in his considerable wake an air of mystery if not confusion.

Two years earlier Durant had tied the board in knots with an injunction procured from Judge Barnard; now it was Fisk's turn. The sheriffs loitered about until the votes were cast, then served an order staying the election until

Fisk's complaint was heard. For an hour the directors clucked anxiously over what to do. Motions were made, then rescinded, to adjourn to Washington, to Boston, or *sine die* until the sheriffs interrupted with warrants to arrest the directors for violating Judge Barnard's order against holding an election. The hot-tempered Dillon tried to shove one of them out the door before he was restrained. Oakes claimed congressional immunity and left the room. Oliver paused long enough to declare the meeting adjourned before the officers led him away with Dillon. Both were held overnight at the Fifth Avenue Hotel and released next morning on twenty thousand dollars' bail.

PRINCE ERIE'S WAR DANCE, blared one headline as the bad press garnered by the Union Pacific in recent months took an ominous new twist. Editors indiscriminately lumped Fisk's notorious escapades in the Erie Railroad with his foray into Union Pacific as birds of a feather. Some applauded with fine irony his attack on the "peculiar relations" between Union Pacific and Crédit Mobilier. The theme of Rogue as Reformer was irresistible to reporters, especially when the rogue was so engaging a chap as Fisk. "This is pretty business," muttered a disgusted John Williams. He believed, as did Oliver, Dillon, Hazard, and others, that Durant was behind the injunction. The Doctor pretended otherwise but Oliver was not fooled. "Durant full of ways to cover it over Fisk," he noted sourly, "which is to cover himself."

The situation was a dangerous one. At a critical time in its affairs the company found itself unable to hold an election or even meet safely in New York. The board had no choice but to go into exile until the lawyers could get the Fisk case out of Barnard's hands and into a federal court. At the same time an effort was launched in Washington to secure legislation allowing the Union Pacific to move its offices permanently to Boston. With the election left dangling, even Oliver agreed that the only alternative was war. "I would sooner lose the whole," he vowed, "than compromise with Fisk."

Or Durant for that matter. On March 11 the stockholders' meeting was reconvened briefly and adjourned to meet in Washington a week later. The board then assembled for a showdown with Durant. The Doctor saw what was coming and immediately resigned all powers conferred him by the resolution of July 1868. Dillon, Duff, and Price were appointed a committee with full power to oversee construction on the road. As a further check to Durant the executive committee was stripped of all power to act without approval of the board. "We have had a lively time of it," Dillon wrote gleefully to Dodge, "but we have beaten the enemy so far & have Bearded the old Lion in his den & if we all stand firm he will have to *remain there.* he seems very tame at this time yet he may be preparing for another leap So we must be careful to watch him close."

The election question still troubled Oliver, who believed the Ames contract remained in force, but Hazard and Williams had an answer: secure legislation to hold a new election as well as move the office. This suited both the Ames brothers. For the next month Oliver and his associates commuted regularly to

Washington to help lobby for a bill. During that time a rump session of the stockholders' meeting was called and adjourned almost daily to keep it alive. Alley offered to help in New York, where Durant and Bushnell were minding the store, but Williams considered them "too smart for JBA." Duff still tacked his own peculiar course, reluctant to break with Durant or join the Ames clique unless they agreed to his terms. "Mr Duff is not so impracticable as he appears," Williams explained to a dubious Hazard. "He may fear to break with TCD for policy sake but if we could get clear—then you would find Mr Duff firm enough." Dillon too insisted that "Duff *is all right.*"

Two battles raged into April, one in Washington and the other in New York. While the courts jousted over the removal question, Fisk got from Barnard an order appointing the namesake son of William M. "Boss" Tweed as receiver for Crédit Mobilier and for certain Union Pacific securities. Young Tweed demanded access to the books and papers in the company's vault, but no one obliged him. Auditor Ham had the combination but was in New Jersey, beyond Barnard's reach; no one else professed to know it. After two weeks of sparring Barnard ordered Tweed to break the vault open. On April 2 Tweed led five brawny "deputies" armed with sledge hammers to the Union Pacific office. The vault was a formidable bastion built into a wall. Durant and his lawyer flapped about the invaders, insisting that they leave at once. Rebuffed, the Doctor calmed down, lit a cigar, and joined the large crowd of clerks, brokers, and other spectators who had gathered to watch the fun.

After vigorous pounding smashed only one layer of plating, Tweed called a halt and sent for the manufacturer of the vault. He came but did not have the combination and could do nothing. Doggedly the hammers resumed their chorus to the cheers of the crowd until at last the battered door was forced. A scuffle broke out between the deputies and clerks for possession of the contents. Aside from some Union Pacific books and securities, nothing of value was found. Bushnell later claimed that four or five hundred thousand dollars' worth of bonds were scattered and lost in the attempt to keep them from the sheriff, but his account borders on the fanciful. For years it was believed that Durant had earlier spirited away the books and papers of Crédit Mobilier. In fact Dillon, as a precaution, had in January removed them to the office of the New Jersey Central, of which he was vice president. Hazard and John Williams knew this, and presumably others did too.

The raid did little more than amuse the spectators and confuse everyone else. For a time it aggravated the company's financial woes by triggering a sharp drop in bond prices. Bushnell asserted that news of the receivership and raid sent the first mortgage bonds tumbling from 102 to 65; Crane estimated a drop from 100 to 70. Although the decline was brief, it came at a bad time. Omaha was pleading for funds while Dillon moaned that "we have all we can do to keep our paper from protest." A bank president in Council Bluffs alerted Dodge that "the failure of the UP to pay is creating considerable excitement west." Dodge fired a telegram to Snyder urging him to "keep good courage. Tell your banks and merchants we are going to see them through all right." But the word was spreading fast. Two of Brigham Young's sons visited New York and, alarmed by what they found, warned their father that the company's credit was weak, its affairs "in a regular muddle," and apprehension widespread "that they will be unable to meet their obligations."

On April 9 eleven directors assembled in Boston and created a committee of five to meet the financial crisis. Next day the committee released a circular offering Union Pacific stockholders the right to take allotted shares of first mortgage and land grant bonds at the bargain prices of 85 and 55 percent, respectively. The urgency of the situation moved Oliver to plead with Hazard, as one of the largest holders, to help out by taking "bonds of the Co at 90 or notes at 4 mos with int at 14½ per cent . . . to relieve Bonds in NY pledged at 2 for 1 and take them out of the hands of Jews and put them into our own." He and Oakes had already loaned the company $1.5 million, Oliver added, "and we cannot raise much more in the channels where we are accustomed to work. Nor should our associates ask us to go in larger." If Hazard and a few others would do their share, he promised, "there will be no doubt of our Success and of putting Durant and his influence out of the Road management."

If successful the offer would realize about $7.7 million on the sale of bonds worth $11.3 million par value. Even at bargain prices subscriptions dragged. Hazard did not rush to embrace Oliver's offer, and Duff lamented that "the Money market is worse than it has been since the road has been building." The end was so near, yet it seemed always to hover beyond their reach, the last forty miles more onerous than the first. For three years they had fought bitterly among themselves, pleading always with one another for harmony while laying the groundwork for strife. The tensions of these dark days inflamed them to new heights of suspicion and acrimony. Somehow Oliver came to the bizarre opinion that Hazard was "eaten up with the desire to be Prest of the Co." Durant let Oliver know that if he were ousted from the board, the Fisk suit would be a fleabite compared to what he would inflict. The belief that Durant was behind Fisk spread rapidly beyond the board to Wall Street. Bushnell told the Doctor bluntly, "You put the injunction in & you had better take it off." Although Durant and his friends talked bravely of taking charge again, a consensus was growing that their days were numbered.

During this clash Duff emerged from the shadows as a pivotal figure. His holdings were modest but crucial in an election, and like Dillon he was an experienced railroad man. So far Duff had borrowed heavily from Seymour's manual of tactics, complaining loudly about the bumbling of others while steering an evasive course himself. He did not change that pattern when events thrust him to the forefront. After refusing to join the Ameses plot against Durant, Duff withdrew a large loan from the company. "Duff wants all things fixed to suit him," noted a disgruntled Oliver, "before he does anything to help us in finances." Yet he joined Duff in suggesting that Durant be put on the new committee to oversee construction as a way of getting the Doctor out of New York!

A startled Hazard argued that the committee would have a hard enough time without having to contend with Durant. He was not alone in finding some of Duff's ideas peculiar. Privately Duff called Durant every name his limited vocabulary could muster, yet he too preferred to keep him on the board until the road was finished. Unless handled gently, he insisted, the Doctor would cause more trouble out of office than in. Duff also feared the new committee would have a hard time ferreting out the swindlers. The members would be watched closely, misled by wrongdoers, and in constant danger of assassination. The thieves were so accustomed to stealing millions, he told an incredulous Hazard, that they would stop at nothing.

Much depended on the outcome of the legal battles. "Cases in NY courts and in Congress look bad," Oliver despaired on March 30, "& [I] fear we shall lose in both." In New York the company's lawyers procured an order from another New York judge removing the Fisk case to the federal court only to have Barnard vacate the order on the grounds that the case belonged in his court. After ten days of jousting Federal Judge Blatchford overruled Barnard and removed the suit to his jurisdiction. Barnard and Fisk's counsel declared angrily they would ignore Blatchford's decision, and young Tweed prolonged the squabble with a new suit. Although the Fisk case took up new quarters in the federal court, where it would reside for years, trouble still lurked in New York.

The papers continued to applaud Fisk's effort, which the *Herald* called "a very good thing, although it does not spring from a very good motive." The *Times,* impressed by tales of "enormous profits" amounting to thirty million dollars, demanded an investigation of Crédit Mobilier. "The truth is," chimed the *Herald,* "there is cheating on the grandest scale in all these railroads, and it is only when sharp managers quarrel over the spoils that the public get at the facts." Nor did the Union Pacific win any friends among the New York dailies by moving its headquarters elsewhere. "The Pacific Railroad gentlemen must keep their money out of this town if they want to retain control of it," sneered the *Tribune.* "They might have known as much when this litigation began. Served 'em right."

* * *

The inauguration of Grant brought dramatic changes in Washington. Browning gave way to Jacob D. Cox, a soldier-politician possessed of uncommon intelligence and literary ability whom Dodge considered "a great friend of the Union Pacific." George S. Boutwell, a former Massachusetts congressman, took charge of the Treasury Department. In the new Congress Oakes relinquished his seat on the Pacific Railroad Committee and Dodge left office altogether, free at last to serve the constituency that mattered most to him. Grant set the tone at once by appointing the new government directors and ordering the two secretaries to suspend action on the issuing of subsidy bonds to both Pacific roads.

Although the new administration was friendly, the battle still had to be won or lost in Congress. The company's lobbyists needed action on three fronts: removal to Boston, sanction for the election of a new board, and settlement of the dispute with the Central Pacific over where the two roads would join. A legal fight with the Central Pacific loomed not only in Washington but in Utah as well. Oakes already had the eminent Caleb Cushing as one of his attorneys; now he also engaged William M. Evarts, former attorney general, who had also been wooed by the Central Pacific. Dodge recruited the services of William E. Chandler, one of the shrewdest lobbyists in Washington. The company would not lack for legal talent or influence, but neither did the enemy. Senator William Stewart of Nevada, a giant of a man once described by Mark Twain as having more brass than the Colossus of Rhodes, picked up quickly on the furor in New York and poured a withering volley of invective on Crédit Mobilier and Union Pacific.

The company's efforts to get a bill before Congress hit more snags in the Senate than Stewart's rhetoric. Oliver was mystified but Bushnell noticed that all the Doctor's old friends had turned against it. "I discovered by this at once," he wrote Durant privately, "your hand as well as Fisk-Huntington & Co." Since the bill would pass anyway, he added, "you might as well have the credit of helping it along—for we kneed [sic] all our united efforts or Huntington will buy himself and lie himself through to Ogden and we shall get no Bonds beyound [sic] that point." Something else bothered Bushnell as well. "I hope," he added pointedly, "you have arranged to get Fisk out of the way."

Secretary Cox lent a hand by urging that Section 8 of the Pacific Act, which allowed the issue of bonds in advance of work, be repealed. On March 29 Bingham of Ohio, one of the congressmen who held Crédit Mobilier stock, introduced a resolution calling for an investigation of the bonds issued to the Central Pacific for work to Echo Canyon. Huntington braced for a "sharp, bitter fight" and lashed back with a stinging attack met in kind by Oliver and Dodge. As recriminations flew, neither side wanted the fight to get out of hand lest it provoke an investigation damaging to both sides. Huntington tried to ram an amendment through the House fixing the junction at Ogden. When that effort failed, he was ready for compromise. Dodge was a man he could deal with, and both men concluded it was better to fix an agreement before Congress imposed one on them. On the evening of April 8 he met Dodge and Hazard at the home of Samuel Hooper. The talks dragged on until 4 A.M., adjourned a few hours, and continued well into the next night.

In Boston Oliver hastily summoned a meeting of the board on the morning of April 9 at which Oakes and Dodge were instructed to fix a junction point "not East of the Eleven hundredth mile Post." Dodge glanced at the telegram from Boston and dismissed it as unrealistic. Unlike Oliver, he had reports from the front on how far the company could build before the roads met.

Snyder thought the Union Pacific "can make Monument Point sure," but in the next breath cried, "Must have help at once to keep going." Morris wired from Promontory that they would be ten days behind the Central Pacific, barring an accident to the latter. Seymour estimated that "with plenty of track material and work driven to utmost on West Slope of Promontory, I think we may reach Monument first. Otherwise not." But ties and other material were not getting through fast enough, and Dodge knew of work stoppages by men demanding their overdue pay. The bleak look of things in Utah led Dodge to conclude that Promontory was the best he could do for the company.

Late in the evening on April 9 a bargain was struck. The roads would connect at some point within eight miles west of Ogden. Both would build to Promontory and the Central Pacific would pay the Union Pacific for construction between the terminus and the summit of Promontory. Huntington also agreed to pay half the cost of the Union Pacific's grading already completed between Promontory and Monument Point. In return the Central Pacific would receive all the government bonds for work west of the terminus. A key to the agreement lay in the belief that an important new town would arise at the terminus. Dodge and Oliver had been scouting town sites for months, not for a junction with the Central Pacific but for the Oregon branch. Now both companies would share equally in the town site, and the Union Pacific would receive half the net proceeds from all land sales up to Bear River.

News of the agreement was rushed to Congress the next morning. A joint resolution, hurriedly prepared, sailed through both Houses within hours. The Union Pacific was granted the right to move its office elsewhere and hold an election on April 22. The agreement on a terminus "at or near Ogden" was confirmed along with the provision that the Union Pacific would build to Promontory and sell that part of the line to the Central Pacific. But there was more. The resolution also authorized the President to appoint a committee of five "eminent citizens" to examine both roads upon completion and report on any deficiencies. Grant was also to withhold enough bonds to ensure completion of the entire line as a first-class road. The report of the eminent citizens would determine what was needed to fulfill this condition.

The long dispute was over at last, and with it the race that had led the two companies into grading two hundred miles of road parallel to each other. Most newspapers hailed the compromise with a sigh of relief, but there was no joy in Boston. Oliver was aghast at the terms, especially the surrender of bonds on the line west of the terminus. In a choleric letter to Dodge he called it "an Outrage upon us and ought never to have been consented to . . . I cant conceive how you should ever have consented to it. If you had known the condition of the Co you would not have done it." Certificates for the bonds had already been sold, which meant raising money at once to redeem them just when everyone on the road was begging for funds. "Our money matters are in a Sad State," he sputtered, and "as it now Stands we Shall have a quarrel with CP to get any pay out of them."

Dodge expected the directors to be unhappy over the lost bonds. In blunt language he wrote a sweeping rebuttal to Oliver's protests. "The great mistake you all labor under," he retorted, "is the supposition that you were to override all the acts of the past administration, revoke what they had done and get a double issue of Bonds over the same ground, none of which would have done." Oakes endorsed the agreement because he knew no better terms could be had, and Oliver came around once his temper cooled. They were all tired, frustrated, and overwrought, and much remained to be done. Money was needed to finish the road, and an office had to be set up in Boston. In Dodge's opinion the most pressing business was to elect a clean board and see that all funds sent west were funneled through Dillon, Duff, or himself to keep the thieves at bay. He turned his lobbying duties over to Chandler and hurried west to take charge of the final push. Oliver provided him with an order discharging Seymour from all duties in the field.

For Dodge it was a bittersweet triumph. Had it come earlier, the order would have vindicated years of frustration. Now it was too late, for without a new board in office it could only disrupt work at the worst possible time. During these last frantic weeks even Seymour would be needed to get everything done. Sorrowfully Dodge laid the order aside, perhaps for use at some later date.

* * *

HAVE WE A PACIFIC RAILROAD? asked the New York *Tribune*. Not if passengers were stranded and mails detained for weeks by a mere snowstorm. The eastern papers were unsparing in their criticism of the blockade as complaints poured in from inconvenienced passengers and shippers. Snyder noticed some of the accounts came from employees of the Central Pacific and launched a counterattack in friendly papers, but the New York dailies refused dispatches or letters favorable to the company. Dan Casement barely survived the ordeal of his trip east along the snowbound line, and the road did not open again until late March. Despite shortages of material, Jack put rails into Ogden on March 7. The Mormons welcomed their first train with artillery salutes, a brass band, and speeches beneath a huge banner proclaiming "Hail to the Highway of Nations! Utah Bids you Welcome!" But there was little joy among the railroad men. Chills and fever plagued many of them and laid Jack low for a time. Warm weather had turned the country into one vast mudhole. As the crews veered north toward Bear River the pace slowed to a crawl; during the next two weeks they managed to lay only another ten miles.

Above all they strained every nerve to learn what progress the enemy was making. For months, even years, the Central Pacific had been an abstraction poking toward them from the remote distance. No longer. By the end of 1868 Charles Crocker's men had finished locating to Ogden and commenced grading on the mud flats and eastern slope of Promontory. Suddenly the two sides were racing not only to close the gap between them but also to seize ground on which both were grading alongside each other. A Union Pacific agent monitoring the enemy's movements reported their line to be 150 miles west of Humboldt Wells on January 28. The burly Crocker then came in person and "stirred up the tracklayers with a stick; told them they must do better or leave the road." A month later his Chinese crews were 40 miles past the Wells and bearing down on Monument Point. By March 23 they were 84 miles from Monument. The Union Pacific was only 70 miles away, but its lead was fast dwindling. "The race," an engineer observed dryly, "is getting exciting & interesting."

It was also becoming lopsided. While the Central Pacific marched across the desert, the Union Pacific bogged down in a quagmire of troubles. Lack of funds threatened to paralyze work. The crews were surly because contractors had no money to pay them. A few went on strike and Dodge warned Oliver that "men will work no longer without pay & a stoppage now is fatal to us." Banks and merchants along the line were, in Jack Casement's words, "loaded with UPRR Paper and if the Company dont send some money here soon they will bust up the whole country." Jack was doing better than most in keeping his men paid, but his urgent appeals brought no response from Dillon or anyone else. The Omaha National Bank advanced Snyder enough money to pay off some discharged men despite carrying vouchers totaling a hundred thousand dollars. "What I am afraid of," admitted Evans, "is that somebody will pitch in and stop the running of the road by attaching rolling stock."

The silence from the East disturbed everyone, especially Seymour. On April 4 the railhead stood a mile short of Bear River but little was being done. "We are being ruined for want of track material," he wired Dodge frantically. If supplies were rushed forward they could beat the Central Pacific to Monument, but the chance was fast slipping away. And ties! Reed said they were plentiful west of Piedmont, yet none came forward and Snyder ignored Seymour's repeated inquiries. "Transportation department cannot be working with us," he hissed, "when fifteen thousand ties await loading between here & Piedmont & private freight comes through freely." Most of all Seymour was anxious about the situation in New York, which had some small bearing on his own future. "I dont hear from the Doctor," he complained to Crane. "Is he still cutting up the Pig?" In desperation he urged Durant to come out at once to get things moving.

The Doctor did not respond but Duff and Dillon were on their way west and so was Dodge. Their presence might not gladden Seymour's heart but Jack Casement was eager to see them. He was annoyed at being stalled for lack of ties with only a few more miles to lay. The money pinch bothered him too, as did the presence of enemy grading parties so near his own camps. He was anxious to get home and see his new son born the previous summer but who could tell when everything would be settled? Glancing over his calendar, he plucked out a date almost at random and wrote Frank, "I am afraid I cannot get away from here before the 10th of May."

Dodge was no less anxious to get out and look things over for himself. Apart from the money troubles he had heard much that made him uneasy. Snyder's complaints about thievery had grown so shrill they alarmed everyone in Boston. Some bridge work had been done contrary to his orders; there were reports that the masonry on the bridges was defective and ugly rumors of poor workmanship on the roadbed. "All track west of Piedmont is poor," Snyder wrote bluntly, "Aspen to Echo *very* poor." To rebuild the road west of Bryan, he estimated, would cost five thousand dollars per mile including snow fences. While the Union Pacific floundered, the Central Pacific rolled onward. On April 10, the day Congress passed the joint resolution fixing the junction point, Seymour wired that the Central Pacific was only twenty-three miles from Monument Point.

There would be no meeting at Monument, though they clung to that hope until news of the compromise arrived from Washington. Caught up in the race, beset by turmoil and anxiety, few paused to realize just how much *had* been accomplished. Ironically it was Seymour who managed to put it all into perspective. Wandering out to end of track on April 16, he reflected that exactly a year earlier he had watched Durant hammer down the last spike atop the summit in the Black Hills. Since that day the road had advanced 519 miles through the heart of the desert and the Rocky Mountains until now it stood at milepost 1,068. The entire Central Pacific line from Sacramento to Promontory was only about 690 miles long. Over 500 miles of railroad built and equipped in one year! As Seymour marveled, "Nothing like it in the world."

11

THE GOLDEN SPIKE

The stockholders' meeting on April 22 was brisk and amiable, a gathering of friends in the State Street sanctuary of Glidden & Williams. The move to Boston was approved and the New York office closed; even the company seal was discarded in favor of a new one. Resolutions were passed confirming the new committees to oversee construction and sell bonds. Brooks, Hazard, and John Williams all gave short speeches that made less impression than a telegram from Dodge: CENTRAL PACIFIC RAILROAD, EIGHTEEN MILES FROM PROMONTORY SUMMIT. WE ARE TWELVE MILES FROM SUMMIT. After Williams's speech the meeting adjourned without transacting its most important piece of business, the election of a new board.

Reporters who expected the election next day were disappointed. Instead the recent pattern resumed of convening and adjourning the meeting almost every day to keep it alive without taking action. Duff's policy of expediency had prevailed: having defanged Durant, a majority of directors deemed it prudent to leave him on the board until the road was completed on the assumption that he could do less harm in the company than outside it. The news dismayed lobbyist William Chandler, who complained that "the internal difficulties of the company affect its standing and its power to accomplish results" in Washington. Chandler was even more bothered by the board's tendency to speak with a divided voice. Important issues were at stake that required prompt and decisive action. Decisions could not be made by a group of directors who would always disagree on one point or another. Chandler wanted authority vested in "some one person with full powers," whose judgment "must be accepted for better or worse as the case may turn out."

This lack of a decisive voice handicapped Chandler's efforts to secure bonds and land patents from the government. It also complicated his handling of less savory matters. Every new administration, even a friendly one, brought in a fresh school of sharks. One of them, Lewis Dent, let Chandler know he and his partner expected to be retained as counsel for the Union Pacific at ten thousand dollars a year. Dent was not a man to be ignored. He was Grant's brother-in-law, and his own brother, Gen. Frederick Dent, served as the President's military secretary. The most influential man in the new administration, General Rawlins, had promised Dent he would receive a "very liberal proposition" from the Union Pacific.

At Dodge's suggestion Chandler offered a flat retainer of five hundred dollars, which Dent dismissed as an insult. Chandler thought he might accept six thousand a year and appealed to Oakes, who said flatly "let them go—we will not pay such sums." But General Dent then told Hiram Price in blunt language that his brother had been treated shabbily. *"It is not the interest of your Co.,"* Price in turn warned Oliver, *"to make enemies in that direction."* Huntington agreed with Chandler that it was better to pay them off long enough "to carry us by the issue of bonds and the settlement of questions to arise within the next six months."

Two other "shysters and black-mailers" harassed Chandler that spring. Chauncey Snow threatened again to publish his damaging report on the road's management unless the company made some "arrangement" with him. When the Ames brothers refused to pay, Snow gave his report to the newspapers. Bushnell countered with a letter revealing Snow's attempt to gain a coal contract, and a war of words ensued with only minimal damage to the company. The second case ultimately proved far more dangerous. In March 1866 McComb had subscribed for 250 shares of Crédit Mobilier on behalf of a friend, H. G. Fant, who decided not to take them. McComb then let them go only to change his mind after the Ames contract was signed. These were the shares at stake in his suit against Crédit Mobilier. Fant now threatened a suit of his own in which he promised to expose the connection of certain congressmen with Crédit Mobilier.

Of these matters Chandler knew little. He thought that "by arranging with Fant the whole claim may be squelched" but did not object when the Ames brothers decided to ignore Fant. "I suppose if you try to conciliate blackmailers there will be no end to their demands," he wrote Oliver. "Only it takes an authoritative decision to keep them off."

* * *

No one knew more about divided authority than Snyder, who considered himself its chief victim. For months his voice had sounded the same shrill note on the subject of corruption. He had hoped a new board would give him license to clean house; instead the election had resulted in what Evans called an "undignified & disgraceful quarrel in New York." As the evidence poured in, Snyder found it hard to distinguish between genuine complaints and those born of grudges or a desire for revenge. One informant called Carmichael "the most accomplished thief in the construction," while another watched with embittered relish the "last scramble" for goods in Utah. Seymour was busily erecting a two-story house for himself with company lumber on a company lot. "Seymour the Colonel looks at these things as his private property," the informant shrugged, "while Mrs. Reed marks all furniture, bedding etc. with S.B.R.—may they long live and prosper."

The irony of it all depressed Snyder. For months, even years, he had flooded New York with complaints about thievery on the road. The response was always the same: cries of outrage tempered by reluctance to act lest it provoke Durant. Management was not only multivoiced but two-faced as well, demanding reform but unwilling to sustain any move that disturbed the fragile truce holding its ranks together. Now Duff, who had remained conveniently aloof from these matters, was on his way west bristling with indignation at the Wendell payoff and the practices of G. W. Frost, the purchasing agent. Durant was informed of Wendell's demand, Snyder insisted, and could have vetoed payment but did not, "yet [he] tells other Directors that he knew nothing about it & holds up his hands in horror at my action." As for Frost, Duff was furious that Snyder had not discharged him months ago. In fact Snyder *had* tried to fire him but was restrained by Oliver and Dillon because it would "raise a row with T.C.D."

Snyder saw what was coming: he was to be the scapegoat for the very depredations he had tried so earnestly to prevent. Once again there was talk of hiring a new superintendent. For Snyder the end could not come too soon. He had been broken on the rack of virtue; his dismissal would merely be the last turn of the wheel. "I am heartily sick of this outfit," he cried, "that talks so much about cleaning out thieves & yet weakens when in presence of the thieves & will let thousands be stolen under their own eyes while looking after old flaws & scrapes."

Dodge was sympathetic but too preoccupied to offer consolation. Bridges were haunting him that April. Durant's blithe dispensing of overlapping contracts to Evans and Boomer had already borne fruit. Boomer complained bitterly that Evans "had done every thing he could to impede my work, and for the purpose of bringing me into disrepute . . . This is I presume because he has turned bridge builder himself." Then Dodge learned that the bridges at Green River and Black's Fork were not being put in on the line originally located. Seymour had changed one of the Black Ford bridges, Evans explained hastily, for no reason "other than such as would be likely to occur to S S." As for Green River, Evans himself preferred the altered line to the old one. Dodge was not mollified; the changes broke up tangents and increased curvature in each case. "I will not agree to or accept any bridge built over Green River or Black's Fork, he wired Evans, "except upon the adopted line."

Even that was not the worst of it. Dodge was besieged with reports of defective masonry on most of the bridges from Bitter Creek west. Boomer found out the hard way; three of his spans crashed when the masonry failed to support their weight. The arches on two culverts at Lodgepole Creek also gave way because of inferior workmanship. After personal inspection Dodge found the abutments on five bridges crumbling and the masonry at Bear River "worthless, the backing is dirt and free stone set on edge, and I doubt if there is a band in any one of Piers." Evans was responsible for overseeing the foundation work but Dodge did not blame him. "Though closely watched it seems we cannot trust masons who have had the reputation of being No. 1 and honest," he wrote Oliver angrily, "unless we employ an engineer to every structure to stand right over them." Oliver promptly warned the contractors that they would not be paid for defective work but the damage was done. Temporary trestles would have to be put in until the foundations could be rebuilt entirely.

* * *

News of crumbling bridges did little to cheer the directors scrounging desperately for cash to finish the road. In their gloomier moments it seemed as if the enterprise was nearer the edge of collapse than of completion. What should have been a triumphal procession toward the fulfillment of a dream had degenerated into a march to the scaffold. Despair had become their constant companion, yet they dared not abandon hope so near the end.

John Williams reported hopefully that since the move to Boston Oliver was "disposed to take more responsibility, than in N Yk." In fact Oliver was exhausted and suffering from headaches so severe that he put aside his teetotaling scruples to seek relief from a bit of whiskey. Duff and Dillon pressed him to come out for the joining of the rails. President Stanford of the Central Pacific would be there, Duff stressed; so should Oliver, to handle any issues arising between the roads. Something else alarmed Duff. Durant was in Omaha and full of noise about being executive officer in Oliver's absence. Everyone feared he might "do something to complicate our affairs, that he could not do if you are present. . . . I shall be much disappointed if the V.P. is to have the finishing of the U.P.R.R."

Oliver was disappointed too, but he was in no mood to share the stage with Durant. Besides, as Bushnell pointed out, it was too late to go out and return in time for the election. The crucial point was to prevent the Doctor from assuming authority as a pretext for paying off his pet contractors. Sidney Bartlett, the company's ablest lawyer in Boston, assured Oliver that Durant had no power to act while the President was on hand at the office. Thus fortified, Oliver telegraphed Dodge that "Duff, Dillon, & Price have full power—no one else." His message to that trio was equally terse: "Must remain here on money matters. You have full power of Board—exercise your authority." Durant might strut and sputter but he could do nothing if they remained vigilant.

Oliver was not the only director held prisoner by the frantic search for money. In New York Bushnell and Oakes struggled to raise funds beneath the shadow of the Fisk suit. When Fisk procured injunctions to attach company funds in local banks, one of his men defected and warned Bushnell in time to clean out the accounts. Although the situation remained explosive, not even the refusal of August Belmont and other bankers to take any Union Pacific securities could dampen Bushnell's optimism. While Oakes importuned the bankers for loans, Bushnell reported cheerfully, "We are all out of trouble financially here and I think we have furnished so much money for the line of road that they must be comparatively easy there."

He was wrong on both counts. The company could leave New York but not Wall Street, and even getting out of town proved an ordeal. When the offices were let go and the sign taken down, Durant promptly rented the rooms and took possession of their contents. Benjamin Ham found himself in a tussle with Crane for the Trustees' books and finally settled for making copies. He found them in dreadful shape, full of inexplicable or suspicious items for which Crane had no explanation. In one case Crane had written a check for ten thousand dollars to pay a note but neglected to reclaim the note and could not remember its date or possessor. Ham could not yet tell if the books were cooked, but he was certain they were underdone. Oakes shared his sense of disgust. "When we can get our Books away from NY and cleaned out from that sink of corruption," he scowled, "we shall feel safe and not until then."

The West was devouring money faster than even Bushnell could imagine. On May 1 Oliver instructed Dillon and Duff to stop drawing on New York. That same day Dillon wired Glidden, WE MUST HAVE FIVE HUNDRED THOUSAND DOLLARS TO PAY CONTRACTORS MEN IMMEDIATELY OR ROAD CANNOT RUN. Glidden tried to arrange the funds in Boston only to be told, "Cant use drafts on Boston." Dillon's incessant demands for money mystified Oakes. "He wants to draw on N. York and Boston both," he puzzled, "and for all kinds of sums and think he must be confused in his operations and the large amounts he wants to draw rather surprises me." It would be weeks before the awful truth was revealed to him.

In the past the company had relied on government bonds for completed sections of road to replenish its coffers, but the bond situation that spring was even more muddled than the financial outlook. The commission appointed by Browning was still busily inspecting the line of road when Grant took office. Until their final report was submitted, no one knew what amount of bonds the government would withhold. Chandler expected the report late in April but bickering over details prolonged the agony. By that time Congress had passed the joint resolution calling for a new commission of five eminent citizens. The existence of two commissions raised some tricky questions. Would the new commission's work supplement or supersede the older one? Would the government wait for its report before deciding on the bonds? If so, more delays would ensue. To complicate matters further, General Warren was on both the original commission and the committee to inspect new sections eligible for bonds. He could not leave Washington to examine sections until the commission's report was wrapped up.

By early May the report still had not appeared. Chandler haunted the departments and learned only that no bonds could be had and it was "of no use to ask anything until Gen. Warren and the others make their report." Nor could he find out who had been appointed to the new commission. When the list was at last disclosed, it disappointed Chandler. "They are not," he told Oliver, "the eminent citizens we could have desired." None of the names he suggested were chosen. One of the appointees was said to have an impaired mind; another was known for "looking after his own interests pretty sharply." Chandler heard that Lewis Dent and his partner had influenced the selection and were cozy with two of the appointees. "I wish we could have made some arrangement with Judge Dent before now," he sighed, "if it is to be made at all."

Chandler was no stranger to men with itchy palms but he could do little on his own. The tangle in Washington reaffirmed his desire for "some one person to decide authoritatively these questions," but little could be done until the company elected a new board. At the moment the feverish efforts to raise money and finish the road took priority over everything else. As the day of connection neared, the press dropped its criticism of the roads and gushed praise for their achievement. Only a few papers like the New York *Herald* maintained a sour tone. "In Congress we see the Union Pacific Railroad ring triumphant," grumped a *Herald* editorial, "and its directors and hangers-on flaunt their corruption and their ill-acquired means in the face of all decency and legislative morality."

* * *

Promontory Point was a mountainous peninsula jutting like a stubby finger into the north side of Great Salt Lake. The heaviest work lay on the eastern approach where the grade rose eight hundred feet in only ten miles and jagged ridges cut by a small river blocked the railroad's path. Carmichael's men were hacking furiously at one particularly long rock cut but did not get it open until May 8. At one rugged ravine Seymour and Reed decided late in March to save time by throwing up a temporary trestle bridge four hundred feet long and eighty-five feet high. But timber for the trestles was slow to arrive, forcing the crews into an extraordinary feat of erecting the structure in only thirty-eight days. Like the Dale Creek bridge it resembled a flimsy bit of cobweb and moved one reporter to predict it would "shake the nerves of the stoutest hearts of railroad travellers."

For a time the rival Irish and Chinese crews toiled alongside each other on both sides of Promontory summit. The mood was tense, even explosive, but the tales of violence between them seem to have originated in the imaginations of later writers. At one point Stanford forbade a Union Pacific contractor from working or moving material within two hundred feet on either side of the Central Pacific line. News of the congressional resolution reached the Union Pacific camp on the evening of April 11. Reed promptly stopped all work west of Promontory but Central Pacific crews kept working the eastern slope. Washington might regard the junction question as settled; the men in Utah were not so sure. The Union Pacific was only twelve miles from the summit. By April 20 the Central Pacific had marched past Monument to within eighteen miles of Promontory, where spring rains turned the flats into quagmire and stalled its progress. That day Stanford met Dillon, Seymour, Reed, and Jack Casement at Promontory for some hard bargaining.

As they rode along inspecting the work, Stanford pointed out that the Central Pacific had nearly completed its line across Promontory. Why not, he suggested to Dillon, abandon your line and lay rails on ours? Dillon was tempted. Both he and Seymour doubted the Union Pacific could finish its grading before May 10 at the earliest. Seymour thought it would save the company a hundred thousand dollars on work yet to be done. After two days of negotiation Dillon promised Stanford nothing and wired for the advice of Oliver and of Dodge, who was in Council Bluffs. "I consider it would interfere greatly with our settlement and would advise you not to do so," Dodge replied. "Duff is here and agrees with me."

So did Oliver. He feared the Central Pacific might try to exert its claim for connection near Ogden before payment was arranged. The junction issue was clouded by the fact that the provision for a joint town site had been discreetly omitted from the congressional resolution. If the Central Pacific was allowed into Ogden, Williams warned, "we may whistle for years for a settlement." Doubts had cropped up "about the agreement made at Hoopers & the Law— both so weak in their provisions—& open to all sorts of criticisms & objections." These were precisely the questions Duff wanted Oliver out West to decide. Dillon and Dodge were still under the impression that he might join them; instead Oliver sent instructions to make no permanent deal with the Central Pacific. "Come home soon," he added, "and let new Board authorize future arrangements."

Dillon had much to do before coming home. He rejected Stanford's offer and told him to pull his men off the eastern slope. Stanford obliged and arranged a demonstration for his rivals. On April 27 he took Dillon, Duff, Dodge, Seymour, and Reed to observe his Chinese track gangs in action. A wager had been made that Crocker's "pets," as they were called, could lay ten miles of track in one day. A derailed engine thwarted the first attempt but on April 28 the Chinese and their Irish foremen performed the feat in eleven hours, thereby setting a new record for track laid in a single day. "They took a week preparing for it, and imbedded all their ties beforehand," Dodge scoffed, but he came away impressed by the Chinese. They were superb rock workers, "very quiet, handy, good cooks and good at almost everything they are put at," he marveled. "Only trouble is, we cannot talk to them." It was a lesson he would remember.

The "Big Day's Work" enabled the Central Pacific to plant its track atop the summit on April 30. Dillon decided to take no chances. While the grading crews toiled day and night, he ordered ties and iron hauled to the summit by wagon around Carmichael's cut and the unfinished trestle. On May 1 Casement's men connected with the Central Pacific and commenced laying track eastward from the summit. In this way the joining came ten days earlier than the ceremony and was meant less as a connection than as a barrier. Plans were made to hold the celebration on Saturday, May 8, but the weather turned wet and blustery. The bridge crew under Leonard Eicholtz opened the big trestle on May 5 only to learn that the storm had washed out a bent on the Devil's Gate bridge and rendered it impassable. Wearily the men picked up camp and hurried to the treacherous narrows.

The downpour, Carmichael's unfinished cut, and the closed bridge at Devil's Gate forced a postponement of the ceremonies until Monday, May 10. Stanford and his guests arrived at Promontory on the seventh only to discover that they had three days of leisure in which to explore the drenched, forlorn landscape. Word was sent back to California but the citizenry were already primed to celebrate on the eighth and ignored the message. Bands played, parades marched, cannon boomed, fireworks exploded, and crowds guzzled champagne amid loud, raucous cheering. In the stillness of the Utah desert Stanford laid plans to surprise his rivals by rushing a construction train forward to put in a siding at Promontory in hopes of gaining an advantage for future settlement. The train was ready to roll but delayed by the storm.

East of Promontory a bizarre incident threatened to delay proceedings even longer. Duff and Durant were aboard a train heading west when some three hundred of Davis's tie cutters blocked the track at Piedmont and vowed to hold the officers prisoner until their overdue wages were paid. No trains would pass, they declared angrily, until their demands were met. The news was flashed to Dillon and Dodge, who were in Echo City. In recent days Boston had responded to Dillon's urgent appeals for money by scraping up several hundred thousand dollars. Now Dillon wired that he must have half a million more at once. Dodge seconded his plea. "If you wait until trains are stopped," he warned Oliver, "it will be too late to release them until we are forced to pay in fact every thing due on line." Word of the hostages had already spread like a prairie fire, but Dodge thought the half million would "relieve necessities and enable us to keep moving." To his wife he wrote, "Duff is in a bad box but we will get them out today."

The hostages were sprung in time to reach Promontory for the ceremonies, but Dodge came away convinced that Durant had arranged the whole affair to force the company to pay off the Davis contract in which he had an interest. Oliver had the same notion. "Durant is so strange a man," he confessed, "that I am prepared to believe any sort of rascality that may be charged agnst him." The incident at Piedmont was not the only thing that put a bad taste in Dodge's mouth. Snyder continued to whine about corruption, but now for the first time Dodge saw it for himself, saw why they had pleaded with him to come out and put a stop to it. The waste appalled him. "I can see plainly," he seethed, "where money has been wasted and in a short six months our entire Construction Dept. has been totally inefficient." His first impulse was to blame not Reed but his old nemesis. "Seymour while here run a fine race," he sneered. "Had his woman, his niggers, and his four black horses hitched to his hack, saddle horses, etc. but did nothing except spend money."

But all this was for private consumption. It was too late to change anything or do anything more than prepare for the joining of rails. At Devil's Gate the bridge crews under Eicholtz struggled for four days to put up a new fifty-foot truss in record time. To their rear the train bearing the officer's car with Duff and Durant aboard waited impatiently to cross, and behind it sat two more trains stuffed with passengers, one of them loaded with troops. By four in the afternoon on Sunday, May 9, the truss was jacked into place and the lead train crawled gingerly across the bridge. Eicholtz climbed aboard for the ride to Promontory, grateful for a night's sleep in a Pullman Palace Car.

The road was clear, and only one piece of unfinished business remained. The notion that a siding in place would stake claim to terminal rights at Promontory had also occurred to Dodge. When the skies cleared Sunday evening, Jack Casement's crews sprang into action. By toiling all night they managed to get in a complete siding and Y-track before dawn. The Central Pacific's construction train hurried forward that same night, timed to reach Promontory at daybreak. It arrived on schedule only to be greeted by hoots from Casement's men, weary but eager to display the fruits of their night's work. The last and shortest race had been won by the Union Pacific.

* * *

Every age creates a symbol that expresses the essence of its character to later generations. For Medieval Europe it was the great cathedrals, for modern times the computer. The nineteenth century found its most potent symbol in the locomotive, that wondrous machine which fired the loftiest visions of its private and national destinies. To disciples of progress the locomotive made possible the first great triumph over time and space. Its raw power was capable of enchanting starry-eyed dreamers and hard-nosed businessmen alike. Daniel Webster proclaimed in 1847 that the railroad "towers above all other inventions of this or the preceding age." Walt Whitman celebrated this new force in his "Passages to India" only a year before the rails joined at Promontory:

> I see over my own continent the Pacific railroad
> surmounting every barrier,

I see continual trains of cars winding along the
    Platte carrying freight and passengers,
I hear the locomotives rushing and roaring, and the
    shrill steam-whistle,
I hear the echoes reverberate through the grandest
    scenery in the world . . .

Whitman's insights were seldom far from the national pulse. If there is one event that symbolized the changing world of the nineteenth century for Americans, it was the driving of the golden spike. Certainly nothing else captured the public imagination so fully or maintained its hold so completely on later generations. Today it still occupies an unchallenged place in our pantheon of national myths, one that embodies the finest of American achievement. So firmly has the myth been encrusted in the national consciousness that, like all myths, it has taken on a life of its own quite apart from the actual events of that Monday in Utah. Nothing will supplant the image of national triumph and perhaps nothing should, but in the cold light of reality the day of the golden spike takes on a different cast from the Myth of the Golden Spike.

Seen in that light, it becomes a ceremony in which the wrong people came to the wrong place for the wrong reason. The three Union Pacific directors at Promontory did not include either of the Ames brothers, who had been so instrumental in pushing the road to completion. Instead the company would be represented by Dillon and Duff, who happened to be out west, and Durant, who was eager to seize the spotlight as the ranking officer present. There was more irony than justice in the presence of Durant and Seymour, who together had done more to confound the road's progress than all other forces of man and nature combined. Enough field officers showed up to offset Seymour. Foremost among them was Dodge, the versatile workhorse whose contribution exceeded that of any other individual. The Casement brothers were there along with Reed, Hoxie, Evans, Morris, Maxwell, Eicholtz, and several of the contractors, including Davis.

So too with the Central Pacific. Stanford was the only one of the California partners who came to Promontory, and by all accounts he had played the smallest role in getting the rails there. Huntington, the driver and mover, was at his desk in New York, the others in California. Nor was any ranking dignitary from Washington present for this fulfillment of a great national project in which the government had played so prominent a role. Grant wanted to come but could not. No representative of his administration was sent in his place—no one from the cabinet or departments, no member of Congress, not even a government director. The lack of a single major government figure at the ceremony is both astounding and puzzling, yet it seems to have gone entirely unnoticed. Here was the realization of a dream that had haunted the nation for decades, a celebration of the sort in which politicians loved to bask, yet only a couple of territorial governors, some military officers, and a superintendent of Indian affairs bothered to come. Even the Mormons, whose isolation was ended with what proved to be fateful consequences, were not represented by their leader. Brigham Young could not make it and sent Bishop John Sharp to represent him.

The great event, then, was made more conspicuous by those who did not attend than by those who did. There was savage irony, too, in the fact that the joining occurred at a place where neither company cared to be or would long stay. The Union Pacific hoped to reach Monument Point if not Humboldt Wells; the Central Pacific coveted Ogden or even the Utah canyons. Promontory was a compromise of conflicting ambitions which, like most compromises, suited neither side. The ceremony alone would attach significance to the site, since the companies had already agreed the Central Pacific would move its terminus to a point nearer Ogden. They met at Promontory not to embrace in joyous harmony but to maneuver for advantage, aware that much remained to be settled between them and with their common nemesis, the government. Nor was either road finished in any real sense of the word. In their haste to win the race both had left much work to be done and a horrendous backlog of bills to be paid. For these reasons the wedding of rails resembled more a shotgun marriage.

What then did the meeting at Promontory signify? It was above all a symbol that far transcended the event. To travel from shore to shore in a week was a stupendous achievement in itself, but there was more: the doorway to a new era of progress that dazzled Americans with the promise of fabulous riches to be gleaned from trade and commerce. The continent was spanned, new lands opened for settlement, the mountains with their treasure trove of ores breached for exploitation. Two great oceans were linked, forging a pathway to the East and its storehouse of wealth that had tantalized imaginations as far back as Marco Polo. Far away, on the other side of the world, another great project, the Suez Canal, was rushing to completion and would open for traffic later that same year. The Darien Canal would soon follow, and telegraph wires would soon connect New York, London, Calcutta, and Canton.

"We are the youngest of the peoples, but we are teaching the world how to march forward," crowed the New York *Herald*. The American century was under way, and its prospects made observers giddy with delight. Corruption there had been and plenty of it, the *Herald* charged, but even so the road would "be cheap to us at a cost of five hundred millions of dollars. Commercially it places the United States in contact with Asia; internally it will make North America sparkle with cities; politically, as a national binding force, it is invaluable." Horace Greeley's *Tribune* was moved to recall Buckle's observation that "Man has succeeded in turning the energies of Nature, bending them to subserve the general purpose of human life. All around us are the traces of this glorious and successful struggle. Indeed it seems as if there were nothing man feared to attempt." George W. Bungay, the most minor of poets, contributed a bit of doggerel with this verse:

> From ocean to ocean the rail
> Runs over the mountain and vale
> Which echo with blows on the *nail,*
>   Now heard by the list'ning races.
> Hail to the pathway of nations here!
> It runs to-day through a hemisphere,
> The good time coming must now be near,
>   It shines on our hope-lighted faces.
>   Hail to the age of steam!
>   Hail to the iron team!
>   Hail to our iron bars!
>   Hail to our flag of stars!

A new era had dawned, the age of industrial progress, and the railroad was its chariot. To "hope-lighted faces" everywhere the transcontinental road was more than the longest ribbon of iron ever built by man; it was an accomplishment that vaulted America to the forefront of this new and exciting world. A frontier of immense possibilities had been crossed, and there could be no turning back whatever the perils. One small step for man, a giant step for mankind. That was it. The exhilaration of a later generation in conquering the moon, planting a first tentative foot in space. This was what Americans felt in reaching out toward a world larger than their own, larger than they had ever imagined, confident of making it smaller through familiarity. The surge of excitement they felt came less from what had been achieved than from contemplation of the leaps to be made beyond it.

* * *

The place itself could not have been more unassuming: a small narrow valley, perhaps a mile wide, bounded on both sides by rounded humps of mountain still patched with snow, its bleak floor broken only by scruffy sagebrush and pools of water glazed with ice. The only buildings consisted of half a dozen tents and "Rum Holes" patronized by the thirsty crews. Down at Blue Run, where the Casements had their camp, one could see in the distance the tent towns of Deadfall and Last Chance, which did a thriving commerce in whiskey. C. R. Savage, a photographer recruited by Seymour for the occasion, heard that twenty-four men had been slain during the past twenty-five days in the whiskey camps. He had never seen a harder set of men. After watching the drunks roll in throughout the night, he muttered, "The men earn their money like horses and spend it like asses."

Sunday night was cold, but brilliant sunshine splashed the valley with warmth through the morning hours. A flag atop the telegraph pole opposite the junction point snapped briskly in the wind. All the preparations had been completed. W. N. Shilling, a telegrapher from Western Union's Ogden office, had rigged a wire from his instrument to the hammer that would drive the last spike. He figured that the hammer's impact would transmit a "dot" that would travel the entire Western Union system; a waiting nation would know the rails were joined at the precise moment it happened. For the ceremony itself Stanford brought with him a spike made of gold, engraved on every side, and a special tie of California laurel, polished and set with an inscribed silver plate. Holes were bored in the tie to receive the spike without damaging the wood. There was also a silver spike, the gift of Nevada, and one of gold, silver, and iron presented by the governor of Arizona. To drive the last spike, the president of Pacific Union Express Company offered a hickory maul with a silver head.

Early Monday morning a crowd began to gather, most of them Irish and Chinese workmen from the two roads. Hunched against the wind, squinting into the sun, they milled about impatiently, waiting for the celebration. Shortly before nine a screeching whistle announced the arrival of an excursion train from Sacramento. The westbound train, after its perilous crossing of Devil's Gate, reached Blue Creek at daybreak but did not chug onto the summit until about 10 A.M. Behind it came two more trains, one filled with dignitaries and reporters, the other with troops from the 21st Infantry. The soldiers brought a band, and Ogden sent along its Tenth Ward Band to enliven the festivities. As they commenced playing the mood of the waiting crowd perked up considerably.

Two other photographers besides Savage lugged their cumbersome equipment about in search of good shots: A. J. Russell, hired by the Union Pacific, and Alfred A. Hart of the Central Pacific. At Russell's request a band of Union Pacific engineers posed in front of the Pullman cars for a group picture in which Dodge found himself alongside Seymour. It was the closest the two men had been in years. The usually ebullient Durant secluded himself in his private car until the last moment, his enthusiasm dampened by a blinding headache. Shortly after eleven Stanford's train, pulled by a locomotive named "Jupiter," rolled onto the summit. After waiting three days, Stanford let the others wait for a time.

Another delay ensued while officials squabbled over who was to deliver which blows to the last spike. The argument grew so heated that at one point the Union Pacific representatives threatened to boycott the ceremony. When tempers cooled, it was decided that Stanford would occupy the south side of the track and strike the first blow; Durant would follow with a second tap from the north side. The crowd shuffled restlessly as the photographers took charge for a brief time. The entire Union Pacific contingent lined up in front of Durant's special train for a group shot, the men doffing their hats at Russell's request to avoid shadows on their faces. Dillon and Duff took places on one side of the track and Durant on the other, his eyes slitted in pain from the merciless sunlight. Between them stood Jenny Reed with her sister and children.

While the bands blared patriotic tunes into the wind, the troops filed into position alongside the track. Reporters, guests, and workmen jostled for places around the last vacant space of roadbed. Shilling took up his post at a table near the track and hunched nervously over his instrument. Two rails remained to be laid. Some of Casement's men deftly dropped the first of them into place, pounding the spikes home with quick, sure blows. The last rail was reserved for a squad of Chinese from the Central Pacific, who would anchor the spikes at one end and leave the other to be used in the ceremony. As they moved forward someone shouted to Savage, "Now's the time, Charlie, take a shot!" The Chinese, knowing only one meaning for the word "shot," dumped their rail and dove for cover. It took considerable negotiating to get them back to the business at hand.

At last all was ready. Inquiries from telegraphers across the nation poured into the Omaha office. TO EVERYBODY: KEEP QUIET, barked an annoyed Omaha operator. WHEN THE LAST SPIKE IS DRIVEN AT PROMONTORY POINT WE WILL SAY "DONE." DON'T BREAK THE CIRCUIT, BUT WATCH FOR THE SIGNALS OF THE BLOWS OF THE HAMMER. A prayer was offered, after which the symbolic spikes were presented to Stanford and Durant. Stanford responded briefly as did Dodge, who concluded with the cry, "This is the way to India." The spectators cheered and pressed forward expectantly as Stanford and Durant took their posts on opposite sides of the last rail. Reed and his Central Pacific counterpart, James H. Strobridge, slid the laurel tie gingerly into place. The president of Pacific Union Express offered Stanford the silver maul.

WE HAVE GOT DONE PRAYING, Shilling tapped out. THE SPIKE IS ABOUT TO BE PRESENTED.

WE UNDERSTAND came the reply from Chicago. ALL ARE READY IN THE EAST.

ALL READY NOW, Shilling added a few moments later. THE SPIKE WILL SOON BE DRIVEN. THE SIGNAL WILL BE THREE DOTS FOR THE COMMENCEMENT OF THE BLOWS.

It was half past noon. As the golden spike was slipped into the waiting hole, the crowd surged closer. Shilling found his view blocked and craned desperately for a sight line. Thwarted, he sent out his three dots on instinct. Stanford took a lusty swipe that missed the spike but caught the rail squarely, producing a solid clang for the telegraph wire. Durant took the maul and followed suit, giving the rail a resounding whang while leaving the spike unscathed. When Dodge and Samuel S. Montague of the Central Pacific gently tapped the spike home, Shilling flashed one word down the line: DONE. The crowd whooped with delight. Durant and Stanford shook hands warmly. The Doctor proposed three cheers for the Central Pacific; Stanford returned the compliment. "There is henceforth but one Pacific Railroad of the United States," cried Durant exuberantly.

The first telegram over Shilling's wire went to Grant, the next to the Associated Press: THE LAST RAIL IS LAID! THE LAST SPIKE IS DRIVEN! THE PACIFIC RAILROAD IS COMPLETED! THE POINT OF JUNCTION IS 1086 MILES WEST OF THE MISSOURI RIVER AND 690 MILES EAST OF SACRAMENTO CITY. Duff and Dillon followed with a message to Oliver as eager crews uncoupled the two locomotives. Workmen and officers alike scrambled for a place on the engines or at the junction. Slowly the Jupiter with its fat funnel stack and Union Pacific's No. 119 with its prim, straight stack crawled slowly toward each other until their pilots touched. At Russell's urging the crews formed a wedge radiating out from the point of contact. Bottles of champagne were held aloft by men clinging to each engine. Below them Dodge and Montague stepped forward to clasp hands, framing the last tie beneath them, their union frozen long enough for Russell to capture the moment for posterity. When time resumed, whistles shrieked and a roar exploded from the men as the champagne bottles were dashed against each engine. Dillon roused the crowd by proposing a cheer for the laborers who had built the road.

Slowly, reluctantly, the cheers faded and the spectators drifted away, leaving the field to those who had to clean up afterward. The photographers were among the last to finish, exhausted from a day of scurrying feverishly about in search of good shots. Savage was so busy that he missed the driving of the golden spike. Soon after the engines parted, some track men replaced the spikes of precious metals and laurel tie with regular stock. Souvenir hunters quickly whittled the new last tie to splinters; in all, six ties would fall victim to their jackknives. Stanford invited the Union Pacific officers and honored guests to a sumptuous luncheon in his car, where there was plenty of California fruit and champagne to go with the speechmaking. The mood grew loud and boisterous, a welcome release from weeks of tension. None relished it more than the Casement brothers. The past year had been hard on Jack. Already his temperance vow had been sent packing like an unwanted guest, at least temporarily, and Frank feared for the worst. "Dear Jack," she had implored, "dont have much of a *jubilee* until you come home to the loved ones here."

But the jubilee, the moment of triumph, was not something to be deferred. Amid the merriment Stanford's speech hit a sour note by launching into a diatribe against the government. The subsidy, he argued, had been more a detriment than a benefit with all the conditions attached to it. Everyone listened in stunned silence except Dan Casement, who by that time was feeling no pain. Impulsively he hoisted himself up on Jack's shoulders and brayed, "Mr. President of the Central Pacific: If this subsidy has been such a detriment to the building of these roads, I move you say that it be returned to the United States Government with our compliments." Cheers and laughter greeted his outburst. Stanford glowered and said nothing. Another round of champagne soothed ruffled feelings but Dan had made his point. It fell, Dodge noted, like a wet blanket on the celebrants.

Late in the afternoon they tumbled out of the car, giddy with champagne and reluctant to let go of the day that filled them with a sense of pride and accomplishment. Nothing could dampen the feelings that infused them. After years of anguish and frustration, bitterness and strife, they had met the greatest challenge of their age, transformed a dream into a national monument. This was their moment, that joyous, fleeting instant of triumph few men are privileged to know in their lifetime. They had done more than build the longest railroad on earth. Every obstacle had been surmounted, every skeptic vanquished. They had made history, become part of one of its indelible chapters. No amount of bickering or scandal, no past or future failures, could take that away from them. Let tomorrow bring its inevitable sorrows and disappointments; today was theirs to cherish always.

* * *

In Washington a large crowd gathered at the Western Union office, where the manager hung a large magnetic ball in position for all to watch the message arrive. At the War Department a more elite gathering headed by Sherman waited expectantly. It was 12:47 Promontory time and 2:47 in the East when word came through. Bells pealed the news to the citizens of every major city, from the Capitol in Washington and Trinity Church in New York to City Hall tower in San Francisco. Even the venerable Liberty Bell in Philadelphia sang a hoarse tone of celebration. Behind the tolling bells came the boom of cannons, the shriek of fire whistles, and auroras of fireworks. The choir and congregation of Trinity Church sang a "Te Deum." Cisco pronounced it "a grand affair" and assured Oliver that the church "was crowded with our best people." Chicago rejoiced with wilder enthusiasm; a parade several miles long snaked exuberantly through the streets. Ogden closed all businesses, and the Tabernacle in Salt Lake City was packed to capacity. There were festivities in Omaha, St. Louis, Buffalo, Scranton, and dozens of other cities.

Congratulations poured in from all sides. Sherman set the tone by wiring Dodge, ALL HONOR TO YOU, DURANT, JACK AND DAN CASEMENT, REED AND THOUSANDS OF BRAVE FELLOWS, WHO HAVE FOUGHT THIS GLORIOUS NATIONAL PROBLEM, IN SPITE OF DESERTS, STORMS, INDIANS AND THE DOUBTS OF THE INCREDULOUS. It was a day of national celebration, yet to some eyes the rejoicing was curiously restrained. "The greatest event of the age," Oliver noted in his diary, adding grumpily, "Boston did nothing." The New York *Herald* wondered why "the greatest marvel of enterprise in the nineteenth century, should not have elicited more of a demonstration than that which marked its triumph in this city yesterday." The answer, it suggested, lay in the spreading taint of scandal and notoriety about its affairs. The air in Washington still reeked of ugly rumors of Crédit Mobilier, and only a month had passed since the assault by Jim Fisk's commandos on the company safe.

In New York Huntington sat at his desk transacting business as usual, indifferent to the pealing bells and roaring guns, brooding perhaps over the lost vision of planting his flag at Green River. There was no taste of victory in his mouth. Nothing impressed him, not even the Central Pacific's big day. "I see by the papers that there was ten miles of track laid in one day," he wrote churlishly to Crocker on May 10, "which was really a great feat, the more particularly when we consider it was done after the necessity for its being done had passed."

The mood in Boston was more celebratory but muted in tone. Oliver was distressed at receiving no news from his associates in Utah about the financial situation or even the ceremonies there. For some reason the telegram sent him after the driving of the golden spike did not arrive until the evening of May 11, too late even to get it into the papers that day. "It would have been just as well here," he huffed to Dodge, "for Duff to have brought it with him in his pocket." He was annoyed too by the lack of festivities in Boston—a few patriotic speeches at Faneuil Hall, nothing more. For himself Oliver honored the occasion with the same restraint that characterized everything he did: He invited a few select friends to join him in a quiet dinner at Young's in Boston.

"Let us rejoice that Last Rail is laid," Oliver wrote Dodge on May 10, but his heart was filled with something less than joy. The finances of the company were still in shambles and the news from the West, when finally it arrived, chilled him to the bone. Two weeks later he confessed to Dodge in a faltering voice, "I am so thoroughly sick of my connection with the Road that I propose to get out of it just as soon as I possibly can. If I could go out to-day I should be a happier man."

(Right) Once the meeting point was determined, the last obstacle was the rugged terrain of Promontory itself. Here a lone workman trudges up the long rise of Carmichael's cut at Promontory. No one examining these cuts is likely to begrudge Carmichael's men their pay.

(Below) Along with the cut there remained one last trestle bridge at Promontory to construct. Shown here with engine 119 working up a head of steam, the bridge looked every bit as fragile and exciting to cross as the one at Dale Creek.

The Great Day Dawns: After three years the Union Pacific track marches into Promontory and stops just short of the last gap in the transcontinental line. Already a crowd has begun to gather for the ceremony. The cars in the distance belong to the Central Pacific. Note the last rails lying on the ties, waiting to be dropped into place.

Workmen from both roads watch eagerly as some Chinese from the Central Pacific lay the last rail in place with a few spikes to hold it prior to the driving of the last, ceremonial, golden spike. Behind the men looms engine number 119 of the Union Pacific.

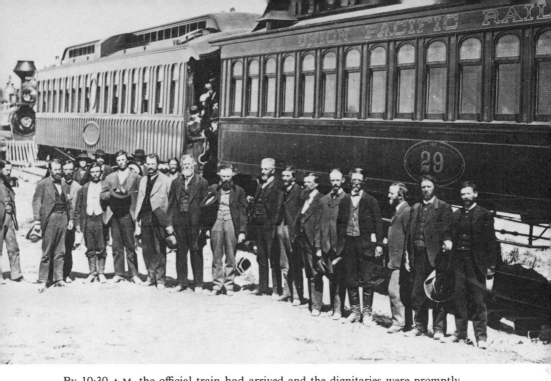

By 10:30 A.M. the official train had arrived and the dignitaries were promptly recruited by the photographers before the official ceremonies began. In this Russell photograph the Union Pacific engineers gathered for a group picture. Unfortunately, the men were not identified. Seymour, clutching his cigar, stands in the center with Dodge on his left and Reed on his right with upturned hat like a man seeking a handout.

With the troops in place on the north side of the track, the Union Pacific dignitaries pose for a group picture, their hats removed to avoid shielding their faces. Durant stands left of the track, wearing long gloves and a pained expression that betrays his headache. Duff and Dillon flank the right side of the track with Seymour just behind Dillon and Dodge the second man to Dillon's left. Reed appears to have been lost in the crowd:

(*Opposite*) Just before the golden spike was driven, the two engines face each other across the last link of rail. This view was taken from the cab of the Union Pacific's engine number 119.

(*Right*) The same scene was captured from atop the Central Pacific's locomotive, named "Jupiter," by A. J. Russell. Note that even the workmen are dressed in their Sunday best for the occasion.

Done! In what is perhaps the most famous Russell photograph of the golden-spike ceremonies, the two engines greet each other while the men christen them with bottles of champagne and Dodge shakes hands with his counterpart on the Central Pacific, Samuel S. Montague.

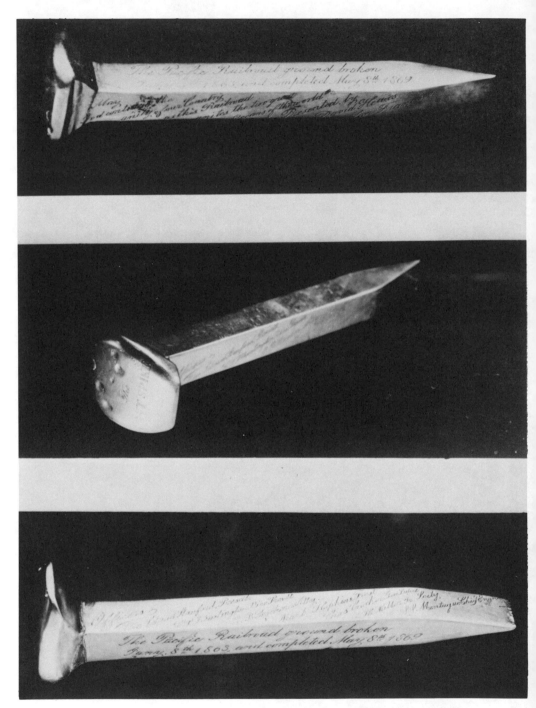

Three views of the golden spike itself, showing the inscriptions on each side.

PART TWO

The Quest for Respectability

1869–84

12

THE MOURNING AFTER

The joy of triumph at laying the last rail proved the most fleeting of moods, a night of revelry followed by a hangover of monumental proportions. For more than a year everyone's energy had been bent, every nerve strained, to completing the road, pushing with blind, almost superhuman effort against the obstacles and complications that barred their way, leaving in their wake an ugly litter of unfinished business and loose ends. Now, on the morning after, collapsed by exhaustion, they awoke bleary-eyed to confront the debris piled high around them and were shocked by the sight. The opening of the road signaled not an end to their labors but only a beginning of the ordeal of cleaning up afterward. As that realization dawned, their hearts sank in dismay at the prospect.

For two weeks after the ceremony Oliver heard nothing from Duff and Dillon except urgent cries for money. Rumors about the appalling state of affairs in the West left him sick with apprehension. Then, on May 22, Duff arrived in Boston and confirmed the worst of Oliver's fears. The situation was desperate, Duff scowled. Everything had been done in the most extravagant and wasteful manner. The unpaid bills were enormous and so scattered that he and Dillon could not even determine the total amount. Still more money was needed to finish the road for the commission, and where was it to come from? Everyone had swindled the company in the most outrageous way and Snyder had done nothing to prevent it. Duff even suspected Dillon of having an interest in some of the contracts.

Oliver listened in disbelief. The Duff-Dillon committee had accomplished nothing expected of it! Economy had not been introduced or corruption weeded out. The organization had not been revamped to improve efficiency and eliminate waste. Piles of excess material and unused tools were stacked up along the road. The bills kept pouring in and Duff could not even tell him how much they would finally come to! Where would they get the money to pay them, let alone finish the road or pay interest on the bonds? They had no more securities with which to raise funds. Oliver had already lent the company all his first mortgage bonds to use as collateral, as had several others. To Dodge he railed at Snyder for allowing expenditures to run unchecked and talked gloomily of leaving the presidency at the first opportunity.

This outburst drew swift response from Dodge, who was all too familiar with Oliver's brand of whimpering. There was always an edge of contempt among former soldiers toward those who had not served. Oliver was a civilian who knew nothing of war and too little of courage. He resembled a general who could not stand fire or take losses, who hesitated at the critical moment. By contrast Dodge was a veteran, the sort of hard-bitten officer who never flinched or faltered in the face of the enemy. He saw what had to be done, and his assessment did not agree with that of Duff and Dillon. In a series of letters he outlined the proper course to Oliver.

Above all, the line had to be put in shape before the committee of eminent citizens went over it. Since the disputed bonds hinged on their report, everything possible must be done to make it favorable. The repairs included not only the bridges, masonry, and hastily built track at the western end but also problems in the Platte Valley, where the cottonwood ties already needed replacing. The untreated wood had begun to rot while the burnettized ties grew brittle and snapped under strain. Money was needed at once to settle with the unpaid men and get them off the line. "It is not very easy," Dodge snapped, "to run a road with a class of discharged men around, growling and looking for the coming of Durant, or some one to give them a new lease of life." Dodge was trying to lure them to Omaha, where they could be handled, but he needed funds.

Once paid off, the Irishmen could be discharged and replaced with Chinese, a move he thought would cut labor costs in half. "The Irish labor," he emphasized, "with its strikes, its dead fall whiskey shops and reckless disregard of all our interests, must be gotten out of the way." A settlement had to be reached with the Central Pacific for the line west of Ogden and on the transfer of passengers and freight at Promontory, where long delays were already raising hackles. The two companies also had to decide on rates. Both wished to maximize returns by keeping tariffs high, but Dodge argued for lower rates to attract more business and deflect criticism from Washington.

On one point Dodge was adamant: to blame Snyder or other officers for allowing extravagance and corruption was unfair if not hypocritical. "You were aware of this state of things for nearly a year," he snapped. Oliver should not find fault with subordinates but "bring it right home to New York where the root of the mischief is, where . . . corruption, dishonesty, extravagance, has been held at a premium. Men out here have only followed the open example set them and none of you can plead ignorance of the state of affairs for you have been told and plead [sic] with to change it." The board alone was responsible, and if it failed to recognize this fact the outcome was certain: "Your hesitating about the establishing of lines, have been, with your business methods, &c. losing you in all quarters what little confidence people might have had in you, and we cannot long even expect to hold the good-will of the powers that be."

This tough talk was too much for Oliver, who brushed aside its truths and chose to take it personally. Blaming the East for frauds perpetrated, he replied with a rare display of pique, was not "a very ready way of correcting abuses." He had "never had any interest in any contract, never any Sallary [sic] or derived any thing but Labor and anxiety from my connection with the Road." Evidently Oliver overlooked the returns from half a dozen dividends which, by his own figures, produced a profit of $512,223 on his investment. Nor did he heed Dodge's trenchant analysis of the situation. In his somber mood it was far easier to believe the tales carried home by Duff, which kept the blame safely west of the Missouri River.

This reaction was typical of Oliver's peculiar moral myopia. His vision of responsibility stopped at the edge of personal involvement. He had taken no salary or share in contracts; he wanted a first-class road as the government stipulated. In his uncomprehending way he saw nothing that he had done wrong. Having desired always to do right, he could not grasp that, by acquiescing again and again in the acts of men like Durant, he had permitted great evils to occur. Failing utterly to see the damage wrought by his policy of appeasement, he now blamed subordinates for the consequences of his own weakness. This narrow, tidy view did more than rationalize past events; it was to distort his vision of what must be done during the coming months. The result would be to prolong indefinitely the vacuum of leadership that had plagued the company from the beginning.

* * *

The return of Duff and Dillon enabled the directors to hold the long deferred election of a new board. Dodge urged that it take place at once, as did Uriah H. Painter, a lobbyist working with Chandler in Washington. If the old crowd was not replaced with "men of honor," Painter warned Oakes, "bankruptcy is inevitable." Privately he told Dodge that *confidence* in the management of the road, is almost entirely destroyed & until it is restored it [is] impossible to get up the credit of the company." Durant was convinced that bankruptcy loomed and knew what fate awaited him in Boston. On the day before the election he submitted his resignation, observing that the great project was completed. "To have been instrumental in its accomplishment is an honor which should gratify any ambition to which I may have aspired," he added grandly. "Since the organization of the Company I have at much personal sacrifice devoted my time and energies to the promotion of its interests."

With this flourish of rhetoric the Doctor severed his formal connection with the Union Pacific. Although he would flit in and out of its affairs for several years, never again would his influence rule except as a threat. His resignation was followed by others from the New York crowd who had been his supporters: Bardwell, Cisco, and Macy. McComb was dropped unceremoniously from the board, and Bates declined reelection because his friend Bardwell had been left out. At the meeting on May 25 Hazard and three Bostonians, Elisha Atkins, Ezra H. Baker, and Oliver Chapman, took their places along with young John R. Duff, who merely kept a seat warm until Dodge could come east and claim it. Despite his misgivings Oliver kept the presidency. The elder Duff replaced Durant as vice president, John Williams succeeded Cisco as treasurer, and E. H. Rollins became assistant treasurer and secretary. A native of New Hampshire like his close friends Chandler and Painter, Rollins joined them in harnessing his considerable ambition to the Union Pacific.

To outward appearances the election routed the dissidents and left the New Englanders in complete control. Only two New Yorkers, Dillon and Cyrus McCormick, remained on the board and both had consistently supported the Ames faction. Chandler was concerned that no one was delegated to take care of business in New York. It was, he noted wryly, "a great road to manage from Boston although it is the *hub*." He was distressed that no one in the East seemed to know anything about the details of construction or equipment. What role was Dodge to assume now that the road was built, and what authority did Snyder possess as superintendent? The old question of who was in charge of what still bothered Chandler, and the election did not provide an immediate answer. Neither did it clarify what direction policy would take in dealing with the problems pressing the company on all sides. In three days of meetings the new board accomplished little more than organizing committees and ratifying the Davis contract belatedly.

After watching this spectacle engineer Fred Hodges sneered that "the present organization lacks *nerve* in its executive affairs. They are so taken aback at the position of affairs that like McClellan, they are deliberating on which flank to strike." Duff was fast emerging as the man eager to take charge. He pounded mercilessly at Snyder and scorned the advice of Dodge and the other engineers, declaring that their professional pride had in his opinion cost the company three or four million dollars. The question of what to do about Snyder split the board badly; a resolution instructing the president not to dismiss him without a vote of the directors was discussed but failed to pass. While Snyder dangled from the rack, Seymour exited with catlike agility, managing to extract some extra pay before following his mentor into obscurity. Those who thought Seymour had more gall than could be found in all of Caesar's commentaries were not disappointed. Six months later he wrote

Oliver asking in hurt tones why the board had not yet acknowledged his services with a resolution of thanks or some other fitting tribute.

Government director Hiram Price, who exchanged sharp words with Duff on the matter, left the board meeting convinced that Snyder's position was safe. Dodge, James F. Wilson, and Hodges all joined Price in praising Snyder's ability to Oliver. Oakes went out to Omaha in June and was favorably impressed by Snyder, but none of these reports matched Duff's incessant drumming in Oliver's ear. With pathetic naïveté Oliver clung to the belief that corruption and inefficiency in the West lay at the root of the company's troubles. Oakes stressed the need to get "out of the hands of the theives [sic] swindlers and Lawyers in N. York and a prudent economical honest administration of affairs on the line of the road." As Duff well knew, there was a limit to how long Oliver would resist a demand before submitting in the name of peace and harmony. Bushnell also wanted Snyder dumped, and the railroad men Oliver consulted assured him a better man could be found. On June 8 the executive committee charged Oliver, Duff, and Bushnell with procuring "the best man that can be obtained as General Superintendent." Two weeks later Duff and Bushnell headed west with full authority to act on all matters.

In effect Duff received the same carte blanche power given Durant with disastrous results on each occasion. The fact that Duff had accomplished nothing on his first western mission did not deter the board. Price was furious at the news. Although the Ames brothers and Dillon had assured him that it would be "impolitic and unjust" to remove Snyder, he had no illusions about what was coming. Late in July Duff replaced Snyder with Col. C. G. Hammond, former superintendent of the Chicago, Burlington & Quincy Railroad. Hoxie was removed as well. Neither accepted the news gracefully, Duff told Oliver with masterful understatement. An embittered Hoxie later wrote that he preferred Durant to Duff because the Doctor "always gave notice when he strikes but John Duff is a *very* bad Copperhead that dont warn." Sullenly Snyder and Hoxie joined the long line of discharged employees applying for overdue pay.

Duff's rash act was poor pay for years of hard work and loyal service. It cost the company two of its most able and experienced operating officers at the very time when operations were commencing along the entire line. Dillon, preoccupied with his own affairs, was stunned but offered little more than platitudes. A disgusted Price wrote Dodge, "I am surprised beyond measure that any set of men can have so little regard for their veracity & consistency, and can so far forget their true interests, as to act as they have done. The struggle seems to be who shall at the present moment get the most dollars, and I am of opinion that if they had 100 geese laying Golden Eggs they would kill them all, thereby proving themselves the greatest geese of the lot." Fellow Iowan James F. Wilson, soon to become a government director, put it more succinctly: "It ought not to have been."

* * *

On May 20 the commission appointed by Browning finally submitted its report to his successor, Secretary Cox. To Chandler's delight the report confirmed the Union Pacific's existing line as the best route and, in examining the roads for defects, bore hardest on the Central Pacific. It estimated that about $6.7 million was required to put the Union Pacific in first-class shape and about $4.4 million for the Central Pacific. "As you may imagine," Chandler wrote Oliver, ". . . the Central people are very much dissatisfied and feel very sore over the report." The commission's work settled the question of location but nothing else. Cox had no intention of issuing bonds on the last sections of road until he heard from the eminent citizens.

In June Cox dispatched the usual commission to inspect the final sections of the Union Pacific. Two of its members, General Warren and James F. Wilson, turned in a favorable report; the third commissioner, Isaac N. Morris, balked at signing and submitted his own version criticizing harshly more than the last sections of road. Coming only weeks after release of the Snow report, Morris's charges reignited the controversy over the road's condition. Wilson dismissed it as "a mere effort to create a sensation" but the jittery directors appealed frantically to their political friends for support. Brooks and Benjamin F. Wade, former senator and now government director, wrote a glowing defense of both Pacific roads after traveling their length. Privately Wade assured Oliver of his desire to counter "malicious representations" and agreed to see the secretaries personally. Senator Roscoe Conkling toured the line in grand style and rewarded his hosts with fulsome praise, confirming Uriah Painter's observation that *"no act of kindness to him is ever lost."*

Painter thought Wade made a "splendid impression upon both Cox and Boutwell" but he could not get either Ames to follow up by visiting the secretaries personally. "If we do not get something fastened now," he urged, "everything will go over to Congress." For two days Painter tried in person to hammer reality home to the Ameses, Williams, and Hazard. He came away discouraged by their inability or refusal to grasp what must be done to get the bonds. "They were delighted with Wades & Conklings reports," he grumbled to Dodge, "& seemed to think they could go to sleep on them." Chandler too insisted that the work in Washington and New York required "one live, active, managing director of breadth and scope but also of integrity." A curious situation had evolved in which the company's lobbyists were pushing its interests harder than were the directors, but the lobbyists had no authority to act.

The absence of a strong voice also hampered negotiations with the Central Pacific. Both companies desperately needed the rest of their bonds but could not get them until the transfer of road west of Ogden was settled. They had also to devise joint rates and resolve other problems arising from the new connection. In this bargaining the committee appointed by the board proved no match for Huntington, who kept them on the defensive all summer. Oliver was anxious to settle, but his notion of a fair price was far more than Huntington cared to pay.

Rather than pay a fair price, Dodge predicted, the Central Pacific intended "to make a row to fight for the bonds to Ogden, go to Congress, lie, howl, and finally steal the road." But Huntington fared no better in Washington than did the Union Pacific. Grudgingly he deposited with the government $4 million worth of first mortgage bonds as security, hoping to get in return bonds on a hundred miles of road; Secretary of the Treasury Boutwell gave him bonds for only sixty miles. Late in July Boutwell informed both companies that no bonds would be given on the line west of Ogden until the junction issue was resolved. Within a week Oliver formally offered to sell Huntington the line six miles west of Ogden for $4.1 million and to buy back the portion east of Corinne for $1.87 million. Huntington rejected both offers. He did not like the price, and he saw through the clumsy attempt to shut his road out of the Salt Lake City trade. The impasse dragged on for months.

Neither could the companies agree on what rates to charge for their new transcontinental service. Oliver wanted them divided on a *pro rata* basis by mileage, but officers of the shorter road objected strenuously to this view. In general Oliver thought rates and fares should be kept high enough "to pay interest & make Dividends on Stock." Even more, he hoped earnings would relieve them of the immense debt still due for construction. Crocker and Huntington protested that high rates would not attract the volume of traffic needed to sustain the road. Dodge agreed with them. Existing rates, he declared, were "prohibitory, ranging from 8½ to 11 cents per ton per mile." Repeatedly he urged Oliver to reduce rates and fares and to make special tariffs as inducements to customers in New York, Chicago, and San Francisco. Dodge understood, as Oliver did not, that business had to be weaned away from ocean vessels. Much of the railroad's expense lay in fixed costs which were the same whether the company ran one train or ten trains. The trick was "to keep all our wheels in motion instead of two-thirds of them lying idle as today, no matter if it does cost us extra for three or six months, it will pay in the end and can be done now for half of what it can be done at some future day."

Unimpressed by this argument, Oliver ordered Snyder to maintain high rates and ignored Dodge's suggestion that he leave the subject to the superintendent's discretion. He soon learned that high rates were also a political liability. Crocker was quick to respond to criticism by proclaiming that his road would put rates as low as the Union Pacific dared. When business remained sluggish, Oliver reluctantly conceded that "we must offer such rates as will lead shippers to favor our line." He continued the policy of allowing Brigham Young half price on Mormon immigrant traffic and began to grapple for the first time with special rates for large shippers and excursion parties. Even as the complexity of rate making dawned on Oliver, he could not shake the belief that the road ought to charge roughly double what eastern roads charged. Nor was he willing to let the superintendent make rates. Hammond wanted to charge whatever rate would "develope [sic] most business and produce most nett [sic] revenue," and asked for "the fullest discretion to operate this road under an elastic tariff suited to develope the country." When Oliver promised shippers special rates, Hammond stressed the "vital necessity that every change in rates should be known here before it is made."

Oliver was slow to grasp the importance of rates in cultivating new business for several reasons. He persisted in applying his experience with eastern roads to the West, where conditions were radically different. In his anxiety to garner immediate income he was reluctant to grant large shippers special rates and doubted whether the law permitted it. "Our charter cannot mean," Hammond felt obliged to remind him, "that we shall carry a single bar of iron at the same figures that we will carry hundreds of tons." During the summer of 1869 he was preoccupied with the company's financial woes and the clashes with the government and the Central Pacific. Until the junction question was settled, the traveling public had to endure a lack of facilities and prolonged delays in the transfer at Promontory. This inconvenience produced ill will and bad publicity for both companies. "We should not let Passengers lay over 20 hours at Promontory to curse the Road," Oliver admitted, and Charlie Crocker was even more blunt. "That connection at Promontory is a d——d nuisance," he growled. The roads ought to be building accommodations before winter set in, he added with a shake of his massive head. "I begin to think the U. P. folks dont want to do business on their road." By any measure of service, the new national highway was off to a fumbling start.

* * *

While the board bickered over who was to blame, the contractors lined up to press for the money owed them. Most would have a long wait. The directors had little money and less inclination to pay because of their conviction that everyone in the West had cheated them blind. In their hysteria over waste and corruption they concluded to pay no contractor until his accounts were verified. Many of the claims were for work over and above the original contracts; others were disputed on various grounds or suspected of having the Doctor as a secret partner. Charges were hurled recklessly that officers responsible for overseeing contracts often had a personal interest in them or, at the very least, had permitted cost overruns through their incompetence. This campaign of malice provoked another savage rejoinder from Dodge, aimed not at Oliver but at the new treasurer, John Williams:

> The fact of the matter is, a man out here discovered to be honest was discharged; if he made $10,000 out of you he was a good fellow and was promoted and many who had worked faithfully and honestly for you saw the situation and accepted it, and the men who did all this, today, . . . cover up their sins by

wholesale Charges against what few honest men there are. . . . I
state here, plainly and openly and defy any man to contradict it,
that all our losses, all our thieving, all our wrongs, come directly
or indirectly from Durant and Seymour's orders and it is no use
trying to charge it off to any one else. They had full, unlimited
power, used it to its full extent, fed the directors with prospects of
big dividends, the press with great ability and took full care personally of themselves. Now they are trying to shift the responsibility to the poor devils who were under them. They may make all of
you down east swallow it but it wont go down here.

Dodge's impassioned outburst made little impression on men fearful of
drowning in a sea of debts. In June a mood of crisis still gripped the management. From Echo Reed warned that the "men are very much excited and
cannot be controlled much longer." Hooper and Brooks, who had gone out to
Promontory, agreed that money was needed at once to curb the "great dissatisfaction & demoralization among men threatening track & bridges there."
Hammond, arriving in Omaha on July 22, found unpaid payrolls as far back
as March totaling $770,090 with another $320,000 due for July. Taken aback
by a "frontier world . . . where municipal state or territorial justice is to a
great extent deficient or unknown," the new superintendent fretted over the
"stoppage if not injury to our trains" by those demanding back wages.

Late in June Bushnell went west with Duff and managed to arrange for
paying off about $2.75 million worth of obligations. Of that amount, he re-
ported, "$750,000 is proffitt [sic] to the contractors, but I do not think there
has been but a very small proportion of dishonesty practiced on us of what I
had expected to unearth." Convinced that the worst was past, he assured
Oliver that no one would take fifty for his stock once he and Duff finished
their work. Bushnell's optimism was, as usual, premature; after his departure
a new flood of debts poured forth. The contractors soon realized that their
claims, however valid, were caught up in an ugly controversy and settled
doggedly into a state of siege. Those with friends in the company appealed to
them for help. The Casements were quick to enlist a sympathetic Dillon, but
even he could not keep their claim from languishing for months.

In this tortuous process Duff played a key role. His pear-shaped body,
snowy beard, and wrinkled face gave him the appearance of a malign Santa
Claus. Having taken no role in the frenzy of contract letting, he was free to
disavow its consequences. On his swing through the West Duff sniffed for
scents of scandal in every contract and distrusted his nose when none appeared. His firing of Snyder was but one part of what Hodges called "the
policy of kicking out *all* the old hands." Reed had already sensed what was
happening and absolved himself of blame with Oliver:

The past year I cannot be held responsible for any extraordinary expenditure. The work has been drove rapidly summer and

winter night & day all the men and teams in the country have been in our servis [sic] and still we wanted more. Labor was not equal to the demand prices ranged far above ordinary times changes have been made in orgina[za]tions which have greatly increased the cost all of which has been beyond my controll[sic].

Nevertheless, in August Reed was summoned to Boston to help the board decide on the flood of claims before it, including his own for salary at twelve thousand dollars per year. That was reason enough to go, but Reed loathed the prospect. Boston was, in his terse observation, "a crooked place and full of crooked men, mentally and physically."

The Doctor was among them, relaxed from a yachting trip, gloating at the discomfort of the Ames group, agile as always in deflecting criticism from himself. Reed saw at once he was "disposed to shift the responsibility of the extraordinary expenses of the last year. I do not propose to shoulder them." In fact the issue became a snare that held him prisoner for months. Not only the board but the Trustees as well had to approve any settlement. Durant and McComb were no longer directors but could influence every decision in their position as Trustees. Much of the controversy involved work done over and above the contracts which Durant or his shadow, Seymour, authorized in the heat of the race. Duff and others took a dark view of these claims, especially where they suspected the Doctor of having an interest in the contract. Their doubts enmeshed every claim in a web of intrigue.

All the contractors bitterly resented the delays and none endured more frustration than Brigham Young, who had been trying since May to get the $1.14 million owed him. In July he sent Bishop John Sharp to meet Bushnell in Ogden, but Bushnell put Sharp off with some blather and hurried on to San Francisco. Undaunted, Young dispatched Sharp to press his claims in Boston. Convinced that the Union Pacific lacked funds to pay in full, he decided to take part of his pay in equipment to build the Utah Central line from Ogden to Salt Lake City. Sharp was instructed to get enough material not merely to reach Salt Lake City but "for 50 or 100 miles," and to do nothing that might give the Union Pacific a hold on the new road.

Sharp and Joseph Young, one of Brigham's sons, found Boston as crooked a place as Reed did. Oliver heard their case patiently and Bushnell admitted that he no longer thought their claim unrealistic, but tales of thieving contractors floated everywhere. Durant seemed resentful at being out of office and determined to embarrass the company if not force it into bankruptcy. His mood worried Oliver enough to extract a promise from Joseph that the Mormons would not join ranks with the Doctor. The Trustees appointed Duff, Dillon, and Durant a committee to settle with the Mormons, but progress was glacial. On August 24 the executive committee offered eight hundred thousand dollars in settlement but Sharp, admonished by Brigham Young to avoid "any compromises that may deprive of us of our just dues," declined.

Newspapers in Utah heaped biting criticism on the Union Pacific that Superintendent Hammond warned, "may at any moment fan a flame that will destroy for a time all use of the line."

A week later the Trustees, empowered by the board to settle the case, assembled to hear the Mormons present their case. The meeting went off pleasantly; Reed verified $730,000 of the claims, leaving about $400,000 in dispute. Sharp and Joseph Young left the room believing a settlement was near. Then McComb stepped out to see them, his jaw set and his face hard. Ten days earlier he had slapped an injunction on his fellow Trustees; now he told the Mormons curtly that the company would pay Reed's estimate and another $100,000, nothing more. Stunned, the Mormons asked for the amount certified by Reed, leaving the rest to debate. *"Not a dollar,"* McComb blustered, *"all* or *nothing."* After some heated words the Mormons rushed in to confront the Trustees, where another stormy exchange followed. Duff snarled a threat to bring the military down on the Mormons. Would the Army, Joseph Young retorted coldly, help the company *"swindle* the *men* who *built* the road out of *their* pay?" Abashed, the others blurted out that the plan had been McComb's and not their own.

That moment of denial captured the essence of the moral and managerial flaws that had marred decision making within the Union Pacific during the past four years. It embodied perfectly the leadership style of Oliver Ames. McComb had conceived a plan to bully the Mormons into submission. The other Trustees had no part in devising it, but neither did they lift a finger to stop him from attempting it. After all, it might work and save them some money; if not, they could simply disassociate themselves from it. As Oliver noted succinctly in his diary, "McCombs [sic] made a push at them by offering ultimatum of his which they rejected and we proceeded on old plans."

Next day, when tempers had cooled, the Trustees retracted their disgraceful performance and fawned on the Mormons, trying to recover with clumsy humor what they had lost by threats. The Mormons stood firm. Duff tried another round of bluster only to be cut short by Joseph Young. He was tired of wasted arguments and ready to try his luck in court where, he vowed, it would be "war to the knife." He offered to accept $940,138 for claims verified by both sides and leave the remaining $198,000 to arbitration. The Trustees agreed and Joseph left Boston satisfied with the arrangement, but his enthusiasm was short-lived. Each side was to send an arbiter to Omaha within thirty days or forfeit all rights to the disputed amount. When Oliver's appointee failed to meet this deadline, a disgusted Brigham Young claimed the balance by default and braced himself for another prolonged siege.

Other contractors showed the same tenacity. October found the Casements still trying to get a majority of the Trustees to approve their claims. When Dillon helped persuade Durant and McComb to sign, Duff was so infuriated he submitted his resignation as Trustee to Oliver and had to be coaxed out of it. Other claimants were not so fortunate and resorted to the courts. Two contractors named Nounnan and Orr went after the company for $175,000 owed them. Nearly a year later they won a decision that Dodge predicted would cause *"untold trouble"* as a precedent. Bates sued the road for nearly $40,000 owed to him, and so did L. D. Bent. The hapless Davis brought suit over his tie contract and found himself snarled in litigation that plagued the company for years.

Reed had no better luck. He remained a month in Boston trying in vain to get his pay and finish up. Not until November was he able to close up his office in Echo and return to his farm in Joliet, Illinois. Other offers awaited him but he could not get free of the Union Pacific. In December he went back to Boston for another round, muttering, "It is almost as much work to settle for, as build the road."

* * *

While Boston fended off its creditors, Dodge undertook to remedy the worst defects in the road before the eminent citizens committee arrived. Wisely he put Tom Morris in charge of all repairs. An able, meticulous engineer, Morris set up headquarters at Wasatch late in May and drove the work vigorously. Two problems absorbed most of his attention: the bridge nightmare and the poor roadbed in Utah, where track had been laid over frozen ground. Grading had to be improved, nearly all the cuts in the snow region widened, and ditching and dams installed to prevent mountain runoffs from flooding the road. A cloudburst in July underscored the latter need by triggering slides that buried three sections of track ten feet deep in rubble. Snow fences had to be installed to prevent another disaster like that of the previous winter, and some points, notably Wasatch, still lacked a reliable water supply.

For seven months Morris toiled at these problems despite shortages of everything. Tools and material were slow to arrive, men were hard to keep because the mines were paying good wages, and money was always scarce. In one case Morris paid the Mormon settlers at Uinta to fix their own ditching. The bridges were his greatest bane. Most needed new masonry, new piles, and more riprap. In his travels Morris turned up eight forty-foot spans ordered by Durant but never used; he promptly put them over the crossings at Sulphur Creek. Thanks to his diligence, Dodge could declare most of the bridges and culverts safe by the end of July, but the work of reconstruction continued long afterward. Slowly the roadbed in Utah was refurbished and cottonwood ties in the Platte Valley replaced, but new problems cropped up as old ones were solved. Morris complained that the Pullman sleeping cars were "ruining the track—it is almost impossible to keep it up under their weight."

By January 1870 an impressive amount of work had been completed. Most of the new bridges were up and reconstruction of the difficult span at Green River was well under way. The roadbed was greatly improved, snow fences were going up rapidly, and most of the cuts in Utah had been widened from twenty to sixty feet. "The cuts which I scraped out do not hold *any snow,*" Morris reported proudly, "it blows through them." There remained "a great deal of work to be done to get ready for cheap & efficient work next spring which should be done this winter," but Morris would not be there to do it. He knew Dodge was about to quit as chief engineer and had no desire to stay on without him. In February he took another position and joined the throng of able men who left the road or were driven out by a management unappreciative of, if not oblivious to, the good work they had done.

* * *

Of all the horrors to be faced on the morning after, the worst by far was the mangled state of the company's finances. The folly of distributing so many of the road's securities in dividends, leaving little or nothing for contingencies, had stripped the board of means to meet the bills that piled up during the mad rush of the past year. On the heels of this short-sighted policy came an improbable series of events that plunged its finances into chaos. The junction controversy tied up sorely needed government bonds and also prevented the company from issuing its mortgage bonds for the disputed mileage. Neither could the three million dollars in mortgage bonds deposited with the government in December be used in the present crisis. The Fisk raid had utterly deranged the company's position in New York. Although the office had left town, young Tweed and his friendly judge stood ready to pounce on any financial activities. In effect the company found itself unable to borrow money, sell securities, or conduct routine transactions in the country's leading money market without the threat of legal harassment. For two years any director wishing access to the books or papers had to summon a man who held the key to the safe and would open it for them. The keeper loitered about until the director finished, then locked everything up again.

The Fisk raid also disrupted the company's records to the point where it literally did not know what it owned or owed. There was confusion enough in the existence of two separate sets of books, one for the Union Pacific and another for the Trustees' accounts. Both were scattered by the raid, and attempts to reassemble them ran afoul of other considerations. Crane, the keeper of the Trustees' books, kept careless accounts and, as Durant's man, was slow to cooperate with the Doctor's enemies. During the raid Bushnell alone did the company's business in New York, buying and selling bonds, dispensing them as collateral for loans, without keeping careful records of his transactions. Auditor Benjamin Ham struggled diligently for two months to piece together Crane's accounts and unravel the mysteries of Bushnell's activities. Bushnell was generous with promises to help but always too busy to deliver; Crane pledged a full accounting but refused to defy the court's injunction. It was all very well for the board to demand books and papers from him, Crane snapped, "but it is out of the question with me—as I have no desire to do anything that will give the Fisk Jr. Crowd any opportunity to send me to the Tombs to spend the Summer."

In the end Ham failed to trace the whereabouts of all the bonds or square the books. "The settlement of the contractors books is a job I dont want," he said in exasperation. "I straightened up the Hoxie books and tried hard to control the books on the Ames contract. I did not succeed, and now I don't care to have anything to do with them." Bushnell's accounts became an object of bitter controversy, raising suspicions that he had pocketed large sums for himself. Ham thought a banker close to Bushnell had been overpaid $250,000. The bond muddle had serious and far-reaching consequences. Several banking houses held certificates for bonds that could not be delivered as promised; Jay Cooke's firm alone was carrying nearly $1 million in certificates. Notes in large amounts fell due and bond coupons had to be paid on July 1, which meant more borrowing. It was an awkward if not embarrassing business trying to raise money with few bonds on hand and no clear sense of what assets were available or what liabilities were due.

The executive committee fumbled for a solution. A call by the Trustees for Crédit Mobilier holders to complete payment on the mortgage bond certificates distributed in July 1868 drew weak response. Oakes and Bushnell struggled to lift the bonds in the market, but tales of the huge debts in the West drove prices steadily downward. "The Banks are afraid of them," young John Duff said of the firsts, "and prefer notes with good names attached." Oakes thought it would help to get Union Pacific securities listed on the New York Stock Exchange, but nothing was done.

Through the long, dreary summer of 1869 Oakes pleaded for his associates to "harmonise matters" and pull together. More than eleven million dollars was paid out but the bills kept coming. The money market tightened steadily, making funds expensive and difficult to get. Falling bond prices erased margins on loans and led to calls for more collateral. A handful of directors kept the company afloat by furnishing money and taking its notes. All were asked to lend their mortgage bonds or exchange them temporarily for land grant bonds so they might be used to fulfill contracts or as collateral. The Ames brothers did their share and more, but others balked or waited to see whether the market improved. McCormick admitted being "concerned about the situation of the Road," while reluctantly signing a note for fifty thousand dollars. Durant and McComb offered nothing more than vague promises. When everything was converted to money, the Doctor predicted cynically, the company would come up six million dollars short of its debts.

To Hazard as chairman of the finance committee fell the task of sorting out a messy situation in New York with three German banking houses. All had lent the company money on certificates but had received no bonds; now they demanded the bonds or repayment. Louis Von Hoffman claimed Bushnell had promised him $1 million in land grants as collateral for his $399,000 loan and was outraged at not receiving them. Each case had its own peculiar complications requiring delicate negotiations; one was so involved that Williams conceded he "would be satisfied to get off losing $40,000." Hazard had also to contend with John Pondir, an erratic broker who demanded exorbitant commissions for arranging several loans despite having so muddled them that Hazard could not determine who held what collateral.

For over a month Hazard labored patiently at the negotiations, shuttling between Boston and New York. He did not have much to work with. The creditors had unassailable cases and could bring the company to protest unless he came to terms. Williams wanted a quick settlement but one favorable to the company; other directors sent him mixed signals on the subject. In this difficult situation Hazard arranged what he thought were reasonable bargains with two of the creditors, taking care to get the opinion of those directors he could find before acting. To placate one creditor, he was obliged to use his own land grants in the transaction because the company did not have enough for the settlement. "I am not willing to sell my bonds at this price," he notified Williams, "but the exigency is such that I shall do it & rely on Co to make up matter equitably."

Hazard got scant thanks for his efforts. Brushing aside the difficulties involved, some directors criticized the settlements as too generous and the executive committee balked at making good his loss on the land grants. Already Hazard was embroiled in disputes over his share of an April bond subscription and the division of bonds between Bushnell and himself. Oliver, Williams, and others also pressed Hazard to have his suit against Durant removed to a federal court. Durant was behind this request, arguing slyly that removal would make a valuable precedent for the Fisk case. A distraught Williams tried to soothe Hazard while conceding none of his demands, reminding him that "you made a good thing in these settlements in N Yk— making some 3% on such large amts of Bonds, without using any money. I dont think you can have heart or Conscience to claim much more."

Years of bitter infighting had hardened Hazard to such pleas, made him if anything more implacable. He watched Bushnell deftly evade an accounting on his bonds and suspected Cisco of using bonds held in trust to protect his own house. Durant and McComb still circled the company like vultures in search of leavings. For himself Hazard had done the company a favor in April by leaving the first mortgage bonds due him for the company to use when it was short. Now it was said he had not subscribed to them and the bonds were needed for others who, in his words, "grabbed all they could lay their hands upon." All this was too much for Hazard's righteous soul. The road would never succeed, he told Williams wrathfully, "except by leasing it to those who can manage it . . . in our hands whatever is not stolen from us at one end will be at the other." Forbidding Williams to use some notes he had just endorsed for the company, he thundered, "This weak and dishonest policy which has thrown millions into the hands of scoundrels and brought disgrace upon the Co. and all connected with it has gone far enough. I will go no farther with it."

Against this dirge Bushnell offered a siren's song extolling the "vast returns we are to secure from our property when we get it into such shape as we will in a few months." But the incurable optimist had no solution for the immediate financial crisis. The strain wore Williams down, left him afraid his health would break under the pressure. In August the Trustees concocted a new plan for raising money. For every two hundred shares held by them Union Pacific stockholders would receive a package of one land grant bond, one certificate for a first mortgage bond, and fifty shares of Union Pacific stock on payment of two thousand dollars. The deadline for accepting the offer was August 20, but on that date McComb stopped the sale with injunctions. Why McComb resorted to this action is unclear; some said he and Durant were angling to regain control or at least force the company into insolvency from which they might take advantage. At the same time McComb assured Oliver that he was willing to do his part if someone would only show him what there was to be done.

The injunctions (in Boston and New York) plunged the company into another morass of confusion. Some Trustees worried that they might be held personally liable for the issue, others that McComb might renew his attack in another guise. At Oliver's request Bartlett devised an arrangement to skirt these objections. Instead of an outright purchase, stockholders were asked on August 26 to *lend* the company two thousand dollars and hold the securities as collateral for six months. This scheme led Williams to dub the transaction the "Evasion Loan." Unfortunately, several holders had already subscribed on the original terms, including Hazard, who took his share on August 18 and left for the West that same day. He returned on the thirty-first to find the terms of the offering changed. What happened next remains in dispute. Hazard and some others insisted on being allowed their bonds under the original terms. Oliver later retorted that Hazard tried both to claim his bonds and subscribe to the loan under the new terms. The only certainty was that yet another wedge of controversy had been driven between the men in charge of Union Pacific, the full impact of which would register in February 1870.

The Evasion Loan failed utterly to relieve the company's distress. Williams crumpled under the strain and retired to a sickbed while the executive committee agonized over a new plan. Some way had to be found for the railroad to pay the Trustees $10 million owed for construction. Apart from other debts, the Trustees needed $2.5 million to redeem certificates issued in July 1868 for first mortgage bonds. The committee decided to issue income bonds but could not agree on terms. After what Oliver called "a great deal of foolish talk" it concluded on September 4 to offer $10 million worth at 7 percent. Next day Oliver left for the West and did not return until September 28. During his absence the executive committee juggled the terms no less than three times before reaching agreement. The final version revealed how desperate the company was for funds by raising interest on the $10-million issue to a whopping 10 percent. Stockholders were offered two income bonds and a bonus of forty shares of stock for $1,600 cash. Those who accepted the offer were also tendered another income bond in exchange for one of the July 1868 certificates.

Despite these attractive terms the incomes met a slow response. They had the bad luck to be offered only two days before Black Friday, the climax to a bold speculation in gold engineered by Jay Gould, threw Wall Street into pandemonium. For weeks the normal channels of business were disrupted and prices fell sharply. The firsts dipped to 82 and money grew tight. Aside from this uproar, some stockholders feared the incomes were part of a new scheme by Durant and McComb to regain control. By October 10 only about $500,000 worth had been subscribed. Ultimately the company issued a total of about $19.8 million in land grant and income bonds on which it realized proceeds of only $12.6 million. Put another way, the board paid an appalling discount of 37 percent on securities that saddled the company with nearly $20 million in long-term debt at high interest rates. Nothing attests more graphically to the dismal state of its credit standing.

In the dark months ahead the company's finances continued to skate the brink of disaster while its managers foundered about in search of remedies. So far only one man had tried to lead by example. "Oakes Ames don't flinch any," Hodges observed, "though it has mostly fallen on him the past summer." Williams was still prostrate and slow to recover. Elsewhere among the divided councils of leadership flinching was in season. Whenever directors huddled to bemoan their fate or hatch new schemes, they talked wistfully of lost opportunities and cursed those responsible for their plight. The energies needed for constructive policy were squandered instead on outbursts of recrimination.

While each had his own stock of scapegoats, all seized on Durant as the arch villain. Former Congressman Ben Wade revealed he first met Durant on one of his grand excursions two years earlier and came home wondering why anyone would entrust his property to him. Bushnell thought anyone going over the road would conclude that the Doctor was a knave or a fool. Duff estimated Durant had cost them five million dollars, then raised it to ten million. Why then, demanded Alley, had Duff introduced the resolution putting Durant in charge again? Because, Duff replied testily, the Doctor had a majority and Duff "wanted to go with him." Oliver suspected Durant of still trying to ruin the company. Probably so that he might profit from the wreckage, Glidden added. Why then, Alley persisted, were Oliver, Duff, and others allowing Durant to wield so much influence in the Trustees' affairs?

For months they traded these snippets of malice, venting their frustrations with glee on shared devils, turning now and then upon one another, as willing to believe the worst of their friends as they were reluctant to look into their own hearts for the reasons why such things had come to pass. Hazard listened intently to this litany of complaint and filled sheets of scrap paper with scribbled memos on its details. They were grist for the mill of his own grievances, fuel for lawsuits that would occupy two decades. In that respect he was but the most persistent among them. The men who built the Union Pacific could not possibly forget the experience; most would spend the rest of their lives fighting over it in court.

* * *

Once the commission of eminent citizens had been appointed, Oakes saw what should be done. "We must have the right men with them to show them all the good points on the road," he wrote Dodge, "and not have them see any bad ones if we can avoid it and where they are bad we must insist that was the best that could be done at the time, and that it is safe and substantial and will be improved as fast as it is necessary for safety." The commissioners did not gather at Omaha until August 23 and were delayed there by one late arrivee. Morris was still working feverishly to get the road in shape for them, but Boston was ready. Some crucial changes in the board were made at a meeting on August 18. Young Duff turned his seat over to Dodge and James F. Wilson became government director in place of Brooks, who was promptly elected a regular director. The board then named Oliver, Dodge, and Wilson to accompany the commission on their tour of inspection.

The commission chose to start its inspection from San Francisco and work eastward. Chandler feared "the Central will get the start of the U.P." with the commissioners but Glidden was in California to counter Stanford's blandishments. When Oliver reached Omaha on September 9, Huntington and Crocker were waiting for him. Mixing pleasure with business, they had brought their families along and hitched their car to Oliver's special train for the ride back to Promontory. At Ogden they paused to inspect the tablelands west of the city and settled on a site five miles west of the town as a suitable junction point. But Huntington would not yield on the price, vowing to pay no more than forty-five thousand dollars a mile. Glidden got a similar message from Stanford, who renewed the threat to build his own road to Ogden if the two sides could not agree on price.

The commission reached Promontory on September 14 and spent nine days inspecting the Union Pacific. To everyone's relief it came away impressed with the road; three of the commissioners even promised to help the company get its bonds. Their report, released on November 1, estimated that about $1.6 million was needed to remedy deficiencies on the road from Omaha to Ogden, and another $206,000 for the stretch from Ogden to Promontory. The Central Pacific was figured at $576,650. "We are out of the woods," cried a jubilant Bushnell. Oliver was in Washington when the report appeared and applied at once for the bonds. He found Boutwell and Cox willing, but one hitch after another developed to prevent delivery. The junction question still hung fire. Bushnell thought Huntington was ready to deal, and the prospect of getting bonds made the Union Pacific men more amenable to compromise. The need for money was too pressing to haggle forever over price.

After some hard bargaining Oliver agreed on November 17 to sell Huntington 48½ miles of road from Promontory to a point about 5½ miles west of Ogden. The price was $2.84 million or about $58,556 per mile, a substantial retreat from the $87,000 per mile Dodge estimated as the cost of construction. The new junction point was a patch of Utah wilderness on which both sides eagerly expected a new metropolis to arise. Huntington dispatched Stanford to buy land there "before it is known that our point of meeting is not Ogden," and the Union Pacific did the same. Then complications began to pile up. A string of technicalities delayed transfer of the road and the issue of bonds to be used as payment for it. Attempts to get the new junction point approved suddenly met with intransigence on the part of Huntington. "He is very exacting," wrote a puzzled E. H. Rollins "and seems determined to yeild [sic] nothing, save on compulsion."

The problem was a split within the Central Pacific ranks over the town site scheme. Three of the partners concluded that it was, as Hopkins later observed, "a fallacy. It can never be realized. There is nothing to build or support a town there—No wood, no water, no agricultural or mineral surroundings, while five miles east of it all these things exist." Stanford saw that the Mormons who owned the land would never permit a competing town to spring up on the outskirts of Ogden. He and Crocker settled on that town as the best alternative, bought some land, and told Duff the junction must be there. But Huntington would not let go of the idea. "I would rather have nothing," he snapped when the news reached him. Early in December the transfer point was moved to Ogden but everything else about the junction remained uncertain. The Central Pacific took possession of the road five miles west of Ogden without paying for it because the bond issue for that stretch still had to be sorted out. The government could not untangle the bond question until Congress designated an official junction point, and a fight loomed over that bill. Meanwhile the Central Pacific was running into Ogden over five miles of track it did not own or lease. A dispirited executive committee braced for another round of intrigues in Washington.

Nothing came easy in Washington. Even in an age when the government was small and intimate, the bureaucracy could be stultifying. "Do you know," groaned one of Rollins's agents, "that a war requisition goes through *forty eight* hands before completion." The astute Chandler understood that much depended on which hands got hold of something, but he could not always get Boston to grasp that fact. In his view the company had dealt carelessly with the Central Pacific and was "liable to be slaughtered by them at any minute." Congress might not oppose the Pacific roads but the departments were another matter. Chandler feared the Treasury would demand that all due interest on bonds be paid "or else stop all transportation dues. Really there is no smart executive officer of the U. P. in this direction."

* * *

"Everything looks fair for a speedy closing up of my affairs," Reed observed on returning to Boston in December. His optimism was soon crushed. Having bungled its handling of large affairs, Boston dug in its heels on smaller ones. So strapped was the company for funds that every petitioner, whether friend or foe, got the same rude treatment. Every claim was doubted, disputed, and delayed. Past arrangements were ignored or disclaimed, an easy matter for directors divided among themselves and, in some cases, doubling as Trustees. Bushnell and Duff grew practiced in their Mutt and Jeff routine, the one promising and the other denying. Their act did not impress men like Bent and Nounnan, who pressed their claims in court. The Mormons too fought stubbornly on for months, as did Davis. Duff was anxious to settle with Davis because he saw "great danger of their getting large sums against us in the courts here [Omaha]" and Poppleton, the company lawyer, doubted the case could be removed to federal court. But Davis spurned his offer.

Unlike the contractors, dismissed employees found themselves at the company's mercy. Duff had promised Snyder his remaining pay by July 28, but the draft for the amount due him was not honored. An embittered Snyder appealed to Oliver for justice, denouncing Duff as "a person of no integrity." Although Oakes vowed that Snyder and Hoxie would get every dollar owed them, Oliver ignored the request. In November a sympathetic Price offered a resolution at a board meeting to pay Snyder's bill only to have it voted down. Hoxie fared no better. He was owed twenty-three hundred dollars in back salary plus the amount due him for assigning the Hoxie contract, which he figured to be forty thousand. Duff had also promised him payment in July and then reneged. "I am going to have my money & that soon or make trouble," Hoxie vowed in cold fury. "I have enough papers in my hands to make some trouble." He was itching to go for Duff, "who is a notorious liar in this country," and knew exactly how to do it. "Wonder if they want Congress to know amt dividends paid on Credit Mobilier," he mused to Dodge. Even with this ammunition Hoxie did not coax terms from Oliver until March 1870.

As for Reed, his settlement too dragged on into the winter. Like so many others hired by Durant, he had worked the whole time without his salary being fixed. Reed wanted twelve thousand a year from the time he took charge of construction; Oliver thought he could be whittled down to ten thousand. The company sorely needed Reed's testimony in all its suits with contractors, yet it gave him the same runaround as any claimant over a difference involving less money than it had spent on advertising a single bond issue. "I am heartily sick and tired of the unbusinesslike way in which I am treated," Reed stormed to his wife. "How such men prosper is beyond my comprehension, unless it be by fraud and dishonesty." When Oliver again rejected his demand on February 5, Reed closed up his construction accounts in Boston and went to New York still unpaid. While there he went one evening to see Edwin Booth perform *Hamlet* and ran into General Dix, with whom he had a long chat at intermission. Had Reed known the right questions to ask, Dix could have given him a lesson or two on how to extract money from the Union Pacific.

*   *   *

As the year of the Golden Spike drew down, the managers of Union Pacific found themselves standing a little deeper in the same old holes. The financial picture looked as bleak as ever, business had been disappointing, problems still loomed in Washington, and the directors continued to feud among themselves. The road had been improved, the management had not; by the year's end it needed ballast more desperately than did the roadbed.

Earnings fell far short of the interest on bonds, prompting frantic calls for Superintendent Hammond to curb expenses and increase remittances to Boston. Bushnell talked confidently of selling the bonds received from the Central Pacific but couldn't deliver. To pay the January interest the company had to arrange sterling loans with Dabney, Morgan and Morton, Bliss at steep terms. Dillon was outraged to learn the Dabney, Morgan loan cost the company 17½ percent and suggested that "our parties should take the loan themselves for about 14 or 15% or less if they can make it," but no one took up his offer. Prospects for the coming winter looked gloomy.

In wrangling over these problems the directors discovered to their dismay that Durant had not been the only source of evil in their universe. Even without him or McComb the board was riddled with antagonisms. Every man had his store of grievances, none more than Hazard, with which Oliver was helpless to contend. Duff's rise to prominence had made him more cantankerous than ever, peevish and resentful of every slight real or imagined. He and Dillon had taken a dislike to each other that daily grew less cordial. Oliver threw up his hands in despair at their bickering, content to record with rare sarcasm an executive committee meeting that exemplified "the very polite way in which Dillon & Duff usually present matters." Floundering in a sea of troubles, the Union Pacific pitched dangerously, a rudderless ship without a captain and possessed of a crew always on the brink of mutiny.

===13===

THE BRIDGE

The driving of the golden spike left only one gap in the rail line between the oceans. The Missouri River had to be bridged, a task as formidable as any that confronted the engineers in the West. At Omaha the meandering river was four miles wide with an adjacent floodplain on which it rose as much as ten feet during the high water season. The bedrock was covered with layers of sand, gravel, and silt deposited by a shifting, treacherous current. Before anything could be done, answers had to be found to three questions: Where should the bridge be located? Should it be a high bridge or a low (draw) bridge? How should it be financed? In deciding these questions the board followed its familiar patterns all too faithfully. The building of the bridge became a miniature version of the building of the road.

As early as October 1863 Dey paused in his surveys to locate a site just south of Omaha he thought ideal for a bridge. "It seems premature to talk of Bridging the Missouri," he admitted to Durant, "but I give you my views for what they are worth." Dey favored a high bridge, arguing that the channel for a draw bridge could not be kept open at all times. He thus anticipated both the location and type of bridge that would ultimately be chosen at a time when most engineers doubted the river's sandy bottom would even support a bridge and when the technology for a high bridge over so great a distance did not yet exist. Although his remarkable foresight has gone entirely unnoticed, at the time it won one important convert, Jesse Williams, who in November 1864 wrote a vigorous defense of Dey's plan to the Secretary of the Interior. Unfortunately, Dey quit in disgust a month later and the project languished for the next year.

Interest revived late in 1865 because of renewed railroad activity in Iowa. The promoters of the Burlington showed fresh interest in building the moribund Burlington & Missouri River across the state. One of them, the indefatigable James F. Joy, was also constructing a road from St. Joseph to Council Bluffs. Both projects wished to connect with any bridge the Union Pacific might erect. That autumn the oxbow controversy ran its course only to have the bridge question rekindle it. In November the board avowed its determination to bridge the river and authorized surveys. A month later Joy announced that the B & M was in the race to connect first with the Union Pacific and would have added incentive if the bridge was located "at *some point lower down than the initial point.*" Joy's plea added an ominous new twist to the location question by tying it to the politics of connection with the roads building across Iowa.

The task of preparing surveys and estimates fell to Dodge, who was not exactly a disinterested party. As a resident of Council Bluffs he was anxious that the bridge and the Iowa roads, notably the M & M, connect there. He also bought some land on speculation, which was but the custom of the country. Dodge produced his report early in December 1866 and added a supplementary report a month later. His surveys boiled the choice down to three locations. The first, a site two miles north of Omaha known as Telegraph Pole Crossing, was especially suitable for a low bridge. The second was Dey's line in south Omaha, which Dodge called the M & M crossing. Finally there was Child's Mill, eight miles south of Omaha, the point of departure for the new route surveyed by Colonel Simpson during the oxbow controversy. In both reports Dodge argued vigorously for a high bridge and for Child's Mill as the best location for it.

Dodge's choice neatly meshed his land speculations with sound engineering. However, the citizens of Bellevue wanted the bridge at their town and had already petitioned the company to put it there. So did Joy, who appeared before the board to urge its adoption. The Northwestern and Rock Island roads favored south Omaha while John Blair wanted a low bridge at the Telegraph Pole for his road. The board created a bridge committee and resolved to form a separate company for constructing the bridge, but it ducked the location question. When it became clear that the prize would go to whichever competitor offered the most financial help in building the bridge, Joy stepped forward at once with a proposal. In typical fashion the bridge committee coyly endorsed it as "the most tangible proposition" but left the door open for other offers. The committee also stumbled on a new complication: since nothing in the company's charter authorized it to build a bridge, new legislation from Congress would be required.

Months of intrigue followed. In December 1867 the committee ordered Dodge to prepare estimates for land needed at Child's Mill and south Omaha. Dodge also had new soundings taken at both crossings. "Heretofore we have been too careless," he scolded House, "and I now want the work done *care-*

fully, accurately and *thoroughly."* Dodge reported in February 1868 that right-of-way had been secured at Child's Mill but not yet at south Omaha. Joy made another powerful appeal before the committee and told Jesse Williams privately that the B & M would probably erect its own bridge at Nebraska City if the Bellevue crossing was rejected. Nevertheless, the committee voted to recommend Child's Mill despite an effort by Duff to switch their choice to Bellevue.

This action not only disgusted Joy but also drew angry protests from interests in Omaha, who threatened war if the bridge was built elsewhere. Omaha reminded Oakes that Durant had been deeded a large tract of land for shops, a depot, and transfer grounds and accused Dodge of pushing Child's Mill because he owned land there. Blair pressured Oakes for a low bridge at Telegraph Pole, arguing that the best policy was "the cheapest kind of a bridge that will stand." Oakes thought him a "pretty good advisor in such matters" but Dodge shredded Blair's argument. He was convinced the river was carving a new channel north of Omaha and would leave a bridge there on dry land. Oliver visited the site during flood season in April 1867 and saw how powerful the current was. "The prospect of building a Bridge at Telegraph Pole as current now is," he observed, "is not favorable." He was also alarmed at the tempest brewing in Omaha.

Dodge was the first to reconsider his position. Reluctantly he concluded that the political and commercial liabilities of Child's Mill outweighed its engineering advantages. It would not do to leave Omaha stranded on a stub branch or force the interchange with Iowa roads to take place at Council Bluffs. In his quick, shrewd way Dodge switched to south Omaha as the most suitable compromise, but the board was slow to follow. McComb proclaimed grandly that Child's Mill was "the point fixed by the God of the Universe, and must be recognized," while others, transfixed by Joy's persuasiveness, leaned toward Bellevue. Dodge had his engineers gather enough information to demolish Joy's argument on the advantages of the Bellevue line, yet Joy persisted and almost carried the board with him.

At a series of meetings in March 1868 the directors resolved the location question by simply throwing it up for auction. The board approved the committee's choice of Child's Mill "unless a satisfactory proposition" was made "to aid in the Construction of Said Bridge at Some other locality." Next day the committee handed its price tag to the Omaha citizens group: land for the depot and right-of-way, enough money to cover the higher cost of the south Omaha line, and a guarantee that its property there would not be taxed by city or county above an evaluation approved by itself. On March 24 the committee received a written proposal from the Omaha group and was promised similar offers within a day by representatives from Council Bluffs and Bellevue. When these were produced, the board obligingly moved to drop Child's Mill from the bidding.

At the meeting Jesse Williams, who had devoted considerable time to the question, presented an extensive report. Seymour countered with a statement urging a low bridge at the Telegraph Pole. When he finished, Williams ripped him to pieces. Had Seymour not noticed that five to seven hundred feet of his proposed site on the east bank had been washed away in only three months? Seymour had not. As for dredging, Williams scoffed, two dredges could work full time for two days "and one day afterward there would not be a hole big enough to bury the bridge committee in." Nothing more was heard about a low bridge. Dodge offered his new data refuting Joy's argument. The directors listened attentively, their ears tuned less to data than to dollars, then invited the delegations to submit their bids. Omaha offered $250,000 and Council Bluffs $200,000 in aid plus the necessary land for a high bridge at south Omaha. When Bellevue could not match those figures, the board voted to build at south Omaha.

Once the location and type of bridge had been settled, Dodge plunged into the engineering problems. Four bridges then under construction on the Mississippi and Missouri rivers were using piles as a foundation. After consulting the engineers on these projects, Dodge and Williams concluded that the depth of quicksand at south Omaha ruled out piling. Only one bridge in the country, over the Harlem River in New York, had been erected using iron piers sunk by forced air. Dodge contacted its engineer, Frederick E. Sickels, and learned enough to convert him to that approach. Several prominent engineers, asked their opinion, assured him that iron piers could not withstand the river's swift current, ice gorges, and masses of driftwood. Only one, William McAlpine, offered encouragement. McAlpine had been in charge of sinking the Harlem's piers and took a keen interest in the Omaha project. He provided Dodge with a steady stream of technical advice.

In May Dodge submitted his plans for an iron-truss structure resting on iron piers at an estimated cost of $1.7 million. Where the money would come from remained a mystery. The pledges from Omaha and Council Bluffs would not be forthcoming for some time, and the company had all it could do to raise money for constructing the road. Nevertheless, in September the board let a contract for the bridge to L. B. Boomer. The committee invited the Iowa roads terminating at Council Bluffs to become partners in the project; all declined and would later regret the decision. By the year's end no solution had been found, but work on the bridge had begun. In October the company hired Theophilus E. Sickels to supervise the work. As an assistant under his brother on the Harlem bridge, Sickels was familiar with the technique of using iron piers. Boomer put his work in the charge of Gen. William Sooy Smith, a splendid engineer and former comrade of Dodge.

Boomer and Smith came to Omaha in November and had their machinery in place by early January 1869. On March 12, despite temperatures below zero, the first column was hoisted into place and driven down all of two feet. Ten days later it reached forty-three feet below the surface. Although Sickels was optimistic, he made little headway. Defective castings broke on column two nearly thirty-five feet below water and were difficult to remove. Boomer had trouble getting men to work inside the columns; above all he had trouble getting money for the project. He could not get the company to pay for bridges he had already put up, let alone advance funds for the Omaha span. No one had yet figured out a way to finance the bridge. The Iowa roads kept aloof, Jesse Williams thought, because "they profess to be afraid of a *Job* inside. They say the UP have commenced it without an arrangement and that they are bound to build it and pay for it any how."

In April Duff replaced McComb as head of the bridge committee, but nothing changed. The company got caught up first in the race to Promontory and then in the financial horrors of its aftermath. Boomer's pleas for funds fell on ears deafened by the cries of contractors for money. While he joined the line of waiting creditors, the work slowed to a trickle, then stopped altogether in July. For months the bridge lay dormant, one more casualty of the crisis in management that threatened the company's very survival.

* * *

In many respects the years 1869–73 were themselves a bridge between two eras. The road had been constructed but still lacked an identity. No one yet possessed a clear vision of its destiny. Immersed in the struggle to stay afloat and distracted by their own squabbling, most directors were slow to formulate policy or even devise an administrative structure. Suspicion and distrust marred every level of decision making. The vacuum of leadership grew even worse without the Doctor, who had at least provided motion if not direction. During these years three different presidents, each more promising than the last, failed to give the company a sense of direction. By 1873 the Union Pacific found itself drifting aimlessly in a depressed economy, a piece of corporate flotsam caught in a whirlpool of scandal that threatened to tear it apart. In the desperate search for an identity it came away stripped of respectability as well.

Amid this turmoil men long associated with the company were forced out or simply left. A disgusted Jesse Williams quit as government director in November 1869. Snyder and Hoxie were long gone, and Evans soon joined Reed in seeking fresh prospects. Of the engineers only House and Morris lingered, and both quit when Dodge resigned as chief engineer. Apart from being ill, Dodge took an intense dislike to Hammond and his methods. One of Hammond's first acts as superintendent was to insist that the engineering department be placed under his control. As Duff's man he took a harsh view of the old hands, an attitude that outraged Dodge. In Dodge's opinion the company was losing the wrong men for the wrong reasons. To Oliver he said only that "no doubt Mr. Hammond prefers his own men"; privately he complained to Dillon about those who "take pleasure in building up the rascalities and corruptions of Durant, rather than say a word commendatory of those who brought the Company to a full knowledge of their condition."

In January 1870 Dodge turned the office of chief engineer over to T. E. Sickels, who had been on hand less than two months. Although he remained on the board, Dodge left with harsh feelings unsalved by testimonials from Oliver and the directors. His departure removed the last of the old guard who had provided continuity since the early construction years. None of their replacements matched their contributions or lasted long in their positions. They too were but a bridge between an old order passing and a new one yet to arrive.

* * *

To Sidney Bartlett the Evasion Loan was a straightforward matter. The terms had been changed to evade McComb's injunction. Under the revised plan the Trustees could not sell the securities but only use them as collateral for a loan. Subscribers were obligated to return them when the loan was repaid in February 1870. To protect the Trustees from personal liability, Bartlett devised an agreement approving all the Trustees' actions that subscribers were to sign before redeeming their loan. Oliver accepted Bartlett's advice and had the forms prepared. Informed of this action, Hazard protested at once. He was still demanding satisfaction for the bonds denied him in 1867 which, he insisted, had cost him a hundred and eighty thousand dollars in profits. The executive committee showed no more sympathy for that claim than the Trustees did for his current one. "The securities must be given up," Williams cried shrilly, *"they cannot be held back* . . . Sidney Bartlett says it may be a *criminal* offense by our laws."

But Hazard would not budge, and this time he was not alone. The securities had gone up in price, and other holders, including some Trustees, had received allotments prior to McComb's injunction. In February virtually everyone except Glidden and Williams refused to surrender their securities. As the fight dragged on, Hazard once again proved the most intractable; by spring he and the Trustees were threatening each other with suits. Another squabble broke out over the income bonds; before it was done the Trustees managed to oversell the incomes by more than two hundred thousand dollars and a rift developed between Benjamin Boyer and Oakes. To Oliver's relief the annual election in March showed only token opposition, but the board was far from united. Although the financial outlook had improved, the directors seemed unable to escape past disputes or rise above their differences.

Suits plagued the company on every side. Fisk served another writ shortly after the election in March, renewing suspicions that Durant and/or McComb had bought into his suit. Bent and Nounnan pressed their cases relentlessly until the company surrendered in the fall of 1870. Oliver called Nounnan's settlement "one of the worst things we have done as I believe the claim was not Just." The Mormons stopped short of court but were no less dogged. In May Brigham Young sent Bishop John Sharp back to Boston for another try at getting the nearly two hundred thousand dollars owed him. Oliver greeted him cordially as did the others, but to his chagrin Durant and Bushnell "laughed heartly[sic] at the idea of me coming hear[sic] for more money." Bushnell tossed out an offer of ten thousand dollars "and call it even." Sharp shrugged it off and provoked another round of guffaws by mentioning the sum he had in mind.

Oliver considered the shrewd, gritty Sharp useful to the company in several ways. After five weeks of waiting and dickering the two men came to a very different agreement than anyone expected. Sharp agreed to go home and persuade Brigham Young to accept seventy thousand dollars in full settlement of the Mormon claims. In return Oliver gave him an annual pass "to look after our interests on Line of Road." When Sharp returned early in July to report his mission a success, Oliver paid him twenty-five hundred dollars "for his Service and influence in bringing about the Settlement." Whether Young knew of this fee is unclear, but the deal did more than resolve the Mormon claims. It marked the beginning of Sharp's lifelong association with the Union Pacific management.

"There are so many of these claims . . . from the Construction Department," Oliver wailed, "that we have no confidence in any of our Settlements." But all the others paled before the Davis suit, which plunged the Union Pacific into complexities it had not yet dreamed of. During their fateful visit to Omaha in July 1869, Duff and Dillon engaged Andrew J. Poppleton as legal counsel for the railroad in the West. It proved a wise appointment. Poppleton served the company well for nineteen years, but he got off to a rocky start with the Davis case. When Davis attached some of the road's property in Omaha, Poppleton managed to dissolve the attachment and had the case removed to federal court. For months Davis tried to arrange a compromise, but Oliver refused to negotiate until the suit was dropped. In desperation Davis's lawyers resorted to an ingenious flank attack.

The new territorial government of Wyoming was already locked in a bitter partisan battle. At its first session in October 1869 the legislature passed a series of measures attacking the Union Pacific, one of which enabled creditors to throw the road into receivership to satisfy a claim. In March 1870 Davis filed suit in Wyoming charging fraud and seeking six hundred thousand dollars, an injunction, and a receiver to pay his claim from the road's earnings. "I should regard the whole thing as an absurdity," Poppleton admitted, ". . . if I were satisfied there was no one but Davis, instigating and pushing it forward." He was right to worry. The old suspicion that Durant was behind Davis proved correct. Through his brother, W. F. Durant, who held a large interest in Davis & Associates, the Doctor had for the past year secretly orchestrated Davis's efforts to obtain a settlement while at the same time advising Oliver on the proper tactics to use against Davis. He also sat with Duff and Dillon as the Trustees' committee to settle with Davis.

Poppleton hurried to Washington, where the Union Pacific lobby was busy promoting bills to settle the junction question and repeal the obnoxious laws in Wyoming. Early in April Judge John H. Howe, who was hearing the Davis case, also turned up in the capital. Oakes promptly took him in hand, doing him some political favors and providing a pass for a sick friend. "I consider it a good investment," he wrote Oliver. Meanwhile Poppleton urged Dodge to use his influence with Wyoming Governor John A. Campbell, an ally of Howe, "putting to him, in as strong terms as possible, the proposition that if any such action should be taken in respect to the road, it would result in a general cleaning out of Wyoming officials—as it most certainly *will,* for it cannot be possible that the Government will consent to allow the road to go into the hands of a Receiver." Oakes was convinced that "we must Control the next Legislature of Wyoming any way."

Poppleton strongly advised settling by arbitration and so did Dodge, who warned Oakes to expect no justice in Wyoming "because Davis owes every body either directly or indirectly and we should stand no chance with a Jury." Oakes thought he had the matter arranged with Judge Howe but was soon undeceived. On May 1 Howe required the company to post five hundred thousand dollars security within twenty days or have a receiver appointed. He refused a bond signed by the directors because they did not live or own property in Wyoming and demanded cash or government bonds instead. Oakes flew into a blind rage at the news. "I would not put up any money they will steal it if you do," he sputtered to Oliver. "Run all the rolling stock off the road into Nebraska and stop running—bring the matter to a head and see if any one horse court will stop the road." The Wyoming laws would soon be repealed, he promised, and meanwhile he would ask Grant to remove the territorial judges "and get a new chief Justice appointed that would be in our interest."

Dodge tried to restore reason. "None of you understand all the bearings of this case," he barked in his curt manner. "We are in a fight, the magnitude of which you do not comprehend; any revolutionary action, on our part, is dangerous." Stopping trains would violate both the charter and all contracts for freight and passengers, which were made for thirty days in advance. How could judges be removed without showing fraud? "To settle, put up bonds, or remove is our only way out," he concluded. "I dont want to put up bonds; I dont believe you can remove." When Poppleton learned that Judge Howe had been promised five thousand dollars for a verdict favorable to Davis, he agreed to the bonds as a way of buying enough time to avert a decision. Hammond supported Poppleton, as did Dillon and Durant. The Doctor offered grandly to furnish proof against Davis and talked wildly of a scheme to throw him into bankruptcy. Alley went to Omaha, investigated the affair, and warned Oliver that "every consideration of policy prudence and interest required its settlement."

Still Oakes would not relent. Denouncing the suit as "an outrage that ought not to be submitted to," he listened willingly to insinuations that Poppleton, and possibly Hammond too, had thrown in with Davis. Hooper and

Attorney General Ebenezer Hoar advised against putting up the bonds. Dodge appealed directly to Grant to investigate the affair. Bewildered by conflicting advice, his wrath spent, Oakes admitted at last, "I dont know what is best to do in this Davis case it is attended with all kinds of complications." He acquiesced in Oliver's decision to post the bonds, but Poppleton's plan for a settlement was ignored and James F. Wilson was dispatched to take charge of the case. The repeal of the territorial laws against the road served notice on Wyoming officials that, in Oakes's stern admonition, "there is a very short & swift retribution here for men who deviate from the paths of rectitude."

Having bungled through the crisis, the company still had to reach some agreement with Davis. Bushnell tried his hand at inducing Davis to settle apart from his associates. When that failed, he joined A. S. Paddock, a prominent Nebraska Republican, in a scheme to buy up Davis's paper and throw him into bankruptcy. The hapless Davis clung to the advice of his lawyer, J. M. Woolworth, who was secretly in league with Durant and holding fast for a settlement that favored the associates. After months of intrigue a compromise was arranged in October 1870 but fell apart soon afterward. Penniless and despondent, Davis was reduced to a pathetic figure, the helpless pawn of his friends and foes alike as his suits dragged on like some ancient feud. The charges of fraud vented in his suit exploded in the company's face during the Crédit Mobilier scandal, but they did Davis no good. Eighteen years later he pleaded for a job with the Union Pacific, claiming he had been "robbed out of $250,000 in its construction."

The Davis suit had an unsavory sequel in Wyoming. Anxious to have a loyal delegate in Congress, Hammond used his influence to secure the Republican nomination for a federal marshal named Church Howe. Unfortunately, Howe was one of the most unpopular men in the territory, and protests soon poured in. Dodge got wind of the complaints and warned Oliver that "our people made a bad mistake." It was unwise to meddle so clumsily in local politics and unforgivable to back a loser. Howe's candidacy flopped and Hammond came away with a bruised reputation, as did the company. Dodge made certain the moral did not go unnoticed. "It is necessary for us sometimes to interfere in matters where we have great interests at stake," he lectured, "but it should be done in such a manner that our action should never be known."

*   *   *

Oakes thought he knew how to break the junction impasse. Huntington was anxious to obtain Goat Island in San Francisco Bay for terminal facilities. When he had a bill to that end introduced in Congress, Oakes planted himself squarely in its path. A bargain was quickly struck: the junction would be settled if Oakes would aid Huntington in getting Goat Island. The two men joined forces behind a bill giving the companies nine sections of land west of Ogden on which the junction would be fixed. Oakes used every influence, including a liberal dispensing of passes to his colleagues. The bill passed early in May and Grant signed it at once, clearing the way for issuing the last government bonds on July 15. All that remained was to fix the exact point of junction and commence work on the new metropolis. Huntington suggested giving Brigham Young some lots in the proposed town to "keep him friendly."

But Young was not so easily appeased. Noting with grim satisfaction that the two companies were slow to leave Ogden, he speculated that "their excitement may subside and they will remain at Ogden, although it is a 'Mormon' city, and they cannot have things entirely their own way." As matters turned out, the railroads got nothing their own way. The junction point was fixed late in June but nothing was done to erect facilities or the new town. With the interchange still at Ogden, the executive committee considered leasing the five miles of track west of town to the Central Pacific. A motion to that effect was tabled on July 12 and not revived. The new metropolis never saw birth, and the lease question drifted in limbo for more than four years.

The bill repealing Wyoming's laws also passed that spring, but the bridge bill ran into unexpected trouble. During the fall of 1869 Dillon resumed negotiations with the Iowa roads and got pledges of support if the Union Pacific agreed to make its transfers at Council Bluffs rather than Omaha. In March 1870 the board voted that concession. Unwilling to ask Congress for a separate charter, the company authorized Dodge to obtain a private charter in which the Iowa roads would share. Stock or bonds would be issued to pay for the bridge and a toll charged to cover the expense. Dodge put his charter bill into the House and quietly bought a thousand acres of land on the Iowa side for the Union Pacific to use as transfer grounds.

Unfortunately the bill got enmeshed in a controversy dating back to Lincoln's "lost order" of 1863: Did the Union Pacific terminate at the eastern or western bank of the Missouri River? The issue arose because the transfer of passengers and freight across the river erupted that spring into a bitter dispute. Without a bridge the transfer had to be made by ferry, with each Iowa road paying the expense for its own cars. In March the Iowa legislature complained that this added cost would turn traffic north or south of Iowa once competing routes were in operation, and it insisted that the Union Pacific absorb the transfer cost because the law fixed its initial point on the Iowa side of the river. Interests in both Omaha and Council Bluffs fought the bill for a private toll bridge, arguing that the transfer should be free of charge as part of the Union Pacific's line.

"I presume that Ames, Duff & Co. will botch the bridge bill," wrote a disgruntled Wilson that spring. He was not far wrong. The bill passed the House in May but with a crippling amendment. Meanwhile the transfer, which was done by an independent company, turned into a nightmare as delays stacked cars up on both sides of the river. By June an estimated seven hundred cars, strung out for miles and clogging every side track, awaited transfer. The Iowa roads screamed in protest as did shippers in the Bluffs, who complained that the delays and high costs amounted to a prohibition on their business. Local newspapers heaped blame on the Union Pacific. Oliver wrung his hands over the outcry but had no solution. Hammond assured Oakes that "there is no accumulation of cars on either side of the River. All are promptly crossed." But Sickels wrote Oliver a detailed report on the blockade and interviewed agents of the four Iowa roads, who told him that *"at no time* that season had the freight been taken across promptly. So much for Hammonds veracity on that subject."

Apart from the ill will generated, the uproar dimmed hopes for getting a suitable bill through the Senate. Dodge quit the fight in disgust but told Oliver forcefully, *"We want a Bridge."* Alley visited Omaha and agreed that "we need that bridge awfully. I had no idea how essential it is, until I came here, and saw for myself." Boomer was eager to resume work and Sickels promised to complete the work in a year if the company would "go on without fear of curtailment." But how to get the money? Bartlett offered the opinion that the company could under its charter build the bridge, issue bonds, and levy tolls to pay for it. Oakes clung briefly to that hope but eventually conceded that the struggle had come full circle; if the company wanted a bridge, it must get a charter from Congress.

* * *

After the golden spike the Union Pacific ran one passenger and two freight trains a day in each direction. Westbound passengers made Promontory in fifty-four hours (an average of about nineteen miles an hour); the same trip eastbound required sixty hours. The usual train of two sleepers, two first-class cars, smoker, baggage, and mail cars could accommodate about 110 passengers, who in August 1869 paid $63.33 apiece for the trip. Second-class or emigrant passengers paid only $26.81 but their spartan coaches were hitched to freight trains, which made the run in about four days going west and five or six days eastbound. An average freight train hauled twenty-two cars and, after shedding four or five of them with way freight, climbed the mountains without help behind a forty-ton locomotive.

Through service to Sacramento took about a hundred hours for passengers, not including the transfer delays at Promontory, and cost $111. A person boarding in New York arrived in San Francisco slightly over a week later for a fare of $150. Along the way trains stopped a half hour or less for meals at eating houses. Although the trip was an ordeal even for first-class passengers, it was rapid transit compared to the horrors of earlier travel between the coasts. By June 1870 fares from New York to San Francisco had dropped to $136 for first class and $110 for emigrants, whose coaches were now attached to passenger trains. The change cut almost in half the time emigrants had to endure the bone-rattling ride in the cabooses or converted boxcars that were their accommodations.

Those who could afford it found some relief in the luxurious trappings of Pullman's Palace Cars. George Pullman came early to the Union Pacific with his newfangled sleepers. In 1867 he joined forces with Andrew Carnegie, who had approached Durant a year earlier about providing the road with sleeping cars. Together they offered the Union Pacific a proposal only to have the Trustees demand an arrangement that kept the service under the road's control. As a result the Pullman Pacific Car Company was formed in January 1868 with the Union Pacific taking 2,600 of its 5,000 shares, Pullman 1,200, and Carnegie 1,200. Carnegie then divided his shares among several associates including Bushnell. A contract was drawn up by which the new company was to provide the Union Pacific with sleepers for fourteen years.

Once the transcontinental line opened, travelers flocked eagerly to the new sleepers. It may be true that Pullman's only real invention was railroad comfort, but on the long ride across the West that was no mean achievement. His cars, with their plush, ornate interiors and exteriors painted in rich browns, especially delighted British tourists, although one parson found it "an odd experience, that going to bed of some thirty ladies, gentlemen, and children, in, practically, one room." Success inspired Pullman to a bold new idea in December 1869, when he persuaded the Pacific roads to run a "Hotel Train." To the sleepers he added new dining, drawing room, and saloon cars, thereby eliminating meal stops. By dropping the transfer as well, the weekly special train advertised that it could make San Francisco from Omaha in only eighty-one hours and, with good connections, New York to San Francisco in five and a half days. Although the Hotel Train ran less than a year, it offered a glimpse of what elegance on wheels could be.

Pullman alone could not make the long journey less of an ordeal. Skeptics still asked whether the Union Pacific could operate in winter, and any accident brought demands for inquiry into the road's condition because "over this railroad, at least, the government has a supervision." Fires razed a machine shop in Omaha and much of Cheyenne. Indian uprisings killed a section hand in May 1870 and kept passengers jittery about an attack or derailment. For most travelers, though, fatigue and discomfort were the worst of it. They endured long delays making connections in Chicago and waited interminably to cross the Missouri in what one called "a rickety old ferry boat." Omaha was a mudhole or a dust bowl, its depot a swirl of confusion from which trains departed abruptly with no more warning than the shriek of a whistle and the cry of "All aboard!" from the conductor, leaving those caught by surprise to jump aboard moving cars. The coaches were freezing in winter, stifling in summer. Open windows caught a rush of smoke and hot cinders from the engine. With few exceptions the food at eating houses ranged from bad to awful, with the same fare of steak, fried potatoes, fried eggs, and tea for every meal.

The pleasures came mainly from the passing spectacle of nature: waving oceans of prairie grass sprinkled with flowers; the bounding tumbleweeds of autumn; the hissing fury of a prairie fire choking the air with smoke above rushing rivers of flame; herds of antelope racing the cars; the playful antics of prairie dogs in their villages; occasional packs of coyotes or wolves, elk or a lone bear, and sometimes even a few buffalo; farther west the snowcapped mountains and soaring profiles of rock looming above Echo and Weber canyons; the forlorn isolation of Thousand Mile Tree, Castle Rock, Hanging Rock, Devil's Slide, and the slashing course of the Weber River through its jagged bed; sudden entry into the forbidding land of the Mormons, and beyond that the barren desert, steep, rugged mountains, and the descent into the lushness of California.

For tourists this glimpse of worlds unknown to them was the thrill of a lifetime. To the railroad's employees it was all in a day's work, part of a constant struggle to keep traffic moving under the harshest of conditions and earn a profit in the bargain. On the 136-mile stretch from Rawlins to Green River, for example, it cost the company a hundred dollars every day for a water train to supply the tanks because no source of usable water had yet been found. By 1870 wear and weather had already taken a toll on the facilities at a time when the company was desperate to cut corners. To save money the engine shops at Wasatch were moved to Evanston, those at Bryan to Green River. The timing of such decisions was crucial, for any work on maintenance or repairs had to be done with an eye toward getting the road in shape to endure the coming winter.

As always the burden of resolving the conflict between economy and efficiency fell chiefly on the general superintendent, who was routinely expected to perform miracles on a shoestring. In nineteenth-century America no man had a tougher or more thankless job than the general superintendent of a railroad. He was forever the man in the middle, the lightning rod for every frustration and discontent among directors, employees, shippers, travelers, journalists, politicians, and competitors. To others he seemed a man of immense power and influence; in fact, he was the prisoner of conflicting demands from a dozen constituencies and subject to the whims of an absentee management. His position was especially difficult on the Union Pacific, where management spoke with a divided voice and changed course more often than the Missouri River.

The shabby treatment accorded Snyder ought to have warned Hammond of what to expect. He took office in 1869 amid lavish praise and high hopes. "The appointment of Hammond certainly adds great confidence to our enterprise," John Williams enthused, "he is so well known & respected every where." Oliver was impressed with him at their first meeting, and the Omaha papers regarded him highly from the start. Yet the cheering stopped so quickly that within a year Hammond found himself in disrepute, suspected of the same charges heaped so carelessly on his predecessor.

Hammond was expected to improve the road's efficiency, but Snyder had run an effective operation despite the madhouse of construction and the chaos that passed for policy, and Hammond could do little better. He was expected to impose economy, but that term meant different things to different people. To the directors it meant spending as little as possible in order to boost net earnings large enough to pay interest and ultimately a dividend. Dillon liked to talk about the need to get down to "hard pan," by which he meant paring expenses to the bone. Every time Oliver went west to inspect the road, he muttered privately that the road had too many clerks, too large a payroll, too much excess material lying about unused. He never conceded that the clerks had a use or that the surplus existed for good reasons. Much of it was left over from the race to Promontory, when the company expected to build farther west. More important, the road's distance from its suppliers forced it to stockpile essential items that could not be obtained quickly.

Hammond took the view that true economy meant spending money on upkeep and not "allowing the road and rolling stock to be run down to a point where it costs more to get it up than to have kept it up in the first instance." This was the policy of well-managed roads, but Boston would not hear of it, especially when earnings proved disappointing in 1870. Oliver insisted that the Union Pacific could be run with the same efficiency and economy as New England roads. When Hammond demolished this fallacy, he found himself criticized for extravagance just as Snyder had been. Oakes grumbled repeatedly that "we are not getting the most economical management on the line," while Oliver questioned every expenditure made by Hammond and grew cold to his explanations.

Above all, Hammond was expected to weed out the corruption that Snyder was wrongly accused of permitting to flourish. By the spring of 1870, however, the same charges were being levied at the men under Hammond. As earnings soured, the directors listened willingly to every rumor about the state of affairs in Omaha. Fred Ames, Oliver's son, visited Omaha and came home with tales of "corruption in the purchasing department fully equal to anything alleged against Frost or Snyder." Hammond's enemies, notably Dodge, Wilson, and lobbyist Uriah Painter, seized gleefully on every chance to turn other directors against the superintendent. They had never forgiven Duff for firing Snyder; Hammond was Duff's man and so deserving of payment in kind. "Keep up the fire!" Painter chortled to Dodge. "It is all coming out right." Oakes tried to reconcile Dodge and Hammond but, forced to choose between them, soon embraced the tales of dishonesty drummed incessantly into his ears by men he trusted. Oliver expressed the wistful hope that a visit to Omaha by Dillon and Duff left them *"so scared out there, they wont steal so openly."*

Against these intrigues Hammond could offer little defense. He had spent money on improvements despite orders to "get along with as Little outlay as possible." He had been caught in a barefaced lie on the pileup of transfer cars and damaged the company with his heavy-handed meddling in Wyoming politics. Late in August 1870 Hammond submitted his resignation. Of the executive committee only Duff and Bushnell defended him; the clash so distressed Oliver that he talked again of quitting the presidency. In October he went to Omaha with Duff and Dillon on an inspection trip. Without even consulting the others Oliver appointed Sickels, who accepted the third job offered him in a year. Duff indignantly termed Oliver's handling of the change an insult to him personally and stormed home on the next train.

The turnover in Omaha obscured the one change of lasting significance there. In March 1870 the board, harassed by the Davis, Nounnan, and Bent suits along with a host of other claims, authorized the hiring of auditors at Omaha and Boston responsible only to the company. The attempts to settle claims, coupled with fresh suspicions of corruption in Omaha, impressed the board anew with the utter lack of system in its handling of accounts, purchasing, and inventory. In June Oliver filled the Omaha position with Joseph W. Gannett, who served the company with a dedication that would have delighted Ebenezer Scrooge. Apart from being honest and able, Gannett was as loyal as a palace guard and fiercely independent. He could not be bought, bullied, or badgered. His acerbic, sometimes testy manner annoyed department heads, who resented his prying into their domain but were helpless against the remorseless logic of his methods. By the year's end Gannett had replaced the loose, disarrayed state of accounts in Omaha with a rigid sense of system. His efforts marked an important step toward the creation of an efficient administration. Like every reformer, Gannett found himself forced to fight for every improvement he demanded.

Hammond's dismissal revealed that the infighting was far from over. The redoubtable Hazard added more proof that summer by taking another swipe at Durant. The Doctor demanded the company's help in removing Hazard's case against him to federal court. "I consider we have no interest in this suit as defendants, and should never have been in it," Oliver replied, adding that hereafter Durant must pay for his own defense. But the matter was not so simple. Hazard's suit hampered efforts by the Trustees to settle their accounts; it also complicated McComb's suit and one brought by the state of Pennsylvania for taxes owed. Aware of the dangers posed by these tangled affairs, Bushnell tried to mediate. If Hazard would concede there was "no valid claim against Durant," he promised grandly to "dispose of all the Mc-Comb humbug Claims against Credit Mobilier and the foolish suit of the Pa authorities against Credit Mobilier so that we can at once close up and divide to the stock holders the assetts [sic] of that Company."

Hazard saw little value in dropping a suit so useful as leverage for all his pending claims. In August 1870, while Durant was yachting in Newport, Hazard had him arrested for violating an injunction still in force. The move galvanized some of the Trustees into bargaining with Hazard. After some legal sparring Dillon arranged a compromise in late September by putting

Hazard in one room, Durant in another, and shuttling terms between them. Durant agreed to have all his accounts with the Union Pacific audited and to arbitrate any differences over them. In return Hazard would discontinue his two suits against the Doctor and lift the injunction, enabling Durant to function as a trustee. To gain this concession the Trustees accepted Hazard's version of the Evasion Loan and relieved his obligation. Everyone left Boston convinced the unpleasantness was at last ended. They soon learned to their dismay that it had merely entered a new phase.

* * *

The financial outlook had been going downhill since winter, when attempts were made to settle accounts between the Trustees and the railroad. In February 1870 the amount still owed the Trustees, estimated to be $3.6 million, was to be paid off with eight hundred income bonds and $3 million in new stock. Three months later, however, the Trustees discovered that they had, in Oliver's words, "Divided among our Stockholders more than we ought and we shall not have enough to meet the debts of the contractors." The executive committee obliged by voting an extra $3 million in stock to cover the shortfall. This final payment by the Union Pacific to the contractors brought the total of stock issued to nearly $36.8 million, an amount that in Painter's opinion was "spreading it out *very thin!*"

The final government bonds received that summer were used to settle with Jay Cooke, who had waited impatiently for more than a year. More bonds went to pay off Bent and Nounnan, leaving the cupboard bare of securities for use as collateral. Earnings from the road dwindled, forcing the company to borrow to meet September interest payments. In desperation the company sold its interest in the sleeping car company to Carnegie and Pullman for four hundred thousand dollars. Oliver tried to raise money by selling some of its surplus material and forcing rigid economy on Omaha.

Although Union Pacific securities were doing well, brokers complained that trading was hampered by their not being listed on the New York Stock Exchange. This was finally done in September 1870, enabling some of the directors to operate actively in the securities. The indefatigable Bushnell had been busy since May trying to lift prices with only marginal success. Once the stock went on 'Change, he formed a pool with Oakes, Dillon, and Durant to bull Union Pacific, then selling at 24. That so strange a set of bedfellows joined together indicates how desperate affairs had become. Oakes and Dillon distrusted no man more than the Doctor, yet in this dark hour they placed the entire operation in his hands. Events soon revealed their timing to be as execrable as their judgment.

One problem was Oakes himself. At sixty-six he showed little sign of slowing down despite periodic bouts with diabetes and distress over the stroke suffered by his wife. Unfortunately, he showed even less prudence. To Oliver's dismay he had ignored their mutual pledge to retrench and, if anything, had grown more reckless in his investments. By November 1870 he was deeply in debt and spread dangerously thin. "He seems crazy almost to involve himself in every new scheme," Oliver groaned privately. Fearful that a sudden loss might threaten the shovel works, he extracted another pledge from Oakes to sell off and "get out of his entanglements."

Scarcely had the promise been uttered when disaster struck from an unexpected quarter. The acts of 1862 and 1864 required the company to repay the principal and interest on the government bonds but said nothing about *when* the interest was due. Should it be paid semiannually as due or could it be deferred until the bonds matured? The company assumed the latter since the government had made no request for payments. The law also provided that the company apply 5 percent of its net earnings and half the earnings on government transportation to this account. Originally Congress expected that these sums would take care of the debt, but they fell far short. Secretary Boutwell calculated that the Union Pacific already owed nearly $2.4 million in interest, then startled everyone by demanding immediate payment from all the Pacific roads and branches.

Boutwell's action hit the Union Pacific at the worst possible time. In their frantic search for money the directors were still chasing Huntington for the Central Pacific bonds owed on the track west of Promontory. The board had already authorized an issue of $2.5 million in bridge bonds on the expectation that Oakes could secure a bridge bill when Congress reconvened. Now the situation in Washington had changed radically. Chandler called on the Secretary and found him "entirely unreasonable" on the subject. An alert Painter warned that Boutwell's demand would be "a stunning blow on your credit" and pleaded for the Ames brothers or Alley or Wilson to come at once to the capital. But Oliver was distracted and worried sick by Oakes's financial plight and sent Rollins instead. Before he could act, Boutwell turned another screw. He asked Attorney General Amos T. Akerman for an opinion on whether he could apply *all* earnings on government transportation toward the interest. Until that opinion was received, he announced, the government would pay nothing on its transportation account.

The crisis had a devastating effect on Wall Street, already jittery from rumblings of war in Europe. A panic in Union Pacific securities sent prices reeling downward. On December 15 Akerman upheld Boutwell's withholding of all transportation earnings. The holes in Akerman's logic made no impression on the bears, who seized on it as ammunition to attack the company's securities. On November 15 Union Pacific was selling at 24; it dropped to 18 early in December and plunged to a low of 9 after Akerman's pronouncement. First mortgage bonds crashed to 72, land grants to 50, and incomes to 30. An avalanche of margin calls descended on the pool members, aggravating the desperate state of Oakes's affairs. Suspicion grew that someone was orchestrating the bear raid, and more than one finger pointed at Durant. Rumors flew of impending default on the January interest.

Through it all Oliver seemed paralyzed, helpless to act. "You do not seem to be aware of the critical situation here," Painter scolded, while a distraught John Cisco asked why Oliver had not responded at once with a strong statement. But Oliver could not shake free of his personal torment. Oakes was floundering, unable to sell off any of his securities because the market was in such disarray. On December 20 Oliver learned that a shovel works in which Oakes had large investments was doomed to fail. "Mr Oakes Ames," he gasped, "must lose a million dollars by this opperation [sic]." Eight days later he bowed to the inevitable as one of the proud firms of a proud family went to protest and Oakes declared insolvency. A sense of humiliation overwhelmed Oliver. "It is," he cried privately, "a terrible blow to me."

For five years the Ames brothers had sustained the Union Pacific through its darkest hours. Even now Oliver gamely joined Bushnell, Dillon, Duff, and Williams in endorsing half a million dollars' worth of notes with only the new bridge bonds as collateral. But more money was needed to meet the January interest and the Ameses could no longer be relied on, at least for a time. Bushnell and Duff went looking for outside help and found it in the men who controlled the strongest railroad in the country.

The Pennsylvania Railroad under J. Edgar Thomson and his charismatic vice president, Thomas A. Scott, had embarked on a whirlwind expansion program in the South and West. Eager to secure a transcontinental line, Scott had recently become a director in the Kansas Pacific and organized a construction company to build a road along the southern route. The chance to acquire control of the Union Pacific proved irresistible to a man of Scott's energy and ambition. Approached by Bushnell, Scott brought his friends Carnegie and Pullman into the negotiations. Together with Thomson they agreed to advance funds to carry securities if Bushnell could work out a scheme to relieve the company's floating debt and provide enough money for the Missouri River bridge, which would ensure direct connection across the continent.

Bushnell hurried back to Boston, where he and Duff hatched an elaborate scheme. Scott's group quietly bought about thirty thousand shares of Union Pacific stock at depressed prices, which Duff carried under his name. The executive committee also sold them through Bushnell large blocks of land grant, income, and bridge bonds at prices well above current market figures. The excessive prices were necessary to realize enough funds to satisfy all the claims of Crédit Mobilier and the Trustees on the Union Pacific (the floating debt) as well as provide for the bridge. The Ameses agreed to give Duff their proxies for a board to be organized by Scott.

Later Bushnell waxed eloquent over his sacrifice in helping to carry so large a load of bonds at inflated figures. In fact the bears were still hammering Union Pacific securities, but most directors recognized that prices were artificially depressed and eagerly anticipated a turnaround once the Pennsylvania connection became known. "In a short time they will want to consolidate with us," Dillon confided to Dodge. "I think our Stock & bonds will go as high as you have seen them and higher." That would be true only if everything went well in Washington, where the Pacific roads assembled what the *Tribune* called a "powerful and persistent lobby." Oakes shook off his depression and joined Alley in Washington. Huntington arrived to lend a hand, as did Scott. Bushnell hired Dodge to exercise his magic on the members. "Dodge is a wonderful worker," Oakes marveled, "in this matter of bringing the members around to our views."

While a war of words raged in the press, the lobbyists exerted pressure in every quarter. The first fruit of their efforts came on February 24 when Congress gave the company a charter to build the bridge, issue bonds, and collect tolls to pay for it. The interest dispute initiated by Secretary Boutwell proved rougher going. When none of the compromise proposals suited the Pacific roads, Senator Stewart of Nevada attached a rider to the army appropriations bill directing Boutwell to repay the amounts withheld. The Senate Judiciary Committee concluded that the roads had no obligation to pay the interest until the bonds matured and that Boutwell had exceeded his authority. After lengthy debate the bill passed on March 3, one day before Congress adjourned.

The act restored the payments on transportation but left the interest question unresolved. It would arise again and again. After a few gestures of defiance Boutwell complied grudgingly with the act. The new measures came on the heels of rumors that the Pennsylvania group had gained control of the Union Pacific. As Dillon had predicted, the road's securities shot upward as rapidly as they had fallen. By March 3 the stock had climbed to 32, the firsts to 85, land grants to 75, and incomes to 71. The swing in mood was breathtaking in its swiftness. The crisis had passed and new prospects loomed; Scott was the coming man, and everyone knew what he was capable of. Giddy with relief, the directors assured one another gleefully that everything would go higher still.

One crucial part of the arrangement fell through. On March 7 the old executive committee rescinded and expunged the settlement with the Trustees and Crédit Mobilier. The reasons for this action are not clear, but events would soon punish all sides for their folly. Nearly two decades passed before the three parties could reach agreement again.

That same day, when the stockholders gathered to elect a new board, a smirking Oliver observed "more of a desire on the part of some to hold their place than I supposed." He and Oakes kept their seats along with Atkins, Brooks, Bushnell, Dexter, Dillon, Dodge, and Duff. But several familiar names departed, never to return: Alley, Chapman, Hazard, McCormick, Lambard, and Nickerson. Their places were taken by the Pennsylvania quartet (Thomson, Scott, Carnegie, and Pullman), Levi P. Morton, and Royal E. Robbins. Oliver yielded the presidency to Scott, with Duff retaining the vice presidency. E. H. Rollins was named secretary and later treasurer as well when John Williams resigned after haggling for a year over his salary. The executive committee was put firmly in the hands of the newcomers and their closest allies among the holdovers.

The new regime took hold with obvious vigor. Executive committee meetings were moved to New York. An auditor was hired for the Boston office and an assistant secretary added to the staff. The result, Oliver hoped, would be a "thorough reform in mode of keeping Books." At Omaha Scott improved the financial administration by installing the system used on the Pennsylvania. Fresh efforts were made to settle with Durant and close out the Fisk suit. A committee was appointed to deal with the "legal expenses" incurred by Bushnell during the fight for legislation in Washington. Above all, work on the bridge would resume. The new charter enabled the company to replace its original 10 percent bonds with an 8 percent issue, which Carnegie took to Europe in search of buyers.

Observers agreed that the change marked the beginning of a new era in Union Pacific. Although the Ames family would remain a major influence, never again would it dominate the company. For the next year the brothers devoted their energies to untangling their own affairs. Meanwhile, Oliver thought, the road was in good hands and the future looked bright. "I like the appearance of Scott," he assured Gannett, "and think he will make an efficient and thorough officer." He was not the first to make this judgment nor the last to be proven wrong in it.

Wisely he refrained from passing judgment on his own presidency, which in most respects had been a failure. As chief executive, Oliver had provided little leadership and less direction. Unwilling to make decisions himself, he also refused to trust the advice of anyone in Omaha. He brought to the road no clear sense of system, no vision of its operations, no ability to seize the initiative in financial affairs. Retiring by nature, he loathed conflict and hesitated to assert his authority. The result was a vacuum which others rushed to fill to the detriment of the company. A poor judge of men and easily led (or misled) by others, Oliver found himself continually forced into the position of siding with his enemies against his friends. No one could fault his intentions; they were good enough to pave his own private road to hell. As a financial supporter willing to pledge his resources in hard times he was staunch and true, but as president he was simply ineffective. To borrow a phrase from Walter Lippmann, Oliver was well meaning but unmeaning.

* * *

There were a dozen piers altogether, eleven of cast iron and one of stone, all grounded in bedrock. The iron piers consisted of two cylinders eight and a half feet in diameter and were braced with cast-iron struts and diagonal ties of wrought iron above water. Once planted, they were packed with concrete for a dozen feet to keep out water and filled above that with rubble masonry. As each pier hit bottom the air pump emptied it of water and men scrambled down inside the cylinders to excavate the sand by filling an endless procession of bags and buckets. Sickels found it hard to recruit men to work inside the piers and tried in vain to get Chinese. All the cylinder men suffered from the bends and endured temporary paralysis; at least one died on the job. Sickels was forced to keep doctors and a hospital unit at the site for months while the columns were sunk.

Work on the bridge resumed in April 1870 but dragged for lack of money. For months the directors haggled with suppliers and with one another over terms. Boomer's contract lapsed and was renewed in amended form that did little to resolve the constant bickering. Passage of the bridge bill and the election of a new board gave the project fresh impetus during the winter of 1871. Carnegie agreed to supply Boomer with iron for the superstructure but fell at once to haggling over prices. In April he went abroad and sold the bridge bonds at 80. By then the piers were nearly all in place, enabling Sickels to concentrate on the spans and the approaches. To reach the bridge he had to construct timber trestles 729 feet long on the Omaha side and 250 feet on the east bank.

It took Sickels another year to complete this last link across the continent. When the bridge opened in March 1872, eleven spans, each 250 feet in length and 60 feet above the water, stretched across the Missouri. The final cost was about $2.87 million including $440,000 discount on the bonds. Some thought it would usher in a new age of travel, but their hopes were dashed when the terminus question flared anew in 1871. In preparation for its transfer business the Union Pacific bought the land in Council Bluffs owned by Crédit Mobilier. Not to be outdone, a citizens' committee let it be known that the bonds and depot grounds pledged by Omaha would be held up until the company promised to make its transfers there. Despite the bitter objection of several directors, Duff persuaded the board to accept these terms in December 1871. The Iowa roads countered by refusing to transfer at Omaha; some even balked at using the bridge. "Iowa roads will stick to the boats as long as possible," Gannett observed sourly, "as their officers are part owners of the transfer."

From this stalemate emerged the infamous Omaha Bridge Transfer, which managed to negate most of the advantages offered by the bridge. Westbound freight and passengers were unloaded in Council Bluffs and run over the bridge in dummy trains to the 20th Street depot in Omaha, where they were put aboard another train. The Transfer was treated as a branch with its accounts kept separate from the railroad. By this ingenious method the bridge became not a boon to faster schedules but an obstacle requiring the same number of transfers as the old ferry. The river had been conquered but not the old habit of bumbling policy. Only in one sense did the bridge usher in a new era: the very month of its opening witnessed another unexpected turnover in the management of Union Pacific.

(Above) Digging out of a blizzard on the Laramie Plains. The camera is sitting on a buried snow fence and shows the top of a work train, depot, and section house.

(Right) Digging into the Wasatch Mountains. The two men on the right are boring a hole to set blasting powder at the start of this tunnel.

(Below) Cutting to support the dig: These men are cutting timbers to support the Echo Tunnel, shown in background.

Home Away from Home: These graders working in Echo Canyon have thrown up temporary cabins.

Mess call for one of the construction gangs. Note the improvised seats. *(Charles Weittle photograph courtesy of the Webster History Collection, Denver Public Library)*

Bring the Family: A work train with its crew and some of their folk pose in front of Green River. The picture was taken by C. R. Savage in 1870.

The Fruits of Labor: When payday arrived, the men gathered about the Paymaster's Car, where the two clerks in the doorway handed out their pay. Here the boys enjoy a rest and a smoke while satisfying the photographer's plea for a shot.

The Bridge: This sequence of pictures shows the progress of work on the Missouri River bridge. In this first one, scaffolding is in place to support work on the superstructure of two spans and preparation for a third. Note the pairs of massive columns that were so controversial.

Here the first span is complete and the scaffolding has been torn down and moved to the fourth span. The base of support for the crews, dimly visible through the scaffolding in the first picture, is seen cleanly here beneath the first span.

The completed bridge and its proud engineer, T. E. Sickels.

This view shows even more of the scaffolding removed and offers a full panorama of the columns and the large fill required on the opposite side of the river.

Nature's Wrath: In 1877 a cyclone blew away two of the bridge's spans. This picture was taken shortly after the storm.

The earliest form of Missouri River bridge. When the river froze over one winter during construction of the road, a bridge was built on the ice and supplies moved across until the spring thaw.

14

THE SCANDAL

The storms that roared in every winter always strained the road's ability to function even if they did not shut it down. Operating men, still haunted by the nightmare of 1869, dreaded nothing more than the appearance of a monster storm. During 1871–72 the blizzards came with a vengeance, raging across the plains with a ferocity even grizzled mountain men had never seen before. The first blockaded the Union Pacific at Rawlins on October 12, and three more followed within a month. Sickels was shocked to find that the snow fences, which had worked well for two years, proved useless this season. They had been erected on the northwest side of the track, but this year's storms attacked from the opposite direction. Hastily Sickels ordered new fences built and installed on the south side. Another howler in November showed their inadequacy by closing the road again.

The worst was yet to come. Beginning in mid-December a succession of blizzards detained virtually every train for two months and stopped the road dead for twenty-eight days. A thousand cars of freight piled up along the line waiting to move. The growing tangle of freight and passenger trains made switching a nightmare. Stranded passengers huddled at remote Wyoming stations for days or weeks at a time, enduring the bitter cold on short rations and scant fuel supplies. Their number included a special hotel train carrying the Japanese legation bound for Washington. Passengers amused themselves with card games, stories, songs, and indignation meetings; at Percy two balls were held to relieve the monotony. As their wait stretched out, some of the men pitched in to help the crews shovel snow. In California the Central Pacific partners, furious at losing so much through business, sneered that their men and equipment had kept the line open under worse conditions.

Sickels did everything he could to clear the track. When the new snow fences failed, he rushed all thirteen of the company's snowplows into action. But the snow was packed so densely that the plows could not budge it, and the effort cost him twenty disabled locomotives in a week. Seven snow trains were then fitted out with accommodations for seventy-five men and two weeks' provisions to go in ahead of the plows. For weeks the crews shoveled wearily at drifts towering fifteen feet high. One exhausted band found itself worse off after six days of hard labor and marooned, their engine in a ditch three miles from the nearest food with night coming on. "One of our party had a photograph of a chicken with him," recalled a survivor, "and the six of us lived on that photograph of a chicken 24 hours." When the first trains finally rolled into Omaha, reporters pounced on tales of suffering by the passengers and their bitter denunciations of the road's management. These reports circulated more in New York than in Omaha, where editors defended the work of Sickels and his men. Passengers from four eastbound trains, including Susan B. Anthony, joined in thanking the crews for their unstinting efforts. Charles Nordhoff survived the trip to San Francisco and wrote an account praising the Pacific roads. As more trains arrived, some New York papers revised their earlier censure of the management's performance.

The controversy demonstrated again the inability of Easterners to fathom the severity of western storms. Those who were stranded on the high plains for days or weeks learned the lesson well. So did the company, which launched a program to widen sixty-seven cuts and protect them with more snow fences and sheds. "I am afraid," Oakes lamented, "that we shall get a bad name for our Road by these snow blockades that we shall be a Long while in getting over." The Union Pacific did not soon forget the winter of 1871–72 even when, a year later, the company and Oakes were saddled with a bad name from quite another kind of storm.

* * *

The vaunted Pennsylvania connection departed as abruptly as it had come, drummed out in disgrace without accomplishing anything. As president, Scott seemed to have everything Oliver lacked. He was energetic, charming, farsighted, a skilled negotiator deft at handling people. Restless, mercurial, driven by ambition, Scott transformed these strengths into weaknesses by constantly overreaching himself. Whatever hopes he had for the Union Pacific could not be realized because he had no time to devote to them. His brief tenure with the road offered an early insight into the habit of dissipating energy that would ultimately ruin Scott.

A dispute over the bridge bonds got the new regime off to a shaky start. Bushnell sold half the bonds, Carnegie the other half in England. Neither liked what the other did. "So far we haven't got a cent out of the Bridge operation," Carnegie complained in July, "& I am out several thousand dollars expenses." Somehow Bushnell failed to have the mortgage recorded properly, an oversight that cost the company sixty thousand dollars. The board promptly assessed an indignant Bushnell this amount and remade the indenture. Doubt then arose over whether the new version constituted a first lien on the bridge. Buyers were assured that it did, but Chandler insisted otherwise and urged the company not to touch the proceeds until the question was resolved. "I think the honor of all of us is involved," he told Dodge, and implored the general to help "prevent a fraud or at any rate to clear our skirts of it."

Controversies also raged over the land grants, the coupon account, and the depot land at Omaha, none of which Scott managed to resolve. Important questions on relations with connecting lines demanded more attention than Scott gave them. All these matters, however, paled before the one action Scott's group found time to take. When the stock soared above 30, they could not resist the temptation to sell out at fat profits to themselves. To the older directors this was an unpardonable sin. They were not above speculating in the company's stock, but all held large blocks as a permanent investment. By disposing of their shares, the Pennsylvania group in effect controlled the management without owning a stake in the company. Carnegie even advised Oakes to sell out above 30 because "it was not worth that."

By January 1872 the old hands were united in their determination to oust Scott. He was, Oliver conceded, "an able man" who might have done the Union Pacific much good, "but he is so loaded with work that we have but very little of his service." Duff and Bushnell shopped around for a replacement and found one in Horace F. Clark, the son-in-law of Cornelius Vanderbilt. Clark was president of the Lake Shore & Michigan Southern, the line connecting Vanderbilt's New York Central with Chicago. He and his friends were eager to take hold of Union Pacific and talked of acquiring the Northwestern as well. If that were done, the Vanderbilt group would control an unbroken line of road from the seaboard to Utah. The Boston associates relished the prospect of delivering their road into the hands of the Pennsylvania's arch rival, to say nothing of another rise in Union Pacific stock once the news leaked out.

The bargain was sealed by forming a pool to give Clark's group an option on twenty-five thousand shares at 30. Outsiders were astonished to see the stock jump sharply despite the awful publicity about the blockade; most of the insiders quietly raked in profits. Oakes and Duff thoughtfully alerted Dodge of the change "to prevent your selling thinking you can get it back at a much lower figure" and assured him of a seat on the new board. At the election in March, Scott, Carnegie, and Thomson gave way to Clark, Augustus Schell, and James H. Banker. Pullman kept his place as did Dodge and Levi P. Morton, whose banking firm acted as agent for the company. Clark assumed the presidency with Duff as vice president.

The same lavish expectations that attended the Pennsylvania connection were cheerfully transferred to the Vanderbilt connection. A lawyer by training, Clark was by nature more prudent and cautious than Scott. Whatever his plans for the future, he had first to deal with ghosts. Although Fisk was shot dead in January 1872, his suit lived on in the hands of his widow and a corollary suit by an associate named Pollard. Hazard was stalking Durant again, the compromise having broken down.

Unable to resolve these cases, the new board managed at least to close out nearly four years of confusion over Bushnell's account. Apart from his bond account fight with Hazard, Bushnell owed the company $255,268 on transactions handled by him during the Fisk raid. There were also questions about the $50,000 he was supposed to have paid Fisk in 1868. One committee after another grappled with the matter until June 1872, when the account was "adjusted" by several credits that left Bushnell owing only $30,000. Bushnell had also received $126,000 from the company in March 1871 for his help in taking bonds above the market price and securing legislation from Congress. Of that amount Bushnell paid $24,500 to Dodge for his services, $19,000 to Scott for advances made by him, and kept the balance for what he delicately called "special expenses."

The Bushnell mess exposed anew the pathetic state of the company's records. A check in September 1871 revealed 110 government and 254 first mortgage bonds for which no one could account. H. B. Wilbur, the auditor in Boston, complained that the books had passed through so many hands "it would almost puzzle a Philadelphia Lawyer to get a familiar understanding of them." He and Gannett struggled manfully to impose a system on the maze of accounting practices they inherited. The purchasing department, in Gannett's opinion, was as slovenly in its methods as during the construction years. "A road a thousand miles long," he snapped, "cannot be safely and economically operated without strict discipline in all departments." When the new administration came up with a plan for centralizing all receipts and disbursements in Boston, Gannett threw up his hands in horror and dismissed it as "entirely impracticable."

Every department cried for systematization. The road had been reorganized into two divisions east and west of Cheyenne, with new shops at Evanston to supplant those at Bryan and Wasatch. After three years of operation, however, debate still raged over what policy the company should pursue to attract business. Hammond had assured Oliver in 1869 that local traffic would not even pay maintenance costs, but Nebraska was starting to fill with settlers, the plains offered choice land for cattle grazing, and a mining industry had begun to develop in the mountain regions. The promise was there, but in 1872 the company's freight agent admitted that the western half of the line was "almost without inhabitants." Very little business originated in the area that offered the road its longest and most lucrative haul.

Until these resources developed, the company had to depend heavily on through traffic. But there were already competitors for this business. The most formidable was Pacific Mail, a steamship line that worked the Far East trade out of San Francisco and connected with Atlantic coastal steamers via the tiny Panama Railroad at the Isthmus. The government still sent much of its business by this route despite repeated protests from the Union Pacific. For years Pacific Mail had been a speculative football, a company "run more in Wall street than on the Pacific." Market coups kept its management in constant turmoil at a time when English competition threatened its China trade. The Pacific roads, anxious to divert part of the traffic in tea and silks to the overland route, signed an agreement with Pacific Mail in November 1870. A year later Union Pacific and the steamship company agreed to pool all California business, but fresh scandals rocked Pacific Mail. The way to end this uncertainty, a friend advised Oakes, was to buy control of the Panama Railroad "and completely shut off our competition between here and California."

Pacific Mail had something else in common with the Union Pacific. As a supplicant for government subsidies it was a familiar presence in Washington. So was another competitor, the Kansas Pacific, which in 1870 completed its line to Denver. From there it reached Cheyenne over a subsidiary road, the Denver Pacific. As a result the Kansas Pacific competed for through traffic between Cheyenne and the Missouri River but depended on the Union Pacific for connections west of Cheyenne. The Act of 1864 stipulated that the several Pacific roads operate "as one continuous line . . . without any discrimination of any kind." On that basis the Kansas Pacific claimed it was entitled to the same rates, time, and facilities that the Union Pacific offered its customers.

Thus began the *pro rata* controversy that would plague the company for years. The Union Pacific had no intention of aiding a competing line. It denied the request on the grounds that the cost of transportation through the mountain country west of Cheyenne was significantly higher and ought to be reflected in the rates charged. The Kansas Pacific sought relief from Congress, where Oakes managed to stall action. In 1872, however, the Burlington & Missouri River (Nebraska) Railroad connected with the Union Pacific at Fort Kearney and raised the same question. Instead of demanding that the Union Pacific prorate through business, it tactfully suggested compromise rates to avoid a fight. Other, smaller lines were sprouting on all sides, however, some of them with money from Union Pacific men. On a grander scale Scott was eager to pursue his dream of a southern transcontinental, and the Northern Pacific was building through Dakota Territory.

The first buds of competition were peeping forth in the West, though no one yet suspected they would grow into a vast, inpenetrable jungle. While others built, the Union Pacific struggled to get enough business to pay its bills. Rate agreements were made with the Central Pacific for fruit, the China trade, and other traffic. The two companies established a joint agency in New York and even talked briefly of consolidation in 1872, but nothing came of it.

A new pact with Pacific Mail was concluded and efforts made to secure part of the traffic moving to Montana. The practice of granting rebates to preferred shippers became so commonplace that agents sometimes got in trouble by offering them in situations where full rates could have been obtained. Between 1870 and 1872 earnings increased steadily but still could not meet the voracious demands of interest payments.

Despite its financial woes, the Union Pacific did not neglect expansion entirely. The company and several of its directors put money into the Mormon roads in Utah and the Colorado Central, a rival line to the Denver Pacific. Some still clung to the vision of controlling their own route to the West Coast. When in 1871 a road called the California Pacific announced plans to build eastward to a junction with the Union Pacific, the board joined eagerly in plans for a joint survey. Huntington and his partners quashed the project by grabbing the California Pacific in a shady transaction. The Union Pacific backed off at once, unwilling, in Oliver's words, to "annoy the CPR when no practical result can be accomplished." Even then some directors gazed wistfully toward Oregon, but they were spread too thin in other projects to consider so vast an undertaking. The Oregon branch remained an idea whose time had not yet come.

* * *

The drop in net earnings alarmed Oliver during the summer of 1872. He expected Omaha to provide $400,000 for the July interest and was crestfallen to receive only a fourth of that. In his anxiety he forgot about the effect of the blockade and overlooked the fact that the road had until recently been living off surplus materials from the construction era. Nor did the sources of increased expenses detain him, though he demanded an explanation from Gannett. Instead he simply informed the auditor that "50 per cent of the Gross earnings is all that the Road ought to spend in opperating [sic] expenses" and that he "must collect and send us $400,000 by July 1st." The company limped along that summer on sterling loans and notes taken by its directors. "To have to carry along a RR of this extent out of our private funds is very discouraging," Oliver moaned. Late in June he went to Omaha and, as usual, did not like what he saw. Every shop yielded signs of what he deemed extravagance. Sickels was traveling most of the time, leaving the office to his assistant, Silas H. H. Clark. From this brief glimpse Oliver surmised that the superintendent was "losing his interest in his business."

Things were no better in Boston. Duff was ill most of the summer, and Horace Clark had done little to make his influence felt except on one issue that did not endear him to the Ames brothers. Once in office Clark was besieged by requests for passes, sometimes exceeding a hundred a day. "I am assailed at my house, in the Street, and in my office, and at all hours," he complained. Apart from the annoyance, the practice cost the road large sums in lost fares. The abuse was an old one and impossible to control, but Clark determined to curtail it. His attempt to limit the "deadhead" traffic complicated life for Oakes, who had always distributed passes freely to win political friends for the road. Congressmen were accustomed to receiving them and did not hesitate to apply for their family and friends as well. Some lent or even sold their passes to others. When Clark took steps in the spring of 1872 to shut down the flow, the protests were loud and unsparing. Laudable as his motives were, he soon discovered that his timing could not have been worse.

* * *

The storm broke without warning on September 4, 1872, when the New York *Sun* thundered in bold headlines:

THE KING OF FRAUDS

How the Credit Mobilier Bought
its Way Through Congress

COLOSSAL BRIBERY

Congressmen who Have Robbed the
People, and who now Support
the National Robber

HOW SOME MEN GET FORTUNES

Princely Gifts by the Chairmen of
Committees in Congress.

Exposés were the fashion that season. For months the *Sun,* like other antiadministration papers, had been hammering away at the corruption in Grant's regime, parading one scandal after another before the public, each juicier than the last. Talk of "rings" was in the air, thanks in large part to the *Times*'s campaign against Boss Tweed launched in July. No one realized even dimly that this latest bit of dirt would soon explode into the most notorious scandal of the century or that its legacy would scar a major enterprise for decades to come.

Although the explosion caught everyone by surprise, it had been simmering for some time. The backlog of suits pending included those of McComb, Fant, Duff Green, Fisk, and the state of Pennsylvania—the last to collect taxes on profits made under the Ames and Davis contracts. Until his death Fisk had been considered the most dangerous of these litigants. Painter averred that McComb and Fisk were *"positively in partnership"* and behind the tax suit together. After endless delays McComb had finally testified on behalf of his own case in June 1871, but nothing had occurred since except an angry spat over who should pay McComb's counsel. The board was more worried about Durant, who in February 1872 filed suit against Crédit Mobilier and the Trustees. In retaliation the company threw its support behind

Hazard's suit against the Doctor. No attention was paid to McComb's case until the *Sun* dropped its bombshell in September.

The *Sun*'s exposé consisted almost entirely of McComb's testimony given *fifteen months earlier.* In recounting his claim for 250 shares of Crédit Mobilier stock McComb unfolded his version of the bitter infight for control of the Union Pacific, the huge dividends and inner machinations of the construction company. To buttress his case McComb furnished the text (but not the originals) of three letters from Oakes discussing the need to spread the disputed shares among certain congressmen. On one letter McComb had jotted the names of thirteen congressmen with the figures "2,000" or "3,000" opposite them, which he claimed Oakes had given him. In publishing this testimony the *Sun* gave the public its first glimpse inside what had earlier been called the "Pacific ring." The letters and figures were by far the most damning evidence; they offered seemingly irrefutable proof of an attempt to bribe members of Congress. With great indignation the *Sun* denounced it as "the most damaging exhibition of official and private villainy and corruption ever laid bare to the gaze of the world."

McComb's version was riddled with errors and distortions that the *Sun* not only accepted at face value but compounded. The most notable example involved the figures, which totaled 30,000. Clearly this represented a dollar figure of stock at par value, but the *Sun* presented it as the number of shares offered even though Crédit Mobilier had outstanding only 37,500 shares in all. Every part of the testimony was twisted about to give it the worst possible interpretation. As the *Sun* intensified its attack, other papers joined the chorus. Ironically, the holders of Crédit Mobilier had been trying for a year to dissolve the corporation; their effort quickly melted away in the heat of controversy. Several of the accused congressmen hastened to deny the allegations, and Oakes himself was moved to publish a statement on September 18. In rebutting McComb's statements he asserted that he had never asked Congress for anything except the Removal Act in 1869 and pronounced his labors for the Union Pacific "among the most creditable and patriotic acts of my life." The *Sun* dismissed his "confession" as a "denial that amounts to an admission of guilt."

For two months the *Sun* pounded relentlessly at its crusade. There was no doubt that the motive for its attack was political. Charles A. Dana of the *Sun,* a liberal Republican bitterly disillusioned with Grant, seized eagerly on any dirt that would help Horace Greeley defeat him in the 1872 election. Crédit Mobilier was but one of many mud pies hurled during the campaign. Its list of alleged bribe takers included former Vice President Colfax and the current nominee, Henry Wilson, Speaker of the House James G. Blaine, Garfield, Boutwell, and other prominent Republicans, but not a single Democrat. Greeley's own paper, the *Tribune,* joined the campaign but felt constrained to add Brooks and some others to the list. Predictably, Republican papers ridiculed the charges and the controversy bogged down in partisan crossfire.

None of it helped Greeley, who was routed at the polls and died shortly afterward.

But the stench of scandal lingered after the election, partly because the charge of corruption had behind it a history reaching back to the Act of 1864. A cloud of public distrust hung over the Pacific roads and would cast a long shadow over the careers of those involved in their construction unless steps were taken to dissipate it. No one realized this more than Blaine, a man fired with presidential ambitions. After the election he offered a resolution in the House for a select committee to investigate the bribery charges. On December 2 a committee of five representatives, all lawyers, was appointed with Luke Poland of Vermont as its chairman.

If Blaine hoped the limited charge would confine the inquiry, he was soon disappointed. The hearings opened on December 12 behind closed doors only to be greeted with howls of protest at the secrecy. Garbled accounts of the testimony leaked out, infuriating those who had given it. When the hearings resumed after the holidays, the House consented to open the sessions. Reporters scrambled frantically to get copies of the testimony already given and jostled one another for seats at the hearings. The uproar had an unexpected effect. On January 6, 1873, Jeremiah M. Wilson of Indiana introduced a resolution for a second committee to investigate whether the government had been defrauded in transactions between Crédit Mobilier and the Union Pacific. The charge was vague and clumsy enough to lay open for inquiry the entire tangle of relations among Union Pacific, Crédit Mobilier, the Trustees, and members of the government. A second committee was appointed with Representative Wilson as chairman and commenced hearings at once. Mark Hopkins, who had deplored the washing of Union Pacific's "very dirty linen" in 1869, now had even more reason to shudder.

Oakes followed these developments as if in a daze, taking no part in them and telling those who asked that he did not know what they meant. Convinced that he had done no wrong, he would not submit to intimidation or blackmail. Months earlier McComb had threatened him with the letters in hopes of getting his claim accepted. Now, fearful that events were getting out of hand, he offered again to settle if the investigation could be stopped. Oakes growled contemptuously that he could do nothing about it. On the stand their testimony clashed head-on and was punctuated with testy exchanges. Elsewhere Durant was busy lighting back fires in the form of suits against those he claimed had defrauded Crédit Mobilier.

The situation was confused and volatile, shifting dangerously from day to day. Worn down by his recent struggles, Oakes was slow to grasp these treacherous currents. For six cold winter weeks the two committees puzzled over the complexities and contradictions furnished them by a parade of witnesses. Each day the rooms were packed with spectators and reporters, whose accounts titillated readers as those of Watergate would a later generation. Every morsel of sensation was relished, every rumor savored for what it might produce later. The press drummed a mounting crescendo of righteous indignation against men long since prejudged as guilty. Under the glare of relentless publicity and condemnation some of the witnesses lost their composure, grew confused, and turned savagely on one another to the delight of their audience. As always in the heat of battle, when everyone was running scared, some resisted panic better than others.

The Wilson Committee, with its broader charge, had the best opportunity to unearth the facts of Crédit Mobilier's complicated history. Like most investigating committees, however, Wilson's group lost its way amid the maze of possibilities offered by witnesses, wandering blindly after this lead or that with no guide to help discriminate between dead ends and paths to further revelations. It was all members could do to comprehend the relationships among the railroad, construction company, and Trustees, let alone penetrate the murky forest of factional disputes and infighting. There was about it all an air of byzantine complexity that made everything seem more sinister and suspicious. As in all investigations, every issue was wrenched out of context and thereby rendered even more inexplicable. The presence of so much smoke argued powerfully for a fire of immense proportions lurking nearby even if it couldn't be seen clearly.

The witnesses did little to help. Anxious to protect themselves or the company, they misled more than they informed. No one could have sorted out in a short time the convolutions within the management during the construction years, especially when bitterness and hatred still galled some of the participants. In recalling events Durant was selective, Oliver vague, Dillon meandering, Bushnell and Alley voluble to an extreme, Duff righteous, Ham reticent, Williams indignant, and Oakes helpful in a limited way. Dodge was simply absent. After several futile attempts to track him down, the committee concluded he was "purposely avoiding the service of the summons." Later Dodge offered a lame defense for his conduct, but Chandler told him bluntly that "your good senses vanished! I am sorry you made this mistake."

Oliver left the witness stand feeling he had said nothing that "can be tortured into any injury to the Road. We made large dividends but not more than we had a right to." He must have been shocked by the conclusions in the committee's report, issued on February 20. Handicapped by incomplete evidence and by their even more imperfect grasp of what had transpired, the members dealt harshly with the builders of the road. Sliding easily over the welter of problems and conflicts that had arisen over the years, they declared that the government had done all it promised to do in aiding the project. In return the builders broke faith with government, deceived and defrauded it, and used illicit means to reap huge profits through the instrument of the construction company. Although the committee acknowledged the difficulties involved in constructing the road, it gave them little weight because it never fully understood what they involved.

Nor did it take into account the drastic change in circumstances between the time the road was chartered and the years it was actually built. Instead it condemned the use of a construction company and insisted that the risk "was wholly that of the Government." As to raising funds, the builders "could easily have represented their difficulty to Congress, which has dealt generously with them from the beginning." This bit of naïveté must have provoked more than one incredulous snort. The argument that large sums had been saved in the transportation of mail and troops was dismissed with the blithe observation that the road had "been built chiefly with the resources of the Government." Its promoters had not carried through a huge enterprise at great personal risks but rather "discovered that the road could be built at vast profit without risk, the resources furnished by the Government being more than ample for the purpose." The thrust of the committee's report fit perfectly the public expectation: a corrupt ring had enriched itself at the public's expense through fraudulent means, leaving in its wake a crippled road "kept from bankruptcy only by the voluntary aid of a few capitalists . . . and liable to fall into the control of shrewd and adroit managers, and to become an appendage to some one of the railroad-lines of the East."

Although the Wilson Report told the public what it wanted to hear, it made little impression at the time. The issues it treated were too complex and technical for casual readers to comprehend, and the only remedy it proposed was a suit by the government to recover the illegal profits siphoned by Crédit Mobilier. Whatever the validity of this position, it was not one likely to grab headlines. Lawsuits were lengthy and involved affairs dealing largely in questions too abstract for most citizens to follow. As a result the Wilson Report found itself upstaged by the spicier proceedings of Poland's committee, which dealt in personalities and the very palpable issue of bribery. The stakes here were not an abstruse suit but direct action against members of Congress, perhaps even the impeachment of a vice president.

The Poland Committee generated considerably more heat if not light. Its task was complicated by the fact that several of those charged with taking bribes were no longer in Congress or were about to leave Congress in March. Others, however, such as Blaine and Garfield, were in the prime of their careers and anxious to clear their names. The ferocity of the attack in the press left all of them no choice but to respond; the crucial question was how best to do it. To a surprising extent the outcome of the hearings was shaped by the posture each man chose to adopt.

Oakes never wavered for a moment in his course. Convinced that he had done no wrong, he was forthright if not always truthful in his testimony. While he impressed observers as being disarmingly frank, there was a calculated edge to his performance. He was an experienced politician who knew how the game was played even when, as seemed to him now, the game was out of joint. There was in his demeanor a veiled contempt for his inquisitors, the scorn of a lion harried by jackals. Between Oakes and his detractors there could be no meeting ground. Men who take great risks tend to be careless of proprieties; those who concern themselves with proprieties seldom expose themselves to great risks and understand little about them. The two types are by nature incompatible and unlikely to fathom each other's purposes or show much sympathy for their ordeals.

Oakes offered the committee a prepared statement before submitting to questions. As always he was vague and loose about details but careful not to divulge information that might embarrass his friends. He saw no impropriety in any of his actions. "There is no law and no reason, legal or moral," he asserted, "why a member of Congress should not own stock in a road any more than why he should not own a sheep when the price of wool is to be affected by the tariff." He and McComb tore into each other on a number of disputed points. Alley joined in on Oakes's side, taking care to inform the committee that McComb "had a bad name in the leather trade, which he and I had been engaged in all our lifetime." Durant went after Alley, who replied in kind. The newspapers loved it.

The clash of personalities did much to enliven the hearings but little to enlighten the members. The fireworks began in earnest when the accused trooped to the stand. Blaine and Colfax testified in December and issued sweeping denials; the others did not appear until after the holiday recess. Boyer alone followed Oakes's lead by admitting his purchases freely. "I had no idea of wrong in the matter," he said defiantly. "Nor do I see how it concerns the public. . . . And as the investment turned out to be profitable, my only regret is that it was no larger in amount." Having left Congress in 1869, Boyer had nothing to lose. Nevertheless, the hearings might have turned out very differently if others had followed his example. Instead they chose to pose as innocents, expecting that Oakes would somehow protect them at his own expense through concealment or even perjury. In that belief they woefully misjudged their man.

On January 16 Patterson, Henry Wilson, Bingham, Kelley, and Schofield paraded before the committee to explain how they had accepted Oakes's advice to invest in Crédit Mobilier only to withdraw at the first hint that something was amiss. Their tone ranged from indignation to sorrowful ignorance. Some denied receiving dividends on the shares or even being aware that dividends had accrued for them. Of course they had no knowledge of Crédit Mobilier or of the road's affairs, and not the slightest inkling that their influence was wanted on its behalf. The stock was an investment recommended by a colleague whose counsel they valued on such matters, nothing more. Kelley sniffed that his self-respect would "not permit me to believe it was proposed to buy my legislative action with the profits I should make on an investment of a thousand dollars."

Oakes listened to this performance in grim, tight-lipped disgust, dumbfounded that they would betray him to save their skins without a flicker of hesitation. "Several of the congressmen testified this morning rather denying my statement that they had received dividends," he wrote Oliver that night; "if I am called again will have to put them in an awkward fix."

Five days later Oakes jolted everyone by announcing that he was tired of hearing evasions and fabrications from men intent on making him their scapegoat. He had consulted his memorandum book and would expose the facts of each case. By that time Brooks and James F. Wilson had joined the chorus of innocents. On January 22 Oakes dropped his bombshell by rattling off the details of transactions he had withheld earlier. He cleared Blaine of any involvement but outlined his dealings with Colfax, Brooks, Garfield, Kelley, and Allison among others. The revelations of "Hoax Ames," as the *Herald* called him, stampeded the accused into a mad rush to issue denials or to amend previous testimony for the sake of "clarity." Colfax, Brooks, and Kelley in particular pulled out all the stops in their desperate attempt to discredit Oakes's version of events. Brooks resorted to pleading his case through his own paper, the New York *Express.* A new tension gripped the hearings as the combatants dropped their masks of civility and lashed into one another's contradictions with biting, frosty remarks.

Throughout the wrathful fight Oakes remained unshaken. No amount of invective, no posture of wounded virtue, could dent the impression he had made. On February 11 he devastated his adversaries by producing the celebrated memorandum book itself for the committee. A shaken Colfax tried feverishly to counter its effect with a heartrending tale verified by members of his family, but this precursor of the "Checkers" speech was to no avail. "If Mr. Colfax's explanation is true," sneered the *Tribune,* "he is the victim of a train of circumstantial evidence almost unparalleled in judicial history."

The Poland Committee managed to follow the most obvious threads without arriving at the most obvious conclusions. By some baffling twist of logic it concluded that Oakes was guilty of offering bribes but that no one was guilty of accepting them. Apparently the members were too naïve or dense to grasp what was tendered them. The committee found they were not "aware of the object of Mr. Ames, or that they had any other purpose in taking this stock than to make a profitable investment." The one exception was Brooks. He was both a congressman and a government director, which barred him from holding stock. Yet he was aggressive in soliciting it and the dividend due on it. To conceal his involvement he had deviously put the shares in the name of his son-in-law. The committee, therefore, took action only against Oakes and Brooks. It recommended that both be expelled from the House.

"The Report itself does not Justify the conclusion to which they arrive at all," Oliver sneered. "It is a poor weak thing all over." Neither the Poland nor the Wilson report satisfied the press. Some papers denounced both as a whitewash; others, especially in Massachusetts, defended Oakes. Attention transferred to Congress, where the House took up the Poland recommendations. The Senate appointed its own committee, which brought in a report calling for the expulsion of Patterson. Throngs of onlookers packed the galleries in anticipation of the fireworks. "I shall beat them I think," Oakes promised his daughter-in-law on February 22, "as there has been no wrong or improper act on my part, and [I] cannot believe that the house will so decide, but we shall see how many cowards there are on the Republican side."

Three days later Oakes offered a lengthy, impassioned defense denying all charges and insisting that "for the first time in the history of any tribunal this body has before it an alleged offender without an offense." In recalling the history of his involvement with Union Pacific and Crédit Mobilier, Oakes asserted yet again the bald lie that he wanted no influence in Congress. "It had never entered my mind that the company would ask for or need additional legislation," he protested, adding that "no legislation at all affecting the pecuniary interests of the company was asked for for three years and a half after the date of the alleged sales by me of Credit Mobilier stock." This was patently untrue, but it had no more effect than the better part of his argument, which exposed some of the fallacies behind the Poland Report. What then were his offenses? Oakes itemized them:

> That I have risked reputation, fortune, everything, in an enter-
> prise of incalculable benefit to the Government, from which the
> capital of the world shrank; . . . that I have had friends, some of
> them in official life, with whom I have been willing to share ad-
> vantageous opportunities of investment; that I have kept to the
> truth through good and evil report, denying nothing, concealing
> nothing, reserving nothing. Who will say that I alone am to be
> offered up a sacrifice to appease a public clamor or expiate the sins
> of others?

Amid the clash of angry rhetoric it became clear that a two-thirds majority could not be mustered for expulsion. One of Huntington's lobbyists reported gleefully that the House was "getting sick of the whole Credit Mobilier business." With adjournment looming, the members settled grudgingly on a compromise to censure Oakes and Brooks. The Senate did even less by declining to act on Patterson because his term expired on March 4 anyway. Colfax escaped when the House rejected impeachment charges by the slim margin of 105–109. Thus did six months of acrimony and sensationalism culminate in two meek resolutions of censure. "Good government has received a deadly stab in the shameful result," roared an angry *Herald.* Unfriendly papers would neither forgive nor forget, but Congress had exhausted its limited store of virtue. With a last flourish of irony it passed the notorious "Salary Grab" Act increasing its own pay and vanished into history.

Oliver found no consolation in the result. "It is a great outrage," he stormed, "and is more of a disgrace to Congress than to Oakes Ames." But the damage had been done. Despite support from Grant and his own frantic efforts, Colfax was ruined politically. Crédit Mobilier became a byword for corruption that would haunt Blaine, Garfield, and others for the rest of their careers. Brooks tried feebly to defend himself, pleading ill health from a fever contracted in India years earlier, but few of his constituents listened. Those who scoffed were startled by his sudden death on April 30. Oakes went home to a testimonial banquet given in his honor by some citizens of North Easton. The affair, with its lavish outpouring of support, pleased Oliver greatly even though the *Herald* ridiculed it as "Oakes giving a dinner in honor of himself."

Whatever comfort Oakes drew from this display was short-lived. On May 5 he suffered a stroke and lingered but three days. "Mr Oakes Ames growing weaker," Oliver noted in his curiously detached way, "and Died at 9 33/60 PM." The passing of both Oakes and Brooks less than three months after the hearings gave rise to the belief that they had been hounded into their graves. If so, they were but the first victims of a scandal that would claim others and attach itself leechlike to the railroad.

True to his name, Oakes stood staunch and unyielding until he toppled, never losing faith in the Union Pacific or in the importance of what he did for it. Although he left it tarnished with disgrace for reasons he never comprehended, the company was much the poorer without him. Especially was his presence missed in Washington where, even as Oakes was laid to rest, the attorney general was readying the suit advocated by the Wilson Report.

* * *

Crédit Mobilier endures in myth as the most notorious scandal of its age, the symbol of a generation condemned for its excesses and corruption. No textbook fails to cite it as prima facie evidence for those most popular of historical clichés, the Gilded Age and the Robber Barons. Yet few Americans have any notion of what it was all about. No history of Crédit Mobilier has been written for the simple reason that no one has ever got the story straight, then or now. Instead, the garbled version of events in the two reports has been passed down largely intact by writers unwilling or unable to grapple with its inconsistencies or give it fresh perspectives. It was much easier to borrow from the reports or from the newspapers, which created their own history of Crédit Mobilier for partisan purposes. Unfortunately, their version has survived with all its errors.

Anyone reading the first chapters of this book will understand the difficulties faced by both committees. They could not grasp or compress the complexities and convolutions, the nuances of conflicting personalities, the influence of forces from within and without the company. Every investigation enters its subject through the door of accident and must consider events lifted out of context. The task would have challenged the most dispassionate of investigators, let alone members of Congress dealing in the glare of relentless publicity with an issue charged with political overtones and subject to intense pressure from all sides. Under the circumstances the result was inevitably a botched job, a mishmash of half-truths and stillborn conclusions. Their failure went beyond a lack of perspective. Amid the confusion they left some questions unanswered, missed the point on others, and overlooked many they should have asked. Sometimes they arrived at the right answer for the wrong reason.

In essence the investigations revolved around two issues, one broad and the other specific. Did the builders of the road defraud the government? And did they attempt to gain influence in Congress through bribery? The evidence suggested that the answer to the first was no, and to the second a qualified yes.

In considering the question of fraud, one must recall how drastically circumstances changed between 1864 and 1873. The Union Pacific had been chartered in wartime as a national necessity worth having at any price. That mood vanished quickly and was followed by the usual reaction to the debts incurred by war. The new zeal for economy was reflected in the growing agitation to cut back military operations in the West, which hampered attempts to build the road through Indian country. It also fueled a growing opposition to giving any more government subsidies to western railroads. The most prominent applicants were the Northern Pacific and Tom Scott's Texas & Pacific, but so many projects had lobbyists clamoring for aid in Washington that *all* Pacific roads got a black eye from the brazen tactics of latecomers trying to elbow their way to the public trough.

All found it hard going against the changed mood of Congress. The advocates of reform and economy were at first a tiny minority, but their ranks swelled as one scandal after another rocked the Grant administration. The Democrats seized on reform as a political issue and were joined in 1872 by liberal Republicans disgusted with Grant's regime. It was this savage conflict that transformed Crédit Mobilier into a political football. Certainly the men of Union Pacific had already done much to blacken the road's reputation with their incessant squabbling. The early outcry against Crédit Mobilier died away after the Golden Spike only to revive with a vengeance in 1872. By then the papers were full of ominous talk about "rings" and could equate the Union Pacific with the outrages of another scandal popularized by Charles Francis Adams, that of the Erie Railroad dominated by Jay Gould and Jim Fisk. The fact that Fisk had injected himself into the Union Pacific muddle only made the fit even neater.

This atmosphere colored the inquiries of both committees. Among other things it led Wilson's group into several wrong assumptions, the most striking of which was the belief that the government had provided ample means to build the road. The history of the construction era utterly refutes that assertion. Two forms of aid were provided: bonds and land. The first was actually a loan and by itself simply not enough. Moreover, the bonds were issued *after* construction, were often slow in coming, and were sometimes held up by disputes. An immense amount of working capital was needed to carry the road, which the builders had to provide. Ultimately the land proved valuable, but it furnished virtually no funds for construction and much of it was tied up by a prolonged squabble over the issuing of patents. Important as the government aid was, it contributed only a portion of what was required to build the road. Many of the practices condemned by the committee, such as skirting the stipulation that stock be sold at par, were born not of fraud but of financial necessity.

A second fallacy lay in the Wilson Committee's horror at the resort to a construction company. This was a common device to attract capital to high-risk enterprises. While subject to abuse, it reflected broader problems inherent in building large railroads through undeveloped country. The committee simply ignored these larger problems, choosing instead to indict the builders personally for practices other roads managed to avoid. But in calling up precedents the committee ignored the fact that there were none—that no enterprise on so grand a scale had ever been attempted, let alone one in partnership with the government. The situation and the difficulties it spawned were unique. From first to last the members never understood how monumental a task it had been to construct the road. To this plea they offered a simplistic reply: "If it was impossible to build the road according to the act of Congress, they had no right to build it. They could easily have represented their difficulty to Congress, which has dealt generously with them from the beginning."

Unquestionably the road could have been built more cheaply than it was. The construction was riddled with costly mistakes, miscalculations, and poor judgment arising from the turmoil among its leaders. The builders were responsible for some of these errors, Congress for others (such as the terminus and junction disputes). But mismanagement is a different thing from fraud, a point the committee missed entirely. It failed to see that the boys were not all crooks or charlatans, though some may have been tinged with larceny. Above all they were inept managers who bungled the job, largely because of their constant infighting. Blinded by spectacular and misleading figures on dividends, the committee never even considered the far more pertinent question of management.

The matter of profits was also handled poorly. As noted earlier, the actual cost of the road can probably never be figured accurately. Neither can the amount of *direct* profits realized from the dividends, which were given in securities of dubious and fluctuating value. How much a man made depended on when he sold which securities at what price, and this varied widely. In their obsession with Crédit Mobilier dividends the committee overlooked the generous returns from a wide range of transactions such as commissions, note endorsements, and interest on loans. The boys bickered endlessly over these rights and for good reason: many of them probably earned more from these transactions than from dividends or any other source. Nor did the committee take any account of sequential profits from investment in land, industry, the sale of goods or supplies to the railroad contractors, or a stake in someone's contract as the Doctor had done with Davis. Little mention was made of these items, and the witnesses did nothing to enlighten the members on them. The impression left of huge profits may well have been correct, but if so the dividends were merely the tip of the iceberg.

What then of the charge of bribery? The committee deserved all the ridicule heaped on it for concluding that Oakes was guilty of offering bribes but no one was guilty of taking them. More precisely, it found Oakes had sold Crédit Mobilier shares to members "for prices much below the true value of such stock, with intent thereby to influence the votes and decisions of such members in matters to be brought before Congress for action."

Apart from procedural objections, there are several fallacies in this charge. Kelley was right to feel insulted at the suggestion that his vote could be bought for so measly a sum. The committee admitted as much and also acknowledged that most of those approached by Oakes were already friends of the Pacific road. If the votes were safe anyway, and if no evidence existed that anyone except Brooks accepted the stock as a bribe, what was Oakes trying to accomplish? The committee suggested lamely that he "desired to stimulate their activity and watchfulness in opposition to unfavorable action by giving them a personal interest in the success of the enterprise." But only a handful of members were offered this interest, hardly enough to make an impact in the House.

If this charge missed the point entirely, so did the premise that Oakes sold the shares below their true value. Oakes rightly pointed out that the stock "was not on the market; it had no market value," but he skirted a crucial issue. Here the case of Brooks is instructive. The committee did well to condemn him without knowing fully just how outrageous his behavior had been. But Brooks was not alone in his dogged pursuit of shares. When Oakes offered stock to members at par in the spring of 1867, he found few takers. Later that year, when word of the impending dividends leaked out, some members repented their inertia and importuned Oakes to fulfill his earlier pledge. It was this dilemma that triggered Oakes's need for the additional shares and the subsequent clash with McComb. In these cases he sold the stock at its original price *at the members' own request,* not to bribe anyone but to avoid alienating men who were friends of the road. Few if any newcomers were invited to take shares.

"We wanted capital and influence," Oakes testified. Certainly he wanted votes for the various pieces of legislation the road needed (despite his repeated denials to the contrary), but above all he needed reliable friends to fend off bills hostile to the road. Already some members had discovered the rewards, political and otherwise, to be had in attacking a company dependent on Congress in so many areas. The Brooks case illuminated a facet of this problem that the committee studiously ducked. It bemoaned the rise of large corporations with their immense resources and unsavory influence on political bodies while ignoring the other side of the coin: the opportunities offered politicians to use their position for what amounted to blackmail. Horace Clark got a small taste of this after announcing in February that the Union Pacific would issue no more free passes. Several congressmen registered their displeasure in private. One sent in his pass for renewal with an insolent letter. "Dont say you dont do such things now days, because I know you do renew them," he snarled. "Do as you please. I dont beg. I have got above that."

Crédit Mobilier raised some important questions, but they hovered always out of reach of the investigators. The real issue behind the bribery charge was one that had begun to trouble men poised on the threshold of the corporate economy: conflict of interest. Where were the boundaries between a politician's public and private roles? At what point did personal interest intrude upon his public duty? The committee gestured lamely at the question and offered no suggestions. Business had its own version of this dilemma. In the emerging corporate economy the close identity between a man and his firm was beginning to dissolve. A corporation could be looted in ways undreamed of in a proprietorship or partnership. What were the personal responsibilities of those who owned and/or managed large, publicly held enterprises? When did self-interest conflict with corporate duty? Clear rules had not yet emerged because the revolutionary role of the corporation in economic life was not yet understood.

The investigators ducked these larger questions entirely except in their choice of scapegoats. Here is another reason why Oakes and Brooks were singled out for punishment, although it remained unspoken. Was it only coincidence that of all the men dragged through the scandal, they were the only two holding dual positions? Oakes was congressman, contractor, director since 1870, and major stockholder; Brooks was government director, congressman, and shareholder. The conflict of interest was obvious to the members even if they did not understand its ramifications. In effect they saw smoke and deduced the presence of fire. This factor may have done more than anything else to seal the fate of the two men.

Although the scandal had virtually no impact on these critical issues in the long run, it left a bitter and enduring legacy. Several notable political careers were ruined or scarred for life. Crédit Mobilier became a catchword for fraud and corruption that newspapers applied indiscriminately to all sorts of purported scandals. Among its later clones could be found the Central Pacific, some banks, Canadian, Illinois, and Vermont Crédit Mobiliers, even a "Colored Crédit Mobilier" concerning an inquiry into the trustees of a black church in New York City. Most damaging of all, the scandal and its publicity deranged the relationship between the Union Pacific and the government for the rest of the century. Every attempt to settle their differences would be poisoned by it. Someone would always be there to raise the old war cry that the company had cheated the people out of millions and deserved nothing from the government. For both sides the result would be an endless ordeal of frustration and failure with all the trappings of an ancient blood feud.

* * *

For the Union Pacific in this season of scandal it was the worst of times. Although Clark gave the road more attention than Scott had, he left little imprint on its destiny. The New York Central connection followed the Pennsylvania connection into the graveyard of dashed expectations. During 1872 Clark and Schell worked vigorously to fulfill their pledge of acquiring the Northwestern. Their effort climaxed in November with a spectacular market fight in which they joined forces with a most improbable ally, Jay Gould, to corner Northwestern stock. The Union Pacific gained little from Vanderbilt control of the Northwestern, but the alliance between Clark and Gould was to have far-reaching consequences.

On a smaller scale the Ames brothers and their friends had been working a pool of their own to boost the price of Union Pacific. Their efforts helped sustain the stock in the high 30s at a time when unfavorable publicity about Crédit Mobilier was only the most conspicuous of the company's woes. In November it was discovered that someone was selling forged income bonds to unwary buyers. Painter took charge of finding the culprits and hired the Pinkerton Agency to track them down.

These difficulties and a prolonged controversy over the bridge bonds suggested to observers what insiders already knew: the Union Pacific's finances were in serious disarray. Despite improved earnings, every quarter witnessed another mad scramble to raise enough money for interest. By December Clark had pledged virtually all available securities as collateral and the company was staying afloat with expensive sterling loans. A report from the finance committee revealed the grim fact that obligations maturing by April 1 totaled nearly four million dollars. To pay this floating debt and redeem the income bonds, which fell due in 1874, the board decided to issue sixteen million dollars in new sinking fund bonds. Tempers flared as directors argued over terms; one meeting broke up after a choleric exchange between Clark and Brooks.

As a stopgap the executive committee assessed ten directors sixty thousand dollars each to fund January coupons. Ever loyal, the Ameses contributed their share but were too distracted by the congressional hearings to do much else. Duff opened his purse grudgingly, and Dillon could not renew notes because he was overextended. In February the board split over whether to pay interest on the income bonds. When another pool was hurriedly formed to pledge the funds, Clark and Schell refused their aid. A curious lethargy seemed to have settled on Clark. Duff and Morton were so upset with him that they made overtures to Oliver about a palace coup to restore him to the presidency. Oliver agreed that Clark did "not take so strong an interest in the road as I think he ought," but Oliver had troubles enough and rebuffed what he deemed an insincere offer. The old officers were reelected without opposition but Dodge, Pullman, Morton, Brooks, and James H. Banker retired from the board. Their successors included such familiar faces from the Boston crowd as Ezra Baker and Oliver Chapman.

After the election the board did little more than protest feebly against the findings of the investigations. Clark, Duff, Oliver, and Bushnell all fell ill and were slow to recover. The sudden deaths of Brooks and Oakes deepened the pall of gloom hanging over the directors. Once again the company's affairs drifted like a ship caught in a storm with no one at the helm. Money was needed for notes maturing in April but Clark seemed completely dispirited and would do nothing. Wearily Oliver, Duff, and some others pledged their own securities to raise the funds. That spring the Attorney General launched the government's suit against the company. Earlier Congress had authorized the withholding of all earnings on government business, thereby reopening that dispute. The dual attack sent Union Pacific stock reeling into the 20s despite the effort of Oliver and his friends to sustain it.

In May Clark shook off a bout with rheumatism to go out over the road. Buoyed by a hero's welcome in Omaha, he came home three weeks later pleased with what he saw. On June 16 he summoned Rollins from Boston to discuss the government suit, adding that "since my return from the West have been some-what unwell with a kind of fever." Three days later he was dead at the age of fifty-eight. The stock dropped to a low of 22 as the guessing game began on who would assume the leadership of Union Pacific. Atkins and Alley pressed Oliver to take the post but age, the loss of Oakes, and other commitments stifled any ambition that might have stirred. He and Atkins went on the executive committee, and Duff filled the role of acting president until the next election.

A week after Clark's death the directors were obliged to lend the company another four hundred thousand dollars for the July coupons. The government enjoined them from paying interest to any of the sixty-two defendants in the Crédit Mobilier suit. In the confusion that followed, all payments were delayed for two days, triggering fears that a default was imminent. Not even in the days when the Doctor held court had the affairs of the company seemed so mixed, the future so unpredictable. Amid the rubble of Crédit Mobilier, with Oakes and Clark gone, who remained to assert leadership? Who would make policy and what would it be? What would become of Clark's large holdings in the company? And always there was the frantic scramble for money, an ominous weakness at a time when the country was heading into the worst depression in its history.

15

THE NEWCOMER

Although prospects for the fall trade looked good in 1873, there were enough contrary signs to make cautious men uneasy. Money grew tight late in August, a few small houses failed in early September, and an insurance company went down. On September 17 stock prices dropped sharply. Two days later, before the Street could catch its breath, the prestigious banking firm of Jay Cooke & Company suspended and was quickly followed by Richard Schell among others. Thirty more houses folded the next day as prices crashed and panic engulfed Wall Street. Several banks, including Union Trust, closed their doors. Overwhelmed by a torrent of desperation selling, the stock exchange suspended trading until further notice. A chorus of cheers greeted the decision. On September 23 the *Tribune* announced that the panic was over; next day the firm of Henry Clews failed.

Alternating currents of gloom and optimism swirled through the financial district. The exchange reopened for trading on September 30, but three days later the house of G. B. Grinnell failed and was summarily expelled from the exchange for "irregularities." This was an ominous development for Union Pacific. Horace Clark had been a special partner in Grinnell's firm, which specialized in Vanderbilt securities, and no one knew for certain what had been done with his Union Pacific shares. In the weeks ahead other houses went down as prices continued their slide. The Street seemed dazed and demoralized, unable to get its bearings. As the wave of panic slowly receded, most observers predicted that business would gradually resume its customary channels. No one dreamed that ahead lay six years of depression, the longest and deepest yet endured by Americans.

Oliver was touring the road when the storm broke. He came home to find the office in chaos. Coupons had to be paid, large sterling loans were due, and no one had money to lend. Augustus Schell, hurt by the failure of his brother's company, could do little. Morton, Bliss pronounced the exchange market dead and grudgingly turned only a part of the sterling loans due. Worn down by the ordeal, a disheartened Duff was ready to let the company go to protest. "I regret that you and some other Gentleman connected with the UP are under the delusion that I have a large amount of money on hand," he snapped in response to Oliver's request for a hundred thousand dollars. The pressure drove him back to the sickbed, leaving Oliver, Atkins, and others to carry the load. By some frantic scrambling they scraped up enough funds, although Oliver was obliged to pay 18 percent for one loan. Gannett was ordered to impose strict economy and rush all available receipts to Boston. The auditor complied readily and even injected a rare note of hope by observing, "I think it has been pretty clearly demonstrated during the past few months that Providence is on the side of Union Pacific RR."

Gannett helped Providence along by delivering enough funds from Omaha to ease the crunch in Boston, but the panic had disrupted markets for the new sixteen-million-dollar mortgage and also broken its trustee, Union Trust Company. Some directors wanted the mortgage redrawn on terms more favorable to the company, which meant more delays in getting the bonds ready. Money had to be found for sorely needed locomotives, and there was the forthcoming election to consider. With the Vanderbilt crowd no longer a factor, Duff was leery of allowing outsiders "who have contributed nothing toward the result reap the reward." The time to buy stock was now, he urged Oliver in November, but no pool was formed to control the election. As late as January 28, 1874, Duff was confident no one was corralling stock.

He could not have been more wrong. Someone was buying heavily, and when the name leaked out in February it was enough to strike terror in conservative hearts. "There seems to be a general impression," Oliver noted, "that Gould has from 100 to 125,000 Shares of Stock in his control—I feel that he will not use his Power adverse to the interests of the Road."

* * *

First it was Tom Scott, the man of irresistible charm and indefatigable energy, who promised to lead the Union Pacific out of the wilderness. Then it was Clark, the staid, sober representative of the Vanderbilt interests, who donned the mantle of savior. The Pennsylvania Railroad and the New York Central—what more powerful or prestigious connections could a company have? But the one slunk off the train in embarrassment at an early stop and the other died enroute on a journey heading nowhere. In their place came a financier looking to come in from the cold.

Irony crackled over the situation like St. Elmo's fire. To the dispirited old guard of Union Pacific it was as if history itself mocked their ambitions. They craved nothing more than respectability, yet found themselves at the mercy of the most notorious man on Wall Street, the former partner of Jim Fisk, who had caused the company no end of grief. Well might they be pardoned for not rushing to embrace a man whose chief reputation was for wrecking properties. Personally he was unknown to any of them except for Oliver, who was still negotiating to buy steamboats from him. Like everyone else, they did not know what to make of him. Jay Gould was the most mysterious and elusive figure on the Street, a loner whose career had at age thirty-seven already become more legendary than real in the minds of those struggling to follow its convolutions.

What happened? A decade later Gould told a simple tale of seeing Clark shortly after the latter's tour of the road. Impressed by his report, he put in an order for some shares from 30 down. When Clark died suddenly, his broker dumped his Union Pacific on the market and Gould's order caught far more of it than he intended. It was a pleasant story but only a prologue. A fuller version surfaced much later from David B. Sickels, a banker and brother of the superintendent, who claimed that Gould had commissioned him to buy secretly all the Union Pacific available in the market. Sickels did his work so well that by February 21 Gould controlled about 132,000 shares. Gould then asked him to bring Dillon and Atkins to his house on Fifth Avenue where, according to Sickels, he met them for the first time. Gould made it clear that he did not wish to fight anyone but was amenable to joining forces with the Bostonians. The suspicious Duff also saw him and was satisfied that Gould was "all right." Dodge had several talks with him and reported that he "intends to stick to road and make it a big thing." But doubts lingered. "I would be more afraid of combinations to buy up some eastern road now than ever before," Dodge added. "Gould is a very *smart man.*"

A bargain was quickly struck to organize the board with Dillon as president and Atkins as vice president. Gould desired only a place on the executive committee, which remained firmly in the Bostonians' hands. Four of his brokers filled seats on the board but did little else. The election went off smoothly, the transition was handled tactfully, and the new arrangement was, in Oliver's words, "quite Satisfactory." The public knew nothing of the change until election day, and papers hostile to Gould responded with biting criticism. The *Times* quoted indignant merchants as deploring "the elevation of Mr. Gould to a social and commercial recognition, following upon the heels of an infamous career. . . . Bankers likewise look upon Mr. Gould as a very shaky individual, with no fixed policy of action beyond self-advantage." There was widespread belief that it would be Erie all over again. An alarmed Buffalo banker railed privately to Rollins about the New York "thieves" who would *"steal* all its available money, run up a large floating debt, and ultimately leave the long bond holders out in the cold."

The vehemence of these reactions suggested that the Union Pacific had fallen into the worst possible hands. Like so many predictions based on an imperfect grasp of past performance, this one was dead wrong. Gould and the company were well matched in that both had tarnished reputations they were anxious to redeem. Just as Crédit Mobilier had dishonored Union Pacific, Erie and the Gold Corner of September 1869 had covered Gould with infamy that would hound him all his life. Both harbored a deep need for respectability in the eyes of a hostile public. Moreover, Gould seemed to possess a magical gift for making money and was generous in sharing opportunities with his associates. This talent appealed greatly to Oliver in his declining years, and his associates were not loath to profit from it.

During the next five years Gould astonished his critics by giving the Union Pacific the strong, unified leadership it had always lacked. He not only stayed with the property but gave it careful, unflagging attention. Everyone knew of his genius for finance but no one suspected his capacity for mastering every phase of railroading. His alert eye caught every detail, grasped every possibility. He did his homework with a thoroughness that astounded less driven men. At heart Gould was a mathematician who thrived on the challenge of knotty problems. His voracious intellect cut through complexities to expose their essence. There was something awesome in his ability to get at the crux of a matter. Everyone who worked with him echoed Andrew Poppleton's recollection that "in quick, clear, intuitive insight into complicated business questions, promptness in decision and celerity in action, I have never met a man who bore any reasonable comparison to him. He was mild, kind and courteous in his intercourse with employees . . . never looked backward in case of disaster or upbraided or made complaint, but bent his entire energies to secure better results in the future."

Some were slow to grasp the full extent of his genius because he was so quiet and unassuming in appearance. Physically he was a caricaturist's delight: a small, frail body with tiny, almost feminine hands and feet crowned by an oversized head from which his dark hair had already begun to recede, exposing a massive forehead. A thick, wiry beard masked his firm jaw. The nose was prominent and overshadowed only by his eyes, deep wells of black radiating intensity and mystery that took in everything while revealing nothing. Gould's voice was light, almost musical in tone. He was a man of few words, spoken so softly they barely rose above a whisper. In meetings he never dominated discussion but let it drone on before expressing succinctly and precisely the point others had been groping for. He did not command or dictate but suggested politely. Far from being an imperious figure, he was content to dwell in shadows and let others take credit. For a man consumed by ambition, he was strikingly unaffected by considerations of ego or vanity.

Yet behind this meek, unpretentious demeanor lay not only genius but a driving force so elemental that death alone could still it. In time the old guard would come to appreciate the full extent of Gould's powers, though even they could not suspect the legacy he would leave. No man did more to shape the railroad map of America or the structure of the industry than Jay Gould. His imprint on the Union Pacific was so profound as to be rivaled only by that of E. H. Harriman, whom some cynics regarded as the second coming of Gould. In fact the two men had far more in common than anyone has ever realized.

*   *   *

Gould's style of managing the Union Pacific was unique in several respects. He held no position other than director and member of the executive committee—not even a seat on the finance committee. Contrary to predictions, the office was not moved back to New York; meetings of the executive committee floated between there and Boston. Gould was content to leave routine business to the Bostonians and attended only those meetings where important policy questions were considered. Dillon performed executive duties but was in New York where he could consult with Gould. Although far from being a figurehead, Dillon decided nothing without first seeking Gould's advice. A close bond between them formed quickly. If Sickels was correct in saying the two men first met only months before, it marked the beginning of a partnership that lasted until Dillon's death.

At sixty-two the tall, handsome Dillon was as rugged as Gould was fragile. A leonine mane of white hair and snowy sideburns framed his chiseled features. Although his approach to business was brisk and all consuming, he lacked Gould's decisiveness. Courteous and pleasant of manner, he also had a hot temper. Like Gould he had risen from humble origins in true Horatio Alger fashion. As a contractor beginning in the 1830s he had virtually grown up with the railroad before drifting into Wall Street. After the death of his partner in 1875, Dillon allied himself with Gould for the rest of his career. Charles Francis Adams later asserted that Gould's word was law within Union Pacific and "Mr. Dillon was his representative. Mr. Dillon never consulted anyone except Mr. Gould, and Mr. Gould was in the custom of giving orders without consulting Mr. Dillon at all."

Adams's observation was only partly correct. Gould possessed authority but did not exercise it in so imperious a manner. He did issue requests or instructions to the treasurer, lawyers, and others on his own, and his orders were followed. No one doubted who was in command, but Adams knew little about Gould's habit of consulting with Dillon, Oliver, and others before he acted. His appetite for information was voracious; he gathered data incessantly from every available source. Like John D. Rockefeller, he preferred decisions reached by consensus. Moreover, he was careful to observe the proprieties of Dillon as president and Oliver as leader of his Boston associates. His delicacy in handling these relationships enabled them to work well together despite occasional disagreements.

If anything Gould resembled a party boss who exerted authority through others while remaining in the background. He relied on a cadre of loyal brokers in Wall Street and on Dillon, Oliver, and other associates for his dealings in a host of enterprises besides Union Pacific. To run the road in this way he needed an able man in the field whose judgment could be trusted by those in the East. He found such a person in Silas H. H. Clark, who was promoted to general superintendent in April 1874. Within a short time Clark became not only Gould's chief operations man but also one of his closest friends.

Clark had much in common with Gould. They were the same age, began life as farmboys, were largely self-educated, and shared a passion for books. Clark started in railroading at the bottom and had worked his way up to conductor when Dillon spotted his ability and put him on a small eastern road as general freight agent. In 1867 he came to the Union Pacific in that position and was promoted a year later to division superintendent. When Sickels made him assistant general superintendent in 1871, Hoxie observed that Clark was "not the man for the place. His head is not big enough." Dillon did not share this opinion, and most likely he was the one who recommended Clark's elevation to superintendent with authority to "make any changes . . . you consider desirable."

A man of striking appearance with luminous eyes and a prominent nose, Clark masked his chin with a long, scraggly beard. Like Gould he was dedicated, reticent, prone to overwork, fragile of health, sensitive yet tough, and above all a survivor. Cautious to an extreme, subject to recurring bouts of insecurity over his position, he required constant reassurance from Gould. He had reason to feel uneasy, for Gould's style of management put him in an awkward position. While his official orders came from Dillon, he also received a constant flow of requests and instructions from Gould by private letter. Clark understood clearly which had priority, but the role of serving two masters was a difficult one. In time it grew even more complex, for as Clark drew closer to Gould he found himself at once the servant of Union Pacific and the trusted agent for Gould's personal interests in the West. If the two roles fell into conflict, as eventually they did, Clark would find himself caught between them.

This triangular relationship could have been disastrous in running a large enterprise, yet paradoxically it produced the most unified management the Union Pacific had ever known. The bitter infighting that had crippled its leadership for a decade vanished almost overnight thanks mainly to Gould, who made a potentially divisive system work through the rapport he achieved with Dillon, Clark, and Oliver. His relationship with Clark marked a particularly dramatic break with past practice. Unlike Durant and Oliver, he trusted the superintendent and relied on his judgment. When differences arose, he did not question Clark's integrity but simply discussed the facts of the case. He knew how to delegate authority and insisted that subordinates use their authority fully.

Here were the supreme ironies. The notorious wrecker of properties provided the Union Pacific with its first taste of effective, cohesive management by giving closer attention to every aspect of its operation than any previous officer had done. The man renowned as a loner showed his new associates how to work together and, in the bargain, cultivated friendships that would last a lifetime.

* * *

"Am glad you are left in," Painter wrote his friend Rollins after the new board was elected. "I hear the future workings of Co are in dark." They were more in a state of limbo. Scott and Clark had inherited bad situations, Gould a desperate one compounded by the repercussions from Crédit Mobilier. The agenda of unfinished business was huge and resisted efforts to impose fresh solutions on old problems. In everything he undertook Gould faced the same challenge: how to free the company from the shackles of its own past.

Aware that the company lacked both credit and credibility, he saw that restoring the one would vastly improve the other. The day after his election Gould brought to a head the acrid debate over the new sinking fund bonds. He proposed redeeming the income bonds at a rate of seven new sinking funds for six incomes; the board argued some more and finally amended the rate to six for five. Neither Gould nor Dillon liked the low rate of exchange, but both were anxious to redeem the incomes before they matured in September and knew delay would be fatal. Wilson denounced the rate as "a speculative movement at the expense of the company. It is wrong, utterly and inexcusably so."

The bond exchange was crucial in two respects. It was Gould's first chance to show what he could do for the company, and for the old guard it became a test of whether Gould was working for Union Pacific or merely using it to advance his own interests. Eventually they would discover that Gould had an uncanny ability to do both at the same time. For now they followed his lead with a reserve of skepticism.

Gould saw other advantages in the exchange apart from replacing a 10 percent bond with an 8 percent one. He wanted to get rid of the large floating debt carried at high interest rates on short-term notes. If the sinking funds could be established as a sound investment, the five million dollars not needed for exchange could be sold at a good price to pay off this debt or used as collateral on better terms than the incomes fetched. Most important, a successful refunding would do much to restore faith in the company's credit, which in turn would help the price of its stock. For these reasons Gould launched an imaginative, carefully orchestrated campaign.

In promoting the exchange Gould utilized all the newspaper contacts at his disposal and urged his associates to bring their influence on prominent bankers. By these means even the Buffalo banker who denounced Gould's accession was induced to convert his bonds, but in mid-August the campaign stalled and some of the associates lost heart. The bonds would come in, Gould promised, once holders realized the true value of the sinking funds. He proposed a pool of a million dollars to buy out dissidents and agreed to take half of it himself.

Although three million dollars' worth of incomes remained unconverted as the deadline neared, Gould insisted that success was assured. The bears would probably "pitch in the stock & sell it down some," he warned Oliver, "but it can only be temporary & as soon as the Income Bonds are fairly out of the way it will go up higher than before. I cannot be frightened into selling a share of my stock and never had more confidence in the future of the property." He would reiterate this theme constantly over the coming months to assuage the doubts of his Boston associates that he was in the fight to stay. "The stock is worth fifty," he added, *"dont be induced to let a share of yours go*—let others sell if they like."

Throughout September Gould promised confidently that the stock would go to 50, the sinking funds to 80. Once at 80, the remaining bonds would easily take care of the floating debt. Most found that hard to swallow since the one hovered in the low 30s and the other in the 60s, but Gould did not recant. To show investors "what security there is behind them," he had a list of the company's assets published in major papers. As more bonds came in and the price inched toward 70, even Atkins became a believer. By September 11 the balance still out had dipped below two million dollars. "We will now all make a pull on the next million," Gould chirped, vowing to get there in ten days.

Gould's optimism was infectious to men whose hopes had been blasted so often. When 1875 opened, the sinking funds were being quoted at 81. In February the exchange was terminated with only $250,000 of incomes still out. Nearly a fourth of the $10.4 million in land grants had also been redeemed and more were being called in. When these were extinguished, the sinking funds would become a first lien on the land grant, making them even more attractive. The floating debt was dried up in March when Gould formed a pool among the associates to pay it off and take sinking funds at 90. These, he told Rollins, "I shall hold for permanent investment."

* * *

The campaign had been a brilliant success, but Gould was never content to operate on one front alone. Already he had formed a strategy for turning the company around. The barometer of its success was the price of Union Pacific securities, which reflected investor confidence in the property. To some extent the market for them could be manipulated, which Gould did not hesitate to do, but over the long haul only sound performance would keep them at respectable levels. "I have no fears about . . . the future of the Union Pacific stock," Gould told his associates repeatedly. "It is really selling at about half its value." This belief spurred him to develop the road's potential, a goal that required more than liquidating the floating debt and restoring the company's credit. Earnings had to be kept high by strict economy and the cultivation of new business. Good performance would in turn enable the company to pay dividends, a sure tonic to security prices. If all this could be done, the company would prosper; so would Gould and the associates who followed his lead.

A disinterested observer might have dismissed these goals as the fantasies of a madman. They were difficult enough to achieve in the best of times, but Gould proposed to restore the credit and boost the earnings of a dishonored corporation in the teeth of a depression. Gould delivered what he promised, and he accomplished much of it within a single year.

Reduced expenses alone were not enough to improve earnings. New sources of business had to be developed, but that took time. Meanwhile the road depended heavily on through traffic, which was at the mercy of competing routes. Maintaining rates at profitable levels on this business required agreements with the Central Pacific at one end and the Iowa roads at the other. These roads bickered constantly with the Union Pacific over the proportion each should receive on through rates. By 1872 the Iowa roads had banded together in a pool to present a united front in the division of rates. For nearly a decade Gould waged a bitter struggle to break the hold of the Iowa Pool, with results that ultimately transformed the railroad map of the country.

The gravest threat to stability was not the Iowa roads but Pacific Mail, which in December 1873 declined to renew the pooling agreement of the past two years. With a management wracked by internal dissension and its traffic threatened by new competitors, the steamship company was a powder keg in search of a match. During the spring of 1874 Gould and Dillon tried to negotiate a new pact but could not get what they deemed reasonable terms. The factions in Pacific Mail were distracted by a rancorous fight for control. One group, associated with the Panama Railroad, wished to compete vigorously with the Pacific road and accused their rivals of being under Gould's influence. The election left both factions entrenched on the board and Russell Sage as president. Later Sage would become Gould's closest ally, but at this time they were not associates. Gould rejected the steamship company's demands as "exorbitant" and resigned himself to a "sharp competition with them which is no doubt one of the principal causes of the decline of earnings of U.P."

As the rate war dragged on unabated through the summer, Gould vowed to find a solution. He tried first to restore the old agreement, the loss of which in his view had cost the Union Pacific a million dollars, but Pacific Mail continued to divert its Far Eastern traffic via the isthmus. "It is outrageous that we have to carry our California business at so low rates," Gould stormed, but the steamship company would not budge. In September he conceded glumly that "we shall have to grin & bear the bad effects of this competition for some time longer." With no hope of peace in sight, he and Huntington explored a new tack: Why not create a rival steamship line owned jointly by the Pacific roads?

Huntington was willing but cautious. He did not yet know Gould well and considered him "a clever fellow, but . . . the most reckless speculator in the world, I think." He agreed to send an agent to charter ships in England but warned Stanford that "if we go into this, it must not get out of our hands. . . . The more I see of these U.P. people the more I am convinced that . . . this steamer company must be controlled by us." When Sage rejected a new settlement proposal, Huntington reluctantly embraced the idea of a new line provided it had a California charter and offices in San Francisco. Gould made no objection and urged Huntington to arrange the details with Dillon as quickly as possible. Huntington thought Gould wanted fast action because he was short of Pacific Mail and eager to knock the price down by publicizing news of the rival line. "I rather Gould were not in," he confided to Crocker, "and I will endeavor . . . to tell him so, of course, in a friendly way."

There was probably some truth in this view, but Gould had a deeper motive. His program to boost Union Pacific securities required a strong performance from the railroad, which was being ruined by the competition with Pacific Mail. Aware that Pacific Mail was in financial trouble, he intrigued through some friends on its board to force its affairs to a crisis. The explosion came in December when the factions pelted each other with charges of fraud and mismanagement. After a stormy session Sage resigned as president of both Pacific Mail and the Panama Railroad. On the heels of this uproar a House committee decided to investigate charges that Pacific Mail had earlier used bribery to obtain an increase in its subsidy. The hearings, like those on Crédit Mobilier, dragged the company's name through the mud for an entire winter. This embarrassment was precisely what Gould wanted, for reasons that would shortly become clear.

Huntington was ready to move on the new company, but a snag developed when Stanford forwarded a charter capitalizing the Occidental & Oriental Steamship Company at $10 million. Gould and Dillon protested the figure as twice what they expected; neither they nor the Boston directors cared to subscribe so large a sum. Huntington had to admit the justice of their complaint. "Just why you made the capital so large as $10,000,000 I do not know," he grumbled to Stanford, "I suppose you do." But he was also losing patience with delays he attributed to Gould's trying to manipulate the stock. "The fact is," he concluded, "I see no other way to have peace and control the China trade than for us to control U.P."

Huntington was wrong. The delays sprang from genuine concerns. Boston grew reluctant after Bartlett advised Oliver that they could not "subscribe safely to so large a capital" and Dillon refused to move without approval from the executive committee. Unwilling to lose more time, Huntington and Gould broke the logjam in January 1875 by asking the Bostonians "to subscribe to $500,000—or more if you desire and we will take the balance."

Oliver alone responded by taking $500,000; of the remainder Gould subscribed for $2.5 million and Dillon $2 million.

The formation of O & O as a rival line, coupled with the investigation in Washington, sent Pacific Mail reeling to 31, its lowest price since 1873. Gould was indeed hammering the stock as Huntington suspected, but for quite another reason. As the bears pounded it down, he switched sides and bought heavily. In one week the price zoomed back to 41 and the Street was startled to learn that Gould controlled the company. He joined the board at once along with Oliver and Dillon, who assumed the presidency. There would be no more wasteful competition, Gould announced, and within days transcontinental rates were raised sharply. The increase, he told Rollins, "ought to add ten per cent to our stock & will help all our securities."

To ensure harmony Gould offered Huntington a seat on the Pacific Mail board. Huntington wavered, then declined. He could not shake the suspicion that all of Gould's maneuvers in Union Pacific and Pacific Mail were another of his classic campaigns to run stocks up and unload them at the top. "I am fearful they will play us false," he admitted, "although I am not sure that I have any reason for thinking so." Until he was more certain about Gould's motives, Huntington treated his friendly overtures gingerly. The thing to do, he counseled an associate, was "avoid a quarrel with him, and watch for the time to come when we are ready to control the U.P., and then go in and get control of it."

* * *

While orchestrating the refunding and Pacific Mail campaigns, Gould kept a close eye on the road's performance. Local business suffered from falling agricultural prices, which also slowed emigration to the plains. An invasion of grasshoppers in 1874 devastated the corn crop in Nebraska, and depressed prices slowed the ore business in the mountains. In September Gould went out with Dillon and Oliver to see for himself. On this first inspection trip Gould set the pattern for those to come. Although welcomed lavishly, he was not one to be whisked through ceremonies with local dignitaries. His alert, restless eye scrutinized the road, the land, farms, ranches, mines, towns—any detail that brought him intelligence. At every stop he pumped employees for information or sought out locals who could tell him what he wanted to know. Officers learned to prepare for his arrival like students cramming for examinations. Local needs interested him, as did the potential for new markets or business, what services were needed and what obstacles loomed.

What he saw on this trip satisfied him that Clark was doing a splendid job despite adverse conditions. He stressed to Clark the need to match if not exceed the previous year's earnings and to curb expenses. "Money is made," he noted tersely, "by saving as well as earning." Before the trip Dillon had talked of spending as much as possible on improvements; afterward he urged Clark to "keep down to hard pan." When fall earnings proved unexpectedly favorable, Gould departed from custom by ordering the figures withheld. "It not only embarrasses you in keeping down expenses," he explained to Clark, "but it gives eastern roads the idea that we are making too much money."

As usual Gould had more than one reason for his request. He wanted favorable news kept in reserve for use at the opportune moment. That winter Clark showed his mettle by keeping trains moving despite a winter that exceeded all previous horrors. During 1872–73 blizzards had again blockaded the road as late as April with temperatures so severe that livestock froze to death in stalled trains. In 1874–75, however, not even forty inches of snow and temperatures of nearly forty below in Wyoming stopped trains from running. To Gould's delight Clark managed not only to overcome winter but also to lower the operating ratio from 48.5 to 44.5 percent for the year. Improved earnings and reduced expenses provided Gould with just the right powder for the bombshell he was preparing.

In one year Gould accomplished more for Union Pacific than had all his predecessors combined. He had succeeded in refunding the income bonds and eliminating the competition of Pacific Mail. Earnings increased sharply in the midst of a depression, expenses had been reduced, and the road was running smoothly under its new superintendent. Gould had taken the first steps toward developing the resources along the road and effecting a settlement of the disputes with the government. A variety of other problems, such as the junction and terminus squabbles, had received his attention. Prospects for the future looked glowing, yet the same nagging question still bothered skeptics: Would Gould stay with the property or was he merely bulling its securities in order to sell out at a fat profit?

Opposition to Gould's control revolved around Duff, who had lost his influence in the road, and Levi P. Morton, whose banking firm was about to lose its position as financial agent for the road in Gould's drive for economy. Early in January 1875 Gould heard that the two men were scheming with Sage to control the next election. Their machinations did not trouble him. "Messrs. Morton & Duff would doubtless like to get back into the controll [sic] of Union Pacific," he told Clark wryly, "but the trouble is the stockholders will not vote for them." His only concern was that Boston stand by him. Gould held 140,000 shares, Oliver 30,000, Dillon 10,000, and the other Bostonians about 20,000, which totaled more than half the stock. "Tell our friends to hold on to their U.P. stock," he exhorted Rollins. "As soon as the mkt is cleared the price will advance above 50. Within two years if I live I mean to plant this stock to par in fact it is worth that to day."

Boston was convinced. Oliver not only stood firm but bought up proxies as well. The avalanche of good news in the company's report buried what little opposition remained. Net earnings amounted to $5.9 million or 7 percent on outstanding stock *and* bonds. Gould's coup in Pacific Mail was timed perfectly to feed the momentum behind his bulling of Union Pacific. At the election on March 10 his ticket swept to victory. Two familiar faces, Dodge and Bishop John Sharp, replaced Duff and Morton on the board. The plum of transfer agent was given to Union Trust, which charged $4,000 compared to the $10,000 paid Morton, Bliss. As a crowning act the directors declared a 6 percent dividend commencing in July.

The rush of events leading to the election, capped by the dividend, created a sensation on Wall Street. Nearly 388,000 shares of Union Pacific changed hands that week as a long depressed market surged upward behind a stock accustomed to leading the retreat. As the price passed 48 the bears counterattacked desperately and knocked it back slightly. Gould saw that the hour of decision had come. Once again he urged Boston not to sell but to place what they could off the New York exchange. Once the market turned, he assured them, the bears would find no shares to cover and push the price above 50. He knew what was on Boston's minds. "I shall not sell a share of my stock at any price," he pledged, "as I can see par for it within the next 18 Months. I shall stand by it."

Gould's associates not only remained loyal but joined him in a pool to lift Union Pacific. Gould had the annual report distributed to bankers and newspapers across the country and managed to generate favorable publicity even in dailies hostile to him personally. The stock left 50 in its wake and by June stood just below 80. Boston was fast coming to appreciate Gould's peculiar genius, especially his magical touch in the market. That spring they were eagerly following his lead into other enterprises, notably Atlantic & Pacific Telegraph and certain railroads in which Union Pacific had an interest. Oliver and his friends discovered too that, contrary to his reputation, Gould was steadfast and reliable. He was meticulous in the way he incurred an obligation, but once his word was given he never went back on it. This was a lesson Huntington had yet to learn. In his experience Gould was "the most difficult man to do anything with that I ever knew." He watched the rise ("which, of course, means unloading") with a jaundiced eye, ready to buy once Gould began to sell.

He would have a long wait.

* * *

The paying of dividends was no mere ploy to bull the stock but an integral part of Gould's program to restore investor confidence. He was sincere in the belief that Union Pacific was worth par and fully aware of the hard work needed to plant it there. Many of the problems confronting him were relics of the past, deposited and accumulated like silt until they threatened to bury the company. To Gould it must have seemed as if the history of Union Pacific was little more than an agenda of unfinished business. He resolved to clear the slate in one concerted effort.

Huntington was among the first of Gould's targets. Four years had passed without any settlement on the five miles of road west of Ogden. Each year the board gestured feebly toward recovering the road but did nothing, leaving the

Central Pacific to use it free of charge. Gould was not so careless with assets. A week after being elected a director he approached Huntington with an offer to lease the five miles to the Central Pacific if agreement could be reached on compensation for past use. In June Dillon, on his first tour of the road, met Stanford at Ogden to discuss a whole range of issues between the two companies. After two days of tough bargaining they came to terms on the lease, although another year passed before it was actually signed.

Gould then turned his attention to the debris left by his old partner, Jim Fisk. A year after Fisk's death his widow revived the suit in new guise. Another suit still pending had been brought by one of Fisk's agents, C. W. Pollard, who had enjoined the company from paying any dividends until his claim was satisfied. The Fisk suit lumbered on in the courts until May 1877, when the Union Pacific paid twenty thousand dollars to dispose of it. Altogether it cost the company nearly fifty thousand to exorcise these ghosts.

By far the hoariest ghost of all was that of Crédit Mobilier. By 1874 it had faded from the public eye, having limped along for five years as a shadow corporation while those who still held its stock tried to figure out a way to wring some value from it. Part of the delay had to do with the inability of the Trustees to wind up their affairs under the Ames and Davis contracts, which made a final settlement with Crédit Mobilier impossible. The Trustees in turn were hopelessly bogged down in a mire of litigation among themselves and erstwhile friends. Many were no longer connected with either Union Pacific or Crédit Mobilier, but still their quarrels persisted, driven by hopes of gain or vengeance or both.

Crédit Mobilier still had assets worth fighting for, notably the two-million-dollar note received from Union Pacific in 1869 and some land in Council Bluffs. The problem was how to cut through the maze of suits that kept everything tied in knots. Hazard was still pursuing Durant, who in turn threatened Union Pacific. In 1874 the Trustees sued Hazard and others who had not surrendered their securities under the Evasion Loan. As the web thickened, even the lawyers were taxed to keep straight who was on what side in which suit.

Well might Gould have preferred to duck these nightmarish complexities. His two closest associates, Dillon and Oliver, were large holders of Crédit Mobilier and Trustees, as was Bates. Atkins, the vice president of Union Pacific, held the disputed two-million-dollar note as trustee. Any move against Crédit Mobilier would force them to choose sides. As Gould saw matters, however, they had no choice and neither did he. The legacy of Crédit Mobilier haunted the company's affairs in a hundred different ways, two of which especially concerned Gould. In trying to arrange a settlement with the government, his credibility would be greatly enhanced if he could present himself as slayer of the Crédit Mobilier dragon. If he could also repudiate the two-million-dollar note, he would rid the company of a large potential liability.

The note caught Gould's attention early. Even before his election in 1874 he demanded assurance from Oliver that no attempt would be made to pay anything on it. Dillon understood that the future held more profit than the past and was anxious to close up Crédit Mobilier. He tried to mollify both Durant and Hazard, who lectured him on his easy gift for accommodation. That was the curse of the Ames brothers, Hazard said wrathfully. "Neither of them were very bad men but instead of contending for principle they were continually yielding to expediency & compromising with the villainy they should have determined to crush." Hazard would not bend as they had done, or retreat from his suits until justice was served. Williams, Bushnell, and Alley all took a turn at importuning Hazard to "put an end to these everlasting fights." Bushnell, who was then deep into oil speculation, pressed hard because he needed money. If the suits were dropped, he pleaded, "we could at once turn our stock in for cash or Bonds."

But Hazard would not budge. The Trustees' suit against him, he raged, was "the most infamous proceeding that I have ever known among businessmen." In 1874 Hazard cut his last official tie by resigning as director of Crédit Mobilier. The Bostonians, heeding Dillon's advice to "keep the control of it in our own hands," filled the board of Crédit Mobilier with their friends. Nothing short of compromise, however, could prevent Hazard or any other adversary from resorting to the courts.

Gould found himself in a delicate situation. In November 1873 the court had dismissed the government suit against Crédit Mobilier. The Union Pacific was free to sue the construction company for recovery of alleged fraudulent profits, but that was unlikely because several of the recipients were still in the road's management. Oliver understood that such a suit would compel them "to answer for all the Stock & Bonds we had recd und the Hoxie Ames & Davis contracts." Gould was reluctant to push his friends into that disclosure, but events forced his hand. In December 1873 the board had passed a motion by Wilson to cancel the two-million-dollar note, but for some reason this was not done. Instead Hazard and other Crédit Mobilier holders mounted a campaign to compel payment of the note. Gould responded by having the Union Pacific prepare suits against Crédit Mobilier "to put Hazard & his party on the defensive."

Alarmed by Gould's action, the executive committee of Crédit Mobilier reacted by filing suit on July 19, 1875, to recover the two million dollars and demanded that Atkins surrender the note to them. That same day the Boston members of Union Pacific's executive committee met without Gould and decided to let Atkins "do as he pleased" with the note. These moves triggered a crisis from which there could be no easy retreat. The Boston group also dominated the Crédit Mobilier executive committee, which included Baker and Fred Ames, Oliver's son who had been put on by his father. By some curious reckoning they estimated their stake in Crédit Mobilier worth a fight against the company they represented as officers and its largest stockholder.

It was a miscalculation of gigantic proportions for themselves and the Union Pacific.

Gould was more disappointed than surprised at the news. "You must on no account surrender possession of note," he wired Atkins the next day. His reproach to Oliver was both stern and sorrowful. The suit would be met in kind and amounted to "stirring up a dirty cesspool just at a time when we want to stand well in Washington—the action will be a serious blunder on the part of the responsible stockholders of the Credit Mobilier who are responsible for all the profits made in constructing the road to the UP treasury . . . *they had better reconsider before it is too late.*" Possibly Oliver resented being lectured on business ethics by Jay Gould; certainly the threat from so dangerous an adversary disturbed him. The suit was not withdrawn. Gould formally requested the executive committee to sue Crédit Mobilier and the Trustees for an accounting of all construction profits and for cancellation of the note. Predictably, the committee rejected his request.

Aware that those with interests in both Union Pacific and Crédit Mobilier were anxious to resolve the dispute amicably, Gould devised a plan to separate friend from foe. When the company refused to bring the suits, he instituted them personally as a stockholder. At the same time he offered releases to Crédit Mobilier holders who agreed to turn their shares over to the Union Pacific. If the railroad could acquire most of the stock, any judgment against it would be ineffective. Gould's terms were, in Dillon's succinct words, for Crédit Mobilier to "give up all its assetts [sic] including the lands at Council Bluffs and call it even."

Most of the Boston directors followed Oliver's lead in accepting Gould's terms. They dared not alienate the man who had led the road out of the wilderness and was making them money in a dozen ways. Crédit Mobilier was a dead end so long as Hazard kept its affairs snarled in litigation, and the old man rebuffed every offer to settle. In December 1875 they signed the release; two months later a similar indenture was executed with those receiving profits under the Trustees' agreement. This clever tactic enabled Gould to protect his friends while pressing his suits against those who refused to sign.

Early in the negotiations Gould discovered "a leak in our proceedings." The leak was undoubtedly Oliver Ames 2d, son of Oakes, who had replaced his father on the Union Pacific board. One might have expected Governor Oliver, as he was later called, to support his uncle and the other Boston directors. Instead he joined Hazard as one of the two most stubborn holdouts from Gould's plan. "Unfortunately," he explained later, "my father's estate lost its Union Pacific stock in the panic, and we had nothing but the Credit Mobilier stock." As executor of Oakes's estate he was determined to extract maximum value from the shares. Besides Hazard and Governor Oliver, a number of old hands were maneuvering for advantage. Durant and Duff both presented large bills for past services as part of their bargaining. McComb showed no eagerness to settle; neither did some smaller holders.

Against all these holdouts Gould proceeded vigorously. Duff's demand, he told Oliver flatly, was "inadmissable. All offers of settlement to Duff & all negotiations should be at once terminated." Gould's zeal made unexpected bedfellows of men who had once fought one another savagely. The committee appointed by Crédit Mobilier to adjust accounts with Union Pacific reported in October that the railroad held valid claims against Crédit Mobilier totaling nearly three million dollars. It recommended a compromise that would offset these claims by canceling the disputed note. Before the stockholders could act, however, Hazard stymied them with an injunction. Gould retaliated with a suit against Hazard for alleged profits made from the construction contracts.

The lines were drawn for another round of battles. Gould hoped for a quick, decisive victory that would rid the company of Crédit Mobilier once and for all. Instead there followed a protracted state of siege in which the enemy proved more stubborn than the gloomiest pessimist would have dared imagine.

Where Thomas A. Scott *(upper left)* failed to revive the Union Pacific, Jay Gould *(upper right)* succeeded with help from his two closest allies, Sidney Dillon *(lower left)* and Silas H. H. Clark *(lower right)*.

16

THE RESOURCES

It was one thing to plant Union Pacific at a high figure, another to keep it there. The first could be achieved by manipulation; the other required sound management and the development of business over the long haul. To accomplish this, Gould immersed himself in Union Pacific until he acquired an encyclopedic knowledge of its affairs. Some railroad managers were expert at finance, others at operations or development; none rivaled Gould at absorbing and integrating all these aspects. That he did this with the most difficult railroad in America to manage only makes his achievement more impressive.

There was no mystery to the program formulated by Gould. The key to success lay in improving the road's performance. Earnings had to be increased through more efficient operation and by developing new business. Branch roads were needed to tap fresh sources of traffic and protect the territory from invading lines. A foreign policy was needed to deal with the growing number of competitors for through traffic. Finally, the labyrinth of conflicts with the government had to be resolved once and for all.

* * *

The most obvious resource possessed by the company was its land grant, which was supposed to help pay for constructing the road. In fact it did little more than serve as security for the land grant bonds. Given the need to develop local business, the Union Pacific had no more urgent business than the sale of land to encourage settlement along the line. Prior to 1874 the land question followed the same dreary pattern as the road's other affairs. It received only sporadic attention, got caught up in personality conflicts, drew charges of corruption, fell prey to mismanagement, and stumbled repeatedly over disputes with the government.

Two months after passage of the Act of 1864 Durant appointed Ebenezer Cook as land commissioner. Cook stressed the importance of having land "selected, listed and put in shape" but resigned in disgust after two futile years of trying to attract the Doctor's attention. For a time the business was done by the resident engineer's office in Omaha. Then in August 1867 a committee headed by Cook emphasized the "many millions of dollars to be derived from the sale of the lands if a proper system of management is adopted" and urged the board to "bring the lands into market for sale to actual settlers at the earliest practicable moment." The board created a land committee to oversee the business and appointed Dodge land agent.

The company received twenty alternate sections of land for each mile built or about 11.3 million acres in all. Before it could get title, however, the land had to be surveyed. The government's progress was so glacial that Dodge's assistant, Oscar F. Davis, feared the surveys would not reach Salt Lake for eight or ten years. On lands already surveyed the government was to issue patents (titles) on completion of each twenty-mile section of road. However, the patents, like the bonds, got caught up in the controversy over whether a first-class road had been built and were withheld for the entire region two hundred miles west of Omaha. The lack of surveys and patents created havoc that took years to unravel. How could the company sell land when it could offer neither surveys nor titles for it? Settlers eager to buy either went away disappointed or took their chances on not being cheated later. Squatters flocked to the lands in Wyoming and Utah, where new towns sprang up as the road moved west. The company itself needed clear title to land for depots and other facilities that spilled over into government sections.

The stage was set for disputes that would occupy the lawyers for years. Dodge sold what land he could and soon found himself snarled in legal technicalities. He had also to accommodate the officers, employees, and friends who wanted lots for speculation, a practice that exposed him to charges of favoritism and corruption. In September 1868 Davis was named head of the new land department; his office did not open until the following July, when the first lands west of Omaha were offered for sale. The government was asked to withdraw from preemption by settlers all the odd-numbered sections claimed by the company to avoid later conflicts, but these efforts bogged down in political intrigues within the Land Office and Interior Department.

When Dodge resigned as engineer in 1870 he also wanted out of his responsibility as agent for land and town lots. He recommended that they be turned over to Davis, but bickering between the two men went on until March 1873, when Davis finally relieved Dodge of his land duties. Oliver inspected Davis's operation and as usual observed only that he was "spending too much on clerks." In fact, the ambitious Davis was working vigorously to expand his operation. Through advertising, promotion, and the assiduous cultivation of agricultural editors, he managed by October 1873 to sell nearly eight hundred thousand acres of land at an average price of $4.50 per acre. However, he was hamstrung by the government's withholding of half the land patents until the dispute over the road's completion date was resolved.

Gould's arrival in 1874 coincided with a low ebb in the sale of agricultural lands. That summer an invasion of grasshoppers cut Nebraska's corn crop in half after four years of tumbling prices. Although the crop made a spectacular recovery the following year, memories of the 'hopper plague and several dry seasons discouraged settlers. The drought prompted some self-proclaimed authorities to revive the old myth of the Great American Desert by casting doubt on the arability of land west of the 100th meridian. Charles Francis Adams, Jr., declared flatly in 1875 that settlers had gone too far west. Such gloomy assertions deflated the campaign to boost the plains as the Garden of the West.

In pondering the debate over rainfall, Gould's thinking was influenced by Dodge, who argued that the country was more suitable for stock growing than farming. "They may write that country up for agricultural purposes, as much as they like," Dodge insisted, "but unless the elements change they cannot west of Grand Island get more than one crop out of five. It is too dry." Although time would prove Dodge wrong, he impressed Gould even more with the assertion that "the man who raises stock, ships three times as much over the road as the man who raises grain." The way to make the land profitable was to "work up your surface on stock and your under strata on coal."

This argument fit Gould's dogged quest for traffic that would give the road a long haul. At first he tried to protect grazing by not selling lands west of North Platte to settlers, but to his surprise the stockmen objected. He then pushed the notion of organizing the land into ranches "to sell the bad with the good & thus locate the cattle more permanently along our road." Dillon echoed the fear that the best grazing land with ample water would be sold off, leaving the company only the poorest sections. "We cannot pay too much attention to stock development on the west end of the road," Gould told Clark. "It is the only business the country is adapted to & it requires some encouragement & inducements to get it started."

Gould was prepared to offer both to local developers with vision. A Wyoming entrepreneur, Judge W. A. Carter, tendered Gould his notion of a cattle-shipping complex near Fort Bridger, where he was post trader. Carter envisioned yards large enough to receive herds from Montana, Idaho, Nevada, Utah, even the Northwest Territories. Most Wyoming cattle were shipped east from Cheyenne; a complex at Fort Bridger would give the Union Pacific a much longer haul. During his inspection tour in June 1877 Gould paused at the fort for a close look. Impressed by what he saw, he promptly offered special rates on all cattle shipped from Fort Bridger, agreed to build extensive yards there, and offered Carter assistance in erecting his own facilities. He also urged Clark to "have plenty of buyers on hand to buy & ship. We ought not to let any cattle be *driven* farther east for shipment. The more of a center we can make Judge Carter's yards . . . the more cattle will be brought in for sale." Carter expanded his yards, put up a hotel for buyers, and erected other facilities. By November he had shipped 250 carloads and had the company scrambling for enough cars to carry cattle.

The same policy was followed in Nebraska, where the Union Pacific built cattle pens at Schuyler, Kearney, and elsewhere to capture northern drives. Ogallala blossomed from an obscure way station into a full-blown cow town. In Omaha Gould encouraged the growth of stockyards through special rates and other concessions to men who, like Carter, took hold vigorously. Those denied his favor cursed Gould roundly for driving them out of business. Elsewhere he searched constantly for new opportunities. The discovery of gold in the Black Hills drew his attention to that region. From a geologist familiar with the area he learned that it was suitable for grazing as well as mining. There was also trouble with the Indians and uncertainty over how much gold there actually was, but the possibilities intrigued Gould enough to contemplate a branch into the Black Hills.

Gould did not neglect farmers in his search for business. "I wish every foot of our lands east of Kearney was sold & in possession of an actual settler," he told Clark. Competition for immigrants was fierce among railroads with land grants. Since the late 1860s the Union Pacific, like other roads, had dispatched agents and a flood of promotional literature to lure settlers. In the struggle for this business Davis had made an indifferent showing. For all his explanations, management regarded his operation as expensive and loosely run at a time when strict economy was wanted. In 1874 Davis was ordered to trim expenses and submit his accounts to Gannett for auditing. He managed to stave off a proposed closing of the Chicago office but could not sell the company on the idea of hiring an agent to recruit emigrants in Europe. While the legacy of "grasshopper times" persisted, Davis admitted having a hard time with land sales and collections. Expenses had been pared to the bone, he insisted, but the crusty Gannett disagreed. Davis, he reported, was inclined "to take things pretty easy himself" and showed no disposition "to reduce the number or salaries of his employees."

Although Davis struggled to boost sales, the results were disappointing. In 1876 Gould paused in Omaha on his tour to install a new accounting system for the land department. When matters did not improve, Dillon grew so discouraged that he proposed selling the company's land back to the government and getting out of the business. By 1877 the depression was lifting, the road was doing a splendid business, and still land sales lagged. "Sales are small & Davis' expenses are too high," Gould told Clark bluntly. "This is the only department of our business that is not satisfactory to me. This one needs a thorough overhauling or a *clean wipe out.*"

Despite his protests, Davis had lost the confidence of his superiors. In February 1878 he was replaced by Leavitt Burnham, a young lawyer in Poppleton's department. Clark supported Burnham warmly because he was bright, able, honest, and lacked the political connections of some other candidates. "For a corporation," Clark declared, "the less politics and out side connections the better for a company." Gould toyed with the idea of abolishing the department altogether but on Clark's advice decided to give Burnham a chance. Davis left on a bitter note, convinced that the company had blighted his efforts through its miserly policies. While he had faced many difficulties beyond his control, notably the muddle over titles, Davis had also run a loose, even careless operation.

As Gould was to discover with so many aspects of the Union Pacific, the land operation could not escape its history. An incredible amount of time and energy was squandered on sorting out the mess left by past confusion and bungling. By 1878 Gould and Dillon had at least systematized the land operation. All lands were appraised by a committee composed of Clark, Gannett, and Poppleton, who set the prices at which Burnham could make sales. A vigorous campaign was launched to reclaim parcels forfeited by nonpayment in order to resell them. Just as prospects for the department brightened, however, the company found itself again locked in combat with the government.

*   *   *

Land was one of two resources Gould regarded as crucial to the Union Pacific's development. The other was coal, which could provide the road with cheap fuel for its trains and supply a region starved for sources of energy. If the market between Ogden and Council Bluffs could be captured, Gould reasoned, the road would not only get a long haul but could earn enough profits from the business to "give the company its own fuel free."

Unfortunately, the coal operation was in shambles when Gould arrived, the victim of its own gothic history. Although the geologist hired by Durant found large deposits in the Black Hills region in 1863, the company could do nothing with them until the road reached the site. In May 1868 an agreement was negotiated with two Missouri coal dealers, Cyrus O. Godfrey and Thomas Wardell, to locate and mine coal along the road. The contract leased the company's coal lands for fifteen years to Godfrey and Wardell, who were to sell coal to the Union Pacific on a sliding scale ranging from six dollars a ton the first two years down to three dollars a ton the last six years. The lessees also received a 25 percent rebate on shipments for other customers, which gave them an enormous advantage over other miners who shipped coal via Union Pacific. Godfrey and Wardell were from the first merely agents for the Union Pacific—or at least some of its representatives. "Made a contract with some parties to mine coal," Oliver noted in his diary on July 16. "They to have 10% of the profits the ballance [sic] to Co."

A month later the Missourians joined Cyrus McCormick, Dyer O. Clark, and the ubiquitous James Davis in chartering the Wyoming Coal and Mining Company. The intention was to assign the coal contract to this corporation just as the construction contracts had been transferred to Crédit Mobilier, but during these same months the Ames contract was being thrashed out and the coal question got sidetracked until December. Although Wyoming Coal was capitalized at a half a million dollars or 5,000 shares, only 3,260 shares were subscribed at first. Ultimately Union Pacific directors held 90 percent of the outstanding stock. Godfrey transferred his interest to Wardell, and on April 1, 1869, their contract was assigned to Wyoming Coal.

By the time the road opened it was obvious that the prices charged the company for coal were exorbitant. The cost of mining coal was only about $2.00 per ton, which gave Wyoming Coal a huge profit besides the rebate allowed it. Hammond protested this arrangement but was overruled by Oliver, who called the contract "as well as anything we can get." The government directors thought otherwise, particularly Wilson, who in November 1869 persuaded the board to disregard the contract. Wardell then offered to sell his interest in Wyoming Coal for $50,000. Oliver foolishly let this chance slip by, thinking he could niggle Wardell down to half that amount. After Wilson's action, Wardell asked Oliver to continue the contract at the price of $3.50 a ton. On this basis the company proceeded to ignore Wilson's resolution. In August 1870 the superintendent was ordered to buy coal only from Wyoming Coal.

An absurd situation had arisen. The Union Pacific was paying excessive prices for coal to a company it was supposed to own but did not, and bore all risks for a business over which it had no control. Those in possession of Wyoming's stock insisted they held it "for the use and benefit" of the road. Durant later asserted that the Union Pacific actually paid only $1.82 per ton of coal, and that all dividends on Wyoming stock went to the railroad. Only Duff defended the arrangement, but no one could find a way out of it. During 1872 the board decided again to annul the contract and create a new organization, but it failed to come to terms with Wardell for his interest. Late in the year the board canceled the rebate provision and left reorganization in the hands of the executive committee, but the onset of Crédit Mobilier hearings buried the issue for most of 1873.

Since Wilson's resolution the government directors had persistently objected to a monopoly that made fuel expensive and prevented the development of mines on sections not owned by the railroad. Not only was the Union Pacific obliged to furnish whatever trackage Wyoming Coal required, but Duff ordered that no side tracks be laid to any other mines. In their report for 1873 the government directors denounced the contract as "unfortunate and unwise." At the December board meeting they backed a resolution opening the coal lands to lease by outside parties but lost by a vote of five to four. Instead it was decided to pay Wyoming Coal nothing more until a settlement between the companies was reached. Wardell dutifully brought his accounts to Boston and, after some dickering, was sent home with little more than promises.

There matters stood when Gould came on board. On the day after the election he cut through five years of confusion and ineptness with one decisive stroke. Poppleton had long believed the contract was invalid and did not hesitate to tell Gould so. His superior, Sidney Bartlett, disagreed and as usual advised caution, but that was not to Gould's taste. At Gould's urging the executive committee repudiated the contract and seized the mines with the intention of operating them as the company's property. Caught by surprise, Wardell surrendered the mines without a fight and took refuge in the court. That was fine with Gould; if nothing else a suit would enable him to discover just who Wardell's partners were. For years he followed the case closely and aided Poppleton with a stream of helpful suggestions.

The government directors applauded this action but did not want the mines managed by the railroad. Gould brushed their objection aside. He regarded coal as the company's most valuable resource and had no intention of sharing its profits with outsiders. "The only thing I have any solicitude about is the coal business," he wrote Clark after his first western tour in October 1874. Gould wanted it "developed to its fullest extent" and resolved to "take hold of this department . . . get the mining and selling of the coal upon the most economical & efficient basis."

The obstacles were formidable. In 1874 the company was new at the mining business. It had yet to create an effective organization or efficient systems for monitoring production, setting prices, or marketing aggressively. Production was low, costs high, and labor scarce. Apart from its own fuel needs, the Union Pacific sold coal to the Central Pacific and to consumers along the route. It also served as carrier for other mines on land not owned by the company, a competitive advantage that had yet to be fully tapped. The company operated seven mines in Wyoming—four at Rock Springs, two at Carbon, and one at Almy, near Evanston. All were besieged with labor unrest, a problem that Gould would shortly convert into an asset.

In Gould's mind the first step was to drive down costs, which in 1874 averaged about $2.13 a ton. For this task he used as a model some bituminous mines he owned in Blossburg, Pennsylvania, which, despite labor trouble, managed to produce coal at a cost of $1.25 per ton. Gould put his target for the coming year at $1.30 a ton and saw clearly how to accomplish it. "Our coal business will never work satisfactorily," he observed, "till we master the labor question." The Rocky Mountain Coal Company near Evanston, owned by the Central Pacific, paid 75 cents a ton and could stockpile as much as it mined, while the miners at neighboring Almy would not permit the Union Pacific to stockpile coal ahead of present needs. One fact accounted for the difference: Rocky Mountain employed Chinese miners, Almy white men exclusively.

This was the key to Gould's plans. As early as 1869 Hammond had urged the company to put Chinese in the mines, but nothing was done. A year later some Chinese were hired as section men despite protests from local editors and displaced workers. The Union Pacific paid them $32.50 a month compared to $52 for white labor, a savings that inspired Gould and Dillon to fill the mines with Chinese at the earliest moment. After a strike in 1871 Wardell had replaced the malcontents with Scandinavian immigrants at a lower wage. By the fall of 1874 the newcomers were disgruntled. When an attempt to organize the miners produced rumblings of another strike, Gould saw that his opportunity had come. In November the first Chinese went into Almy and the white miners retaliated by walking out.

The strike occurred at a time when Gould was desperate to improve earnings. Dillon feared the walkout would spread and fretted that "it would be very bad to have a general strike of miners this winter." Nevertheless, Gould understood that the paramount issue was to bludgeon down labor costs whatever the short-term consequences, and he urged Clark to take a hard line. If coal ran short, it could be purchased from Rocky Mountain. "I would not make any concessions to the miners," Gould suggested, "but fight it out with them even at the cost you mention for the purchase of coal & in the spring I would let Mr Serat fill up his mines with Chinese labor and thus settle the status permanently."

The strike ended in a truce that resolved nothing. In the spring Gould instructed Clark to fill a new mine at Almy and all other vacancies with Chinese labor. Superintendent Serat managed to reduce the cost per ton at Almy by 25 cents, saving the company nearly $40,000. Gould wanted the figure cut by twice that amount but conceded that "it is better to come down gradually." Within a year, he promised Oliver, the cost could be reduced to $1.25 a ton. That summer eastern miners lost a prolonged strike and suffered a cut in wages. With Gould's approval Clark promptly reduced wages at both Carbon and Rock Springs. "With Chinese at Almy & native miners at the other point," Gould observed shrewdly, "you can play one against the other & thus keep master of the situation." The miners understood the cost of provisions and clothing would also be lowered. When that did not occur, they went out on strike.

This was the moment Gould awaited. Clark moved to crush the strike by replacing the strikers with Chinese, whipping up public sentiment against the miners, and recruiting the help of Governor John M. Thayer, who sent troops to protect the company's property. Thayer was an old Union Pacific hand as senator from Nebraska before his appointment as territorial governor. The outmanned miners never had a chance. As the strike collapsed they begged Clark to take them back at lower wages, but Clark turned a deaf ear to their pleas. He had the Chinese in place and with them another 25-cent cut in costs. "Every-thing lovely & the goose hangs high!" he chortled. Gould and Dillon showered him with praise for routing a "dangerous labor combination." There were protests in the territory about displacing white labor, enough to prompt Wyoming's Republicans to warn "that the introduction of Chinese labor into this country is fraught with serious and dangerous consequences." More Chinese were brought into Rock Springs, nurturing a legacy of bitterness and prejudice that would one day explode into violence.

With labor costs sharply reduced, Gould moved at once to perfect the coal operation. "I shall be disappointed," he declared, "if we do not reduce the cost of our coal to not much over $1 per ton." It was a theme he would hammer incessantly for years. He wanted the coal business put in a separate department under an efficient head. To monopolize the coal trade, rival operators had to be driven out through rate discrimination. New mines had to be opened on company land and existing ones acquired from other interests. Gould fixed his sights on the commercial market. "What I want," he stressed, "is to gain so large a local trade that we can keep our mines & rolling stock busy all the time."

Part of that trade would have to be wrested from Huntington and his cronies, who had similar ambitions for their mines. In May 1874 Rocky Mountain tried to snatch one of the most valuable coal tracts at Evanston, but the land belonged to the Union Pacific grant and Gould thwarted the attempt. Huntington hoped to pressure Gould into a long-term contract at favorable rates. Instead Gould startled him by suggesting that the Pacific roads form a joint company to control all the mines at Evanston. His plan was to provide both roads fuel at cost, transport coal at cost, and supply the entire market from Evanston to California. The proposal intrigued Huntington, but the old fears held him back. "Now, I think Gould is very much in earnest about this," he wrote David D. Colton, ". . . but I do not like to be mixed up with Gould in anything of which it is possible for him to get control." Once again his caution prevailed, and the idea was dropped.

If the Central Pacific insisted on competing, Gould intended to beat them. "I think we should so regulate the rates of transportation & the price of the coal delivered as to monopolise the coal trade of Utah," he told Clark. To do that required an organization capable of running the mines efficiently and seizing business through aggressive marketing. In typical fashion Gould immersed himself in the details of coal operation until he mastered them thoroughly. His style was not to issue orders but to pepper Clark with advice on every aspect of the business. "To mine coal cheaply in the long run," he stressed, "you want to have the best of machinery mines always kept in good shape concentrated as much as possible as you can mine much more cheaply on a large scale." He offered precise suggestions on where and how to market coal, how best to use machinery, where to locate storage sheds, how to maintain quality control, when to offer special rates, ways to monitor costs and avoid false weighing—anything that caught his ever watchful eye.

"You know this coal business is a sort of hobby of mine," he noted almost apologetically in August 1876. "I will hardly be satisfied until we get the cost

TABLE 1

UNION PACIFIC COAL OPERATIONS 1875-1883

Year	Tons Mined	Per cent Increase[a]	Cost Per Ton[c]	Sales to Individuals	Carbon		Rock Springs		Almy	
					Tons Mined[c]	Cost Per Ton[c]	Tons Mined	Cost Per Ton[c]	Tons Mined	Cost Per Ton[c]
1875	208,222	—	1.88	—	61,750	2.05	104,667	1.84	41,805	1.73
1876	264,771	27	1.42	65,042	69,062	1.58	134,953	1.38	60,756	1.33
1877	275,480	4	1.14	92,290	74,343	1.26	146,494	1.11	54,643	1.05
1878	275,795	0	1.04	102,341	62,418	1.25	154,281	.99	59,096	1.01
1879	340,152	23	1.07	125,662	75,325	1.19	193,251	.99	71,576	1.17
1880	445,129	31	1.23	137,119	100,434	1.36	244,460	1.25	100,235	1.08
1881	587,493[b]	32[b]	1.39[b]	193,032	156,820	1.51	279,908	1.27	110,157	1.21
1882	728,210[b]	26[b]	1.50[b]	238,891	200,124	1.41	276,589	1.39	116,548	1.37
1883	904,454[b]	23[b]	1.43[b]	265,114	248,366	1.20	301,711	1.53	111,300	1.33

Notes: a) Figures rounded to nearest per cent

b) Figure includes production at other sites besides the three listed.
For those three the tons mined and per cent increase are as follows:

Year	Tons Mined	Per cent Inc.
1881	546,885	23
1882	593,261	8
1883	661,377	11

c) Figures rounded to nearest penny.

Source: Poor, *Manual 1884*, 779.

of mining reduced to $1.00 per ton & mine & ship about 1,000,000 tons per year." Ten days later the receipt of some disappointing coal returns prompted the hobbyist to blister Clark's ear on the subject. *"It ought to be thoroughly advertised,"* he lectured, *"& a good sales agent should be at work pressing & advertising the coal & introducing it into new markets."* A few days later Gould followed up with a detailed outline on improving quality of coal, service, and marketing. Why did the Echo mines produce twice as much as Rock Springs and Almy together? The figures could be reversed, he insisted, if his suggestions were heeded and if the department were put "in the hands of an *efficient & driving head."*

Despite Gould's efforts production lagged, costs dropped slower than he hoped, and efforts to seize commercial markets sometimes stumbled. The situation at Council Bluffs was a case in point. As early as October 1874 Gould suggested selling coal in the Bluffs at Omaha prices, which meant waiving the bridge toll. For fifteen months he urged this policy on Clark, which reveals his sensitivity to the question of Clark's authority. In most cases Gould deemed it more important to maintain Clark's trust by deferring to his judgment than to impose policy by mandate. In later years Gould would be portrayed as a friendless loner, cold and ruthless in his dealings with others. Actually his problem was more the opposite one of allowing his friendship and consideration for Clark (and others) to sway his better judgment. As a result he did not capture the Bluffs market and failed to effect larger changes quickly.

The intensity of Gould's attention to coal matters diminished after 1878. Larger strategical questions absorbed more of his time, the proliferation of his own interests divided his energies among a number of properties, and his involvement in the Union Pacific's affairs lessened. Nevertheless, by 1880 the coal department had become a profitable operation. Gould deserves much of the credit for its development. As Table 1 indicates, he never realized his goals for cost or output, and commercial sales never fulfilled his lofty expectations. Yet between 1875 and 1880 production more than doubled and the cost per ton dropped 65 cents. Gould's drive and vision laid the foundation for future expansion.

How important was the coal operation? Charles Francis Adams, Jr., called it "the salvation of the Union Pacific; those mines saved it. Otherwise the Union Pacific would not have been worth picking up."

* * *

"We must develop our local resources to the fullest extent," Gould told Oliver, "soda—coal—oil—cattle." Every mining strike aroused his hopes for thriving new industries to swell the road's traffic. He searched tirelessly for new mineral deposits to exploit and hired scientists to research untried areas. The possibility of producing coke from the company's coal especially intrigued him. In April 1875 a load of Rock Springs coal was sent to Pennsylvania for testing. When the results looked promising, Gould engaged specialists to experiment with different processes. "If we can successfully turn our coal into coke which we can," he enthused in 1878, "it will revolutionize the silver industry in Utah." Undaunted by setbacks, he sustained the research for several years.

Gould showed the same keen interest in soda, perhaps the most unlikely of the resources he sought to develop. Soda exists in natural deposits at evaporated lakes and can also be made through a process of conversion. The discovery of large deposits in some lakes twelve miles west of Laramie lured Gould to the site on his first western tour in 1874. He came home enthused over their potential and asked Dillon to explore the feasibility of erecting a refinery at the lakes. When a chemist reported favorably, Gould followed his usual pattern of seeking private parties to build the refinery. "We shall get the business," he explained, "& our hands are left free for other matters," but when the project lagged, he took it up. Eager to exploit the natural deposits and produce soda through conversion, Gould hired a geologist to survey the lakes and, as he had done with coking, asked scientists about every known conversion process. Sickels was dispatched to Europe to study the techniques used there, procure machinery, and recruit skilled workmen. Davis was ordered to perfect the company's land titles in the lake region.

Sickels returned from his tour convinced that "we shall furnish from our road all the Soda consumed in this country, and possibly we may supply Europe." But Dillon learned that the best conversion processes required salt water and seaweed, both in scant supply at Laramie, and some directors wondered if the deposits were large enough to warrant building a refinery and a spur line to it. In the spring of 1876 Sickels and a geologist headed west to measure the lakes and confirmed that the deposits were more than ample. Then it was discovered belatedly that settlers had preempted part of the site and had to be bought out. The project languished another seven years before reviving in 1883. Gould never saw the returns he hoped for from the soda business in his lifetime. That he had stumbled onto something big did not become apparent until the 1960s, when the mining and refining of trona developed into a major industry in Wyoming.

Setbacks never diminished Gould's enthusiasm. On every tour he roamed the line searching for new enterprises to develop as sources of business. Especially was he eager to promote the growth of industries in Omaha that drew their raw materials from the mountains so as to give the road a long haul. A prime example was smelting, which utilized ores mined in the Rockies. Despite protests from Colorado smelters, Gould encouraged the Omaha and Grant Smelting Company to extend its works. When the company floundered because of poor management and other problems, he toyed with the notion of taking it over or building a new facility. Instead Omaha and Grant was merged with a Colorado company in 1882, with Dillon and Fred Ames providing capital for the reorganization.

As early as 1873 the Union Pacific talked of erecting a rolling mill in Wyoming. Within a month after Gould's arrival the project sprang to life. Plans were drawn, bids solicited, and the prize given to Laramie, which had no industry except the railroad. Despite Dillon's constant prodding, the work bogged down in delays. Cold weather slowed the work, as did the lack of enough old iron to roll. In April 1875 the mill finally opened; a year later it was producing thirteen hundred tons of rail a month. The company had no intention of operating the mill itself but leased it to private parties two months before it started up. Here was a classic example of what Gould thought local development should be. The mill provided cheap rails utilizing the road's scrap iron and ran on coal from the company's own mines. Laramie got one of the state's largest plants, employing about a hundred men, to bolster its depressed economy. In return it provided generous tax concessions to help make the operation profitable.

In promoting development Gould understood the crucial role of rates, saw that an inflexible tariff hampered business. The long view required the road to charge not merely what the traffic would bear but also what it would bring. His formula, like most others, was to charge high rates for captive through and local traffic, match or beat competitive rates, and encourage new business with special tariffs to keep cars filled in both directions. When ore traffic between Rawlins and Utah dwindled, he reminded Clark that "the trade gives us a long haul & is important that it not only be held but increased." He suggested that the company mine its own ore "to supply the market the same as we do with coal."

Gould's ability to weave disparate details together was uncanny. In scanning the mountain of data that crossed his desk he noticed a market in Baltimore for low-grade Utah copper ore if shipped at the low rate of $6.00 per ton. "This ore is worth in Baltimore $2.80 for each 1% per ton," he reported. "Ore carrying 15% will therefore be worth in Baltimore $42 per ton or $420 per car load. Copper ores as low as 8% are brought to Baltimore." He also prodded the road's freight agent, E. P. Vining, to bring out Utah barley "at a *concession* if necessary as the cars will go back loaded with corn." Tea from the Orient posed a special challenge in finding a rate low enough to wean it away from the water route. A week after the golden spike, analysts predicted confidently that it would never pay to ship tea overland. The Pacific roads soon proved them wrong, and Gould was anxious to get a larger share of the business. He urged Vining to issue time bills "for early tea crop say guaranteeing 45 days from Yokahama—this allows you about 22 days from Frisco to N.Y. We could get for this 1¢ per pound additional."

In his quest to increase income Gould left no corner unswept. Pullman's contract for sleeping cars annoyed him because he resented the company being "deprived of so large a source of revenue for the benefit of outsiders." The company had run its own express service since October 1869, when Wells, Fargo abandoned its fight to keep the business. Gould made certain that the Union Pacific Express was put on every branch the company acquired and by 1876 looked to extending the service to Chicago and St. Louis. This desire reflected one of Gould's most distinctive talents, an ability to make a single action serve several purposes at once. At the time he was trying to cement an alliance with the Baltimore & Ohio, which had decided to operate its own express service. At Chicago and St. Louis the Union Pacific could exchange both traffic and express business with the B & O.

Nowhere did Gould display this talent more brilliantly than in his handling of the company's telegraph business. The charter required the Pacific roads to build a telegraph as well as a railroad. Like most roads, the Union Pacific went out of the telegraph business early; unlike most, it did not sign on with Western Union, already the industry giant. Dodge raised so many objections to Western Union's proposal that it was rejected. In 1869 the company got much better terms from a small firm called Atlantic & Pacific Telegraph and received twenty-four thousand shares of A & P stock in the bargain. Three years later it made peace with Western Union through an agreement giving Union Pacific and A & P a wire from Omaha to Chicago in return for allowing Western Union one from Omaha to Ogden.

Until 1874 A & P limped along in obscurity. Morton, Bliss held the Union Pacific's shares as collateral for an exchange loan made during the hard times of 1873. The company thought so little of the stock it gave Morton, Bliss an option to purchase twelve thousand of the shares at 12 when the loan matured. Morton conceived the notion of using A & P as the basis for an independent line to challenge Western Union. To that end he had A & P listed on the New York Exchange in February 1874. A month later, however, Gould took charge of Union Pacific. Duff and Morton soon found themselves opposed to the new regime, partly because of friction over the telegraph stock.

Gould's keen eye seized at once on the telegraph stock as too valuable an asset to let go. After a stiff fight he compelled a reluctant Morton to surrender his option on the A & P shares. Duff and Morton then tried to buy control of A & P in hopes of selling it to Western Union. Gould thwarted their attempt and in March 1875 crushed their feeble effort to challenge his control of Union Pacific. With his two adversaries routed from the field, Gould launched his own campaign to transform A & P into a serious competitor of Western Union. His Boston associates lent their support on the promise that he would perform no less a miracle with A & P than he had with Union Pacific. In May 1875 the executive committee authorized Gould to sell the company's shares at 25, the current market price. Gould personally took sixteen thousand of the shares while the Bostonians divided the remaining eight thousand. "I dont think an amalgamation of the WU & A&P. T. Co's far off," Gould noted hopefully in July.

In fact, it took Gould another two years of grinding struggle to force a merger with Western Union in August 1877. Western Union bought a majority interest in A & P at 25, the same price Gould had paid Union Pacific for its shares and considerably more than the stock had ever been worth before his arrival on the scene. In this campaign Gould realized handsome profits for himself, the railroad, and those who followed his lead, along with some important fringe benefits. The money paid Union Pacific for its A & P stock was loaned to O & O Steamship, which needed funds badly. During the fight Gould struck an alliance with John W. Garrett of the Baltimore & Ohio, whose help he also needed for Union Pacific's fight against the Iowa Pool. Finally, the successful outcome cemented the relationship between Gould and the Boston directors, who now realized he seldom promised anything he could not ultimately deliver.

* * *

The key to success, observed Gannett in 1872, was "a strong organization *working harmoniously and effectively* for the best interests of this Co." This was the philosophy of management Gould followed throughout his career. He believed in the simplest possible organization staffed by capable men who were delegated authority and expected to exercise it fully. In his view the most valuable resource a railroad could have was a corps of officers who were loyal, worked hard, and did not squander their energies scheming against one another. While Gould demanded much of his lieutenants, he treated them well, paid them handsomely, and looked after their interests.

Gould's emphasis on personnel left him somewhat indifferent to structure, which could not have been more elemental. He and Dillon handled finances with the help of the Boston directors. All matters of operations, rates, traffic, equipment, maintenance, personnel, and dealings with other roads were managed by Clark, to whom all department heads reported except the auditor. In 1875 Clark maneuvered to bring Gannett's department under his control but was thwarted by the Boston directors, who appreciated fully the importance of an independent auditor. Dillon agreed with that view but rebuffed a suggestion in 1874 that the road needed a general manager in Omaha by noting, "Mr. Clark is now really General Manager and has . . . full charge of the entire road and all its departments." If a general manager were appointed, he added curtly, "what need have the company of a President or General Superintendant [sic]?"

This remark showed how fully Dillon shared Gould's belief in a lean organization manned by a few good men in the right places. In 1878 the government directors, all but one of them new to their position, criticized the road's administration as "simple even to crudeness, and quite lacking in system." The tone and style of the report suggests that it was drafted by Charles Francis Adams, Jr., who would ultimately succeed Dillon as president. Later events would prove him something less than a master in the creating of efficient structures or the handling of personnel. In 1878 he found nothing "in the present shape of the organization, as regards division of labor and study of detail, which would indicate that it is the work of any superior organizing mind."

While there was some truth in this observation, it reflected more a different philosophy of organization than an analysis of whether or not the existing one worked effectively. The men who headed the departments did good service in a time of turbulent change. Sickels had never been comfortable as superintendent and surrendered the post willingly. He stayed on as chief engineer until 1876, when the loss of his wife and a daughter left him anxious to remain in his native Pennsylvania. Dillon obliged by making him a consulting engineer. Vining, the freight agent, and Thomas L. Kimball, the passenger agent, occupied two of the most difficult positions a railroad offered. Both were tough, effective officers under pressure. Vining made enemies freely and could be stiff-necked on occasion, but no one denied his ability in a job filled with pitfalls. Kimball was a shrewd, steady professional whose career would skirt the shoals of change within the Union Pacific management for many years.

In the end performance depended chiefly on Clark, who occupied one of the most difficult jobs America had to offer in the nineteenth century. The superintendent of a major railroad had crushing responsibilities, not merely in operations but also in such areas as expansion, development, personnel, labor relations, political activity and diplomatic relations with other roads. He was the lightning rod that caught every flash of discontent from those above and beneath him. In the realm of policy he had the dual task of making recommendations to those who formulated it and then of implementing the final product. His was the desk at which every buck stopped except in the area of finance. No manager in the country had more duties to perform or constituencies to satisfy than a general superintendent.

Small wonder, then, that Clark approached his job with extreme caution. He had also to contend with his triangular relationship with Gould and Dillon, both of whom showered him freely with advice. The perils of his position reinforced Clark's native insecurities. Reluctant to delegate responsibility lest some part of his authority be snatched away, he also hesitated to make decisions on his own initiative. His way was to oversee everything while taking no action on important matters without instructions from Gould or Dillon. Gould assured him repeatedly that he had the power to act. "You must not hesitate to take *responsibility* of doing what in your judgment is best for the interest of the road on the *spot,*" Gould emphasized in 1877. *"Your acts will be sustained."*

No amount of prodding, even by Gould, could budge Clark. He moved slowly and tested the ground carefully before every step. Periodically he would wilt under the pressure, plead illness, and take to his couch. "Don't go out on the line this winter to expose yourself," advised Dillon, whose rugged constitution belied his age, "but give the orders and have it done by others." Gould too urged Clark to find a capable man for the operating department "to relieve yourself of the ugly wear & tear of details." It was advice better saved for himself; not yet forty, he was fast working himself into an early grave. In December 1875 he fell seriously ill and was confined for nearly a month. But Gould would not slow his pace and Clark would not accelerate his. The suggestion of an assistant to handle detail work did not appeal to Clark because it would create one more pretender to his position. In that sense Clark's idiosyncrasies worked against the creation of an efficient administration.

Whatever its deficiencies, Clark's operation was widely believed to be a clean one. Even Oliver thought as much. Since construction days he had been rabid about thievery on the road; he had dumped Hammond because of his conviction that the superintendent was stealing. Although he did not always agree with Clark, he admitted the road "has been in its Management I think thoroughly honest." When Gannett exposed a defalcation by some agents at Ogden in 1876, Oliver observed mildly that it was "the First Steal of importance that we have had among our Employees—if we except Frost & Hammond and Associates who cover their Steals by the claims of their position." Credit for this record went to Gannett, whose gruff loyalty and devotion to duty endeared him to the Boston directors. They thought far too well of Gannett to promote him. In 1876 Rollins was elected to the Senate and reluctantly surrendered his post as secretary-treasurer. Gannett coveted the position but had no chance for it. The major problem, sympathized the Boston auditor, Wilbur, "would be to show the Directors how they could get along without you at Omaha." The position went instead to Henry McFarland.

Although the Union Pacific was a large and growing enterprise, its administration remained a personal one to a remarkable degree. This was true of most railroads prior to the 1880s, when the rise of systems forced changes in their internal organization. The unique feature of the Union Pacific was the peculiar arrangement whereby the dominant figure in its management exercised power without holding any office beyond director and member of the executive committee. Gould's influence was felt not merely in financial policy but in every aspect of the road's affairs. He worked tirelessly to promote harmony and cooperation within a management notorious for its long history of acrimony and prickly personalities. His approach was an intensely personal one that, in less gifted hands, might have failed miserably. It succeeded because of his brilliance and his utter lack of ego, which enabled him to work smoothly with men of all types. While his incredible range of talents has been appreciated even by his critics, one has gone virtually unnoticed—his skill at human relations. Within the Union Pacific it was one of his most important contributions.

By 1877 the company's management bore little resemblance to what it had been only half a dozen years earlier. An important link to the past was severed in March with the death of Oliver Ames, whose role as leader of the Bostonians supporting Gould exceeded anything he had done as president.

"Mr Ames death is a serious loss to us," Gould mourned. "He was always ready to do his full share & both liberal & enterprising just such a friend as the Union Pacific Rd needs for the next few years." Oliver's death left Dillon as the sole surviving figure from the construction years, but it did not remove the Ames influence from the company. Fred Ames replaced his father on the board, just as earlier Oakes's son, Governor Oliver, took his seat. In the coming years Fred would support Gould as staunchly as Governor Oliver opposed him.

At the annual election in 1875, when Gould sent Duff and Morton into permanent exile, the directors paused briefly to honor the past with a resolution to erect a monument in tribute to Oakes for his contribution to the road. The intention was to retrieve his memory from the stigma cast upon it by Crédit Mobilier. Work on the monument did not begin until September 1880, which permitted a worthy addition. When the finished structure was unveiled two years later, it enshrined the memory of both the Ames brothers. In death as in life, Oliver found himself following the lead of his brother.

17

THE BRANCHES

"I have a dread of branches," Gould told Clark in 1875, "but . . . it is a very important matter to the future of the road." He was wise to approach the subject with caution. Railroad managers agonized interminably over the question of whether to build or not to build. Branch lines tapped sources of local business beyond the main line and discouraged invasions from rival roads. Gould regarded these as vital functions, but he shrank from the expense of building and maintaining branches. They were costly and clumsy weapons in a railroad's arsenal; once employed, they could not be withdrawn. Their location had to be planned with great care because a branch in the wrong place at the wrong time became what was called a "sucker" road instead of a feeder and saddled the parent road with indebtedness.

To make matters worse, the Union Pacific's charter did not permit it to build branches. It could assist in the construction process and acquire control through purchase of securities, but the road's managers or "friends" had to undertake projects as personal investments. The completed branch might be leased or sold to the Union Pacific, but that outcome was not guaranteed. The costs were high, the risks great, and the returns uncertain, but the alternative was to leave a huge, undeveloped domain with enormous resources at the mercy of competing interests. There were ways to lessen the risk by encouraging local parties to help shoulder the financial load and by seeking local subsidies. Oliver and his friends resorted to these devices only to discover that they produced unexpected complications. Their handling of the branch question prior to 1874 proved as inept as their management of the main line.

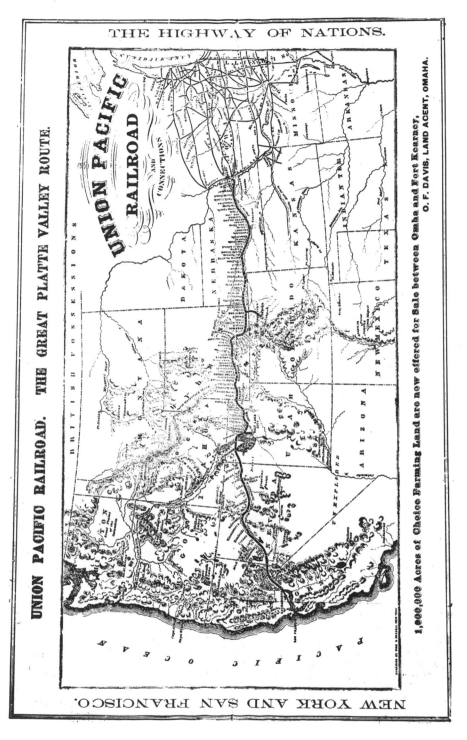

An early map of the new transcontinental route used by the land agents.

* * *

The branch question arose the moment the Union Pacific had decided to build through Wyoming instead of Colorado. From the first it was assumed that the road's most lucrative traffic would be the mineral trade from the mountain region. During the 1860s the center of the mining industry was Colorado, which made a branch to Denver imperative. Once Colorado interests swallowed their disappointment at being left off the main line, they rushed to promote construction of the north-south branch. The Colorado Central, chartered in 1865, originally planned to build through Berthoud Pass as part of the main line. When that hope vanished, its promoter, William Loveland of Golden, blithely announced his intention of building to Cheyenne. Eager Denverites put some money into the project before learning that Loveland intended to make Golden his terminus, with only a branch to Denver. Outraged, they withdrew their support and Loveland's project soon collapsed.

The Union Pacific's policy in Colorado was simply to dominate the Denver branch whoever built it. Oliver Ames and others subscribed to the Colorado Central's stock while Durant and Dodge schemed with former Governor John Evans to obtain a charter for another project, the Denver Pacific. After several attempts Evans secured the charter in November 1867 and signed an agreement with Durant and Dillon the following April to build the road. This dual approach set the stage as early as 1866 for what proved a long and bitter rivalry between Loveland and Evans in Colorado railroads. It also planted the first seeds of a policy that would reap utter confusion and disaster for the Union Pacific in Colorado. There too every twist and turn in the management left its imprint on what was done. The bungled state of affairs in the Rockies was but a reflection of the board's own internal convolutions.

Although grading contracts were let in May 1868, the Denver Pacific bogged down with problems in selling bonds and a dispute over its northern terminus. Durant, who had just thrown the Union Pacific into turmoil with his infamous General Order No. 1, was scheming with the Denver Pacific's engineer to divert the terminus from Cheyenne to Pine Bluffs. Governor Evans and Dodge managed to thwart this move, but the fight over the Ames contract shut off funds for work on the Denver line. The Union Pacific would pay dearly for this blunder. Disgusted by the delays and broken promises, Evans turned to the Kansas Pacific and in March 1869 got from Congress an act enabling the Kansas Pacific to contract with the Denver Pacific for building "one continuous line" from Kansas City to Cheyenne. By this act the Denver Pacific moved into the orbit not of Union Pacific but of its only rival on the plains.

During the summer of 1869 Evans bought some construction material from Union Pacific, hired the Casement brothers' track gangs, and started work in earnest. The line reached Denver in June 1870, three months ahead of the Kansas Pacific. Hammond grasped at once the danger to which his superiors seemed oblivious. "The loss of the Colorado business which now seems quite inevitable unless we bestir ourselves," he warned, "will be followed by the immediate loss of some portion of our Salt Lake and California business between Omaha and Cheyenne which is by far the easiest and cheapest portion of our road to run." The Kansas Pacific was now in position to divert traffic from Cheyenne to Kansas City. Already it had requested the Union Pacific to adhere to the "one continuous line" provision of the Pacific Act by giving it the same rate between Ogden and Cheyenne charged its own customers. Thus was born the *pro rata* controversy that would haunt the Union Pacific for a decade. By carelessly letting the Denver Pacific fall into the hands of its only rival, the Union Pacific acquired both a competitor and yet another controversy to be thrashed out in Washington.

This embarrassment pushed the Union Pacific back into the waiting arms of the Central for what amounted to the most awkward of embraces. An old friend, former government director T. J. Carter, was president of the Central, but the dominant figures in the road continued to be Loveland and H. M. Teller. In March 1870 the Union Pacific agreed to furnish money for construction only to have Sidney Bartlett stall the work by questioning the legality of this course. Irritated by the delays and legal wrangling, the Colorado interests dumped Carter as president. Boston complained that they were putting up the money but Colorado controlled the company; Colorado retorted that the promised funds were not forthcoming. For two years no progress was made. F. Gordon Dexter visited Colorado in May 1872 and came home with the impression that both Loveland and Teller were sharpsters not to be trusted.

Trapped in this labyrinth of distrust, Boston could find neither a way in nor a way out. Duff proposed making the Colorado group an offer and suing them if they refused, but Oliver concluded the safest course was for outside "friends" to build the road and lease it to the Union Pacific. To that end Oliver was made president of the Central and a new corporation, the Colorado Improvement Company, was created to extend the road from Golden to Julesburg on the Union Pacific line. To skirt the *pro rata* danger, the Union Pacific and Central signed an agreement giving the former control over all through rates and the latter power to make local rates on its line. The Improvement Company got off to a rocky start despite liberal subscriptions from the Boston associates. Teller took no shares, pleading a lack not of confidence but of cash. More ominously, George Pullman declined because he still doubted that Boston had control of the Central.

Pullman was entirely correct. The influence of Loveland's group created another serious problem which auditor Gannett, of all people, seemed to grasp more clearly than Oliver. Why, Gannett wondered, was the company building to Julesburg on a circuitous route via Golden, which was due west of Denver:

To control the business of Colorado we want a *short line to the railroad and commercial centre of the Territory.* Denver is that today, and will continue to be for years to come; it is the natural distributing point for the territory south and west, and I regard all attempts to build up Golden at the expense of Denver as impolitic. What we want is a short line from Julesburg to Denver.

The reason was Loveland, whose interests lay in developing Golden. The Central ran into Golden and would favor that town as long as Loveland had a voice in its affairs. If the Union Pacific used the Central as its entry into Colorado, it would incur the wrath of Denver interests, who feared the rise of Golden and had never forgiven Loveland for his earlier perfidy. To get the line Gannett wanted, the Union Pacific would have to start from scratch with a new company. While that may well have been the wisest course, it did not take into account one factor that proved decisive. Oliver and his friends had large investments in the Central and were anxious not to lose them. This alone was enough to dismiss consideration of any alternative.

The route chosen crossed rugged terrain that made for slow, expensive work. In April 1873 the Central crawled into Longmont but within a few months the financial panic stalled its progress. By the year's end the Central was starved for cash and its management as divided as ever. The goal of the Colorado men, Gannett noted sourly, was "to get the largest amount of money out of the pockets of eastern men and into their own."

This was the situation Gould inherited in 1874. He was quick to grasp its perils and pitfalls. Both the company and his Boston associates had large investments in a road they did not control. The Central was in the wrong place for an efficient line to Julesburg and better suited for an extension to Cheyenne, but that meant paralleling the Denver Pacific. The Kansas Pacific had barely survived default; if the road went bankrupt it could cut rates with impunity. Already it was pressing the *pro rata* issue hard in Washington, where the aftertaste of Crédit Mobilier still lingered. In June 1874 Congress obliged by passing an act requiring the Union Pacific not to discriminate against other roads. Never had the situation in Colorado looked darker or prospects for a solution more remote.

In typical fashion Gould searched for a way to attack all these problems at once with a minimum of resources. He opened negotiations with Robert E. Carr, president of the Kansas Pacific, for a rate agreement even before Congress acted. When the Bostonians tried to interest Gould in the Improvement Company, he appeased them by having Union Pacific buy their interest in the company. He wanted the Central as a club to bludgeon Carr into an agreement similar to one Scott had forged with the Kansas Pacific in 1871. At the same time Gould wondered privately to Clark whether the best course was to build "direct to Cheyenne by the easiest & most practicable route (& the shortest) our own independent road . . . I should like your views as to the

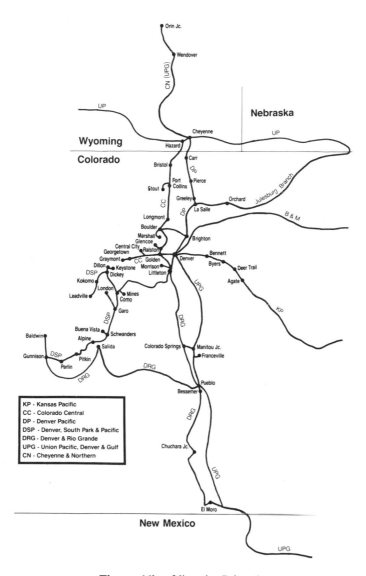

The muddle of lines in Colorado.

true interest of the Union Pacific Rd in making a Colorado connection—it is important that we make no mistake." Meanwhile, Clark was given charge of the Central and told to pare its expenses to the bone.

Through long and tedious negotiations Gould tried to interest Carr in a consolidation of the Central and Denver Pacific. Carr countered with the proposal that Gould buy the Kansas Pacific as well. Gould was intrigued by the possibility but not on Carr's terms. "We have exhausted the subject of an arrangement with K.P.," he told Clark in January, "& I think any further time spent with that view is thrown away." Once again he agonized over where to build a Colorado branch. Clark advocated Cheyenne and observed with remarkable foresight that the only virtue of a line to Julesburg was that it "might prevent the B & M from building into Denver. But that line undoubtedly will go there any way, sooner or later."

But Gould did not discourage easily. Wielding the threat of extension, he nursed the negotiations along until Carr agreed in April to consolidating the Kansas Pacific and both Colorado roads into a new company capitalized at twenty million dollars. The Union Pacific was to receive half its stock and control all the roads. The deal appeared to resolve the whole Colorado tangle in one package. It gave the Union Pacific a line into Denver, removed the Kansas Pacific as a competitor, allowed the Central to extend in a manner suited to its location, and eliminated a dangerous political issue. "Our arrangement with the Kansas Pacific I consider of great value to us," Gould beamed. "It settles forever the question of *pro rata* & as the UP owns a majority of the KP stock we can so shape the policy of that company as to promote harmony & profit." As a bonus the agreement also helped fuel Gould's bulling of Union Pacific stock in the spring of 1875.

Already Gould was envisioning a through route to the Atlantic seaboard via the Kansas Pacific and four connecting lines. While he looked toward the horizon, the merger came unwound at his feet. The Kansas Pacific promptly elected four Union Pacific men to its board, but the counties owning Denver Pacific stock were reluctant to sell their shares or approve the merger. Local interests in Colorado also protested loudly. Within the Central Loveland complained bitterly of being sold out even though Union Pacific owned three fourths of the Central's stock. As the delays piled up Gould insisted repeatedly that the matter be finalized. "The Kansas Pacific have completed their part," he stressed at one point, "& we should now do ours."

In December Gould fell ill and was laid up for over a month. Once recovered, he and Dillon disposed of the last obstacles and obtained the board's approval in March. All that remained was action by the Central's board at its annual meeting in May. However, Rollins carelessly forgot to put the official seal on the company's proxies forwarded to Golden. Loveland pounced on this blunder and had the Union Pacific's 9,350 shares thrown out. With support from the counties owning stock, Loveland elected his own board, assumed the presidency, and enjoined the Union Pacific from any transactions with the Kansas Pacific. A shocked Teller hurried to see Loveland and reported that "his temper is up & he means to make all the trouble he can and he is well aware that in this controversy he has support of the people of the Counties holding stock."

Furious at this maneuver, Gould decided to force the Central into foreclosure and have a receiver appointed. When suit was brought, Loveland stalled the case with procedural snags and rebuffed overtures from Dillon, who went to Colorado to negotiate peace. Poppleton then filed a bill for a receiver, who was appointed on August 12. The court agreed to convene in Boulder a few days later to approve the receiver's bond. Aware that the court's term expired the day after this session, Loveland resorted to a spectacular maneuver. As the train carrying the judge neared Boulder, it was stopped by masked men who seized the judge and drove him blindfolded toward the mountains for a brief vacation. Three days later the judge was put in a carriage, blindfolded again, and released in downtown Denver.

The excitement aroused by this incident did not stop the receiver from taking possession of the Central, but Loveland had so inflamed local opinion against Eastern Moguls that the receiver could do nothing. Poppleton tried to get the case removed. "This State is too full of thieves for non-residents property to have any chance except in the U.S. Courts," he snapped. "If Oliver Ames or any body else puts more into this Country, he ought to loose [sic] it." Loveland spurned another offer from Dillon, leaving no alternative except to press the suits vigorously. The problem was that Loveland could rally local sentiment against the Union Pacific regardless of what the courts ruled. Even Poppleton had to concede that "Loveland controls the Colorado side of this controversy and whatever he agrees to will be done."

During this lengthy struggle two major developments forced Gould into rethinking his tactics. The Denver & Rio Grande under General William J. Palmer opened its narrow-gauge road from Denver to Pueblo. In March 1876 the Atchison, Topeka & Santa Fe reached Pueblo, which enabled Denver traffic to reach Kansas City via either the Kansas Pacific or the combined Rio Grande-Atchison line. This dramatic change in the competitive picture transformed Colorado into a hothouse of intrigue. All three roads were eager to build south to Trinidad and west along the Arkansas River to the mining region beyond Canon City. None had the money to expand, which made them eager for peace. After prolonged negotiations the three roads agreed in August 1876 to pool Colorado business. It was at best a fragile truce, liable to fly apart at the first strain.

The second development was no less ominous. In September 1876 Gould realized that the Kansas Pacific would default before the consolidation was perfected. Together with the road's leading investors, he prepared a plan of reorganization that preserved the intent of the merger. Gould hoped to get control of the Denver Pacific cheaply, but in November the court dealt him a blow by appointing Carlos S. Greeley and Henry Villard joint receivers for the Kansas Pacific. Gould now had to deal with three distinct groups: Carr represented the stockholders, Greeley the bondholders on the main line, and Villard the bondholders on the Denver extension (Denver Pacific). Carr and Greeley still favored the consolidation; Villard was more concerned about the need "to save the road from losing the Denv Pacif stock."

Amid these treacherous currents of change Gould decided on a radical change in tactics. Few men rivaled his ability to reverse course when necessity demanded or his skill at opening several fronts at once and shifting deftly among them. Like a chess master he plotted every move not in isolation but as part of some larger scheme designed to serve several objectives at once. In February 1877 he ended the stalemate in Colorado by coming to terms with Loveland and putting him in charge of the Central. "I dont think it will work," wrote a dubious Oliver Ames, who missed its finer points. The deal restored the Central as a bargaining chip in the Kansas Pacific negotiations. Moreover, as Palmer noted astutely, it enabled Gould to "have control as thoroughly as before [while] allowing Loveland to claim victory to make him right before his neighbors & the counties."

Gould still wanted control of the Denver Pacific with or (preferably) without its parent road. As part of the original agreement the Kansas Pacific had issued a $1.5 million mortgage to secure the floating debt, half of which was held by the Union Pacific. When the loan matured, the Union Pacific was to receive the collateral held by it, which included the Denver Pacific's stock. Villard sought to prevent this by raising enough money to pay interest on the funding bonds. But Gould had also loaned the Kansas Pacific $85,000 on notes maturing in February 1877. As a prod he unexpectedly sued to collect when these notes expired and talked of selling off the funding bonds. In Denver John Evans stirred up sentiment for placing the Denver Pacific under local management while Loveland inflamed the county officials against the high rates caused by Kansas Pacific control of the road.

These moves caught the Kansas Pacific by surprise. Carr had recently suspended his *pro rata* suits as a gesture of goodwill only to find fresh evidence of discrimination at Cheyenne. Convinced that Gould was "at the bottom of the Denver Pacific troubles in Denver" by "using Gov Evans as an instrument," he warned Villard to prepare for war and turned all negotiations with Gould over to him. But the Kansas Pacific bondholders were squabbling among themselves and agreed only to press the *pro rata* suits anew. Gould compounded their confusion by asserting his desire to proceed with the plan for consolidation. In May he worked out a revised version of the plan with the bondholders committee, raising new hopes for a final settlement.

Once again the plan fell through. The Colorado scene had grown more complex. Loveland was anxious to extend the Central westward to Georgetown, and for some time Evans had been trying to interest Gould in his pet project, the Denver, South Park & Pacific, which was to curl through the mining region southwest of Denver. Possibly Gould saw that if these roads formed a system to tap the Colorado mines, they would need a reliable connection to the Union Pacific. If he could not get the Denver Pacific on his terms, the Central would do as well or better, since it lay west of Denver. Work on the Georgetown branch was already underway when Gould announced in June that the Central would build at once to Cheyenne via Longmont.

Villard responded by breaking off negotiations with Gould. A journalist turned financier, Villard had the support of the foreign bondholders who had large holdings in Denver Pacific. Their leader, who dismissed the Central extension as a bluff, urged Villard not to trust "men like Gould who avail of every chance to ignore an agreement that does not suit them for the time." As the fight warmed, Villard showed himself a dangerous adversary. He set about devising a new reorganization plan to eliminate the influence exerted by Gould through his holdings in Kansas Pacific junior securities. At the same time Villard opened a vigorous lobby in Washington for a new *pro rata* bill introduced by his ally, Senator Jerome B. Chaffee of Colorado. In this campaign he got quick support from Charles E. Perkins of the B & M.

None of this surprised Gould. "I dont believe the KP will ever get *pro rata,*" he assured Clark, "& we must so effectively clean them out in Colorado that they will sue for terms." With Clark prodding Loveland, the Central entered Cheyenne in November 1877 amid fanfares of oratory in Denver about cheaper, competitive rates. To intensify pressure on the Denver Pacific, Loveland was given discretionary power on rates for all eastbound Colorado traffic. That winter Gould and Dodge managed to throttle *pro rata* in Congress and thwart the Kansas Pacific in court as well. Villard, lamenting that "the U.P. seems to be now making war on us in earnest," tried desperately to enlist John Murray Forbes of the Burlington and Thomas H. Nickerson of the Atchison in the Kansas Pacific reorganization. Both limited their investment to moral support. Forbes conceded that Villard needed "somebody behind him to fight Gould," but he was far too conservative to shoulder a bankrupt road.

Gould recognized that the advantage he had gained was only temporary. The hostile mood of Congress to all the Pacific roads turned events there against him. A long battle over refunding the government loan culminated in the punitive Thurman bill, which was marching steadily toward passage. *Pro rata* revived unexpectedly when the House agreed to consider a report advocated by the Kansas Pacific. The House was also under pressure to investigate the Kansas Pacific for past irregularities trumpeted by the New York *Sun* as "The New Credit Mobilier." These threats prompted Gould to switch tactics again while his bargaining position was strong. Dropping his warlike mask, he formed a pool in Kansas Pacific junior securities with most of the St. Louis stockholders and many of the bondholders represented by Greeley. In the process he induced some directors to deposit their holdings by assuming personally about $313,000 of the floating debt carried by them.

By this maneuver Gould gained equity control of the Kansas Pacific and wedded the interests of Greeley and the St. Louis directors to his own. Having isolated Villard, Gould proceeded to offer him a new reorganization plan with concessions favorable to the Denver extension bondholders. Its terms amounted to a *status quo ante bellum* in which the Union Pacific would manage the Kansas Pacific and Central. Villard accepted and signed a traffic agreement on June 1, 1878. With a sigh of relief he turned the road over to Dillon on June 20 and prepared eagerly for a trip to Europe. That same day, however, the new Kansas Pacific board met in Lawrence. Gould and Dillon were there, having paused on the return leg of an inspection tour. The board decided to offer the Denver extension bondholders a new plan with less favorable terms and took steps to foreclose under one of the junior mortgages before the first mortgage holders could act under their prior lien.

"The scamp Gould is again going back on us," Villard raged after learning that "he and the rascally St Louis people, including my colleagues Carr & Usher, had formed a regular conspiracy in the West to break the contract and cheat the bond holders." Instead of a soothing European spa Villard found himself in the wilting summer heat of St. Louis, tossing fitfully in his bed while a relentless downpour battered the hotel roof. The bondholders rallied behind him and a bitter struggle ensued for control of the reorganization. Gould wanted it dominated by the members of his securities pool and insisted that the Union Pacific operate the Kansas Pacific under the June agreement. When the latter's superintendent, Thomas F. Oakes, refused to acknowledge Clark's authority, Gould filed suit to remove Villard as receiver.

In October the court removed both receivers and appointed the Kansas Pacific's auditor in their place. The bondholders spurned all overtures to negotiate on any terms short of the original agreement. They distrusted Gould and were tired of following him "through endless mazes." Villard prepared a new reorganization plan, pressed relentlessly for foreclosure, and even talked of extending the road to Ogden. Fred Ames tried to intervene and was told bluntly by the head of the bondholders' committee that "certain parties are very shy of entering on any negotiations . . . where it is known, Mr Gould has a predominating Interest." Villard put it more bluntly. The bondholders, he declared, "are trying to overcome Gould & Gould is trying to overcome us."

By the autumn of 1878, the struggle for Colorado had wound its tortuous way to a stalemate. Thus far the failures of Gould's policy outweighed its successes. Having inherited a dismal situation, he tried diligently to cut through its complexities only to find himself bogged down in yet another labyrinth. The Union Pacific had wedged its way into Colorado but on costly terms. It had built the parallel road from Denver to Cheyenne that Gould hoped to avoid and still found itself at the mercy of Colorado interests who were as treacherous as they had been in Oliver's day.

During 1878 ominous tales about Loveland had begun to surface. J. M. Eddy, the young axman whose pluck had saved the survey party in 1867 after Hills had been slain by Indians, was general agent in Denver and wrote Dodge a lengthy indictment of Loveland's deceit and mismanagement. The Central was poorly built, he charged angrily, its operation bungled, its equipment run down, and its managers hostile to the Union Pacific. The overt favoring of Golden had outraged Denver shippers and ruined the Central's business. Anxious that Gould and the Union Pacific not be blamed for the fiasco but helpless to effect a change, Eddy resigned in disgust and took a position with the Atchison.

Eddy was not alone in his protest. An engineer confided to Dodge that Loveland and his cronies were silent partners in the grading contract for the Cheyenne extension and had falsified much of the work. As for the line itself, "There is scarcely a place . . . where *a better and cheaper line to build and operate is not in sight.*" In the summer of 1878 Gould and Dillon toured the Central and were "terrible mad at what they saw & heard," but by then it was too late. In trying to resolve a messy situation Gould put his confidence in the wrong man. For that mistake the Union Pacific found itself saddled with the wrong road in the wrong place for the wrong reason.

* * *

The flaw that plagued Gould in the Colorado arrangement was having to share control of the Central with men he was obliged to trust and could not watch constantly. A similar pattern unfolded wherever the company looked to develop feeder lines. To some extent this was inevitable in a policy that relied on local promoters for branch building. The Union Pacific could support their effort but not dominate it, and was always at the mercy of conflicts and rivalries among competing local interests. In that awkward role it did not so much shape events as become an unwilling prisoner of them, pitched and hauled by the crosscurrents of regional passions and politics. This was another of the liabilities inherited by Gould, and it forced him repeatedly into a role he was reluctant to assume. When progress on a branch stalled, he took up the work himself.

The situation in Utah resembled that in Colorado with one crucial difference. There the company had as partners not Loveland's venal group but the Mormons, whose passion for railroad building knew no bounds. Like Colorado, the great potential for wealth in Utah was mining, which required an efficient rail system to tap on a large scale. The long and bitter squabble over settling accounts had left the Mormons distrustful of the Union Pacific, but they lacked the capital to build railroads and were far too practical to shun their most logical source of aid. After his futile attempt to prevent the Union Pacific from going north to Salt Lake, Brigham Young used loans and material from the company to build his Utah Central between Ogden and Salt Lake City.

Completion of the Utah Central in January 1870 left Young weary, deeply in debt, and still wrangling with the Union Pacific over his accounts. That summer Bishop Sharp sounded Duff on the company's interest in leasing or buying the new road or providing it a loan. The directors were far too absorbed in their own woes to offer Young any comfort. Only when Huntington put in a bid for the Utah Central did Dillon and Dodge alert Oliver Ames to the danger of losing the Utah trade to the Central Pacific and persuade him to lend the Mormons enough money to hang onto their road. The bargain struck in February 1871 taught both sides a useful lesson. The company realized that its Utah connections were too valuable to ignore, while the Mormons discovered the value of playing one Pacific road against the other.

During 1871 an expansionist mood swept through Utah. The railroad's presence encouraged the opening of several smelters. As word of Utah's mining potential spread, gentile promoters began investing in the region south of Salt Lake City. If rails could be extended southward, a thriving mineral industry would develop. To the north lay scattered Mormon communities in the Cache Valley and beyond them the vast mining potential of Idaho and Wyoming. The early reluctance of the Mormons gave way to euphoria over what more trackage could accomplish. That year two new projects were chartered, the Utah Southern and Utah Northern, to extend the Utah Central in both directions. The Union Pacific provided loans to help the Southern get under way, while the Northern was in the hands of John Young and Joseph Richardson of Connecticut, who was friendly to the Union Pacific and anxious to keep the project under its influence.

In Utah the Union Pacific had also to deal with a complication not found anywhere else. The first transcontinental transformed every part of the country it traversed, but in Utah it had a unique social impact. By opening the region to travel and commerce, it exposed the Mormons anew to a nation that had reviled them and driven them into exile decades earlier. This fresh glimpse at Mormon institutions brought grudging praise for their wondrous development of the Utah wilderness along with a new wave of violent anti-Mormon sentiment aimed chiefly at what the New York *Times* called "a hideous excrescence," polygamy. By 1871 the issue was fast boiling into a political crisis as pressure grew for Congress to ban the practice. Aware that the conflict had grave implications for the Union Pacific's role in Utah, Richardson urged Dodge to "keep Grant cool on Mormonism."

Dodge needed little prodding. He was alarmed by the tendency of government officials in Utah to force a confrontation. "The Mormons are determined not to be the aggressors, and are submitting," he stressed, "but this overhauling crimes committed years ago . . . only brings harm instead of good." If left alone, Dodge predicted, public opinion and the weight of emigration would bring the Mormons to abandon polygamy without a fight. He was adamant that "a conflict should not be allowed under any circumstances" because of the disastrous effects it would have on both the country and the railroad. The immediate crisis passed but the tensions lingered for years. Not until 1890, when the Mormons at last abolished polygamy, was Utah admitted to the Union. Through those difficult years the Union Pacific maintained close relations with the Mormons despite criticism for doing so.

During the early 1870s, however, the relationship was strained for reasons that had nothing to do with Mormonism. Brigham Young was anxious to push construction of the Southern to open up the mining region and sent Bishop Sharp to badger the Union Pacific for aid. Boston was sympathetic but preoccupied with its own problems and the muddle in Colorado, which had first priority. For more than a year Sharp made repeated pilgrimages east to plead for money, iron, supplies, and rolling stock. The company put him off with a trickle of material, most of it old and worn out. On one occasion Sharp waited months and was rewarded with less than a mile of iron with no spikes. Rails were expensive and hard to obtain, and the company was wallowing in debt. The persistent Sharp declared he would rather trust in God than the Union Pacific, but he was shrewd enough to know which was more likely to provide immediate capital.

An exasperated Brigham Young flatly refused to accept any more used material and declared that if the Union Pacific would not deliver, "we shall have to form connection with some other company." Sharp dutifully visited Huntington and was told the Central Pacific did not lend money but might be willing to buy a controlling interest in the Utah Central. The Union Pacific's Horace Clark also asserted that it was his policy "never to invest where he could not control." In June 1872 Sharp got some money by selling the Union Pacific three thousand shares of Utah Central stock, but the *"everlasting board"* continued to drag its heels on furnishing material despite Sharp's constant prodding. In his relentless search for aid Sharp approached the Kansas Pacific and even the truncated Central Branch, which had ambitions of building to Utah. The Kansas Pacific eagerly made Sharp a proposal even though its finances were in worse shape than those of the Union Pacific.

Young talked hopefully of "settling up and looking elsewhere," but times were hard and there was nowhere else to turn. The Mormons managed to push the Southern to Lehi in 1872, then suspended work for lack of funds. During the next year the Union Pacific was prevented by its own woes from rendering any help. On their own the Mormons brought the Southern into Provo by parceling out work to the faithful in exchange for shares in the road. To eyes capable of looking past the obvious, Utah was ripe with promise by the end of 1873. It already possessed thirty ore-reduction furnaces, eleven of them within a dozen miles of Salt Lake City, and a swelling traffic in coal and coke. Although the Mormons controlled nearly all the local railroads, 90 percent of the mining property was owned by gentiles. Beyond Provo lay a large mineral region waiting to be developed.

Gould was fully alive to the possibilities but he wanted control of the Utah roads and he needed the right man with whom to deal. Sharp satisfied him on both counts. In October 1874 Gould reversed years of ambivalent policy toward Utah by arranging the sort of package deal that was his trademark. Sharp agreed to sell him enough stock in both the Utah Central and Southern to assure a half interest in the roads. Gould in turn sold these shares at cost to the Union Pacific, which then loaned the Southern two hundred thousand dollars to build another twenty-five miles of road. The Utah Southern bonds already owned by the company were then used to pay Oliver Ames and his friends for their stock in the Colorado Improvement Company. All this was at first too fast for Oliver. "I do not feel that is a proper thing for Impt Co or UP to do," he muttered, but a few months' reflection changed his mind.

This chain reaction cemented the company's position in both Colorado and Utah. Gould regarded both as crucial in the grand scheme of things. Never mind that a depression loomed on the horizon; the results would show, he predicted, "when times get good & when we get our Colorado Central & Utah Southern systems developed & in full accord with the trunk line." His decisiveness erased years of company lethargy in Utah and galvanized the Mormons, who completed the new track in only four months. Gould showed his appreciation of Sharp by putting him on the Union Pacific board. The canny Sharp, who had come to Utah from the coal pits of Scotland, was to hold that seat the rest of his life.

The Mormons had another budding project, the Utah Western, organized in June 1874 to reach the Pioche mines across the desert in Nevada. Starved for funds, John Young in October 1875 first approached Huntington, then went to Dillon with the same proposal. However, the old trick of playing the Pacific roads off against one another backfired this time. Huntington had other fish to fry, while an annoyed Gould asked Clark to have an agent quietly purchase some shares of Southern to give the Union Pacific a majority. "I dont like to be in the controll [sic] of the Mormons," he explained. His reason had nothing to do with Mormonism but rather with his distaste for shared control, the same bugaboo that plagued him in Colorado and, on a grander scale, with the federal government. Clark picked up enough shares to reorganize the Southern's board in January 1876 with Sharp as president and superintendent.

By early 1876 the company had both Utah roads under firm control and in reliable hands. When an ailing Brigham Young offered to sell another small mining road, the Summit County, Gould picked it up for sixty thousand dollars. Although he remained aloof from John Young's Western, his acquisitions spurred rumors in Utah that new branch extensions would soon be built. Gould did nothing to squelch such talk but he was in no hurry. "I dont think we want to extend the U. S. Rd.," he told Clark privately, "till we know whether it will *hurt* or help UP." Later he would find expansion of the Southern useful as a pawn in his duel with Huntington.

Before Gould extended the Southern he had to resolve the problem of what to do with the Northern. By February 1874 John Young and Richardson had managed to build seventy-seven miles from Ogden to the village of Franklin on the Idaho border. Young viewed the road as a feeder to the Mormon farmers in the Cache Valley, but their thrifty habits did not support it. Wells, Fargo agents had already learned the harsh lesson that "one Gentile makes as much business as a hundred Mormons." Richardson saw that his investment could be salvaged only by extending northward to Montana, where railroad mania had reached fever pitch, but Young looked no farther than the Mormon settlement at Soda Springs. In March 1875 Young tried to arouse Huntington's interest in the Northern. Huntington refused because he was "satisfied that the U.P., and not J. M. Young, controlled that road." A few months later Young resigned as president of the road, leaving Richardson free to woo the Union Pacific for assistance.

Huntington was wrong. The Union Pacific owned some securities in the Northern but not the road itself. Gould was receptive to Richardson's pleas because the Northern intersected a number of possibilities. He knew Montana had been starved for railroads since its great hope, the Northern Pacific, had gone bankrupt before reaching the territorial border. The north country was in the same position as the West before the coming of the Union Pacific. It had to be supplied by Missouri River steamers and overland wagons. Farmers and stockmen lacked access to markets, and placer mining was about played out. Low-grade ores could not be mined because the cost of importing heavy machinery and hauling ore to reduction plants was prohibitive without a railroad. The Northern could open the entire region to development and funnel traffic down for the long haul on the main line. There was another, less obvious angle that intrigued Gould: the Northern might also be used as part of a branch to Oregon and/or the Black Hills, where discoveries of gold had begun to attract miners.

In mulling over these considerations Gould concluded that the project was feasible if he could get the right location for the line and a suitable subsidy from the territory. Since 1872 the legislature had been locked in fierce battle over the subsidy question. One group, headed by Governor B. F. Potts, favored the Northern Pacific's east-west route; another, led by Samuel Hauser, wanted aid for the north-south Northern line. The fight grew even more desperate after the Panic of 1873 brought railroad building to a standstill. In January 1876 the legislature tried to satisfy everyone by approving subsidies for the two major roads and a small local line, but Richardson promptly declined the offer as too much of a good thing. A flood of bonds from a territory with modest resources, he pointed out, would not sell in eastern markets.

Bloodied but unbowed, Hauser and Martin Maginnis, the congressional delegate from Montana, worked feverishly for a new subsidy package. They saw that Richardson could not go it alone and took their case directly to Gould and Dillon. Maginnis came away impressed by Gould as "a bright little fellow . . . who has the clearest idea of the advantage of a Montana connection to their road." After lengthy negotiations Gould put together a syndicate to extend the Northern, asked the legislature for a new subsidy, and signed an agreement with Richardson, who would act as contractor for the work. The legislature complied in February 1877 and Montana seemed destined at last to get the railroad it had awaited for so long.

However, the "bright little fellow" had second thoughts. To Hauser's chagrin the syndicate rejected the new subsidy, ostensibly because of an unfavorable tax provision but also because Gould considered the Northern the wrong road in the wrong place. He wanted a standard rather than a narrow gauge road, preferably built from Evanston where grades were easier and coal abundant. That autumn he and Dillon looked the Northern over on their western tour. Convinced that further delay would prove fatal, Gould reluctantly abandoned his Evanston line and let a contract to extend the Northern twenty miles. At once Richardson objected to Gould's choice of route north of Franklin. A perplexed engineer on the scene appealed to Dillon, "Gould says let work Richardson says dont let it." Once again the problem of shared control rose to haunt Gould. When neither his friends nor the company showed any desire to put more money into the Northern, Gould bought Richardson out and personally assumed the contract. The road was foreclosed in April 1878 and reorganized as the Utah & Northern. Gould ordered Clark to prepare for laying fifty miles of track at once. "I feel that we should make a strong pull to get & keep the Montana business," he added, "otherwise it feeds & strengthens the Northern Pacific & is an incentive to their pushing ahead."

Once the decision was made, Gould drove the work vigorously. Even before work started on the fifty miles he concluded to build twice that amount to reach the Snake River at Blackfoot. To draw business from western Idaho he spent money to improve the wagon road from Boise to the Snake River. By late summer he was looking beyond Blackfoot to Montana. "The more I hear of & from Montana & Northern Idaho," he enthused, "the more I am impressed with the wonderful mineral wealth in gold & silver of that region & when the U & N is once extended so as to give them a chance to mine the lower grades of ore . . . it will be Colorado over again."

While urging the work crews forward Gould applied to the legislature for another subsidy. Unlike many railroad men, however, Gould did not wait for the subsidy to build. The Montana branch was too important to the Union Pacific to suffer delays. It would pay, he was certain of it. In one season he had swept away the indecision over the north country; the Union Pacific was going to Montana. Here as elsewhere, Gould left an indelible imprint on the destiny of the Union Pacific. By extending the Utah roads in both directions, he forged a north-south branch system through the mineral region that would play a vital role in the company's future.

*   *   *

The enthusiasm Gould showed for building branches in the mineral region did not extend to the plains, partly because of his belief that "as a general rule railroads that depend for support on agriculture never pay." Mining provided immediate traffic for long haul, farming a slow and uncertain business. The presence of other roads also imposed restraints. Competition scarcely existed in the mountains, but on the plains it created a delicate web of diplomacy in which branch building was tantamount to mobilization. Gould also found the provisions of a new state constitution passed by Nebraska in 1875 "so obnoxious I dont want to build much RRds subject to them in that state." For these reasons the company did little in Nebraska beyond fending off projects seeking subsidies that it might want later.

The twin factors of diplomacy and subsidy were responsible for the one agricultural branch that was built. The tier of counties south of the Platte River between Omaha and Grand Island occupied sensitive ground between the Union Pacific and the B & M. Gould thought the new constitution forbade counties from issuing bonds for railroads. When it became clear that a subsidy could be obtained, he approved construction of a narrow-gauge line in 1876. Known as the Omaha & Republican Valley, the road was built to Wahoo by January 1877, then later extended that year to David City, sixty miles from the main line. Although county bonds helped finance the work, the market for them was so poor that Gould was obliged to take most of them personally. It took him more than a year of concerted effort to dispose of them. In time the Republican Valley would expand into a modest system of feeders. During the 1870s it served mostly as a club wielded by Gould in his negotiations with the B & M.

The restraints that tempered Gould's approach to branch building were most strikingly evident in his handling of the Black Hills question. In 1874 scientists accompanying Gen. George Custer's expedition to the Black Hills returned with glowing accounts of gold in the Bighorn region. Newspapers picked up the scent, especially in Omaha, which hoped to capture the travel and outfitting business of a gold rush. The following summer a scientific expedition headed by Professor Walter P. Janney undertook a careful study of the Black Hills region. By then the first wave of prospectors had flocked eagerly into Indian country, rummaging everywhere for gold in violation of existing treaties. Grant ordered the miners off Indian land but the Army was overrun by sheer numbers. Janney found his own movements shadowed by men eager to cash in on whatever the scientists found. He reported finds of gold in paying quantities but was careful to emphasize that "no matter how valuable the mines may be, the future great wealth of the Black Hills will be its grass lands, farms, and timber."

By 1876 the gold craze had drawn twenty thousand people into the Hills, creating an explosive situation. Those hungry for quick riches ignored Janney's prudent words. Gould was among the few who read the professor's report closely. Any promising mineral strike aroused his interest, but he was not a man to follow his enthusiasms blindly. In February 1876 he invited Janney to spend an evening discussing the Black Hills in depth. This conversation satisfied Gould that the potential for a profitable branch was there, but the Indian conflict had to be resolved and the starting point for a branch weighed carefully. Gould's object was not merely to exploit the gold rush but also to cultivate a traffic in livestock and farm products as well. Janney thought the best approach to the Hills was from Cheyenne because the route offered "splendid grazing country."

Although Janney assured him that the mineral prospects of the region were enormous, Gould moved cautiously. To capture the flow of prospectors, he ordered Clark to open a stagecoach service between Cheyenne and the mining district but did nothing about a branch line. In July the country was shocked by the massacre at Little Bighorn. Clark fretted that the outbreak of war would destroy the mining boom, but Gould looked further ahead. "The ultimate result," he predicted shrewdly, "will be to annihilate the Indians & open up the Big Horn & Black Hills to development & settlement & in this way greatly benefit us." He was content to watch and wait while the war played itself out. Dillon talked of building a hundred miles the following year and commenced surveys that winter, but Gould would not be hurried. He wanted the road in the right place, and he demanded a suitable charter. "We can get what we want before the road is built," he reminded Clark, "but not afterwards."

A charter was prepared and rumor spread that construction would begin, but Gould decided to wait until Cheyenne delivered on its promise of a $250,000 subsidy. Then his uncertainty over the starting point got entangled with his ruminations over where to put the Northern and with Loveland's desire to make the Black Hills road an extension of the Colorado Central north of Cheyenne. During the summer of 1877 Dillon brought James Evans back to run some surveys. "I think Evanston is the route," he told Evans. "Can the Black Hills line be continued into Montana and is it practicable?" Before Evans finished his work Gould mused that "this Black Hills line when built will have to start from some point east of Cheyenne—though I would not wish to say that out loud." Once convinced that a single route could not serve both roads, Gould's interest in a Wyoming subsidy waned.

Evans confirmed Gould's hunch by reporting that a line from Cheyenne would be inferior in every respect and "any money spent in that way will be thrown away." The board then accepted Gould's plan for an alternate route that would drastically shorten the wagon haul to the Black Hills and permit competition with the overland route via Bismarck. However, this line required a charter to cross government land and allow the company to build such a branch. Loveland continued to scheme for a way to extend the Central to the Black Hills despite Evans's findings and even ran surveys on his own. Another season passed without a rail going down. Gould still advocated the branch, which he called a "necessity," and a chat with General Phil Sheridan renewed his enthusiasm. "The Genl is full of Black Hills," he reported, "& says there is business enough there now to make a railroad pay."

But its time had gone by. After two more years of talk the project was shelved. The Union Pacific declined the bonds offered by Laramie County and instead chartered a branch with the imposing name of Omaha, Niobrara & Black Hills. This line left the main stem a hundred miles west of Omaha and got no closer to the Hills than the village of Norfolk, Nebraska. By 1880 the company's and Gould's own situation had changed dramatically. In their scheme of priorities the Black Hills could not compete with other projects for funds.

Some years later, amid the competitive wars of the 1880s, Dillon told a government commission grandly, "We, on the Union Pacific, are like an apple tree without a limb; unless we have branches there will be no fruit. We must build branch roads." In their quest for traffic it was the way of many railroads to grow branches as indiscriminately as did the apple tree. That was not Gould's style. During his Union Pacific years he did not simply promote expansion but worked hard to give it a focus and cohesion it had always lacked. He did not always succeed, but his failures resulted more often from the legacy of past policies, political pressures, or competitive forces than from his own mistakes of judgment. His sure grasp of the need for growth was tempered by caution and patience, a determination to get precisely what his analysis revealed was needed. As his handling of the Black Hills line illustrates, he understood that it was better to build no line at all than to build the wrong line in the wrong place.

Bear with us, please: The largest and most elegant structure on the line was at its terminus. The transfer station at Council Bluffs received passengers from the Iowa lines and moved them to the Union Pacific depot across the river. In this scene, taken during the flood of 1881, the river has the best of the railroad.

Starting Point: This photograph from the late 1860s shows Omaha looking north from the hill on South Eleventh Street. The large brick building at right is the Herndon House. The river appears to be in flood. *(Courtesy of the Bostwick-Frohardt Collection, KMTV, Omaha, Nebraska)*

A view of Omaha in 1871, looking east down the hill from Seventeenth and Farnam streets.

The first headquarters of the Union Pacific was the old Herndon House, built in 1857 and shown here in its original form.

The Union Pacific acquired the Herndon House in 1870 and enlarged it to the extent shown in this picture.

Men at Work: The machine shops at Omaha, which served as supply base during the construction years.

The shops at Laramie. Note the elaborate belting required to run machinery.

Men at Play: *(Above)* The Union Pacific band in 1871, decked out in their uniforms and ready to show their stuff.

(Left) The Union Pacific baseball team in 1886, which a year earlier had boasted of being "World Champions."

(Below) The Boys at the Office: a section gang at Elm Creek in 1884.

═══ 18 ═══

THE ANCIENT FEUD

The political role of railroads has long been misrepresented as a morality play in which powerful, ruthless corporations trampled the public interest underfoot until regulation curbed their depredations. In the folklore of reform the struggle between the railroads and "the people," like most myths, contains enough truth to mislead. All railroads had an economic impact on the regions they served, which thrust them into state and local politics to protect their interests. The Union Pacific as a mixed enterprise had also to contend with the federal government. This perpetual battle at so many levels of government drained the company of resources and vitality it could ill afford during these years.

Myth has a way of distorting conflicts into simplistic clashes between good and evil from which a proper moral can be drawn. In reality the struggle was far too complex for either side to possess a monopoly of virtue. Like any corporation, the Union Pacific did not hesitate to use its considerable power on behalf of its interests, but even its worst abuses were more often born of weakness than of strength. Outsiders tended to view the company as a corporate leviathan and ignored the extent to which size made it a target as well as a force. Its enemies might be smaller and weaker, but their number was legion and their demands incessant. Who were "the people" opposing the railroad's power? They were not disinterested spectators but a collage of individuals, firms, interest groups, rival lines, speculators, politicians, whole communities, each seeking some advantage in the form of contracts, jobs, payoffs, lower rates, rebates, services, branch or spur lines, profits from the rise or fall of security prices, and many more.

Within its territory the Union Pacific functioned as queen on the chessboard of economic development. The most enlightened or disinterested policy could not have satisfied the whole range of interests clamoring for its services. Decisions favoring one group invariably disappointed others, who were quick to blame their misfortunes on the malevolence and greed of the railroad. Farmers could attribute their distress to high rates and unfair classification policies, businessmen to rebates or other discriminatory practices that gave rivals an advantage. Communities not located on the line condemned the railroad for sentencing them to economic stagnation, while those on the line complained bitterly if they did not receive tariffs favoring their growth at the expense of rival towns. That the railroad made decisions to serve its own interest did not impress those whose self-interest suffered from the results.

All these conflicts were played out in the political arena, where size made the Union Pacific vulnerable though it loomed like a juggernaut in the eyes of adversaries. The company could not wield influence everywhere all the time. From the first it had to contend with three legislatures, municipal authorities, town councils, and county courthouses as well as the federal government. To transact business it needed the assistance of governors, congressmen, judges, legislators, mayors, aldermen, sheriffs, editors, bankers, and merchants. Contrary to myth, the company seldom got as good as it gave from friends or foes. For every favor granted a dozen were demanded in return—passes, payment, investments, securities, contracts, agencies, jobs, and political contributions, to name but a few.

Predators swarmed the company like flies tormenting a bull. The corporation might not have a soul to damn or a body to kick, but it had a pocket to pick and the art of venality was not confined to its own officers. For the Union Pacific, politics was an exercise in self-defense. It worked hard to elect friends to office, harder still to defeat foes. More effort went to resisting hostile legislation than to obtaining favorable bills. Ever sensitive to publicity, the company was more intent on punishing unfriendly editors than rewarding sympathetic ones. In the courts it had to defend against many more suits than it brought. Local juries and judges were often hostile to the railroad. The tactic of appealing lost decisions was effective but expensive, which made for rich pickings among lawyers who feasted on the railroad business.

As resentment against the railroad swelled, the clashes multiplied and the price of victory soared. All roads faced this same dilemma but most did not also have to grapple with the federal government. In one way or another the Union Pacific made its peace with local agencies, but the dispute with Washington dragged on through the century like some ancient family feud, a ritual of acrimony that had long since lost touch with the realities of changing times. Ultimately the fight brought the company to its knees but, as with all ancient feuds, the outcome produced many casualties and no winners.

* * *

"The belief prevails here," Peter Dey wrote from Omaha in 1865, "that the influence of the Company is, and is likely always to be overshaddowing [sic]." In Nebraska the Union Pacific was present at the creation. At the company's request Poppleton drew up the territory's first general railroad law in 1864 and was its lobbyist when the first constitution was drafted two years later. In Wyoming the railroad was actually creator; the territory was, as one historian noted, "the child of the Union Pacific." The company did not create Utah but it opened the Mormon enclave to the outside world. As the chief instrument of economic development, the Union Pacific exerted a profound influence throughout the region it served. It was usually the largest employer and certainly the largest customer in the towns along its line. As the largest property owner, it furnished a major share of local tax revenues.

Inevitably the company's dominant economic position thrust it into state and local politics, where it did not hesitate to promote or defend its interests with all the power at its disposal. In 1887 Edward Rosewater, founder of the Omaha *Bee,* denounced the Union Pacific for meddling in politics and painted a lurid picture of "droves of men taken from the shop to vote." If the company wanted a candidate elected or a bill defeated, Rosewater charged, it set up "oil rooms" in Omaha hotels to lubricate legislators and public officials with liquor, cigars, and other amenities. His account fit all too neatly the stereotype of powerful corporations wielding political clout through corrupt means, but how true was it? The evidence suggests that Rosewater was accurate in some details but misleading in his conclusions, partly because of what he discreetly chose to leave out of his statement. To get at the truth one must ask not only what role in politics the company tried to play but also to what extent it succeeded or failed to obtain what it wanted.

Most of the time the Union Pacific was on the defensive, if only because the political scene in Nebraska was so volatile. Early in the 1870s scandal enmeshed the state government without any help from the company. A governor was impeached, his successor was accused of taking a bribe, and the state's revenue system wallowed in disarray. Granger sentiment swept the state on a wave of hard times and corruption. In 1875 voters were offered a new constitution with a provision for regulating railroads. By that time the Union Pacific had already fought two major battles with Nebraska, which tried to impose taxes first on its roadbed and then on that portion of the land grant in Nebraska. The company carried both levies to the Supreme Court, losing the first and winning the second. Apart from these issues, it did little in state politics beyond a feeble gesture toward relocating the state capital along its line. The new constitution shook the company from its inertia.

But not at once. The Union Pacific was slow to react because opinion differed over whether the new provision applied to a railroad with a federal charter. Dodge warned Gould that "the whole article appears to be aimed directly at us" and thought it could be beaten if Clark kept his lobbying as covert as possible. Gould doubted the measure could be used against the company but disliked it as a dangerous precedent and asked Clark to "lay the pipes for its defeat." Despite railroad opposition the new constitution won overwhelming approval. Gould had no intention of complying without a legal fight, but he could not refrain from asking Clark, "Where are the friends whom we helped so liberally last fall & winter by money aid & free transportation?"

As Gould implied, friends in high places cost a lot of money and yielded uncertain returns. In protecting its interests state officials mattered less to the company than the congressional delegation, who were needed as allies in the Thirty Years' War with the federal government. But efforts to elect helpmates gained only limited success. In 1874 the Union Pacific supported John M. Thayer's bid to reclaim a Senate seat lost three years earlier. Territorial pioneer, Indian fighter, Civil War veteran, and staunch friend of the Union Pacific, Thayer did nothing to conceal his ties to the railroad. He went to New York "to borrow money with half Nebraska well informed as to his mission," Gould reported to Clark, "and while we all feel friendly to him we thought it indiscreet to advance money to aid him further than had already been done." Thayer lost the election but was later appointed governor of Wyoming, in which position he remained useful to the company.

Nor was Union Pacific influence strong enough to prolong the career of Phineas W. Hitchcock, one of its best friends in the Senate. As author of the Timber Culture Act Hitchcock was considerably more than senator from Union Pacific, but in 1877 he lost his seat to former governor Alvin Saunders. "Sorry H is defeated," Gould responded to the news, "but of all the other candidates prefer Gov Saunders. I see no reason why he should not be friendly to us." Saunders did not disappoint him, but the lesson was plain. Railroad support alone could not put or keep a man in office; often it was as divided as any other constituency. Part of Hitchcock's problem was opposition from the B & M, which wanted a senator friendly to its interests.

It was not the first political clash between the rival roads. During the summer of 1876 Gould was bent on removing Lorenzo Crounse from Congress, where he had taken the B & M's side on such issues as *pro rata* and the bridge controversy. Gould instructed Clark to "defeat him at all hazard" and "get a good friend of the road nominated in his place." Rosewater recalled a "four days' pitched battle" at the state Republican convention in which Gould and Dillon personally led the campaign to get John C. Corwin nominated in place of Crounse. In fact Gould and Dillon paused for a week at Omaha during an inspection tour to orchestrate the attack. "We have had a big fight here with the B & M Rd over the nomination of Crounse," Gould informed Oliver Ames. "We have defeated them handsomely and nominated our man." Rosewater charged that delegates were bribed to secure Corwin's victory. Although his evidence was only hearsay, there was probably some truth in his allegation. As his career with Erie demonstrated, Gould knew how to bring politicians around to a proper point of view.

At the local level no issue aroused the company's wrath more than bond proposals for rival roads. It was an axiom of the age that towns or counties without a railroad wanted one, and those with a railroad wanted another one. Promoters understood this and were adept at wooing local officials for bonds to support construction. Of course the Union Pacific did not object to such bonds for itself, but it bristled when a county it ran through offered help for a competing line. In effect, the Union Pacific would be taxed to help build a rival road. On this question Gould was adamant. When Lone Tree, a forlorn village west of Columbus, entertained a bonding proposal, he advised Clark to "fight out even if in doing so nothing but the one Lone Tree was left to mark the present town site."

The most sensitive spot was Douglas County, since Omaha was the logical terminus for any line threatening the Union Pacific. In 1875 some Omaha businessmen sought bonds for a narrow-gauge project called the Nebraska Central. "Is it true that all our Omaha friends are going in to build a competing road to us West?" Gould wired George Miller of the *Herald*. "If so, I will vote for the immediate removal of our shops and all our works to Council Bluffs." The startled Miller tried to reassure Gould that the road posed no threat but was told curtly, "the injurious effect of the proposed scheme is too evident to require discussion." The bond issue was defeated amid rumblings from Rosewater that the company had "thumb-screwed" its own workers and men from the smelting plant into voting against the proposition. Later Rosewater asserted that the company had purchased a building from Phineas Hitchcock and some stock in the Omaha *Republican* in return for the senator's help in the fight against the bonds.

In this case more was at stake than the tax issue. A few months later the Union Pacific obtained bonds from the same counties solicited by the Nebraska Central to commence work on its Republican Valley branch. Clark advised Dillon that "any Railroad running through Saunders County and the southwest will control the balance of power in Nebraska both politically & commercially." The city of Omaha also issued bonds for the branch, then tried to repudiate them a year later. Gould promptly renewed his threat to move the shops and this time furnished Clark a detailed analysis of where they should go.

Clearly there was more than a germ of truth in Rosewater's charges that the railroad resorted to coercion and corruption to get what it wanted. A maverick Republican, he had good reason for believing the worst about the Union Pacific. Where Miller's *Herald* and the Omaha *Republican* got in bed early with the company, Rosewater's *Bee* became its most implacable critic. His stridence drew a savage response from Gould. Muttering that "Rosewater ought to be *squelched,*" he denied the *Bee* any of the company's printing or advertising business and refused to allow the paper on Union Pacific trains. When that did not suffice, Gould used his control of the telegraph to shut off eastern dispatches from Rosewater. The company bought stock in the *Repub-*

lican and tried to build it up in hopes of draining circulation from the *Bee.* All these tactics accomplished nothing. The *Bee* kept its readers and Rosewater continued hammering at the Union Pacific.

In denouncing the company's influence on the local press Rosewater's eloquence and righteousness knew no bounds. He condemned Miller and his *Republican* counterpart as lackeys of the railroad fattening their purses on its favor, omitting all mention of the fact that he had himself tried and failed to cut a deal with the Union Pacific. Rosewater had no monopoly on virtue; he drifted into opposition partly because he could not get his share of the company's largess. The problem in Omaha was that the Union Pacific had too many editors to placate, and Rosewater arrived late at the trough.

No one was a more persistent or voracious feeder than Miller, who had been the road's "friend" since construction days. Along the way he asked for a warehouse concession, stock in the Wyoming Coal Company, and especially the company's printing business. "I have perhaps done more," he noted modestly, "to settle conflicts between the line and Omaha . . . than any other ten men in Omaha." The company did three hundred thousand dollars' worth of printing in New York and Chicago, he complained, even though the *Herald* did so much on its behalf. Miller thought he should be rewarded "not in *bribes,* not in *favors* as such, but in the simple privilege of doing your printing, say $50,000." While Snyder was superintendent Miller got the work because both were ardent Democrats. The *Republican* cried foul and demanded its share on frankly partisan grounds. Hammond put the printing contracts out for bid and thereby offended both papers.

When Scott took charge, Miller grumbled that the Republican management deprived the *Herald* of its patronage because the paper was a Democratic organ. Gannett replied curtly that the company was not happy with "the quality and price" of work done by either paper, but Miller did not relent. In 1875 he asked Oliver to put in a good word with Gould. "I want nothing from the company," he said solemnly. "I merely wish to get close to Mr. Gould." In fact he wanted not only printing but a lengthy contract for selling books and periodicals on trains. "I took a contract eleven years ago to educate the people of this state to keep their hands off the Union Pacific Railroad," he pleaded. "The corporation . . . would not miss this pittance which I ask for on a purely business basis. Let them let me have this thing for $4000 a year, no matter what change may occur. No management can complain of it and if they do, who the devil cares? I am kicked and knocked around here . . . and I am entitled to the only protection you can give."

"It is [sic] always been our aim," proclaimed Oliver Ames in 1876, "to keep the Management of the Road entirely aloof from Party Bias or Dictation." But even with the best of intentions it could not avoid entanglement in local affairs or with newspapers that sought to enlist it in their fiercely partisan wars. During the bitter struggle of 1876, Gannett admitted that "unusual trouble seems to have been taken to inform employees which parties it is supposed will best serve the interest of the R. R. Co.," but he doubted that "coercion or intimidation has been used." The company's role elsewhere differed from Nebraska only in degree. Like other corporations, the Union Pacific's political activity was focused laserlike on those specific issues that affected it, such as bond propositions, taxation, and regulation. Sometimes it joined forces with other roads; more frequently conflicting interests had them lunging at each other's throats. As competition grew, the clash between rival lines spread to the political cockpit in state capitals and Washington. The vaunted "railroad lobby" was several different lobbies as suspicious of one another as of their common enemies.

Over the years the Union Pacific lost more political battles than it won. Time and again it demonstrated that a powerful corporation could be as inept as the littlest lobbyist. In Wyoming the company accomplished little more than arousing public sentiment against it. As the Davis case showed, no solution was found to the problem of "translating its economic power into political effectiveness." Ham-handed influence often backfired into hostile legislation. Subsidies were nice to have but only under the right conditions; Gould turned down more offers than he accepted for just that reason. When he asked again for Montana aid in 1878, he advised Clark that "Exemption from taxation & county bonds are all I would ask for." Montana balked at giving even that much help, and in the end Gould built without it.

Expansion aggravated the political problem by swelling the ranks of the enemy. Within a few years the Union Pacific would penetrate five more states or territories. That meant five more legislatures and governors, five sets of officials, interest groups, judges, editors, lawyers, politicians, and the whole swarm of "friends" seeking a free ride of one kind or another. By then the clash had grown uglier because of mounting public hostility against the railroads. Like other roads, indeed like nations, the Union Pacific learned that victory was not always worth the price of war.

* * *

From the first, Gould realized that the ultimate fate of the Union Pacific rested in two places: Wall Street and Capitol Hill. For half a dozen years he fought both campaigns with consummate skill and tenacity against terrible odds. His financial abilities were widely known, his political prowess less so. Yet he came within a whisker of victory only to be beaten by forces beyond his control. Had he won, the history of the Union Pacific and all railroads west of the Missouri River would have turned out very differently. His defeat set in motion a series of developments that not only sealed the doom of the Union Pacific but reshaped the railroad map of America.

By 1874 the Union Pacific was embroiled in a dozen disputes with the government, all of which preceded Gould's arrival. Several pitted the company against other roads and interests as well. In the treacherous crosscurrents of Washington alliances formed and parted with breathtaking rapidity.

The company needed an alert, astute presence on duty there at all times, but Oliver's penny-wise, pound-foolish policy had alienated its best lobbyists. His haggling over bills drove Painter and Chandler from the road's service, leaving Chandler so embittered he vowed to oppose the Union Pacific "whenever an honorable opportunity offers." Gould moved at once to repair this damage and reacquire the services of both men. His appreciation of their value showed itself thereafter in prompt payment.

One issue caught up both local interests and the Iowa roads in its complexities. The terminus question was not a legal abstraction to Omaha and Council Bluffs, which viewed its outcome as decisive in their fight for commercial supremacy. The company hesitated to fulfill a long-standing promise of a new depot and general offices in Omaha until it knew for certain where the road began. Omaha regarded the new facilities as both moral collateral for its bonds and proof that it was the chosen city. After stalling for a year, the Union Pacific opened a new brick depot in May 1874 that featured a dining hall complete with soda fountain. That same month another bill went into the House to fix the terminus at Council Bluffs, reviving the old argument that the road and bridge should be run as "one continuous line." Despite Omaha's howls, work on the depot and office building was suspended. The bill was postponed and the fight went into court.

In May 1875 Dillon's own nephew, Federal Judge John F. Dillon, ruled that Iowa was the road's initial point and the bridge must be operated as part of the line. While his decision was appealed in vain to the Supreme Court, a new fight erupted over the bridge tolls. Judge Dillon upheld the company's right to charge "reasonable" tolls, but Crounse quickly introduced a bill to put the tolls on a *pro rata* basis with other parts of the line. Since the tolls were used to pay interest on the bridge bonds, any attack on them put those bonds in serious jeopardy. On the transfer question the Iowa lines split along what would soon become familiar lines: the Northwestern and Rock Island agreed to use the Omaha depot, the Burlington objected. As Clark well knew, Perkins was behind the Crounse bill and was also working against the Union Pacific in the Nebraska legislature, but he was thwarted in both cases.

Perkins's intervention on the toll issue was a flanking maneuver in the larger fight over *pro rata*. Every session of Congress was greeted by fresh bills to compel the Union Pacific to prorate with the Kansas Pacific and B & M. The company managed to frustrate these efforts until the winter of 1874, when the Kansas Pacific launched its most vigorous campaign at a time when the stench of Crédit Mobilier still lingered in Congress. The rival lobbies were already deep into their intrigues when Gould joined the board in March. A senate version known as the Ingalls bill was especially repugnant to the Union Pacific, while an alternative House bill, Rollins thought, would "more than give us the chance to have the question determined in the Courts." When the lawyers and lobbyists all agreed this was better than risking passage of the Ingalls bill, Gould gave his consent and the House version sailed through in June 1874.

As expected, the Union Pacific evaded the act's rather vague provisions and the Kansas Pacific brought suit. Gould then deflected the issue for over a year with his negotiations for a merger of the Kansas Pacific and Colorado roads. The B & M tried to push the fight alone but got nowhere until the clash between Gould and Villard broke out in 1877. At once Perkins offered his help in the fight at Washington, where he joined with Villard in support of the Chaffee *pro rata* bill. Gould enlisted support from other railway men by warning that passage of the Chaffee bill would "render it impossible to defeat pro-rata legislation in every state in the Union." The whole notion was, in his opinion, "revolutionary and dangerous to railway interests and ought to be squelched."

These tactics succeeded in defeating the Chaffee bill after a vigorous fight. A disappointed Perkins paid grudging tribute to Gould's ability to persuade "so many persons commonly regarded as of sound mind to declare that black is white, and to pull his chestnuts out of the fire, believing them to be their own." But the battle was far from over. A new bill providing for a commission to investigate the cost and present condition of the Pacific roads surfaced and slipped through at the session's end. The act also created a new bureau under an Auditor of Railroad Accounts. Theophilus French, who had just been exonerated from charges of impropriety in his previous position, was appointed auditor. Gould thought the act unconstitutional and the company stalled French's request to see its books. Huntington went even further by flatly denying him access to Central Pacific records.

The bridge, terminus, and *pro rata* fights were but one front on a confused battlefield where different clashes overlapped one another. Gould was also endeavoring to get increased pay on government mail, resolve the long squabble over land patents, and beat back a Crounse bill to tax unpatented lands. Each of these matters was vital to the company's interest, yet all paled in importance before the government loan. It was there, Gould realized, that the battle would be lost or won. By 1874 three crucial issues spawned by the ambiguities of the Pacific acts had already found their way into the courts: When were the interest payments due? When was the road actually completed? How should net earnings be defined?

Since February 1873 the government had withheld all earnings on its transportation account pending a court decision on when interest was due. Interest was to accrue from the date of the road's completion which, the government contended, was July 15, 1869, when the last subsidy bonds were issued. The Union Pacific countered that the government had refused patents to half the land grants of both Pacific roads until they corrected deficiencies itemized by the commission of eminent citizens. Not until October 1874 was this work certified as completed, and that, asserted the company, ought to be the proper date. As for the clause requiring the company to apply at least 5 percent of its net earnings to the interest account, there existed no standard definition of net earnings. Was it the amount left after deducting operating expenses alone or fixed charges such as bond interest as well? What about expenditures for new construction or equipment? Earnings withheld by the government? Receipts from land sales?

These issues were not mere legal abstractions to Gould. Huge sums were at stake, to say nothing of his program to restore the company's credit. A favorable decision would boost its securities; an unfavorable one would devastate them. Any legislation passed or threatened by Congress would have a similar effect, and Capitol Hill swarmed every winter with lobbyists eager to profit from waving the bloody shirt of Crédit Mobilier at the Union Pacific. The infighting grew both fierce and expensive; during the winter of 1873–74 Dodge alone turned in twenty-five thousand dollars' worth of "Washington drafts."

The conclusion impressed on Gould was inescapable: the Union Pacific could never attain stability so long as its destiny was tied to the vagaries of governmental action. Every suit or court decision, every unfriendly bill, every departmental order disturbed the market, forcing Gould and his friends to sustain the price with large purchases. The bears pounced gleefully on every rumor and did not hesitate to invent plenty of their own. Speculators had their own agents in Washington ready to make mischief for a fee. Convinced that a settlement with the government was imperative, Gould bent every effort toward devising a compromise even though it meant dealing with a hostile Congress.

By 1875 the time was ripe for fresh proposals. Anxious to get a decision on when the interest was due, Gould pressed the suit to recover the funds withheld on government transportation. A new commission had reported in October 1874 that the Union Pacific had complied with the recommendations of the eminent citizens, whereupon Grant revoked the order withholding land patents. A month later Secretary Bristow made the first attempt to collect the 5 percent of net earnings dating back to 1869. Both Huntington and Dillon pointed to the October report as the proper date of the roads' completion. Bristow tried to get legislation supporting his position but the indefatigable Dodge corralled enough votes to defeat it. While this fight raged, help arrived from an unexpected quarter. The government had argued persistently that net earnings should be defined as the balance left after deducting only operating expenses. In February 1875, however, the Supreme Court decreed in a case unrelated to Union Pacific that net earnings comprised what remained after operating expenses, interest, construction expenses, and rent on leased roads had been deducted.

The decision, wrote an ecstatic Gould, was "as full & complete as though we had had it prepared by our own lawyers." He grasped at once its importance to the company and its value in strengthening his effort to forge a compromise settlement. Already he had prepared a proposal to pay the government five hundred thousand dollars per year as a sinking fund with interest compounded semiannually. By Gould's reckoning, this amount would pay off the government loan with simple interest in forty years. It would also eliminate in one stroke all bickering over the 5 percent clause, net earnings, payment on government transportation, and the interest due date. The chief source of friction between the road and the government would be removed forever.

Here at last was a concrete proposal to stabilize relations with the government and get the company out of the political cockpit in Washington. Dodge quietly showed it to Grant, who suggested that the payments be increased to seven hundred fifty thousand dollars after twenty years. Gould agreed readily and the revised terms were submitted to Bristow. Until that moment Dodge took care to keep the offer secret. "If we put it in the papers and began to run up stock on it," he noted, "they would be suspicious of its being a stock jobbing operation and . . . would keep hands off." Dodge knew nothing of the sort was intended because he had sounded Gould explicitly on that point. "From your letter," he verified, "I understand that you don't care anything about any temporary effect; that if anything is done, you wish it to be something to base permanent operations upon and I am acting upon that supposition."

Bristow took the proposal to the cabinet, which demanded several changes in the government's favor. Although Gould could be the toughest of bargainers, he complied at once "in order to get the strong endorsement of the Prest & Cabinet." When all but one member of the cabinet approved the revised version, Grant drafted a message to Congress in support of the bill. But the message never materialized, and within days all hope of settlement vanished like a mirage. The Senate Republicans advised Grant that any new legislation would require a special session. In his phlegmatic way Grant decided to put the message off until the next session, or so he explained to Dodge. "I think that the action of the Republican Caucus this morning is the cause and nothing else," Dodge reported glumly. "No one can be more disappointed than I am as I think I never worked anything up with so much satisfaction."

Dodge was right to mourn, for never again would the two sides come so close to an amicable settlement. A decade later, Charles Francis Adams looked back on Gould's proposal as "the most beneficial, the most businesslike and the most financially sound of all the plans to meet the obligation of the Government." A golden opportunity had been lost by a matter of days.

No one suspected that their last, best chance had slipped away. The recovery of Union Pacific seemed assured that summer as the stock reached unprecedented figures and the company began paying dividends. In May the Court of Claims ruled that the government could not withhold all payments on transportation and ordered it to pay the company $512,632 due on account. In November the Supreme Court sustained the decision by unanimous verdict. Even observers hostile to the company conceded that the Attorney

General had not a shred of law behind his case. Gould was elated. This was a decision he wanted desperately, for it also decreed finally that interest on the government loan was not due until the bonds matured. Here surely was the impetus needed to force a compromise.

But the battle had only begun. Instead of releasing the funds, the government launched a new suit to define net earnings and settle the date of the road's completion. Gould did everything possible to move the case along, but without success. In Congress the mood was hardening for reasons that had nothing to do with Union Pacific. An election was approaching and fresh scandals had disgraced the Grant administration, giving rise to a movement for retrenchment and reform. Feelings ran high against anything that smelled of subsidies, which to some wary congressmen included any settlement of the government loan on terms favorable to the railroad. Against this tide of reform Tom Scott was lobbying feverishly to wrest government aid for his southern transcontinental project, the Texas & Pacific, which allowed foes of a settlement to smear Union Pacific with his efforts.

So far the Union Pacific had gone the fight alone. Gould was anxious to enlist Huntington's help, but there was a complication. Huntington wanted to build his own road from El Paso to New Orleans and was bent on defeating the Texas & Pacific subsidy bill. For years he and Scott had been sparring; now they were embroiled in a pitched battle that put Gould in an awkward position. No rival line across the continent was palatable to the Union Pacific, whether in Scott's or Huntington's hands. The trick was to beat one and deal later with the other. Scott was the obvious target because his clamor for aid was hurting the Union Pacific's cause. Huntington was eager to throttle Scott and obtain a favorable settlement from the government. That made him a natural ally, except that Scott's chief engineer and lobbyist was none other than Dodge, whose talents Gould also required. Dodge had returned to the Union Pacific board in 1875 and somehow managed to keep his allegiances disentangled enough to work for both Scott and Gould.

Gould had learned that Huntington could be dealt with in a no-nonsense manner. Accordingly, on a cold Sunday in January 1876, he went to Huntington's home and startled his host with a proposition to merge the Pacific roads. As part of the arrangement Gould thought the Union Pacific should have the eastern end of the Southern Pacific. Huntington grasped at once that "it was the S.P. that brought him to see me." He saw too that Gould's proposal would eliminate the threat of extending the Utah Southern to the Pacific. Experience had begun to soften Huntington's view of Gould, whom he now regarded as "a very able man, although his methods may not be always right." He had also come to believe that "a better way than for the C.P. and U.P. to divide would be to consolidate on almost any terms."

As a first step they could unite to crush Scott and obtain a settlement with the government. That same January Dillon renewed his settlement offer to the government and was joined this time by Huntington. To their surprise, the House responded by directing its judiciary committee to determine what legislation was needed to secure payment of the debt. In March the committee presented what became known as the Lawrence bill calling for payments to a new sinking fund *in addition* to those already required by law. It also forbade the roads from paying dividends until these obligations had been met. Protests that the Lawrence bill simply ignored the recent Supreme Court decision went unheeded. While Gould mulled over this development, Huntington devised a scheme to sweeten the proposal by offering to sell most of the land grant back to the government at $2.50 an acre. So confident was Huntington of success that Gould reluctantly let him take charge of the fight. On March 27 Dillon dutifully made the land offer on behalf of the Union Pacific.

A few days earlier Gould and Dillon had told Huntington bluntly that the Southern Pacific must be shared between them. When Huntington pledged his support on that basis, Gould summoned Oliver Ames from Boston for a conference on March 25. After lengthy discussion the Union Pacific men agreed not to oppose Huntington's bill in return for a share of the Southern Pacific and Huntington's aid in obtaining a settlement. Within a week, however, it became clear that Huntington was more intent on getting his bill than on pushing the settlement. The fight with Scott had taxed him to the limit. "Scott is making a very dirty fight," he noted grimly, ". . . and if I do not live to see the grass growing over him I shall be mistaken."

Gould thought this obsession sheer folly. If Huntington "really wants to pass his compromise," he told Oliver Ames, "it is unwise to press this scheme." But Huntington would not relent and even asked Gould's help, insisting that it was part of their bargain. Meanwhile Scott, aware that his bill was all but dead for the session, was recklessly slinging the mud of past scandals at both Pacific roads. A perplexed Gould saw Huntington again and came to a new understanding. The Union Pacific would actively support the Southern Pacific bill in Senate committee but no attempt to report it out would be made without mutual consent. That done, all sides would drop everything else to force through the government settlement. The sinking fund bill was placed in the hands of a Senate subcommittee under Senator Hitchcock's care, where it ran into difficulty at once. Hostile newspapers pounced on the land offer as a scam to sell worthless lands back to the government at inflated prices.

Too late Huntington realized the danger inherent in his obsession with the Southern Pacific bill. With the sinking fund bill foundering and the Lawrence bill gaining ground, the Pacific roads found themselves forced gradually but inexorably on the defensive. Not until the end of April did Huntington finally consent to drop his bill if Scott would do the same. With Gould acting as intermediary, all sides agreed to close ranks against the Lawrence bill. Gould surmised that if the right bill could not be had, it was best to wait until after the presidential election, but Huntington made a determined if belated attempt to get the Senate bill reported out. As the fight raged on through the spring, Huntington abandoned the land offer and tried for a sinking fund alone.

His attempt failed miserably. While Huntington's bill languished, the House overrode intense lobbying to pass the Lawrence bill by a landslide vote of 153–9. The severity of its terms alarmed even conservative financial editors, and the Senate quickly buried it in committee. On July 12, however, Senator Allen G. Thurman of Ohio reported out a bill with similar provisions and an even harsher repayment plan. Like the Lawrence bill, it demanded that earnings on government transportation be withheld despite the Supreme Court decision. Along with this sum and the amount owed under the 5 percent requirement, the Pacific roads were to pay another 25 percent of their net earnings up to $1.5 million a year. No dividends could be paid until these obligations were met.

Thurman's bill did not pass, but it loomed like an avenging angel over the forthcoming session. Instead of a settlement the company faced the prospect of another prolonged struggle on its hands. "This is a great deal worse than the House bill," complained Oliver Ames. He had no doubt where the fault lay. "We have failed in Congress by trying to drive too Sharp a Bargain . . . we have followed Huntington's lead." But Huntington had miscalculated badly, and now there was more to worry about than the Thurman bill. Despite Gould's efforts at mediation, Huntington and Scott would renew their suicidal clash, and the presidential campaign was already poisoning the atmosphere with its frenzied rhetoric. The embittered legacy of Grant's scandal-pocked administration and acrid controversies over Reconstruction policy split both parties, making it difficult for the railroad lobbies to line up support for their interests.

Bartlett offered the opinion that Thurman's bill would not hold up in court. Gould believed it repudiated "existing contracts between the Govt & the Company," and thought its revival would trigger a desperate battle at a time when the mood of the country was hostile to railroads. With uncanny perception he sensed that a major storm was brewing. What he could not foresee was that its fury would be unleashed in the aftermath of the most controversial election in American history.

So close was the presidential contest between Samuel J. Tilden and Rutherford B. Hayes that its outcome hinged on disputed returns from three southern states. No formula existed for resolving the matter. Congress convened on December 4 and plunged at once into a fiercely partisan debate on the question. Tension and uncertainty gripped the country as it had not since the secession crisis. Charges of fraud and coercion led quickly to ugly threats of violence, even of secession. The mood in Washington, stirred by bitter memories of war and reconstruction, was explosive.

The storm did not prevent lobbyists from prowling their haunts with their usual intensity. Scott and Dodge were working the committees so effectively that Huntington admitted to "having the roughest fight with Scott that I ever had." Gould had the *pro rata* and bridge bills to contend with as well as a revised version of the sinking fund bill, which Huntington had put in the hands of Senator John B. Gordon of Georgia. The Northern Pacific also had a bill it wanted passed. To Gould and Dillon it looked like a long, cold, grinding, and very expensive winter. Dillon implored Oliver Ames to send him ten thousand dollars "for the same purpose as before." Again Huntington turned to Gould for help against Scott, and again Gould accepted. Despite the failures of the previous session, he could find no better course than to follow the same tactics in this one by allowing Huntington to lead the charge.

Within a week the Scott steamroller clanked to a halt. After two futile attempts to wrest his subsidy bill out of committee, Scott went to Huntington's room and came to terms. Overnight the two antagonists became allies behind a compromise bill described by Huntington as "nothing like what we want but as good as we can get." The spectacle of a warm embrace between two foes who had for months been alerting the Republic to the venality of the other was hardly convincing. "The two great schemers have joined hands," sneered the *Times* in a typical response. Reformers were outraged that so sordid a piece of business should brazen its way into the midst of a national crisis. For his part, Dillon had the opposite complaint. "The Presidential question," he wrote mournfully, "absorbs all other business for the present."

Time was running out. If the election tangle was not sorted out by March 4, the country would find itself without a President. The congressional calendar overflowed with business, and lobbyists swarmed the floors of both houses like clouds of locusts. Under such intense pressure the Gordon bill would have an uphill struggle at best, but it also had to compete with Thurman's bill. The burly Huntington was confident he could ram it through despite warnings from Dodge that its enemies would try to gut it with amendments. Too late Huntington realized that Dodge knew his way around the corridors better than most men. The amendments poured forth and consumed what little time the Senate could give the subject. By late February the Gordon bill and Scott-Huntington grab-bag compromise were both dead. Thurman's bill reached the Senate floor and touched off an impassioned debate cut short only when a motion to postpone carried by the slender margin of 29–28.

Sorrowfully Gould watched the election crisis play itself out, his hopes blasted by the political imbroglio and Huntington's miscalculations. Only gradually did he realize how much damage had been done. A reform-minded Rutherford B. Hayes took office along with a large number of new faces in both chambers, which meant restructured committees. The Thurman bill was sure to return, and no one expected the new Congress would even glance at an alternative proposal. The depression that still gripped the country exploded that summer in a wave of strikes and violence against the railroads. After their brief fling at peace, Scott and Huntington braced for yet another savage fight over the southern route. Gould's Washington policy lay in shambles. He had neither obtained a settlement nor blocked the rival transcontinental route. Although some hostile bills had been defeated, he now found himself forced entirely on the defensive with the issue that mattered most, the government loan. Prospects looked bleak for the coming session.

In November Gould and Huntington wearily put their case again before the Senate Judiciary Committee, but the Senate preferred the Thurman bill. Things were no better in the House, where the Pacific Railroad Committee, that former bastion of Oakes Ames, had eight new members and a new chairman who resigned shortly after being appointed, throwing its affairs into turmoil. The settlement offer to the government was the largest ever, but it was too little too late; Congress and the press were hostile to the Pacific roads. Huntington and Scott were slashing each other to pieces again, leading Dodge to observe shrewdly that "The complications are such that either can do a great deal more mischief than both together can do good."

Gould and Huntington hoped to substitute their bill for Thurman's during the Senate debate or, failing that, weaken the Thurman bill with amendments. As late as March Gould predicted success, but his hopes were shattered with brutal swiftness. Despite intense lobbying, the Thurman bill passed the Senate intact by a vote of 40–19 and swept through the House in the same form with only two votes against it. Hayes signed it into law on May 8, 1878. The Texas & Pacific bill was scuttled again, leaving Huntington a sort of victor by default. Gould's only consolation from the session was the defeat of a determined effort to get a *pro rata* bill.

The Thurman Act incorporated virtually every feature the Pacific roads tried to avoid. It defined net earnings as the sum left after deducting operating expenses and interest on the first mortgage bonds alone. A sinking fund would be established and its balance invested in government bonds. All earnings on government transportation would be retained, with half the amount applied to current interest and the other half to the sinking fund. The Union Pacific and Central Pacific would also pay annually into the fund 5 percent of their net earnings up to $850,000 and $1.2 million respectively. In addition, the companies would pay annually a sum equal to the difference between the amounts required above and 25 percent of their net earnings. No dividends were allowed until these obligations were met.

Opinions differed on what the act's effect would be. "I think we can manage to get along under it if compelled to," Crocker grumped, but added sourly, "it seems to be almost a crime to own any property." An enraged Huntington labeled Thurman a demogogue, and said of him, "lying was his best forte." No one was more embittered than Dodge, whose resentment still smoldered a decade later. "When we needed help from them to take care of the property," he said wrathfully of the government, "they did not pay much attention to us; but as soon as we got the road up so that it appeared to be a success, we were attacked constantly." Gould too was deeply disappointed but in his usual manner wasted few tears over spilled milk.

The reasons for failure were not hard to find. Much of it was simply bad luck, notably the missed opportunity in the spring of 1875 and the complications wrought by the election in 1876. The odds were always against success, but in mounting the campaign almost everything had gone wrong. Throughout the fight Gould was caught helplessly in the crossfire between Scott and Huntington, which not only damaged his efforts but dissipated Huntington's energies at a time when he was badly needed. Without the imbroglio over the southern route, Huntington could have given the settlement his undivided attention. As it was, Gould miscalculated in relying so heavily upon a distracted Huntington to push the compromise through. Nor did it help that the company paid handsome dividends during the years it pleaded an inability to meet the payments demanded by Thurman. The fact that its initial offer in 1875 had been made *before* any dividends had been paid was ignored entirely. Ironically, the road's splendid performance through these depression years worked against its efforts in Washington.

Although no one yet realized it, the Thurman Act marked a turning point in the company's long struggle with the government. The failure of each year's campaign made the next attempt that much more difficult. Slowly, inexorably, the initiative seized by Gould in 1875 was lost and the Union Pacific was forced on the defensive. The passage of the Thurman Act plunged even incurable optimists like Gould into gloom. Most observers regarded the act as punitive legislation despite the insistence of some hostile papers that the company could meet its requirements and still pay a dividend. To more astute minds, however, the Thurman Act was not merely a lost battle but a portent that the tide of war had changed. More attacks would follow, threatening or even rolling back successes achieved earlier.

There was reason to fear the worst. On the heels of the Thurman Act came the legislation creating an auditor of railroad accounts. That same summer Carl Schurz, the new Secretary of the Interior, unexpectedly ruled that all land granted to the Pacific railroads and not yet sold were open to preemption under the Homestead Act at $1.25 an acre. Impartial analysts assailed this decision as both spurious and unwise, but settlers flocked onto the lands in hopes of acquiring them below the prices charged by the company. The result was another messy legal tangle that wound its way to the Supreme Court, which overruled Schurz in April 1879. Once the verdict was rendered, the company had to sort out the status of those who had claimed land under the Secretary's edict.

So far the courts had been the company's best refuge against Congress and the departments, but that too was changing. In June 1878 the Court of Claims stunned the Union Pacific with an adverse decision on two crucial issues. It ruled that the road was completed on November 6, 1869, when the eminent citizens made their final report, and interest was therefore due from that date. At the same time it defined net earnings as the balance left after deducting *only* operating expenses. This not only reversed the earlier decision but also imposed a definition even narrower than that contained in the Thurman Act. In May 1879 the Supreme Court delivered another blow by upholding the validity of the Thurman Act.

The devastating impact of these defeats would not be fully realized for years. Routed by every branch of government, the company soon discovered that its position in Washington had changed radically. Any future attempt at a settlement would be confined within the parameters imposed by these actions. All along it had been assumed that the Thurman Act and the court decisions would finally resolve the questions that had blighted relations between the combatants for years; instead they insured that the struggle would continue unabated. Conceived as a final solution, they succeeded only in carrying both sides farther away from a rational settlement.

The Supreme Court could declare the Thurman Act constitutional but could not make it workable. When its defects became clear, attempts to modify the terms merely reopened old wounds. Victory stiffened the sense of righteousness in Congress, which at best was slow to grasp the changing realities of railroad competition. Defeat reinforced the feelings of persecution that infused the company's officials. Washington was for them a bottomless pit that sucked up enormous amounts of time, energy, and money with nothing to show for it. Since Crédit Mobilier the government and hostile newspapers had fixed in the public mind an image of the Union Pacific as a tainted property run by crooks and thieves bent on swindling the country. The New York *Times* typified this attitude when it charged in December 1877 that "There is not, and never has been, on its part, the first intention of honorably dealing with the Treasury, by the aid of which this splendid property was built up."

One other effect of the Thurman Act has gone unnoticed, yet it did more to shape the railroad map of America than any other action of Congress: it drove Jay Gould from the Union Pacific to seek his destiny elsewhere.

19

THE COMPETITION

To eyes unfamiliar with the nineteenth century it would appear as if society had found in railroads a substitute for war. The correspondence of railroad men rang with the clang of arms. They fought wars, launched or repelled invasions, made treaties and broke them, forged alliances, claimed suzerainty over territories, disputed boundaries, and squandered their resources in hopes of gaining the spoils of victory. Other roads were referred to as foreign lines or simply the enemy, who must be "slaughtered" or "crushed" or "routed" if they would not agree to terms. Every road was a sovereign state whose officials ruled their domain with possessive zeal, providing services, granting favors, collecting taxes, punishing dissidents, and regarding outsiders with suspicion. Relations between companies were a form of diplomacy of which war was, as always, the last extension.

It is not at all strange that railroad men used the images and metaphors of war and peace to define their world. The central, indeed overwhelming, experience of their lives was the Civil War. Many of them had been soldiers or civil servants of war; the rest had spent four years reading in graphic detail the accounts of bloody battles, the grand maneuvers of armies and the machinations of diplomacy, the tragic grandeur and sordid inequities, heroic deeds and petty squabbles. Who could have passed through those fearful years without absorbing their language and imagery, and to what later experience did these apply more neatly than to the railroads? A railroad company occupied a large territory and was organized much like an army, which in fact provided the model for its administration. As the nation's first big business the railroad had to find inspiration somewhere for a structure to govern its sprawling domain and unprecedented number of employees. Only the military, swollen to gargantuan size by the demands of war, offered a comparable example of how to organize everything from supplies to accounts, from labor forces to administrative procedures. The military model not only fit the railroad's needs but was familiar to railroad men.

As railroads grew in size and number, the lessons of wartime became even more useful to men who had been weaned on them. The competition for business was a struggle not unlike war, in which victory usually went to the biggest battalions and/or cleverest commanders. In the early postwar years certain constraints of geography and resources fixed the rules of war. Each road had its own territory with boundaries defined by its terminuses and connecting points. The most basic rule was that of one road for one territory. Every road regarded its tributary region as "natural" territory like a sovereign state, the invasion of which by another line usually led to war. But the territorial rule, like a vow of chastity, was easiest to keep where the temptation to violate it did not exist.

In the railroad-starved West no sane promoter would build a second line where there was not yet business enough to sustain one. Early diplomacy, therefore, dealt more with problems of connecting than of competing. To move traffic beyond their own lines, roads had to cooperate in such matters as physical connections, transfers, creating rate and classification structures, devising uniform operating and accounting procedures, standardizing technology, and coordinating schedules. These questions dominated the early relationship between the Pacific roads. Gradually there emerged a network of independent lines integrated by a series of cooperative agreements reached through a process of continuous negotiation. These arrangements expedited the flow of through traffic, which at first provided western roads with most of their income.

Since through rates were at the mercy of competitive pressures, rival roads often formed alliances to avoid rate slashing by dividing business. In 1870 the three Iowa roads created the Iowa Pool, an informal arrangement for sharing eastbound traffic from the Union Pacific. The alternative to cooperation revealed itself in the bitter rate wars between the Pacific roads and Pacific Mail after their failure to maintain agreements. While anxious to increase through traffic, railroad managers were more intent on cultivating local business. Since local rates were immune from competition and could be kept at high levels, managers recognized early that local business must form the backbone of their road's earnings. This need made defense and expansion of the territory even more imperative, which meant building branches into untapped regions. Branch lines were costly and risky ventures at best, but if a company did not undertake them someone else might. The West swarmed with promoters playing on the hunger of every village for a rail connection. These local projects preempted a piece of the territory and loomed as potential menaces if they should fall into the hands of a rival or evolve into larger lines.

During the 1870s changing conditions steadily eroded territorial integrity and the cooperative agreements that sustained it. One new road after another appeared, slicing up domain, multiplying points of dispute, and tangling the calculus of diplomacy with Byzantine complexities. Every new competitor clamored for its share of traffic and posed the threat of becoming a link in some new through line, a beachhead for invasion. Five years of depression intensified the struggle and exposed certain grim truths about competition among railroads. For the first time Americans witnessed the spectacle of a few very large enterprises vying for the same business. Every road needed a steady flow of traffic to remain solvent because fixed costs (especially interest) comprised so large a proportion of its total costs. It made sense, therefore, to fill empty cars with freight at reduced rates even at the cost of violating agreements. Once a road succumbed to this temptation, war usually followed.

The delicate fabric of cooperation crumbled beneath the relentless pressure of costs and proliferation of roads. When war broke out, the combatants could resort to a limited arsenal of weapons. They could cut rates or divert business if the enemy was a connecting line. Sometimes alliances could be formed with other roads on which the enemy depended. The territory could be defended by constructing branches and threatening the enemy with retaliatory invasion. The problem was that all these weapons inflicted heavy casualties on both sides and seldom gained a decisive victory. To hammer a rival into bankruptcy only made it a more formidable foe in that a bankrupt road need not pay interest on its bonds and could therefore slash rates with impunity.

The diplomacy and war of railroads baffled the logic of ordinary minds. Bitter, unsparing conflicts persisted even though only Pyrrhic victories seemed possible. Rate wars and invasions drained both sides. Defeated foes did not go out of business but sprang up in new guise, ready to fight again. The weak were less a victim of the strong than a menace to them as nuisances or pawns for some stronger enemy. They could be eliminated by purchase, which meant saddling solvent roads with insolvent ones. Buying "suckers" made no sense financially, yet it was done again and again, always to prevent rivals from getting them. Defense became the supreme rationale for rate wars, branch building, and invasion by construction of new lines or acquisition of existing ones. No aggression was intended; it was merely a matter of protecting the territory, and railway managers took an expansive view of what constituted "their" territory.

There were always voices who counseled peace, and they grew louder as the wars raged on with growing ferocity. But even the wisest diplomats could not find ways to counteract the underlying forces that fueled their conflicts. Their failure, like those of nations, doomed the industry to a ritual of self-destruction that would have enormous repercussions for the future. If nothing else, the railroad men of the nineteenth century succeeded to a shocking degree in fulfilling their own metaphors.

* * *

In 1874 the Union Pacific still owned the middle of the continent. The Northern Pacific was a floundering bankrupt on the upper Missouri and the southern routes merely glimmers in the eyes of Huntington and Scott. Pacific Mail and Kansas Pacific remained its only competitors for through business along with some small roads in southern Nebraska, most of them controlled by the Burlington. Since all these roads connected with Union Pacific, they could not compete effectively as long as the company imposed discriminatory rates. It was the attempt to break this stranglehold that gave rise to the long and bitter fight over *pro rata.*

Gould's strategic objectives for the Union Pacific were plain. Through rates must be kept high, which required either an agreement with or control of Pacific Mail. On overland traffic he wanted a larger proportion of the through rate, which meant perpetual conflict with the Iowa Pool. Above all, he was intent on protecting and expanding the territory, and he was not modest in his view of what constituted its "natural" territory. These goals were to keep him embroiled in conflict for nearly a decade.

The capture of Pacific Mail in March 1875 ended years of debilitating rate wars, but fresh trouble arose from an unexpected quarter. That same winter a speculator named Trenor Park surprised Gould by gaining control of the Panama Railroad, the tiny but vital rail link across the Isthmus on which Pacific Mail was dependent for its coastal traffic. Once in control, Park abrogated Panama's contract with Pacific Mail only days after Gould had enthused about the "advanced rates recently established under the harmonious relation with Pacific Mail." When Gould threatened to move oriental traffic overland, Park countered by announcing plans for a rival steamship line. Through the summer and autumn of 1875 the two men sparred, announcing new agreements with a fanfare only to repudiate them before the ink had dried. Park stood firm because he knew Pacific Mail needed funds to meet $1.35 million in payments on new steamers, $500,000 of which was owed to the Panama Railroad. In November the Panama board approved the purchase of ships for its new line. Gould enjoined the road from going into the steamship business and bought Pacific Mail heavily as a precaution. "It is important to keep controll of Pacific Mail," he told Oliver Ames, "it is the key to our China & Japan and Australian trade."

Although Gould talked bravely, he held a weak hand. The Union Pacific and its leading directors had been obliged to advance funds to both steamship lines. Park realized that a rate war with Panama would transform joint ownership of Union Pacific and Pacific Mail into a liability. Freight carried at low rates would have to be divided between the two routes; since Gould was strongest in Union Pacific, he would favor it at the expense of Pacific Mail. To make matters worse, Gould was ill much of the winter and could do little. While he recuperated, the confident Park organized his new steamship company to begin operations on April 1, 1876, when his contract with Pacific Mail expired.

In March the Supreme Court tossed out Gould's injunction, and Pacific Mail found itself desperate for cash to meet its obligations. When the company defaulted on its note to Panama, Park twisted the knife by attaching the steamers. Gould, Dillon, Oliver Ames, and the Union Pacific had already advanced the steamship company large sums to stay afloat; now more was needed to protect its ships. Huntington agreed to furnish the necessary security in San Francisco if the Union Pacific board would indemnify him against loss. To Gould's chagrin, the executive committee lost heart for the fight. "I fear trouble in San Francisco within a week if this bond is not arranged," Dillon warned Oliver, but the committee would not budge. Without its help Gould could do nothing. Wasting no time with laments, he moved at once to protect everyone's investment by reversing his position.

It was an inspired move, one Gould had used before to extricate himself from a tight corner. He and Dillon sold Park's group twenty-five thousand shares of Pacific Mail, giving them control of the company. In return Park agreed to pay off the notes and advances made by the Union Pacific men, who retired from the Pacific Mail board. This clever change of front did more than save Gould and his friends from financial loss. The whole point to controlling Pacific Mail was to eliminate competition. When Park thwarted this objective, Gould managed to salvage it through a brilliant retreat. The new owner of the floundering steamship line found a rate war no more palatable than Gould had. As Dillon noted gleefully, the new owners were "so loaded up with Pacific Mail & Panama stocks that they fear a fight as much as we do."

While hostile papers trumpeted the defeat of monopoly, Gould and Huntington negotiated a new agreement with Park that virtually restored the old contract between the Pacific roads and the steamship company. This arrangement brought peace until 1878 when Henry Hart, Pacific Mail's largest stockholder, seized control of the company and terminated the contract on the grounds that it was too favorable to the railroads. Gould and Huntington countered by doubling their rate to San Francisco and then organizing a new transcontinental fast freight line. The rate hike affected merchants who sent only valuable cargoes by rail and bulk shipments by clipper ship. The sea route was cheaper but much longer; the clippers delivered transcontinental goods in about a hundred days compared to thirty days for Pacific Mail and fourteen for the railroads. In effect the increase invited merchants to make contracts a year in advance for shipping all their goods by rail at some average rate or else pay higher premiums for sending their valuable cargoes alone.

To move these goods efficiently, Gould persuaded the eastern trunk lines and Iowa roads to cooperate in a new fast freight line which, he predicted, would "solve the question of water competition." All California freight was to be loaded in separate cars and moved from New York to Omaha without breaking bulk. If done properly, Gould reckoned, the system would cut four days off schedules from the eastern seaboard to Omaha. On passenger business the Union Pacific paid Pacific Mail a subsidy of five dollars per traveler, and passenger agent Thomas L. Kimball thought it a bargain. "In paying it we lose nothing," he argued, "as we would otherwise be forced to pay the same as commissions to ticket sellers to hold our travel if in competition with the Steamer line."

The snag in negotiations for a new contract was not over whether to pay a subsidy but how much it should be. Pacific Mail demanded $30,000 a month for passengers and $25,000 for freight; Union Pacific offered $25,000 and $19,000. Unable to close this gap, both sides were content to drift along on a temporary agreement until January 1880, when Pacific Mail accused the railroads of stalling and launched a rate war. The fight lasted only a month before terms were reached on a new pact. By that time the volume of business had swelled to the point where the railroads agreed to pay Pacific Mail $110,000 a month and to buy for O & O two steamers that made the China run for Pacific Mail, giving O & O a monopoly on the China trade.

The reason for so rapid a settlement became clear at the next Pacific Mail election when Gould, Dillon, Huntington, and Park returned to the board in place of Henry Hart and his friends. A new deal had been struck between erstwhile opponents to run Pacific Mail on behalf of the Pacific roads and Panama. Five years of struggle had brought the conflict full circle, but much had happened during that time. Although Pacific Mail remained a thorn in Union Pacific's side, it was reduced to a sideshow upstaged by the fierce competitive struggles among emerging overland routes.

* * *

Defense of the territory was for the Union Pacific a two-front war. At the eastern end clashes raged with the Iowa Pool roads and local poachers. In the West Huntington posed the threat of a flanking movement with his Southern Pacific, and other roads, notably the Atchison and Denver & Rio Grande, were eager to grab a share of the lucrative mountain trade in Colorado. During the 1870s these two fronts remained entirely separate, but within a shockingly short time they would merge into one battleground.

At the Omaha gateway relations between the Union Pacific and the Iowa roads had been strained long before Gould arrived. They had quarreled over the terminus, transfer, and bridge tolls along with the perpetual clash over how to apportion through rates. The Burlington dominated the Iowa Pool and soon emerged as the chief antagonist to Gould. Like the Union Pacific, it was controlled by a group of Boston capitalists led by John Murray Forbes, who had cut his business teeth on the China trade before venturing into railroads during the 1840s. Well connected and possessed of inherited wealth, Forbes preached the gospel of sound construction, conservative financing, and cautious (some said timid) management. While not above an occasional plunge, his contempt for speculators in general and Gould in particular knew

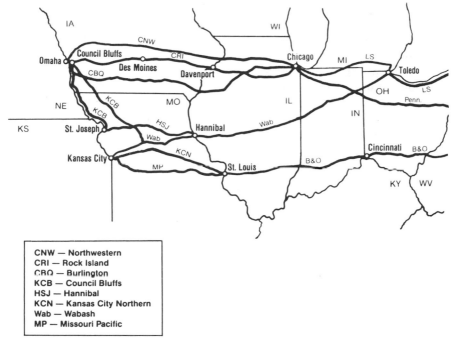

CNW — Northwestern
CRI — Rock Island
CBQ — Burlington
KCB — Council Bluffs
HSJ — Hannibal
KCN — Kansas City Northern
Wab — Wabash
MP — Missouri Pacific

The Iowa Pool roads and connecting lines.

no bounds. Although only a year younger than Dillon, Forbes had lost none of his acumen, energy, or acerbic wit. Above a gaunt frame his patrician features were dominated by an outsized nose and sardonic mouth.

Forbes came to power within the Burlington during the mid-1870s, when muddled finances and a tainted construction contract led to the ouster of another Burlington patriarch, James F. Joy. In March 1876 Robert Harris was elevated to the presidency with Charles E. Perkins as vice president. An intelligent, vigorous executive, Perkins was also vice president of the B & M and Forbes's cousin. Mutual respect even more than blood bound the two men together. Stocky, bull-necked, his face clean-shaven beneath a walrus moustache and close-cropped hair, Perkins looked the part of bulldog he played so well. Four years younger than Gould, he shared Forbes's conservatism but not his cautious tactics. No man would oppose Gould and the Union Pacific with the relentless tenacity displayed by Perkins.

During the lean years after 1873, the Burlington did little more than absorb its Iowa subsidiary and lease two small lines. By 1874, however, competition at the Omaha gateway had grown more complex for the Iowa roads. Through an assortment of smaller lines the Union Pacific could route eastbound traffic away from the Pool via six alternative routes for avoiding the Pool roads, all of them cumbersome and roundabout but useful in times of war.

The history of these smaller roads was interwoven with that of the Burlington and reflected the divergent views of its two chief architects. Where Forbes believed the Burlington's destiny lay westward, his predecessor, James Joy, placed his faith in the north-south route along the Missouri River. Joy controlled both the Kansas City, St. Joseph & Council Bluffs and the Atchison & Nebraska, which kept them friendly so long as he remained in charge of the Burlington. He and his Boston friends had also dominated the Hannibal & St. Joseph before leaving its management in 1871. Although Burlington directors owned a majority interest in the B & M, which extended from East Plattsmouth to Kearney, Perkins insisted on running it on behalf of all the stockholders. He favored the Burlington on traffic arrangements but refused adamantly to serve the needs of the Pool roads at the expense of the B & M.

Here was precisely the sort of complicated situation on which Gould's genius thrived. Since 1870 the Union Pacific had been striving in vain to break the stranglehold of the Iowa Pool. Gould made that goal a cornerstone of his policy, shifting deftly from one tactic to another. In January 1874 the Union Pacific offered the Council Bluffs a share of its through traffic if it would accept a rate division spurned by the Pool. The road's superintendent jumped eagerly at the offer until Joy intervened to protect the pool by ordering full rates restored. "The eastern roads and Union Pacific are in a quarrel," Joy explained. "The quarrel will be short and you can gain nothing permanently by playing into their [UP] hands with low rates." Joy also closed the route via the A & N.

Undaunted, Gould approached Perkins with an offer to throw business over the B & M. Perkins too was eager for the business but could not accept because Joy had shut off his outlets. "I am unable to see," he snapped, "why the interests of the B. & M. in Nebraska should be made to suffer in order that the Pool lines may be victorious in the present controversy with the U. P." His protest underscored Joy's inability to find a policy reconciling the Pool's needs with those of smaller roads crying for more business from the Union Pacific. In searching for ways to exploit these internal rifts, Gould turned to a new eastern connection. The Baltimore & Ohio owned a line to Chicago and one between Cincinnati and St. Louis. Its president, John W. Garrett, sought business by slashing rates and combining with the Union Pacific against the Pool roads. Another maverick road, the Chicago & Alton, extended from Chicago to St. Louis and reached Kansas City via the Kansas City, St. Louis & Northern. In April 1874 Gould startled the Pool by diverting traffic onto a circuitous route via the B & M, St. Joseph, Hannibal, Alton, and B & O.

This tactic deprived the Union Pacific of both the rate between Kearney and Omaha and the bridge toll, but it brought the Pool roads to terms by the end of May. Gould's action revealed in stark outline the growing competitive muddle in the region between the Missouri and Mississippi rivers. For two years savage rate wars raged as alliances rose and fell in rapid succession. The Pool roads maintained their unity but could neither curb the smaller roads nor prevent encroachments by new rivals. Joy's ouster from the Burlington in 1875 placed the Council Bluffs and A & N in hands no longer friendly to the Pool. The Hannibal wallowed in debt, a threat if it should fall into the wrong hands. Unable to secure peace, the Burlington acquired its own line to St. Louis but still found its position deteriorating. "We must do something at all Missouri points," pleaded one official, "or lose our business."

Although everyone admitted the need to restore rates, no one seemed in a hurry to do it. Tortuous negotiations during 1876 produced a new pool on southwestern business, but it was too fragile to end the fighting. By then Perkins suspected that Gould had been using him as a wedge to split the Iowa Pool; this revelation led him to join the Kansas Pacific in the *pro rata* fight. Clark opposed a new pact with the Iowa roads and advised keeping "open an outside line otherwise when the pool shall have got us committed they will squeeze us sure." Gould assured him that no exclusive tie to the Pool would be made "or any that would exclude the Alton line. I think we ought to strengthen that line & if possible break up the Pool of the Iowa Lines."

By autumn the Union Pacific and Burlington were inching toward open war. The key to a solution, Gould surmised, lay with the B & M's ties to the Burlington, the only Pool road with a Nebraska affiliate. Traffic moving across the Union Pacific had to be shared among all the Pool roads, while that shipped via East Plattsmouth went exclusively to the Burlington in return for a rebate. To the extent that *pro rata* would increase the flow of traffic along this route, it would profit the Burlington at the expense of the Union Pacific and other Iowa roads. Perkins had made himself a driving force behind *pro rata* and was fast emerging as the most truculent of Gould's adversaries. Although the Rock Island and Northwestern nursed other grievances against the Burlington, the B & M had become the lightning rod of conflict west of the Missouri. For that reason Gould determined to remove it as a source of friction.

His proposal, advanced by Dillon in December 1876, was for the Pool roads and Union Pacific to lease the B & M in perpetuity "and have the B & M business all go to Omaha and let all the roads have a share of the business." At first glance the offer appeared to be a clever thrust at the solidarity of the Pool, but there is every reason to believe the offer was sincere. In typical Gould fashion it was designed to solve several problems at once. It would neutralize the company's most dangerous competitor in Nebraska, restore rates, and minimize the danger posed by smaller roads. A harmony of interests would eliminate the threat of costly wars and retaliatory invasions. At the same time it would remove Perkins as an ally of the Kansas Pacific in the *pro rata* campaign. This was a major consideration early in 1877, when the disputed election made affairs in Washington unpredictable.

Predictably, the offer split the Burlington management. Perkins and Forbes saw "great difficulties" in the arrangement while the vision of peace appealed to President Harris and other directors. Unlike Perkins, Harris saw nothing wrong in attaining peace through compromise, and unlike Forbes, he did not regard Gould as the devil incarnate. In March 1877 he met with Gould and representatives of the other Pool roads to consider the whole question of Nebraska business. Gould's proposal was well received and all sides agreed to meet again within a week, this time with Forbes and Perkins present.

To strengthen his hand, Gould bought enough stock in the Rock Island and Northwestern to arrange an exchange of directors. He, Dillon, and Fred Ames joined both boards while representatives of the two roads were elected to the Union Pacific board. Gould also took steps to bring the Council Bluffs and Hannibal roads into alliance with the Union Pacific. Although these moves were viewed as an attempt to isolate the Burlington, Harris determined not to mobilize for war unless the negotiations fell through. "As to 'throat cutting' as applied to operating Railroads," he asserted, "count me out first, last and always. I object to murder in all forms and especially to suicide."

The next round of negotiations blossomed into a comprehensive settlement of all outstanding differences between the Pool roads, Union Pacific, and B & M. Perkins's views of this so-called "Quintuple Contract" and of Harris bordered on contempt. "I know Harris takes the ground that west of the Missouri is common territory," he said derisively, "& that we ought to pool B. & M. in Neb. but that is to my mind absurd." Perkins wanted war to the knife with the Union Pacific. "We can damage them quite as much, & I think more than they can us," he argued. Gould was in his opinion more bluff than substance. "The C.B. & Q.," he declared confidently, "is not in position to be 'bulldosed' by anybody or any combination."

These views made an impression on Forbes but not on the rest of the Burlington board. By the end of March the basis for an agreement had been hammered out. Gould called it "a good thing for UP & a wise arrangement" in that "all parties agree to build no more railroads in Neb." An elated Dillon instructed Clark to halt all construction in Nebraska the moment agreement was reached. Fortunately Clark did not hold his breath; the dickering dragged on for three months. While Perkins interposed one objection after another, Harris pleaded the case for the agreement. The Northwestern, Harris warned, "would yield to the pressure that Gould can bring to bear to take the U.P. business in common with [Rock Island] and break the pool, and all my action is based upon this idea." In his opinion the Burlington could "better afford to lose two thirds of the B&M Neb. business than to lose its one third of the U.P. business."

In this campaign Harris was no match for the truculent Perkins or the sharp-tongued Forbes, who railed against "the grasping monopoly of the U.P." A conference between the Pool roads and the B & M to settle details of the agreement broke up when Perkins demanded (and received) so many concessions that the other roads began to reconsider the overall contract. Although Harris tried to nurse the negotiations along with fresh proposals, the stillborn Quintuple pact was quietly buried in June with results for the future no one could yet foresee. The Burlington and B & M closed a new traffic agreement while Gould tried unsuccessfully to arrange a pact with the Northwestern and Rock Island. When it became clear that the Iowa roads would not break rank, Clark negotiated an agreement with them and the B & M in which the Union Pacific agreed to build branches north of the Platte while the B & M stayed south of the river.

The period of peace that followed would later be called the "golden age" of the Iowa Pool. In fact it proved little more than an interlude. Gould had failed either to break the Pool or negotiate terms with it. In the process he had aroused the enmity of Forbes and Perkins, whose future dealings with him would be colored by their personal dislike of him. "My objection to him is chiefly personal," Forbes admitted privately, "but goes deeper to the manner in which he is likely to use any power he gets." The significance of their feelings became apparent when Perkins forced the Burlington to choose between Harris and himself. The result was a turnover in May 1878 that elevated Forbes to the presidency with Perkins as his right hand. Their dominance insured that Gould would face tough, unfriendly bargainers in future conflicts.

* * *

On the western front Gould was anxious to maintain good relations with the Central Pacific, if only because the two roads had more enemies in common than differences between themselves. By 1875 most of the early disputes between the two companies had been resolved. Huntington's growing obsession with the Southern Pacific posed a threat if he succeeded in flanking the Union Pacific, but his progress was slow and Gould had taken steps to counter the movement. There was also bickering over division of rates for through traffic, an issue inflamed by the abrasive personality of the Union Pacific's freight agent, E. P. Vining. At both ends of the road Vining had shown himself a tough, inflexible bargainer; some said he was unscrupulous as well. A Chicago agent considered him "so despised here that not *one* of the RR men want any further business relations with him."

But Vining also had his defenders, notably those who thought he worked unswervingly to protect Omaha's interests. For all the controversy he spawned, Vining negotiated an agreement with his Central Pacific counterpart in May 1875 that was satisfactory to both sides. Eighteen months later, Dillon reminded Clark that policy was still not to "take any action selfishly that may disturb the present pleasant relations between the two companies."

The most dangerous battleground in the West was Colorado, where Gould's hope of dominating traffic hinged on his ability to resolve the Kansas Pacific muddle. South of Denver the pooling agreement of August 1876 was crumbling beneath the pressures of mutual distrust and conflicting ambitions. General William J. Palmer was anxious to extend the Rio Grande southward to Trinidad and westward to the mining region around Leadville. The Atchison harbored similar designs and, like the Rio Grande, was strapped for funds to push the work. Both watched the fight for control of the Kansas Pacific with keen interest, aware that its outcome would deeply affect their plans. During 1877 the three companies schemed and intrigued with one another, jockeying for terms that would give them the best position in the race to come. In November the Atchison hired a new vice president, William B. Strong, whose forceful personality gave its expansionist plans vigorous new leadership.

Before Strong's arrival there was already bad blood between the Rio Grande and Atchison. One of Strong's first moves was to propose an alliance through merger or lease of the Rio Grande. Palmer rejected the overture, setting the stage for a spectacular battle. In February 1878 Strong's crews seized the vital Raton Pass in a bold commando raid, shutting the Rio Grande out of Trinidad. Palmer grudgingly conceded the loss and turned his attention toward the difficult route to Leadville, which lay at the tip of a bulging triangle southwest of Denver and northwest of Pueblo. The doughty John Evans was already pushing his Denver, South Park & Pacific road toward Leadville from the northwest, and Palmer feared that the Atchison might attempt to build from the southwest along the Arkansas River valley.

Here too nature provided a strategic site in the form of the Royal Gorge, which was crucial to any rail line to Leadville. In April both Palmer and Strong dispatched men to occupy this canyon. Feelings ran high as the "armies" of both sides milled about the disputed ground claiming prior possession. The fight spilled over into the courts until October, when Palmer agreed reluctantly to lease his road to the Atchison. This proved little more than a truce, for the distrust between the leaders of both roads was too intense for peace to endure. By spring Palmer was hard at work seeking ways to reclaim his road from the Atchison.

The battle for southern Colorado complicated Gould's efforts to extend the Union Pacific's influence there. The collapse of the pool triggered a rate war during 1878 described as "the most bitter fight ever known in the west." Gould concluded that the brawl was likely to continue for some time and clothed Loveland with discretionary power to make rates for eastbound business. An unimpressed observer called the Union Pacific freight department "the most unpopular of any line in the West any-where." Attempts to form a new pool failed in part because all sides were awaiting the outcome of the Atchison's attempt to control the Rio Grande and the Union Pacific's attempt to control the Kansas Pacific.

Even the Iowa roads had a stake in the struggle. The Northwestern and Rock Island wished to see the Rio Grande allied with the Union Pacific, since all their Colorado business came via that route. However, the Burlington had become friendly with the Atchison and wanted it kept in harmony with the Rio Grande. Forbes was concerned that the personal antagonism between

Palmer and Strong might drive the Rio Grande to "renew their alliance with Jay Gould, which I think is not their natural alliance." The Rio Grande lease salved his fears by blocking Union Pacific access to southern Colorado. Gould was obliged to make a new pool with the Atchison, conceding that "so long as the D&RG is under Strong's controll & we have no line of our own into that country it is better to submit than fight. When rates are once down as they would go in a fight it is hard to get them up. The public clamor to have them kept down."

This apparent surrender was merely Gould's way of signaling a switch in tactics. There were other ways to reach the Leadville mineral region; he could build his own road or buy into Evans's South Park line. Strong also showed an interest in the South Park, which gave the wily Evans a chance to play him off against Gould. This tactic did not impress a veteran trader like Gould. "The Gov is on record in the past," he noted sardonically to Clark, "as selling us out whenever he gets a good chance. Our access to south west Colorado is too important to be placed in jeopardy." He was convinced the Union Pacific needed its own line to Leadville; the only question was how best to get it. With a show of indifference he declined Evans's offer and ordered a line surveyed west of Colorado Springs. The final decision, he declared, would depend on the outcome of Palmer's effort to pry the Rio Grande loose from the Atchison.

And on his own struggle to obtain the Kansas Pacific. All these factors affected Gould's fight with Villard as well. By the fall of 1878 Villard appeared to hold a winning hand. As representative of the Denver extension bondholders he prepared to foreclose, smash the pool, and take control of the property. Conceding that "it may take years to bring the foreclosure proceedings to a final determination," he advised members of Gould's pool in junior securities that "the best thing they & Gould could do would be to sell out to us." These threats shook some pool members but left Gould unmoved. He had no intention of selling out or waiting years. Financial reverses during 1878 crippled his ability to fight until the year's end, when he had enough cash on hand to act. The question was where and how to strike.

The first step, he concluded, was to resolve the Colorado muddle once and for all. He approached Loveland with the notion that leasing the Colorado Central to the Union Pacific would secure the road and neutralize opposition. "It would take them a long time to get the lease annulled," Dillon observed, "& in the meantime we could take action to control the road in some other way." Gould was looking even farther ahead; he wanted control of both lines to Cheyenne. With the lease in hand, he predicted, "then if we close with the KP the DP will fall into our hands." To that end he paid Captain E. L. Berthoud five thousand dollars for "services" in bringing Loveland to terms. After weeks of hard bargaining the lease was signed on March 1, 1879.

While trading with Loveland, Gould also resumed negotiations with Villard. Confident of victory, Villard approached the junior security holders in hopes of persuading them to desert Gould. The Atchison was also sniffing about the Kansas Pacific, which gave Villard another card to play against Gould. The extension bondholders demanded nothing less than terms equal to the original agreement between Gould and Villard. To their surprise, Gould offered to pay back interest to August on their bonds if they would accept a new issue with interest reduced from 7 to 5 percent. The bondholders were tempted but hesitated when Villard opposed the proposal. Gould promptly raised the interest to 6 percent and promised to pay the back interest in cash. These concessions coincided with the bombshell that Gould had just sold a large block of his Union Pacific stock.

This rush of events puzzled the St. Louis interests in Gould's securities pool. On March 2 two of their representatives, John D. Perry and Carlos S. Greeley, arrived in New York to meet with Villard. After a long talk Villard expressed doubt that the bondholders would accept Gould's latest proposal. Alarmed, Greeley hurried the news to Gould next morning. To his dismay, Gould merely said he was tired of the whole affair and would go no higher. "Suppose they refuse to yield," Greeley asked. "What then?" We will fight them, Gould replied. "Mr Gould that is ruin to our property," Greeley whined, "& to our St. Louis friends." Why don't you sell out, Gould suggested. "I cant sell unless all sell," Greeley asserted. In that case, Gould said blandly, why don't I buy you all out?

Gould agreed to take the pool's holdings at the valuations fixed in the original agreement. Dillon, Fred Ames, and Russell Sage took small shares in the purchase, giving it the appearance of being on behalf of Union Pacific. For some time Gould and his friends had quietly been buying up Kansas Pacific stock at prices ranging between 11 and 22, putting Gould in position to control the reorganization if he could come to terms with the bondholders. Villard's intransigence made that seem unlikely; the pool members sold because prospects of a settlement seemed remote. Only a few days later, however, Wall Street was stunned by the news that Gould had reached agreement with the bondholders, gained control of Kansas Pacific, and planned to reorganize it "as substantially a tributary to the Union Pacific."

Analysts heaped praise on Villard as the Denver extension bonds, which had sold at 35 two years earlier, soared past 102. To smooth the path of reorganization, Gould made his peace with Villard, assuring him of his "entire good faith" and his willingness "to advance *at once* the requisite amt to pay the bank interest & also the $125,000 to the committee." Originally Gould had offered the bondholders committee one hundred thousand dollars for expenses, but, wise to the ways of such negotiations, he was quick to sweeten the pot when it yielded the results he desired. Another issue that same spring brought Gould and Villard closer together and may have been decisive in the Kansas Pacific settlement. Villard had embarked on an ambitious project in Oregon. Gould subscribed to his construction company and discussed with Villard the possibility of extending the Utah Northern to connect, perhaps even consolidate with the proposed road.

Early in May Union Pacific men took over the Kansas Pacific board and installed Dillon as president. Observers assumed that the takeover closed the long struggle between the two roads; events would soon cure their naïveté. In tracking its course they missed entirely one aspect that was vital to Gould's plans. Once he had reached agreement with Villard, Gould moved at once to replace the trustees of the Kansas Pacific funding mortgage. "They hold the stock in the Denver Pacific," Dillon explained, "and . . . we wish to have it transferred to Messrs. Gould and Sage so that they can control the election." The mortgage was foreclosed and replaced by a new thirty-million-dollar consolidated mortgage with Gould and Sage as trustees. Among the collateral deposited for this new issue were nearly thirty thousand shares of Denver Pacific stock. At the time this seemed a trivial detail, an impression Gould was careful to leave undisturbed.

Possession of the Kansas Pacific transformed a rival into a useful ally. It also gave Gould two lines across the plains, a firm foothold in Colorado, and a monopoly on the Denver–Cheyenne connection. Perkins was left a lone voice crying for *pro rata.* As always, Gould had large ambitions for his new road. "I want to build it up & make it good," he told Clark. "It seems to me that worked in harmony with U.P. there will be no trouble in making it good." A pool was arranged to divide all business coming over the two lines. Gould had reasons for wanting the Kansas Pacific to prosper; he had laid out $1.5 million to become its only creditor outside the bondholders. "Until I am reimbursed I would like to give the KP all it can fairly earn," he stressed. "I have regarded it as of the greatest importance to controll that road & of course the whole load comes on my shoulders."

That importance was in Gould's eyes primarily strategic. "Now that we have the KP firmly in our hands," he declared, "there is no reason why we should not . . . smash the Omaha pool which is hanging like a millstone around Nebraska." Already that spring he had set in motion a plan of gigantic dimensions, opening several fronts at once in his secretive way, masking them so that no one could fit the disparate pieces together. Only Gould knew the pattern, and he moved toward it with the irresistible fury of a tornado. Deploying his forces with a unique blend of genius and energy, Gould was about to remake the railroad map of America.

The air was charged with mystery and anticipation, an eerie stillness before the coming storm. Perkins sensed its approach. "Since the Kansas Pacific surrender, we are about the only fighting enemies left against him," he warned. "In short, he is more dangerous than ever." But not even Perkins's wildest fears imagined the force of the blow that was about to strike.

20

THE
CONSOLIDATION

Between 1879 and 1881 Gould erected a business empire of such magnitude and with such breathtaking swiftness that the railroad industry would never be the same again. Of all the business titans of his age, none managed to accomplish so much with so little so quickly. The extraordinary chain of events that would elevate Gould into a legendary figure began with his attempt to restore the fortunes of the Union Pacific.

For six years Gould toiled unremittingly to make the Union Pacific the dominant railroad in the West. As the largest stockholder he reaped the largest rewards from advances in its price, from improvements in the company's credit, and from his dividend policy. But Gould earned his pay. By transforming a road riddled with debt, dissension, and scandal into a stable, prosperous enterprise he performed a minor miracle. How did he do it? Largely through a combination of original methods and close attention to detail. Gould was widely acknowledged as the foremost market manipulator of his age, but few observers recognized his ability as a corporate leader or in the volatile arena of railroad diplomacy. This blindness led them repeatedly to misinterpret his actions. His associates within Union Pacific knew better. They did not always grasp his thinking, but they saw firsthand the blend of brilliance and dedication others missed.

As the road's chief creditor Gould aimed to avoid a large floating debt that could hurt the stock and increase the cost of borrowing. This was no easy task when the Union Pacific embarked on an expansion program and also commenced paying dividends. Gould's solution was to provide most of the loans the company needed himself or arrange them with friendly brokers.

From the first he formed the habit of leaving his own dividend in the treasury as a loan until the quarterly payments were met. Oliver (and later Fred) Ames did the same, as did Dillon. Since together they owned about two thirds of the stock, this amounted to three hundred thousand or four hundred thousand dollars on call before other borrowing was required. Loans made by directors were at the lowest prevailing rate of interest.

When the company acquired county or branch road bonds in payment for construction work, it often could not sell them at a suitable price. Gould first persuaded Oliver and Dillon to join him in buying bonds "rather than to borrow money on the Bonds & have a floating debt under foot." Then he hit on the notion of having major stockholders take their dividends in bonds at a higher price than could be realized in the market. This policy disposed of the bonds, avoided a floating debt, and eased the paying of dividends when cash was short. Gould always took the largest share and was often obliged to advance funds personally for construction or other needs.

Gould's creativity extended beyond finance to accounting. The Union Pacific offered a unique challenge because of the dispute over the definition of net earnings. For years it followed the practice used by other roads. "The general theory," as Dillon explained it, "is that the entire cost of an enterprise includes all expenditure to the time of completion including any discount on Stock or Bonds . . . and any interest paid on the Bonds." But the 5 percent clause put a premium on reducing net earnings to the lowest possible figure. One obvious way was to include construction costs as part of operating expenses.

The favorable Supreme Court decision in 1875 convinced Gould that net earnings on the Union Pacific should be "the residue left after deducting operating expenses, necessary construction, all interest charges whether on funded debt or floating debt, all rents paid." For that reason he wanted the books kept to reflect two separate statements on net earnings. One for the government would lump these categories together to show the lowest possible net; the other would itemize them separately to offer stockholders a more favorable set of figures. This was done until the court surprised him by imposing a much narrower definition of net earnings. Gould never missed a trick to dress the income account for public consumption, which is why he worked hard to avoid a floating debt. Year after year he urged a policy of turning "enough of our assetts [sic] into money to meet our new construction a/cs without treading on 'Nett [sic] earnings.' "

Gould's uncanny grasp of details astonished associates and subordinates alike. Nothing seemed to escape his eye. He caught discrepancies in the accounts, offered shrewd advice on fine points of law to the lawyers, and searched constantly for novel solutions to thorny problems. On one occasion he pinpointed a flaw in the sinking-fund mortgage and suggested a remedy; on another he resolved a difficulty hampering the function of the land trustee. In each case he did not issue orders but offered suggestions and sought advice to avoid friction with sensitive officers. His reasoning had a steely quality that was hard to resist, yet he did not always get his way. For two years he argued in vain that registering the sinking-fund bonds would make them more attractive to investors.

Much of Gould's time was consumed by his role as watchdog of the stock and money markets. He followed trends in the latter closely to get the cheapest possible rates for borrowing. The stock had to be protected from speculators who exploited every twist and turn in the company's fight with the government. These repeated bear attacks challenged even Gould's unequaled skills as a manipulator. His task was complicated by the recurring fear among his associates that Gould would one day sell out his interest without warning and exit with his profits. His performance demonstrated otherwise, but such was his reputation as a speculator and wrecker of properties that no amount of reassurance could entirely rid the Bostonians of their anxieties. They peered uneasily over their shoulders even as they grew rich following his lead in Union Pacific and other enterprises.

During 1875 Gould and his associates formed several stock pools to maintain or advance the price of Union Pacific. These were handled by two of the brokers who had come onto the board with Gould, Charles J. Osborn and Samuel M. Mills. Together Gould and his friends owned about 210,000 of the 367,450 shares outstanding. Dillon estimated that only about 43,000 of the remaining shares were in the hands of outside speculators. The pools pledged to buy various amounts, usually 20,000 to 30,000 shares, with Gould and Oliver the chief buyers. Gould monitored the transfer books closely for signs of shares changing hands. If the pool did not beat off an attack, he bought more on his own account. In this work Oliver proved his staunchest ally, following his lead even though they did not always agree. "You & I together have over a majority," Gould reminded him in November 1875, "which makes it easy to manage & lay out a definite policy without consulting any body else."

Their alliance assured the Union Pacific of a stability it had never known. When Oliver Ames died in March 1877, his son Fred stepped into the same role. During these years Gould kept his pledge not to sell his stock. In 1875 he owned about 140,000 shares. The following summer Cornelius Bushnell concocted a scheme to recapture Union Pacific and offered to buy 100,000 of Gould's shares. Gould refused even to quote a price and confided to Clark, "I long since decided to hold my interest in the road permanently & would not sell a share of my stock at par." An uneasy Clark wondered if the Bostonians were using Bushnell to force Gould out of the management. Gould assured him that *"Oliver Ames is & would be no party to the scheme I am certain."* Bushnell had in fact approached Oliver, who observed cryptically, "I think Gould dont wish to sell."

By the spring of 1878, however, events forced Gould to rethink his position. The long fight in Washington had worn him down and snuffed out his last hope of resolving the government tangle. It rankled him to own a majority of Union Pacific stock and still be deprived of absolute control. To make matters worse, Gould ran short of money just as his financial load was increasing. In March he loaned the company his dividend as usual, but by June circumstances had changed drastically. After the twin disasters of the Thurman Act and the Supreme Court decision the board reluctantly passed the July dividend, which triggered a bear raid on the stock. Forced to buy heavily, Gould had to borrow two hundred thousand dollars from the company to meet an expiring note. The attack eased, then revived a month later after the Schurz decision on land preemption. Stripped of his dividend income, Gould asked for another two hundred fifty thousand dollars. "After the storm blows over," he promised treasurer McFarland, "I can reborrow & let you have what you want."

As the selling continued, Gould learned from a broker that much of it was coming from Boston. He urged Clark to "make this six months the best possible nett [sic] so that dividends could be resumed. The Schurz edict, he explained, had "frightened some of our stockholders & I have had to become a large buyer but if I can have my next two dividends I will run out of debt." Unfortunately, at this critical juncture Gould misread the market. Convinced that it would decline through the rest of the year, he decided to sustain Union Pacific while selling the granger roads short. There followed a long and bitter struggle in which his enemies hammered Union Pacific down, hoping to ruin his credit by destroying its value as collateral, while boosting the granger stocks.

Battered by these attacks, Gould saw no alternative to raising cash by selling some of his Union Pacific. In November he sold thirty thousand shares of Union Pacific to Sage and James Keene, one of Wall Street's leading operators. As part of the deal they insisted that Gould sell the Utah Northern to the Union Pacific. With gold fever raging along the Snake River, Dillon had changed his opinion of the road and now considered it vital to the company's interest. "Our directors seemed to think the U & N ought to belong to the U. P.," Gould reported, "& I have acquiesced."

One of Gould's favorite devices was to arrange transactions in a way that he appeared to surrender reluctantly to the outcome he desired most. In this case, however, his regret was genuine. He knew the Utah Northern was a valuable property, but he was starved for cash. His friends knew this and were not above driving a hard bargain. Gould agreed to complete the road to Blackfoot and sell at the cost to him. Within a few years the Utah Northern became the company's most valuable branch as well as its link to the Northwest.

Gould was forced to sell to lighten his load, but the relief proved only temporary. In January 1879 the market battle surged toward a climax in which, Dodge observed, "the entire street is fighting Mr. Gould." The New York *Times* asserted that Gould was losing a hundred thousand dollars a week, while a banker told Forbes privately, "Goulds cash means are, I think, very much reduced. I am told that he is no longer feared or followed." Perkins rejoiced at the news. "If Gould shd burst as we all ought to hope, and UP should take a big tumble," he mused, "it might not be a bad thing to go into."

Hard decisions faced Gould, not only about his market position but also his future in the railroad industry. His large block of Union Pacific stock had become a millstone about his neck, inviting attack from his enemies and allowing him no flexibility to respond. The obvious solution was to sell some of the stock, which would cost him control of the company. Reluctant as he was to part with it, Gould could not avoid certain harsh realities. By 1879 his grand design for the Union Pacific had been smashed. The Thurman Act ruined all hopes of settling with the government, without which he could never free the company from the clutch of politics and the financial marauding it spawned. He longed above all else to create not merely a road but a system of his own. That was not possible with the Union Pacific where control had to be shared with the government and with Boston.

If Gould entertained doubts about selling, an old specter helped nudge him along. For nearly five years he hacked furiously at Crédit Mobilier, which proved less a dragon than a hydra on which two fresh heads of dispute grew in the place of every one lopped off. The government suit against Crédit Mobilier lingered, as did McComb's, which had triggered the infamous hearings. Hazard still chased Durant and had another suit in Pennsylvania. Crédit Mobilier's suit to recover the two million dollars from Union Pacific still loomed in a Massachusetts court. Duff continued to use his position as trustee for the land grant mortgage to exact a compromise on his own terms. A host of other individuals pressed claims for their services as trustees or officers, each of them posing another obstacle to a final settlement.

How to cut through the thicket? Gould's amnesty offer brought in a substantial amount of Crédit Mobilier stock but not enough. Early in 1876 he diligently amassed evidence for the suits against those who still held out. Durant, now on the verge of bankruptcy, offered his help in settling up the Trustees' affairs, but the Doctor was as slippery as ever on particulars. The centers of opposition remained Hazard and Governor Oliver Ames. Enough stock had come in for Gould to control the Crédit Mobilier board, and in June he filed suit to recover one of its last remaining assets, the land at Council Bluffs.

There was in Gould a remarkable blend of patience and tenacity that stood him well in a protracted fight. Unfortunately, he was well matched in this case. Governor Oliver held firm, arguing that he would be charged with squandering his father's estate if he let the stock go; in March 1877 he was dumped from the Union Pacific board. Hazard, whose family owned 2,416 shares of Crédit Mobilier, clung to his belief that the stock was worth two thirds of its cost, prompting a friend to ask, "*Who* will purchase at that price?" Ironically the fight flung those two ancient foes, Hazard and Mc-Comb, into each other's arms against Gould. The Doctor reversed himself abruptly and accused Gould of working against his interests. His secretary, Henry Crane, refused to surrender the Trustees' books until his claim for back salary was satisfied. Even Cyrus McCormick protested that he had not been paid for his services and joined forces with Hazard and McComb. The dissident holders raised funds to push their suit for the two-million-dollar note.

Against this array of foes Gould proceeded with grim determination. He staunchly refused any payment to the Trustees and did not settle with Duff until February 1877, eighteen months after negotiations began. The government's suit was denied by the Supreme Court only to revive on a technicality; Gould feared it would "stir up old matters" and ruin their last chance for a funding bill. By agreement the land in Council Bluffs was sold to the Union Pacific and Crane was appeased with some back pay. Gould refused to negotiate with Hazard, insisting the old man could be beaten in court. As the war of litigation dragged on in half a dozen cities, Dillon let McComb know that the company was in deadly earnest about winning its suit against Hazard. John B. Alley got the same message and warned Hazard that he was "in very serious danger" unless he relented.

Hazard's own son, Rowland, also urged him to settle, arguing that "whether it is closed by receiving a few thousand dollars more or less is of no consequence." Durant was bankrupt and could pay nothing even if the suit against him prevailed, while the Union Pacific's suits could damage Hazard badly. By July 1878 McComb too was weary of war and added his voice to the chorus pleading for compromise. In November Hazard signed an agreement with both the Trustees and the Union Pacific that seemingly ended more than a decade of litigation. Shortly afterward the Supreme Court finally disposed of the government's suit, raising hopes anew that Crédit Mobilier might at last be relegated to oblivion.

Scarcely had the ink dried when the agreement ran into trouble. The snag involved that last tangible asset of Crédit Mobilier, the two-million-dollar note, that the stockholders of the construction company had sued to collect. Once in command of Crédit Mobilier, Gould had tried to discontinue that suit only to be enjoined by Hazard and others, including Governor Oliver. Hazard's agreement to drop this injunction did not extend to his colitigants, who moved at once to keep the suit alive. After some legal maneuvering Governor Oliver got himself appointed as receiver of Crédit Mobilier and assured Hazard, "I mean to press the suit with vigor." At seventy-eight Hazard still had not lost his stomach for battle. He wavered, then reneged on his agreement and talked of bringing a new suit against the Trustees. McComb bristled anew when his claim was denied, and the Doctor pondered another suit to rebuild his shattered fortune. The fight was far from over.

These discouraging events took place during the winter of 1879, just when

Gould's market fight reached its crisis point. If he needed one more reason to sell his Union Pacific, the morass of Crédit Mobilier provided it. To extricate himself from trouble, Gould resorted to the same tactics he had used in Pacific Mail. He disarmed the enemy by bringing them into the very company they were attacking. In mid-February he sold seventy thousand shares of Union Pacific to a syndicate that included Sage and such formidable bears as James Keene, Addison Cammack, and W. L. Scott, all of whom went onto the board. The stock bounded up fourteen points at the news, and no more was heard of bear attacks on Union Pacific.

The sale created a sensation on Wall Street, but it was not sprung as a surprise on Gould's associates. For the past year he had discussed with them his desire "of relieving himself as much as possible from the load." His own explanation of the sale was disarmingly simple. He assured Clark, who was stricken with anxiety at the news, that shared ownership would leave the company "less open to attack than when it was all 'Jay Goulds.' " The buyers were all his "personal friends" whose presence would enable the company "to get any amt of fresh capital for the perfection of our system of branches." He wanted rest but would not leave the board. His secretary confided to Clark that Gould had "no idea of severing his connection with the Union Pacific for her prosperity is identified with his own. It was only for strategic reasons best known here in Wall Street than any where else that he has let others in."

Eight years later Gould gave virtually the same explanation to the Pacific Railway Commission. Like so much of what Gould said, it was the truth without being the whole truth. The sale was in fact a brilliant and daring gambit played for deeper reasons than he cared to reveal. In effect, he sacrificed control of the Union Pacific for enough cash to realign his position in the railroad game. Few of his contemporaries understood what he was doing or where he was heading. Historians, blinded by the frenzy of what followed, overlooked his continuing presence within the Union Pacific. At the March election he voted 123,700 shares in his own name. Although he began quietly to dispose of more stock that spring, he remained active in the company's affairs.

Gould had no intention of abandoning a company in which he had so large a financial and emotional investment. Every action he took on its behalf was genuine and useful. He began again to lend it money and push for expansion. "We must build toward the Black Hills to retain that trade & keep out roads," he wrote Clark only days before the sale, "also press on in Utah & Colorado. Truly we have a great field to develop and we must move ahead vigorously or [others] will get the start of us." All seemed as before, yet with every act, every gesture, Gould was also preparing the ground for a radical shift in his own position. The subtle complexity of his maneuvers was revealed only a few days after the Union Pacific election, when Wall Street was stunned by the revelation that Gould had gained control of the Kansas Pacific and would reorganize it as "substantially a tributary to the Union Pacific."

While the implications of the deal were digested, Gould wrapped up the details of the reorganization and set sail in July for Europe, leaving in his wake whole cadres of puzzled and bewildered observers.

* * *

At least two men grasped that a new competitive age had dawned and would revolutionize the railroad industry. One of them was Charles Perkins. "I have long been of the opinion," he proclaimed, "that sooner or later the railroads of the country would group themselves into systems and that each system would be self-sustaining . . . any system not self sustaining would cease to exist & be absorbed by those systems near at hand & strong enough to live alone." The other was Gould, whose quick mind and quicker moves alarmed Perkins. "If Gould's combinations turn out to be solid—& more than mere stock operations," he predicted, "the general tendency in the direction of consolidation will be hastened. The crystallizing process is going on faster & faster & what seemed a year ago far distant has come & gone."

Perkins believed that Gould was what one historian called a "competitive bull thrown into the stabilized china shops, overturning rate compacts from the Rockies to the seaboard." They were wrong. Gould was not the source of change but rather its catalyst, one of the first to recognize the forces of a new age and harness them to his own purposes. Like Perkins he realized that competition had rendered the territorial concept obsolete. The Union Pacific had long since lost its monopoly position. Too many roads jostled against one another and more were coming. Fearful of isolation, they eyed each other warily and searched for ways to neutralize the threat posed by each newcomer as a link in some fresh combination.

Logic pointed to self-contained systems as the surest refuge. If the territory could not be defended, then it must be expanded and key outlets secured without reliance on outsiders. Weak foes must be subdued and strong ones cowed into that higher form of cooperation practiced by monarchs who divide neighboring realms on an amicable basis. An age infatuated with Darwin could appreciate the spectacle of strong roads devouring weak ones until only the fittest survived, and the dangers inherent in a policy of indiscriminate gorging were not yet apparent.

Perkins had reason to be wary of Gould as competitive pressures eroded the peace imposed in 1877. The Burlington responded to Union Pacific's Republican Valley branch with its own line to tap the valley. After Clark and Perkins exchanged the obligatory threats, Gould conceded the region along the Republican. "If the B & M & ourselves can work in harmony," he told Clark, "it is money in both our pockets." Gould wanted peace because he was already plotting to free the Union Pacific from the iron grip of the Iowa Pool. To do that he needed access to St. Joseph or Kansas City without relying on the B & M. The territory east of the Missouri River was a tinderbox of weak, vulnerable roads that could be acquired cheaply. During 1878 and early 1879, while everyone watched his market struggle and traded tales of his downfall, Gould moved stealthily to obtain the lines he needed.

Since 1876 Gould had been dickering for the St. Joseph, which was in fact two companies, a railroad and a bridge. In January 1879, the very time he was supposed to be in deep financial trouble, Gould secretly picked up both. "With this line in our hands," he beamed, "we will be independent of the Pool lines." Traffic could soon flow over the Union Pacific branch under construction from Grand Island to Hastings and from there into St. Joseph for connection with the Hannibal and points east. The trick was to find a route into Kansas City, from which lines reaching St. Louis and Chicago would enable him to outflank the Pool. Gould's mind teemed with schemes of vast combinations of which the public learned nothing and his associates only those bits and fragments he chose to reveal.

For months rumors of a grand combination had swept Wall Street, the most prominent figures being William Vanderbilt and C. K. Garrison, who sat atop the Missouri Pacific and Wabash roads. Little attention was paid Gould because of his financial difficulties. By the spring of 1879, however, a startling reversal had occurred. Gould had sold his block of Union Pacific, taken charge of the Kansas Pacific (which sent its stock soaring from 22 to 60), and captured the St. Joseph. He also stunned the Street by buying Garrison's interest in the Wabash, which ran between St. Louis and Toledo. As part of the deal Gould received use of the Kansas City Northern between that city and St. Louis. All these moves looked to be on behalf of Union Pacific. As Gould explained to Clark, Wabash would provide "a direct line from Kansas City & St. Jo to Toledo *independent of the Pool Lines. . . .* When our Grand Island connection is completed we can take care of ourselves."

Even during his stay in Europe Gould was not idle. In a lightning transaction he relieved the Dutch interests of their Denver extension bonds. These enabled him to control the foreclosure ordered by the court, but apart from that fact no one could imagine why he wanted them; the reason would not emerge for months. The Wabash was merged with the Kansas City Northern, creating a line from that city to Toledo with extensions planned to Omaha, Chicago, and Detroit. Once completed, the new system would outflank the Iowa Pool roads between Chicago and the Missouri River. Dodge thought Gould was trying to put together a line all the way to the Atlantic seaboard. Analysts excited by this development overlooked another possibility: the same system, run in tandem with the Kansas Pacific, would also parallel the Union Pacific all the way to Denver.

Meanwhile, Dillon and Perkins were squabbling over rates and expansion threats in the sensitive region between their roads. Forbes blanched at the danger posed by what he called "this carnival of bankrupt roads" and feared Gould might grab the Hannibal. The hardnosed Perkins was ready to fight fire with fire by extending the B & M to Denver. For months he had tried to forge an alliance with the Atchison; failing that, he told Forbes, *"I should favor a consolidation there also."* This was far too much for the conservative Burlington management, which could not even bring itself to bid for the Hannibal. When Gould returned from Europe late in August, they watched and waited to see what he would do next. While their anxious eyes glanced toward the Omaha gateway, Gould struck unexpectedly in the West.

After a bitter fight, the court had thrown out the Rio Grande lease and appointed a receiver for the road. The Atchison countered with an appeal and plans for a parallel road into Denver. Gould viewed the Atchison as a threat to the Union Pacific and even more to the Kansas Pacific, which vied directly with it in Kansas. Before the Atchison could move, Gould and Sage bought from Palmer a half interest in the Rio Grande and loaned it money for construction toward Leadville. The obstacle there was Evans's South Park road, which the Atchison coveted. Although Gould distrusted Evans, he made peace with him as easily as he had earlier with Loveland, filling his ear with flattery and his pocket with funds for the construction company building the road. In October 1879 he persuaded Evans and Palmer to stop fighting and construct the line to Leadville jointly. Privately Gould encouraged Evans to push the South Park on toward Gunnison. "We ought to extend this road at least 100 Miles per year," he exhorted, "till we reach Utah."

Why Utah? Gould was playing too deep a game for anyone to fathom its intricacies. The timing of his moves in Colorado was superb. Once the Rio Grande lease had been overturned, his swift response had shut the Atchison not only out of Leadville but out of the two key independent lines with access to the mining region. When the mining boom reached its peak that fall, the securities of both the Rio Grande and South Park soared in value. After tying the two lines up in traffic agreements with the Union Pacific and Kansas Pacific, Gould approached the Atchison with overtures of peace. If the Atchison would abandon its claim to the Royal Gorge line, Gould offered to pay all its expenses and a four-hundred-thousand-dollar bonus. In addition, the Rio Grande would drop its proposed line into New Mexico.

The Atchison was tempted but hung back. Preoccupied with expansion plans, its aggressive management still eyed Denver and had just concluded an agreement with the St. Louis & San Francisco to build a line to the Pacific coast. The Union Pacific, B & M, and Atchison arranged a meeting to discuss "the question of territorial division." Before it convened, Gould announced plans for a new road paralleling the Atchison from Fort Dodge, Kansas, to Pueblo, with extensions to Utah and Arizona. This bombshell hit the Atchison shortly after it learned that the court had awarded the Royal Gorge route to the Rio Grande. A chastened Thomas Nickerson, the road's president, signed a treaty with the Rio Grande in February on the original terms proposed by Gould. The new road was never built, but its shadow had done good service in more ways than one. If constructed it would, with the Rio Grande, parallel not only the Atchison but the Union Pacific as well.

* * *

As mystery piled upon mystery, one question continued to elude even the shrewdest of observers. What did Gould want? Clearly he was gathering pieces for an immense transcontinental system, but how were they to be put together? Everyone assumed the Union Pacific would be its cornerstone except for one astute analyst who noted as early as September 1879 that Gould's "recent acquisitions . . . have made him comparatively indifferent about the control of the Union Pacific, that no longer being a prime necessity for his transcontinental scheme."

This insight touched closer to the answer than anyone realized. The crowning ambition of Gould's life was to develop a rail system of his own, free from shared control with the government or anyone else. Events had ruled out the Union Pacific as a possibility, and the Kansas Pacific was no more palatable. Apart from its heritage of debt and mismanagement, a system built around the Kansas Pacific would force Gould into direct competition with the men who had been his closest associates for years. Contrary to legend, Gould was never a man to go back on his friends, and it made no sense to alienate his most valuable allies. There was another alternative, one he chose with characteristic boldness and vision. He could merge the two roads and use the proceeds to move into another competitive arena. In that way he could retain his friends and his influence in Union Pacific, both of which would prove useful in the competitive wars.

The idea of a consolidation was hardly new. It had been pursued in one form or another since 1875, when Gould first broached the scheme as a way of resolving the Colorado muddle. There followed a lengthy struggle for control from which Gould emerged victorious. In September 1879, shortly after returning from Europe, Gould proposed merging the Union Pacific, Kansas Pacific, and Denver Pacific through an equal exchange of stock. The major directors were willing to consolidate but rejected Gould's terms as too steep. "Gentlemen, you are making a mistake," Gould told them. Gordon Dexter thought he was irritated, that he headed west with "his war paint on and his trunk in hand." Gould left on an inspection trip over the Kansas Pacific and took time to look over the Central Branch and Missouri Pacific as well.

Negotiations resumed after his return in October but made no progress. Finally, on October 23, the board appointed Dodge and banker Solon Humphreys a committee "to prepare a plan for the equitable consolidation." To Gould's surprise, Dillon strenuously opposed his offer and told Sage that the only fair terms were two shares of Union Pacific for three of Kansas Pacific. "I feel very much hurt that Mr D should not have frankly expressed his views to me rather than behind my back," Gould lamented after Sage passed the remarks along. "I really think the value comparatively is the other way." If his friends disagreed, Gould added, "I shall withdraw the offer to consolidate & shall close my connection with UP & let the future demonstrate whether my offer & my plan was a wise one."

These were words dipped equally in sorrow and menace. The situation was a delicate one. The hapless Clark, distraught at being forced to choose between his patron and his company, refused to act on anything concerning the merger and took to his couch. Dillon was distracted by the illness of his wife and by threats elsewhere. He and the Bostonians feared the Burlington might build to Denver after merging with its subsidiary, the B & M. The Atchison had the same notion, Commodore Garrison owned some small roads in Kansas that could be used to extend the Missouri Pacific toward Denver, and Governor Oliver Ames was already pushing the Central Branch westward. They assumed the Kansas Pacific would remain friendly while in Gould's hands, but Dillon reminded Fred Ames that the merger should be disposed of quickly because "the longer it stands the more complicated it may get."

Scarcely had Dillon uttered these words when Gould jolted his friends with another series of lightning moves. He relieved Governor Oliver of the Central Branch for the steep price of $240 per share. The next day he and Sage gained seats on the Hannibal's board. Before the impact registered, Gould met Garrison for what he later described as a "stormy interview or two" and after some tough trading, agreed to pay $950 per share for half the stock (four thousand shares) of the Missouri Pacific. Garrison threw in the Kansas Central and another small Kansas road as well. The deal ignited rumors that half a dozen other roads would soon fall. "Just where this Gould combination is going to stop," wrote an alarmed Perkins, "it is not easy to see."

In November Gould headed west again, moving like a whirlwind, leaving his imprint wherever he stopped. He promised to bring the Missouri Pacific to St. Joseph, the St. Joseph to Atchison, the Central Branch to the Kansas Pacific, creating the "shortest and most direct route from Denver to the Missouri River." In Colorado he picked up the Denver Pacific and South Park stock owned by Arapahoe County. Clark, who had recently been made a vice president of Union Pacific, was also appointed general manager of the Missouri Pacific, which deepened the anomaly of his position.

Rumors that only months earlier would have seemed the ravings of a madman now flew wildly in all directions. Gould was after the Atchison, the Frisco, even Tom Scott's floundering Texas & Pacific. He was already into the Northwestern and would draw the Rock Island and Alton into his sphere of influence. Perkins had been burned too often to ignore such tales. "The acquisition of so much Railroad property ought to make Gould conservative," he said hopefully, "but how far he will try to use his power to whip the B. & M. & the Atchison into subjection I do not feel sure." He feared the "rapidity & brilliancy" of Gould's movements would cow the trunk lines into an alliance with him and urged Forbes to recruit allies for a coalition to withstand the onslaught.

Forbes too felt the ring closing about the Burlington, but the collar was not yet tight enough to squeeze the caution out of him. He dickered for control of the bankrupt Missouri, Kansas & Texas but balked at the price, and rejected the Council Bluffs as more sucker than feeder. Buying into the Atchison was altogether too grand a project for him; the Burlington board had taken months merely to approve consolidation with the B & M. Old habits died hard even in an age of breathless change. Nevertheless, even Forbes could not ignore Perkins's ominous reminder that "Gould moves so rapidly it is impossible to keep up with him with Boards of Directors . . ."

* * *

"It was always a bugbear, this Kansas Pacific," lamented Vice President Elisha Atkins later, and now it held them fast. The same noose tightening around the Burlington could also be drawn about the neck of the Union Pacific. Gould had pieced together the skeleton of a system stretching from coast to coast. "I saw Sidney Dillon and Dexter and Fred Ames as gloomy and unhappy a set of men as I ever saw," recalled Governor Oliver Ames, whose fat profits from the Central Branch deal allowed him to watch the show with detached amusement. "Mr. Gould had them in his power." The report submitted by Dodge and Humphreys endorsed Gould's original terms of an equal trade, but Gould no longer needed their support. He was in position to dictate terms regardless of what the report said. As he put it so succinctly, "My interest had changed."

His timing could not have been better. Earnings on the western roads were swollen from the mining boom and bumper crops coupled with short harvests abroad. Early in January, Kansas Pacific soared to 97½, eleven points higher than Union Pacific, making it hard to dispute Gould's claim for an equal exchange. The Burlington completed its merger with the B & M and renewed its threat of extending to Denver, hoping to curb Gould. Instead it alarmed Dillon into summoning Fred Ames and Dexter to New York "to do something immediately and to determine upon some plan to meet them." Dillon had in mind the consolidation, which now seemed imperative to avoid having two powerful competitors south of the Union Pacific.

For generations the consolidation has been universally condemned as a fraudulent transaction that fattened Gould's purse while ruining the Union Pacific. Even historians who conceded the technical brilliance of Gould's maneuver have dismissed it as a grab for profits. Like the Golden Spike and Crédit Mobilier, it has become part of a myth that bears little resemblance to reality. Taken in context, the decision was both rational and sound. In the long run it proved a blessing, although a mixed one, for the company.

Dillon and the Boston directors understood with painful clarity what later critics persist in ignoring, that the danger confronting them was very real.

Gould was not one to bluff. If the consolidation failed, he would either complete his own line and compete with the Union Pacific or sell the Kansas Pacific to someone else. They recalled the time after passage of the Thurman Act when a wrathful Gould proposed building another road parallel to the Union Pacific. Now he owned the better part of such a line, and no one doubted he would construct the rest. While the directors welcomed Gould as a friend, they shrank in terror from the prospect of him as an enemy. "A man of Mr. Gould's ability," explained Dexter, "—for he is the first man of the country on that subject—with such a weapon as the Kansas Pacific, let alone his Missouri Pacific, could have built branches and cut rates and cut us all to pieces."

Gould did not even have to renew his offer. In their anxiety, the directors came to him, which was precisely what Gould wanted. On the evening of January 14 Dillon, Sage, Fred Ames, Baker, and Dexter went to Gould's home and did not leave until midnight. Although their versions of what occurred differ in detail, all agreed that the discussions were protracted but not bitter. Gould's earlier annoyance had given way to a "pleasanter frame of mind." The consolidation, he said coyly, was no longer in his best interest. He now had only about twenty seven thousand shares of Union Pacific, a pittance compared to his holdings in the other lines. Four days earlier he had resigned as a Union Pacific director and was intent on erecting his own system. His friends would not hear of such a thing. As Gould put it, "they would not let me go out of the room until I had signed a paper that I would carry that consolidation through."

"I do not remember anybody keeping him in," snorted Fred Ames, but he was more literal than accurate. The Bostonians reminded Gould of their long association together in Union Pacific and insisted he was "bound by previous conversations" to go through with the consolidation. Gould always enjoyed being forced into doing exactly what he wished to do; on this night he relished yielding graciously to the pleas of his friends for the very terms they had rejected earlier. When at last he agreed, Dexter dashed off a memorandum of terms that everyone signed. It stipulated that Union Pacific, Kansas Pacific, and Denver Pacific stock be exchanged at par for shares in a new Union Pacific *Railway* Company. After conversion the four million dollars in Denver Pacific stock would be used to buy from Gould the St. Joseph road and bridge at par for the bonds and 20 for the stock. Pressed hard to sell the Central Branch and the Kansas Central as well, Gould agreed to let them go at cost on condition that the roads were leased back to his Missouri Pacific. In this way he could use but not extend them into competing lines.

The mystery of Gould's pursuit of the Denver Pacific securities stood revealed at last. In one stroke the agreement gave them a value no one ever dreamed they would have, provided certain legal obstacles could be removed. The stock was still deposited as collateral for the Kansas Pacific mortgage, of which Gould and Sage were trustees, and could not be used without first being released from trust. Ordinarily such proceedings took weeks, even months, but in this case they moved with the speed of light. Early in January the Kansas Pacific formally asked Gould and Sage for the release. When the trustees dutifully refused to comply, the company brought suit against them on January 22. The court appointed a referee, who heard testimony and filed his report recommending release in *one day.* On January 23 Judge Donohue of the New York Supreme Court accepted the referee's report and signed a decree releasing the stock. Then it was discovered that the Union Pacific's lease of the Colorado Central barred acquisition of the Denver Pacific. Since Gould, Dillon, and Fred Ames dominated the Central's boards, the lease was canceled as if by magic.

On the morning after the meeting at Gould's home the newspapers were already buzzing with rumors. Sage dismissed them as "made out of whole cloth" but the *Times* insisted that Gould had induced the Bostonians "to take the pill after sugar-coating it." The directors convened on the afternoon of January 24 to consider the matter. Two weeks earlier Gould had resigned from the board; now he sat down the hall in his own office, fidgeting while the deliberations proceeded. In short order Gould's resignation as director was formally accepted and cancellation of the Central lease approved. The Dodge-Humphreys report was then received, followed by the proposed articles of consolidations. There was no need for debate except among the government directors, who found themselves in a peculiar position. All ten directors present voted in favor, as did three of the government directors. One of the latter voted against; the fifth abstained.

On Wall Street traders, already panting over the rumors, greeted the news by kiting Kansas Pacific to 98 and Union Pacific to 94½. Only a year earlier Kansas Pacific, still bogged down in the fight between Gould and Villard, stood at 9⅛. The consolidation articles provided a board for the new company that included Gould; two days later it met for the first time to formally approve the transaction. A question arose as to the effect of the consolidation on the government directors, who were allowed to remain until the legal details were worked out. The new Union Pacific Railway Company, controlling 2,300 miles of road, was born.

For a century this transaction has been universally condemned. In 1887 the Pacific Railway Commission took thousands of pages of testimony and concluded that Gould and his associates had done it chiefly to profit themselves. Historians have echoed this theme and charged Gould with foisting a motley group of unprofitable roads on the Union Pacific and swelling its capitalization to fatal proportions. These assertions endure even though they have never been proven and rest largely on circumstantial evidence. Like Crédit Mobilier, the consolidation has been more assailed than analyzed. Looked at closely, it turns out to be something quite different from what critics have denounced so loudly over the years.

For all the talk about huge profits, no one has ever bothered to calculate even roughly what Gould actually made in the transaction. Henry Villard gave later generations a benchmark by asserting that Gould "cleared more than ten millions of dollars by the operation." While a precise figure is not possible, there is enough data to amend the wild numbers thrown about over the years. Gould insisted that "no director or individual . . . made a dollar" out of the Denver Pacific stock, and he was right. The shares he bought, along with his holdings in Central Branch, were turned in at the cost to him. His Denver Pacific profits came from the bonds. He bought about two million dollars' worth in Amsterdam at 74 and later exchanged them at par for Kansas Pacific consols. The difference in value was Gould's profit, but he did not keep the entire $2 million for himself. In his customary way he let Sage have $353,000 of the bonds and probably sold more of them to other friends as well.

Four other properties were involved in the transaction. Gould shared the St. Joseph road and bridge with his associates, who together took 30 percent of his holdings. For his shares of the St. Joseph, the Kansas Central, and the Hastings & Grand Island, Gould's own records show he paid $1.55 million and exchanged them for 24,502 shares of Union Pacific. At the market price on February 16, when Gould received this stock, the Union Pacific shares were worth about $2.25 million. On the branch roads, then, he garnered a profit of about $700,000, an impressive sum but hardly the stuff of legend.

On the Kansas Pacific itself, Gould bought 43,393 shares at 12½ or $542,416 and exchanged them for 40,382 shares of Union Pacific with a market value of slightly more than $3.7 million. He also owned about $1.25 million in Kansas Pacific securities from the pool of 1878 and bought another $1.35 million in junior bonds from pool members for $598,284. These were later exchanged for Kansas Pacific consols, presumably at par. On these trades Gould cleared nearly $3.2 million on the stock and an unknown but probably sizable amount on the bonds, but here too the profits were shared. Sage held a sixth interest in the pool securities and others had lesser amounts. Even so, Gould reaped a rich harvest on these holdings, possibly as much as $5 million. Yet he shrugged it off with the observation that he "did not make any [money] out of the consolidation, because these securities were worth as much before the consolidation as they were after."

Critics blinded by their obsession with profits have ignored this remark completely, an oversight that has led them to miss the most crucial point of the transaction. The true source of Gould's profits was not the consolidation but the astonishing rise in value of Kansas Pacific securities during 1879. In effect the agreement was merely a vehicle that enabled Gould to sell his holdings at peak prices. A more relevant question, then, is who or what created this fabulous rise in value?

By any measure the credit belongs to Gould. The fight over Kansas Pacific had dragged on for five years. As it progressed, Gould bought the road's securities from men who would never have sold so cheaply had they believed them worth anything more. After a difficult struggle he reorganized the road and, by acquiring other properties, transformed it into the nucleus of a formidable new transcontinental line. The road may have been financially weak but, in Julius Grodinsky's words, "as a threat to its competitor it had the strength of Samson." Gould understood this and so did other investors. The Kansas Pacific soared in value not for what it was but for what it could become in the hands of a man with Gould's ability. Critics who attribute the rise to the consolidation rumors overlook the fact that the stock reached 85 by the end of October, well before the rumors surfaced. Gould the market magician may have nudged the stock upward, but it was Gould the railroad man who pumped life into a dead property and made it a force to be feared.

His associates were eager to buy simply because, as Fred Ames admitted, "We all felt it was a matter of life and death to the Union Pacific." Efforts to charge them with conflict of interest, like the furor over Gould's profits, miss the point of what was at stake in the consolidation. All of them had some holdings in both the Kansas Pacific and St. Joseph, but these were small compared to their interest in Union Pacific. Fred Ames himself owned $4.83 million in Union Pacific securities and $828,000 in Kansas Pacific. The Bostonians would hardly approve a transaction that earned profits on a small interest at the expense of crippling a much larger one.

To a man the Bostonians agreed that they had acted to protect the Union Pacific, that the price paid was reasonable, and that, as Atkins put it, "without the consolidation, the road to-day would not have been worth a great deal of money." They also shared Ezra Baker's view that the transaction was "not forced upon us by Mr. Gould." Baker defended Gould's conduct as "very proper" because "the rest of us were trying to bring about exactly what we persuaded him to do." Gould understood perfectly the threat posed by the roads under his command. Asked later what effect his system would have on the Union Pacific, he replied bluntly, "It would have destroyed it." Perhaps he was bluffing, but the Bostonians, aware that he possessed the ability and the means to carry out his threat, were unwilling to gamble their large stake in Union Pacific that he was. In retrospect it is hard to dispute their judgment, for everything in Gould's later career suggests that he would have done precisely what they feared he would do.

Seen in the context of how matters stood in January 1880, then, the consolidation was no greedy grab for profits but a sound and rational choice. Far from being the disaster portrayed by critics, it turned out reasonably well for the company. In the short run it averted a dangerous competition at the cost of a swollen capitalization that would plague the road during the competitive wars of the next decade. It became customary to blame the consolidation for the financial woes that ultimately brought the Union Pacific to its knees, but in fact those problems had much deeper and more complex roots tracing back to the construction era. The road had always been overcapitalized, like most pioneer roads, and it suffered more harm from the endless dispute with the government than from any acquisition it ever made. No one could have foreseen the savage forces of expansionism that would put the company at such a disadvantage during the next decade. In that atmosphere the presence of the Kansas Pacific as an enemy probably would have done the Union Pacific more harm than the burden of debt imposed by the consolidation.

In the long run the consolidation turned out far better than anyone might have expected. The policy of buying rival lines in self-defense had by 1880 already become standard practice among American railroads and would long continue. The Union Pacific started early and did not do badly at all with its acquisitions. The Central Branch and Kansas Central ultimately proved of little value, but the St. Joseph properties, after a slow start, prospered as part of a short line to St. Louis. As for the Kansas Pacific and Denver Pacific, they remain an integral part of the Union Pacific system a century later. That fact alone offers a telling judgment on the wisdom of the decision.

A far more pleasant terminus than Omaha could be found in Salt Lake City, the Mormon capital, which amazed and delighted visitors with its beauty and lushness of landscape after the long haul across the plains. The house of many gables in this scene is the residence of Brigham Young.

Those traveling to the Northwest were treated to quite another landscape. This photograph, taken in 1890, shows a graceful arc in the Oregon Railway & Navigation's line between Pendleton and Walla Walla.

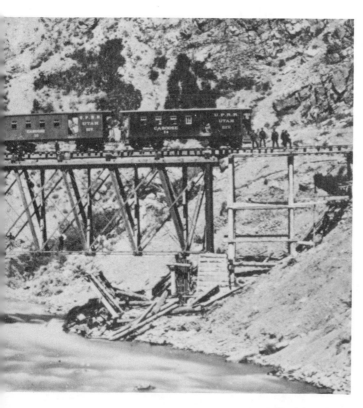

The new permanent bridge at Devil's Gate, built in 1869, is tested by putting as much weight as possible on the span. Happily for those on the engines, it held.

A double-headed passenger train crosses the new bridge at Dale Creek. Built in 1885, the new bridge of girders looks even more fragile and spidery than the original span. It was dismantled in 1901.

The transfer at Ogden. The Central Pacific train left of the depot has just arrived from the west and will transfer its passengers and baggage to the Union Pacific train on the right side of the depot.

The new roundhouse at Denver, built to accommodate the growing crush of traffic at what had by 1890 become the most overworked facility on the system.

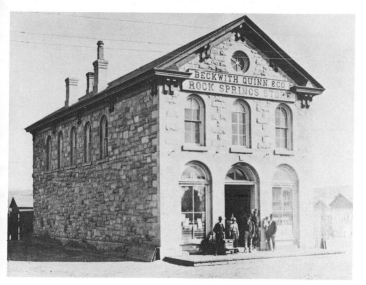

Trouble Spot: The Beckwith,
Quinn store at Rock Springs.

(Right) From tiny
acorns: the original
depot at Cheyenne.
(Below) The new
Cheyenne depot soon
after its completion
in 1890.

21

THE EXPLOSION

The men who actually operated the railroad fought battles quite unlike those seen in Wall Street or Washington. Their foes were more elemental and their struggle against them perpetual. In the winter came the snowstorms, in the spring threats of flooding at a dozen different rivers. Summer's drought shriveled crops and the water supply for thirsty engines. Lightning ignited fires and an occasional tornado flattened company property; one twister in August 1877 ripped two spans off the Missouri River bridge. Apart from these spectacles, nature had slower, more methodical ways of grinding a railroad down. Rails wore, ties rotted, trestles weakened beneath the strain of heavier loads, telegraph wires leaked or blew down, locomotives wheezed from overuse, rolling stock strayed onto other lines or sagged from exhaustion like overworked animals. To the men in the field the railroad was a living organism, an intricate complex of life cycles, each requiring close attention and renewal to keep the whole functioning properly.

Maintenance and improvements were the terms accountants used to describe the process. In a ledger or report they were quiet, placid words that reflected nothing of the hellish, unceasing struggle to keep the road running or make it better than it was before. The cliché that English railroads were better built than American ones was true but irrelevant to western roads, which covered much greater distances through undeveloped regions that could not support an expensive line. It made sense to build a lighter line until enough traffic arose to warrant a better one. Moreover, the technology of railroads was changing so rapidly that a heavy initial investment in plant and equipment worked to a company's disadvantage. The Union Pacific learned this the hard way when it erected the Laramie mill to reroll iron rails only to discover that steel rails were the wave of the future. Although no one could have foreseen it, the fall in prices for labor and material during the late nineteenth century would make a new or renewed line much cheaper than the original.

Like other Americans, railroad men found progress to be a paradox that caught them up in a vicious cycle. They toiled slavishly at getting more business only to cringe at the pressure it put on all their facilities. As traffic increased, larger cars were needed and more of them. Heavier trains required more powerful locomotives to haul them, stronger rails to sustain their weight, and improved bridges to bear loads for which older wooden or even iron spans were inadequate. Maintenance became a frantic struggle to keep traffic moving, improvements a desperate scramble to keep plant and equipment equal to the demands of a swelling flow of traffic. Since both cost money, the matter always came down to how much the company was willing to spend. To superintendents grappling firsthand with inadequate power or shortages of rolling stock, needs always looked more palpable and pressing than they did to financial officers whose concern was to keep expenditures from eating up the earnings.

The standard policy was to spend when the money was there and scrimp when it was not. Ever cautious, Clark was slow to embrace any change until its worth was demonstrated or his hand was forced. When a nightmare winter and heavy traffic in 1875 wore out his track in the Platte Valley, he shunned laying steel on such easy grade and used iron rail instead. Two years later, however, the company recognized the superior durability of steel and adopted a policy of substituting it for iron "as fast as it can economically be done." By 1879 the road had 485 miles of steel including the entire western division and all curves and grades in the mountain country. The old iron was picked up, rerolled at Laramie, and used as rail on new branches where traffic was lighter. In this way the need for iron to build branches quickly and cheaply spurred the process of converting the main line to steel.

Bridges were another matter because of the danger posed by collapse under heavier loads. As a first step the company found a happy solution to two problems at once. During 1873 several of the cuts where snow tended to gather were widened and the dirt used to fill several high trestle bridges; six years later all twenty-four bridges on the Mountain Division were filled in the same manner. On larger bridges the company had no choice but to replace wooden spans with iron trusses. Dale Creek was the first to be refitted in 1876, followed by Loup Fork and North Platte two years later. The Missouri River bridge was threatened by the river's shifting course, which threatened both the company's shops on the Omaha lowlands and the bridge's approach on the eastern bank. In July 1877, a month before the tornado hit the bridge, the Missouri cut a new channel through the western side, shortening its course by three miles but leaving the shops untouched. The change relieved pressure on the east bank, but large sums had to be spent on riprap to protect the piers from the breakup of ice.

To handle the expected flow of traffic in 1875, the company bought twelve new locomotives, forty-one passenger cars, and eighty-five freight cars. They proved a wise investment. "Stock, tea, coal & merchandise are giving us all we can handle," Clark reported happily. Despite a slight downturn in business, earnings stayed firm and the amount of freight carried increased steadily through 1879. Nevertheless, little money went to renew the equipment during these years. Of the twenty-four locomotives acquired, ten were replacements for worn-out engines retired to branch lines. Two new passenger cars were bought but four were destroyed. Although 260 new freight cars joined the fleet, the Union Pacific entered the 1880s with an aging and undersized roster of equipment.

To house its expanding Omaha operation, the company in 1875 bought a building known as the Herndon House and some adjoining lots. In Boston it continued to lease rooms in the Equitable Building while maintaining an office in New York. During these years the administrative structure underwent little change. Both Gould and Dillon believed that simple structures produced the most efficient management; the trick was to get the right men in the key positions. The Bostonians kept their hold on the executive committee by succession as Fred Ames took Oliver's place and Ezra Baker, Jr., that of his father, who died in 1879. Rollins resigned as secretary-treasurer in 1877 after winning a Senate seat and was replaced by Henry McFarland. That same year McFarland was given an assistant by the promotion of Oliver W. Mink, who had come to the office as a clerk five years earlier and shown exceptional diligence. In the turbulent years ahead Mink would prove an anchor of stability.

The consolidation expanded everyone's workload. Clerks in every department worked overtime to handle the increased paperwork, and more responsibilities were delegated to every officer. The two key men in Omaha remained Clark and Gannett, the crusty watchdog over accounts who held everyone's confidence. Aware that Gannett's strict devotion to duty was wearing him down, Dillon urged him to give up routine work "and look after matters generally." He offered to provide Gannett a stenographer and suggested that he "take some fresh air exercise instead of staying too much in the office." But Gannett could not shake the habits of a lifetime and continued to grind away until the winter of 1881, when his health began to fail. A concerned Dillon pressed him again to "be the captain or the general of that department."

Clark was a similar but more complex case. He too suffered from fragile health and, like Gannett, had a compulsion to do everything himself. His constant anxiety about his position caused him to keep all the reins in his own hands lest someone else seize them to his detriment. In his cautious, reticent way Clark trod a delicate path through his tangle of allegiances to Gould, the company, and the Boston directors, who did not fully share Gould's confidence in his ability. Thoughtful and deliberate, Clark was fond of saying that "65 percent of things would naturally settle themselves if left alone—the remaining 35 percent now and then demanded prompt and determined action." He moved at only one speed, slow, and admitted that his attempts at hollering failed because he could not use his voice like other men. One friend called him "an anomalous mixture of weakness and efficiency."

Gould knew all too well that Clark's desire for power was exceeded only by his reluctance to use it lest he displease his masters. From time to time he prodded Clark to show more initiative, aware that Clark was eager for promotion and longed to be made a vice president. Gould made an effort in 1877 but was thwarted by the death of Oliver Ames. A year later he tried again and found that "any change would likely lead to a jar with our Boston directors." In 1879 Clark was tendered the office of general manager as a consolation prize.

Possibly Clark's peculiar blend of ambition and insecurity accounted for the bouts of neurasthenia that plagued him throughout his career. The attacks seemed always to strike at pivotal times in the company's affairs. One felled him in December 1879 during the consolidation negotiations and disabled him until spring. Gould and Dillon both lectured him regularly to take care of himself. "It is of the first importance you should look after your health," Gould scolded. "If you could unload the details of the operating department so as to devote more of your time to the general commercial business of the company, you could do us most good & at the same time relieve yourself of the ugly wear & tear of details." Dillon told him bluntly not to "go out on the line this winter to expose yourself. Give the orders and have it done by others."

Clark had no intention of surrendering an ounce of authority to any potential rival, but he had no choice. For months he was incapable of work and had to entrust it to his superintendents. When he returned in the spring of 1880, the strain broke him down again by November. After hesitating for months, Dillon appointed Thomas L. Kimball assistant general manager and put him in charge while Clark went to California on extended convalescence. He also brought back as chief engineer the venerable Jake Blickensderfer, who had been overseeing branch construction in Colorado. At sixty-four the Dutchman was still an alert, methodical engineer, but he hardly added vitality to an organization already debilitated by age and illness in key offices. Although no one yet realized it, the Omaha administration was veering toward a crisis that would hit at the worst possible time.

* * *

By far the most significant change, and the one least obvious to outsiders, was the withdrawal of Gould from a dominant role in the company's affairs. During the years 1879–81 Gould ripped through the railroad world like a whirlwind, buying properties in all parts of the country as pieces in an elaborate puzzle that would one day shake out into a new business empire. No one yet knew what that empire would be or whether Union Pacific would be a part of it, and Gould did little to enlighten them. Selling off the securities received in the consolidation gave him the means to operate at a breathtaking pace. That same winter, with the Wabash and Missouri Pacific already in hand, he picked up the Missouri, Kansas & Texas (Katy) and Tom Scott's moribund Texas & Pacific, which he planned to complete eastward to New Orleans and westward to El Paso.

Suddenly Gould possessed the skeleton of another transcontinental road. Huntington was pushing his Southern Pacific toward El Paso, and the Atchison joined the Frisco in an effort to create still another line. All these directly threatened Union Pacific, yet Dodge and Fred Ames were associated with Gould in his new roads. In January 1880 the California partners decided to offer fifty thousand shares of Central Pacific to the public. When Gould joined the syndicate to dispose of them, talk revived of a merger between the Pacific roads. Both sides were serious enough to pursue negotiations for a year and seek the views of the government auditor, who expressed warm approval. But terms could not be reached and Huntington withdrew his offer, partly because Gould informed him that he had sold his Union Pacific stock and was no longer involved. "This is to be regretted," Huntington told a reporter, "because I have always found Mr. Gould a good man to meet . . . He always knows what he wants, and so do I."

While observers puzzled over his intentions, Gould launched a campaign that would shatter traffic agreements on both sides of the Missouri River. His first target was the Iowa Pool, where his probing mind found a weakness in the Burlington's policy of not sharing its B & M business with other Pool members. He proposed doing the same for traffic moving along the Union Pacific–St. Joseph–Wabash route unless the Pool admitted the Wabash as a member and agreed to divide *all* business west of the river. This demand struck a raw nerve in Pool relations. The Burlington owned a large feeder west of the Missouri, the Northwestern a small one, and the Rock Island none. Without an agreement the entire territory to the Rockies could explode into a war of rate slashing and construction. Perkins was convinced that "the law of Railroad nature" required "that each line must own its feeders," but how to acquire them without transforming friends into bitter rivals? Gould's thrust forced railroad men to confront this nasty dilemma.

Perkins also believed Gould's demand was designed "to trade with us on the basis of our not going to Denver." On that premise he closed an agreement with the Union Pacific in which the Burlington pledged not to build westward if "existing Missouri River pools . . . continue undisturbed." The Burlington would retain its monopoly on B & M traffic while the Union Pacific, Katy, and Hannibal would not discriminate in favor of Wabash. This was possible, Perkins reasoned, because Gould controlled these roads. The flaw in his thinking lay in a fine but crucial distinction: the agreement was with Union Pacific, not with Gould personally.

To Perkins's chagrin, the Wabash went on cutting rates while the Union Pacific honored its pledge. Through some clever maneuvers by Gould, the Wabash snatched two small roads in Burlington territory and announced plans to extend one westward to Council Bluffs and the other eastward to connect with the Wabash. The result would be a road parallel to the Burlington through what was described as "one of the most productive districts in the world." Poised to strike at the heart of the Burlington's lucrative local traffic, the Wabash renewed its demand for admission to the Iowa Pool.

These moves shocked the Burlington into a fateful change of strategy. Forbes had dickered for both the Hannibal and the Katy only to see Gould snatch them while he hesitated. Now he conceded that the old conservatism must be abandoned in favor of defensive expansion. Reluctantly he embraced the policy he despised most, buying "sucker" roads at inflated prices to keep Gould from getting them. Forbes never forgave Gould for forcing this practice on him; his blind, almost irrational dislike of Gould would hamper efforts to resolve disputes in the West for a decade. The B & M had already leased the A & N; in May 1880 Forbes bought the Council Bluffs at a fancy price and soon afterward acquired a small road for use as a connector to the Atchison. For all his misgivings, Forbes served notice that the Burlington would not be bulldozed (a favorite term of railroad men) by anyone.

Gould responded with a masterful display of his new role as corporate chameleon. The Union Pacific again diverted traffic to the Wabash, which continued cutting rates. Then the Hannibal announced plans for a line to Chicago in retaliation for the Burlington's purchase of the Council Bluffs. Gould, Sage, and Dillon were among the incorporators of this project, yet Gould took pains to warn Perkins of the move in advance, suggesting that the Wabash and Burlington join to "protect this business fairly in the future." Baffled as to which hat Gould was wearing, Perkins countered that if the Hannibal went to Chicago, the Burlington would go to Kansas City. By August war seemed imminent. A rate war engulfed the region southwest of Chicago and the truce west of the Missouri neared collapse.

The time to talk had come. Gould and Dillon met with Perkins to settle all differences between the Burlington and Union Pacific. Afterward Gould informed T. J. Coolidge, a Burlington director who had recently become president of the Atchison, that agreement was reached "in a very friendly spirit." The two of them agreed that the Union Pacific and Atchison should treat lines east of the Missouri "all fairly and they should stay on their own side of the river . . . otherwise if they come into your and our territory we should retaliate and build our own lines to Chicago—a free fight that would in the end ruin every line west of Chicago." Having assumed the voice of Union Pacific, Gould offered to use his influence with the Wabash and Hannibal but added blandly that he could not control their destinies.

Prolonged negotiations accomplished nothing. The Hannibal told Perkins it had rejected Gould's advice and suggested that the Burlington buy the road. The Wabash entered Chicago and promptly slashed passenger rates. Union Pacific was again accused of diverting business to the Wabash. In Iowa Perkins threatened to parallel the Wabash all the way to Toledo if the new road was built. In that case, retorted Wabash president Solon Humphreys, the Wabash would build into Nebraska. By September the war drums had grown loud enough to alarm even neighboring roads. Forbes was beside himself, his conservative soul tormented by memories of the crash that followed the orgy of construction in the early 1870s. He longed for peace but could not bring himself to negotiate with men he held in contempt or worse. Instead he asked fellow Bostonian Fred Ames to intervene with Gould, pleading that "the last time we met only mischief came of it. I know he dont like me and I certainly dont like him."

Ames was eager to "do anything in my power to prevent a disturbance," but he could do nothing. In careful language Gould told him the Hannibal had agreed to settle but not the Wabash. The January agreement had been made expressly to narrow the dispute to the Burlington and the Wabash. "I am doing all I can to secure peace and good fellowship between these large interests," he insisted, "but if I fail I object to having the C.B. & Q. inflict a punishment on the innocent Bond holders of the U. P. *Two wrongs will not make one right.*" This remark confirmed Perkins's belief that "the only way to get peace with the Wabash is to make Gould understand that war means injury to his Pacific Roads." But how to "tie Gould East of the Missouri where he operates under so many aliases?" The answer, Perkins thought, was that "he personally should also be party to such a contract if practicable."

Gould was far too shrewd for that. Except when signing contracts or agreements that served some purpose of his own, he operated through the instrumentality of bankers, brokers, or corporations. A crucial part of his style was to define obligations precisely and allow careless minds to believe he had committed himself when in fact he had not. To Gould this was merely part of the business game where alertness and perception scored points. Operating through others permitted him to roam freely, shift course without warning, conceal his true intentions from others. This tactic worked too well with Perkins, who in his confusion clung to the notion that "When he becomes really convinced that we intend to hold him responsible he may move." Perkins searched for a compromise proposal that would lure Gould to the bargaining table and came up with the idea of having the Wabash and Burlington build the Iowa line jointly and divide the local business equally, with a provision forbidding branches. The Wabash would stay out of Nebraska and the Burlington would not extend to Denver or Toledo. Gould and Coolidge could mediate the negotiations personally.

Even that concession nettled Perkins. "To let the Wabash come into our Iowa Country even on joint ownership," he growled, *"without our building any thing in retaliation is a dangerous precedent—& a backdown.*" But he could find no better solution. By his own admission the Burlington as well as the Wabash had already violated the territorial principle; a war would shatter the last pretense of its validity. A general treaty could restore harmony, end the construction race, and, above all, restore rates. By coincidence Gould made a similar proposition to Coolidge; this discovery of common ground led to a series of meetings in October. Although the Wabash remained belligerent, agreement was finally reached on the terms suggested by Perkins and Gould. In a separate pack the Southwestern Pool mollified the Wabash by admitting it as a member with an equal share of the passenger business.

The compromise was a reasonable one, yet one observer dismissed it as "a complete surrender of essential points in dispute" by the Burlington. Nor was he impressed by attempts to salvage the concept of territorial integrity. "The truth is," he argued, "that no railroad has any right or claim to the traffic of any tract of country, into which any other persons may see fit to build another railroad." These words chilled the souls of railroad managers. To their dismay the passenger rate agreement collapsed before the ink had dried and war raged for nearly two years; in November the fare between Chicago and St. Louis shrank to one dollar. Despite this breach, the other provisions held firm. Peace had been restored, but how long would it last?

The answer depended largely on what Gould had in mind. "I believe Gould must have some . . . plan for eventually putting all of his lines together," Perkins mused, but neither he nor Dillon nor anyone else could divine it. Gould was moving too fast in too many places for even quick minds to follow. In the East he bought into the Lackawanna and extended it to Buffalo. Another upheaval in Pacific Mail obliged him to recapture that company with Sage's help and impose a new pooling contract. Shortly after making peace with the Burlington, Gould settled the dangling status of the South Park road by urging its consolidation with the Rio Grande. The Rio Grande made a bid that suited Evans and Gould, but a snag developed over the method of payment. Gould then sounded the Union Pacific, which agreed to pay cash for the stock as Evans and his friends demanded. A brisk exchange of telegrams with Evans closed the deal in only two days.

Although the South Park depended on a trackage agreement with the Rio Grande to reach Leadville, the mining boom made its prospects seem brighter than ever. Its entire stock of 35,000 shares had been distributed to the construction companies that built the road. Of that amount Gould already owned 5,716 shares. From Evans's group he purchased another 25,908 shares at par and two months later sold a total of 30,993 shares to the Union Pacific for the same price. Later Gould would be accused of unloading this stock on the company for a fat profit. In fact he made money only on 5,085 of his original shares, and he sold to a willing, even eager, buyer. The Union Pacific wanted the road to shut out the Rio Grande and complete its hold on every line north, east, and west of Denver. For two years the South Park did well enough to pay its interest and a dividend as well.

While consummating the South Park transaction, Gould was also busy with the negotiations to merge the Pacific roads. "Our Boston people are opposed to it & so is Mr Dillon," he sighed wearily after his efforts failed, "& so I guess the UP will have to fight her own battles." Their failure to support Gould's plan was to leave a fateful legacy to the history of Union Pacific and western railroads. In both these operations Gould appeared to represent the Union Pacific's interest, yet at the same time he was also fashioning a new system in the Southwest. With Dodge as chief engineer, he pushed the Texas & Pacific toward El Paso and the Gulf. After perfecting his hold on the Katy, he leased it to the Missouri Pacific and announced plans for six hundred miles of extensions, including a connector to the Texas & Pacific. Then, in December 1880, Gould stunned the railroad world again by acquiring the St. Louis, Iron Mountain & Southern, which ran from St. Louis to Texarkana. Two weeks later he scooped the International & Great Northern, a ramshackle project that, if completed, would extend from Texarkana to the Rio Grande.

Early in 1881 the cloud of mystery surrounding Gould's intentions began to dissolve. Through the mist emerged a potential system stretching from El Paso to New Orleans and from St. Louis to the Rio Grande. Gould had staked claim to a vast territory, largely undeveloped and crying for railroads. It competed with Huntington's Southern Pacific but not directly with the Union Pacific. That spring Gould relieved a dying Tom Scott of his holdings in Texas & Pacific and announced plans to complete his unfinished roads and unite them into a southwestern system with the Missouri Pacific as parent road. He would devote the rest of his life to the mission of creating and integrating a system that, ironically, would merge with the Union Pacific a century later. Although Gould kept his seat on the Union Pacific executive committee, he withdrew entirely from an active role in the company's affairs. By April 1882 Dillon no longer thought it even necessary to send him monthly statements. Given Gould's voracious appetite for data, this was a sure sign that his attention had turned elsewhere.

What was obvious to Dillon was not so evident to the managers of other roads. Gould's presence in so many companies left them as baffled as ever over his intentions. During 1881 his genius at playing the role of chameleon came back to haunt him, triggering a crisis that would engulf the western roads into the war of expansion they had dreaded for so long.

In the West there had been peace or at least an uneasy truce since the agreement of March 1880. Dillon was on good terms with the Atchison and Rio Grande and anxious to stay that way, but no one was sitting still. The Atchison and Frisco joined rails in Kansas and laid plans for building into California. Late in 1880 the Atchison also inched toward a connection with Huntington's Southern Pacific in New Mexico. The Rio Grande extended its line into New Mexico and eyed new branches in Colorado, where it ran afoul of the Union Pacific. The March agreement contained provisions prohibiting the Atchison, Rio Grande, and Union Pacific from building into each other's territory. These restrictions did not apply to the South Park, which was at that time an independent road. Now it belonged to the Union Pacific and was intent on extending into regions covered by the agreement.

Palmer denounced this plan as a violation of the agreement only to be reminded stiffly by Dillon that the March treaty allowed the South Park to build branches regardless of who owned it. Dillon left the negotiations to Clark, who found Palmer implacable. Losing patience, Dillon warned that "unless something definite can be arranged with Palmer, we shall have to adapt a very vigorous course." Palmer responded by putting graders on a line parallel to the South Park and threatening branches to Cheyenne and elsewhere. In August 1881 he chartered a new line, the Denver & Rio Grande Western, to connect his Colorado lines with Salt Lake City. Once again the threat of war in the Rockies flared. The logical man to intervene was Gould, who owned a half interest in the Rio Grande and was presumed to dominate the Union Pacific. Instead of moving to ease tensions in the West, however, Gould startled observers by precipitating a crisis at the Omaha gateway.

Although the passenger war still raged and sporadic bouts of rate slashing kept the region on both sides of the Missouri in upheaval, railroad men and observers alike clung to the hope that the October agreement would endure. As late as April 1881 one analyst concluded that the Burlington would not extend to Denver "in the immediate future." These forecasts did not reckon with Gould, whose ultimate intentions still mystified everyone. In June Gould finally unmasked his priorities by organizing a company to extend the Missouri Pacific to Omaha on the Nebraska side of the river. The Wabash already had a line to Omaha, but Gould was anxious for the Missouri Pacific to tap directly the flow of traffic from the Union Pacific. He also secretly explored the feasibility of a line to San Francisco serving both the Union Pacific and Texas & Pacific.

Since the extension would penetrate the counties regarded as Burlington territory, it violated the spirit if not the letter of the October agreement. Perkins sounded Gould on his intentions and was told the rumor was true. The extension was needed, Gould explained, because the Burlington had absorbed two former connectors, the Council Bluffs and A & N. "We simply project a direct through line to Omaha," to which Perkins could have no objection. Even Rosewater's *Bee* hailed the extension as "of incalculable benefit to the entire eastern portion of the state," but Perkins was not impressed. He saw Gould at his old game of walking the tightrope of an obligation. Neither Gould nor the Missouri Pacific was a party to the October agreement, yet Perkins considered Gould the real power behind two of the signees, Union Pacific and Wabash.

To unclouded eyes the extension hinted strongly that Gould's interest lay more with the Missouri Pacific than with Union Pacific. But Perkins's eyes were clouded by his past dealings with Gould, which narrowed his vision and stiffened his resolve. Unable to shake his belief that the Union Pacific was of primary importance to Gould, he saw only that Gould was "building his Missouri Pacific into Nebraska, notwithstanding his agreement last summer as head of the Union Pacific not to do so." An alarmed Coolidge, fearing the outbreak of war, warned Dillon that the Burlington might ally with Palmer against the Union Pacific. The hapless Dillon found himself in a quandary. "I regret very much that the Missouri Pacific extension should have been projected at this time," he confided to Clark. A war would ruin them all, none more than the Union Pacific, which depended heavily on high rates. But, Dillon added with the truculence typical of railroad managers, "let it be understood that if it is war, it is war to the knife."

Perkins stood poised with his own knife, ready to slash the Union Pacific if he could not get at the Missouri Pacific. The extension posed so many threats to the Burlington that on July 20 its board formally abrogated the October agreement. "It looks a little now," Perkins alerted his vice president, T. J. Potter, "as if we should go to Denver at an early day."

Dillon was aghast that Perkins proposed to punish his road for the sins of another because he assumed they were puppets of the same guiding hand. "I never consented to the building of that Road," he protested hotly, "but earnestly objected to it from the first." He considered it "highly unjust to the Union Pacific to hold it responsible for action taken which it could not and can not prevent, and which it did not and does not favor." William Vanderbilt, as holder of a "very large interest in both Companies," pressed similar views on Forbes and offered his services as mediator to no avail. The point that Gould and Sage controlled Missouri Pacific but owned little stock in Union Pacific was lost on Forbes and Perkins, who shared a fixed view of the relationship between men and the corporations they served.

To them, whatever the legal niceties, Gould had promoted and accepted the October agreement that curbed building in eastern Nebraska, and his new line violated that agreement regardless of what alias it assumed. Gould, Sage, and Dillon all sat on the boards of Missouri Pacific, Union Pacific, and Wabash; Clark was an officer in the first two roads. Whom did they represent in a given negotiation? If directors could skirt an agreement simply by changing hats, how could responsibility ever be fixed? Agreements must depend, Forbes lectured Vanderbilt, "not upon their legal or technical validity, but upon the honest purpose and determination of all persons participating in their formation to live up to them." In short, Forbes and Perkins believed agreements were made by individuals, not corporations.

But the interests of individuals changed, and so did circumstances. Forbes's view belonged to an earlier age when firms were closely identified with the men who founded or ran them. The practice still lingered as a habit and was still useful for smaller businesses, but as corporations grew larger they outlived their founders and took on an identity of their own. The corporation allowed individuals to float easily from one company to another or among several companies at once. Gould belonged to this new, mobile type of businessman and pioneered its possibilities. The ethics of this new method had yet to be explored, but more than ethical differences separated men like Gould and Forbes. They held radically different views of what businessmen should be and what they should do.

In this conflict, however, the only choices left were to make concessions or war. Gould told Perkins curtly that "the Union Pacific had, and has, nothing to do with building of this line" and took complete responsibility on behalf of Missouri Pacific. He condemned Perkins's action as "unprecedented among Railroad men" and warned that if the Burlington built to Denver, the Missouri Pacific would go to Chicago, throw out branches in Nebraska, and shift its business to rival lines. "We want peace but are ready for war if you insist on making it," Gould asserted. "Carrying out your menaces or extending your line to Denver means war."

Dillon reinforced this view with a letter of his own, but the threats left Perkins unmoved. In a lengthy reply he noted acidly that the Burlington would not "remain with our hands tied while the other party insists on being free." Diplomacy had reached another dead end with the usual result. On August 19 the Burlington board authorized the Denver extension, which opened for business nine months later. It also elevated Perkins to the presidency and put Forbes back in as chairman.

The Denver extension did more than merely widen the field of conflict. It ushered in an age of expansionist wars fought with unprecedented fury on a scale never seen before. There would be few winners, many losers, and heavy casualties inflicted on all sides. While all the roads would feel the consequences for decades to come, none suffered more immediate losses than the Union Pacific. It no longer owned the continent and would find it hard to compete with newer, cheaper, more efficient routes.

* * *

Within a remarkably short time the two-front war merged into one as once isolated battles became separate engagements in a larger transcontinental conflict. Palmer decided to build his new Rio Grande Western all the way to Ogden, which it reached in May 1883. Together with the Burlington's Denver extension it formed a line that paralleled the entire length of the Union Pacific. Utah papers hailed their emancipation from the Union Pacific monopoly, which in effect meant lower rates for everyone if agreements could not be made. Throughout most of 1882 Dillon and Perkins haggled over terms for a Colorado pool.

To counter the threats posed by Perkins and Palmer, the Union Pacific accelerated its own expansion program in Colorado. During 1881 it completed the Julesburg branch, which left the main line at the fork of the Platte River and followed the South Platte to a connection with the Denver Pacific.

Surveys commenced on lines from Denver to Longmont and from Fort Collins up the Cache La Poudre into the North Park. The most daring and costly project extended the Georgetown branch through Loveland Pass to Leadville along the so-called "high line," with other spurs planned to tap mineral districts. All this work was expensive and depended on continued growth of the mining boom. Nearly all of it was designed to shut out lines projected by the Burlington or Rio Grande. "We will not give way," Dillon barked defiantly in one case, "even if we have to build a parallel road." Despite the costs and the construction difficulties, the high line to Leadville went forward and was opened early in 1884.

West of Colorado the Union Pacific pursued an even more aggressive expansion policy as a defense against invading rivals. In Utah a season of depression caused by falling lead prices during 1878 slowed progress only for a short time. The Utah Southern extension pushed steadily across the desert to the mines at Frisco, 280 miles from Ogden. Taking care to coordinate his plans with Bishop Sharp and his Mormon partners, Dillon swept the Utah Central, Utah Southern, and the latter's extension together into a single company in June 1881. To protect the territory he favored taking "at least one half interest in all new roads" seeking to penetrate Utah. The Western shattered that hope abruptly, as did the expansionist aims of other large systems erecting new transcontinental lines. By 1881 the Southern Pacific and Atchison posed threats to the south that could no longer be ignored.

As a weapon the Union Pacific had the old Utah Western, which ran from Lehi Junction fifty-seven miles to the Tintic mining district. Beyond it lay a forlorn derelict called the Nevada Central that connected only with the Central Pacific. In 1881 Dillon bought this line and laid plans to extend the Utah Western toward it. Later he claimed that Rio Grande engineers were nosing about Salt Lake Valley and he grabbed the Nevada Central "to keep it out of their hands, whether it was good for anything or not. . . . I was mistaken. Everyone is mistaken some time."

This was disingenuous at best. In fact, the Nevada Central was a pawn in some elaborate diplomacy by Gould. As part of a proposed line to San Francisco he organized in cooperation with the Atchison and the Frisco it could be wielded against both Palmer and Huntington. Gould was also dueling with Huntington in the Southwest, where the Southern Pacific and Texas & Pacific were heading toward each other. This shadow line permitted Gould to attack Huntington in the guise of protecting Union Pacific when his true interest was actually the Texas & Pacific. The California partners took these threats seriously. "I hope you will give Mr. Dillon pretty square talk," the flinty Crocker advised Huntington, "and tell him that all this stuff and talk about building parallel to us will not be tolerated." Crocker suggested countering with a threat to build the Central Pacific eastward to Denver. "If Dillon thought for a moment we would connect with the C. B. & Q.," he cackled, "it would scare him out of his boots."

Nothing illustrated the changing dynamics of competition more dramatically than the fact that clashes between lines could no longer be confined to one region. Apart from the Rockies and the Southwest, Crocker and Huntington had also to worry about the Northwest, where the Union Pacific posed yet another threat. In March 1880 the Utah Northern crossed the Montana border, the first railroad to reach that territory. By October the line had advanced to Dillon, where it was expected to remain for a time. Normally the adventures of a narrow gauge venturing into the wilderness held little interest for Huntington, but two striking developments drew his attention to this one: Henry Villard was breathing life into the moribund northern transcontinental route, and the Union Pacific decided to build its long cherished line to Oregon.

Huntington was painfully aware that the two activities were rooted in common soil. After their long struggle over Kansas Pacific, Villard and Gould had not only reconciled in 1879 but gone partners in Villard's scheme to capture railroad and steamship lines in Oregon. As part of the deal a new company would be formed to build a road connecting the Utah Northern with Villard's lines. Dillon and the Boston associates planned to invest in both projects, but the Central Pacific got wind of the venture and, as Villard reported in July 1879, "remonstrated with and threatened the Union Pacific people to such an extent that the latter were disinclined to commit themselves openly." Gould and his friends withdrew from the project, leaving Villard to organize it in his own way with the private understanding that the Utah Northern connection would still be constructed.

A man infused with grand ambitions and a bullish temperament, Villard pushed his enterprises with a speed that astonished even jaded promoters. He swept the Oregon lines into a new company called Oregon Railway & Navigation and organized another firm, Oregon Improvement Company, to exploit the region's resources. Work began on a rail line up the Columbia River to connect with the Northern Pacific at Wallula. Villard was not the only promoter seized by Oregon fever, but no one was more infectious in spreading it through the investment community. His efforts caught a rising tide of prosperity that flung his enthusiasm to unbounded heights. "It is a large thing now," he enthused, "but the growth of it in the next few years will be positively astounding."

While Villard pursued his grand design, the long dormant Northern Pacific sprang to life under new leadership intent on constructing the road not to Wallula but all the way to Portland. For months Villard sparred and dickered with Frederick Billings of the Northern Pacific. Their clash marked the first shots in what would prove a long and bitter war for dominance of the Northwest. A treaty signed in October 1880 left neither side satisfied. The Northern Pacific laid plans to invade Oregon only to be outflanked by one of the boldest schemes ever devised. During the spring of 1881 Villard raised a war chest of eight million dollars through his famous "blind pool" in which he refused to tell investors what he intended doing with the money. They found out only when Villard used it to buy control of the Northern Pacific. A new holding company, Oregon & Transcontinental, was organized as the parent of both Northern Pacific and Oregon Navigation.

The sudden emergence of a new transcontinental system to the north forced the Union Pacific to rethink its strategy. Villard was a friend who counted on an early connection with the Union Pacific. With the Northern Pacific laying rails across the Northwest, it no longer made sense to use the Utah Northern as a starting point for reaching Oregon. That route was far too roundabout to compete efficiently. Instead the company decided to extend the Utah Northern to Butte and worked out an agreement with the Northern Pacific to build a joint road from Butte to the latter's main line. The Utah Northern thus remained purely a north-south road, 462 miles long and firmly planted in the mineral regions of Idaho and Montana as Gould had envisioned.

To reach Oregon the company dusted off the survey made by Hudnutt in 1868. Even then Oliver Ames considered the Oregon line a "first rate opperation [sic]" if a subsidy could be obtained. McComb too thought it "worth all our combined strength," but all their efforts to get a subsidy bill out of Congress failed and the project languished for a decade. In 1879 Dillon had a new survey run between the Boise and Snake rivers, then turned the results along with Hudnutt's survey over to Blickensderfer, who chose the final line. The route selected left the Union Pacific at Granger, intersected the Utah Northern at McCammon, utilized its track to Pocatello, and followed a line north of the Snake River to connection with the Oregon Navigation at Huntington.

In February 1881 the executive committee accepted the route and voted to build the line "as rapidly as practicable." At once the old problem arose of how to get around the charter's lack of provision for building branches. On other projects the company worked through subsidiary corporations, using its own construction department to build the road and taking as pay securities in the subsidiary company. This time it worked a variation on the theme by organizing a new company, the Oregon Short Line, and offering its bonds along with half the stock to Union Pacific holders. The subscription went well and work commenced on the line, but legal complications arose. The company needed permission to build through an Indian reservation and could not even organize in Idaho because the territory had no law on its books authorizing the formation of railroads. To surmount these obstacles Dillon managed to procure legislation from Congress.

By the end of 1881 the whole region west of the Mississippi River seemed caught up in a frenzy of expansion, diplomacy, and war from which no road could escape or isolate itself. It was as if the forces underlying the railroad industry had suddenly exploded, throwing every company into motion at a greater velocity than ever before. Change came so rapidly that managers no longer had the luxury of time to contemplate their effects. A major source of the explosion was the return of prosperity in 1879 after a half dozen years of depression, which unleashed a torrent of pent-up ambitions and frustrations among railroad men. Another was the blitzkrieg operation by Gould, who stunned rivals with one unpredictable coup after another and forced them to respond or be overrun. Gould's lightning moves changed the competitive map so rapidly that other managers had no choice but to follow suit. Such was the impact of the explosion that no one had time to digest the implications of what was taking place. Only later would they discover what devastation had been wrought and learn the true price of progress.

On this surging wave of change the Union Pacific pitched and bobbed as helplessly as other roads. Gould did what he could to give it a secure destiny. The combined weight of his threats enabled him to strike a peace treaty with Huntington in November 1881 that proved remarkably enduring. The Gould-Huntington agreement resolved their differences in the Southwest, but the negotiations soared beyond that region to a package solution of all outstanding problems. Both sides agreed it was more profitable to join forces than to fight everywhere at once. For that reason the heart of their scheme was the long-awaited consolidation of the two original Pacific roads, a notion so inherently logical and natural that only human ingenuity had thwarted it over the years. Gould and Dillon favored it; so did Huntington and Crocker, who thought there was "but one way out of these difficulties, and that is by consolidating the two roads."

But that was only the beginning. Gould and his Union Pacific associates would also take a half interest in Southern Pacific, the Californians a like interest in Utah Central and (if Huntington got his way) the Utah Northern as well. The Utah Western would be extended to California under joint ownership. Huntington also wanted the Union Pacific to stop work on the Short Line but Dillon rejected that demand as "out of the question." Here truly was a plan of breathtaking scope and vision, one that would have created the Harriman system a generation before Harriman. It is fascinating to speculate on how western rail systems might have evolved had the plan been carried out, but too many obstacles stood in the way. The biggest stumbling block remained the opposition of the Ames family. Crocker recognized glumly that the scheme "cannot be brought about as long as the Ames' have such a large block of the stock." He was prepared to organize a syndicate to buy out the Ameses, but Gould could not induce Fred either to sell or support the plan and so it died aborning.

As a consolation prize Gould and Huntington joined forces in January 1882 to buy a half interest in the Frisco, which itself owned a half interest in the Atlantic & Pacific Railroad. This stalled the Atchison's drive to reach California but left the Union Pacific out of whatever larger plans they had in mind. That spring Huntington demanded a share of the Utah Northern's

Montana business for the Central Pacific. With all the roads nervously eyeing one another's moves and Gould busily piecing together his new system, relations in the West seemed certain to explode again. The only question was where and when.

22

THE CRISIS

Everyone knew that expansion costs money and could be paid for only by a significant increase in business which, it was assumed, would come from the opening of new territory to settlers, industrialists, and merchants. More important, each road realized that if it did not seize untapped regions, someone else would. This reasoning doomed the territorial doctrine to extinction even though railroad men still paid lip service to it. Bitter experience had taught them that the surest connections were roads owned by themselves. Having lost faith in cooperation as a means of resolving disputes, they turned increasingly to construction and consolidation. This shift triggered the greatest explosion of railroad building in the nation's history. In the dozen years after 1878 railroad mileage leaped from 80,832 to 163,359. The country marveled at the fact that 40,692 miles of rail had been laid during the 1870s, but that achievement paled before the 71,212 miles put down during the next decade. Much of this was branch line into new territory, but a surprising amount consisted of extensions that opened new through lines to areas already served by one or more roads.

Creating a system meant possessing a line to every point a company wished to serve. The object of a self-contained system was to eliminate uncertainty by assuring connections, expediting the flow of traffic, maintaining rates, garnering a larger share of through rates, and penetrating new local territory. But this rationale did not reckon with two vital forces on which it was dependent. To sustain their heavy investment in new track, companies needed a bullish economy that kept traffic flowing over their lines, and they needed to carry this traffic at rates high enough to pay for their expansion programs. Unfortunately, events of the 1880s reduced both of these underlying assumptions to shambles.

The first omen of disaster came on a pleasant July day in 1881, when a demented office seeker gunned down President James A. Garfield. Although the assassination in no way caused the rush of events that followed, it unleashed forces long welling up behind the façade of prosperity. The bull market of 1879–81 staggered and fell, never to regain its former momentum. The economy continued to expand in fits and starts, but its very growth put insatiable demands on the money market. The more mileage railroads built or bought, the more borrowing they had to do. To finance their expansion, companies flooded the market with new issues of securities until it was saturated by the decade's end. As their bonds grew harder to sell, one road after another accumulated large floating debts that threatened them with bankruptcy if a sharp downturn occurred.

Competition among systems provided a rude shock to those who thought it would stabilize rates. The effect of more roads vying for business at the same points was to intensify the struggle for business and ignite a series of wars that drove rates inexorably downward. Too late railroad managers discovered that hauling more traffic at lower rates increased maintenance and equipment costs without producing more income, let alone paying for new mileage. This was perhaps the bitterest irony of all. The business was there and growing fast, but they could not stop fighting each other long enough to carry it at remunerative rates. The savage rate wars of the 1880s undid their best intentions and, ironically, drove them in desperation to explore new avenues of cooperation. As the toll of battle mounted and cost of expansion strained their resources, the strong cut or eliminated dividends while the weak flirted with bankruptcy. By 1890 not only individual railroads but the industry itself was in deep trouble.

*   *   *

"It is simply *damnable* the way the Railroads in the west are handling their passenger business," grumbled T. J. Potter of the Burlington. "We ought to get the rates up before the spring travel, and not flitter away another years business." But that was easier said than done. By 1882 rate structures everywhere were falling to pieces as newly opened lines upset old agreements. The Southwestern Pool broke apart in June 1881 and, though patched up, wobbled uncertainly from one crisis to the next. From the Missouri River to the Rockies an uneasy truce kept war barely at arm's length. The Missouri Pacific completed its Omaha connection in May 1882, the same month that the Burlington reached Denver. Although Forbes talked of using money for "making peace rather than in building new Roads this year," the Burlington did not slow its plans for expansion.

In Colorado the presence of the Burlington forced all roads to negotiate a new pool. The Burlington accepted terms before entering Denver, then changed its mind when it found more business than expected. "I would rather see all the pools go to pieces," snorted Potter, "rather than stay in the Colorado Pool with our present percentage." A new division was reached in July but foundered when the Union Pacific insisted abruptly that any pool must be preceded by a pledge that the B & M would not invade northern Colorado. Perkins laughed at this demand as "about the most absurd proposition that could be made." The Burlington held fast to a policy that "We will not mix up our traffic agreements with the territorial question." There followed three months of posturing spiced with threats and diversions of traffic to other lines. "We want nothing but what is justice in that country," Dillon proclaimed, but one man's justice was another's outrage. One analyst predicted that war in Colorado would ruin the Union Pacific. "The striking weakness of the Union Pacific system," he noted, "is its high-rate policy."

That weakness was greater than anyone yet realized. Unable to budge Perkins, Dillon withdrew his demand and agreed to a pool in October. The relief proved temporary because the forces of expansion had also battered the Iowa Pool itself. As new lines reached Council Bluffs, they demanded a share of the business. The Pool admitted the Wabash in December 1881 only to find two new applicants, the Missouri Pacific and the St. Paul, at its door a few months later. The Iowa Pool was reorganized with six members and an elaborate administrative structure that could not conceal or defuse its inner tensions. Gould had long since set the tone for expansion with the roads under his control, and once the Burlington launched its expansion drive the other roads could hardly sit idle. The Rock Island had a bellicose new president in Ransom R. Cable, who was already pushing a vigorous building program. The Northwestern was staking out the territory north of Nebraska, and the St. Paul would triple its mileage within five years.

Although these changes reduced the Iowa Pool to a shadow of its former self, no one was prepared for the brutal swiftness with which the old order crumbled on both fronts. Yet another new line between Chicago and Omaha, formed by the Illinois Central and Chicago, St. Paul, Minneapolis & Omaha (known popularly as the Omaha road), emerged late in 1882 and deranged rates until it too was accepted into the Pool. The other members could not resist cutting rates or seeking advantages through secret ties with connecting lines such as the Union Pacific, which itself tried to break the Pool's stranglehold through an alliance with Gould's roads.

The sheer number of lines involved transformed negotiations into tangled intrigues. Bitter accusations, aggravated by personality conflicts among some of the leaders, flew back and forth. During the spring of 1883 Gould unexpectedly grabbed the Hannibal and, in a complicated transaction, sold it to the Burlington. This maneuver did little to ease tensions on the larger battlefield, where the animosity between the Union Pacific and the Burlington, as the only Iowa Pool road with a line to the Rockies, poisoned efforts to reach a settlement. Perkins resisted every plea to throw his Nebraska traffic into the general pool or give the Union Pacific a larger share of Colorado business. Dillon retaliated by diverting traffic at Omaha to other lines. While this battle raged, the St. Paul infuriated all the other Iowa Pool roads by slashing rates.

In April 1883 Palmer's Rio Grande Western commenced running trains to Salt Lake City. Five months later the Northern Pacific drove its golden spike in Montana, opening yet another route to the seaboard. Both roads ran into problems at once. Palmer leased the Rio Grande Western to the Rio Grande, then fell into a violent dispute with the board over his expansion policy. In August he surrendered the presidency to Frederick Lovejoy, leaving the Rio Grande paralyzed with internal strife. Villard too was in trouble, as his incomparable gift for raising funds was diminished by a tendency to buy properties indiscriminately at inflated prices. The perceptive Forbes described him as "an *honest* 'wild man' " with a habit of acquiring "extravagant & lengthy tails *to feed a short system."* So disarrayed were the Northern Pacific's finances that some thought Villard would not last out the year.

The Union Pacific found little solace in the distractions of its rivals because it too was under fire. Since 1880 the floating debt had been on the rise, fed by the insatiable demands of the Short Line and other expansion projects. Gould and Dillon tried to get out of debt by selling off bonds in branch lines and issuing collateral trust bonds, but a lawsuit blocked the new issue and the debt mounted faster than funds could be raised to shrink it. During 1882 rumors circulated that "the corporation was rotten," that bankruptcy loomed despite large loans from Gould, and that Vanderbilt was about to gain control. Friction was reported between Gould and Dillon, between Dillon and Fred Ames.

Dillon dismissed such tales as rubbish, but controversy raged over the size of the floating debt and the bears pressed their attacks relentlessly. Anxious stockholders besieged Dillon with inquiries and were assured the company's affairs were sound. Personally Dillon was demoralized by losses in the market and distracted by the prolonged illness of his wife which, he admitted to Clark, "has a very depressing effect upon me." While he drifted, an improbable figure did what he could to allay public fears about the Union Pacific. Charles Francis Adams, Jr., the heir of presidents and a national authority on railroads in his own right, had in recent years caught a fever for business and enhanced his fortune through a series of investments. During 1878 he served a year as government director for the Union Pacific and afterward bought some stock in the road. On his advice other friends also made purchases and now beseeched him for an explanation of the rumors chasing the company.

A concerned Adams applied at once to his old friend Fred Ames for the inside story and was promptly shown the company's private papers and books. Satisfied by what he saw, Adams published a letter in the newspaper assuring investors of his confidence in the road's financial condition. "The results of my all inquiries," he concluded, "have been a curious insight not into the weak spots of the Union Pacific" but rather "into the ways and operations of Wall-street" which had produced "one grand organized raid of a successful bear campaign." Adams praised the company's policies as sound and its value as an investment high. He urged that control of the company be planted firmly in New England hands.

Although this letter would come back to haunt Adams, it made a favorable impression in December 1882. Some considered him the rising star in the company; certainly his ascendance came at a time when its management was crippled by age and infirmity. Gould was preoccupied with his other affairs, Dillon with his wife's deteriorating condition. Her death late in 1883 left the old lion, now seventy-one, crushed with grief. Clark suffered another relapse and was forced to convalesce for several months in California, leaving his duties in the hands of Kimball. For a time Dillon doubted Clark would ever be able to resume his position. In May 1883 Gannett's ill health finally obliged him to resign the post he had held for fourteen years. "We have looked upon you, in all times, as being our sheet anchor," wrote a sorrowful Fred Ames. Although his successor, Erastus Young, proved able and even more cantankerous, he could not match the experience and authority of one who had served loyally since the year of the Golden Spike.

Adams looked to be just the tonic for a management in disarray or transition at every level. His expertise and reputation for integrity commanded a large following among New England investors, whose influence helped put him on the Union Pacific board in March 1883. The election confirmed a shift toward control by New England investors, who by then owned about a third of the company's stock. Since Gould had reduced his holdings to only twenty-five hundred shares, Fred Ames suggested dropping his ally, Russell Sage, from the board. Dillon balked at once, pointing out that he served on a dozen boards with Gould and Sage and wished to avoid any "rupture of our relations with Mr. Gould. As you are aware Gould and Sage are bosom friends (although some times they talk about each other) and I am satisfied that if we should turn out Mr. Sage, it would be in effect the turning out of Mr. Gould also."

No one cared to antagonize Gould, and Sage kept his seat, but Gould's withdrawal from an active role had created a vacuum in leadership that the Boston interests had not yet filled. With the board divided and Dillon in no condition to exert a guiding influence, a sense of drift permeated the management at this critical time in the company's affairs. During 1883 the rate wars and appearance of rival lines took their toll on earnings. The Union Pacific actually carried half a million tons *more* freight than in 1882 but received $1.1 million less in earnings. Passenger earnings also fell sharply, and the business depression in the mining states showed no signs of easing. The price of steel rails dropped so rapidly that in June 1883 the company stopped rerolling iron rails at the Laramie mill because it no longer paid.

All year long Dillon prodded Clark and Kimball to hold down expenses "so that we may be in position to hedge off the various roads that are threat-

ening to invade our territory, and to pay off . . . our floating indebtedness."
By autumn his voice had grown shrill. Earnings continued to decline and
expenses to rise, partly because the company had to put on more trains to
meet competitors. The Colorado pool fell apart before the negotiators reached
home, while in Kansas rates were slashed 25 percent for most of the year. In
Utah a four-dollar rate was knocked down to fifty cents and then to twenty-
five cents a month later. Completion of the Northern Pacific cut the Union
Pacific's business in Montana "right in two." A cataclysmic war threatened
to engulf the entire region west of the Missouri.

"We want peace," Dillon pleaded, "and . . . by peace we will all make
money." But how to get it? As the fight in Utah worsened, Lovejoy of the Rio
Grande appealed to Adams to intervene. The renowned theorist jolted
Lovejoy with the truculent view that, while war was distasteful, the greatest
waste was an inconclusive war in which "at the end of six months we should
have this thing over again." Accordingly, Adams thought the best policy was
to "force the fighting until some results of a permanent nature were reached"
and "one party or the other was thoroughly worsted." Eventually one side
would crush the other and dictate terms, which would be "much better than
the indecisive closing of the present difficulty at this time, which would only
lead to its renewal hereafter."

While Lovejoy retreated in confusion, Adams offered Perkins the same
cold comfort. The Burlington, he declared, had forced the Union Pacific to
seek new allies by joining forces with the Rio Grande in a "thoroughly aggressive way." Perkins denied this charge and blamed the trouble in Utah on
Union Pacific belligerence. "Clark has always seemed to regard the building
of a Railroad anywhere near the Union Pacific as a high crime for which
somebody ought to be punished," he snapped, "and as a personal grievance of
which he had a just right to complain." Yet this was precisely the attitude
Perkins took in retaliating against Gould by building the Denver extension. It
was an attitude endemic among railroad leaders, who rivaled politicians in
their ability to justify for themselves the same behavior they condemned in
others.

Perkins might dismiss "this absurd theory of Adams'," but he could find
no way to stave off war. By November not only the Colorado pool but the
Iowa Pool itself was on the brink of collapse. For a time it appeared that the
Union Pacific, Burlington, and Rio Grande might come to terms on traffic
west of the Missouri over a proposal offered by the Burlington. Before it was
finalized, however, a series of startling developments threw relations among
the roads into pandemonium. The Rock Island and St. Paul, which had been
locked in a fierce dispute, abruptly made peace, whereupon the St. Paul announced it would leave the Iowa Pool at the year's end. In a stunning reversal
the Union Pacific dropped its negotiations with the Burlington and opened
talks for a separate treaty with the Rock Island and St. Paul.

A bewildered Perkins could not conceive why the Union Pacific should sacrifice a chance for peace west of the river to ally itself "with our enemies east of the Missouri." The result could only be a demoralization of rates and the building of lines by the Burlington and Northwestern in the region "now controlled wholly by the Union Pacific." Surely, he thought, Ames and Adams realized that "The stronghold of the Union Pacific is to make peace with us; because we can do them more good and more harm than anybody else can." In typical fashion Perkins dismissed the explanation advanced by Clark because it did not square with his own reasoning. "The record is clear enough to put the responsibility of war, if it occurs, where it belongs," he declared righteously, "and that is not upon our shoulders."

Events did much to shock Perkins but little to enlighten him. On December 5 the Union Pacific, Rock Island, and St. Paul signed the Tripartite Agreement, described as "an offensive and defensive agreement for 25 years." The Iowa Pool was dead along with the principle that had always governed railroad relations. "The question of territorial rights no longer exists," proclaimed Cable of the Rock Island. "Each road will build when and where it pleases." Clark defined the pact as "the outgrowth of the Burlington extension to Denver" and "the necessary outcome of the roads building into the territory of the Union Pacific." Confusion reigned no less among observers than participants. One analyst called it an alliance "thought before to be incredible." Another sneered that the Union Pacific "shrinks into the position of a local road."

Because no one could imagine what the new order of things would be, the mood everywhere was ominous, apprehensive. Perkins simply could not bring himself to believe it. "I am often struck with the truth of the remark," he muttered to Adams, "that men are but children of a larger growth." Like some newspaper editors, he thought the Union Pacific board would not ratify the agreement and was wrong again; on December 20 nineteen of the twenty directors voted unanimous approval. Gould had his doubts about the pact but saw Dillon meant to have it and fell in line, saying with a laugh that it would "be a good thing for the Union Pacific." Always quick to accept changed realities, he had the Missouri Pacific and Wabash apply for admission to the new pool. *"The advantages of the contract are all on the side of the UP,"* he told Clark privately. "No one knows that better than you & me." Only Gould could appreciate the irony of the Iowa Pool's demise without any effort by the man who had worked longest and hardest to destroy it.

The Union Pacific took care to invite the other roads to join the new Western Trunk Line Association, thereby reorganizing the Iowa Pool on new terms. After some hesitation the Northwestern agreed to come in, leaving only the Burlington outside. "This whole thing is a ridiculous farce," stormed Perkins, "and the action of the Union Pacific and the other roads is simply an outrage upon the owners of the properties." It was in his view the revival of an old argument by E. P. Vining "which nobody has, heretofore, paid any attention to," a suspicion reinforced when the new pool made Vining its

commissioner. Righteousness and obstinacy blinded him to the grievances
that had driven the other pool roads into the new alliance. On one point he
was adamant: the Burlington had more to lose than to gain by joining the
pool. For that reason Perkins was prepared to go it alone.

Gould hoped fervently the new association would "result in a long and
permanent peace and . . . help all our stocks," but peace was not to be
found that season. Through the dark months of a bleak winter, the bickering
raged on without letup. The expected collapse in the Northwest climaxed in
January when Villard resigned the last of his presidencies, assigned his
properties, and fled to Europe a sick and broken man. The Oregon Short Line
was by then only about forty miles from Huntington, where it would find
only the debris of Villard's shattered empire. The blow of Villard's downfall
sent the market reeling. Already the securities, grain, cotton, and provisions
markets were in turmoil, with shrinkages in stock and bond values exceeding
anything witnessed since 1873. Rumors persisted that the Union Pacific
"would not see the end of its trouble until President Dillon went out." A
distressed Clark suggested to Gould that he buy into the company again. "I
dont think it practicable to take the controll [sic] of the road away from New
England," Gould demurred, "and you know how jealously they have always
held onto it. Besides just now I have my hands full & in these uncertain times
it is always best to go slow and shure [sic]."

The best tonic for both the railroads and the markets would be an end to
the rate wars, but the squabbling only grew worse. The Transcontinental
Association, created a few months earlier to pool California business, tried
desperately to square its agreements with those embodied in the Tripartite
pact. Suddenly, painfully, all sides realized that rate agreements could no
longer be segregated by territory. The growth of systems had so intertwined
them that one could not be settled without affecting others. Clark rammed
the message home by refusing to consider differences on transcontinental
matters unless the association first admitted the Union Pacific's new allies
east of the Missouri into the pool. When the vote split evenly on the question,
the Union Pacific served notice that it would withdraw from the association.

All sides agreed the present fight was suicidal but no one could find a way
to escape it. Clark hastily patched up agreements on Utah rates and his
differences with the Rio Grande only to have the other Tripartite roads balk
at the terms. Trouble then arose on the Colorado pool and in Nebraska,
where a war of expansion loomed unless the Tripartite roads could resolve
their differences with the Burlington. Late in January Clark fell ill and went
to California, leaving Kimball to negotiate. "Kimball is an abler man than
Clark," noted Perkins hopefully, "and the Tripartite calf is not of his getting,
so I should expect his advice to his Directors would be better than that of
Clark, who is the father, or mother, of the deformed creature."

A conference between the Union Pacific and Burlington was arranged but
scuttled by a fresh crisis before it even met. On his own initiative Commis-

sioner Vining ordered rate cuts on Colorado business and hired an agent empowered to make special rates in Nebraska, where the Burlington had been slashing tariffs at points reached by Union Pacific. "We want to annoy and demoralize the B. & M. and their business as much as possible," Vining told the agent, who was also instructed to "stir things up" and "do all that you can to increase the ill-will." Somehow Perkins got hold of these orders; later he was informed that Vining had "a letter or contract from Clark authorizing his recent assumption of power properly belonging to UPR." Reacting in cold fury, Perkins denounced Vining as "about the worst man that could have been selected for the position he occupies" and threatened in retaliation to "knock the bottom out of Colorado rates" and "terminate existing pools east of the Missouri River" with the Tripartite roads.

This belligerence surprised even the hapless Dillon, who agreed that Vining's rate cuts were both rash and unwise. "He should not have the power to do anything he pleases," Dillon objected, "but should act under proper authority from the . . . association." When Perkins talked angrily of building more branches in Nebraska, however, Dillon bristled. "We can not afford to have the C. B. & Q. trample us in the dust," he growled. "I for one am willing to put in my individual funds to meet them in any fight." Fred Ames tried to appease Perkins with the suggestion of selling the St. Joseph & Western road and bridge, and perhaps the Central Branch as well, to the Burlington. Both sides agreed to halt all cuts in Nebraska pending a conference, but Dillon continued to prepare for war. "We can open their veins wider than they can ours," he insisted, "and take more business from them than they can from us."

Neither side was anxious to bleed without another effort to settle their differences. A series of meetings in April produced a basis for agreement that ran afoul of a familiar obstacle. Clark found he could not sell the terms to his Tripartite partners and tried to back-pedal with the Burlington's Potter, who would have none of it. When Clark offered to arrange Colorado rates instead, Potter replied curtly that he "would not have anything to do with Colorado until Nebraska was out of the way." The Burlington adamantly refused to deal with the Tripartite pool or even acknowledge its existence. Perkins was intent on holding Clark to the original terms as the only basis for peace. "Where we can hurt them most in a fight is in Colorado," Potter advised, "and that is where I propose to let them have it."

Already it was clear that Tripartite had not solved the Union Pacific's problems with neighboring roads. Relations with the Burlington had never been worse and seemed ready to explode into an unrestricted war from the Missouri to the Rockies. For all of Dillon's bluster, the company was in no position to fight. Even Perkins was slow to grasp just how weak his adversary was until events during the spring of 1884 disclosed that fact with shocking clarity.

* * *

Since March 1883 the company had been short of money and scrounging to meet its payments. As the floating debt rose and the stock fell, shrinking its value as collateral, Dillon vowed with Fred Ames to reduce the debt as rapidly as possible. But business remained depressed, and a declining market was no place to sell bonds. For three years after the consolidation Union Pacific stood well above par, and it remained in the 90s during most of 1883. When the bears hit Union Pacific hard in December, knocking the price into the 70s, Gould helped organize a pool to lift the stock. The price steadied and even climbed back into the 80s during February, but by then a far more serious problem had emerged.

Contrary to Dillon's hopes, the slide in earnings during the fall of 1883 did not slow but accelerated during the winter at an alarming rate. Apart from causing severe cash-flow problems, the decline exposed a basic flaw in the Thurman Act. As earnings fell, so did the amount on which payments to the government were based. Long before 1884 it was apparent that the Thurman Act had failed to meet expectations. The government worsened matters by leaving large portions of the sum collected uninvested for long periods and by investing the remainder in its own bonds at absurdly high premiums averaging 20 percent. By 1883 more than $850,000 of Union Pacific payments were still uninvested, while another $650,100 had been invested at premiums totaling $124,065. This gave the sinking fund an annual yield of only about 2 percent. As early as August 1880 Dillon strenuously protested this policy without avail.

Nor had the act done anything to stop the bitter wrangling between the government and the Pacific roads. The Attorney General continued to insist that *all* earnings on government transportation should be withheld, and that the provision applied to all leased or branch lines of the consolidated Union Pacific, including those that received no government aid. The company rejected this notion and applied to the courts for relief. Despite the Supreme Court ruling on net earnings, a new dispute erupted over the issue when the Union Pacific claimed the right to deduct amounts expended for some construction and new equipment. The long controversy over pay for mail service dragged on with no sign of resolution, even though the Supreme Court had ruled in the company's favor. In short, time had not healed old wounds but merely deepened them.

After 1881 the Union Pacific refused to make payments into the sinking fund until the court settled these disputes. As Dillon put it tersely, "They owe us several hundred thousand dollars more than we owe them." However, critics like the New York *Sun* still clung to the belief that "the capital for the Pacific roads came out of the public treasury," and insisted that "No such liberality was ever before exhibited by any Government." The Pacific roads were portrayed as greedy ingrates who had "enlisted for another long war against the Government" and were spoiling to overturn the Thurman Act. During 1883 the administration prepared a new suit to collect the overdue sums while Congress waded through a raft of bills to toughen the Thurman Act. Dillon pleaded his case to the Secretary of the Interior with no effect. His cause was not helped by the Massachusetts legislature, which chose this inopportune moment to ask Congress to restore the good name of Oakes Ames, or by a lawsuit that provided newspapers with some ripe samples of Huntington's correspondence during his imbroglios with Scott in the 1870s.

The Huntington sensation broke late in December 1883, just as the slide in Union Pacific earnings gathered momentum, the Tripartite fight was heating up, and the situation in Washington was deteriorating. "In Congress efforts are not wanting to depress Union Pacific," observed one analyst, "and whether the bills are being offered with that purpose in view or not they give evidence of the fact that a pretty hot fight is coming on the question of the rights and duties of Pacific railroads." Some thought the company had erred badly in refusing payments and awaiting a court decision. Too late Judge Dillon discovered that "the impression is current that we are not acting in good faith with the Government . . . that the excuse that the Govt owes us for transportation is not valid in law or in fact."

As the annual meeting approached, Dillon was at his wit's end. He and Fred Ames had for months nagged Kimball to "stick the knife in everywhere there is a chance and cut down expenses." So dreadful were the earnings figures that he balked even at giving them privately to Dodge, but he could not ignore the shrill rumors sweeping Wall Street. "If the same state of affairs continue," he fretted, "I fear there will be danger of our having to suspend the payment of the dividend, which would be a sad calamity to the Union Pacific." A record crowd of anxious stockholders flooded the annual meeting and forced its removal to a larger hall. The old board was reelected and a dividend declared even though it had not been earned. Dillon tried to conceal the true state of things by issuing as uninformative data as he dared, but no one was fooled. Analysts heaped withering criticism on his report and his staunch refusal to give out monthly earnings. When the January figures leaked out late in March, they showed a shocking decrease in net earnings of over $664,000 from the previous year. "The statement is considered all the worse at this time," noted one analyst, "because the road is known to have had a poor business since January."

Into this valley of despair rushed the quixotic Adams. No one was more anxious to revive the company's standing than the man who had assured New Englanders that it was a sound investment. To his mind more than its finances were in disarray; at the organizational meeting of the board he moved to create a special committee to examine the entire management. Adams wanted not only to revamp the organizational structure, which had not changed significantly since the golden spike, but also to pump fresh blood into the officers' corps. He already found Clark inadequate and would soon consign him to that peculiar blend of contempt and ridicule in which the Adams family so excelled. Even Dillon conceded that "something should be done, and in a very short time to strengthen our organization." The executive committee complied by appointing Adams, Hugh Riddle, and government director Isaac Bromley to the special committee.

Although the road had grown tremendously in recent years, Boston had done little more than enlarge the duties of officers and centralize the general manager's authority. This approach suited Clark, who liked power concentrated in his hands and was possessed of what Dillon delicately called "a jealous mind." However, his recurring bouts of ill health thrust his duties on Kimball. Predictably, the result was friction between the two men on whom rested the entire responsibility of operating the road. Dillon recognized that Clark's weakness was "wanting to do things too much his own way" without consulting anyone, but like most railroad men he hesitated to look beyond those he knew and trusted. When the general superintendent resigned in May 1882, Dillon's first thought was to bring back Webster Snyder. He backed off when Fred Ames objected, but no amount of difficulty or dissension could shake his loyalty to Clark.

As a newcomer unfettered by any such loyalties, Adams's critical eye scanned the organization and saw only horrors of inefficiency. The Union Pacific system had grown much larger, but the organization had done nothing to meet its new demands. In fact it had grown smaller through attrition. The general superintendent had not been replaced, and neither had freight agent Vining when he left to become commissioner of the new pool; instead their duties had merely devolved on subordinate officers. Kimball was still nominally in charge of the passenger department even though he had his hands full as assistant general manager and, during Clark's absences, as acting general manager. The construction department, busy with all the extension work, was in the charge of Blickensderfer, "whose advancing years," in Adams's opinion, "disqualify him in a greater or less degree from the severe work which the head of that department has necessarily to perform."

The Adams committee recognized that a modern rail system should have five distinct departments: finance, operating, commercial (traffic), construction, and law. On April 29 it presented a report recommending changes in three of them. Operations should be placed in charge of a new general superintendent and the whole commercial department, including the coal business, entrusted to Kimball, who would be promoted to general traffic manager. Clark would be elevated to the new office of second vice president with authority over all the departments. The committee stopped short of proposing a specific revamping of construction but suggested that Clark, once relieved of some current duties, might take it under his wing temporarily. It also recommended creation of a new office, "assistant and confidential advisor of the President and Board of Directors at the East . . . the duties of which it is not necessary to at present define." This was an obvious attempt by Adams to strip Clark of his absolute authority over the system. Indeed, three weeks before the report appeared, the company hired S. R. Callaway of the Chicago & Grand Trunk at a salary higher than Dillon's to fill a post yet to be defined. Although Clark was duly promoted to second vice president, rumors swirled that he would soon be replaced by Callaway.

In its report the Adams committee seized on glaring weaknesses in the company's organization. To some extent these were the natural product of sudden growth wrought by expansion and the consolidation. There was, however, another cause that Adams was in no position to grasp. A vacuum of leadership had plagued the road since Gould's withdrawal from an active role in its management. No one had assumed his role in guiding its affairs or providing direction. In effect Dillon and Fred Ames divided responsibility, but they did not possess Gould's ability and vision together or separately. Both were men who tended to react to situations rather than shape them. They were more earnest than energetic and more inclined to deal with issues piecemeal than as part of some larger design. Never was this weakness more glaring than in their handling of a crisis that erupted only a few days after the committee offered its report.

As part of its effort to reduce expenses the company resorted to that old standby, a wage cut, to take effect May 1. A similar effort in 1877 had been met by a threatened strike that forced Clark to back down; seven years later the workers reacted to the news with the same vehemence. Afterward Kimball declared that Clark had bungled his opportunity. Comparisons satisfied him that Union Pacific workers got better pay than those on other western roads. Well before the strike, one superintendent told Kimball he could scale his payroll down about 10 percent at once without opposition, but Clark showed no interest. Instead he announced the reductions without warning and found himself embroiled in another angry confrontation.

"If we had taken the men into our confidence," Kimball argued, "by explaining to their leaders . . . the pressing necessity for them to share for the time being the company's misfortunes," then the cuts could have been imposed without trouble. But that was not Clark's way. "To flash a telegraphic order in the faces of sixteen thousand men—cutting their wages from ten to fifteen per cent—without previous explanation or warning," Kimball sighed, "was to invite just what happened. It was a grave blunder on Mr. Clark's part, not the thing itself, but the manner of doing it."

Kimball was right, but he did not have the whole story. In urging the cut Clark had been prodded by Fred Ames. "Employees are considerably dissatisfied and possibly may object seriously," Clark reported after issuing the order. He told the men the reduction was not his idea, and that he opposed it. When nearly all of them turned out to protest the cut, Clark appealed to New York and Boston for instructions. That *was* Clark's way. Both Dillon and Fred Ames well knew that he always hesitated to act without authority from above, yet neither lifted a finger. Dillon replied, "Have no suggestions to offer. Use your own judgment." Fred Ames too said, "I can't give you any advice," but added, "Should hate very much to yield to the strike if it can be avoided. You on the spot should be able to form better idea of what could be done." He urged Clark to negotiate a compromise, perhaps in the form of arbitration.

The situation was critical. On May 1 one group of employees after another in Omaha voted to strike until wages were restored. At a mass meeting held that evening telegrams arrived with news that the strike was spreading rapidly along the entire system. Clark pleaded frantically with his superiors for instructions on how far he should go. "I cannot assume responsibility of deciding whether to rescind the order or fight to the end," he asserted with considerable justice. Three times on May 2 he wired urgent appeals to Dillon and Fred Ames, stressing that "delay only makes matters worse." No response was forthcoming. Disheartened by the silence, Clark summoned his courage and revoked the cuts on his own. To Dillon he explained that "unless the order was rescinded, a strike would have occurred which in its results would have been most disastrous to our company." The evidence confirms his gloomy view of the situation.

Dillon gave his approval freely, Fred Ames with reluctance. Both were distracted by a crisis brewing in the East, where the financial situation was deteriorating rapidly. The continued fall in earnings and fight with the Burlington kept the stock weak, as did the discovery in April that the road had run a deficit of nearly $450,000 during the first quarter. This figure did not include the dividend paid, which swelled the deficit to $1.5 million. A discouraged Dillon talked bravely of earning a dividend in 1884 but could not keep the stock from sliding downward in heavy trading. Neither could he find buyers for the bonds he needed desperately to peddle to reduce the floating debt. The strike encouraged the bears to batter Union Pacific so badly that Dillon stayed afloat only by raising funds on his own securities, but their value as collateral was shrinking fast. After advancing $700,000 to the company, he appealed to Boston for help. "I must be kept strong," he warned Fred Ames, "or else there will be trouble."

At this critical moment the storm that had been hovering over Wall Street for months suddenly unleashed its full fury. On the morning of May 6 the firm of Grant & Ward suspended and the Marine National Bank soon followed. Before Wall Street could recover from these shocks, it learned that the president of the Second National Bank had squandered $4 million of the bank's funds in speculations and fled to Canada. That same day, May 14, the Metropolitan National Bank closed its doors after the brokerage headed by · its president announced bankruptcy. Panic engulfed the financial district and brought down more firms, including the prominent house of Fisk & Hatch. Those with long memories recalled the horrors of 1873 as prices crumbled, the money market tightened, and margin calls pelted borrowers like hail.

Early in May Union Pacific still hovered around 60; the convulsion started it on a downward slide to a low of 35¼ by the month's end.

Only days before the panic broke, Dillon admitted to feeling "very much depressed . . . with all my troubles." The storm crashing over his head left him no time to gather his wits. In his anxiety he hedged even at revealing to Gould the size of the company's floating debt, fearing that in the hands of "outsiders" it might be "used to our disadvantage." While Dillon scrambled frantically for funds, Fred Ames and Adams were traveling west on an inspection trip. In Chicago Adams gave out an interview in which he was quoted as admitting that earnings had shown no improvement in March or April, and the next dividend might well be passed. Papers across the country picked up the dispatch. Dillon read it and was appalled at what he deemed "serious admissions regarding the poor condition of the property." He wired Fred Ames, urging him to "have it contradicted at once." Already Wall Street boiled with rumors that large stockholders were dumping their shares on the market and that a change in management was imminent.

The financial crisis erupted just as affairs in Washington came to a head. While the House bill to stiffen the Thurman Act progressed, the Senate Judiciary Committee, chaired by George F. Edmunds of Vermont, offered its own bill. Considered the ablest constitutional lawyer in Congress, Edmunds had long served as watchdog over the Pacific roads and was considered the true author of the Thurman Act. In an age stained with scandal he enjoyed a reputation for unblemished integrity, but Adams soon came to think otherwise. A few years later he reviled the "sea-green immaculate from Vermont" as the "most thoroughly corrupt and dishonest, and the most insidiously dangerous man, when balked of his bribe, that there is to-day in Washington."

The company's lobbyists tried first to derail the Edmunds bill with a similar but more favorable version. When that effort failed, Dillon and Fred Ames huddled with Edmunds to thrash out a compromise. To their dismay Edmunds would not budge from the position that the company should "pay up, and then, if it is not all due, get it back by suit." Instead he prepared a report asking the Attorney General to enforce the penalties against Union Pacific for evading payments to the sinking fund and paying unauthorized dividends. Directors who had voted for the dividends would also be charged with a misdemeanor. If this report was released, it would devastate the company and its stock at the worst possible time.

For months fierce clashes on three fronts—the competitive, financial, and political—had kept the Union Pacific in turmoil. A major defeat on any one of these fronts was enough to put the company in grave danger, but late in May the full weight of all three crashed down with devastating force. The rate wars had knocked the bottom out of earnings, the panic made borrowing impossible at a time when money was urgently needed, and Congress seemed intent on passing punitive legislation and issuing a report that would destroy what little remained of the company's credit. Like streams converging into a mighty river, once separate difficulties combined into a major crisis that threatened to overwhelm the Union Pacific.

The hapless Dillon had long dreaded this moment and was wholly unequal to its demands. The strain had worn down his nerves, left him overwrought at "the serious depreciation of securities, and especially of the stock of our company, which I hold very heavily." On top of these woes his wife's mother suffered a paralytic stroke and died a few days later. Borne down by his afflictions, Dillon longed for release from the presidency if some way out of the crisis could be found. The most pressing task was to stave off the Edmunds report and placate Congress with enough concessions to give the company some breathing room. When Dillon and Fred Ames failed to move Edmunds, Adams was chosen to try his luck in Washington.

He was the logical man for the job. Apart from his reputation for integrity and expertise in railroad affairs, Adams was relatively new to the board and therefore untainted by past policies. No one else could muster the authority his argument would carry with Congress. Moreover, Adams had compelling reasons of his own for resolving the crisis. As Perkins noted wryly, he had "induced a lot of people to buy Union Pacific, and does not know how to get himself out of the scrape." To redeem himself along with the company, Adams hurried to Washington to persuade Edmunds and the Judiciary Committee that any measure against the Union Pacific would prove disastrous to the public interest. A reporter following his movements considered it "the hardest day's work that he ever did for the road."

To Edmunds and his colleagues, Adams protested his own innocence of any wrongdoing; everything he had heard or seen convinced him that the property was sound. He had voted for dividends the past year unaware that his action violated the law. Deftly sidestepping the question of how he could have urged the stock on investors for two years without knowing any details of the controversy over the Thurman Act, he emphasized the drastic consequences that would flow from adverse legislation. The tumbling stock would destroy an army of small investors who had bought it in good faith, perhaps even trigger a new panic that would devastate not only Wall Street but the national economy. This argument deeply impressed senators in an election year. Adams pleaded for enough time to negotiate terms satisfactory to both sides. To men still uneasy over the recent panic, this seemed a reasonable request. The committee agreed to defer action until Congress reconvened if the company accepted certain conditions.

There followed one of the most extraordinary arrangements ever made by Congress. The committee insisted on terms amounting to unconditional surrender. It demanded that the company cease its dividends and pay at once to the government $718,815, the amount claimed under the Thurman Act for 1883. All receipts on government transportation, including those from lines not involved in the subsidy, were to be applied to the sinking fund even though the law required only half that amount. Another $69,259 deposited in the treasury earlier was also to be surrendered to the sinking fund. Finally, the committee wanted the road run in the interest of the government. As a first step it wanted Dillon replaced by none other than Adams.

In effect the committee went beyond making law to enforcing it, ignoring both the Attorney General and the Justice Department. No congressional body had such power, yet the company submitted because it saw no choice. On June 11 Adams consented to take the presidency; a week later the board voted its approval. Dillon submitted his resignation and was given a place on the executive committee. Adams was elected in his place by unanimous vote.

"The past year has been a trying one for corporate property," sighed Gould, who had taken advantage of the drop in prices to buy a large block of Union Pacific. Nevertheless, he would leave the board at the next election. Dillon was grateful for the relief but insisted that "were it not for my health and my age I would not resign the Presidency of the road." Never would he admit that events had forced him from office. He wrote Clark a lengthy explanation and asked him to place the news before "the people of Omaha in the right light." That done, Dillon fled to Long Island for a summer of fishing and sailing. Clark dutifully offered his resignation but withdrew it at Dillon's request. No one could guess what changes the coming of Adams portended. The only certainty was that the government had not thrust him into office for the purpose of continuing past policies and practices. No one doubted Adams's intelligence or his intentions, but did he know how to run a railroad? That remained to be seen.

PART THREE

The Road to Hell
1884–93

23

THE MAN
ON HORSEBACK

The new president seemed the most unlikely of figures to take charge of a western railroad. Urbane, cultured, Harvard-bred, the heir to Presidents and ministers of state, Charles Francis Adams, Jr., survived the immense burden of his heritage better than most of his brothers and was the only one to venture into business. After service in the Union cavalry, he abandoned his original plans to read law on the premise that the country needed "trained thinkers,—men capable of directing public sentiment." His future would be "business and literature," hitched not to a star but "to a locomotive-engine" in the belief that he could earn a living "by wedding railroads with reform."

The creation of a Massachusetts railroad commission in 1869 gave Adams his start along with a series of articles, including "A Chapter of Erie" and another piece in which he warned of a Pacific railway ring. In 1878 Adams summarized his experience with the commission in *Railroads, Their Origins and Problems,* a book that earned him a national reputation as an expert on the subject. A year later he accepted a post as arbitrator for the trunk line commission headed by one of the foremost railroad men in America, Albert Fink. He remained in that position five years and also did a brief stint as government director for the Union Pacific, which introduced him to railways in what he called "the dreary prairie states." His summons to the Union Pacific presidency gave Adams his first chance to deal with the problems of railroad management from the inside.

This unique blend of personality and experience made Adams unlike any other railroad president. Bright, witty, acerbic, Adams prided himself on being an intellectual, a philosopher capable of taking the broad view of affairs.

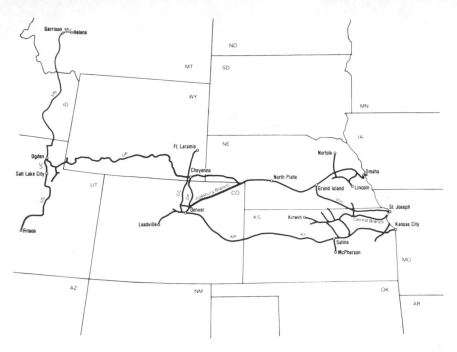

The Union Pacific and its branches. KEY: KP (Kansas Pacific; SGI (St. Joseph & Grand Island); DP (Denver Pacific); CC (Colorado Central); UC (Utah Central); US (Utah Southern); UN (Utah & Northern); MU (Montana Union).

He wrote and spoke exceptionally well, perhaps too well for the position he now held. Railroad management had long been dominated by men who had worked their way up through the ranks and learned the trade piece by piece. Adams came to office not from the bottom up but from the top down, a renowned theorist eager to impose his ideas on a specific road to demonstrate their feasibility. That he had never worked a day of his life on an actual railroad did not trouble him. He had nothing but contempt for what he called "practical" railroad men and their narrow, "rule of thumb" approach to problems. In his view they were by nature incapable of recognizing the "philosophy of events," but dealt with everything on a piecemeal basis. Above all, they lacked vision.

The solution to the railroad problem, Adams believed, was to create a better class of officials, men of culture and education who could bring not only greater vision but a higher tone to business. Adams determined to make the Union Pacific a greenhouse for such men and to introduce a new style of management. He would not rule but lead; above all, he would manage in a proper way. His would be an open administration, as any model must be. Detailed reports would be issued and the public kept fully informed. Honesty would be restored to all departments. Adams would not merely save the company but make an honest woman of what many regarded as a strumpet. It was the perfect role for the aspiring reformer.

And a delicate one. A century ago railroading was already an industry hidebound by tradition. Its officers and men did not warm easily to change or to outsiders with fancy notions. Most regarded Adams with a mixture of curiosity and suspicion. Perkins took his measure early. "An entirely honest man himself, morally speaking," he noted shrewdly, "he, nevertheless, suspects everybody less stupid than himself of not being honest."

In many ways Adams's weaknesses were but the reverse image of his strengths. He talked and wrote so well that he tended to overwhelm others without convincing them; out of frustration his tongue became a weapon that lashed without enlightening its victim. He thought everything through to the point where, like Hamlet, he was paralyzed by choices. Adams also suffered grievously from that ancient disease of his family, chronic introspection, which transformed every decision, every crisis, into a torment of the soul. In the business arena he was a nervous Nellie, an incessant worrier who shrank from conflict and could not stand fire in battle. Finally, for all his insight into the vagaries of human nature, he was a poor judge of men. Ultimately this proved to be his Achilles heel.

None of these shortcomings were apparent in June 1884. Although Adams took office under difficult circumstances, he commanded universal respect. The company staggered under the legacy of its past, but he was free to tackle its problems with a clean slate. Even critics recognized that the challenge facing him was immense and were content to wait and watch, at least for a time. The destiny of the Union Pacific was firmly in his hands.

* * *

From the first Adams had a clear sense of his objectives. To make the Union Pacific a success, he must effect a settlement with the government, restore the company to a dividend-paying basis, reorganize its administration with efficient officers, and develop the system to a point where it could compete with rival lines. During all his struggles he never lost sight of these goals or the fact that he would sink or swim on his ability to achieve them. He could not know how long this would take, but two days before taking office he vowed to hold the position for only two years.

Tactically Adams saw the value not merely of detaching his administration from the past regime but of stressing the contrast between them. The press helped immensely by painting overdrawn comparisons between the corrupt, secretive Gould ring and the open, straightforward practices of the new leader. What could be more natural than the author of "A Chapter of Erie" disassociating himself from the villain of that piece? Adams milked this campaign for all it was worth, especially in his dealings with Congress. The comparison suited his own temperament nicely as well; that it was a false and misleading image seemed rarely to intrude on his conscience and was easily explained away by necessity.

To carry out his reforms, Adams needed men he could rely on. That would not be easy for one who was by nature demanding of subordinates and quick to point out their faults. The Boston office first impressed him as a "circus of hopeless incompetency," although he soon came to regard its staff as his most reliable officers. The worst horror stories came from the field and told tales of an undermaintained road, demoralized and bickering officers, restless workers, disorganization, odors of corruption, and a vacuum of leadership. Two weeks after going "on deck" Adams headed west with Fred Ames on a lengthy inspection trip. At Chicago they picked up S. R. Callaway, the new officer without portfolio, and Hugh Riddle, the retired president of the Rock Island, whom Adams liked and respected as a railroad man. On the way home Riddle offered an insight that deeply impressed Adams. "Your trouble is that you have got nothing to work with," he said bluntly. "There are no men on the Union Pacific who amount to anything at all; the dearth of material is simply inexplicable."

Although Riddle exaggerated the case, there was some truth in his assertion. The blame rested squarely with Clark, whose dark sense of insecurity impelled him to keep down or drive off potential challengers to his authority. Adams took an immediate dislike to Clark, whom he caricatured as a "narrow, tricky, dishonest and treacherous promoted railroad conductor, utterly unequal to his position." Clark was in his view the worst type of "practical" railroad man. A "henchman of Gould . . . tall, thin, dyspeptic, with a long beard and narrow forehead, he knows neither what a good railroad or a good man is." Since June Clark had been rumored on his way out, but in Omaha Adams struck a deal with him that was less than decisive. Clark resigned as vice president and general manager in favor of Callaway but was retained as an advisor to the board at a salary of ten thousand dollars a year. Possibly the older directors forced this arrangement on Adams despite his pledge to cut expenses in every quarter. For obvious reasons news of the advisory post was not made public, and Clark held it only a short time.

Other changes soon followed. The freight, passenger, coal, and stone departments were swept together into the new commercial department under Thomas L. Kimball. The man in charge of the Kansas division, S. T. Smith, was made general superintendent for the entire system. The supply department was overhauled and a study made of all other departments. In the East the company headquarters, which had bounced like a Ping-Pong ball between New York and Boston since the Fisk suit, changed sites again. Adams closed the New York offices except for a small one manned by James Ham and moved the operation back to Boston. He also hired two new assistants for himself, Howard Hinckley and Gardiner M. Lane, who assumed the duties of auditor in Boston when Wilbur resigned in March 1885. That same month Gould and Clark left the board, leaving Dillon as the last remnant of the old regime.

Adams and his reorganization committee delayed action on the auditor's position until they had a chance to study the systems used by other large railroads. In September 1885 the committee revamped the structure by replacing the auditor with a new office, the comptroller, who reported directly to the president and board. Whereas the treasurer was responsible for disbursements, the comptroller was to oversee all accounts and auditing. He was also to have charge of all accounts with the government, a task that had already become herculean in the piles of paperwork it generated. The new post went not to Gannett's replacement but to assistant treasurer Oliver Mink, whom Adams came to regard as his most indispensable financial officer. With the restructuring of the accounting department, Adams's committee closed its work in the belief that it had given the company an efficient, modern organization.

Important as these internal changes were, they paled before the external problems facing the company. The morass at Washington was as confused and menacing as ever. Three suits were still pending in the court of claims, the last residue of the company's stand against the Thurman Act. Two of them concerned old and bitterly contested issues, net earnings and the amount of payment for carrying the mail. There was talk that Congress might revive the Thompson bill, which required that *all* net earnings be applied to the sinking fund. A new and dangerous question burst into the debate over the government debt when critics charged that the money spent by Union Pacific on its branch and auxiliary lines should have been applied to the sinking fund. An official of the Railway Bureau toured the Union Pacific system and declared that most of the branches were a drag on its earnings.

The usual coalition hostile to the company was gathering in Congress, spurred on by Senator C. H. Van Wyck of Nebraska. After gaining office as a Burlington man, Van Wyck turned maverick and joined Rosewater in an alliance that made him the despair of regular Republicans in Nebraska and of the Union Pacific. Unimpressed by the new regime, Van Wyck sneered that Boston too had its "bunko men" and dismissed Adams's supporters as "the same crowd of gamblers." With this rhetoric Van Wyck set the tone for the debate that followed.

Like Gould before him, Adams saw that the only hope for Union Pacific lay in a permanent solution. Everyone knew the Thurman Act had been a dismal failure which the dreaded Thompson bill merely carried to its logical absurdity. In Adams's view the government debt must be refunded over an extended period at the lower rates then current in the bond market. There must be fixed annual payments instead of sums based on earnings, so that everyone knew what to expect. In November Adams went to Washington and, together with the company lobbyist, Moorfield Storey, arranged a bill refunding the bonds for sixty years at 3 percent, the same rate offered on some other government bonds. The bill was introduced in January 1885 and guided through the Senate Judiciary Committee by Senator Hoar of Massachusetts.

To prepare the ground, Adams stated the company's position forcefully in a series of open letters to banker Colgate Hoyt, a government director. Any attempt to apply all earnings to the sinking fund or to bar the paying of dividends, he argued, would succeed only in driving the stock out of the hands of permanent investors and into those of speculators. Even more, it would strip the Union Pacific of capital urgently needed to improve the road and build branch lines. Gould's policy had all along been to sink surplus earnings into developing an auxiliary system that would secure the traffic of a vast territory. This system would in turn open new areas for settlement, ensure the company's continued prosperity, and provide the income to pay the government debt. Adams defended this policy as "the most beneficent, the most business-like, and the most financially sound of all the plans to meet the obligations of the Government which have yet been suggested."

The Thurman Act had superseded this program with disastrous results. Far from being "suckers," the branch lines were feeders that enabled the parent road to survive in a competitive age. Money needed for new mileage languished instead in the sinking fund, where it earned a pitiful return of about 2 percent. Any settlement, Adams insisted, must give the road's managers the same power as its rivals. "To retain their traffic they must be able to extend their system when occasion requires. The exercise of this power on their part in the past has given the company its present value." Without it, the Union Pacific would not be worth "the amount of the first-mortgage bonds upon it." One of two things should be done, Adams concluded: "Either the Government should take this property and manage it, or else the Government should leave the stockholders to manage it."

Unfortunately, Congress was inclined to do neither. Adams made a valiant effort to inject reason into a dispute that had long ceased to be reasonable. Critics would not let go of the past or shake free of the notion that any settlement would benefit the Gould and Crédit Mobilier gangs; at the very least it would sanction their plunders. The debt question had become not a matter of equity or an issue demanding resolution but a symbol for public indignation against the devious machinations of businessmen and the overweening power of corporations. The extent to which the facts of the case actually fit this description no longer mattered except to a small body of moderate opinion whose views got trampled in the political arena. More than a decade had passed since Crédit Mobilier, but in that time the rapid growth of corporations had roused cries of alarm against their influence. The debt dispute was a perfect outlet for such frustrations, for here was a company over which the government actually had power. In that sense the conflict had a most unexpected effect: it helped arouse public sentiment behind the concept of government regulation of business.

The hostile Omaha *Bee* expressed in inflammatory terms a widely held view of Hoar's bill. "Apparently it is fair and reasonable," sneered the *Bee,* "but upon close examination it will be found to be a measure for the purpose of legalizing the robberies of the wreckers and permitting them to continue their extortions upon the people. It is based upon the false assumption . . . that the obligations of the Union and Central Pacific railroads were incurred honestly." The New York *Times* suggested that Adams's connection with the Union Pacific "appears to have had a peculiar effect upon his mind. He seems to think that the Government ought to let the company alone and leave it to provide for meeting its obligations in its own way, although it has thus far been engaged in no effort whatsoever to make such provisions."

Adams did what he could to counter these misconceptions. He had his assistant Gardiner Lane circulate a letter asking stockholders to urge their congressmen to support the Hoar bill. Concessions were offered on applying the earnings of certain branches to the sinking fund. That winter the court handed the company a split decision, ruling for it in the net earnings case and against it in the postal service case. As a show of good faith, Adams elected not to appeal the postal decision but remitted the amount of difference ($916,704) two hours after being notified of the figure. By this unusual promptness, he hoped to demonstrate the company's desire to "establish complete harmony" with the government.

It was to no avail. The net earnings decision moved the *Times* to complain that "it seems to be impossible to get from any branch of the Government straight-forward dealing with these great corporations which have already swindled the country out of many millions of dollars." The Hoar bill went nowhere despite Adams's dogged efforts to enlist support for it. Even a sympathetic journal admitted late in April that "the ultimate disposition of the Government debt question is as much involved in doubt as ever." Reluctantly conceding defeat, Adams looked at once to the next session. To reinforce his lobby, he hired another assistant, Isaac H. Bromley, a newspaperman whose sharp mind and facile pen made him an invaluable aide.

The new President, Grover Cleveland, encouraged Adams by appointing an unusually able corps of government directors headed by E. P. Alexander, a former Confederate general with impressive credentials as a railroad man. But that fall Adams got a taste of what lay ahead. The railroad commissioner questioned the way net earnings had been figured for the Kansas Pacific and demanded a recalculation going back to the company's origins. A market fight over Pacific Mail prompted some speculators to make sensational charges about the subsidy paid the steamships by the Pacific roads. The outcry moved the new administration to investigate charges that had already been thrashed over repeatedly in public. Both issues concerned the amount due the government under the Thurman Act and promised still more litigation.

In November another threat loomed in the naming of Major Thomas Reddington as chief clerk in the railroad commissioner's office. Reddington was a veteran railroad lobbyist whose appointment was interpreted in Wall Street as a sign of hostility toward the Pacific roads. Ten days later the commissioner's office requested all subsidized roads to submit a staggering list of reports and paperwork. Adams protested the demand as "physically difficult, if not impossible, to be literally complied with," as well as a violation of the privacy enjoyed by rival roads. To Adams it was but the opening of a new chapter in an old game whereby "the Government is used as a lever with which to put prices up or down on the stock exchange."

Adams had taken his first bold strides into the murky labyrinth of Washington politics where Gould had wandered for years without finding a suitable way out. Doubtless his brother Henry provided him a lesson or two about its vagaries and pitfalls, but Charles's education was to be a slow and painful one. Like Gould before him, Adams found that the deeper he penetrated, the darker grew the path and the less confident his step.

*   *   *

"The bugbear of the period is a railway floating debt," observed one analyst in the fall of 1884. For Adams this was especially true; he had inherited a large floating debt and could do little with the road until it was discharged. To do that he had to cut through an old and vicious cycle: the debt discouraged investors and kept the price of Union Pacific securities low, which in turn made it difficult to market the bonds that would pay off the debt. Prudent management could reduce expenses but not necessarily boost earnings, which were at the mercy of rate wars and other factors. Adams soon discovered how utterly dependent he was on the monthly report from Omaha. He watched the returns with the nervous, uneasy eye of a politician aware that his future dangled on the thread of unpredictable whims of fate. "Life in U.P. certainly has ups and downs!" he sighed that fall. In time that remark would seem to him a massive understatement.

Help arrived from an unexpected and unwanted quarter that summer when Gould, in an effort to improve his weakened financial position, bulled Union Pacific as a lever to push stocks upward. Analysts who labeled the stock "a safe target for bears" in July were dumbfounded as it surged from a low of 28 to 57 in August. Privately Gould expressed confidence in the road's future, arguing that "its large land grant and its assetts [sic] must bring it out in the end." Although the stock sank back into the 40s and 50s that fall, it stayed firmly within that range through 1885. Gould's operation gave Adams breathing room to put the company's finances in order. His activity made Adams more uneasy than grateful, even though Adams could not resist turning some shares on speculation for himself.

Improved earnings helped sustain what Gould had begun, as did the quarterly statements issued by Adams on the company's performance. As the impact of the spring panic receded, analysts revised their gloomy views of Union Pacific. Its finances, conceded one, "are more closely supervised and scrutinized than are those of any other corporation in the United States, and yet are the most misunderstood and most unjustly criticised." Through 1885 Adams felt the brunt of that criticism as he groped for a way to shake free of the debt and of Gould's shadow. The impression lingered that Gould was still the *eminence grise* in Union Pacific affairs, and that Adams lacked the backbone to resist his influence. Although Adams did consult Gould on financial matters, the rumors had no basis in fact. "I dont understand the policy of the new administration," Gould admitted privately, "as I am not in the confidence of the new President." What he saw did not impress him. "It looks," he noted, "very much like an attempt to run the road on *theory.*"

In his battle against the debt Adams enlisted as allies the major banking houses of Boston. Both Lee, Higginson, with whom Gardiner Lane was associated, and Kidder, Peabody showed their willingness early to lend money to the new management. During March 1885, as part of Adams's concerted effort to wean the Union Pacific away from dependence on Wall Street, the company obtained $1.2 million in loans from New England banks outside of New York. The stock too was leaving New York; by 1886 about 18 percent of the shares were held by foreigners. As the company's finances improved, the holders grew restive for a renewal of dividends. When a petition circulated in May 1885 asking the company to sell enough assets to pay off the floating debt and place the stock on a dividend basis, wary analysts were quick to suspect Gould of being behind the drive.

The petition fizzled out, but its basic premise had already occurred to Adams. His problem was finding suitable assets to peddle at decent prices. He toyed with the idea of selling the Central Branch to Gould's Missouri Pacific and the St. Joseph & Western to the Rock Island but hesitated when Perkins raised vehement objections. During a lengthy tour of the system in the summer of 1885, Adams evolved a plan utilizing the St. Joseph in quite another fashion. Originally part of Gould's scheme to outflank the Iowa Pool, the road had become a derelict since the consolidation. In 1883 suits by minority holders put it in the hands of a receiver. Both the road and the bridge sorely needed repair, but neither the Union Pacific nor the minority holders cared to invest anything until they reached some understanding.

In October 1884 Dillon had a long session with financier E. C. Benedict, who controlled the minority holdings and came away muttering, "The more I talked, the less I knew." Not until the following April was a bargain struck with Benedict to reorganize the road as the St. Joseph & Grand Island, an independent company owned by the Union Pacific with Benedict and his son James at its head. The reorganization put into the Union Pacific treasury a new batch of bonds which as yet had little market value. Adams tried to boost them through a traffic alliance with the Grand Island that was interpreted as a virtual guarantee of the latter's bonds. He then borrowed $3 million from his Boston banking friends, using the Grand Islands as part of the collateral even though they had yet to show a market value.

The loan was intended merely to tide the company over until the bonds could be sold. By autumn the rise in Union Pacific securities encouraged Adams to believe he could dispose of the entire floating debt. Lee, Higginson took over $1 million of Short Line bonds and Kansas Pacific consols. As the stock soared into the high 50s, Adams bought another thousand shares in his exuberance only to sell eight hundred of them in December when a bear attack forced the price down. Already he had climbed aboard the emotional rollercoaster he would ride throughout his presidency. In October the man on horseback felt himself "getting firmer in my seat"; by January he confessed to "going through an awfully blue streak."

His friend Charles Whittier of Lee, Higginson prodded Adams that the time had come to sell bonds because the market was turning dull and might soon be flooded with new issues. Adams made the effort but found Ames and Atkins cold to the idea. The bear attack renewed with growing ferocity on rumors that insiders were selling out. Shaken by the assault, Adams managed to sell another $1.3 million in Short Line and Kansas Pacific bonds but hesitated to try the unproven Grand Islands. The attack slowed in March when the annual report revealed a better showing than expected despite a drop of nearly 9.5 percent in net earnings. Gross earnings had actually increased but were shriveled by the rate wars and heavy expenditures to improve the Short Line and Utah Northern. Asked pointedly about dividends at the annual meeting, Adams replied they would be forthcoming only when the debt was settled and the long war in Washington was brought to a conclusion.

Encouraged by the report's reception, Adams sent Lane to Europe with Henry Higginson in May 1886 to seek buyers for the Grand Islands and some other bonds he was anxious to sell. A new bridge over the Missouri was needed, the Utah Northern had to be changed to standard gauge, and money was required for new branches elsewhere. New bonds could not be issued for these projects until the floating debt was erased. In his anxiety Adams let the untried Grand Islands go cheaply to a syndicate headed by Kidder, Peabody and by Lee, Higginson. To everyone's astonishment the bonds sold well from the start, giving the bankers a fat profit. "We sold them at too low a price," Adams admitted, but he showed little regret because the rise in Union Pacific securities was "paving the way to a loan at a lower rate of interest. That is what I am looking to."

The proceeds from the Grand Islands enabled Adams to wipe out the entire floating debt. On the morning of August 24 he paid the last due note and in his exuberance gave the clerks the rest of the day off. "We are overflowing with money," he chortled to Lane, "and will have no occasion to borrow during the remainder of this year." Basking in the praise of financial journals, Adams sensed that a high-water mark had been reached. If he could only resolve the government dispute, his work in Union Pacific would be complete. Slowly, reluctantly, he would learn that getting the road out of debt was easier than keeping it out.

*   *   *

Adams realized that the other railroad presidents considered him an oddball who did not think as they did or even speak their language. He was content at first to play the part of greenhorn and even to use it for advantage. "Am afraid to venture into your country alone," he teased Perkins shortly before taking office. "It's a dangerous region for green country lads." Lack of experience did not deter Adams from considering himself intellectually and morally superior to the other presidents, however, or from taking their measure as mercilessly as they took his. Huntington was "a regular old man of the sea" who used "words with a good deal of skill to hide thoughts." Strong of the Atchison was narrow but "logical in a small way,—a bargainer by nature and training, and cold-blooded to the last possible degree in matters of business." Adams liked Perkins and got on well with him, but he limned his portrait in harsh, precise lines as a "typical head of a small independent state" who would "jealously reserve his petty independence, and always go in earnestly for peace and two-thirds of the traffic."

In 1884 Adams found himself at war with all of them. On one front he was torn between the intransigence of Perkins and the truculence of his Tripartite partner, Ransom Cable of the Rock Island. Attempts to reach peace in Colorado were threatened by Strong's expansionist policy. Huntington's Southern Pacific was already capturing much of the transcontinental business; nevertheless, the old bear looked darkly on the opening of the Oregon Short Line, which would siphon traffic from the Central Pacific. All the major lines were edgy and suspicious, ready to explode in an orgy of tracklaying to protect themselves. Faced with war clouds on every side, Adams typically sought the high ground by undertaking the role of peacemaker.

Since the Atchison connected with the Rock Island and Wabash at its eastern end and was affected when those roads cut rates, it could retaliate only by cutting Colorado rates. All these slashes hurt the Union Pacific, which prompted Adams to sound Strong on a peace conference. Strong refused to negotiate unless the Union Pacific freed itself from the Tripartite roads. When Adams bristled at his sharp rebuff in "the 'God Almighty to a black beetle' style," Strong protested that his message had been garbled. With Perkins's help feelings were soothed enough to hold a meeting in July. In those discussions Adams offered his pet notion of a personal agreement among himself, Perkins, and Strong to keep rates firm. The three men agreed to do so until the year's end, with a proviso that the truce could be canceled on five days' notice.

In Nebraska Adams groped for some way to reconcile the conflicts among the partner lines or curb their influence on the Colorado fight. As the rate war and bickering worsened, the Northwestern quit the Tripartite pool in August and resumed relations with the Burlington. There followed a month of frenzied negotiations that managed to piece together some temporary rate agreements hailed by most observers as an abandonment of Tripartite. To gain this truce, both the Burlington and the Northwestern made concessions. For them, as for the Union Pacific, one issue loomed above all others: some way had to be found to keep the Rock Island and St. Paul from building lines west of the Missouri River. If those roads joined the scramble for territory, no chance of a permanent peace seemed possible.

Tripartite limped along like a crippled bird, alive but unable to fly. That winter Perkins explored with Adams the possibility of an alliance, but nothing could be done so long as Union Pacific clung to Tripartite. Adams recognized that the pact had failed but could not decide what to put in its place. "Adams does not know what he wants," sneered Perkins, "but he has a vague feeling that he wants something." Both cringed at the Northwestern's expansion north of the Platte River and feared that the other Iowa roads would soon follow. If the Burlington, Northwestern, and Union Pacific could keep the other lines east of the Missouri for a period of five years, Perkins figured, they could "so thoroughly occupy that country that the temptation will be very slight to anybody else to build over there."

The outbreak of a long-smoldering rate war in April added urgency to their deliberations. A series of tense meetings in Chicago finally produced a comprehensive settlement that appeared to stabilize the whole region between Chicago and Colorado. Tripartite and other pools were scrapped in favor of a new one, the Western Freight Association. Rates between Chicago and Omaha were restored to former levels and equalized with those between Chicago and Kansas City. Agreement was also reached on Colorado rates and on those between Chicago and the Twin Cities. A satisfied Perkins believed rates would be "reasonably well maintained west of Chicago for some time to come" and regarded the adjustment on Union Pacific traffic as a "pretty good one for us." Adams was no less pleased. "For the first time," he noted happily, "I feel some assurance of the future."

Even as Adams breathed a sigh of relief, another crisis was brewing. During the fall of 1884 the Transcontinental Association, which now had thirteen members, was reorganized into two pools, one dealing with traffic east of the Missouri and the other with traffic west of the river. In December, however, Huntington's roads refused to accept the arbitrator's decision on percentages, and the rate wars resumed. Three months later the Central Pacific startled everyone by refusing to participate in rate cuts made by its connecting roads. Adams took this action as a declaration of war but joined in efforts to save the association. A lengthy meeting in June produced little more than a reprieve.

Attempts to thrash out a transcontinental agreement ran afoul of an old nemesis, Pacific Mail. For some years the Pacific roads had bought peace by paying the steamship line a subsidy to maintain rates. Since 1880, however, complications had arisen. There were wrangles over the amount of subsidy and the settling of old accounts. Foes of the Pacific roads pounced on the subsidy as an Achilles heel for political attack. As new transcontinental lines emerged, the Pacific roads balked at paying the entire subsidy themselves. A dispute over the size of the payments led Adams and Huntington to withdraw from the contract in March 1885, amid the transcontinental clash. Gould, acting as a director of Pacific Mail, then devised a proposal that produced a new contract with a slightly lower subsidy. A rate war with the steamship line had been averted, but at the cost of thrusting the subsidy question back into the political limelight, where enemies of the Pacific roads quickly made it a target.

No sooner had the Pacific Mail threat subsided than the transcontinental agreement fell apart again. As always Huntington professed his desire for peace while his roads refused adamantly to honor the claims against them that were the crux of the June compromise. The glaring weakness of all pools was exposed anew as the Association passed resolutions against the Southern Pacific and Central Pacific without any means of enforcing them. The strategic position of Huntington's roads at the western end of the route enabled them to defy all threats with impunity. The Central Pacific further outraged the Union Pacific and the Iowa roads by imposing obstacles on their through service to California, the California Fast Freight Line, and then withdrawing from it altogether in October 1885. As bitterness against Huntington mounted, fresh cuts drove rates down by 40 percent during the last quarter of 1885.

Adams must have felt like the little Dutch boy, watching the dike spring leaks faster than he could plug them. In his view the problem was that the presidents were "so afraid of each other, and will not come together" because they feared "any civility they may show each other will be misconstrued." One solution, he mused, would be to give them all houses "on Fifth Avenue or Commonwealth Avenue, or where not, in some block;—a sort of Presidents' Road. Then they would walk down to their offices together in the morning, and I would be willing, I think, to wager my head that there would not be one quarrel then where there are five quarrels now." This bit of fancy held more appeal for real estate brokers than for his peers, but Adams persisted in advocating the personal approach and in pursuing what he called "my high mission among the railroads of the country . . . acting simply as the friend of peace."

Huntington was willing, even eager, to talk, but Adams found the discussion aimless. Early in 1886 the Atchison triggered a passenger-rate war. Frantic meetings in New York bogged down over pool percentages, and on February 18 the Transcontinental Association formally dissolved; next day the rate slashing began in earnest. "Things look worse and worse," moaned Adams, "to me almost hopeless." Within a month the war reduced first-class fares between Missouri River points and the Pacific coast from ninety dollars to twenty-three dollars and second-class or emigrant fares from forty-five dollars to thirteen dollars. This was a bonanza for the traveling public but disaster for the railroads, especially when the war spread to freight. Unlike passenger fares, where lower rates might attract more customers and cover some of the loss, lower freight rates amounted to a dead loss. Gamely Callaway instructed his agents to accept no business below half a cent a ton, but the Central Pacific bristled and the Atchison took business at any price. Convinced that the Atchison "have in mind simply the making of a tonnage record," Callaway reluctantly ordered their rates met. Even that would be difficult. Kimball reported that the Atchison told its agents "to go below any rate quoted by their competitors, no matter what it may be."

In desperation Adams appealed to his old friend Albert Fink, the trunk line pool commissioner, to intervene with Huntington and Strong. Fink was amenable but predicted that "as usual in such case, they will have to go on and exhaust themselves before they can be brought to reason." He was right. Huntington made his usual cooings about peace but refused to pool westbound business except on his own terms. Meanwhile Kimball alerted headquarters to a new danger: the Southern Pacific, Atchison, B & M, and Rio Grande were not merely slashing rates but offering them with six-month guarantees. "This matter of guaranteeing cut rates for weeks and months ahead is the most serious phase, to my mind, this quarrel has yet taken," he warned. Nothing would make it harder to form a new pool than "the knowledge that a large amount of future traffic in such pool is tied up [in] time contracts at cut rates."

Through most of the fight a vast majority of passengers bought limited tickets which, through rebates, enabled them to travel from Omaha to San Francisco for just $5. The Union Pacific's share of that amount was $2.93, compared to $32.63 it received on a $60 unlimited ticket. On first-class freight the rate had dropped from $4 per hundred pounds to $1, and the Union Pacific's share from $1.82 to 16 cents. Other lines suffered equal or heavier losses and, more important, carried much more traffic to earn as much or less than they formerly earned with considerably less wear and tear on their equipment. An ominous pattern was emerging.

In April 1886 Adams, Huntington, and Strong managed a patchwork truce, but the Pacific Mail contract was due for renewal in June. The steamship company wanted the subsidy increased to one hundred thousand dollars per month; Huntington offered only seventy thousand dollars because of the reduced earnings wrought by the rate war. Pacific Mail's board suggested it could do better "by acting independently." The threat of renewed cuts by the water line meant the Transcontinental Association members could do nothing among themselves until Pacific Mail was brought in tow. Adams and Strong thought Pacific Mail should become a regular member of the Association and receive a percentage of traffic instead of a subsidy, but that was wishful thinking so long as the Association itself lay in tatters.

As the summer wore on with no agreement in sight, the transcontinental roads veered ever closer to an outright war of expansion. The same threat faced Adams on the eastern front as the truce of April 1885, like so many others, proved a hollow shell. There seemed no way, no device of reason, to bring the bickering heads of state to compromise. Every president denounced the building of new road as a waste of capital, and every one itched to lay rails before his rivals got the jump. Forbes had his usual churlish explanation for this unhappy situation. "The tribe of Hinckleys, Cranes, Graves, Villards, and other cranks and thieves led by Hopkins and Gould," he stormed, "have built and will build Roads wherever fools with money will follow, and where three Roads, stimulated by contracts, are thus built to do the work of one, it . . . leads right up to a necessity for the nearest solvent Railroad to buy the other useless ones."

There were more compelling and less sinister motives behind expansion, notably the desire to seize new territory, increase traffic volume, and eliminate the problems posed by multiline service. Such things as schedules, division of rates, types of equipment, transfer time, and handling efficiency all required constant adjustment among roads sharing a route. A one-haul system did away with all these complications and gave the company the entire rate. Moreover, by 1886 the time was ripe for expansion. Interest rates were low (3 percent on corporate bonds), and the market for good bonds was apparently insatiable. Construction costs were cheaper than they had ever been and likely to advance before long. Every president knew these factors and weighed them carefully, but there was something more—an influence no less powerful for being intangible. Each president had in his own way caught the fever of empire, the drive to leave his stamp on the country in the form of a dominant system where, only twenty years earlier, there existed not a single road across the continent or even to the Missouri.

The country was growing, filling up with settlers as plentiful rainfall made for bumper crops on the plains. Once-empty stretches of land were dotted with farms, settlements, and towns, all clamoring for rails. Another boom was underway, and its prospects aroused in the presidents the hunger of miners lusting for a rich new vein. No amount of rhetoric about moderation could stay their ambitions once the fever took; the only question was how to expand without precipitating a wholesale war. Two events unleashed the crisis they had long feared and freed them from the restraints against which they had long chafed. The irrepressible Gould once again took the lead by expanding vigorously in Kansas and southern Nebraska, while the Burlington stunned everyone by constructing a line to the Twin Cities.

Gould's move posed a direct threat to the Kansas division of the Union Pacific, the Atchison, and the B & M. An alarmed Adams warned Perkins that the situation west of the river was "becoming very serious. Owing to the aggressive course of the Missouri Pacific, a railroad-building mania has arisen in Kansas, and will spread into Nebraska. We will be cutting and slashing at each other like fiends before long." He hastened to secure charters for some Kansas extensions and at the same time approached Gould, who was building through the territory of the Central Branch. Adams was shocked to find the usually placid Gould "mad all the way through" over stories that the Union Pacific intended to terminate the Central Branch lease. After lengthy discussion Gould calmed down and offered to curb expansion in its territory if the lease was renewed.

A relieved Adams agreed to extend the lease for twenty-five years on condition that Gould undertake no construction competitive with the Union Pacific except for a branch to Lincoln already underway. When the bargain was sealed, he tried to defuse Perkins's suspicions by disclosing the facts to him. He had done it, Adams said, to halt a "Kansas mania" that would not cease "while there is a point on the map which has not got a railroad, and which can vote bonds." Perkins was not appeased. Hughitt of the Northwestern assailed him for upsetting the balance by building to St. Paul, but Perkins shrugged off the charges with his usual stiff-necked righteousness. What he had done in the Northwest was exactly what Gould had done in Kansas, but to Perkins the one was justifiable policy and the other an aggressive if not hostile act. That Adams should concede privileges to Gould in a territory vital to the Burlington's interest infuriated him.

Hughitt threatened to retaliate by building southward across the Union Pacific into Lincoln, thereby invading Burlington territory below the North Platte. Thus Perkins saw Gould marching on him from one flank and the Northwestern from the other. By some curious twist of logic, he decided to hold Adams responsible if either enemy struck him through Union Pacific territory. Adams found Perkins's indignation more than he could bear and pounced on the absurdity of his position. "When you built into St. Paul," he chided, "you certainly did not expect that the shot-gun you fired into the hornet's nest was going to produce no commotion." That extension was "as aggressive a move as any railroad company probably ever made. It set the whole circus going." If the Burlington could build to St. Paul, he asked, why should the Northwestern and Missouri Pacific not build to Lincoln, or anywhere else for that matter? Adams would inform Hughitt that any line put across the Union Pacific would be considered an "act of aggression," but he warned that the St. Paul line had "set a ball in motion which is going to knock the spots out of every railroad company West of the Missouri."

Adams won the war of words handily, but Perkins's intransigence dashed his hopes of playing peacemaker. Nothing could be done, he noted sadly, "while the long record of the past is to be overhauled in order to see whether every one is even with every one else." The presidents nursed grudges like feudal barons or mountain clans. There would never be peace "unless we all agree to separate the future from the past." These were words of wisdom, but they fell on deaf ears. Perkins merely told Adams that his attitude did not "evince a proper spirit" and laid plans to expand in all directions. Forbes was sent a map penciled with "lines where the B. & M. ought to build railroads; *when* to do it, is the question." In defense of his actions Perkins offered Adams the familiar justification:

The attitude by the Union Pacific toward us and the threatened invasion of the South Platte country by the Rock Island and Northwestern, as well as the danger, since your sale[!] of the Central Branch, that Gould may think it expedient to build north, all combine to make us feel that the completion of our system in that region cannot be safely delayed any longer.

Although negotiations continued, a war of expansion seemed inevitable by the end of 1885. The worst had come, and Adams was ill-prepared for the fight. He had done little to mobilize for expansion because it conflicted sharply with two of his most cherished goals, paying off the floating debt and promoting peace among the roads. Now that war loomed, the Union Pacific found itself at a disadvantage. It had not been aggressive in protecting markets or territory. Months earlier former agent J. M. Eddy had warned Dodge that "the Colorado traffic history of the UP *has been repeated* in Montana, and is today being repeated in Idaho & Oregon you mark my words. Simply burnishing up old muskets and having dress parades never yet won a battle, and attending Pool meetings and printing tariffs will never create business for a Ry or even hold what they already have."

These words would have stung Adams, for during the first half of 1886 it became painfully evident that old muskets would no longer do service. On every front he found rival lines pushing their expansion programs with zeal. Gould was constructing lines all over Kansas and talked of going to Pueblo. The Atchison, which had done little building since 1883, responded with a vigorous program of its own in Kansas as Strong, like Perkins, accused Adams of violating old agreements by joining hands with Gould. The Rock Island was eager to jump the river once Cable determined where to strike. For years the cautious Hugh Riddle had kept the expansion beast caged, but now he was gone and Cable dreamed gaudy visions of empire. He tried to badger Adams into selling him the Grand Island and, together with the St. Paul, demanded use of the new Missouri River bridge once the Union Pacific completed it. Both roads vowed to erect their own bridge if denied, thus opening a controversy that would plague the Union Pacific for a decade.

The St. Paul built to Kansas City in retaliation for the Burlington line to the Twin Cities and was looking westward. The Northwestern had already snatched the Black Hills country from the Union Pacific, and some feared it might continue on to Ogden. As for the Lincoln line, Hughitt apologized to Adams for crossing his line but insisted he must smite the Burlington even if the Union Pacific suffered in the bargain. Competition in the Northwest was heating up, and in Colorado a new road, the Colorado Midland, triggered a fresh fight in the mining region. The Burlington pursued its extension program relentlessly. If Perkins had any doubts about his course, they were dispelled when he went to order rails and found the mills clogged with orders from other lines. The Atchison then stunned everyone by acquiring the strategic Gulf, Colorado & Santa Fe and announcing plans for a line to Chicago. A startled Perkins began eyeing St. Louis.

The rage for construction blasted all hopes of stabilizing rates. How could the long-cherished hope for a "permanent arrangement" be realized when the competitive map changed almost daily? "If everybody who can patch up a roundabout line of railroad communication between two points is justified in cutting the rates," Perkins snapped, the result could only be "great injury to *all* the roads." A feeble effort to renew part of the Tripartite agreement flopped miserably, and the Western Freight Association limped along under what amounted to a stay of execution. Progress was made toward curbing the passenger war, but the truce was tenuous at best.

"Let us have peace," cried Charles Whittier of Lee, Higginson, a close friend of Adams. But how to achieve it? Adams admitted to being "terribly perplexed by situation." There seemed no alternative response to these threats except an expansion program of his own. Because that was the last thing he wanted, he came slowly, grudgingly to accept its inevitability.

After much thought Adams outlined to Dodge in September 1886 what he deemed the best strategy. The true arena for development, he argued, was the unoccupied country west of Cheyenne and Denver. Adams wanted to run lines down the western side of the continental divide toward the coal and coke fields near Aspen; up the Malheur River in eastern Oregon; down the Little Salmon and Salmon rivers in Idaho, toward Lewiston on the Snake River. East of the mountains he would build only to protect existing business because the Union Pacific did not have a long enough haul to compete with roads running to Chicago. By contrast the far country would give the road a haul five hundred miles longer than the plains, which was already crowded with railroads anyway.

This letter was written only a week after Adams had paid off the last of the floating debt. The irony could not have been crueler or the signs more portentous of what lay in store for him. An expansion program would of course swell anew the very debt he had toiled so hard to eliminate. Two disparate areas of policy, the financial and the strategic, were headed on a collision course despite Adams's best intentions. The man on horseback found himself not leading the charge but dragged in directions he did not wish to go by forces he was helpless to counteract.

The Man on Horseback, his vice president, and two of his tormentors: Charles Francis Adams *(top left)*, Elisha Atkins *(top right)*, Henry Villard *(bottom left)*, and Samuel Callaway *(bottom right)*. *(Henry Villard courtesy of Fogg Museum)*

THE MASSACRE

From the day Adams first took office, the "labor question" occupied his mind. Twice in recent months the company had tried to impose wage cuts or force reductions only to back down at the threat of a strike. All along the line the men were organizing, growing confident of their ability to make their weight felt. The government directors believed the company's need to drive costs down to survive in the new competitive wars had forced workers to combine in self-defense. "There is no method now," they lamented, "by which alleged grievances of the employe [sic] may be amicably and intelligently discussed, nor the real exigencies of the company brought to his knowledge." Until some way was found, confrontation was inevitable.

Adams understood this dilemma but had no remedy. His impulse was to blame Clark for the ugly state of affairs that existed. On his first trip to Omaha in May 1884, Adams found the impression prevailing that the wage cut had been ordered from the East and repealed at Clark's insistent pleas. This was Clark's version of events, and it did not square with what Adams knew. Clark himself had strongly urged the reduction in March and assured the directors that the men would accept it. When the attempt backfired, Clark cried for help and was left to find his own way out of the hole he had dug. Doubtless that misrepresentation did much to fuel Adams's contempt for the "long bearded conductor of the monkey head."

In August 1884 another strike threat loomed just as the new president was grappling with the financial muddle and relations with the government. The walkout began in Denver and spread to Cheyenne in protest of layoffs that were supposed to have been nullified by the spring agreement. Adams moved gingerly and managed to convince the men that there had been a misunderstanding. Once the crisis passed, he issued a policy statement on labor relations. A personal investigation satisfied him that Union Pacific employees were better paid than men on other western roads. Everyone must realize that "reductions of wages and of working force are at this time being made throughout the country." Nevertheless, he would impose no cuts at least through the coming winter; if work in the shops went slack, the company would reduce hours rather than the work force. If layoffs became necessary, they would be made on the basis of seniority. Callaway was instructed to "personally cultivate the most open, honest and direct relations with the employes" and to hear any grievance brought to his attention.

In fact, the Union Pacific hired extra men for the Omaha shops that January, but the labor issue did not disappear. Railroad workers had been growing more restless since the outburst of strikes in 1877, and they were organized if not unified. In 1884 the New York *Tribune* published census figures showing that railroad workers earned far more than their counterparts in Europe, but few firemen or yardmen read the *Tribune* or accepted it as gospel. The same figures revealed that in Chicago engineers earned an average of twenty-seven dollars a week, firemen fifteen dollars, and trackmen and laborers about nine dollars. However, western railroads had unusual problems. Adams acknowledged that "the character of the country" through which the Union Pacific ran often left its workers "wholly dependent on the company for employment; they have nowhere else to turn."

Engineers, firemen, and conductors had all organized by 1873 and were joined a decade later by the Brotherhood of Railroad Trainmen. Known as the Four Brotherhoods, these unions were dubbed the "aristocrats of the labor world" and usually opposed strikes. By contrast, the Knights of Labor appealed to workers of every kind in any industry. Their success in organizing railroad workers not included in the brotherhoods left all the presidents nervous about a possible strike in 1885. They recognized that unionism had transformed the labor question into an industry problem rather than one unique to each road. In their zeal to suppress discontent they achieved a level of cooperation utterly lacking in their other affairs. Every manager hoped a strike would hit someone else; when the Northern Pacific was struck in March 1885, a relieved Adams observed that "they at least lead off." The danger then was that a strike launched against a neighboring line would spread to one's own men, perhaps even lead to a general strike.

To Adams and his peers the labor issue in 1885 was a storm waiting to happen. In May trouble arose in Denver but, to Adams's surprise, passed quickly. Three months later the Knights talked of extending a strike against the Wabash to the Union Pacific and managed to stir up the Omaha shops. For days the situation looked bleak, then brightened so suddenly that on August 29 Adams noted in his diary, "The labor trouble is now quiescent and promises to remain so for some months." A few days later his optimism would be shattered by a burst of gunfire.

* * *

For some time tensions had been growing at the coal mines, which, like so much else, had been largely neglected during the tired last years of Dillon's reign. In addition to the original mines in Wyoming, the company also had operations in Colorado along its lines there. The Knights were working hard to organize miners in both places. Wages in Colorado rose 15 to 20 percent above those in Wyoming, which angered the Wyoming miners almost as much as their old nemesis, the Chinese presence. In January 1885 the miners in Carbon, Wyoming, struck over wages and the importing of Chinese miners. The company agreed to arbitrate the pay question and the men returned without pressing the other matter. In both states, however, the men were still restless, and officers feared more trouble might erupt at any moment. The threat of a general strike worried Andrew Poppleton enough to explore with Judge Dillon a basis for invoking federal help in that event. "I am unable to discover any law of the United States," he confessed, "under which the federal military authority can be brought to bear in our favor."

Judge Dillon was also stumped on how to deal with strikes in a territory. Early in February the matter grew more urgent when some Colorado miners walked out and asked the men in Carbon and Rock Springs to join them. In his insecurity Callaway badly misread their action. He rejected their demands out of hand and saw behind the move a plot by "Clark's friends both in & out of the Service to do everything possible to down me." The schemers were "moving heaven & earth to raise a rumpus & think if they can bring on a strike before the March meeting, they will succeed in bringing Clark back into the management."

Two weeks later the Colorado miners returned to work without winning any concessions, but rumblings of a general strike persisted. During the spring the Knights were preoccupied by their strike against Gould's roads. Their unexpected success in that struggle brought a rush of fresh members to their ranks and emboldened local chapters to extend the conflict beyond the more cautious approach of the national leadership. For months the mines remained quiet, but old grievances still smoldered. The most volatile situation was at Rock Springs, where there were 331 Chinese and only 150 white miners. That summer eighty new Chinese were brought in to replace a like number who had left the mines. Although no new men were added, the superintendent of mines, D. O. Clark, admitted that "if a White miner came along and we did not give him employment, he naturally complained about the 'Heathen Chinese,' taking the bread from American citizens."

The situation was complicated by the fact that in 1875 the Union Pacific had arranged with two contractors named Beckwith and Quinn to provide all labor for the mines. It was a peculiar contract, neither a lease nor a delegation of power to work the mines, probably hedged to avoid a repetition of the Wardell fiasco. Gradually it evolved into a practical arrangement whereby Beckwith and Quinn procured Chinese labor and also served as paymaster for the white miners. In effect they became agents for the company and the contract a technicality which, in Isaac Bromley's opinion, left the company "fully responsible for the employment of the Chinese."

Over the years the white miners had accumulated a number of specific grievances. Most shared the common theme that superintendents gave the Chinese preferred treatment, probably as a way of keeping whites in the minority. However, no one was prepared for the events of September 2, and when the violence had ceased, no one would admit to what had started it. The immediate causes of the Rock Springs massacre remain as obscure as its origins are obvious. Bromley, who as Adams's assistant conducted a partisan but clear-eyed investigation at the scene, concluded that the explosion began without premeditation "except in the most vague and general way" and that the "bloodshed and pillage following the outbreak were partly the effects of passion and impulse; but to a considerable degree they were deliberate and cold-blooded."

On the morning of September 2 two white miners clashed with two Chinese in Mine No. 6. The Chinese were beaten up and carried off in a buckboard. According to mine inspector W. H. Brown, a general meeting was called for that afternoon "to see whether the white men or Chinamen were to run the camp." At 2 P.M. Brown saw men gathering on the track leading to Mine No. 3, some of them with guns. After their numbers increased, the men headed toward Chinatown. At half past three Brown heard gunfire. He dispatched a telegram to Callaway and ran outside in time to see Chinese fleeing across the tracks toward the hills. Smoke was rising from one of the houses, about half of which belonged to the company, the rest to the Chinese. Brown hurried toward the smoke and told the crowd they were going too far. They assured him that no company property would be burned, and Brown left to check on the engine house.

Suddenly he saw more Chinese racing toward a bridge over the creek with the mob in pursuit. Shots were fired into houses, including that of a laundryman who was later found dead. Some Chinese miners emerging from No. 1 were greeted with gunfire and fled in panic to the hills. The crowd did not give chase but gathered in front of O'Donnell's store, where they slowly quieted down. O'Donnell, who kept the store for Beckwith and Quinn, was handed a notice saying, "You must not bring any more Chinamen to this town—Leave as soon as possible." He was aboard the evening train. Brown thought the worst had passed, but more shots were fired and buildings set ablaze after dark. A hundred houses were burned; in the morning only one belonging to the Chinese remained standing. The Chinese huddled somewhere in the hills, shivering from the night cold. No one knew how many lay dead in the smoldering ruins and how many were in hiding.

The territorial governor, Francis E. Warren, a forceful, energetic figure, hurried to Rock Springs the next day with Superintendent Edward Dickinson. After inspecting the scene Warren asked President Cleveland for federal troops to restore order. That day fifteen bodies were pulled out of the debris; a coroner's jury attributed their deaths to "causes unknown." Callaway informed Adams that the armed men roaming the town would not allow any Chinese to return. "The local authorities are wholly powerless," he added, "and the City is in the hands of a mob." The men closed the mines and sent the local superintendent packing. At Grass Creek the Chinese were told to leave town in twenty minutes. Callaway feared the next blow would fall in Evanston.

Adams appealed to the Secretary of War for help and ordered Callaway to "yield nothing to the rioters." Troops arrived in Rock Springs on September 5 but with orders only to protect the mails. The sheriff at Evanston warned that the outrage would be repeated there unless help was sent; at Warren's and Callaway's urging two companies were dispatched there. The next day Beckwith was notified that he would be shot if he did not "clean out all Chinese at Evanston within three days." At Almy the men threatened to fire on the Chinese if they attempted to enter the mines. Warren took a tough stand. Since Wyoming had no territorial militia, he asked that the troops protect not only the mails but the Chinese, and that they help civil authorities find the perpetrators of the riot.

The white miners held a meeting and decided the Chinese "must go at once." They also issued a demand for higher wages. Callaway saw no choice but to close the mines at Almy. Warren was adamant that order could not be restored without the Army's help. After a frenzied exchange of telegrams Washington ordered the troops on September 8 to "protect the Chinese at all hazards." The survivors were rounded up and escorted back to Rock Springs, where they were housed in boxcars guarded by the troops. The body count continued to rise and ultimately reached twenty-eight; more may have gone undiscovered in the scorched ruins of the houses. Adams sent Bromley to investigate the affair and manage the press coverage. A veteran journalist with a shrewd eye and cool head, Bromley handled the assignment deftly. His account did much to shape Adams's view of events.

By the time Bromley reached Omaha on September 12, order had been restored at Rock Springs. The men were "talking very loud," Dickinson reported, but showed no inclination for more violence. After taking testimony from all sides, Bromley confirmed his early impression that "the outbreak was accidental in its origin, and not preconcerted." But he found something more that disturbed him. The crowd had given the Chinese an hour to leave town. Hurriedly they gathered up belongings to take with them, and that, Bromley surmised, "was not according to the purpose of the mob." Before half an hour had expired, the men suddenly opened fire on the Chinese and looted their houses before setting them ablaze. This was no maddened or drunken crowd but one bent on finishing its work "in a deliberate and orderly manner," and that work involved pillage no less than arson and murder.

Three of the government directors headed by General Alexander arrived shortly after Bromley to conduct their own investigation. Their findings coincided with his. Neither held out much hope of identifying or convicting those responsible for the slaughter. Bromley could find "no one in Rock Springs or elsewhere in the Territory who had the slightest expectation that the perpetrators of the outrages would be punished," and they were not. Despite strenuous efforts by Warren and the Union Pacific, no one was indicted; in the end the government compensated the Chinese for their property losses. Meanwhile, the confrontation over the mines remained tense as both sides maneuvered for position. The massacre proved but a prelude to the real battle of Rock Springs which, although far less publicized, lasted much longer than the spasm of brutality that triggered it.

In that larger struggle both the company and the Knights of Labor saw a chance to turn the event to their own advantage. The massacre inflamed anti-Chinese sentiment already raging in the West. Rosewater of the Omaha *Bee* echoed editors in Wyoming and elsewhere in deploring the bloodshed while insisting that "The Chinese Must Go." Bromley reminded Adams that "the universal sentiment along the line of the road is anti-Chinese" and that the company "cannot defy public opinion or undertake organized defence of Chinese labor." The verdict of public opinion had been rendered three years earlier by passage of the Exclusion Act, and the conviction was widespread in the West that the company used the Chinese to beat down the cost of white labor. The massacre gave the Knights an opportunity to use these sentiments as a wedge for organizing the miners.

On the day after the massacre Callaway wired Adams, "I have no doubt trouble at Rock Springs was instigated by Knights of Labor." Two days later he heard that an attempt would be made to "clean out all mormon miners because they will not join Knights of Labor." His suspicions were confirmed when an officer of the Knights' executive committee in Denver protested against "driving white miners away from Rock Springs." When Bromley arrived to hear testimony, he was soon joined by Thomas Neasham, a Union Pacific employee and Knights officer who acted as counsel for the committee. Neasham informed Bromley that "the greatest point is to prove wherein the white man has been imposed upon for the sake of giving the Chinese miners their places." Bromley came away convinced that Neasham was intent on "making a case against the Company which should justify the massacre."

With two mines closed, the road was fast running out of coal to operate its trains. So intense was feeling against the company that Callaway feared a general strike if he attempted to reopen the mines. The miners insisted on negotiating their grievances, which included barring all Chinese from resuming work; Callaway refused adamantly to negotiate on that basis. The company could not retreat from that position, he told Adams, "unless it is prepared to hand over its property to a lot of lawless ruffians." The normally placid Poppleton was even more shrill, crying that it was "part of a general plan to take the control of employees & their wages out of the hands of the Company." He urged Callaway to hold no talks and make no concessions "to the rioters or their friends until order is restored & the men driven away by violence are allowed to resume work."

Adams needed little convincing that the Knights were behind the affair, and he had no intention of yielding to the union. Since the coal business was in need of reorganization anyway, he suggested that Callaway close the mines and arrange to get coal elsewhere. Callaway doubted enough coal could be found to feed the road and the large smelters dependent on it. He advised making every effort to open the mines; if a general strike broke out, the mines could be closed and the "odium will then rest with the strikers." Adams left the decision with Callaway but instructed him to stand firm, get all demands in writing, and have "a shrewd lawyer with political instincts . . . at your elbow." Everything depended on "so shaping demands and answers that those making an issue with us will be clearly in the wrong."

The stalemate was fast pushing Adams toward a harder line. For some time the company had wanted to experiment with cutting machines to reduce their work force at the mines; Adams wondered if the shutdown did not offer the ideal circumstances to install them. The cagey Dr. Miller handled the labor issue gingerly in his Omaha *Herald* but insisted privately that there was "nothing to arbitrate. These savages put things beyond debate; the issue must be met, and the sooner the better." On the eighteenth Callaway learned that the Knights' Denver committee had issued orders for all miners and carpenters to stop work. That move settled it for Adams. "Dismiss every man who stops work on order from Denver," he wired Callaway. "In case of a general strike at any mine close the mine and do not open it until you get orders from here." The company was ready to sustain the fight. "I shall be greatly disappointed," he said pointedly, "unless issue is made now and matter is brought to a head. In my opinion it is useless to go on as we have been doing for the past six months. An explosion will clear the air."

Adams acted on his own initiative, believing that his directors were "wholly ignorant of the situation." Callaway notified the miners that the mines would reopen on Monday the twenty-first. Those who had not been dismissed for taking part in the riot could have their jobs, but anyone who did not show up for work would be paid off and never rehired by the company. The next day someone burned the snowsheds at Archer. Word went out for all Knight lodges to stand ready for a general strike. Governor Warren exhorted Adams to "under no circumstances recede in the slightest degree from the stand taken that Chinese shall work and criminals shall not. I believe that law and order in the territory as well as discipline of rates are at stake." All hope of catching or punishing those guilty of the massacre had faded. General Alexander McCook, who was in Rock Springs, informed his superiors heatedly that any attempt to hold a trial "will prove a burlesque and farce." He wanted martial law declared and the murderers tried by military commission.

On Monday morning the Chinese, under army protection, went back into the mines while all the white miners and most of the white laborers stayed out. Callaway offered the strikers free transportation to Omaha and ordered some cutting machines. Bishop Sharp promised to furnish replacements, but the Mormons were harvesting and could not easily spare the manpower. Neasham and the executive committee of the Knights reiterated their demand that the Chinese be removed along with Beckwith, Quinn, and D. O. Clark. The company would investigate any charges brought, Callaway replied, but refused to "ostracise any one class of its employes at the dictation of another." Privately he denounced Neasham as a "pestilential demagogue" and suspected that the call for a general strike had broken down.

Governor Warren again urged him to fight "to the bitter end and win fully without compromise . . . *everything* is propitious for a thorough shaking up and purging out of objectionable characters." From Boston Adams reaffirmed that "the most unyielding firmness is expected from you. No concessions of any description are to be made except on authority from this office. We believe that . . . no equally good opportunity will present itself." The company's interest, he emphasized, was to "have Rock Springs worked entirely by Chinese and machinery. The mines worked by white labor should, in my judgment, be closed."

From this position there could be no retreat. The Army assured Callaway that it would protect the Chinese. Few white miners left Rock Springs, however, and most of the new men hired were frightened off within a day or so. Neasham made an impassioned speech at Omaha, and a supply of blasting powder was stolen at Ogden. On October 1 the miners at Carbon walked out on demands similar to those at Rock Springs. Callaway promptly closed the mines and braced for the explosion. None came. There were some beatings and sporadic acts of violence but no general strike. A petition was circulated asking the company to discharge all Chinese. Neasham tried to rouse the men, with little effect; some Union Pacific employees withdrew from the union. Having earlier proposed that Neasham be fired, Callaway now urged Adams not to dismiss him, because "he is just aching for an opportunity to poise [sic] as a martyr." Callaway also concluded to make Rock Springs a Chinese and Evanston a white mine when the strike ended.

Late in October the Knights' national leader, Terence V. Powderly, tried to intervene with Adams. It proved a futile gesture. On November 11 the Carbon miners trudged back to work with no concessions; the others followed within days. Callaway promptly ordered Clark to be "more than ordinarily careful in seeing that they are fairly dealt with in every respect. . . . I would have the Co. err on the side of liberality and demonstrate to the men that we intend to be just and fair." With the strike broken, the mines resumed work with a changed labor force. By the end of November the number of miners at Carbon had dwindled from 295 to 225, while at Rock Springs there were 343 Chinese and only 81 whites. A year later Clark reported that some of the men who had refused to go back to work had been rehired, but none of the men blacklisted for participating in the riot had been taken back. Although the revolt faded, some troops remained at Rock Springs for thirteen years.

The outcome did not satisfy Adams, who was sorely disappointed that the explosion he desired so ardently had not occurred. "We never will have such another opportunity," he lamented to Callaway. "If the Knights of Labor could have been compelled to stand before the country with their organization in direct alliance with murderers, desperadoes and robbers, it would have been worth to us almost anything." With the air of a schoolmaster he explained his reasoning to Callaway:

> Anything which brings about a remedy has got to be radical in its character. It is useless to talk of quelling these men, or of dismissing them. It can not be done. They constitute almost the entire region in which our road is operated. They are at present thoroughly demoralized. We have got to meet them squarely and educate them. . . . A condition of paralysis cannot continue long and when the explosion has taken place I am strongly inclined to believe that the better portion of our employes will gradually assert themselves over the worst portion. Under proper rules and regulations the weeding out process might then be entered upon. We can get rid of the drunken, the immoral and the dishonest.

Here as in the rate wars Adams revealed again his itch for achieving radical change through quick, forceful, even violent means. Unlike other presidents he was not bound by the traditions and shibboleths that made them prisoners of past policies. But neither did he possess the ability to cut through the inertia of this most conservative of industries. He did not get his explosion or clear the debris of custom that blocked his path to reform and enlightened policy. The theorist found reality unyielding and so turned grudgingly to slower paths of change in dealing with labor. Rock Springs passed into history as a shocking and disgraceful massacre, which it was, but not as the first major confrontation on the Union Pacific between management and unionism, which it also was. The first shots had been fired in a long and bitter battle that would ultimately dwarf even the tragedy of the Chinese.

* * *

As the fight petered out in the mines it shifted to the railroad, where the Knights were anxious to organize every class of worker, even clerks, and win an eight-hour day for all of them. During the fall of 1885 the company tried the eight-hour day in the shops but returned to nine hours in late October.

The *Bee* quoted one official as saying, "The eight hour system is played out so far as our experience with it is concerned." In March 1886 the pay of trackmen was cut, sparking another protest from the Knights. With wages falling and discontent rising, every road in the West braced for a confrontation with the Knights, whose victory in the Wabash strike a year earlier had filled them with confidence. No one knew where the first blow would strike, not even the Knights as it turned out. In March the union's leadership found itself dragged unexpectedly by one of its locals into an ill-conceived strike against the Gould roads in the Southwest.

When the Knights on the Union Pacific talked of boycotting Missouri Pacific trains, Adams ordered Callaway to take "an entirely firm stand." The boycott threat passed, but trouble arose at Kansas City, where the switchmen demanded Chicago rates and schedules. As a connecting point between the Union Pacific and the Missouri Pacific, Kansas City might easily become a tinderbox if, as Adams and others feared, the clash escalated to a general strike. Dodge for one advised Adams that "I do not believe that the discharge of half our employes would hurt our road." The men walked out, halted some trains, then returned and struck an agreement with Callaway. A month later they went out again and were soon followed by the trainmen and the brakemen on the Wyoming division. Although the conductors stood by the company and Neasham tried ordering the men back to work, the strike spread to the Utah Northern and turned ugly.

At Laramie the men seized the yard and stopped all trains, pulling pins, killing engines, abducting conductors who tried to move the trains. Dickinson hurried to the scene, saw that the deputy sheriffs were helpless to control the mob, and waited for the arrival of fifty Pinkertons. "Confronted with large number [of] six footers with Winchester rifles," Callaway reported gleefully, "they gracefully retired." Dickinson posted five armed men at the Dale Creek Bridge with orders to kill anyone who tried to tamper with it. Despite a huge crowd milling about the yard, Dickinson tried again to start trains. Two brakemen were caught pulling pins. Dickinson chased another through the yard ("for awhile it looked like old times," he laughed later) and had him arrested only to have the charge dismissed by a court sympathetic to the strikers. "You have no idea of the way things are conducted in Wyoming," he reported, "and particularly in Laramie City." The crowd, including some deputies, blocked attempts to seize other brakemen tampering with air hoses.

The next day, with a full contingent of armed guards, Dickinson got the trains moving. "We quit," cried the brakemen. "We know when we've had enough." The Wyoming strike was over, "a complete fizzle," Dickinson sneered, "petered out, collapsed without a struggle. The sickest lot of strikers I ever saw." Neasham admitted the brakemen had been in the wrong and pleaded for leniency, but thirty were discharged. The Knights were further embarrassed when some of the men in Denver ran a member of the executive committee out of town for attempting sodomy. Elsewhere the men were filing back to work. At Butte, where "the hardest people to be found anywhere are congregated," cars had been derailed, air hoses cut, and valves smashed before order was restored. The United States marshal in Idaho refused to deputize the Pinkertons sent to Eagle Rock, and several of them were later arrested by local authorities for impersonating federal officers. Although the strike ended early in May, a controversy with local businessmen raged for months when Adams threatened to remove company facilities from Laramie and Eagle Rock.

The Wyoming and the Idaho divisions had always been the toughest on the road and would remain so for decades. The country was rough, living conditions harsh, and the men a challenge for any superintendent to control. Adams tried to understand their situation as best he could and, like a good Brahmin reformer, searched for ways to improve their lot. His approach to labor policy was to undercut the appeal of unionism by treating the men well and furnishing means to better themselves. Any attention would have been an improvement over past neglect. In Omaha the men had early formed a band and a baseball team, both of which were popular with the townspeople. Dillon took a dim view of anything that cut into company time, however, and was "outraged that such an organization should have been tolerated." During the crisis of 1884 he decreed that "under no circumstances should the clerks be allowed to play base ball this year during office hours." When the auditor in charge of the team resigned at the season's end, the *Bee* charged that he had been forced to quit.

The change in management saved the baseball team, but Adams had more uplifting ideas in mind. Even before the labor crisis had cooled he took up the project of creating libraries along the line. Callaway suggested putting one at each large terminal point. The company would erect and maintain the buildings and provide some books; the men would provide more volumes through a small subscription. Each library would be managed by the master mechanic and a committee selected by the men. Stocking the libraries became a pleasant hobby for some of the officers. In 1887 some Omaha employees formed the Union Pacific Railway Club and Library Association, which heard papers and debated current issues. In one meeting the members enjoyed a presentation on the railroads of Peru before discussing the question of whether manual training should be introduced into grade schools.

In the area of reading matter, the Knights within the company got the jump on Adams by starting in February 1886 the *Union Pacific Employes' Magazine*. "Now that the growth of our organization is so rapid," proclaimed the first issue, "it is time to prove to our brothers that the springs of their improvement are to be found in our Organization." Adams and the union leaders both knew that the worst enemies of men on the line were boredom and idleness, which drove many to bars, whorehouses, and gambling joints. Adams was no less adamant than Dillon about the use of liquor by employees, who obtained it easily from the bars of the hotels run by the company for its passengers. In 1889 Adams ordered the hotel bars closed and other arrangements made to provide liquor for the public.

In the West the change hit home at once. One officer reported happily that "on the last pay day there was not a drunken employe at Green River on the Wyoming division, and so far as can be ascertained, not a single case of drunkenness among our employes on the Idaho division." The company also worked with the YMCA to provide facilities for the men on the Wyoming and the Idaho divisions. At Rawlins, where more than half the town's population of 2,300 were railroad people (450 of them Union Pacific employees), the Y competed with the saloons and gambling houses by opening a reading room with a library of four hundred volumes, a game room, and two baths. Similar facilities were installed at Ogden and Pocatello as well. Although the men paid a small membership fee, most of the expense was picked up by the company. Adams considered it a good investment; so did the men who frequented them. It was, declared a fireman, "one place (outside a saloon) where a railroad man was welcome." A brakeman called the rooms "a blessing in many ways. They keep men from saloons and places of vice."

Apart from making the men more comfortable and providing constructive ways to use leisure time, the company had to deal with bread-and-butter issues such as medical expenses and pensions. No organized system existed to handle these matters. The federal government did not enter these fields until well into the twentieth century, the last major industrial nation to do so. Every company treated them in its own way, with no obligation to do anything at all. In September 1886, for example, the Knights called Adams's attention to the case of an employee with an incurable disease. Finding his record to be "regular," Adams had the superintendent send the man to Los Angeles and "provide for his needs in such manner as commends itself to your discretion."

Medical attention for employees was an issue railroads could not evade, given the dangers inherent in the work and the high rate of injury among certain classes of workers such as brakemen. As early as 1871 the officers and men of the Kansas Pacific in Colorado and western Kansas created their own hospital fund by contributing fifty cents a month. Plans were made to build a small hospital near Denver, but the project was shelved. The Union Pacific, like other roads, left medical care to the individual. Sick or injured men used local physicians at their own expense or did without. After the merger the Union Pacific was impressed by the existing fund and in January 1882 extended it to cover the entire system. The company used part of this fund to open a hospital in Denver and employ a chief surgeon. Other doctors were hired at strategic points to handle cases as company physician for a given territory.

This medical plan worked so well that in January 1884 Clark expanded it to all departments and lowered the assessment to forty cents a month. Patients would be treated only at company hospitals, which were "open at all times for disabled employes of the Union Pacific Railway, whether from sickness or injury, free of expense to themselves, other than the monthly assessment." The fund also covered temporary treatment by another doctor if a company surgeon was not available. Any hospital stay beyond ninety days had to be approved by the chief surgeon or general manager. The chief surgeon also had to authorize the use of drugs, nurses, and board accounts. In case of death the fund allowed a small sum for funeral expenses. The hospital would not keep patients with contagious diseases, but the fund paid for treatment elsewhere. Workers "sick from Venereal disease, the results of intemperance, or other vicious habits" were not entitled to benefits, and any employee known to be infected with a social or chronic disease likely to "render him a burden to the Fund to an extent unjust to others," could be dropped from the assessment rolls on advice of the chief surgeon.

Except for this moralistic restriction, the hospital fund provided remarkable coverage in an age when medical plans and fringe benefits were unknown. Apparently the plan was borrowed from the Missouri Pacific, which had operated a hospital under the assessment system since 1879. It was a practical solution to a difficult problem, yet some men objected to the assessment and resented having to be treated at a hospital on terms dictated entirely by the chief surgeon. Shortly after Adams took command, the chief surgeon resigned because the board would not raise his salary of four thousand dollars. On advice from the Harvard Medical School Adams appointed a young Vienna-born surgeon, Dr. Oscar J. Pfeiffer, and moved his office to the Union Depot in Denver. Apart from the company hospital there, Pfeiffer established temporary hospitals at Omaha, Ogden, Kansas City, Laramie, St. Joseph, and later Portland and Fort Worth.

Curiously, the plan won far more support from the company than from the men it served. The fund was expected to be self-sustaining, but Callaway reported so many protests over the assessment that Adams was induced in 1884 to lower the amount to twenty-five cents a month. Some workers, perhaps goaded by the Knights, argued that the company should pay part of surgeons' salaries because they were "necessary for the company's interest as well as those of the employes." As a result, the fund ran a deficit of $47,326 between 1884 and 1888, and Callaway's successor, Thomas J. Potter, advised Adams to "go out of the hospital business." Potter had come over from the Burlington, which had tried a similar plan and given it up as "a bad job." He objected to forcing men to pay even a small assessment and proposed having instead one medical officer in Omaha who would pass on all charges for services and medicines by outside doctors and fix a fee schedule. Adams agreed that the company hospitals now stood "in the way of development of private and public hospitals." He authorized a gradual withdrawal from the business, then reversed himself. Instead the company in 1889 restored the forty-cent rate, which was still a dime below that on most other western roads.

The primitive state of medicine in the 1880s was matched by the primitive attitude of many patients. Pfeiffer complained regularly of the inadequacies at Denver, but his laments paled before those of the division surgeon at Ogden. Local surgeons resented the company physicians everywhere, but Dr. G. W. Perkins found that in Ogden "Mormon boycotting extends to the Profession and it is a part of the creed never to pay a Gentile if they can help it." Perkins's hospital was a "wretchedly constructed building," overcrowded, hot in the summer, ill-heated in the winter, and impossible to keep clean. The men spat tobacco juice everywhere but in the spittoons and refused to stop, braying that "we paid our dues and can do what we please." They heaped curses and abuse on the hapless male nurses, whom they held in utter contempt. Female nurses might gain more respect, Perkins noted wistfully, but "no woman would remain a week in the present accommodations." Any patient above the rank of section hand demanded special treatment and threatened letters to Omaha if it was not forthcoming. And, of course, nobody liked the food.

By 1892 the company had built a new hospital to relieve the congestion in Ogden. The high-minded Pfeiffer struggled with his position until 1891, when he resigned and was succeeded by Dr. W. J. Galbraith, who found the medical department "very loosely managed and disorganized." Although Galbraith reduced the debt and made some improvements, the fund continued to operate at a deficit. For all the complaints, however, it performed an invaluable service for the company and its employees. During 1890 and 1891 alone it treated more than forty thousand sick and injured workers.

No comparable progress was achieved in devising a pension plan despite Adams's keen interest in the idea. Here Adams was not merely a theorist but a visionary far ahead of his time. In his usual thoughtful way he responded to the labor strife of 1885–86 not with piecemeal solutions but with a bold, comprehensive plan to prevent strikes altogether. Created during the summer of 1886, it was unlike anything produced by a railroad officer. The company then employed some fifteen thousand men, more than any American army put in the field before the Civil War. About fourteen thousand of these were in the operating departments, of which 20 percent moved trains, 30 percent worked in shops or took care of equipment, and the rest were flagmen, switchmen, section men, station agents, and the like. All labor conflicts involved these men. The public scarcely noticed if the clerks struck, but the operating men could shut down the road and paralyze the communities it served. The key to labor harmony, therefore, was to bring this vital body of workers into harmony with management.

Everyone knew the railroads had mushroomed into the nation's leading industry, but Adams was struck by how little adjustment the roads had made to their changed position. The larger they grew, the more specialized they became. Of necessity the organization divided into departments, each with its own officers, yet companies persisted in treating their huge work forces in the old manner of individuals to be hired or fired at will. "No rationally organized railroad service—that is, no service in which the employer and employed occupy definite relations toward each other, . . . no such service exists," Adams observed. The dawn of organizational management had not yet illuminated labor relations. Some plan was needed to end the recurring cycle of strikes that plunged railroads and large parts of the country into chaos. Adams offered one of breathtaking scope.

All railroads, he noted, had two classes of employees, permanent and temporary. On the Union Pacific, for example, the operating force shrank to about twelve thousand during the winter months when the field work dwindled. As a first step companies could recognize this distinction by treating the two classes differently. Before being accepted as a permanent employee, every man might serve a sort of apprenticeship as a temporary worker, during which time he would be on probation. Once promoted to permanent employee, he would gain certain privileges. He could not be dismissed except for good cause, which would require the creation of a tribunal to hear and decide such cases impartially. Both labor and management had always regarded any such body with suspicion. Workers looked to their unions to protect them; officers protested that they could not maintain discipline without the right to dismiss men arbitrarily. The chief effect of these attitudes, Adams stressed, was to "divide the railroad service into hostile camps."

Permanent employees should also have seniority rights, be assured of regular increases in pay for satisfactory service, and be entitled to certain benefits. Adams proposed the creation of a fund on every road to provide for hospital service, retirement pensions, illness or disablement pensions, and accident or death insurance. The money would be "contributed partly by the company and partly by the voluntary action" of permanent employees only. The proceeds of such a fund would assure the social welfare of every employee and bind his loyalty to the company. If that were not enough, Adams suggested that the company also fund schools to educate the children of employees in railroad service. "From those thus educated," he asserted, "the higher positions in the company would thereafter be filled." This would actually save the company money in the long run.

None of it would work, Adams believed, unless the employees were "allowed a voice in its management." No road had faced squarely the question of how to accomplish this, because it ran against the grain of all past practice. It would be impossible, he predicted, "to establish perfectly good faith and the highest morale in the service of the companies until the problem of giving this voice to employees, and giving it effectively, is solved. It can be solved in but one way: that is, by representation. To solve it may mean industrial peace." In true New England fashion he thought the town meeting might serve as a useful model. However it was done, the object was to bring management and labor "into direct and immediate contact through a representative system." Problems would be tackled through cooperation rather than the conflict of hostile camps.

Adams circulated this imaginative paper among his officers, the "practical" railroad men he would later come to despise as a body. Those worthies shrank in horror from his heresies and were quick to offer all sorts of reasons why it could not be done. The general superintendent was certain its effect would be "directly opposite to that intended" and was adamant that "no tribunal or official should be permitted to interfere in questions arising between the superintendent and his subordinates." A district superintendent agreed it would "lead to demoralization, and destroy the entire discipline of our service." Another declared that "a majority of these men are working for their pay, and . . . take no special interest in the company's welfare, except in so far as it assures them support and good wages." Most would "become careless if they understood that the head of the department in which they are working did not have full power to dismiss them for neglect of duty, or other good and sufficient cause."

All of them viewed shared power as a threat to their own position, of which they were as reluctant to surrender an inch as most officers were to pay a dime toward social welfare programs. The traditionalists had their way. Adams glumly abandoned the notion and stuffed his paper into a drawer. In 1889, stirred by the disastrous Burlington strike a year earlier, he pulled it out and had it published. Nothing had changed in that time. Decades later his entire program would be enacted, but for now he remained a lone visionary among men comfortable with the belief that tomorrow must always be more of the same.

* * *

In practice Adams did what he could to ameliorate relations with labor or at least budge his officers from their dour inflexibility. "Nothing is gained in this life," he scolded General Superintendent S. T. Smith, "by being pig headed over trifles." Despite the legacy of Rock Springs, the union appealed regularly to him for arbitration of grievances and were gratified by his cooperation. When the company moved its shops from Eagle Rock to Pocatello, the union protested that men who had bought homes in Eagle Rock would suffer losses. Adams ordered an investigation and, satisfied that the value of the homes depended on the shops being located there, agreed to compensate the men for their loss. The union praised his "spirit of fairness and good will" as "unprecedented in the history of American railroading."

But small victories made little impression on the course of the war. When the strike against the Burlington erupted in February 1888, the Union Pacific again found itself on the edge of a tempest. The source this time was not the Knights but one of the conservative brotherhoods, the engineers. As other unions supported the action, the threat of a boycott against connecting roads grew. Even before the strike there were rumbles of discontent in Denver, the company's most crowded and overworked yard. The Knights warned that another reduction of pay was imminent and urged the men to unite. Dodge barked anew that the company must stand fast and yield nothing. A familiar pattern was unfolding, and it caught Adams at the worst possible time. He was busy with the fight in Washington, and his general manager was too desperately ill even to read correspondence.

The brotherhood forced the issue by asking Union Pacific engineers to refuse any business from the Burlington. Kimball tried to persuade the men that the order violated national law. A harried Adams asked Dodge to act as advisor to Kimball, but Kimball wanted no part of Dodge's hard line. "We should hold the good will of old engineers," he told Adams, "but this cant be done by leading off in a contest with them as General Dodge suggests." The general attorney in Omaha, John M. Thurston, found the men he interviewed anxious not to harm the company but bound to obey the dictates of their leadership in the belief that the union's existence was at stake. Thurston came away amazed and disgusted by "the blind character of their allegiance to their order."

Late in March the brotherhood recalled their boycott order on Burlington freight and the immediate crisis passed, but the strike straggled along for the rest of the year. The situation in Denver remained volatile, and reports from detectives who infiltrated the Knights confirmed that Neasham was using the Burlington strike as a lever to revive his own order. "I only regret we have not cleaned out the Denver gang long ago on general principles," growled the Colorado superintendent, J. K. Choate. "We will never have our men contented until we do." Kimball agreed with this sentiment but thought *"now* is not the time to attempt it. It must be accomplished gradually and for reasons which conceal the Company's real purpose. If closely watched, such men will generally furnish ample excuse for lifting their scalps."

In the heat of battle even Adams came grudgingly to the view that "now is the time to settle the strike question," but he could not have been pleased at the outcome. Hostility between the camps had not diminished, and the road to an enlightened policy seemed more distant than ever. The sticky labor question would go its way without the benefit of Adams's wisdom. This experience, like so many others, reinforced his image as a missionary among the most ungrateful of savages and isolated him still more from those with whom he must deal. He was never a man who cared for a future that promised more of the same, and labor relations promised exactly that.

25

THE SERVICE

War and expansion placed enormous demands on every western railroad. Like a nation mobilizing for war, the Union Pacific harnessed its resources to fight as efficiently and effectively as possible. The first imperative of the new competitive order was that every road do more for less, and none dared shirk that challenge. It was not an easy task. The problems were immense, the solutions expensive. Old attitudes and technologies had to be revised, a difficult adjustment for this most conservative of industries. Money had to be raised and defects of organization corrected. The work of integrating the system was both physical and psychological, financial and organizational.

Important steps toward integration at the national level had already occurred by the mid-1880s. All railroads adopted standard time in 1883 and standard gauge three years later. A uniform gauge facilitated the interchange of cars and pushed roads toward standardizing their motive power and rolling stock, which in turn improved efficiency in the shops. The development of block signals and interlocking signal systems allowed trains to travel more safely at higher speeds. Automatic couplers and air brakes drastically reduced not only delays but the accident rate among brakemen. By 1890 steel rail had replaced iron on about 80 percent of the nation's mileage. Rails also increased in weight and length to handle the strain of swelling traffic. Technical innovations produced new breeds of locomotives capable of hauling heavier and longer trains. The cars themselves grew steadily larger and more specialized to handle diverse loads in immense quantities.

In every department the Union Pacific suffered from a familiar handicap: it competed with roads that were newer and therefore possessed more modern facilities. To bring the road up to standard required more money than Adams could possibly raise, but he determined to make a vigorous start. Unfamiliar with technical matters himself and loath to rely on the judgment of officers he had inherited, Adams adopted the practice of hiring experts to study problem areas and make recommendations. In the fall of 1885 Charles Blackwell, an experienced engineer, investigated the mechanical department and shocked management with a wholesale indictment of its facilities and practices.

The Union Pacific shops, Blackwell concluded, lacked adequate facilities, machinery, and tools, had no standards, and were incompetently managed. Stocking parts for seventy-four different designs of locomotives meant costly and wasteful inventories. Some of the power was exhausted; the rest was driven so hard that neither running nor general repairs were made on schedule. Shop machinery was obsolete, and too much work was done by hand that could be better done by machine. Water quality was so poor on some sections that fireboxes and tubes were corroded and clogged with scale. Coal facilities for engine service were primitive and expensive to operate. Small wonder that the cost figures for shop work on the Union Pacific far exceeded that of other western roads.

Blackwell suggested concentrating general repairs at a few well-equipped points and confining running repairs to outlying terminals. Standard designs and practices should be adopted, water and coal facilities improved, machinery upgraded, and the management overhauled. Superintendent I. H. Congdon had served the company well since construction days and had devised both a new type of smokestack and an improved brake shoe; Adams retired him with a testimonial and a bonus of $2,500 before replacing him with Clem Hackney. The shops in Eagle Rock and Shoshone were moved to Pocatello, and in 1889 work started on new shops in Cheyenne. That same year electric lights were installed in the Omaha shops. Adams hoped to make improvements on a large scale but could not reconcile his desire to spend with his constant exhortations to reduce expenses. The old dilemma of whether economy was best served by spending or cutting still puzzled railroad officers. In hard times, when earnings sagged, events settled the issue for them, but the longer improvements were delayed, the harder it was to catch up again.

Scars of neglect from the frantic cutbacks of 1884 still marred the road. The Idaho division, which had endured years of undermaintenance, suffered drastic reductions just as business increased sharply from the opening of the Anaconda mine and the dizzying growth of the Butte mining region. The result was a nightmare to conscientious officers. Trains and crews alike were run mercilessly until they dropped. Tired men grew indifferent to safety, and the supply of oil allotted crews was cut so severely that they lacked enough for proper signals. Trainmen flocked to a road where, Robert Blickensderfer noted, "they could steal with impunity. Freight cars were pilfered at the rate of from $500 to $2000 worth of freight per month, and cash fares taken as a rule."

The track was worn to the point of danger, and so was the equipment. Callaway inspected the line and admitted that the locomotives "could barely pull themselves," and that "the whole thing seemed to be dropping to pieces." Wrecks and derailments occurred with depressing regularity. Maintenance was a farce with inadequate material and too few men. Engines were never wiped and so went uninspected; some ran without ash pans, exposing bridges to the threat of fire. The list of defects was appalling and compounded by the use of green firemen. The division was, Blickensderfer moaned, "short of power, cars, shops, engine houses, side tracks, coal platforms, water tanks, and everything else necessary to run a railroad with."

The service suffered dearly from this wretched state of affairs. On the Oregon Short Line trains had to move so slowly—eighteen miles an hour at most—that shippers complained bitterly. The lack of side track and equipment in Idaho and the mining region bottlenecked traffic to a point that kept the mining and railroad people constantly at each other's throats. During heavy storms the superintendent had to concentrate all his power on snowplows, which left freight sitting idle for days. No one could have anticipated the spectacular growth of the mining region, but local officers warned repeatedly that the division was crashing into ruin. Unfortunately, the company had plunged into a financial crisis and could not respond even though the Idaho division fetched handsome earnings.

Adams moved to correct the worst abuses but simply lacked the money to accomplish everything at once. He had to wait until 1887 to begin the crucial work of widening the Utah Northern's gauge to standard. Despite a heavy flow of traffic, the division remained the most substandard on the line, always short of power and cars, lacking in shops, facilities, and maintenance. The demands of the system simply overwhelmed the resources available to meet them. Competition forced the company to divert funds to construction that were badly needed for upkeep and equipment. The addition of new mileage to the system aggravated an already serious problem.

To this dilemma Adams could find no answer, although at first he had high hopes. In 1885 he instructed Callaway to bring two sections, one in Nebraska and the other in Kansas, up to "the highest standard of railroad work." Both were to be ballasted, fenced, ditched, equipped with sixty-five-pound rail, supplied with proper signal switches, and screened with trees or hedges. All station buildings or eating houses were to be repaired, painted, and landscaped tastefully. The two sections would then serve as models for section work on the rest of the line. "Standards of everything must first be prepared," he added, and the work must be done "without undue cost." How this could be done cheaply, Adams did not elaborate. Apparently Callaway did not solve that riddle or was preoccupied by more immediate problems, for when Adams inspected the road a year later he found nothing had been done. This disappointment was one of many that soured him toward Callaway.

The main line west of Omaha had no ballast. Since broken stone cost the company half again as much as coal, Adams thought it necessary only along the first hundred miles west of the river and "wherever the track is low and wet with a clay soil." In those places heavier equipment wore down the steel and roadbed at an alarming rate. With proper ballast, Adams argued, the road could be maintained "for a fractional proportion of what it now costs." Despite the steep cost, an estimated $338,000 for ninety-six miles west of Omaha, Adams launched a gradual program of ballasting in 1889. Fencing posed a similar problem. During the years 1884–87 the company paid $111,215 for stock killed along the line, and the figure was rising steadily. Wire fencing cost about $375 a mile, which made it profitable to fence the most exposed sections where cattle grazed. Adams got the work underway, but here too needs outran resources. In 1891 claims for stock killed reached $221,000, which prompted the board to authorize the expenditure of $148,000 for more fencing.

Large quantities of rails and ties were needed to renew the line against the wear of nature and the weight of heavier traffic. On the main line the early thirty- and forty-pound rail was gradually replaced by sixty-pound steel after 1881. Adams purchased some seventy-five pound rail in 1888 but four years later, after he left the presidency, the standard weight for the road was set at seventy pounds. Along with a standing contract in 1889 to buy two hundred fifty thousand or more ties for five years, Adams also made special purchases. That same year he bought six hundred thousand ties for the Kansas division and another half million for the Utah & Northern. The price of ties varied widely, depending on the wood and available supply. In 1890, for example, the company bought almost a million oak ties for 53⅓ cents each and a like number of pine ties at prices ranging from thirty-four to forty-two cents.

The demand for more and larger rolling stock was insatiable. As the traffic grew more diverse, so did the cars hauling it. By the late 1880s the Union Pacific employed box cars, flat cars, stock cars, coal cars, fruit cars (fitted with platforms, hooks, and swivel trucks), refrigerator cars, dump cars, and even furniture cars. For passenger traffic there were chair cars, diners, Pullman sleepers, and emigrant sleepers along with baggage, express, and mail cars. The explosion of traffic in the 1880s utterly swamped the company's ability to supply cars. Expansion aggravated the problem by forcing the same fleet of equipment to serve a growing mileage; Adams estimated that in 1887 alone the road needed 75 new locomotives, 20 passenger cars, and 1,500 freight cars just to service new branch lines. That November the general manager warned that he must have at least 50 engines and 2,635 cars for the coming year "or else we will be the loser." Five months later an officer in Oregon pleaded that his supply of box cars was "entirely inadequate to take care of the business of the road."

Faced with this crisis, the board in 1888 resorted to an issue of equipment trust bonds to buy 50 locomotives and 1,735 cars of various types. On his inspection tour that summer, however, Adams saw that even this large addition was not enough and ordered another 50 locomotives and 2,125 cars. The total cost exceeded $3.1 million (not including 100 dump cars for the Montana Union), and still the company strained to cope with its swelling traffic. A shortage of power posed the most serious threat. "Should we have a severe winter," Edward Dickinson warned, "our power will be reduced from 20 to 50% in very short time on our mountain districts." The reason, explained another officer, was that "considerable of the power is in bad condition and engines cannot pull full trains, and give out on the road, making it necessary to send other engines to relieve them."

Adams recognized that the Union Pacific was the least innovative of western roads. The company approached any change with conservatism if not outright suspicion and did not lead rival lines so much as react to their moves. It was the last to adopt standard time in Omaha and one of the slowest to convert wholesale to air brakes. George Westinghouse devised his triple-valve system in 1872 but not until January 1883 did Dillon consider an offer from Westinghouse, and only then after learning that Huntington had contracted to put the brake on all his freight cars. Since the brakes cost forty dollars per car, Dillon suggested buying them gradually to spread the outlay. However, Clark advised against installing the brakes and the matter was dropped until Adams took charge.

Grasping their value at once, Adams arranged in February 1885 to equip the entire rolling stock at a rate of fifteen sets a day. When the triple valve proved inadequate for heavy freight trains, the Burlington gave Westinghouse a chance to run exhaustive tests on West Burlington hill for two summers. The result was a radically improved brake which Westinghouse offered to his customers for forty-five dollars a car, claiming that it would work with "equipment you already have, and the old brakes will in a measure be improved in their action when coupled with it." The Burlington's historian asserts that the improvement "revolutionized train operation," but Charles S. Mellen, then general purchasing agent of the Union Pacific, spurned the new brake, arguing among other things that the original version "has worked very satisfactorily, and it is Westinghouse and not the Rail Road that is worrying about the adoption of the improved." In 1890 another firm muddled the issue by offering the company its new air brake. By then money was so short that the question had become academic.

In a few select areas the company was quick to embrace new technology. In 1886 it established a weather service for the system modeled after that used by the government. The perpetual fight against blizzards led it to experiment in January 1887 with a new gadget known as the rotary snowplow. Tests on the Short Line, conducted under the eye of the inventor, proved so successful that Dickinson praised the device as "worth most any reasonable amount of money." Adams promptly ordered three of the plows that spring and later bought another for the narrow-gauge South Park line. A new type of locomotive known as the "Wooten" (sometimes called "dirt burner"), equipped with a wide firebox and large grate area, was tested on the Wyoming division. Impressed by the results, Adams bought ten of the engines to utilize the low-grade slack coal from the Wyoming mines. Unfortunately, they did not perform well and were abandoned.

One major improvement could not be deferred. The swelling traffic across the Missouri River had swamped the capacity of the bridge to handle it. In February 1885 Adams commissioned George S. Morison, a New York engineer, to examine the bridge. Morison's lengthy report, submitted in May, forced the company to act sooner than it had anticipated by declaring the bridge unsafe. All the cast-iron cylinders had cracked from frost the first winter, and the patches were weakening. One of the two spans blown down in 1877 had been replaced only with a wooden trestle, which remained a serious fire hazard on so heavily traveled a bridge. Morison found the cylinders too small in proportion to their height, forcing an excessive use of riprap to keep the piers stable. The top chord of the superstructure was made of flawed cast iron and the lateral system was defective, rendering it dangerous in high winds. The floor system could not withstand the strains imposed by the heavier traffic of the 1880s. In short, there were danger points everywhere. Morison warned that "the breakage of a chord section would result in the immediate fall of an entire span, and might come without warning."

Jake Blickensderfer and an officer of the Detroit Bridge Company also inspected the bridge and agreed with Morison that it was not only inadequate but unsafe as well. Their views convinced Adams that a new bridge was needed at once; the responsibility for a disaster, he declared, was "more than I am willing to assume." Morison offered him four alternative plans, one of which was for a double-tracked bridge with room for a street railway as well as for wagon and foot traffic. It replaced four of the original spans on the Iowa side with a long, earth-filled trestle and would, Morison predicted, "accommodate an almost unlimited traffic." The board accepted that version in September, and work began a month later. Adams instructed Callaway to explain the decision publicly "on the grounds of inadequacy—wholly ignoring the question of safety in our statement." With a new bond issue providing the million dollars needed for construction, the work proceeded rapidly enough to open the bridge for traffic in October 1887.

For all of Adams's efforts, the problems mounted faster than he could field them. In May 1887 he toured the road and found its condition "very discouraging." Denver cried desperately for more yard room, a new terminal, and better water. A company chemist informed Adams that, despite his warnings three years earlier, the East Denver shop continued to use water "taken from the cistern below the shops near the river, and fed by what is practically the sewerage of the whole neighborhood." The foundry at Omaha had outgrown its facilities, and the clocks along the line were not being properly regulated. In Wyoming the power shortage reached crisis proportions. A rash of accidents in 1888 alarmed Adams about the shape of the road even though Dickinson assured him that "fully 90% of railway derailments and wrecks are caused by the careless, or rather the wilful, disobedience of well-defined rules and regulations on the part of some employe [sic]."

The schizophrenic character of railroad operations never revealed itself more clearly than in the 1880s. While Dr. Jekyll toiled diligently to bring the road up to highest standards, Mr. Hyde drove the plant and equipment for all it was worth or decreed radical cutbacks to slash expenses. This was not wholly the fault of officers or their policies. The industry had entered a new phase in which business simply outran the capacity of roads to handle it. A large amount of investment capital was raised, but most of it was funneled into new construction rather than into the upgrading of existing lines. As a result rail managers met the challenge in the only way they could, by running men and equipment until they dropped from exhaustion.

This situation badly strained the relationship between traffic officers and the other departments. The former were responsible for obtaining business, the latter for delivering it. Important changes in the nature of that business occurred during the 1880s, the most striking of which was a radical shift in the ratio of through and local traffic. Gould had stressed the need to cultivate local business as an offset to the through business siphoned away by competing lines. The fruits of this policy became evident by mid-decade. In 1881 through traffic produced 54 percent of the system's earnings, 59 percent of its freight ton-miles, and 66 percent of its passengers carried one mile. By 1885 those figures had plummeted to 23 percent of earnings, 31 percent of freight ton-miles, and 24 percent of passengers carried one mile. Local business increased as dramatically as through business declined. Although through business improved in later years, it never regained the dominant position of earlier times.

Adams singled out the development of local business as the most pressing problem of his administration. Unfortunately, that policy exposed a traditional weakness of the company. "A striking feature regarding the Union Pacific," noted the government directors in 1884, "is the unpopular, bitterly hostile feeling toward the road in the communities generally through which it passes, and by many of its patrons." This attitude was attributed to the road's monopoly position, which allowed it to treat shippers with high-handed indifference. Once new lines appeared, customers "embraced the first and earliest opportunity to divert patronage to any competitor." In consequence the company now had to "bear the load of aggravated ill-will, not only along its line but at commercial centers."

But the problem was not that simple. While the railroad was guilty of abuses, traffic was a two-way relationship in which neither side held a monopoly in virtue. If roads wanted all the traffic would bear, shippers and travelers sought the lowest possible rates regardless of the effects on the road's ability to provide efficient service. The fixing of rates was in practice less an accounting than a political exercise. All shippers desired special rates or services, but only the largest had enough clout to obtain them. There were exceptions, notably for new enterprises that promised a large traffic if they thrived. Once a competing line appeared, shippers did not hesitate to play one road against another to wring a lower tariff. Nor were rival firms slow to use the railroad as a weapon against each other.

It was not difficult to explain the traffic bonanza of the 1880s. Above average rainfall sent immigrants streaming onto the plains and produced huge crops. The mining and cattle kingdoms were in their heyday, and rapid settlement was opening up new local industries everywhere. All these sources were volatile, subject to abrupt and massive shifts in output. The Horn silver mine, for example, was a major reason why Gould extended the Utah Southern to Frisco and for several years gave the Union Pacific an enormous business. In 1884 it shipped more bullion than all other Utah smelters combined; the next year it failed and was the leading factor behind a drop of fourteen thousand tons in bullion shipments from Utah.

Gould's strategy had been to favor local development in those areas promising the road a long haul. It was a sound policy for the 1870s and would become so again at a much later date. Unfortunately, the traffic department often interpreted this goal as a mandate to stifle local development so that supplies could be brought into communities rather than produced locally. As the road's territory filled with settlers and new competitors emerged for traffic at distant points, Adams properly shifted the emphasis from the haul to cultivating on the line "a thriving local community with all its numerous railroad requirements." Local industry meant not merely traffic but growing populations with shipping needs of all kinds. These settlements, Adams argued, were "worth infinitely more to a railroad than the freights upon a very large amount of raw material."

Adams did what he could to implement this policy in practice and in the minds of his traffic officers. He pushed the production of sulfur, salt, paint, and other products native to regions along the line. In the arid stretches crossed by the Short Line, he encouraged irrigation projects to transform wasteland into potential sources of traffic. The building of shops at Cheyenne not only improved efficiency but also boosted an ailing local economy at a time when the cattle boom had gone bust, people were leaving the area in droves, and businesses were failing or hanging by the slenderest threads of hope. Here as elsewhere the railroad did not merely assist the development of local industry; it was a major local industry.

These efforts thrust Adams onto the horns of an old dilemma, the giving of rebates. Like other roads the Union Pacific had long paid drawbacks to certain customers, usually for one of three reasons: as a bonus for large, regular shipments; to meet lower tariffs offered by competing rail or water lines; or to assist new industries that promised a large traffic but could not at first afford full rates. No other issue aroused more bitterness or hostility toward railroads, particularly among shippers who were not favored with special rates and who cried discrimination. On the surface the question seemed purely one of equity; in practice it was filled with complexities that defied easy analysis because every aspect was layered with strata of conflicting interests.

Adams loathed the practice and longed to do away with it, but he could not. In this area he was at the mercy of the traffic officers, who had power to offer rebates and pay them. The arrangements were often informal or disguised; Boston learned only about them after the fact if at all. The slippery ways of freight agents led Adams to hold them in utter contempt, but all managements were two-faced on this point. The same agents whose methods were deplored also endured constant pressure to get business at any cost as competition intensified and rates dropped. Moreover, Adams's own policy stood in the way of reform. A new local industry in one place competed with others elsewhere and was quick to demand special rates or services to gain an edge over rivals. The policy of development thrust a railroad squarely into the cockpit of competing interests.

Adams made some gestures at change. He took the auditing of rebates away from the traffic department and gave it to the auditor, Erastus Young. In July 1886 he had Comptroller Oliver Mink issue a warning that anyone paying an unauthorized rebate would have the amount deducted from his salary. None of it helped much, because the demands from shippers were insatiable and Adams dared not refuse them all. Standard Oil's western affiliate, Continental Oil, agreed to ship via rail only in return for large drawbacks. After complaining about poor service, it shifted some of its business to Pacific Mail. F. H. Peavey, owner of a string of grain elevators, induced the Union Pacific to give him a penny a bushel on all grain shipped to the Missouri River, including that handled by rival elevators. Every smelter in Union Pacific territory wanted concessions to meet its competitors; one in Colorado also asked the company to give its banking business to a bank owned by the smelter's officers. Even the Omaha and Grant Company, which the road had helped repeatedly, filed a claim in 1888 for $55,000, charging that in the past three years it had paid higher rates on shipments than other smelters.

Few shippers liked the rates offered them, and some told Adams so in blunt language. H. H. Porter, a steel manufacturer long associated with the Northwestern and one-time director of the Union Pacific, was refused a special rate on rails because it violated the Colorado pool agreement. Porter asked Adams if he thought the rate fair and was referred to the pool officer. "I tell you frankly," blustered Porter, "that in all the railroads I have ever dealt with, the mode of procedure, arbitrariness of manner and price shown by the Union Pacific towards every company, always has been the very worst." In his wrath Porter let the correspondence go public in the New York *Times.*

One incident typified the frustrations Adams felt in dealing with the problem. A freight agent, anxious to get tonnage, secretly contracted for a shipment of rails at a rate much lower than that offered by the Northern Pacific.

This move directly violated instructions recently given traffic officers and obliged the Union Pacific to carry freight that did not pay when it was already short of motive power. It also infuriated the Northern Pacific at a time of delicate negotiations. "They will of course 'get even' with us," growled Adams. "The freight agents do not realize," he added, "how angry and worked up the owners of railroad properties at the east now are. The tomfoolery of rate cutting and traffic stealing will not be tolerated much more." If it happened again, Adams warned, the transgressor would be fired without being permitted to resign.

Dillon supported Adams's response fully. In earlier times, he observed, business was so scarce that "it seemed necessary to meet the other roads with their own weapons or else to lose a great part of the outside business." Now the roads had more traffic than they could handle, and true policy was to "cultivate and take care of our home business and secure that which pays the best." The most revealing response came from Dodge, who wanted the agent dismissed outright. The Union Pacific, he asserted, "never need haul a ton of freight that it does not get paid for." But only a few months earlier Dodge complained of not getting a low enough rate on the road for some construction material he had ordered.

The same frustrations carried over into the passenger service, where rate cutting was more direct and no less savage. Here too competition had intensified the struggle. The Union Pacific competed with the Northern Pacific for passengers to the Northwest and with the Burlington for Denver customers. The immigrant business dwindled as the better lands filled up, leaving the Northern Pacific as the lone road with an Immigration Bureau. Idaho had possibilities but, as Kimball noted, needed "irrigating ditches first, and the farmer later." In the race for transcontinental business the Union Pacific had not distinguished itself for either speed or service. Adams got a glimmer of the latter problem when one of his officers, responding to a complaint, assured him that "most of the station agents and almost all of the travelling public are simple barbarians."

Competition in the passenger trade was as curious as it was costly. Since most roads bought their coaches from the same manufacturers and their sleepers from Pullman, there was little difference in equipment. The Union Pacific got its sleepers under what was known as the Pullman Association plan, whereby the road paid 75 percent of the cost of cars and equipment, Pullman the other 25 percent, and the profits or losses were shared in like proportion. Travelers using the sleeper paid regular coach fare plus a fee per day to Pullman. Passengers still took their meals in eating rooms at stops along the route. The uneven quality of fare and cleanliness were a source of constant complaint, but no diners had been run since the short-lived Hotel Train of 1869–70 because everyone knew they lost money.

The growth of systems forced all roads to rethink their handling of the passenger trade in the 1880s. Two factors held the key to gaining a larger slice of the business: improved service and shorter schedules. To upgrade service Adams bought new equipment and in November 1887 inaugurated a new train, the Overland Flyer, which ran from Omaha to San Francisco in seventy-one hours and Portland in seventy-seven hours. At first the Flyer carried both coaches and Pullmans, but after four months it was changed to Pullman Palace Sleeping Cars exclusively. Adams also tried to provide for uniform quality of meals by leasing the eating houses to the men who ran the Millard House in Omaha. To keep abreast of their efforts, Adams was not content to rely solely on his officers. He also asked friends traveling over the road to send him detailed reports of the conditions at each stop. The eating houses improved but never approached the quality of Fred Harvey's legendary system on the Atchison.

Meal stops also posed a major obstacle in shortening schedules, as did the need to make connections at terminal points. One problem could be solved by putting on diners, the other by running through trains. Both solutions were effective but costly. For years George Pullman had advocated a limited special between Omaha and San Francisco—in effect an updated version of the old Hotel Train. The Central Pacific opposed the idea for the same reason it resented the Overland Flyer. Any through train obliterated the separate identity of the Central Pacific, which was preserved by having passengers change trains at Ogden. After some tough bargaining Pullman got his special train in December 1888. The Golden Gate Special was the ultimate luxury train, running four trips monthly with Pullman cars that featured ornate decors, electric lights, a gentleman's bath, barber shop, diner, sleepers with large lounges, desks, a library, and enlarged windows for enjoying the scenery.

The Golden Gate Special pleased those travelers who could afford to ride it, but the train lasted only five months. In withdrawing it the general manager at Omaha complained that "the Central Pacific have not been favorable to this train at any time since it has been put on," and that Pullman favored "honoring passes on this train solely for the purpose of giving his dining-cars and sleepers more business." Instead the Overland Flyer was put on a new schedule which made the run eleven hours slower than the Golden Gate westbound and four hours slower eastbound. However, the Overland ran daily instead of once a week and, with improved connections at Omaha, actually got passengers to New York faster.

By 1888 the passenger service still lagged behind that of competing roads. Adams's assistant, L. S. Anderson, found many of the Pullman cars "simply disgraceful" and "not fit for firstclass passengers to ride in." Some Pullman cars were being replaced with newer vestibule cars, which enclosed the frames at both ends of the car with elastic diaphragms. This eliminated dust, cinders, and the weather, made movement between cars easier, and helped prevent cars from telescoping in an accident. Adams's officers wanted more and better equipment to fight rival lines; their persistence triggered the Great Dining Car War of 1888–89.

So anathema was dining car service that in 1881 the Union Pacific, Atchison, and Burlington signed a pact not to use it on the Denver route. However, the Northern Pacific threw down the gauntlet in 1887 by putting a diner on its Portland trains. The Rock Island contemplated running a train of vestibuled cars with diner from Chicago to Denver. At once Adams's subordinates bombarded him with requests to meet the challenge. "I dont believe we can afford to furnish less facilities than our competitors," argued Charles S. Mellen, "and again I don't think the question of whether the direct income from the dining cars pays us a profit or not, the all important one." A passenger agent was even more blunt. "If the Union Pacific is to continue in the future as in the past," he growled, "to be like the cow's tail, always behind because it belongs there, we can continue to run our trains without dining cars."

After lengthy debate Adams agreed to begin dining car service west of the Missouri on May 12. Perkins heard the news in dismay and tried earnestly to change Adams's mind. It would, he reminded Adams, "increase Expenses all round at a time when the reduction of Expenses seems so essential." To Adams's surprise, Cable of the Rock Island, whose road was supposed to have launched the fight, bitterly protested an "expenditure of money that to my mind is useless." Adams tried to limit the conflict but could not persuade his leading officers. The Burlington made better time to Denver, argued the general manager, and refused to schedule connections at Omaha so that passengers could "reach either of our dining stations at a seasonable hour." A new vestibuled train run with the Northwestern had done quite well; the choice, therefore, was "to put up more dining stations, or put on diners, or see our travel gradually drift away from us again." Hughitt of the Northwestern agreed it would "be a mistake not to meet them fully with all the facilities offered by them . . . including dining cars."

Helpless to resist the advice of his best officers and allies, Adams agreed to implement the service. The passenger war, like the arms race, escalated to new levels of cost with no advantage gained by anyone. Each side protested righteously that its hand had been forced by the others. Mellen assured Adams that Pullman would build diners under the Association plan, but Pullman denied saying any such thing and offered several alternative proposals, all of them less favorable than the Association plan. The general manager recommended that the company build fourteen diners at a cost of $210,000, but Adams cringed at that large outlay. Instead he accepted a modified version of the Association plan under which Pullman ultimately built and operated thirteen diners for the company.

The results were predictable. During the next few years the wars in both freight and passenger service grew steadily worse despite repeated efforts to contain them. Improvements in equipment and service merely increased costs that could not be recovered so long as every road followed suit. By 1893 the Union Pacific dining service was running "a dead loss of over 100,000 per year" and management was groping for a way to get out of the agreement with Pullman.

Passes were another form of necessary evil. Rail managers agreed they were a curse and longed to be rid of their abuse, but how to do it? The worst offender was the "family pass," given to traffic agents as an inducement to secure business from them. The family pass was transferable, and since anyone presenting them might be a family member, the conductor dared not challenge them. Congressmen and other politicians also demanded their usual right to free transportation, not only for themselves but for relatives, friends, and constituents. So did editors and journalists, who seemed to have as many constituents as politicians. Railroad managers could not easily refuse requests from men who had something to offer in return. Traffic agents could provide the road business, politicians influence, and journalists favorable publicity.

At one point Adams learned that passes frequently cost the road as much as twenty thousand dollars a week in lost revenues. "In the larger part of the west," he told a friend in exasperation, "I find that few persons pay fares on the railroads except those who have neither friends nor money." A decade earlier Dillon and Huntington had tried to limit political passes to those congressmen who asked for them, but that hardly stemmed the flow. Dillon took the position that congressmen who received passes "should deal with us fairly," a view Adams found repugnant but too realistic to ignore. Despite an agreement to consult with Huntington before issuing passes over their lines, Adams could not avoid violating this pledge on occasion. He explained one offense as "in accordance with a plan I have adopted of submitting to what I consider congressional blackmail in view of the circumstances."

During 1885 Adams asked his fellow presidents to join in banning the family pass. Hughitt was willing, Perkins and Robert Harris of the Northern Pacific evasive, and Strong was flatly opposed. A year later Perkins was more amenable, but the officers of each road insisted as always that the worst fault lay with their rivals. Traffic men defended the practice as an unavoidable necessity because of competition. After one futile effort to hammer out an agreement, Callaway threw up his hands and complained that "the whole subject gives me more annoyance and worry than anything else I have to deal with." Still Adams persisted in his quest, with discouraging results. In December 1889 W. H. Holcomb, then vice president, advised Adams that the Burlington was "flooding Nebraska with passes, ostensibly on political account; but they are given where they influence trade in almost every instance." The company had lost heavily, Holcomb added, "by attempting to do away with the issuing of passes and live honestly. So long as the general situation remains as it is now, this cannot be done, and I think the only course that will result in net earnings for the Union Pacific is for you to shut your eyes at Boston and only look to net results."

Journalists posed a special problem because they usually sought passes in return for future considerations. When one reporter requested a pass for his brother, the astute Mark Hanna, then a government director and good friend of the Union Pacific, urged Adams to comply because the applicant was "an *influential* newspaper correspondent at W[ashington] and has been of some service to me in U.P. matters there." Banker R. S. Grant supported a request by a *Sun* reporter, deeming him a "powerful writer" who could "do much good by what he will say and write, and having been a member of the last Congress he may be useful in the future." Some journalists were not content with passes alone. N. W. Josselyn of the New York *Daily Indicator* asked Adams to buy and carry for six months five hundred shares of Union Pacific on his account as "a proper way of recompensing me for what I have done." Adams put him off by saying he was powerless to do any such thing.

No amount of indignation on Adams's part could curb the endless stream of requests for free transportation. The abuse, like so many others, blunted his zeal for reform because it was so pervasive throughout the industry. Over the years it gained momentum, a rolling snowball fast becoming an avalanche. To cite but one small example, in February 1892 the Union Pacific issued 4,985 trip passes serving 8,133 customers at a loss of $52,982 in revenue. Of that number 3,690 were employee passes, 466 foreign road passes, 194 editorial passes, and the other 635 "stock" passes. In addition, unclassified time passes cost the company another $35,940 in fares, making a total of $88,922. Data for other months of different years suggest that these figures were typical.

Railroad men continued to deplore the pass problem and to shrug it off as merely one more of the necessary evils with which they were forced to contend. Conventional wisdom could find no solution to these evils, and earnest reformers like Adams soon abandoned all hope of persuading others that radical surgery was needed to eliminate the cancer. Too late the industry's leaders realized that the combined weight of so many necessary evils was pushing them toward a rendezvous with disaster.

26

THE ASSETS

The policy of development involved more than generating new sources of traffic. Adams was eager to press the work begun by Gould of cultivating the resources throughout the territory occupied by the Union Pacific system. The financial pressures wrought by unbridled competition made it imperative to transform these resources into assets for the company, both as sources of traffic and as separate bases of income. In his zeal to promote local industry Adams did not neglect the opportunities offered by raw materials and new services, but he was not as quick as Gould to exploit them. As the system expanded, so did the variety of possibilities and the demand for capital to develop them. Although no one realized it at the time, these efforts laid the foundation for the later transformation of the Union Pacific from a railroad to a company of multiple enterprises.

From the first the two most obvious assets had been land and coal, both of which filled basic needs on the western frontier. Like the railroad itself, these departments were caught up in the throes of change and were in urgent need of revamping. Expansion brought the company more land in the grants belonging to the Kansas Pacific, but its disposal, too, was at the mercy of the government. Although the Supreme Court reversed the infamous Schurz decree allowing preemption of unclaimed lands, Congress continued to view the handling of all land grants with dark suspicion. The lengthy struggle to obtain patents dragged on without relief and got entangled with the issue of whether unpatented lands were taxable.

By 1884 the Union Pacific had sold about 2.8 million acres of land. All the agricultural land was gone; of the 8.4 million acres that remained, most of it in Wyoming and Utah, 1.8 million were labeled arid and the rest deemed suitable for grazing. The Kansas Pacific had another 5.3 million acres still unsold, most of it grazing land. Dillon was anxious to dispose of the grazing lands but rejected a suggestion to let them go for ten cents an acre, saying, "we should hesitate about giving them away entirely." He had also to contend with the old problem of alternating sections with the government, which frustrated attempts to sell large parcels to stockmen. The cattle boom was underway, and large herds had already been put on the open range. Some cattlemen were willing to buy the land if Dillon could persuade the government to split the land in some equitable way.

When Adams took office, the policy was for the land commissioner to secure authority for sales contracts directly from Fred Ames, the trustee for the land grant mortgage. A committee of appraisers, consisting usually of Poppleton, Young, and Kimball, was supposed to certify all sale prices, but their endorsement was perfunctory. The appraisers never met as a committee and relied entirely on the advice of local agents. There was a general policy that no lands were to be appraised below a dollar an acre, but that figure clashed with the desire to sell grazing lands in large amounts. During 1884 the land department sold a record 4.3 million acres, far more than the combined sales of all previous years. A closer look at this astounding performance revealed a radical shift in the disposal of lands. The average price per acre was only $1.52 compared with $3.11 the previous year. Only 1,517 buyers were involved, whereas in 1883 a total of 805,834 acres had been sold to 2,606 buyers.

The trend was obvious: more land was being sold for less money to fewer buyers, most of them cattlemen. At first the mammoth sales of 1884, which fetched nearly $6.6 million in net proceeds, delighted Adams. The company badly needed the money and could reduce its land operation as the acreage dwindled. During the next year, however, certain facts dribbled out that chilled Adams's enthusiasm enough to launch an investigation of the department and its head, Leavitt Burnham.

Two large transactions especially caught Adams's attention. Burnham had sold 473,616 acres to the Swan Land and Cattle Company and another 267,895 acres to S. W. Downey, all at fifty cents an acre. Since the price was below the usual minimum, Burnham in July 1884 took the offer to Fred Ames, who was then in Omaha. Their discussion produced a misunderstanding that was to have serious repercussions. Burnham insisted later that Ames authorized the sale, saying, "if that was the best that could be done, better let it go at 50¢." Fifteen minutes after the conversation Burnham wired Swan that the sale had been approved; later he negotiated the sale to Downey on the same assumption. In October Ames and Adams summoned Burnham to explain these transactions at so low a price. At this meeting Ames flatly denied he had authorized the sale. Since no written record existed, the matter boiled down to Burnham's word versus that of Ames. Given the latter's stature, it was no contest.

The issue lapsed until September 1885 when Ames, asked to approve certain documents for the sale, replied that he had "never approved any sales at less than $1.00 and still hold that position, but as the matter has gone so far, I am advised the company will be held by the contract you have made." Two days later he abruptly reversed his position. By that time a new wrinkle had appeared in the form of a report charging that Burnham had promised earlier to reserve certain lands for Swan and had then sold them to another party. A furious Alex Swan promptly visited Burnham and threatened to expose certain questionable transactions by Burnham and J. G. Pratt, the land agent at Cheyenne. To placate Swan, Burnham agreed to sell him a large tract of land at fifty cents an acre.

Disturbed by this muddle, Adams sent Lane in December to investigate the Omaha land office. Lane in turn engaged Henry Rothert, an experienced land man, to probe not only the office operation but reports of dishonesty by Pratt and another agent at Overton. After a two-month investigation Rothert uncovered damning evidence of fraud and extortion against the two agents, and both were discharged. He found nothing to taint Burnham's reputation but condemned the "want of system, order, business tact, supervision, regulation and instruction in every local office I have visited." Poppleton and another member of the legal department vigorously defended Burnham's character. Lane agreed that Burnham was personally honest but concluded that he was "too small a man for too big a place."

Although his integrity remained intact, Burnham had run an operation as loose and careless of details as his predecessor, Davis. The best of administrators could not have survived the clash with Ames, however, and in May 1886 Burnham was dumped in favor of George M. Cumming, a Duluth lawyer who had worked in the land department of the Northern Pacific. Apart from cleaning up the department, Cumming took a novel approach to land policy. He was anxious to put all agricultural land in the hands of settlers but not eager to let the rest go. "The company seems to pride itself on its immense land sales during the past few years," he told Adams, "whereas I am persuaded that they were mistakes; and my desire is to manage the remnant of your land grant in such a way as to do the least harm to the company's permanent interests." The notion of conserving rather than selling off the land must have startled Boston, as did Cumming's observation that "land grants have in many cases proved to be a misfortune for the companies, and a great injury to the region affected by them."

The novelty of Cumming's notions did not make them repugnant, for Boston was already revising its attitude toward land policy. With most of the agricultural land gone, the company recognized that the remainder must be sold at lower prices. Whatever ultimate value these lands might have could only be in whatever coal and other minerals they might possess. For that reason the executive committee decided in March 1886 to insert a clause reserving to the company all mineral rights in future conveyances. This step, which passed virtually unnoticed at the time, would assume immense significance in the development of resources along the route.

Cumming moved to tighten the operation by reducing the list of agents who received passes, cutting commissions, and choosing outside agents more selectively. To encourage purchases in Kansas by actual settlers instead of speculators, a new policy was adopted of offering rebates of 20 percent to buyers who broke ground for cultivation within two years. The separate operations of the Union Pacific and Kansas Pacific land departments were consolidated in hopes of running them more efficiently at less expense. After seven months Cumming was promoted to the new position of assistant general manager and his place given to Benjamin McAllaster, former head of the Kansas Pacific land department. Cumming regarded his successor as "neither a very active nor a very intelligent man; but he understands the land business of the Kansas Division thoroughly, is perfectly honest, succeeds in selling a great deal of land, gets very high prices for the land and has made a great deal of money for the company."

In changing jobs Cumming urged Adams to leave the land department under his control, arguing that it had been "a mistake in the past to separate the land dept. from the operating dept." Instead Adams chose to appoint Charles J. Smith to the new position of general land commissioner, a place with few duties other than overseeing McAllaster's operation. Why Adams felt the need for another layer of management at a time when the business of the land department was dwindling is not clear. Two years later Smith was made general manager of the Pacific Division, and a few months after Adams left the presidency in November 1890 the office of general land commissioner was abolished.

Through this constant shuffling McAllaster remained the anchor of stability; after his death in May 1890 he was succeeded by his son, B. A. McAllaster, who would tend the department well into the next century. The collapse of the cattle kingdom in 1887–88 slowed sales of grazing land, and passage of the Interstate Commerce Act hurt efforts in Kansas by eliminating the special reduced fares given to prospective buyers. McAllaster considered the loss of these fares the chief reason for diminished immigration and a sharp decrease in values. The company sold 574,024 acres in 1887, the year the law was passed; the next year it sold only 146,474 acres and a total of 872,628 acres for the period 1888–92. When hard times spread across the country in 1893 and payments on land purchases lagged, McAllaster informed his superiors that "it has come to a point where we have either got to give them more time or cancel their contracts." At his urging the company granted extensions on its land contracts.

By 1892, thirty years after its creation, the land grant remained what it had always been, a creature of superb if unwitting irony. Nearly 3.3 million acres were still unsold on the Union Pacific and another 3.2 million on the Kansas Pacific. A large segment of public opinion believed erroneously that proceeds from land sales had, along with the government bonds, paid for building the road. They did serve as collateral for the land grant bonds, but these played only a small role in funding construction. Over the years the returns from land sales provided a useful but not impressive income for the company. As a source of endless dispute and litigation the land grant did more to build the legal profession than it did the Union Pacific Railroad. The struggle to get lands patented was as frustrating as ever. By 1886 the company had sold more than 8.6 million acres for which patents had not yet been received. Of this amount 5.2 million acres had already been sold to buyers who could not get clear title. In March 1893 McAllaster noted optimistically that the government was "only three years behind on our Patents instead of eight," although some lists had been pending since 1882.

Through these early years the land grant had proven a mixed blessing. On one occasion Dillon had tried to sell it back to the government. Fortunately the offer was rebuffed, for decades later the land would yield the company a return beyond its wildest hopes. Changing times would reveal beneath its surface the fabulous riches that only dreamers suspected was there in the nineteenth century.

*   *   *

The nightmare at Rock Springs was but the most spectacular evidence of trouble at the mines. As a source of fuel and traffic, coal was a vital asset to the company. There had always been problems in operating the mines, most of which had been neglected or sloughed off until changing conditions in the 1880s made them impossible to ignore. Even at these remote, dreary slashes in the Wyoming crust, the new competitive environment helped bring matters to a crisis point for the beleaguered Adams.

Gould had resolved one major problem before his departure. The long battle over the Wardell suit finally reached the Supreme Court in 1880 after a journey filled with pitfalls. Gould never slackened his efforts to dump the odious contract that had ensnarled the coal operation. In 1875 he reached a settlement with Wardell only to have it fall through. Two years later Wardell won a judgment against the company, which was promptly appealed. Durant filed suit claiming that the profits on his shares in the Wyoming Coal Company belonged to him and not the company. Bushnell agreed to cooperate with Gould in the litigation and collected a fee of ten thousand dollars for "services." Only the fight over Crédit Mobilier proved longer and nastier, but in the end Gould prevailed. In April 1881 the court decided in favor of the company.

When Adams took office, the company had undisputed control of its mines. The consolidation had given it mines along the Denver Pacific, and Dillon had acquired other Colorado coal properties as well. In 1883 most of these Colorado holdings were swept together into the Union Coal Company, of which the Union Pacific held a large interest. During Adams's first year the Wyoming mines did well, increasing output by 106,048 tons to 882,608 and lowering the cost per ton from $1.42 to $1.32. Whatever pleasure Adams drew from this impressive performance was short-lived. The Rock Springs upheaval called national attention to the labor strife in the mines. In January 1886 a gas explosion at Almy killed eleven men and raised questions about whether the mines were properly ventilated.

These tragedies underscored a growing welter of problems in the mines, of which labor unrest was only one. Some mines were played out and no longer economical to work. New veins had been located but would be costly to develop. As productive mines burrowed deeper, longer hauls were required, thereby hiking costs. Labor was scarce, coal cars even scarcer. Machinery wore down faster than expected, and some proved too light for the work demanded of it. The new machinery performed well but was expensive. To improve ventilation new fans were installed at several mines; the one at the mine where the explosion occurred cost nearly six thousand dollars. As a precaution the superintendent, D. O. Clark, experimented with new ways to break down the coal without resorting to powder.

In short, the mines were becoming less efficient and more costly to operate at a time when the demand for coal was growing rapidly. As the expanded system ran more trains with heavier loads over longer distances, fuel consumption increased. New industries and settlers along the route provided a surging market for commercial sales if enough coal could be produced. The conditions envisioned by Gould a decade earlier had arrived, but the mines were in no shape to meet them. Between 1880 and 1885 commercial sales soared from 137,119 to 361,521 tons. The market had by no means peaked, but some feared production had; after a decade of steady growth output declined for three straight years from a high of 904,454 tons in 1883 to 784,587 tons in 1886. If the trend continued, the mines might soon fall short of feeding the insatiable appetites of the locomotives.

Despite the uproar created by the Rock Springs affair, Adams was too distracted by other problems to tackle the coal crisis. Fortunately, one of his government directors was Mark Hanna, the shrewd, intelligent coal dealer from Cleveland who would later carve as impressive a career in politics as he had in business. Hanna inspected the Wyoming mines in October 1886 to investigate complaints made by the miners. Among other things he found that Beckwith was hiring Finnish miners because they did not "fraternize with other miners" and resisted organizing. A strike in Colorado, provoked by a pay reduction, prompted officials there to seek Hungarians as replacements for the same reason. No more Chinese were imported, but the object was still to find men who would not join the union. As a result labor tensions remained high at all the mines.

A few months after coming to the Union Pacific as general manager, T. J.

Potter asked mining expert John Kangley to make a thorough investigation. Kangley's report threw the coal crisis in bold relief. He was impressed by the quality of Rock Springs coal, which he called "the best domestic coal on this continent. It is more lasting than Pittsburgh or any Eastern coal, and not so smoky, and should be sold in every town from Rock Springs to the Missouri River." To mine it efficiently, however, required new shafts that would cost about three hundred thousand dollars. The labor situation appalled Kangley. Rock Springs betrayed "the effect of a long reign of weak management. The miners have complete possession of the place." So too at Carbon, where the miners "order the Supt. what to do," and at Evanston, where the quality of coal was abysmal and production methods sloppy. At each place the superintendent had the same explanation: if they tried to crack down, the men "would stop work, and the President or some other official of the road would settle with the men, and have them resume work without consulting him." Often the superintendents were not even informed of the terms.

With Kangley's report in hand, Potter put the issue squarely to Adams. The company must move at once to improve the mines and increase output or run the risk of not being able to supply its own fuel needs. The question as Potter saw it was, "Shall the Company go ahead and expend within the next two years half a million dollars to put the mines in condition to increase their output, or will they lease them on some fair basis to responsible parties?" Potter favored a lease, perhaps to Beckwith, which would take the company out of the coal business at least until it settled the funding dispute with the government. The board responded by naming Adams, Fred Ames, and Hanna a committee to take up Potter's recommendation. Early in 1888 Beckwith was given charge of the Colorado coal and stone properties, but Adams wanted Hanna to run the Wyoming mines. When Potter died unexpectedly, the matter fell once more into confusion. Thomas Kimball urged that a policy be "promptly determined and all plans necessary to carry it out promptly adopted."

Adams was willing but distracted by too many other problems. He needed to find the right man to take charge of the mines. D. O. Clark, who had been superintendent since the mines opened, was not a mining expert but an office man whose strength was commercial sales. In June 1888 Hanna toured the mines with an engineer, J. F. Jones, whom he touted as a supervisor if Adams wished to separate operations from sales. At Carbon Hanna examined some coal fields north of the existing mines which he thought could meet fuel and commercial needs for years to come. He suggested a method of expanding output at Rock Springs at far less cost than Kangley's proposal but dismissed Almy as hopeless because it had "been opened and worked on an incorrect principle from the beginning."

Adams believed in taking advice from men he thought knew something, and Hanna had become his guru on coal. The proposed expenditures were made at Rock Springs and steps taken to develop the fields north of Carbon, which were later given Hanna's name. A new branch, the Carbon Cut-off, was incorporated to reach the fields. Some officers opposed this expansion policy. Cumming thought the company should "withdraw from all business, except that of transportation, as rapidly as circumstances will permit, and encourage the development of private enterprises" to avoid criticism from the government. W. H. Holcomb, who succeeded Potter, came around to the latter's old argument that the company should lease its coal operation to private parties. Had these suggestions been adopted, the history of the Union Pacific would have turned out far differently.

But they were not adopted. Hanna inspected the mines again in June 1889 and urged that another two hundred thousand dollars be spent to develop new mines. The executive committee approved the outlay despite Holcomb's protest and created a standing committee on coal. Adams himself toured the mines that August and came home more inclined to Hanna's belief that the company should "build up a 'Reading RR' for the West." To transform the Union Pacific into a major coal carrier, however, required a major reorganization of the coal department. The labor situation was still sticky. Chinese and white miners still shared Rock Springs. Holcomb wanted to use only Mormons at Almy and Pleasant Valley, and suggested trying black miners in the new shafts at Hanna and Dana for the usual reason that they were "clannish and will not associate with other miners," thereby reducing the threat of unionism and strikes.

The coal problem was, Adams admitted, "a hard conundrum for me to crack." He had three basic options: get out of the business altogether, put it in the hands of outside parties, or continue to work it in some reorganized form. The first two options had serious drawbacks. Could a railroad so utterly dependent on coal for fuel afford to place its supply in independent hands? Adams thought not, and many of his officers agreed. Moreover, the road could in many instances "influence the course of general traffic through its control of coal." That is, the company could, and often did, sell coal below market prices to obtain the business of select customers such as the smelters or Anaconda. If outside investors owned the mines, they would hardly be willing to sacrifice income for the railroad's benefit.

In Adams's view the only sound choice was to keep the business, but how to reorganize it? The answer came partly from Hanna and partly from the model offered by Pacific Express. "Problem solved!" Adams rejoiced in April 1890. The coal properties would all be transferred to a new, wholly owned subsidiary, Union Pacific Coal Company, and run separately but in harmony with the railroad. Adams wanted Governor Francis Warren to manage the new company, but Wyoming was about to become a state and Warren was reluctant to leave politics. Instead Adams chose J. S. Tebbets, a young freight agent at Omaha, to be general manager reporting directly to the president. All the coal interests, Adams declared, would "be maintained separately from the Omaha offices, and nothing can be done which is not approved here." To emphasize his independence, Tebbets set up headquarters in Denver.

Most of the Colorado properties did not go into the new company because the Union Pacific did not own them outright. Two companies, Colorado Fuel and Colorado Coal & Iron, dominated the coal trade and were angling to keep the Union Pacific out or to enlist it on their side against the other. Both also wanted to be rid of two mines Dodge had acquired near Trinidad to supply his Panhandle road. Dodge appealed to Adams for help against Colorado Fuel and Colorado Coal. Since both firms gave the Union Pacific considerable traffic, Adams heeded the advice of Hanna and Holcomb to maintain amicable relations with both and to decline "any part in the contest by helping one at the expense of the other."

Although Adams could not know it, the formation of the coal company had a significance far beyond the improvement of coal operations. It marked the first step toward a strategy that would make the Union Pacific a powerful influence in areas outside transportation in the next century. As the first subsidiary it would provide a model not so much for diversification as for a rational method of harnessing other resources that would become more crucial to the company's prosperity. Although the vision of the Union Pacific as something more than a railroad was but dimly perceived, the seed had been planted.

* * *

Coal was not the only resource Adams tried to develop or the only attempt to derive earnings from ancillary enterprises. Gould and Oliver Ames had worked diligently to build traffic by promoting industries utilizing such raw materials as precious ores, soda, and even oil. As early as 1872 the company conducted extensive tests on shale oil found in the rock ledges along Green River to determine its value for lubrication and illumination. The geologist who found the oil thought it might also be useful for preserving ties. When careful analysis revealed that the oil was not pure enough to be extracted and marketed profitably, the project was reluctantly shelved. More than half a century would pass before oil emerged as a major resource for the Union Pacific to develop.

So too with the soda works near Laramie, which Gould had pushed so vigorously. A curse seemed to hang over the entire project. Development was delayed by a prolonged effort to get clear title to the deposits. In 1881 the Union Pacific finally purchased the lakes, but little was done toward converting the sulfate of soda into caustic soda until 1883, when Dillon put Frederick Sickels in charge of erecting works. Dillon was anxious to get the enterprise started, yet he appointed a man who was, by his own admission, "no driver or manager of work." The facility was completed just in time for the financial crisis that brought Adams to the presidency and lay idle until 1885.

Adams was at a loss over what to do. The company had spent nearly seventy thousand dollars with nothing to show for it. Unlike coal or even oil, this venture had nothing to do with what Adams called the "legitimate functions" of the railroad. No one even knew whether caustic soda could be manufactured profitably at the works. However, the town of Laramie badly needed new industry, and the road was eager for new sources of traffic. One of Adams's assistants, Howard Hinckley, took up the challenge in March 1885 by leasing the soda works from the company and moving energetically to get production going. His determination was exceeded only by his run of bad luck.

Hinckley took possession of the plant in June and discovered at once that Fred Sickels knew more about bridges than soda works. All the pipes had been laid above the frost line and had burst. There were defects in the machinery, and no bins for coal, lime, or raw soda. It took Hinckley six weeks of hard work to lay new pipes and get everything in working order. On July 15 he fired the furnaces for the first time only to shut them down five days later when he found that the black ash furnace, used in the crucial process of drying the wet sulfate, was instead destroying it. After repeated experiments he found a solution that enabled him in late August to produce the first batch of caustic soda equal to the higher grades of English soda. Unfortunately, the furnaces proved too small and could turn out only about half the amount needed.

Undaunted, Hinckley introduced some labor-saving devices to cut operating costs and started up again. To his dismay, the first two runs of ten tons each refused to clarify. Then the "boat pan" collapsed, causing a loss of another ten tons. Hinckley shut down again, tore out the masonry, and repaired the pan. After work resumed, the pan failed again and could not be fixed. Close inspection revealed that the pan was made of cast iron only half as thick as the lightest pans used in England, and that no attention had been paid to the composition of the iron. Hinckley had no choice but to get an English pan or one that duplicated its composition, which meant another large expense.

Afer six months Hinckley had invested $23,354 in the soda works and received from the sale of his first batch the magnificent sum of $144. Still he clung to his belief that the enterprise could be made profitable. A new steel pan was ordered and other improvements made. In May 1886, before the pan arrived, a fire destroyed several buildings including the laboratory with all its records of the year's research. Hinckley replaced his losses and managed to start production in October. At last he was able to produce soda of good quality and the market took all he could make at good prices, but his fixed costs had increased so much that he could not manufacture enough soda to turn a profit. Needing another $13,000 to expand output, a desperate Hinckley pleaded for help. The company obliged with a new lease on more lenient terms and agreed to pay for half the cost of the new facilities.

By the summer of 1887 the Laramie Chemical Works was in full swing, producing caustic soda, salt cake, soda ash, and crushed lye. Then disaster struck again. In May 1885 a land company had opened an irrigation ditch not far from the soda lakes. Within a short time the lakes, which had always been dry during the summer and fall, began filling with water. An alarmed Hinckley installed pumps in July 1887, but even by removing a million gallons per day he could not keep the lakes dry enough to get soda before winter crusted the beds with snow and ice. Dejectedly he closed the works in December and tried to bring legal pressure on the land company. But that would take time, and Hinckley could not afford a long wait. He held out a few months longer before abandoning the lease in June 1888, with little to show for the three years and $120,000 he had invested in the venture.

Hinckley's experience offered a painful lesson in the perils of new enterprises on the frontier. He lost heavily and so did the Union Pacific, not only in its financial stake in the soda works but in traffic it would have received if all had gone well. Several parties inquired about taking over the lease, but in 1891 the company was still searching for a buyer or tenant. Economist Robert W. Fogel has called the Union Pacific a case study in premature enterprise. If so, it was a necessary one, for without the railroad the West would never have been developed. The term applies more aptly to such ventures as those attempted in oil and soda, where no amount of energy and diligence could yet transform these resources into profitable enterprises. Their time would come with changes in technology and market circumstances. Those who pioneered their development, however, found them to be costly experiments.

Conventional wisdom stated that railroads had no business venturing outside the field of transportation, but in the volatile competitive arena of the late nineteenth century it would have been foolish to neglect potential assets or new sources of traffic. Although the soda works proved a failure, the Union Pacific continued to search for new opportunities. It sponsored attempts to find mineral water suitable for bottling at Soda Springs, Idaho, and assigned the company chemist to analyze samples from various springs. In 1889 the executive committee referred to Adams the "question of further investigation of the mineral resources of the company's arid land." Years earlier the company had entered three other fields as natural extensions of its work as a carrier. At first the telegraph, express, and hotel operations were all contracted to outside firms. This arrangement made more sense for the telegraph than for the other two, which the company reclaimed and transformed into subsidiary enterprises.

In two of these areas Gould was the decisive influence. Once he gained control of Western Union, it suited his interests to have that company hold contracts with as many railroads as possible. By contrast no company dominated the express field nationally as Western Union did the telegraph. Gould's objective, therefore, was to secure the express business for roads under his control. After terminating the Union Pacific's contract with Wells, Fargo in 1879, he organized a new company, Pacific Express, under the management of E. M. Morsman, a veteran express officer, to serve three Gould roads, the Union Pacific, Missouri Pacific, and Wabash. Gould subscribed for nearly all the stock, but none was issued and nothing paid in for it. The railroads simply divided the net earnings of the express company on an agreed basis.

This move triggered a bitter competition during the early 1880s as rival companies vied for the express business of roads expanding west of the Missouri River. Amid these clashes Pacific Express had to cope with the problem of its rather casual organization, which became a thorn after Gould left the Union Pacific. In 1886, after prolonged negotiations, the stock was finally issued and divided among the three roads. The Union Pacific and Missouri Pacific each received 40 percent and the Wabash 20 percent. Pacific Express signed contracts to handle express for the roads for ten years. Two years later the Rock Island's expansion across the Missouri threatened to sweep the express companies into the larger railroad war.

Heretofore Pacific had enjoyed good relations with United States Express Company, which stayed east of the river and hauled Pacific's business to Chicago. Once across the Missouri with the Rock Island, however, it would become a competitor. Morsman warned that Pacific would suffer in a fight unless it could get a more efficient outlet to Chicago than the Wabash. Of the Iowa roads, only the St. Paul was in a position to work with Pacific. Since Wells, Fargo had recently contracted for lines reaching New York, Gould suggested a consolidation between Pacific and United States. Negotiations were opened but nothing came of them. A few months later Adams Express opened a campaign to acquire Pacific.

If the Union Pacific wished to go out of the express business, here was the perfect chance. Morsman thought it a good idea. Noting that "wonderful improvements have been made in handling 'less than car load shipments' by Freight trains," he argued that the express business had "reached its maximum, in fact passed it, and is now declining." Improved freight service meant decreased tonnage and earnings for express, and with it a drop in the 7 percent dividend paid by Pacific for the past four years. Even if Pacific did better than expected, its contracts would expire in 1896, forcing Adams Express or any other buyer to make new arrangements. Morsman's argument was persuasive but did not convince Adams. The Union Pacific kept its stock in Pacific, and the express business, contrary to Morsman's prediction, continued to grow. By 1893 Pacific operated over twenty thousand miles of road.

One of the company's greatest assets in luring travelers to the road was the country itself. The line passed through scenery of spectacular beauty and gave the public access to regions once as remote as the interior of the Amazon. The Great Salt Lake itself was a popular attraction to tourists, which prompted the Union Pacific to install a modest resort facility at a point called Garfield Beach. It was nothing special—a few bathhouses, a pavilion, and a lunch counter at the nearby depot—but the beach drew well in the summer. Had competition not reared its ugly head, Garfield might have remained a quiet, pleasant oasis in the Utah desert. In 1886, however, the Rio Grande Western decided to build its own resort halfway between Salt Lake City and Ogden. Lake Park boasted the most modern bathhouses and other facilities; what it lacked was a decent beach. To remedy its muddy shore and clay bottom, the Western dumped carloads of sand in hopes of creating an artificial bottom.

Despite this handicap, Lake Park did well its first summer. Palmer invited Adams to join him in developing one grand facility instead of two rival ones. Adams declined the offer and the Great Resort War was on. W. W. Riter, the Utah superintendent, pleaded at once for escalation. The company should build a proper hotel with a pavilion for concerts and dancing, new bath-houses, and some other improvements. "We have an unscrupulous, and I might say dastardly competitor," Riter sputtered. "No trick or lie is too contemptible for their employment." Adams took a less dark view, especially after Riter estimated that the improvements would cost nearly twenty-eight thousand dollars, not including a new hotel. He agreed only to run a new side track to the lake to serve both the resort and the shipment of salt from some manufacturers who had located nearby.

Competition aside, the issue again boiled down to the question of whether the railroad should go into other enterprises. Shortly after becoming presi-dent, Adams had leased all the company's hotels and eating houses to the Pacific Hotel Company, owned by two partners named Markel and Swobe, who ran the Millard House in Omaha. In May 1887 he turned the Garfield resort over to them as well. New bathhouses were erected, but construction delays caused the resort to open later than usual. Although the first season was a disaster, it did so well the following year that Holcomb recommended putting in a large new dining room, pipes for fresh water, and a hotel if possible. In 1889 the company went so far as to cancel the contract with Pacific Hotel and resume management of its hotel and eating facilities.

Another magnificent tourist attraction lay in the territory of the Union Pacific line. As early as 1884 the company explored the possibility of running a branch into Yellowstone Park, but the financial crisis put the idea in limbo. Since the park was in the far northwest corner of Wyoming, it could most easily be reached from the north by the Northern Pacific. In 1887 Arnold Hague, a government geologist, urged Adams to tap Yellowstone from the south via a short branch from the Utah Northern. Few tourists entered the park that way because it required a rugged stage ride of more than a hundred miles from the railroad. Jake Blickensderfer was sent to examine possible lines to the park and reported in favor of one running from Eagle Rock. T. F. Oakes of the Northern Pacific suggested joining forces, arguing that it was "better to share in a very large business than to have the monopoly of a small business." Oakes asked Adams to buy one hundred thousand dollars worth of stock in the Yellowstone Park Association to build three more hotels.

Young J. S. Tebbets tugged at Adams to put up the money, promising revenue "in sight of from $30,000 to $50,000" if the railroad built "within *easy distance* of the park." Hague was busy in Washington lobbying for a bill to have the government construct a wagon road from the Upper Geyser Basin to the southwest corner of the park. The bill did not pass, but a version of it reappeared each year. Adams was tempted, but the Yellowstone fever came just when more critical expansion projects elsewhere were draining all the funds he could muster. The idea was sound, the timing wrong. Not until 1905 did the company build its branch to Yellowstone Park.

These early ventures into the tourist trade were small and somewhat fleeting, yet they too planted seeds that in the next century would blossom into one of the finest tourist operations in America. Men like Oliver Ames, Gould, and Adams understood that the company's assets went far beyond its function as a carrier. The trick was to find these assets and then discover ways to utilize them profitably. This was part of what they meant when they talked of developing the country. In much of this work they were ahead of their time, so much so that they did not live to see it realized. They always regarded the Union Pacific as a multifaceted enterprise even though their vision was not fulfilled until the next century.

Pride of Place: The good engineer gave as much care to his locomotive as a cowboy did to his horse. The crew's devotion to their machine shines through these early pictures.

(Above) Engine number 5, a more ornamental version of the first Union Pacific locomotive. The crew and their ladies display an obvious relish in this carefully posed family portrait.

(Below) Four eager engines and their crews pose for another kind of family portrait.

Engine number 74 shows far more spit and polish and a decorative bird atop the bell. The wooden parts of the wheels were painted red and the brass bands on the boiler were shined to a brilliant gleam. Number 74 also has a Congdon smokestack designed by the Union Pacific's chief mechanical officer, I. H. Congdon.

(Above) Engine number 924, a 4-6-0, shown here with a combination baggage-passenger car, is flanked by its proud and confident crew. Note the little boy peeping out of the cab.

(Left) Engine number 23 was polished and shined to gleaming perfection to have its portrait taken at this small stop on the Little Laramie River, fifteen miles west of Laramie. Note the decorative antlers, a common ornament on the Union Pacific's early locomotives.

Sign of Things to Come: This fast fruit train carried a solid load of fruit about 1890 and may be considered a forerunner of the unit train. The first of these fast fruit trains ran in June 1886.

Digging Out: An early snowplow, which often proved overmatched against Wyoming blizzards even with all this power behind it.

A new rotary snowplow, shown here in 1887.

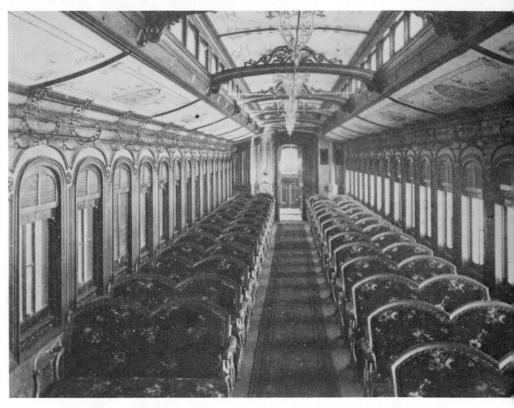

Traveler's Fare: The interior of an early coach. Note the stove at right rear.

The interior of a Pullman Palace Car. The panels above the seats are upper berths.

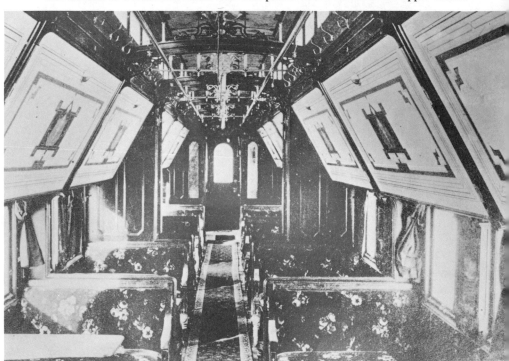

27

THE LABYRINTH

The deeper Adams plunged into the labyrinth of politics, the more distressed he felt. If there was one place an Adams should have been at home, it was Washington, yet Charles found it a dark, foreboding maze where pitfalls and predators lurked at the bend of every unmarked path. There were two classes of citizens with whom Adams never grew comfortable: politicians and Wall Street men. Both offended his genteel sensibilities with their coarse manners and moral slovenliness and sly ways. Like the class of railroad officers he despised, they were hard-bitten, practical men who were surefooted in slippery, treacherous places where the high-minded flailed helplessly. Unfortunately for Adams, they were both groups pivotal to his mission of leading Union Pacific to safety.

Major Thomas Reddington gave Adams an early taste of what to expect in Washington. In January 1886 the newly appointed chief clerk of the Railroad Commission arrived in Boston brandishing a letter of instructions drawn up by himself. Reddington was on a fishing expedition into the Union Pacific's books, seeking information on a dozen points and promising "to preserve in absolute secrecy all information obtained." Instead Reddington put his findings into the hands of Wall Street operators who used it to bear the stock. A henchman in Congress then demanded an investigation into recent charges of fraudulent transactions by the company. The major attacked with the finesse of an elephant, however, and his clumsy fraud was quickly exposed. He was abruptly dismissed from office in March, only five months after being hired. Driven to cover by a fusillade of ridicule, he would return to haunt Adams with the most improbable of sponsors.

The Reddington charade occurred just as Adams was girding for another campaign to resolve the government debt. Apart from raids by bears fomenting rumors, Adams had also to worry about Huntington, who advocated a "bold and ringing denunciation" of the government for their treatment of the Pacific roads, because the "other course has been held for years without favorable result." There was a certain logic in Huntington's wrath, but Adams preferred to give reason another try. Each house had its own bill to consider that winter. Senator Hoar of Massachusetts reported his version to the Judiciary Committee without allowing anyone from the Union Pacific to see a draft of it. When the company's lobbyist, Moorfield Storey, finally saw the bill, he warned Adams that it contained fatal errors of computation. Aware that enemies would blame the company for the defects, Adams persuaded Hoar not to press the bill and shifted his attention to the House version.

Isaac Bromley surveyed the new Pacific Railroads Committee and concluded it had a majority favorable to settlement. As usual everyone agreed the Thurman Act had failed miserably, but confusion reigned over what to put in its place. Late in February Adams appeared before the committee and tried once again to exorcise the "nursery goblin" of Crédit Mobilier. Conceding that "there is nothing so hopeless to contend with as an intangible phrase, when once it gets hold of the public mind," he lectured the committee at length on the company's history, stressing at every turn the importance of a settlement to both the company and the government. Adams was forceful, earnest, lucid, and compelling in his presentation, but in vain. He might as well have preached the virtues of chastity to the inmates of a brothel.

The bill was referred to a House subcommittee headed by Joseph H. Outhwaite, a new member from Ohio who happened to be a close friend of Thurman. The shrewd Hanna invited Thurman to join the ranks of former foes retained by the Union Pacific and succeeded at least in gaining his support for fresh legislation. Outhwaite attacked the problem with diligence and sincerity: on April 26 he produced a bill that won unanimous backing from the committee. His approach was precisely what Adams and others had long advocated. It called for fixed payments of about $903,000 semiannually until 1921, when all principal and interest would be paid off. The term was extended, but payments were to begin at once instead of 1895, when the first bonds matured. Interest would be reduced from 6 to 3 percent.

By any measure, the Outhwaite bill offered a reasonable solution to a thorny problem. As a compromise it won enough support to convince Adams that passage by a large majority was assured. "My own feeling," he told Dodge, "is that things are going so well that it is very dangerous to interfere with them." He was about to receive an education that probably amused brother Henry more than it did him. His tutor in the art of obfuscation was none other than that "low down knave," Major Reddington.

The House set aside June 5 to take up the Outhwaite bill. Consumed by his thirst for revenge, Reddington toiled furiously to churn up another dust storm of rumor and allegation. Charges and stories were circulated on the House floor and planted in the press, all of them variations on old themes: the proposed settlement gave the Union Pacific enormous benefits at the expense of the government and ought not be approved until a thorough investigation of the company's affairs was made. The road was mired in debt if not insolvent, its officers corrupt, and its directors poised to reap huge fortunes if the bill passed. The ghosts of Crédit Mobilier were conjured up again as evidence of the company's bad faith. "It seems to us," concluded one planted editorial, "that a little more delay as to the compromise, and a little more activity in the investigation of the charges submitted, would just now be especially becoming in members of Congress."

The connection to ghosts of Crédit Mobilier was closer than anyone knew. Reddington had found a new patron in Rowland G. Hazard, who at eighty-five still burned with resentment at his treatment by the Union Pacific. Crédit Mobilier still lived, at least in the courts, and creaked toward extinction at a glacial pace. Hazard's wrath had long since displaced his judgment to the point where he was willing to offer encouragement if not pay to a charlatan. Reddington gloated at being told he "had done more to defeat the Roads than all their opponents" and promised Hazard that "if I live long enough I will have a receiver for the Union Pacific. This crowd have always treated me outrageously, and I shall pay them with compound interest." In the next breath he importuned Hazard to help him find a good railroad job.

Reddington appealed to Hazard because he had cleverly seized on what he called the "Kansas Pacific steal" as an issue. One of Reddington's cronies, a California representative named Henley, had already introduced a resolution demanding an investigation of the consolidation. It lay in committee, a smoldering ember waiting to ignite if the bill faltered. By the eve of battle it was evident that the bill was in trouble. "I do not see how anyone with common sense can disagree with you," a cynical John Hay wrote Adams, "but Congressmen may." Reddington's campaign had made supporters timid and given even reasonable men pause. Abram S. Hewitt, a bulwark of integrity, conceded that the House was "unanimously in favor" of an investigation.

Caught in this web of intrigue, the bill was talked to death. Henley led the charge along with James B. Weaver of Iowa and other granger congressmen who opposed any concession to railroads. Dodge tried to rally his Iowa allies but was stymied by a flare-up of the old dispute between Omaha and Council Bluffs interests. At every turn the Union Pacific seemed blocked by its own history and forced, as Dodge grumbled, "to have ones friends tied up so that they become the enemy." Too late Adams realized who had throttled the bill. "Mr. Reddington, of course, is at the bottom of the whole thing," he scowled. "He has certainly scored a success against us."

Not all the damage came from Reddington's hands. In the Senate, Preston B. Plumb of Kansas offered a resolution to investigate the Union Pacific's affairs. A maverick Republican popular with farmers, Plumb was the sort who concealed his own dirty hands in the white gloves of reform and indignation against corporate oppression. For months he had been pressuring Adams to sell a branch road in Kansas to himself and the Atchison so that it might be extended. Adams wanted no part of the deal and tried instead to interest the Missouri Pacific, but Gould recognized Plumb as dangerous and did not care to antagonize him. The resolution was Plumb's way of expressing displeasure at not getting what he wanted.

Adams responded with a biting protest to Senator Edmunds, head of the Judiciary Committee. No corporation on earth, he complained, had its affairs "subjected to such incessant and wearisome supervision and investigation as those of this company during the last sixteen years." The Union Pacific had nothing to hide and would cooperate with any new investigation, but if there was to be one, Adams wanted it done at once, without delay. The charges and rumors made it impossible "to conduct the business of the company on ordinary business principles." In particular Adams wanted the investigation completed before the next session of Congress, to prevent it from delaying action on the funding bill.

In the House Henley pressed his accusations with a recklessness that provoked Adams into a public rebuke. The Pacific Railroad Committee affirmed their support of the funding bill but hesitated to push it. Henley and Reddington bombarded the committee with more charges filled with obvious errors. Reddington handed out the same misinformation to the New York *World* and other papers. To Hazard he promised that criminal charges would be brought against all directors who took part in the consolidation. Insiders knew what was going on. "Everybody here who knows Henley," sneered one, "believes that he is using his place in Congress to feather his nest." Nevertheless the publicity campaign threw the House into confusion. On July 23 its judiciary committee reported back the Henley resolution calling for an investigation during the summer recess. At once Adams urged immediate passage, but Congress adjourned without taking action and hurried home to the more pressing business of reelection campaigns.

The funding bill was not the only piece of legislation at stake that tortuous season. The company also wanted relief from all restrictions on its power to build or acquire branch lines, which also meant assurance that such acquisitions would not be subject to the financial load placed by the government on the subsidized lines. This had become a touchy issue because of charges that the Union Pacific funneled large sums away from repayment of the government debt to investment in branches. The company countered that branches were vital to protecting its territory and developing new sources of business. Here again the anomaly of a federal charter, and a vague one at that, rose to plague the company.

During the winter of 1886 the company tried first to get what it wanted as a rider on an appropriation bill. When that failed, a bill was put forth not by a friend but by one of the company's loudest foes, Senator Van Wyck of Nebraska. While Adams contemplated this irony, Senator Plumb registered his disapproval that Van Wyck "now represents your Co." He had the last laugh when Van Wyck joined the chorus denouncing the Kansas Pacific steal and backed away from the branch bill, whose adoption, Plumb sneered, he "never had any serious purpose of securing." The bill dropped into limbo to await a better day while Adams puzzled over the question of who were his friends and who his enemies in "that incapable and mischievous body, the U.S. Congress."

As winter approached, the clash renewed over not only the funding bill but another controversial measure. Years of debate over federal regulation of railroads had by 1886 boiled down to a dogfight between the Senate's Cullom bill and the House's Reagan bill. This battle too had ended in stalemate and was expected to be resolved early in the new session. A Supreme Court decision in the *Wabash* case added pressure by denying states the right to regulate interstate commerce. Most railroad men favored the Cullom bill, but sentiment was swinging toward the Reagan bill. In the Senate the ubiquitous Edmunds solemnly invoked the people's need to "emancipate themselves from the tyranny of this corporate management and corporate combination that now exists." The outlook for rational consideration of a funding bill did not look promising in an atmosphere soured by the battle over federal regulation.

A clique of prominent bears greeted the new session by pouncing on a misinformed rumor to send the stock tumbling. Bromley tried to "enforce the lesson on Congress" by sending every member a copy of the story. Although Outhwaite survived a rugged reelection campaign, he complained to Hanna that "a bitter fight has been made upon me here, on account of the bill, ever since I spoke upon the subject in the House." Hanna hurried to Washington to lobby along with Franklin MacVeagh, a government director and prominent Democrat. MacVeagh sounded President Cleveland on the question and came away satisfied that he "simply cared to know what it was right to do and seemed never to entertain a thought about the political effect of his action." Outhwaite remained steadfast and Abram Hewitt now favored the bill, but he was about to resign his seat and warned Adams that "The prejudice against corporations, and especially those which have received land grants, is so great in the House that reason has lost its sway."

In December Bromley surveyed the prospects and drew a gloomy prognosis. "The average member of Congress," he noted, "does not view this bill as an ordinary measure affecting the public generally or his constituents particularly. He sees in it a measure for the benefit of a great corporation." No bill would be passed unless "we can bring together a sufficient number of members of Congress worked up to a pitch almost of enthusiasm for it, and push it. How to do this is the question." The company had obtained committee approval and qualified support from both the departments and the President.

"We have reached the point," Bromley concluded, "where the only thing that is necessary . . . is to overcome the *vis inertiae* of Congress." The only hope lay in an intensive lobby to convince members that their constituents would benefit from the bill.

Bromley was stumped over how to deal with the incestuous relationship between certain Wall Street bears and the papers. Joseph Pulitzer of the New York *World* had lent his ear to Josiah C. Reiff, a scavenger who vowed revenge on the Union Pacific because Gould had supposedly cheated him out of four hundred thousand dollars in the Kansas Pacific consolidation. Reiff was dismissed as a blackmailer or "striker" not worth paying off even though he had joined forces with Reddington. Another familiar predator, Theophilus French, threatened to disclose sensational charges against the Central Pacific unless salved with cash. Helpless to deflect these rogues and their access to willing editors, Adams made the mistake of underestimating the damage they could inflict.

When the Outhwaite bill came up, opponents cleverly substituted a resolution for investigation and got it passed. This procedural end run forced another struggle to get the funding bill back on the calendar. The consensus among knowing observers was that the bill had enough votes to pass but that its foes were "strong enough to prevent that by filibustering." Meanwhile, the Senate asked the Treasury to inform it on the practical effects of the long-dormant Hoar bill. The Secretary pointed out the defects already known to Hoar, who had an amendment ready to correct them. Before he could act, however, Adams's worst fears were confirmed. The New York *World* blasted the bill as a cunning device by the Union Pacific to rob the government and whipped up another rehash of old scandals. Once again the demand for investigation began to snowball. Adams's friend Charles Dana of the New York *Sun,* who had scourged the Union Pacific in past years, tried this time to counteract the *World's* fulminations. Explanations were planted in other friendly journals but made little impression.

The House asked Treasury for a similar opinion on the Outhwaite bill and was promptly told it had no defects and would accomplish its ends. This reassurance could not offset the clamor aroused by the *World* or the agitation of anticorporate crusaders. Dodge confirmed that the rumors "demoralized a *good many* members," and John G. Carlisle, the House Speaker, confided privately that passage was "not at all probable during the present session." A dispirited Adams conceded that "the lick they put in on us on the Hoar bill was certainly a masterpiece." He watched glumly as the Interstate Commerce Act sailed through Congress by large majorities on January 21. "Whichever way I turn," he groaned, "Congress and Congressional restrictions stand across my path." Reluctantly he abandoned all hope of passing the bill and pushed for an investigation to clear the air by the next session.

Nothing seemed easier than bringing on an investigation, but in the Senate Judiciary Committee Edmunds struck again with an amendment to broaden the inquiry to embrace the *World*'s charges, extend payments under the Thurman Act to include the Kansas Pacific and the Central Branch, and hike the amount to 40 percent of net income. The bears took their cue and battered Union Pacific again. "No corporation could stand this sort of thing," muttered an outraged Adams. Edmunds's resolution, he told Dodge, "stretches us on the rack for an indefinite period. Three men would be paid $750. a month to probe continually into our affairs, and use their information for stock operations."

Adams responded with a lengthy protest to the Senate. After a heated debate the amendment was beaten back. The final act suited Adams's original hopes, but he found little solace in salvaging one small victory in a lost campaign he had directed personally. A friend, General James H. Wilson, assured him the fault was not his, but Adams was not appeased. The man on horseback had been driven from the field and, like a true Adams, blamed himself too much. There had been blunders, but large forces determined the outcome. The true obstacle, reiterated a lawyer, was "a vague, ill-defined, but yet discernible feeling in many quarters that no arrangement should be made unless it were more or less punitory in its character." No one could figure out what Edmunds was after or what Congress would do. The investigation provided a reprieve, perhaps a fatal one. Wilson thought it meant "the end of legislation for two or three years, unless you can get a capable commission appointed to conduct and hurry up the investigation."

* * *

Everything depended now on the choice of commissioners. President Cleveland, stung by criticism on some of his nominations to the Interstate Commerce Commission, moved cautiously. Dodge wanted W. P. Hepburn of Iowa, arguing that it was "best for us to have a first class Politician in the Committee." Adams agreed it would be "a very great thing for us to get some man put on that commission familiar with Congressional ways and Congressional action, and who might possibly, after the service on the commission was done, enter our employ as our agent at Washington." Distasteful as the game was to him, Adams was learning its rules.

But he was still a novice. After a month of deliberation Cleveland appointed E. Ellery Anderson, an able New York corporation lawyer, former Governor Robert E. Pattison of Pennsylvania, and David T. Littler, an Illinois lawyer and legislator. None of them were household names beyond their own thresholds or expert in railroad affairs. Anderson and Pattison were Democrats, Littler a Republican said to owe his appointment to Senator Cullom, who had boosted Littler unsuccessfully for a place on the Interstate Commerce Commission. Of Littler the *World* observed that "What he does not know about the machine is not worth knowing."

Wilson advised Adams to take the initiative and not "place too much confidence in the fairness of the Commission." Adams needed little prodding on that point. The stockholders approved a resolution instructing the board to formulate and submit a plan of settlement to the government. Adams hoped this plan might give the commission "an 'objective' to steer for from the start." When he tried to present the plan, however, the commission informed him that it preferred formulating its own proposal without outside help. Adams would soon discover that the members needed more help than he could provide.

From late April until October the commission toiled, amassing more than five thousand pages of testimony, statistics, and exhibits. After lengthy hearings in New York and Boston, the members took to the road for a month, listening to anyone with something to say along the route from Omaha and Kansas City to San Francisco. Nearly all the living ghosts of the roads' past were summoned forth to tell their tale: Dillon, Dodge, Gould, Huntington, Stanford, Crocker, Fred Ames, Atkins, Dexter, Sage, Sharp, Dey, Governor Oliver Ames, Evans, even the venerable John Blair. Huge amounts of data were demanded from the Pacific roads and certain individuals, and the government accountants supplied still more. In length and depth the probe dwarfed that of Crédit Mobilier. It was by far the most extensive investigation of a private corporation prior to the age of wholesale federal regulation.

Reporters flocked to every session in anticipation of the juicy revelations their editors had promised the public. If nothing else the event was a rare opportunity to watch celebrities of business squirm beneath the inquisitor's glare. The prospect of glimpsing such shadowy and elusive figures in full daylight guaranteed overflow crowds at most of the hearings. Throughout the sittings in New York and Boston the indefatigable Bromley monitored the testimony and newspaper accounts of it, providing Adams with a box score of points gained or lost and by whom. A nervous Moorfield Storey suggested that Bromley try to influence the Associated Press reports, but Bromley did not think it could be done and assumed that Adams wished "to avoid the appearance of an attempt to control" newspaper accounts.

Early in the proceedings, Bromley took the commissioners' measure. He considered both Anderson and Pattison as "at the bottom self-seekers." Littler he regarded as "of a coarser grain and something of a demagogue, but upon the whole, with better impulses and a sounder man at bottom, than either of the other two." The real menace on the commission was its expert, John Norris, editor of the Philadelphia *Record,* who apparently owed his appointment to Pattison. The *Record* had long been hostile to the Union Pacific, and Bromley sized up Norris as "a crank, but a very industrious and persistent one, filled full of anti-railroad prejudice, and saturated with suspicion of everybody who has any connection with railroads."

Although the inquiry roamed indiscriminately over a broad landscape, it pursued two issues with a vengeance: the Kansas Pacific consolidation and certain charges against the Central Pacific. Adams held an important advantage in heading a reform administration that had no part in the consolidation, while the Central Pacific remained in the hands of its originators. At every turn he did what he could to emphasize the distance between himself and the Huntington crowd, hoping that the latter would draw most of the commission's fire.

But Adams could not dodge the consolidation controversy, especially the removal of the Denver Pacific stock from trust with what appeared to be indecent if not illegal haste. The commission grilled every participant mercilessly in hopes of sparking fireworks. The proceedings on the consolidation, Bromley observed, were "in the nature of an inquisition. The minds of the three commissioners are clearly made up, and they are bent on making something out of this feature of the investigation to justify the inquiry." Most of the witnesses shrank from the assault and retreated behind defensive testimony. Judge Dillon was "sphinx-like," his uncle Sidney vague, picturesque, and rambling, James Ham reticent, Sage nervous like a man fearful of betraying secrets, and others simply timid. Only lawyer Artemas Holmes spoke freely about the transaction, but he was too peripheral a figure to sway opinions. One man alone could make a decisive impression if he chose, and that was Gould.

Gould was not only willing but anxious to set the record straight on the consolidation. A week before going on the stand he recited his case to Bromley and Mink, who found it "very forceful and effective." Just before he was called, Gould suffered a severe attack of facial neuralgia, but so remarkable was his self-control that no one even suspected the excruciating pain that wracked him during three days of relentless questioning. Since the sensation created by Huntington's appearance, public interest had flagged for want of lurid exposures. Gould's presence restored attention at once; it was the highlight of the investigation, a confrontation long and eagerly awaited. An overflow crowd jammed the room to witness the fireworks.

They were not disappointed. Anderson sensed his moment in the spotlight had come and determined to make the most of it. His tough, probing questions had reduced Sage to a fidgeting wreck and intimidated others, but Gould was not easily cowed or cornered. Speaking as always in a voice so soft the reporters strained to hear it, he talked easily and frankly. Anderson interrupted repeatedly with questions to throw Gould off his prepared text, but the little man took it all in stride. The commission had pressed his partner and secretary for Gould's books, only to be met with evasion. Confronted by the demand, Gould astonished everyone by offering them willingly. Through it all Pattison and Littler listened intently to everything Gould had to say and were impressed by his candor.

If the commission hoped to uncover fraud in the consolidation, here was their best chance. Anderson bore in on the Denver Pacific transaction and struck bedrock. Gould grew more animated and his voice louder as, with a defiant shake of his oversized head, he took full responsibility for the transaction and defended it as both honest and sound policy. "It was quite refreshing," noted an admiring Bromley, "to find anybody among those concerned in this transaction who acted as though he believed in it and was willing to stand up for it." For two more days Anderson matched wits with Gould and got nowhere. Gradually his tone softened, as did that of his colleagues. A delighted Bromley reported that even Norris began "to have rather a discouraged and melancholy look." No shocking revelations or hints of iniquities emerged. For every question, Gould had an answer that was direct and plausible. He retired from the stand leaving the inquisitors deflated if not demolished in their quest.

Gould's virtuoso performance took the sting out of the commission's probe into the consolidation. The scene shifted to Boston, where the sessions dragged wearily on until Adams muttered, "I am sick of it." His exasperation mounted when he was obliged to accompany the commission on its tour through the West. At every stop an assortment of railroad men, shippers, bankers, city fathers, politicians, and editors vented their grievances. The commissioners found themselves utterly at sea in the intricacies of rail operations and rate structures. In their ignorance they seized on the most obvious details of rebates and pools in hopes of making the case that had so far eluded them. The investigation grated on Adams, who resented having to run a "railroad kindergarten for uninformed inquisitors." At Ogden he turned the whole crowd over to the Central Pacific and breathed a sigh of relief at escaping from the "repulsive journey."

By that time a split had occurred in the commission between Anderson and Littler, who had softened their views, and Pattison who clung doggedly to the dark suspicions favored by Norris. The obstinacy of Stanford and the Central Pacific people also helped the Union Pacific. Where Adams had opened his records freely, Stanford resisted the commission's every demand and exchanged angry words with Pattison. "These people," smiled Bromley, "have a whole lot of fight in them." Their resistance confirmed at last the belief that wrongdoing lay just beneath the surface, and resulted in criminal charges. Bromley did what he could to ingratiate himself with both Anderson and Littler, who assured him that the Union Pacific would not be ill-treated in the final report.

The fireworks in the West fed the New York *World*'s relentless campaign against the Pacific roads. It complained of Cleveland's "apathy" on the question but, as Adams learned, the President had no intention of acting until the commission submitted its report. The New York *Herald* joined the crusade by encouraging a move to bring criminal charges against Gould and Sage for their role in the Denver Pacific transaction. James Gordon Bennett had his own reasons for a vendetta against Gould, which reached a spectacular climax in March 1888. Although Bennett's incessant drumming was a sideshow, it kept the Union Pacific's past in the headlines for six months at a time when Adams sought desperately to focus attention on the settlement question. When suit was brought against Gould and Sage, Judge Dillon advised that the company had little choice but to "uphold and sustain the trustees in the defence."

The split during the hearings remained to the end; Anderson and Littler submitted a majority report, Pattison a minority dissent. All agreed the government should get out of the railroad business but differed strongly over how to do it. The majority preferred a modified version of the funding bill as the basis for settlement, while Pattison argued that "a mere money recovery is the least of benefits" the government should consider. He wanted the road thrown into receivership as "the direct path to the complete solution of a tangle into which the Government should never have been drawn." The government could thereby "recover its debt and put its seal of condemnation upon the multiplied wrongs that have marked the administration of that trust." Criminal charges should be brought against those officers or directors suspected of illicit transactions. Once reorganized, the new line should be prohibited from investing in competing or parallel roads and from engaging in any other business.

Pattison was unabashedly vindictive in demanding that the company be punished for its past crimes. The majority condemned the consolidation as indefensible but conceded that its results had been "beneficial." Its harsh words for past policy were softened by insistence that Adams had ushered in a new era of honest and intelligent management deserving of consideration from the government. Pattison rejected any such distinction in urging "a speedy and absolute divorce" between the government and the Pacific roads. The most striking aspect of both reports was the extent to which the ghost of Crédit Mobilier haunted the reasoning behind them. Pattison was brutally explicit on that point. He denounced any funding proposal because it amounted to "an additional subsidy" and would "recognize as valid the Crédit Mobilier wrongs and the extravagant mismanagement" of past boards. "It would validate the results of fraud," he added savagely, "and be a condonation of monstrous iniquities which the Government cannot afford."

Adams dismissed Pattison's report as the "dyspeptic utterance of an untruthful, dishonest political crank," but he could not ignore the problems it posed. To save time in their deliberations all three commissioners had agreed to accept the earlier Wilson and Poland reports at face value and refused to replow old ground. As one historian observed, their decision to accept these investigations as "infallible and nonpartisan put error at compound interest." The specter of the past infused not only their reports but the public response to them. "I have yet to see any newspaper article," mourned Bromley, "that does not devote more space to the iniquities of the past management of the roads than to the proposition for settlement." The *Herald* led the charge in blasting what it called "ROBBER RAILWAYS."

Convinced that Norris had actually dictated Pattison's report, Bromley prepared a response and showed it to Anderson, who found it too much a "display of solemn and somewhat melancholy indignation." He suggested a lighter touch, a playful satire on "Don Quixote Pattison and Sancho Panza Norris." But neither Bromley nor Adams was in a playful mood. In his message to Congress, Cleveland rejected Pattison's argument in favor of the majority report with its reasoned approach to a settlement. He urged "prompt and efficient action," which was all Adams could ask. The question, as always, was what the Congress would do. That winter, Adams stepped gingerly into another uncharted pathway of the labyrinth. He would find it darker and more sordid than any into which he had yet ventured.

* * *

On January 16 Outhwaite introduced a revised version of his bill to a reshuffled Pacific Railroads Committee with only four holdovers from the previous session. In the Senate Hoar managed to get his bill referred to a special committee. Adams trudged dutifully to Washington to make the rounds, calling on the President, submitting himself to both committees, and doing what he could to lobby the cause in private. The commissioners also appeared before the committees to reiterate their views. Adams had reached an "understanding" with Littler, and Anderson was sympathetic, but nothing could be done about Pattison. The genial Hanna also lent his considerable influence to the cause among his wide circle of friends in Congress. In March the House committee reported out Outhwaite's bill by unanimous vote.

Everything seemed to be moving smoothly, or was it? Moorfield Storey kept returning from Washington with the report that became his theme song: "Everything looking well but nothing accomplished." The executive committee exasperated Adams with its inability to grasp a "glimmering conception of the position of affairs." The aged Elisha Atkins, hobbled by a stroke, drove Adams to distraction with his "snarling criticisms of senility." Only Fred Ames seemed to comprehend the bold plan Adams had conceived of seizing control of the Northern Pacific, forging an alliance with the Burlington, and using that combination to raise enough cash to pay off the government outright. Adams broached the scheme to Perkins and found him not only cold to the idea but implacably hostile to the funding bill. Instead of a grand coalition, Adams found himself bogged down in a petty, bickering correspondence with Perkins.

Through the spring and summer, Adams doggedly pursued the "dreary Washington process." In the House Anderson and Weaver of Iowa led a drive to filibuster Outhwaite's bill to death. Every pressure was brought to bear without success; the filibuster could not be broken. The Burlington was using its influence well. A disgusted Hanna suspected that "there is something else besides politics in this. I believe that other Railroads are paying some of these fellows to do this and I believe that Redington [sic] is the medium."

Thwarted in the House, Adams shifted his attention to the Senate. In an effort to break the deadlock, the special committee on July 31 unanimously endorsed the Outhwaite bill. Passage by the Senate would put pressure on the

House to act, but every effort to bring it to a vote failed. Someone was blocking the path, and Adams soon learned it was his old nemesis Plumb. The news came through the company's other Washington lobbyist, E. W. Ayres, who had been hired by the Union Pacific in 1882 as a favor to Plumb. Since then Ayres had become a valuable agent and had gradually broken with Plumb. He was at a loss to explain Plumb's constant attacks on the company. Adams received several intimations that Plumb wanted something, but what? When all attempts to appease him failed, he sent Ayres in August to ask the senator bluntly where he stood on the Outhwaite bill. After a heated exchange Ayres learned only that Plumb saw nothing for himself in the bill's passage and thought the Union Pacific management a selfish crowd.

Adams realized that Plumb was a master obstructionist who could bottle up the bill indefinitely. To soften him, Adams built a station at Lawrence, leased a small Kansas road, built some track for his constituents. None of it impressed Plumb. Congress adjourned without taking action and went home to fight the campaign of 1888. After the election Adams sent Ayres to Kansas to sound Plumb again, using Morrison Mumford, editor of the Kansas City *Times,* as his intermediary. Plumb told Mumford that he wanted "money,— and 'big money.' " Washington, he complained, was an expensive place to live on a small salary. He suggested a meeting with Adams, but Charles shied away from "compromising myself or the company with him in any way."

When Congress met in December, the same mysterious forces kept the funding bill off the calendar. Cleveland's defeat in the election left Adams depressed in the belief that his "whole work for U. P. [had] to be done over again." Huntington worsened matters by shoving forward his own bill for settling the Central Pacific's account with the government. To Adams he was all sweetness and light, offering him drafts of two bills and vowing to work together on either one. In fact he had impaled the Union Pacific on the horns of an ugly dilemma. One bill was a substitute for the Outhwaite bill, the other an amendment of it to include the Central Pacific. Adams thought it out of the question to abandon Outhwaite's bill at that late date, but he also saw what a "heavy load" the amendments would be. "Nevertheless," he told Dodge glumly, "if we had opposed it, it would have been the end of our bill. It would certainly have been in his power to have destroyed us." The only chance left was to hope that Congress might reject the amendments but accept the Outhwaite bill itself.

An uphill battle loomed which, Ayres reported, could be smoothed if Plumb was defanged. Adams grew less squeamish about a deal and had in fact already lost some of his innocence. In August, during the election campaign, W. H. Barnum of the Democratic National Committee had approached Adams with an offer to get the funding bill passed for a contribution of fifty thousand dollars. "I can get your bill passed if any man can," Barnum boasted, "and you can rest assured, if I can't get it passed, it cannot be passed." The offer moved Adams to a cynical experiment. He related it to

Fred Ames and suggested that he make a similar offer to Matthew Quay of the Republican National Committee. "We would soon in this way," he observed, "learn what political influence money could buy."

If this seemed strange behavior for a Brahmin reformer, Adams was quick to rationalize it. In the delightful phrase of his biographer, he portrayed Ames and himself as "white-coated scientists conducting a laboratory experiment in political science." Each party received twenty thousand dollars at once, with the remainder promised after the bill was passed. The money, it turned out, bought nothing. Neither side could deliver on their promise, yet Adams and Ames agreed it was "worth the $40,000 it actually cost to have tested the matter so thoroughly."

From this experience it was but one more step downward to dealing with Plumb. Adams admitted being out of his league in handling "western men," and Ames wanted no part of it. He returned from Washington early in December and said bluntly he would not go there again. Adams hit upon the idea of summoning John M. Thurston, the company counsel at Omaha and himself a politician. Thurston went on to Washington, struck Plumb's trail, and backed off at once, saying Plumb was "too dangerous a man." At Adams's prodding he persisted, however, until he got what he had come for. In January 1889 he hurried back to New York and disclosed the details to Adams, who had by then been approached by Plumb's Kansas partner.

The wily Plumb conveyed his terms to Thurston not personally but through his colleague J. J. Ingalls, then acting vice president. After assuring Thurston that he personally favored the bill, Ingalls emphasized the need to placate Plumb. That could be done for fifty thousand dollars, half in advance and the rest when the bill passed the Senate. Adams was struck dumb at the spectacle of one senator arranging the sale of another. Here was the "most dangerous kind of political black-mail," for Ingalls hinted that unless Plumb was satisfied, he, too, would be obliged to oppose the bill. What to do? Once again Adams agonized his way to a convenient rationale. If the bill could be passed by paying fifty thousand dollars in blackmail, he would be unfit as a president if he did not agree. In his view "morally it was no case of bribery" but of duty to his stockholders. He decided, therefore, to "fling the dirty dog his bone, provided I could do so in safety."

Everything was arranged through negotiations between Thurston and Ingalls but, for reasons Adams does not make clear, the deal was never consummated. Apparently Plumb could not deliver the goods, and no money changed hands. Adams came away satisfied that "the measure was not to be carried by the use of money," which left open the question of how it *was* to be carried. Weaver continued to block action in the House, and behind Plumb in the Senate stood Edmunds, as malign and sanctimonious as ever. "Unlike Plumb he never allows a direct bribe to reach him," Adams sneered; "he only takes retainers as a counsel in the Supreme Court, but when retained in the Supreme Court, he takes the best of care of his client in the Senate Chamber."

Gould, Huntington, Perkins, and Villard learned this early and were quick to hire Edmunds, but years earlier the Union Pacific had for some reason ignored the "sea-green immaculate from Vermont." Since that time Edmunds had injured the company at every opportunity.

Or so Adams heard. He also believed Edmunds was addicted to the bottle, and that his drinking was what ultimately forced him to quit the Senate in 1891. Whatever the truth, Edmunds excelled at the art of pious obstructionism. Adams watched in helpless rage the "bribe-taking old drunkard . . . bushwacking us with infinite adroitness." By late February the bill was dead and the future looked bleak. Littler picked that unhappy time to ask Adams for the ten thousand dollars and expenses owed him by the company for "services" during the campaign. Adams responded churlishly that the payment was contingent on the bill being passed, obliging Dodge to referee the squabble.

Everything had turned out badly for Adams. Virtue had failed to get a settlement, and so had vice. He had mired himself in muck with nothing to show for it beyond a soiled self-image. Curiously, what distressed him most afterward was not lapsed virtue but inadequate technique. "I simply didn't know how to go to work," he lamented. "Not that I'm above it; I'm not. I would have bought Plumb, just as I would have bought a horse or a hog,— and there would to me have been a perfect and intense satisfaction in slipping the dollars into the greedy hands of the Vermont immaculate."

Routed from the field and broken in spirit, Adams quietly abandoned the fight. After five years he was no closer to a settlement than Gould had been. During 1889–90 yet another version of the bill came before Congress. The Senate committee toured the Union Pacific and came home impressed; Adams found its chairman, William P. Frye of Maine, "an enlightened and changed man,—a friend of the U.P." But Frye's conversion was not enough to offset the rising tide of the farm revolt on the plains. "This Congress is frightened to death by the farmers' league in the west," Adams observed, and antirailroad sentiment was gospel to the farmers. In Nebraska the farmers got up a monster petition against the funding bill. Nor did it help that the bill gave the Central Pacific much better terms than the Union Pacific. A discouraged Adams went before the Senate committee and startled everyone by flatly opposing the bill for that reason.

The loyal Hanna again declared his willingness to "take a hand in the scrimmage," but the game was lost. Congress had more important measures to consider, including the Sherman antitrust bill. The funding bill was not even allowed to die a quiet death; in June the New York *World* levied another blast at the "Union Pacific Barons" and charged that Gould was behind the scheme. Adams had long since abandoned hope and become a mere spectator to what he called the "everlasting Washington business." Such was his disillusionment that, after meeting a senator who wanted nothing from him, he proclaimed, "for a wonder, a U. S. Senator not on the make." The hurt in

Adams ran deeper than anyone knew. From the first he had made a settlement with the government one of his chief objectives, and he had failed utterly to achieve it. By 1890 the first bonds were only a few years from maturing, and Adams was no nearer a solution than the company had been two decades earlier.

* * *

Throughout the interminable struggle in Washington, Crédit Mobilier was a specter that haunted the Union Pacific at every turn. It was also a living creature, deformed beyond recognition, defying every attempt to kill it. The public had long since forgotten Crédit Mobilier except as a symbol of corruption, but to certain lawyers and litigants it remained all too palpable. Since the winter of 1879, when the agreement with Hazard had come apart, the struggle had taken more twists than a soap opera. Gould's drive had brought nearly two thirds of Crédit Mobilier's stock into the Union Pacific treasury, but most of the outstanding shares remained in fighting hands. The state of Pennsylvania pressed its suit for unpaid taxes against Crédit Mobilier, which was in receivership under Governor Oliver Ames. Durant and McComb had yet to settle, and the two-million-dollar-note suit was still pending.

All these complications paled before the wrath of old Hazard, whose thirst for vengeance knew no bounds. Hazard still had suits against Dillon and others in Massachusetts and in the New York Circuit Court, against McComb and others in the Delaware Circuit Court, against the Ames estate in the probate court of Bristol County, Massachusetts, against the Ames executors in the Massachusetts Circuit Court, and against Durant in the Rhode Island courts. When a suit failed in the lower court he promptly appealed to a higher one; for every action taken against him, he launched a countersuit. The moment anyone seemed ready to compromise with what he called "the Jay Gould gang," he moved to block the settlement. Although he haggled constantly with his lawyers over their fees, his obsession overrode all considerations of cost or reason.

As Gould's attention turned elsewhere, Dillon was obliged to push the fight. In December 1879 the company formally wrote off $107,082 worth of items in the suspense account, including the long-disputed charge of nearly $70,000 against Bushnell. Durant filed a new suit against the Trustees but showed some willingness to negotiate. Early in 1881 Dillon managed at last to reach agreement with both the Doctor and McComb. For a small consideration and a full release, McComb surrendered his Crédit Mobilier stock only months before his death in December 1881. The Doctor was too broke to give in so cheaply. After some tough bargaining he agreed in March 1881 to accept for all claims $75,000 and cancellation of a loan for $21,000 held by Dillon. The deal required a release from the receiver of Crédit Mobilier; when Governor Oliver granted it, Hazard promptly sued to have it set aside. The court granted Hazard's petition and threw part of the arrangement back into a tangle of litigation.

The settlement finally eliminated Durant as an adversary. The Doctor walked away with money in his pocket and without having to restore a penny of what he had taken or misused. Dillon tried to wind up the affairs of the Trustees as well and succeeded in having their claim against Crédit Mobilier transferred to the Union Pacific in August 1881. Since this claim plus accrued interest amounted to nearly $1.3 million, Governor Oliver, Hazard, and other Crédit Mobilier stockholders asked the court to set it aside as collusive. The request was granted and the case appealed to the New York Supreme Court, where it remained pending for years. Staving off this suit kept the opposition of Hazard and Governor Oliver alive. If the Union Pacific had won, the entire settlement would have fallen on the diehard band of Crédit Mobilier holders who had not yet surrendered their stock.

The importance of this stalemate soon became evident. Hazard continued to stalk Durant with his two suits in Rhode Island, unmoved by the argument that the Doctor was bankrupt and could pay nothing anyway. An embittered John Williams agreed to help but at the same time offered his 314 shares of Crédit Mobilier to Hazard at fifty dollars per share. "Some tell me that it is worth much more than that," he said hopefully. When Hazard added Ebenezer Hoar to the team of lawyers pressing the suits, Hoar looked over the papers and admitted to being in doubt whether Hazard was plaintiff or defendant "or trying to be a little of both, which is a novelty." Unable to get at Hazard, the Union Pacific took steps to remove Governor Oliver as receiver of Crédit Mobilier.

In December 1882 the Rhode Island Supreme Court handed Hazard an adverse decision on one of his suits. Undaunted, Hazard filed a new suit in Massachusetts a few days later against Durant and the other trustees or their estates. The Union Pacific then assigned Sidney Bartlett to help Durant defend the second Rhode Island suit. Before it was decided, however, another ruling dealt the company a severe setback. After hearing the two-million-dollar-note case three times, the Massachusetts Supreme Court threw out the Union Pacific's equity suit on the grounds that there was insufficient proof of actual fraud. This decision left the company open to Crédit Mobilier's suit to collect the two million dollars for its stockholders. About 13,700 shares were still outstanding, most of them belonging to Hazard and Governor Oliver. The company now had little choice but to settle with them.

On the heels of this blow came a victory by Hazard in his suit against Durant in Massachusetts. This decision struck the Union Pacific during the dismal winter of 1884, when the financial crisis was boiling to a head. A distraught Dillon appealed the Hazard ruling and made overtures to settle with Governor Oliver, who was willing to bargain but uncertain as to whether he could negotiate for Crédit Mobilier as well as himself. The opportunistic Bushnell got wind of this dilemma and hurriedly thrust in his oar, claiming that he could get control of ten thousand of the outstanding shares. Dillon regarded Bushnell as a schemer who was "as usual in want of money," but he agreed to pay him a commission of twenty thousand dollars if he could acquire the shares at a price of about 20. Unaware of this deal, Elisha Atkins negotiated with Governor Oliver for his holdings and agreed to terms that muddled Dillon's arrangement with Bushnell.

As usual Bushnell talked a better game than he played. He produced only about 583 shares at 20, for which he managed to wheedle three thousand dollars of the commission out of Dillon. When some of the holders he approached wrote Hazard asking if Bushnell was his agent, it did not take the old Rhode Islander long to figure out what was going on. He advised them to bid the price up, and later made a counteroffer. Hazard learned too that Governor Oliver was trading with the enemy and moved to oust him as receiver. Protesting that he was willing to quit the post but not "under apparent compulsion or as if . . . turned out for some fault or misconduct," the governor sold his Crédit Mobilier shares to Atkins for 20 plus seventy-five thousand dollars for expenses and surrendered the receivership to Samuel R. Shipley, a Philadelphia banker.

In the midst of these events Adams took office. The deal with Governor Oliver left only one obstacle to settlement: the implacable Hazard, who continued to press his one live suit against Durant. Shipley was anxious to wind up the affairs of Crédit Mobilier, from which the patient H. C. Crane still drew a salary. Dillon felt obliged to stay out of Massachusetts to avoid being served papers in Hazard's suit there. He asked Adams's opinion of when it would be safe to come to Boston "in a public way" and was told solemnly, "I think it will be safe for you to do so the day after you read of Hazard's death in the newspapers." In October 1885 Durant, the chief object of Hazard's wrath, died, transferring his judgment to a higher authority. Five months later the Union Pacific formally released the Trustees from all pending litigation, including the two-million-dollar note. By then only two of the seven (Bushnell and Dillon) were still alive.

Still Hazard persisted, opening yet another suit in 1886 and gaining a victory in his suit against Durant. His target in the latter was not the departed Doctor but his bondsman. There was left to him only his share of the two-million-dollar-note suit, which he was willing to negotiate. On June 22, 1888, his son Rowland agreed to take $125,000 for 347 shares of Crédit Mobilier, which included the 314 shares purchased from Williams. He also agreed to transfer 152 shares of Union Pacific stock and accrued dividends for $25,000. The bulk of the cost was paid by the Union Pacific, the rest by Fred Ames, Dillon, and McComb's estate.

The agreement was signed on June 23. On the very next day, at his home in Peace Dale, Rhode Island, the indomitable Hazard died, a few months shy of his eighty-seventh birthday. The papers thought his death sudden and perhaps it was, but the select few who knew of his obsession over the Union Pacific suits surely realized that he had lived just long enough.

It took Judge Dillon another two years to untangle the legal snarls and lay Crédit Mobilier to rest. Rowland Hazard executed two supplemental agreements to thrash out some details. The state of Pennsylvania accepted forty thousand dollars in settlement of its tax case. Crédit Mobilier released the two-million-dollar note to the Union Pacific, and title to the lands in Council Bluffs was finally perfected. Amid the sorting out, a smiling Bushnell came away with another seventy-five hundred dollars for "commissions and expenses." The question remained of what to do with the charter itself. Judge Dillon pointed out that its liberal terms made it "exceedingly valuable," but Adams countered that the "taint of its past history" demanded that it be dissolved, rather than sold. Not until June 1890, more than twenty-one years after completion of the road it helped to build, was Crédit Mobilier finally interred. "Peace to its ashes!" intoned Judge Dillon. "It ought to have a long rest for it had a stormy existence."

28

THE NORTHWEST PASSAGE

The good commander chooses his battles wisely and avoids a fight until his army is ready. During the expansion wars of the 1880s Adams tried to live by this maxim. He was in no position to fight everyone and everywhere at once. In many respects the Union Pacific was the Russia of railroads, large but weak, hobbled by ancient debilities, unable to harness its size or strength effectively against smaller but more nimble enemies. For Adams personally, the analogy carried one step further. Like the czar, he found himself a prisoner of advisors whose capacity he was helpless to judge and whose conflicting counsel he was slow to reconcile.

The basic strategy Adams chose was sound in theory. By 1886 he recognized that the Union Pacific could not avoid the wars of expansion raging on every front. If the company must build, it made sense to seize the region beyond the Rockies and fight a holding action on the plains where the Iowa roads, the Atchison, and the Missouri Pacific were all laying track at a furious pace. The original line in Nebraska and Kansas was the most vulnerable to rivals because of its excessive capitalization, which could not be improved until the government debt was settled. The newer branches, in better shape and beyond Washington's clutches, might be developed into a system powerful enough to carry the older lines through their financial ordeal. "The child will be greater than its father," Adams mused, "and may yet buy him out of his slavery to the government."

This vision was reinforced by Dodge, whose influence on Adams grew steadily during the late 1880s. In October 1886 Dodge returned from a tour of the Union Pacific and Northern Pacific roads, much of it through country he had once crossed as explorer and surveyor. Expansive as always, Dodge outlined an agenda for future growth. Above all else he stressed the importance of reaching the Pacific coast, preferably by buying or leasing the Oregon Railway & Navigation Company. This would plant the Union Pacific in the Northwest on equal terms with the Northern Pacific. The Utah & Northern should be widened to standard gauge and a line built to Helena. Dodge also favored construction west of the Rockies to the coal deposits below Fort Steele. He wanted the revived Cheyenne & Northern project pushed to a connection with the Northern Pacific somewhere between the Tongue and the Big Horn rivers in Montana. By contrast, Dodge saw nothing worth doing on the plains except a line from the North Platte to Sioux City.

Dodge's support did much to bolster Adams's confidence. Along with this expansion program, Adams had also to weld the sprawling lines of the Union Pacific into a cohesive system. Little had been done since the consolidation to unify or harmonize disparate pieces; the Kansas Pacific had simply been attached as the Kansas division. In 1884 the Union Pacific operated 4,476 miles of road, and the race for empire had just dawned. Here too the military analogy applied: the larger the army grew, the more imperative it was to organize and administer it efficiently if battles and wars were to be won.

* * *

Adams did well to stay out of the cross fire on the plains, where the fight grew both intense and ugly. Gould, moving like a whirlwind to erect his Missouri Pacific system, built or bought 2,975 miles of road in six states and Indian Territory. The Atchison did even better, throwing out track in every direction like a bull maddened by the matador's cape until its mileage swelled from 2,799 in 1884 to 7,010 in 1888. The Rock Island, spurred by Cable's grandiose vision of empire, mushroomed from 1,400 to 3,000 miles, most of it in territory contested by the Missouri Pacific and the Atchison.

The chief battleground was Kansas, which by 1890 would possess more railroad mileage than any other state except Illinois, but no territory went uncontested. The Northwestern swarmed across northern Nebraska and Dakota into Wyoming and talked of reaching the coast. Since it had also penetrated south of the Platte River, the Burlington retaliated by marching north of the Platte at Grand Island. Gould and Cable both built into Colorado, the Atchison was in Chicago, the Burlington in St. Paul, and two other companies were constructing roads between Chicago and the Twin Cities. To punish the Burlington for its invasion, the St. Paul built to Kansas City. Perkins toyed with the idea of attacking Kansas but decided to go slow.

No one could predict when or how the carnage would cease. A fearful John Murray Forbes, who had a longer memory than most, urged the creation of a cash reserve "against the next 1873, which is sure to come, if this lunacy as to Railroad building extends much farther." Adams shared Forbes's uneasiness. As the newest combatant he was also the one least sure of himself. By nature a disciple of reason, he was slow to respond to forces that seemed to sweep all reason aside. Many thought him indecisive, but there was method in his lack of haste. Having to contend with the government as well as rival roads acted as a brake on the temptation to plunge headlong into expansion. Adams was in no position to lead the construction race; he could but watch and mediate until a course of restraint was no longer possible.

In Nebraska and Kansas, Adams made elaborate preparations to do more building than actually took place. What seemed a defensive policy against invaders was in fact part of a deeper contingency plan. Years earlier Gould had threatened to parallel the Union Pacific with the Kansas Pacific. Adams now looked to parallel both roads with new track if negotiations with the government fell through. For about $20 million, he thought, "the company could easily duplicate the entire subsidized portions of its line," which currently owed the government over $80 million. In Nebraska some extensions planned for the Republican Valley could quickly become a through line by filling a few gaps. As for Kansas, Adams considered the newly chartered Salina, Lincoln & Western a better line than the original Kansas Pacific. Several other branches were chartered to extend the road in both directions.

Adams did not think it would come to that, but he wanted to be ready. The Union Pacific added only about 50 miles of track to the Republican Valley and built about 128 miles in Kansas. Even this small amount was enough to disturb Perkins. For some time he and Adams had an agreement not to build any competing road without prior notification. The construction mania in Kansas unsettled both of them. In Adams's view the Atchison was "striking out right and left, and apparently determined to own the whole earth." An agent in Plainville lamented that "Every man, woman and child, even the dogs howled 'Santa Fee' [sic] at me." With tensions mounting, not even the threat of common enemies could disarm the mutual suspicions between Adams and Perkins. After an exchange of snide letters, Perkins declared the notification agreement terminated at once.

Perkins was especially bothered by attempts to revive the moribund St. Joseph & Western. Originally acquired by Gould as the key link in flanking the Iowa roads, the Western had gone bust and was reorganized in 1885 as the St. Joseph & Grand Island. The Union Pacific retained control with the Grand Island's chief minority bondholder, James H. Benedict, as president. For Adams the new arrangement did not solve the problem of what to do with the road. When the Rock Island crossed the river in 1886, he tried to appease Cable with the Grand Island and some joint ventures in branches. Cable spurned Adams's overtures and pushed ahead with his own construction program. His aggressiveness forced Adams and Benedict to defend the Grand Island by constructing a system of branches for it. A new company, the Kansas City & Omaha, was created in July for that purpose.

Adams knew Perkins would interpret these moves as a declaration of war and hit back in some way. Fred Ames agreed it would "bring on a row with

Perkins, but we might as well face it now as later on, after the Rock Island has occupied the country and shut the St. Joseph and Grand Island out entirely." In all, the new company built 194 miles of branch line, most of which passed into the Burlington's hands a decade later. Relations with the Grand Island were never smooth, because Adams did not trust Benedict, who was in his mind a typical Wall Street man. "I greatly fear that his methods would not bear the strictest inquiry," he confided to Fred Ames, "and that too close association with him is dangerous."

No sooner did Adams decide to protect the Grand Island than another complication presented itself in the form of the Kansas City, Wyandotte & Northwestern, a new line building from Kansas City to Seneca, Kansas. Newman Erb, its vice president, invited Adams to buy into the road and link it to the Grand Island. Adams was tempted. The connection would give the Grand Island (and therefore the main line) a direct line to Kansas City without relying on the Missouri Pacific. This would help retain the livestock traffic, which was fast shifting from St. Joseph to Kansas City. The general manager of the Grand Island favored the acquisition but Thomas Kimball opposed it. Unable to resolve the conflicting advice, Adams made no move to acquire control.

While Adams hesitated, A. B. Stickney bought some of Erb's bonds. The volatile Stickney was throwing together an odd line connecting St. Paul, Chicago, and Kansas City and needed Erb's road to reach Kansas City from Leavenworth. A nasty dispute arose when Stickney and Erb tried to force entrance into Leavenworth over Union Pacific tracks. When Erb sought to placate Adams and offered to lease or buy the Grand Island, the vituperative G. M. Cumming, who had taken charge of the road, urged Adams not to deal with "this little Jewish scamp" and his "Hebrew retainers." Adams needed little prompting. He denounced Stickney's action as a form of "railroad fraud" and closed a trackage agreement while rebuffing all offers for the Grand Island. In 1890 the Wyandotte passed into Gould's hands and was absorbed by the Missouri Pacific. The Grand Island's future remained for Adams an unsolved puzzle to the end of his presidency.

To curb Burlington aggression north of the Platte River, T. J. Potter in 1887 unfolded an ambitious plan calling for 465 miles of construction, but little of this was undertaken. In Kansas Adams struck a deal whereby Gould protected the territory south of the Kansas Pacific while Adams defended the ground north of it. Unlike the agreement with Perkins, this one endured despite the inevitable bouts of suspicion. Except for some minor projects, Adams laid no more track on the plains where rival lines multiplied like rabbits and, thanks to the cheap cost of construction, undercut the Union Pacific at will.

The situation was no better in the mountain region, where every traffic arrangement hung by the frailest of threads and new roads fought savagely for the mineral business. In Colorado the fabled riches of Leadville had become a snare for both the Rio Grande and the Union Pacific, which found themselves dueling for dubious gains. The traffic, Adams noted acidly in 1884, "would hardly suffice to support one line, much less two lines in large part parallel and . . . most difficult to construct and expensive to operate." There were, he added, "few regions in the world where more acts of costly folly, in the way of railroad building, have been committed, than in Colorado." But the folly was far from over, for in September 1886 a new company, the Colorado Midland, built into Leadville and headed toward the boom town of Aspen.

In May 1886 director Ezra Baker, Jr., inspected the South Park and sent Adams a bleak report. He found 200 of its 322 miles nearly "destitute of local business" except for some lumber and coal from mines that were near exhaustion. He doubted the line was worth keeping; yet, in typical fashion, he feared what might happen if an aggressive rival got hold of it. Adams waited another year before deciding to let the road default on its interest. At once Potter urged him to reconsider, arguing that the company could not afford to lose the South Park's business or "the prestige with the Denver merchants that the control of that property gives it." This advice from a source he respected led Adams to reverse himself. Once again he advanced funds for the interest, hoping against hope for better times.

Instead times grew worse. By 1888 the Union Pacific had advanced over $2.65 million to a road that in 1887 earned a paltry $19,563. The drain was becoming intolerable, yet Adams still hesitated. This time banker Colgate Hoyt pressed him to continue the interest for quite another reason. "Some of our friends in Washington hold some of these bonds," Hoyt cautioned, "and I think it would be very unwise just now to have any question about the prompt payment of interest." Here was another, more subtle form of political blackmail. Adams dared not do anything to queer his last chance at a funding bill; reluctantly he advanced the funds.

The funding bill went nowhere and so did the South Park, which by October had become for Adams a "very dreary tea-party." No one ventured to suggest that he keep the line afloat again. After transferring its major assets to the Union Pacific, notably some land, quarries, and stock in the Union Depot (Denver), he let the South Park slide into bankruptcy. Within a few months the minority bondholders came to terms and the road was reorganized into the Denver, Leadville & Gunnison.

The South Park debacle was yet another in a series of disappointments in Colorado, where nothing seemed to go right for the Union Pacific. That experience left Fred Ames dubious about Adams's projected line from Fort Steele through the North Park country. "We have made a great many mistakes in Colorado by hasty and ill-considered railroad building," he told Adams. "In fact, a large part of our troubles there proceed from that one cause." Still Adams persisted, arguing that the new line could be united with the other Colorado roads in one company. A charter was procured for the

Union Pacific & Western Colorado, and surveys were made for about 350 miles of road. Some grading was done at Fort Steele before work was suspended in March 1887. It was never resumed.

The Boston directors hesitated to build more mileage in Colorado because they had been burned so often there. They showed the same reluctance toward the north country despite its potential for mineral and grazing traffic. Even Gould's ardor for a line to the Black Hills and Montana had cooled when he could not find a route that suited him; he forfeited the right to subsidy bonds rather than undertake the Cheyenne & Northern. By 1886, however, the Northwestern had penetrated eastern Wyoming, and some feared it might seek bonds to build into Cheyenne as well as Casper. Governor Warren, who had cattle interests north of Cheyenne, urged the Union Pacific to stake its claim to that region first.

The Wyoming legislature obliged in February 1886 with a law allowing counties to pledge bonds for construction. Early in March Warren and other friends of the Union Pacific incorporated the Cheyenne & Northern, which received four hundred thousand dollars in county bonds. As the track snaked northward 125 miles, speculation arose over where it was heading. The expansive Potter wanted to keep building once the road intersected the Northwestern at Orin (152 miles), to hold the north cattle country and perhaps strike the Northern Pacific. He dispatched Jake Blickensderfer to examine the region from Douglas to the Powder River Valley. After poking about that bleak terrain for a month, however, the venerable engineer told Potter what he didn't want to hear: the country was no good for agriculture, passable for grazing, and had no mineral resources except coal. Even worse, the best approach to it was from the northeast, which made it "tributary to the Northern Pacific Railway."

"The old gentleman does not seem to take as favorable a view of that country as I hoped he would," Potter scowled. "I believe it is a good country, and that we ought to go in there when we have money enough to do so." But livestock was the one traffic it promised, and the killer winters of 1886–87 devastated the cattle industry. Although Wyoming interests kept pressing Adams to cover both sides of the Bighorn Mountains with branches, he did not respond. The Cheyenne & Northern was not even extended to meet the Northwestern until 1891.

The same caution prevailed in Montana, where Adams finally found an opportunity to invoke his cherished doctrine of cooperation. To protect the rich mining region, Dodge wanted the Utah & Northern widened to standard gauge and extended to Helena. The Northern Pacific contemplated a branch from its main line at Garrison to Butte, but its president, Robert Harris, was amenable to compromise. This quality, which had cost him his place as head of the Burlington, endeared him to Adams. In 1886 they agreed on a plan for a joint line between Garrison and Butte. Adams surrendered forty-four miles of the Utah & Northern and Harris nine miles of his branch line to a new company, the Montana Union, which would be jointly owned. The Utah & Northern would be changed to standard gauge and the Union Pacific given trackage rights over the Northern Pacific from Garrison to Helena.

Here was a model of how to avoid what Adams called "a system of duplicating lines which cannot but result in disaster." The two roads shared one line instead of building two and trying to cut each other's throat. "I find myself exceptional among railroad men in that I believe in this sort of thing," Adams told Harris. He fully expected to be "gravely censured by the superficial" and "told that it is the work of a 'theorist in railroads.'"

Appealing as this model was, it did not reflect certain harsh realities. The big prize for the Montana Union was the Anaconda complex, which was locked in a savage fight for markets with copper mines in Michigan, Arizona, and overseas. Victory depended on their ability to increase production and drive costs down until the opposition crumbled. From the railroad they needed low rates and reliable service to move a steadily expanding output. Neither was forthcoming. As a joint road the Montana Union was able to keep its rates high despite repeated complaints by the mine owners. Service was never adequate, because the Utah & Northern was the weakest link in the Union Pacific system and wholly unable to handle the business thrust upon it by the copper mines. The result was a running battle between the mine owners and the railroad, and between the two railroads, that grew steadily more bitter.

The mine owners at Butte were bright, energetic, tough bargainers. William A. Clark's genius at business was exceeded only by his relentless ambition. A detractor once called him "about as magnetic as last year's bird's nest," but even those chilled by his aloof personality were quick to court his favor. Marcus Daly, a genial, unpretentious Irishman whose disposition was as sunny as Clark's was dour, had no equal as a practical miner and developer. James Ben Ali Haggin showed his Turkish ancestry in his swarthy complexion and dark, piercing eyes. Beneath his exotic physical presence lay a talent for business that enabled Haggin to invest in a wide variety of ventures without ever failing.

This formidable array of talent was not one to deal gently with the railroad's shortcomings. The Montana Union never possessed enough power or cars to meet the mine's demands. With the Utah & Northern also short of equipment, the superintendents bickered constantly over its use. To help pay for the gauge change, Adams decreed that expenses on the Idaho division be slashed in 1886. This forced Robert Blickensderfer, the division superintendent and one of Jake's sons, to lay in a smaller supply of coal than usual. A series of fierce storms that winter forced him to use coal consigned for Anaconda to move his locomotives. Caught short of coal, Anaconda had to shut down its mines. Daly protested hotly that this negligence cost him fifty thousand dollars, threw a thousand men out of work, and utterly demoralized business in the town of Anaconda. He blamed not the Montana Union's officers but Boston for its shortsighted policy.

This was but one example of the growing rancor between the mine owners and the railroad. Relations between the Montana Union's parent roads were also strained. The Interstate Commerce Act's ban on pooling scotched the arrangement for the Union Pacific's share of business between Garrison and Helena. Each side blamed the other for the dissatisfaction at Butte and Anaconda. Potter looked into the matter and was convinced the Union Pacific should break the agreement and run the Montana Union on its own. When Adams balked, Potter brought in a new superintendent for the Montana Union and promised "a big improvement" in its management. Unfortunately, the dismissed officer was one in whom Daly had confidence, which did nothing to ease tensions.

While recriminations flew back and forth, a new element loomed up in the form of James J. Hill, who was driving his St. Paul, Minneapolis & Manitoba road across the continent north of the Northern Pacific. A whirlwind of energy and intelligence, Hill had emerged from nowhere to become a decisive new force in the transcontinental clash. He was practiced at the art of exploiting the weaknesses of his rivals, and the muddle in Montana offered him all the weakness he could digest. In one blazing summer (1887) Hill's crews laid a record 643 miles of track from Dakota Territory to Helena. From there he threw a line called the Montana Central southward into Butte. When the new line opened, Hill promised his friend Daly "all the transportation you want, at rates as will enable you to largely increase your business. What we want over our low grades is heavy tonnage, and the heavier it is *the lower we can make the rates.*"

Hill entered Butte in mid-1888 and promptly sent rates tumbling. If Daly or Haggin persuaded Hill to build to Anaconda as well, he could carve the heart out of the mineral traffic. Thomas F. Oakes, vice president of the Northern Pacific, invited Adams to join him in building a branch from Butte east to the Northern Pacific main line, but Adams saw no value in it. W. H. Holcomb, Potter's successor, suggested getting out of the Montana Union agreement, then negotiating trackage rights with the Montana Central that would "let us into Helena and prevent their constructing from Butte to Anaconda." Both Daly and Haggin were expanding their operations at Anaconda, which prompted Dodge to advocate a new road, with low grades, to their mills. Anaconda, he predicted confidently, was growing fast and would soon become the capital of Montana.

Butte was, Adams noted ruefully, "the weak point in our system," where "we have to meet other competitors with shorter lines than our own, and Messrs. Haggin and Daly are amply able to take care of themselves under those circumstances." The laboratory experiment in cooperation between railroads had turned into a fiasco. Hill had demonstrated what an aggressive driver could do while others talked peace. Harris gave way to his truculent vice president, Oakes, who schemed to parallel the Montana Union from Butte to Anaconda and snatch the business for himself. The situation at Anaconda went from bad to worse. During 1889 another operations debacle forced Adams to shove one of his bright young men, William H. Baldwin, Jr., into the Montana Union superintendency. The change provoked Daly into reckless charges that the Union Pacific "purposely wrecked trains and refused to handle his business satisfactorily in order to help out the Lake Superior lines."

Haggin was just as furious. "It looks to me," he snapped, "as if your new man, Mr. Baldwin, was starting out to make war on Anaconda." He greeted one rate hike by threatening to build his own railroad, a step he had taken once before in Utah. Unabashedly he worked the Northern Pacific then Union Pacific, trying to wring concessions from one to use against the other. Adams left one meeting convinced that Haggin was "bluffing us intolerably" but conceded that the Anaconda crowd had "played the game of our customers with almost incomparable skill." In their trading, however, Adams had one decisive card to play. The copper works needed huge quantities of top-quality coal, and that supplied from Rock Springs was far superior to anything Hill or Oakes could offer from Duluth.

This advantage enabled Dodge to reach agreement with Hill on Montana business. Adams and Haggin "looked each other in the eye" and saw little more than their own reflections. The old quarrels over rates and service grew worse, with Baldwin proving the toughest bargainer the Anaconda owners had yet encountered. When the mines refused on one occasion to pay some switching bills, Baldwin simply cut off all switching. Daly shut down the mines to arouse sentiment against the Montana Union, and in the furor threats were made to hang Baldwin if work did not resume. Baldwin coolly faced the miners down, after which Daly's agent agreed to pay the bills "to avoid personal violence" against Baldwin.

Although both sides had legitimate grievances, a neutral party investigating one rate dispute found that Haggin had "no definite knowledge either as to the cost of the transportation service performed for him, or the conditions under which it is rendered." However, Baldwin recognized that the Montana Union had performed miserably. Appalled at the state of its management, he cleaned house from top to bottom. "Whiskey, dishonesty and jealousies were the source of trouble," he told Adams tersely. No improvement sufficed to heal the differences between the Montana Union and the mine owners. The old fights raged on until Adams left the presidency in 1890. Daly was quick to court the new management in hopes of repairing the damage done by "the wrecker Mr. Adams," but no amount of good intention or concessions could placate the Anaconda interests. In 1892 Haggin offered to buy or lease the Montana Union, declaring that he would build his own road if refused.

Through these same years the Union Pacific also battled with the Northern Pacific over the latter's unpaid accounts for the Montana Union. In 1892 the fight went into litigation and the last pretense of cooperation between the roads was abandoned. Practical railroad men were not surprised at the utter failure of Adams's dream of harmony; they knew all along it was a chimerical hope. What few if any of them paused to consider was the extent to which the Montana Union debacle resembled a self-fulfilling prophecy.

* * *

For centuries explorers roamed the frozen north in search of the fabled Northwest Passage to the riches of the East. When at last one was found, it turned out to be not worth having. No such disappointment awaited the quest for an overland northwest passage. The railroad men who coveted the Pacific Northwest were confident it would reward them with a lucrative traffic. Dodge had been impressed with the potential of Oregon since 1867, and Hudnutt's survey had shown the feasibility of a railroad to the coast. Despite the Union Pacific's keen interest in the region, the company's endless travails left it helpless to do more than watch early developments there. Instead the leadership in Oregon transportation fell to Henry Villard.

For a decade the fiery Villard blazed across the Northwest like a comet. Between 1873 and 1876, as agent for certain German interests, he wrested control of the Oregon & California Railroad, the Oregon Central, and the Oregon Steamship Company from the corrupt hands of Ben Holladay. This triumph cemented the faith of German financial circles in Villard's ability. After becoming president of the O & C and Oregon Steamship, he formed an ambitious plan to unite the latter with another steamer line, Oregon Steam Navigation, in a new company empowered to build a railroad connecting with the Pacific roads. Villard learned of Hudnutt's survey through Dodge and approached Gould and Dillon with a plan to go partners in a construction company. These negotiations took place during 1878, when Villard and Gould were resolving their lengthy clash over the Kansas Pacific.

Had Gould thrown in with Villard, the history of the Northwest might have turned out very differently. Instead Gould backed away to placate Huntington and because he was already looking to the Southwest as his seat of empire. Villard raised the funds he needed among his financial friends and in 1879 organized the Oregon Railway & Navigation Company. The new company took charge of both steamship lines and two years later added a third, giving it a virtual monopoly on steamer traffic. To this Villard added more than four hundred miles of rail centered on a main line along the south bank of the Columbia River from Portland to Walla Walla. One branch reached northeast to Colfax in the Palouse country; another left the Columbia at Umatilla and headed southeast toward a connection with the Union Pacific.

Villard's rapid movements compelled the Union Pacific to build the Oregon branch it had wanted for a decade. While a joint line saved the company an enormous sum of money, it also created another symbiont like the Central Pacific by leaving the Union Pacific dependent on Villard for an outlet to the coast. Dillon hoped to push his road as far as Baker but had to settle for a meeting at Huntington, just across the Snake River, where the ceremonial last spike was driven in November 1884. The Oregon Short Line traversed country still barren of local traffic. It was a stake in the future, not a source of immediate returns to cover the large costs of construction.

To the north Villard had to fend off the Northern Pacific, which coveted a line to the coast along the north bank of the Columbia River. In 1880 he persuaded the Northern Pacific to run its trains into Portland over the Navigation's tracks, but a few months later the Northern Pacific managed to sell enough bonds to build its own line to the coast. This threat forced Villard into attempting his spectacular "blind pool." Having astonished Wall Street, Villard proceeded to organize a new company, Oregon & Transcontinental, which bought control of the Northern Pacific and completed its road to connection with the Navigation at Wallula, Washington, in September 1883.

One of the nation's first holding companies, Transcontinental became the vehicle for Villard's profligate expansion program. It owned a majority interest in Navigation and about a third of Northern Pacific's stock, enough to dominate that company with the help of shares in friendly hands. Besides completing the Northern Pacific, Transcontinental leased the O & C, merged some smaller roads south of Portland into it, and started work on an extension to meet the Central Pacific at the California border. It also pushed the branch toward the Union Pacific and commenced a line north of Portland toward Puget Sound. In all this activity Villard inspired his followers to blind faith in his judgment. "I feel absolutely confident," he told one, "that we shall be able to work results out of this combination of interests that will astonish every participant."

He was more right than he knew. As a financier Villard was reckless and careless of details as only a visionary can be. In his haste he paid exorbitant prices for properties and scant attention to costs, which invariably proved higher than he anticipated. His roads ran through thinly settled or empty country. No matter; they would pay, sooner or later, he was sure of it. "I begin to believe," he sighed to banker W. J. Endicott, "that there is something enchanting in the name of Oregon." The rude awakening came in 1883, when the magic disappeared from Villard's stocks and all broke sharply. Villard threw his personal fortune into a desperate attempt to stem the tide. Early in 1884 he was compelled to put his affairs in the hands of friendly receivers and pledge even his mansion on Madison Avenue against his debts. Distraught, broken in health and spirit, Villard resigned from all his companies and fled to Europe, leaving a trail of disillusionment in his wake.

The mess was colossal for the bankers who had to sweep up afterward. Losses to many of Villard's followers were heavy. Endicott took temporary charge of Transcontinental and T. J. Coolidge of Navigation, which had halted all its construction work. Coolidge later admitted finding things "in a much greater state of confusion than I had expected." Villard left behind a formidable backlog of debts, unpaid bills, muddled contracts, and ill-advised purchases. Massive loans from such diverse figures as Morgan, Gould, and Sage kept Transcontinental afloat, but only at the expense of selling off some of its holdings.

Amid this sorting out, Adams came to office. With the Oregon Short Line nearing completion, some arrangement had to be made with Navigation. Coolidge and Endicott hoped to lease the road to the Union Pacific or the Northern Pacific or both. In July 1884, however, Coolidge resigned as president of Navigation and was succeeded by Elijah Smith, a veteran financier known, with something less than reverence, as the "Prophet." Smith was cool to the idea of a lease but changed his mind when it became clear that Navigation could not survive as an independent line. Dillon met with Smith and reported an agreement on terms in May 1885; Adams completed a separate traffic pact with the Northern Pacific. All looked well, yet the proposed joint lease hung fire for two years.

Without realizing it Adams had wandered into another labyrinth, one that would confound and exasperate him for four years. Villard's downfall shattered the last semblance of harmony among the companies he dominated. As president of Navigation and later of Transcontinental as well, Smith looked to take care of the Portland interests on his boards. This meant protecting Transcontinental's investment in Northern Pacific and ensuring that the latter continued to use the Navigation's road to the coast. However, Northern Pacific had fallen under the influence of a faction headed by C. B. Wright, whose large holdings in the Tacoma Land Company made him anxious to build across the Cascades. If Northern Pacific laid its own rails to the sea, it would deal a severe blow to Navigation and put Transcontinental in an impossible situation. The opening of the Oregon Short Line aggravated the problem by enabling Navigation to divide its eastbound business between two rival lines, the Northern Pacific and the Union Pacific.

These complications made the Northwest a hothouse of intrigues spiced with treachery and personal animosity. Smith viewed the lease as a way of binding the Northern Pacific to Navigation, yet he pursued a myopic policy on through business. Using the Oregon Short Line connection as a lever, he forced the Northern Pacific to accept the same rate for its 1,700-mile haul from Wallula to St. Paul as Navigation received for the 213 miles from Wallula to Portland. If Smith hoped to pressure Wright and Harris into the lease, he drove them instead to a firm conviction to breach the Cascades. With Navigation prospering, Smith tried to wrangle better terms on a lease from Adams and talked of building deeper into the Palouse.

Wright and Harris retaliated by limiting Smith's representation on the Northern Pacific board despite Transcontinental's large block of its stock. Within his own companies Smith was opposed by a group headed by financier Brayton Ives. Apart from policy differences, Ives loathed Smith and considered him dishonest; on one occasion Smith roused Ives to a frenzy by accusing him of not paying for wine used in a business car. In 1885 Ives launched a campaign to oust Smith from the Oregon companies. An unwilling Adams soon found himself dragged into the brawl, from which he emerged bruised, bloodied, and warier if not wiser.

The clash took place at a time when Villard was striving to settle his accounts with the Oregon companies and Morgan was anxious to fund Transcontinental's $7.5-million debt. Early in 1886, after strenuous negotiations, Villard's agents arranged terms with both Oregon companies. Artemas Holmes, his attorney, suggested that if Villard wished to regain control of the companies, "Smith is very weak. He has no friends, no following of any consequence . . . it would be easy to oust him." Villard was not yet ready to leave Berlin; however, Smith was aware that he lacked sufficient friends or resources to stave off a determined attack by Ives. Lacking a strong voice on the Northern Pacific board to oppose the Cascade branch, Smith tried to promote harmony through two other issues: the proposed lease and the O & C.

Amid the debris of Villard's collapse Transcontinental had lost control of the O & C. The fear arose that Huntington might seize it and complete his own road from San Francisco to the Oregon border. The prospect of the Central Pacific draining traffic southward from Portland alarmed all the roads with a stake in Oregon. Unable to buy or lease the O & C himself, Smith asked the other roads to join him in acquiring it. Harris was cool to the idea because, Smith told Villard gloomily, he had "only one mania that seems predominant—*Cascade Branch.*" Not even Oakes's prediction that the presence of the Central Pacific in Portland would cost the other lines "from $500,000 to $750,000 yearly" could budge Harris. Adams was interested but in his cautious way wanted assurance that Huntington would not construct his own line anyway.

In 1885 Adams still clung to his faith in cooperation and his repugnance toward duplicate building. The O & C was allowed to pass into Huntington's grasp and was later used by him to force a division of Northwest business. The proposed Navigation lease bogged down in legal problems and Wright's passion to breach the Cascades. Harris expressed interest only in an outright lease to the Northern Pacific, which would put the Union Pacific at his mercy. By the end of 1885 it was clear that the Northern Pacific's Cascades branch would go forward. Unable to draw the other lines together in a community of interest and faced with Ives's attack, Smith saw his options dwindle to a hard choice: Transcontinental could try to regain control of the Northern Pacific, or it could sell its shares in that company and lease Navigation outright to the Union Pacific.

Events led Smith to conclude that his best chance lay with the Union Pacific. The Northern Pacific had dropped him from its board and repaid his dawdling over the lease by starting work on its Cascades branch. In May 1886, as the Transcontinental election neared, Smith bought all the stock of that company he could afford before appealing to Adams for help. The situation was not one Adams could take lightly. He dared not let Navigation fall into hostile hands, and he needed an ally willing to make a lease. Moreover, Transcontinental was a prize worth having for its broad charter, which could be used for building branches. Adams, Dillon, Fred Ames, and other "friends" of Union Pacific agreed to help Smith by forming a pool to buy enough Transcontinental stock to control the forthcoming election.

The struggle for proxies threw the clash into Wall Street, where Adams always felt like a mullet swimming among sharks. For that reason he willingly let Dillon take charge of the pool, but an unexpected complication arose. Unaware that Adams had committed himself to Smith, Colgate Hoyt pledged the shares controlled by his brokerage firm to Ives and sent him to Adams with a letter urging support for his campaign. When Hoyt learned to his chagrin that Adams had taken the other side, he showered Adams with assurances that he wished only to serve the Union Pacific. But, Hoyt added, he was "simply a broker in this matter" and could not go back on his clients. He was bound also to protect his friend Charles Colby and admitted to having "no confidence in either Smith's integrity or ability."

Despite Hoyt's dogged efforts to mend his fences, the episode soured his relations with Adams. Dillon was indignant that a Union Pacific director should support the enemy. "He professes to be a great friend of yours," he told Adams. "Cannot you control him." Adams could not. Ives had also secured the support of Drexel, Morgan. Reluctantly the pool increased its purchases to forty thousand shares and made overtures to the Northern Pacific for a joint lease of Navigation if its officers would drop their support of Ives. Then, early in June, Hoyt discovered that Ives's strength was much less than he had represented. The opposition suddenly wilted. When Ives meekly surrendered his proxies to Smith, a scornful Artemas Holmes informed his friend and client Villard that "Ives lost his courage. You could have won for him if you had cared to."

A jubilant Adams proclaimed the victory "one of the most significant developments that have taken place since I have been in control." The earthier Dillon hailed it as "a ten strike for the Union Pacific," whose representatives joined the boards of both Oregon companies. Adams looked to an early lease of Navigation and use of the Transcontinental's liberal charter "to build freely in western Idaho and in Oregon, and not impossibly elsewhere." His elation proved premature. A battle had been won, but the war went on with renewed intensity. Two factors gave it wrinkles Adams could not have foreseen: the fierce commercial rivalry between Portland and Tacoma, and the stunning reemergence of Villard in Northwest affairs.

Although rumors of a lease were rampant, Adams did not come to terms with Smith until November. Even then he hesitated because of his desire to include an agreement with the Northern Pacific as part of the package. He recognized that once its Cascades branch opened, the Northern Pacific could compete for Portland traffic via Tacoma and shut Navigation out of Puget Sound business altogether. Eager to avoid a rate war, Adams sounded Harris anew on the possibility of a joint lease. Harris responded with a proposal to resolve all outstanding differences. He offered to lease Navigation trackage rights from Portland to Tacoma in return for a lease of Navigation's Palouse road. The Northern Pacific would stay north of the Snake River if Navigation agreed to keep south of it. All business to points east of the Missouri River would be pooled on an equal basis.

This was the sort of treaty Adams liked, but Smith bridled at once. He urged Adams not to surrender the Palouse country so easily because it was "worth vastly more for future development than the Walla Walla country which they propose to allow us." A perplexed Adams sent Franklin MacVeagh to inspect the Navigation's road and received a glowing endorsement of the country's potential. MacVeagh emphasized the importance of a secure line to the coast. At present, he noted, "The U.P. seems to neither begin at any beginning nor end at any ending." Every one of its terminuses was at best a meeting point, giving the system the appearance of "a hand without final joints to the fingers."

In January 1887 the Northern Pacific helped Adams decide by rejecting his counteroffer for a joint lease and asking instead for a traffic contract. A Portland paper predicted the lease would "concentrate in Oregon the interests of the Union Pacific, and it would be much to have the commercial and industrial interests of our state backed and supported by so powerful a company." Sentiments of this kind doubtless led Adams to assume that the Portland business community was behind him. Even so, it took three more months of tough bargaining before the Navigation lease was finally executed in April 1887, two years after Dillon reported he had reached agreement on terms.

The Union Pacific seemed at last to be firmly planted on the Pacific coast. Unfortunately, the lease did nothing to resolve the problems facing the company there. In July 1887 the first Northern Pacific train reached Tacoma. Completion of the Cascades branch meant an immediate loss of business for Navigation. A subordinate warned T. J. Potter that the Northern Pacific was "the skeleton that may be developed into a great earning property," while Navigation was "being cut down" by the Cascades branch on one side and the rapid progress of Huntington's O & C on the other. Potter responded by advocating a host of branches from the Navigation line in Oregon, Washington, and Idaho as a way to offset these losses.

A building program would be expensive and provoke certain retaliation from the Northern Pacific. Although Adams favored expansion, his impulse as always was to avoid needless duplication of lines by seeking a rapprochement with Harris. However, the ground was far trickier than he yet realized. The legacy of personal animosities and conflicting financial interests left by Villard was far from healed. The Northern Pacific's board was split into two factions, one favoring and the other adamantly opposed to close relations with the two Oregon companies. The latter faction held the upper hand and continued to deny Transcontinental more than token representation on the board despite its large holding of Northern Pacific securities. Smith and his friends returned this hostility and scorned all talk of peace. They preferred buying enough Northern Pacific shares to force their way onto its board and secure a policy favorable to their interests.

If Smith got his way, the old Villard policy of uniting all the properties under one ownership would be revived. But times had changed in a way that neither Smith nor Villard nor Adams yet grasped. Where earlier there had been only one line to the Northwest, now there were three, with a fourth on the way. The proliferation of roads fed the growth of commercial rivalry between Puget Sound and the Columbia River Basin. Both of these outlets also had to contend with the aspirations of local communities, Tacoma with Seattle and Portland with the Walla Walla-Pendleton area. As always, every city regarded the railroad as a weapon to be used for or against it in these fights for supremacy. The appearance of a new line, or a change in relations among existing ones, was inevitably viewed by local businessmen through the narrow lens of their own interests.

Any step Adams took to harmonize relations with the Northern Pacific would have to cross the shifting sands of these rivalries. The situation was delicate and complicated even before an unexpected turn threw it into utter confusion: Villard was coming back. After a long swing through the spas of Europe to renew its strength, the comet was hurtling again toward the United States to fill the Northwest with its blinding light.

THE SYSTEM

In his grudging way Adams respected Villard, who was, among the jaded inmates of Wall Street, "a wholly different and interesting type." He was an intellectual of sorts, a fellow member of the American Social Science Association, "the only man who can take an idea and work persistently to it." Adams considered him the "biggest man of the crowd," at least compared to the "crafty, dishonest, and grasping" Huntington or the "weak, garrulous and well-meaning" Harris. The fact that he was not a financier by trade made Villard attractive to Adams, gave them a kinship that would in the end prove a fatal flaw in both men.

By 1886 the Deutsche Bank had renewed its faith in Villard's advice and asked him again to represent it in New York. For several months he did nothing but study the investment situation. The German bankers grew impatient, then ecstatic when Villard made a profitable turn of some railroad bonds in the spring. This refurbishing of his financial reputation coincided with the onset of fresh intrigues in the Northwest. In August 1887 Villard found Elijah Smith at his door with an appeal to take command again of those properties with which he had been identified for so long.

A difficult situation had grown worse. Unsure of his way, Adams moved cautiously. He approved the construction of some mileage and the purchase of a small road in the Palouse. These activities brought immediate protests from Harris, who invoked the terms of a traffic contract between Navigation and the Northern Pacific made by Villard in 1880. This squabble impressed Adams anew with the need to make a comprehensive treaty with the Northern Pacific. A joint lease of Navigation was still possible even though the

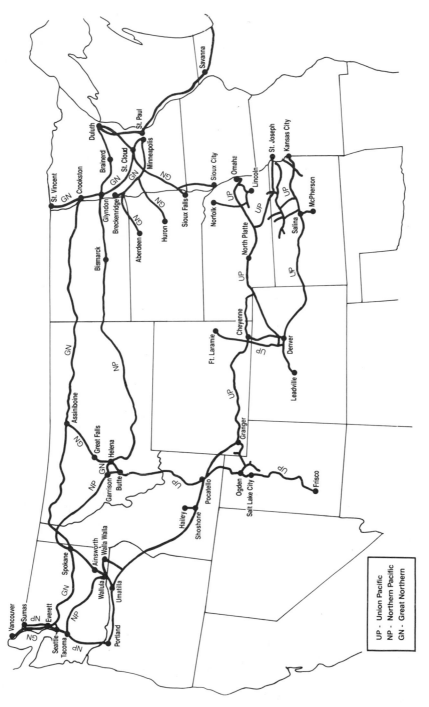

A map of the Union Pacific system showing its lines in the
Northwest along with connecting and rival roads.

Interstate Commerce Act knocked out the pooling provision. Adams was willing, but he knew Harris could not carry his splintered board. His uncertainty opened the door for Smith, who invited the Boston parties to join him in a pool to buy Northern Pacific stock and put in directors who favored the lease.

Adams did not relish another plunge into the cesspool of Wall Street, but a successful campaign could solve several problems at once. He was anxious to avoid a costly war of construction in the Northwest, and the question of viable terminuses was very much on his mind. Adams was thinking in grand terms of sweeping the Union Pacific's disparate lines together into a cohesive system anchored on the Pacific coast and in Chicago, perhaps by a lease or some other tie with the Burlington. Surely, he concluded, it was worth a dirty fight or two to realize this bold vision. In June 1887 Adams, Dillon, Fred Ames, and other Boston parties formed a pool with Colgate Hoyt, who cheerfully switched sides to work as vigorously for Smith as he had against him a year earlier. At the same time Adams resumed talks with Harris on the joint lease.

Hoyt sought to induce some Northern Pacific directors to change sides and managed to recruit none other than Brayton Ives. He and Smith then sounded Villard, who expressed interest but kept discreetly in the background. In Wall Street everything went wrong. A panic sent stock prices tumbling and strangled the money market. The opposition pounced gleefully on the fall to hammer down the Oregon stocks. Transcontinental had loans falling due which it could not meet or renew. The prospect of failure loomed, and with it the collapse of Navigation as well. A distraught Smith dumped his holdings in a frantic effort to stave off failure. In desperation he appealed to Villard for $5 million to save the Oregon companies, promising him control of them and enough proxies to choose his own board for the Northern Pacific.

"What a revolution in the wheel of fortune!" Villard later observed. He cabled the offer to his German clients and, to his astonishment, received the entire $5 million in thirty-six hours. Suddenly, unexpectedly, he found himself again in the driver's seat. Adams was profoundly grateful, for he and his friends were scrambling to meet margin calls before news of Villard's relief galvanized Wall Street. After a lengthy meeting with Villard Adams declined a place on the Northern Pacific board and left the choice of directors to Hoyt, insisting only that "it is understood the lease is to be made joint with no further nonsense." Villard, too, refused a seat but changed his mind after both factions pleaded with him. He would later rue the decision as "the greatest mistake he ever made."

Trouble arose at once. The slithery Ives reneged on his pledge to support Villard and delivered his votes to Wright, who controlled the Northern Pacific election. The best Villard could get was five of thirteen seats and the assurance that three of the opposition directors—Billings, Oakes, and August Belmont—favored the joint lease. There followed three months of hard trading to thrash out terms for a lease. Tempers flashed, then subsided as each side realized the stakes were too high to let the lease slip away. The Union Pacific and the Northern Pacific were already at loggerheads in Butte and could not afford to expand the war to the Northwest. Both were also looking over their shoulders at Hill, whose Manitoba road marched inexorably westward.

Unlike his rivals Hill built cheaply and carefully, taking care to strike markets that would support his advancing line from the start. He was known as a tough bargainer who, in the words of one rail officer, was "most dangerous . . . when he wears his most winning smile." Adams recognized the threat posed by Hill and his low-cost, efficient line to the older roads. Compared to the Manitoba, he lamented, "all our properties are in very bad shape. The Northern Pacific, no less than the Navigation Company and the Union Pacific, is heavily over-capitalized. We have to pay more for money than the Manitoba, and we will have to hold our own in a struggle for existence against it." If they fought among themselves, Hill would cut them to pieces and bankrupt them. It made sense to Adams for the three companies to work together, so that "each of them can carry its load."

The joint lease was a logical solution if agreement could be reached. Although Villard's deal provided a bare majority on the Northern Pacific board, Smith remained implacable. Adams found him "sodden and sullen" and "disposed to stick" as president of Transcontinental despite the desire of both sides to remove him. Ives wanted the job but no one wanted him. When Villard declined the office, Adams persuaded a reluctant Dillon to accept it. Every attempt was made to promote harmony for another reason that escaped the public eye. The pool formed to buy Northern Pacific for the election still staggered beneath a heavy load of stock carried in a weak market. To avoid disaster the participants had to maintain its price; anything that jarred the lease negotiations sent it tumbling and triggered fresh margin calls. Adams felt this pinch dearly and later wailed that he "foolishly and unnecessarily" lost over three hundred thousand dollars in this operation. The experience did not enhance his opinion of Wall Street.

A draft agreement was finally thrashed out late in October 1887. Although modified by later negotiations, the basic terms were incorporated in the final lease. The Union Pacific and the Northern Pacific jointly guaranteed a 6 percent dividend on Navigation stock. The Northern Pacific would develop that part of Washington and Idaho north of the Clearwater and the Snake rivers, leaving the region south of the rivers to the Union Pacific. As part of this arrangement Navigation would surrender its Columbia & Palouse line to the Northern Pacific but retain the right to build from Wallula along the Snake to Lewiston. Rates on Portland and Tacoma traffic were to be equalized, eliminating competition between the two cities.

Although these terms appeared to settle all issues between the roads, final agreement seemed always just out of reach. A serious problem loomed in the form of the so-called "Hunt System." These roads under construction by a local promoter, George W. Hunt, threatened Navigation territory, especially one line between Wallula and Pendleton. The Northern Pacific had no direct investment in these roads, but Adams learned that Hunt was financed by Wright. At a showdown meeting Adams threatened to break off negotiations, throw up all Montana arrangements, and commence building north of the Snake unless Wright and Hunt sold the line to Navigation for a reasonable sum. After some heated sessions he got the Northern Pacific to agree only that it would not control the Hunt roads and would allow Navigation to acquire them on whatever terms it could make.

This compromise satisfied neither Fred Ames nor Potter, who insisted that no lease be signed until Hunt's road was sold to Navigation "without any conditions whatever." Their opposition put Adams in a quandary. At heart he agreed with them, but he deemed the lease too important to risk over this issue. It took all his skills of rhetoric to convince the directors that if they let the lease slide, Wright and Hunt would only take advantage. On January 18, 1888, the board ratified the joint lease. As its champion Adams had in effect made himself hostage to its success; if it failed, he would have few excuses and fewer options. Hopefully he reminded Harris that "the thing will not hold together unless the most absolute good faith prevails between the parties. If there is the slightest attempt . . . to take undue advantage a quarrel and consequent catastrophe will come about at a very early day."

Two weeks later controversy erupted over Navigation's right to build north of the Snake. A furious Adams called it a "cool attempt on the part of Harris, this blundering gas-bag, to cheat me!" Judge Dillon added another wrinkle by casting doubt on whether the Northern Pacific had any legal right to sign the lease. Both these difficulties paled before the explosive reaction of Portland's business community, which denounced the lease as a scheme to perpetuate monopoly by keeping rates high and preventing the construction of competing roads. The Board of Trade issued a sharp protest with a veiled threat. A year earlier it had helped secure legislation to sanction the original lease to the Oregon Short Line; now it might seek to repeal that authority.

Despite these obstacles, Adams pushed doggedly forward. The dispute over construction north of the Snake River was resolved by inserting a new clause in the lease. As a safeguard Adams insisted on signing the lease in the presence of Villard and Hoyt, who approved a memorandum stipulating those terms agreed to verbally. Villard brushed aside Portland's objections with the observation that when its people "properly understood the question involved the opposition would quickly die out." He would soon swallow that prediction. The Portland directors of Navigation managed to delay action on the lease, then joined with local businessmen to procure an injunction restraining the board from executing it. These moves forced Adams and Villard to meet with a deputation from the Board of Trade, which submitted a list of demands calling for blatant rate discrimination in favor of Portland.

Adams and Villard offered enough concessions to placate these demands, and the deputation went home mollified. Or so the presidents thought. The injunction remained alive, and the Navigation board delayed action on some bonds contracted to Villard for sale in Germany. "This sad business," noted a disgusted Villard, "is hourly getting into a worse mess." Adams put the blame squarely on Smith's influence behind the scenes. "Foolishness should stop," he wired Gardiner Lane, "and the prophet if he will neither fish nor cut bait, must go ashore." In April 1888 an ailing Villard sailed for Europe to consult with his clients and take the waters for his gout. During his absence the situation grew steadily darker. Like so many other railroad agreements, the joint lease had crawled to creation and was speeding toward demise.

* * *

The joint lease was scheduled to take effect on July 1. Early in May, however, Navigation's general manager reported that Hunt was pushing work on new branches in the wheat country around Walla Walla. The general manager was anxious not only to block this threat to Navigation but also to steal a march toward what many deemed the richest prize of all: the Palouse and Coeur d'Alene regions. A move in that direction would bring howls of protest from the Northern Pacific, but if, as Adams suspected, directors of that company were in league with Hunt, some defensive steps were justified. Adams ordered surveys made and deflected an inquiry from Harris by saying that Villard had approved them before his departure for Europe. On May 31 the Navigation board, dominated by its Portland members, approved construction projects totaling nearly two hundred miles of new road and branches north of the Snake.

Before this dispute was resolved, another one erupted over the election of boards for the Oregon companies. Adams let Villard convince him that the best way to ensure the lease was to buy enough Transcontinental stock to control the Navigation election. Villard himself would then replace Smith as president and the Portland directors opposed to the lease would be ousted. A pool was formed with Hoyt and his friend Charles Colby in charge, and Adams foolishly left them to arrange the new Transcontinental board despite a warning from Dillon that the loss of Smith would cost Union Pacific "one of its firmest friends." The folly of this oversight was soon revealed when Hoyt proposed himself, Villard, Colby, Ives, William Bull, and Gardiner Lane for the Navigation board without even consulting Adams on the matter.

An oversight, Hoyt assured Adams blandly. "Union Pacific," he added, "is safe with this Board of your friends." Adams didn't think so. Furious over the slight and shocked by the choices, he fired off an indignant protest to Hoyt. How, he asked coldly, could Hoyt presume to select a board for a company still controlled by Union Pacific until the joint lease went into effect? And why were the choices nearly all men with primary interests in Northern Pacific? He suspected a plot to replace Smith with "the man who of all men living is most offensive to him,—that is, Mr. Ives." Nor could Adams fathom why Villard had put himself in the hands of "a Wall Street gang."

The grizzled Dillon examined a copy of Adams's letter to Hoyt with a knowing smirk. He was not surprised to see Adams so annoyed. "The great mistake you made," he observed, ". . . was to concede to them the right to elect a majority of the directors as they saw fit." Once elected, they would control both Northern Pacific and Navigation through the pool's holdings in Transcontinental. "Another unwise thing I think you did," Dillon added pointedly, "was to arrange with them without consulting me about it. . . . If I had had anything to do with it, I think we could have controlled the election." He was right. Adams had conceded too much because of his distaste for Wall Street and their ways. He was not the man to deal with such matters, which is why he desperately needed someone like Dillon or Hoyt or Dodge, who were willing and able to get their hands dirty.

While Hoyt tried to placate Adams, Colby assured him that Wright had long since cut his ties with Hunt. Unappeased, Adams instructed Lane, who was in London peddling securities, to carry a message directly to Villard in Germany. Adams warned Villard that the proposed inclusion of Wright in the Transcontinental board alarmed Union Pacific and that the complications piling up might compel him to disavow the joint lease. Lane also tried to impress on Villard "what was thought in Boston of the men he is associated with." Villard suggested holding matters in limbo until his return, but he did not reach New York until late in July. By then events had pushed Adams into a painful decision to withdraw from the lease.

At the board elections in June 1888, Hoyt's faction captured Transcontinental and installed Ives as vice president under Villard. In Navigation, however, Adams abruptly threw his support to Smith, who retained the presidency and most of his old board. Adams also announced his withdrawal from the lease until it was modified to resolve Portland's objections, the Hunt muddle, and the dispute over construction north of the Snake. Hoyt retaliated angrily by resigning from the Union Pacific board and severing relations with Adams. In July Ives brought suit to stop Navigation from building its branch lines. By the time Villard met with Adams on August 1, he was livid. He knew nothing of these developments until his return and was furious at Adams for reneging on the lease without telling him directly.

Adams's handling of this tangle was as revealing as it was typical. The more insecure he felt in dealing with Wall Street men, the more vitriolic grew his denunciation of them as a class. His prickly ego found salve in taking the high ground with those who exploited his shortcomings. Ironically, he shared this characteristic with Villard, whose own ego was as vulnerable as it was massive. Once arrived in New York, Villard declared grandly that he would see no one and would appoint a meeting as soon as possible. Adams refused to come to him, huffing that Villard had "come back after interviews with the potentates of Europe, sufficiently possessed of an idea of his own importance." In sharp, blustering language Adams outlined his views for Lane to carry to Villard:

> Give him to understand that we feel perfectly strong and satisfied with our position. We have possession, and we have all the means at our disposal which are required to assure it to us. . . . I should not pretend for a moment to deny that his course at this time is of very considerable importance to us, and to me personally. I am equally clear that I cannot greatly influence his course. My own is equally clear to me. I will have nothing to do with these Wall Street feather-weights, and I will not be drawn into their complications.

Privately, however, Adams sounded a different note. "In this Oregon business," he lamented to his diary, "I have in truth got myself out of my depth. I have not known my own mind clearly."

Lane's meeting with Villard went poorly and was followed by an exchange of long, recriminating letters. Adams always had a tendency to personalize conflicts, and nowhere was this flaw more fatal than in his business dealings. The Northwest situation was baffling in its own right and riddled with personal intrigues; now it was to be complicated by a clash of temperament between two men obsessed with the notion of self-vindication. While admitting his mistake in handing Villard "a club with which he at once proceeded to harm me," Adams put the blame for his fix squarely on Villard and Smith. His righteous soul burned with resentment at the misery inflicted on him by "a vagabond Teuton and a Yankee swine." Humiliation was for him at once a sackcloth and a vendetta, yet he told Lane with a straight face that "temper has nothing to do with business. For myself I can truthfully say that I do not feel the slightest degree of irritation over all these charges."

The break with Villard threatened to plunge the Northwest again into the chaos of unbridled construction. Ives's injunction led to a prolonged bout of what Smith called "legal fiddling" over Navigation's right to build north of the Snake. Despite their chilled relations, both Adams and Villard searched for a way to avoid outright war. Dillon suggested that the joint lease be restored with all differences left to arbitration, but Judge Dillon reaffirmed his opinion that the Northern Pacific had no legal power to sign such a lease. As an alternative he proposed "a division of territory." Adams put the two ideas together in what became known as the "arbitration contract." This pact created a neutral zone between the Columbia and the Snake rivers in which the two roads would submit all issues to a board of five managers, the fifth member to be an experienced railroad man hired to serve as arbitrator. There was also formulated a "financial plan" which, among other provisions, called for the sale of Transcontinental's $12 million worth of Navigation stock jointly to Union Pacific and Northern Pacific.

The road to reconciliation proved rocky. Villard offered the newspapers his version of the lease dispute and used the affidavits in the Ives suit to wash more dirty linen in public. This "morbid desire to rush into print" appalled Adams. Villard's course, he cried in exasperation, "has been simply inexplicable to me, and I can only attribute it to his having lost his head. It looks to me as if there was danger that he will before long be the inmate of an insane asylum." As early as August 1888 he had Lane quietly picking up shares of Transcontinental stock in case negotiations collapsed. The threat of war was real. Oakes delivered an ultimatum on traffic matters, growling that "The time for mincing matters has passed." Villard demanded the Union Pacific's proxies for the Northern Pacific election and threatened to abandon all hopes of a settlement in the Northwest if they were not given.

Unable to sway his foes, Adams also failed to enlist his friends. Smith fought the new proposals vigorously and was promoted to the rank of "dirty, low down cur!" in Adams's private inferno. In his despair Adams found a new ally, banker R. Suydam Grant, to mediate with the Northern Pacific. Grant had influence with the large Standard Oil interests in Northern Pacific and thought he could induce the "Messrs. Rockafeller [sic] to urge upon the Northern Pacific management the necessity of an adjustment." Four days later Ives, Harris, and Oakes changed front and agreed to support the arbitration and financial contracts. Within a week the terms were fixed and Adams rejoiced at what he called "my railroad monument!"

The new arrangement was scheduled to take effect July 1, 1889, but problems arose long before that. On the same day in December 1888 that Adams and Harris came to terms, the court sustained Ives's injunction against construction north of the Snake. Smith and the Portland directors struck back with a suit to restrain Transcontinental from interfering in Navigation's management. Villard angrily suggested to Adams that the new agreement include the dumping of Smith and the Portland directors from Navigation's board. Adams was eager to be rid of Smith but realized that Smith's suit was useful in protecting Union Pacific's interests until everything was settled. As the intrigues deepened, Adams grew more hesitant over his course. Early in 1889 Dillon offered him the perceptive advice that the only sure solution was for Union Pacific and Northern Pacific to buy Navigation's stock outright.

The legal tangle was but a skirmish in the larger battle for possession of the rich territory of eastern Washington and western Idaho. Both sides knew the prize; the question all along had been whether they would divide it or fight for it. On the outcome hinged the future of each road in the whole region from Montana to Puget Sound. The Ives injunction was aimed at Navigation's Washington & Idaho line pushing northward through the Coeur d'Alene country toward Spokane, where it would intersect the Northern Pacific and, Adams thought, connect with Hill's road when it moved that far west. To counter this threat, the Northern Pacific diverted traffic from Portland over its Cascades line and encouraged Hunt's building of track in Navigation territory south of the Snake. Harris and Wright persistently denied that they were aiding Hunt, but Adams remained unconvinced.

In March 1889 the fight turned ugly when the Northern Pacific sent men to physically block work on the W & I at Jefferson Canyon. W. H. Holcomb, then Navigation's general manager, wanted to meet force with force but settled for a court order. Adams retaliated by postponing action on the arbitration contract, which solved nothing. Events were fast pushing him into a corner from which there seemed no escape. The lawyers warned him that the Northern Pacific interests in Transcontinental might elect a new Navigation board in June and have it stop all construction. Smith was dragging his heels on certain financial matters crucial to the arbitration agreement. Rate cuts and diversion of business by the Northern Pacific hurt Navigation earnings so badly that the lease payments ran a deficit. There was fear that Transcontinental might even try to abrogate Navigation's lease to the Union Pacific and shut that road out of the Northwest altogether.

It was, Adams sighed, all "very perplexing and tedious." Through Artemas Holmes, who served as intermediary between Villard and Adams, Villard offered new proposals to handle the financial questions and force Hunt to sell his roads to Transcontinental. The slippery Ives also pledged his support, as did Smith. On March 19 the Union Pacific executive committee endorsed the arbitration contract, but the Northern Pacific and Transcontinental boards were slow to act. Adams protested the endless delays and hinted that Villard was stalling; Villard in turn accused Adams of plotting with the Portland directors against Transcontinental. The Hunt dilemma continued to defy solution, and Villard fell ill in April.

Adams was at his wit's end. Complications piled up faster than they could be untangled, and he despaired of ever resolving the intrigues within the boards. His cherished peace plan was slipping away and there seemed no way to save it. Matters had reached the point where negotiations could no longer bring about the results he desired, and he had no alternative policy to pursue despite long, aching hours devoted to the search. There seemed no choice but a radical change of front. To Ives and William Bull he wrote ominously that "the long and provoking delays to which this negotiation has been subjected have probably already committed the Union Pacific to action which heretofore might have been avoided."

But what was that action to be? Holcomb stressed the importance of having "our own rails in Couer [sic] d'Alene country. Any other agreement might deprive us of taking out these ores, and they are absolutely essential to the smelters on our lines." Dillon was convinced there could never be peace until the Union Pacific controlled Transcontinental, and Dodge agreed with him. Ives suggested forming a pool to buy enough stock to dominate the forthcoming election. If that was done, Dillon added, "the Northern Pacific directors would see the handwriting on the wall and come down like the coon did when he saw Davy Crockett's gun."

Adams disagreed, partly because he cringed at the prospect of another Wall Street imbroglio. However, he recognized that both the joint lease and the arbitration contract were no longer possible or even desirable. Like it or not, the time had come to force the fighting. Adams evolved a bold plan to plant Navigation in Coeur d'Alene, Spokane, and Puget Sound with or without the help of the Northern Pacific. Already he had suggested to Harris that the existing arrangement in Montana be extended to the Northwest; to avoid duplicate construction, each company would sell the other trackage rights to any desired competitive point. If the Northern Pacific refused, Adams was ready to dismantle the Montana Union, ally himself with Hill, and let competition rage from Butte to Puget Sound. He would also dump the Navigation lease if the Portland interests did not fulfill their obligations under it, reasoning that Navigation needed Union Pacific as badly as Union Pacific needed it.

This show of belligerence was too much for Fred Ames and the Boston directors, who feared Adams was going too fast without consulting them. Dodge reaffirmed his belief that "the key to the whole situation is for us to capture the O. T." Gardiner Lane offered a clever variation on this theme by suggesting that the best course was to surrender Transcontinental entirely to Villard, who would then worry that "Union Pacific intends to injure the O & T Co. seriously through the O. R. & N. Co's stock." This would lead him to sell off large amounts of Transcontinental, which could then be bought back by the Union Pacific crowd at prices well below what they had sold for earlier.

Dodge found this notion too oblique; by temperament he preferred a frontal assault. On April 23 Adams, Fred Ames, Dexter, Dodge, and Dillon devoted the entire day to debating their course of action. When it became clear that no one cared for his plan, Adams reluctantly dropped it and agreed to let Dillon and Dodge wage their market campaign to seize control of Transcontinental and oust Villard. Victory would at least give Adams personal satisfaction; for months he had seethed with resentment over what he called "Villards attempt at 'disciplining' me." But Adams declined any role in the fight. "So far as these Wall Street complications are concerned," he told Dodge, "I consider myself worse than useless." Privately his language was less delicate. "A man stands about the same chance" in Wall Street, he noted acidly, "that a woman would stand in a brothel."

Grant and Harris assured Adams that many Northern Pacific directors, including Billings, Ives, and Harris, wanted Villard out of that company as well. Sensing the forces arrayed against him, Villard resorted to bold measures. He squeezed the Union Pacific members off Transcontinental's executive committee and tried to issue $10 million worth of new preferred stock. By selling these shares to friends in Germany, Villard could assure his hold on Transcontinental and use the proceeds to secure firm control of Northern Pacific. Adams countered with suits to block the issue and force the liquidation of Transcontinental. As the suit progressed, Adams regretted not following Lane's plan. It would be vastly cheaper, he thought, to destroy Transcontinental in the courts before buying it.

Instead Adams watched from the sidelines, noting sourly that "the hyenas are eating each other up." Lane, who served as his liaison in the fight, was no less priggish. This sort of work, he complained, "cannot but disgust a gentleman. It is low and dirty and like all Wall Street intrigues—perfectly disgusting and loath-some." Despite heroic efforts, Dodge and Dillon failed to acquire a majority of Transcontinental shares. Villard could control the election, but the storm of opposition aroused in Oregon by the liquidation suit threatened to render the holding company useless to him. He controlled all and commanded nothing. Tired and nervous, pressured from all sides, Villard was fast losing his taste for battle. Huge sums had been thrown into the contest and the outcome remained as uncertain as ever.

During the market fight Adams nursed along the negotiations with Harris for a trackage agreement based on the Montana Union model. If he could forge such an agreement and liquidate Transcontinental, the result would be not only peace but vindication of his policy. "We never will have any peace or quiet," he reiterated, "until the Transcontinental is liquidated." Harris came to terms early in May and circulated the proposal among select directors of Northern Pacific. The election stalemate boosted his efforts as all sides realized they could suffer heavy losses unless some way out was found. A prolonged legal battle could cost millions, and the Union Pacific still had a potent card to play in the form of an alliance with Hill.

The major obstacle, of course, was that both sides were so loaded up with Transcontinental stock as to face ruin if the market took the liquidation threat seriously. After several more days of "fighting, quarrelling and wasting time," Villard on May 27 sent overtures through Charles Fairchild of Lee, Higginson for a settlement on terms virtually identical to those proposed earlier by Adams. This sudden change of front to pose as statesman fooled Villard's biographer but not Adams, who was both elated and outraged by what he deemed a blatant attempt to steal his thunder and "blast me with my own lightning." Nevertheless, Adams was quick to grasp that Villard had yielded every essential point; the trick now was to convince his friends that Villard had opened the door to a settlement. Dodge, for one, doubted that the Northern Pacific would accept any agreement "until they are absolutely forced into it for their own protection." He was also wary of any arrangement that did not include Hill's Manitoba road as well.

On June 4 Adams signed a preliminary agreement with Oakes in which they agreed to elect a Navigation board to be selected by Villard and Dodge in Portland two weeks later. The agreement resolved most differences over the lease and gave Navigation control of the extensions under construction north of the Snake, including the W & I. This was crucial to Adams, for he had earlier extracted from Smith a signed pledge assuring control of these projects by the Union Pacific. Since Adams and Villard were not on speaking terms, Dodge was obliged to undertake the long journey to Portland even though he was hobbled by gout. Smith would also be there, and everyone feared he would do something to disrupt the proceedings; already he had offended Villard by attacking him in the papers. Lane went along too but stayed discreetly in the background, observing that "Villard will talk much more freely if I am not present."

The meetings went better than Dodge dared hope. A chastened Villard was willing, even anxious, to settle the Oregon muddle and surprised Dodge with an offer to sell the Navigation stock held by Transcontinental at 90, somewhat below the market price. Dodge accepted at once and wrote Adams, "When I arrived here and looked the field over I thought we were in a very bad hole. I think we are out of it." In short order he and Villard put together a broad agreement. Villard accepted the Adams-Oakes agreement of June 4 and promised to form a syndicate to take up the Transcontinental stock held by the Union Pacific crowd. The holding company would be reduced in size and taken out of Oregon. All litigation would be dismissed. A new board for Navigation was agreed on and elected despite dogged efforts by Smith to scuttle the compromise. All sides heaped praise on Dodge for his skillful handling of the matter.

Adams breathed a loud sigh of relief even though the inevitable snarls arose. Smith knew he was a marked man and tried to sweeten his exit with a little blackmail. He struck a deal with Dodge and surrendered the Navigation presidency to Edmund Smith (no relation), whom Adams considered "a crank." Villard's attempt to form a syndicate was blocked by Hoyt, Colby, and other Northern Pacific directors who resented what they considered his "generosity to the Union Pacific." Fresh intrigues within that board stalled action on the trackage agreement as Oakes broke with Villard and cooled toward the pact he had signed. So long as the fight for control of Northern Pacific raged, there was little hope of ratifying the peace plan. The threat of an expansion war loomed anew.

Adams was content to let the agreement drag out. Privately he admitted that his own course had "not been above criticism." He had reneged on the joint lease and ignored a ruling by his own arbitrator on Puget Sound traffic. His construction program north of the Snake went relentlessly forward, and in July he opened negotiations with Hill for trackage rights over the Navigation system once both companies reached Spokane. This move alarmed both Villard and Oakes, who feared the trackage agreement with Union Pacific would let Hill into Puget Sound over their road. "If Mr. Hill wishes to get into that country he must build his own line," Oakes growled; "our Company will never take him there." By the year's end Adams and Hill were mulling just that possibility, and the trackage agreement died a quiet death.

The final sale of Navigation stock took months of tortuous negotiation and was not completed until November 1889. In a complex transaction the Union Pacific acquired half of Navigation's stock for about $12 million, mostly in short-term notes. Adams planned to relieve this large new floating debt with an issue of collateral trust bonds, but finances seemed in good enough shape that he decided to go slow with the sale. His caution would soon come back to haunt him. Although Dodge had done the company good service, Lane found his aggressive tactics disquieting in so volatile a theater. "If we had followed General Dodge's plans to the end," he confided to Adams, "it would result in financial disaster and ruin to the Union Pacific system. This is what has already happened to the Atchison and Rock Island, and God forbid that we follow in their footsteps."

But not even Lane suspected the scope of Dodge's vision. Since 1886 the old general had plotted broad strategy with Adams; now he was maturing plans that astonished even the man on horseback. Adams's growing confidence in Dodge's counsel was to prove decisive in his bold campaign to forge a large and powerful system out of the Union Pacific's disparate lines.

* * *

Outright possession of Navigation assured the Union Pacific a connection to the Pacific coast. It also left the company saddled with the sort of floating debt Adams had vowed to eliminate. By 1889 Adams recognized the incompatibility of his original goals. The failure to obtain a settlement with the government reinforced his belief that salvation lay in erecting a solid, unified rail system beyond the Rockies capable of hauling enough traffic to carry the financial burden of the original line. As the Navigation purchase demonstrated, this could not be done without incurring a large floating debt. If Adams had any qualms about the choice, the fierce expansion wars of the 1880s laid them to rest. He dared not stand still lest he be swallowed by his competitors. To stay in the fight, the system had to expand and run the risk of another debt. With luck the growth of business would bring it out.

An obvious first step was to reorganize the jumble of existing lines into one company. During 1889, while the Transcontinental fight raged, Adams swept the Oregon Short Line, Utah Central, Utah & Northern, and five branches west of Granger into a new company with the cumbersome title Oregon Short Line & Utah Northern. At the same time, he prepared to merge half a dozen Colorado lines into the new Union Pacific, Denver & Gulf. The name of this company, created in 1890, reflected a fateful shift in strategy for which Dodge was again the mainspring.

Ever the optimist, Dodge believed ardently in the Northwest's future. The drift of emigration to the Puget Sound region, he predicted, would make it "a second California, in its magnitude." But Dodge was also looking to the Southwest, where he had long been an active promoter. He had built the Texas & Pacific for Gould, and since 1881 he had been immersed in a line from Denver to Fort Worth together with another grizzled railroad veteran, Governor John Evans. Their uneasy, often tempestuous partnership resulted in the construction of the so-called "Panhandle" road after a seven-year struggle. With Evans starting from Denver and Dodge from Fort Worth, the 805-mile line opened in March 1888. Through connecting roads it could reach the Gulf at New Orleans or Galveston.

Dodge enlisted his Union Pacific friends in the venture as investors, and Dillon served as president of the Texas company. Since both roads reached Denver, Dodge always regarded them as natural allies against a host of common rivals. With Gould, Huntington, and the Atchison dominating business in the Southwest, the Panhandle needed a strong friend to give it traffic. The rapid shifts in the railroad map wrought by the expansion wars convinced Dodge that a more permanent bond was required. He had always plotted strategy on a grand scale; by the late 1880s the twin forces of construction and consolidation were fast transforming fantasies of empire into reality. His influence with Adams enabled Dodge to weld his vision to the road that had always been his first love, the Union Pacific. While Adams bore responsibility for its creation, the true architect of the emerging Union Pacific system was the engineer who had originally built it.

Except for the Utah roads, the Union Pacific had always been an east–west line. As the growth of systems shattered old barriers between territories, rail managers were forced to rethink their strategies. The Union Pacific reached the Pacific coast but stopped at the Missouri River, where it was dependent on the Iowa lines. Why, reasoned Dodge, should it not also seek an outlet at the Gulf over the Panhandle? C. F. Meek, the road's general manager, offered Dodge an even more audacious plan, whereby the companies could even throw a line into southern California.

Adams spurned this proposal, but his vision of system exploded to breathtaking dimensions. Control of Panhandle would create a diagonal line from Puget Sound to the Gulf; a pact with Hill could put Union Pacific traffic into Duluth; the company might later build into California and/or forge new ties with one of the Iowa lines. In July 1889 Adams offered Hughitt of the Northwestern a close traffic alliance. Uneasy over Adams's dickering with Hill, Hughitt jumped at the idea. Two months later they worked out the terms but deferred final action until Adams closed with Dodge over the Panhandle. While the papers showered attention on the Panhandle maneuvers, the Northwestern sessions proceeded in utter secrecy. Adams and Hughitt signed the final agreement on October 21; the public did not receive its first inkling until three days later.

Although the pact was billed as a traffic agreement, most observers interpreted it as unifying two powerful roads. Adams declared that they became "in all essential through traffic respects one company." The Northwestern was dominated by the Vanderbilts, whose control of the New York Central created a through line from Omaha to New York. The new arrangement forged a harmonious line from coast to coast. It would, Adams predicted, "do away finally with the Missouri River as an artificial barrier in western railroad traffic."

Buoyed by this success, Adams moved briskly to bring the Panhandle in tow. The two roads already had a traffic agreement, but Dodge wanted the Panhandle integrated fully into the Union Pacific system. The Northwestern pact added urgency to his belief. Adams agreed that the best interests of both companies would be served by acquiring the Panhandle outright. Only Evans held back, his views scarred by past experience with the Union Pacific. Dodge had a harder time selling the idea to him and some other associates in the Panhandle than he did in striking a deal with Adams. On November 13 they signed a provisional agreement to merge the Panhandle with the Colorado Central, the Cheyenne & Northern, and all the smaller Colorado branches except the South Park into the new Union Pacific, Denver & Gulf.

"The Union Pacific system," noted one reporter, "is now, next to the Pennsylvania, the largest railroad system in the United States." By the year's end the details were wrapped up and Dodge could crow to his brother, "This will make all the securities and stocks very much better." However, integrating the Panhandle into the Union Pacific organization proved far more tricky than anyone suspected. Evans and others still harbored doubts over the merger's effect on his beloved Colorado. The governor's tenacity prompted Adams to approve a traffic agreement filled with ambiguities lest the clashes over specific issues break up the consolidation. When Lane ventured to observe that the agreement was "very crude," Adams lectured him on the virtues of leaving "many questions somewhat vaguely disposed of in language somewhat vague in its character." He would soon learn that ambiguity was a two-edged sword.

The new corporation finally got underway in April 1890. Meanwhile Adams pushed construction in the Northwest and in Utah, where an extension to Pioche, Nevada, was finally begun three years after Bishop Sharp urged it. Two problems especially bedeviled Adams in the Northwest: an entry into Puget Sound and the Hunt system, which defied all efforts to swallow it. Dodge had examined Washington Territory countless times only to confess that "which point is going to be *the point* is beyond my comprehension." As early as August 1889 Lane warned Adams that the trackage agreement would never get the Union Pacific into Tacoma. "We must begin construction to the sound at once," he argued, "or better still join with the Central Pacific and Manitoba in such construction. *The Northern Pacific will never come to terms until we do this.*"

Lane's warning proved prophetic, but Adams was not yet convinced. In September 1889 he closed a loose agreement with Hill which, he quipped, committed the Union Pacific "to absolutely nothing except giving Hill power to fight the Northern Pacific at his own expense as much as he liked." For months he pondered the best course to pursue. Hunt was scrounging for money to extend his roads and approached the Portland Board of Trade with an offer to build into that city. Another small but critical road, the Seattle, Lake Shore & Eastern, was offered to Adams for a rental of twenty-three hundred dollars a month even though its net earnings were scarcely a thousand dollars a month. Nevertheless, Adams had to watch the road, for Seattle was an ambitious city and no one yet knew whether it or Tacoma would be the dominant port on Puget Sound. Hill talked of building to Seattle and was after concessions there; the Northern Pacific eyed developments warily, hoping to pick up Hill's leavings in case Seattle outstripped Tacoma in the race for commercial supremacy.

"It is hardly possible," enthused W. H. Holcomb in April 1890, "to express the excitement and development in the Puget Sound Country." But how to get there? The best way, Holcomb argued, was for Union Pacific, Southern Pacific, and Manitoba to build jointly a line from Portland to Puget Sound points. The chief engineer looked over the ground and came to the same conclusion, as did other officers. Adams was not impressed by the call to parallel the Northern Pacific. It was "after the manner of all 'practical' railroad men that I have ever met," he sneered, and the only thing practical railroad officers knew how to do was "to spend the largest possible money for the doing of any given amount of work."

Three weeks later, on his western tour, Adams arrived in Tacoma to examine the situation for himself. "After a very careful survey of the whole field here," he reported to Lane, "Mr. Ames and I both reached the conclusion that the Union Pacific must have its own line to Puget Sound and Seattle."

It could be done, he reasoned, by constructing a road that would put the Northern Pacific "at a hopeless disadvantage," one that shortened the time between Portland and Seattle from twelve to five hours. This meant an expensive line with superior alignment, 75-ton rails, and a costly bridge over the Columbia River. Adams wished to avoid all the mistakes made by the Northern Pacific in its original line. The price tag would be $8 million (including $1 million for the bridge), or about thirty-five thousand dollars per mile. A new company, the Portland & Puget Sound, was formed to undertake the project. Adams ordered a financial plan prepared and bids solicited at once.

By July a plan to finance the project was perfected and a partner found to share the cost. The Southern Pacific dropped out, but the indomitable Hill had reorganized his company under a new name, the Great Northern, and was ready to undertake the boldest gamble of his career, a line through the mountains to the coast. He was willing to take a half interest in the Puget Sound road and, as always, wanted the best possible line. "If there was one thing which gave Hill nightmares," his biographer observed, "it was the thought that he might, after putting everything he had into the greatest work of his life, build the railroad in the wrong place." So it was with the Puget Sound line. Through an associate Hill sent detailed instructions on where and how it should be built.

On October 13 Adams paused at St. Paul on another western swing to sit down with Hill. He was surprised at how easy the negotiations went with so intractable a bargainer. Hill was not only fair and reasonable with him but uncharacteristically prompt. "I do not think that much more than twice the necessary time was required," Adams reported wryly. "In the case of Mr. Hill this is a very low average." Yet Adams was not entirely pleased with the results, for he would have preferred owning the line outright and renting Hill trackage rights. The partnership, he observed pointedly, was "a case of two cats with one mouse."

But there was no choice. Even with Hill's help the Puget Sound was a financial load to be carried at a time when Adams had already shouldered the Navigation purchase and several smaller projects. In doing so he had driven the floating debt up to where it had been when he first took office. As architects of the new Union Pacific system, he and Dodge were taking an enormous gamble which, like all gambles, required a dose of good luck to bring them out. Above all, they needed strong earnings and healthy financial markets for the next year or two, to support construction and enable them to sell enough bonds to erase the floating debt.

But fortune's dice were rolling against them. The competitive wars raged on, a monster whose voracious appetite was fast swallowing weaker roads and draining the strength of stronger ones. By 1890 the financial skies were darkening ominously, and cautious souls were already scurrying for cover against the coming storm. As early as December 1889 Adams detected signs of a "financial crisis." Not even his worst fears prepared him for the upheaval that lay ahead.

30

THE WARS

"I tell you," a disgusted rail official lectured his fellow victims, "a war of rates is about as catching a disease as ever was seen. You gentlemen may think that you can make a barrier of the Mississippi and think that you can cut the rates there, but I tell you that it will creep beyond the Mississippi and will then go to the Rocky Mountains."

These words proved more than a prophecy; they became an epitaph for a generation of rail leaders who discovered too late that it was no more possible to fight a limited war than it was to have a limited epidemic. Expansion spread the scourge like a deadly virus as every new connecting link carried it from one region to the next. What began as territorial fights had by the late 1880s escalated into intersectional wars that infected more and more roads. Companies formed the habit of retaliating against invasions in one region by striking back in another. At first only through rates were demoralized, but the explosion of new track threw competition into once protected points and blasted local rates as well. Nothing alarmed railroad managers more than the prospect of losing control over most if not all of their tariff schedules.

What could be done? If war failed, the only resort left was diplomacy, an art in which rail presidents had already set new records for futility. They were not stupid men, although their exaggerated sense of independence caused them to behave like petty feudal barons. They did not want war but could find no way to peace. Every attempt to resolve disputes through diplomacy bogged down in mutual suspicion and distrust. There was something comical in their childlike way of patching up each quarrel, however violent; yet they dared not do otherwise. Like it or not, they had to live with one another.

"Misery is so fond of company," quipped Perkins, "that we are pretty sure to be driven together like quails in a snow storm."

But how? For two decades the pool had been their refuge, but its weaknesses were many and glaring. There was no way to enforce its rules if a member violated them, which was often, and no way to prevent cheating in the form of rebates or other secret arrangements. As the number of lines swelled, there were more pools and more roads in each pool than ever before. By 1887 the Transcontinental Association had *nineteen* members and was supplemented by pools for Pacific-coast business and Colorado/Utah business. The Iowa Pool evolved gradually into the Western Traffic Association, which had more lines and far less cohesion. There was a Northwestern pool and a Southwestern pool and smaller pools on specific kinds of traffic. In each one, arrangements for freight business were separate from those for passenger business. Their mechanisms were elaborate and often ingenious; the problem was that none of it worked. Despite long, tortuous hours of negotiation, agreements broke down faster than they could be patched up, leading to more frustration and bitterness.

The pool lacked any standing in law and, after the Interstate Commerce Act of 1887, became an outlaw. This ban occurred on the eve of the most virulent outbreak of expansion yet witnessed and stripped rail leaders of their most familiar remedy for adjusting differences just as competition reached new levels of intensity. One by one the fragile pools disintegrated as wars of unparalleled ferocity erupted everywhere. By the winter of 1888 disheartened observers described rates as totally demoralized and in chaos. The value of rail securities plummeted, forcing another round of dividend cuts. As the wars raged on with little relief in sight, public hostility toward the railroads mounted steadily even among friends of the industry. The New York *Sun,* long sympathetic to its problems, published a sweeping denunciation, while the conservative *Commercial and Financial Chronicle* charged that the "controlling power in each corporation has been wholly selfish."

A fear of anarchy haunted railroad leaders. The state of affairs had grown desperate enough to convince them that they were fast losing control of their own industry. They needed a remedy that was both workable and within the restraints of the Interstate act, but what was it to be? The past offered no useful models; they were in a new game, unwilling participants in a world struggling to be born. The *Chronicle* hinted at its contours by suggesting that "some authority over and above these differing managements strong enough to force a permanent arrangement of present rivalries . . . must come in before lasting order can be brought out of the Western chaos."

Like his peers, Adams was eager for order if it could be had at the right price. The wars were bleeding Union Pacific dry on every front. In Colorado he tried to fend off the budding Colorado Midland, then snarled that negotiations were "definitely off, and we are going in to cut their throats." The Transcontinental Association, dangling as usual by threads, faced a new menace in the Canadian Pacific, which cut rates on through traffic with impunity and could ignore the Interstate act. Reductions in the Northwest and the Southwest were so frequent, noted the *Chronicle,* that it was impossible to keep track of them all. A missionary would have been hard put to find a single road at peace with its neighbors. "There is no end to the fights we have got on our hands on rates," wrote an exasperated Dodge.

One clash in the Northwest epitomized the dilemma. The Burlington and the St. Paul were locked in a battle that caught the other Iowa roads in its cross fire. Hughitt tried to mediate and was told by Roswell Miller of the St. Paul that his policy was to "follow in the West and Southwest the action of the Burlington line in the Northwest. . . . We cannot make an agreement in the West without having one in the Northwest." At the same time both Perkins and Frank Bond of the St. Paul blamed the Interstate act for the demoralization of rates. "The Interstate Law is responsible for the existing rate war," Perkins said loftily. "Pooling, or self-regulation, has been prohibited and nothing provided to take its place." Nor had the law's ban on rebates proved effective. "I am inclined to think," Perkins snapped, "there is more cheating going on to-day than ever before in the way of secret rebates of one kind or another." On that point Adams had to agree. Every road was still paying rebates, including the Union Pacific despite his instructions to the contrary.

As usual railroad officers looked everywhere for the source of trouble except in their own offices. Perkins knew that pools had been utterly ineffective in curbing rate wars. The chief difficulty was the same one that plagued politics. Everyone recognized the need for some power greater than themselves but feared the creation of any agency that impinged on the autonomy each president guarded so jealously. They could work together only by giving up part of that authority they were least willing to surrender. "Like you I am anxious to secure a permanent peace," wrote one discouraged banker. "How to aid a bringing about I don't know."

Perkins had at least one idea. So devastating were the rate wars of February 1888 that he quietly appealed to Albert Fink, the Trunk Line commissioner, for help. "I have been unable, so far, to think of any plan for maintaining rates west of Chicago," Perkins admitted, "unless we can agree upon some common agency, representing all the lines, which shall have the sole rate making power." T. J. Coolidge agreed the large roads should "make an arrangement by which rates would be kept up and money payments made to equalize trade in any way which would not be contrary to the Interstate Commerce law against Pooling." Although Fink could do little, other rail leaders took up the question of how to end the wars that were ruining them all. To the surprise of many, the leader of this movement was Gould. The man maligned as the most notorious wrecker of his age emerged unexpectedly as a railroad statesman.

In November 1888 Gould hosted some meetings attended by Huntington,

Strong of the Atchison, E. F. Winslow of the Frisco, J. W. Midgley of the Western Freight Association, and representatives from the Iowa roads. Ostensibly Gould was attempting to mediate the wars west of Chicago; in fact the group debated the merits of several broad plans, each more sweeping than the last. Huntington and Gould offered proposals that, in Winslow's words, "were so comprehensive as to require further time" to study. Strong, for one, blanched at them as too radical. Instead the conferees drew together behind a plan favored by Winslow, who chaired the committee to thrash out its details. Known as the "clearing house" plan, the Winslow approach was more conservative but still departed sharply from past practice.

Under this plan the roads west of Chicago would create a new agency empowered to prescribe and maintain rates, rules, regulations, and services. These would be established by a board of managers composed of one representative from each road. All disputes would be arbitrated by an executive board of three men elected by unanimous vote. At least two of the three were to be "experienced in traffic matters"; they would have charge of freight and passenger affairs. The third would serve as chairman and administer the organization. The power to make all rates would be "vested absolutely" in the managers, who would appoint committees for the task. Divisions of through rates would also be made by the board, with rebating flatly prohibited. The clearinghouse auditor would have authority to examine the books of all member roads.

In effect, member roads surrendered all authority over rate making. This delegation of power alone was the most radical step yet proposed. Violators were to be fined $250 or, in more serious cases, an amount equal to the "entire lot thus contracted." Any agent or officer found guilty of willful violation was to be fired by his company. This provision was aimed at the slithery relationship between presidents, who signed agreements pledging to maintain rates, and traffic officers, whose jobs depended on the amount of business they procured. While traffic men resorted to any means foul or fair to obtain business, presidents pleaded their innocence of such practices. These protests amounted to the hypocrisy of one who turns the screws only to profess astonishment that they dug deeper. Traffic agents had always been known for their barnyard ethics, and the desperate competition of recent years had eroded the last pretense of scruples. Adams complained of "a depth of railroad morals among freight agents lower than had ever previously existed, and that is saying much."

The clearinghouse plan sought to uproot this evil by eliminating the competition among traffic agents. By any measure the plan was innovative, yet it paled before those offered by Gould and Huntington. Gould advanced a proposal based on the creation of an "Operating Company," Huntington one on the notion of an "Owning Company." The former proposed centralizing all traffic work in one giant company; the latter advocated a form of interlocking ownership that would consolidate the major roads into one huge company.

Unable to gain support for such radical propositions, Gould and Huntington reluctantly agreed to try the clearinghouse in hopes that it might serve as a stepping-stone to something more comprehensive.

Adams endorsed the plan at once, but other presidents wavered. The cautious Hughitt thought it too strong, the Alton's executive too weak, and Cable dismissed it as "insufficient or lacking in permanency." Perkins, suspecting wrongly that the clearinghouse was Gould's invention, sneered that "Its Parentage is bad" but conceded that it "certainly has good features however & it may be worth trying if all come in—But there is the rub." The public knew nothing of these activities until someone leaked the plan to the press, which climbed all over it as a "R. R. TRUST." Like Perkins, some papers labeled it Gould's plan despite his persistent denials. Given Gould's position as the favorite whipping boy for several New York dailies, that association guaranteed bad publicity, but in fact the recalcitrant presidents had already scotched the proposal. The committee took up alternatives but feared that "Probably there will be more objections to other plans than to this one."

Winslow suggested that everyone agree to restore rates until something more could be done. Gould ordered the Missouri Pacific to do so at once and was quickly followed by the Iowa road presidents. Midgley tried to arrange an informal meeting of the presidents to consider a revised version of the clearinghouse, but hostile interests sabotaged his efforts by scheduling a meeting of the Western Freight Association in Chicago for the same day the proposed meeting was to take place in New York. As one of the association's commissioners Midgley was obliged to attend. Charging that Midgley was Gould's puppet, some western railway officers declared loudly that they would "not be at the [New York] meeting, nor join in any agreement Mr. Gould may propose."

A mere truce did nothing to dispel the sense of rage and frustration. "While we are hesitating," Winslow despaired, "rates in many places are continually dropping. How much lower can we see them go before we waive personal views and fears of some inequalities which might attach to a tentative agreement." Perkins wondered grimly whether it might "not be best in the end for the strong Roads to let *palliatives* alone & just let the disease run its course?" In a speech before the Boston Commercial Club Adams defended the clearinghouse scheme and predicted that more railroad consolidation was inevitable. Huntington went even further. "When there is only one railroad company in the United States," he scowled, "it will be better for everybody concerned, and the sooner this takes place the better."

What Gould or Midgley couldn't do, the bankers might. On December 14 three prominent houses with large interests in rail securities, J. P. Morgan, Brown Brothers, and Kidder, Peabody, issued a call for a secret meeting at Morgan's home on December 20. As representatives of large holdings in the squabbling companies, the bankers exerted a powerful influence beyond the industry's own officers. By 1888 Morgan was emerging as the banker in whom most railroad men had confidence. His appeal drew an impressive response, a summit conference unlike anything witnessed before. Seated around the giant table in Morgan's ornate dining room on Madison Avenue were himself, John Crosby Brown of Brown Brothers, George Magoun of Kidder, Peabody, Gould, Adams, Perkins, Hughitt, Winslow, Bond, and Cable. In Strong's absence Magoun, a director, represented the Atchison.

Adams sat quietly while Cable and Hughitt did most of the talking. Finally Cable offered a scheme to maintain rates which, Adams sneered privately, was "merely the old story . . . to bind the railroads together with a rope of sand." Everyone signed it with what Adams called "expressions of contempt and a good deal of suppressed wrangling, especially between Cable and Gould." The meeting adjourned until the next morning. Afterward Adams walked up Madison Avenue with Gould and complained of the futility of "going round and round in this old circle." A new organization was needed, something powerful enough to compel obedience and still fit within the strictures of the Interstate act. The bankers could be of immense use in such a scheme, and so could the Interstate Commerce Commission itself.

"Yes," Gould shot back, "and why not call the Commissioners in now; invite them to meet us, and co-operate with us in developing a scheme." In a flash Gould saw that involving the commissioners would disarm the charges of "trust" and "conspiracy" that had poisoned earlier efforts. He agreed to present the idea next morning, and they shook hands on it. If the irony of this *rapprochement* between Adams and the man he had vilified in *Chapters of Erie,* struck the Brahmin, he left no hint of it. He had in fact come to admire much about Gould, especially his mind. Despite his roots in the black hole of Wall Street, Gould was one of the few railroad men whose vision and intelligence, if not his ethics, suited Adams.

But next morning the frail, diminutive Gould arrived late for the meeting and seemed on the brink of collapse. Adams noticed earlier how "dreadfully sick and worn" Gould looked; he did not know that Gould was already ill with the tuberculosis that would kill him, and exhausted from weeks of vigil at the bedside of his dying wife. His feeble attempt to present the idea failed so badly that Adams stepped in at once with a vigorous plea for utilizing "the power of the bankers against recalcitrants and . . . the machinery of the Interstate Commerce Act against every violator of law." To his surprise, only Perkins balked at the suggestion to bring in the commissioners. The presidents agreed to maintain rates for sixty days and to reassemble at Morgan's house after the holidays to hammer out the specifics of a plan with the commissioners present.

During the interval rates held surprisingly firm. Privately, some influential parties raised doubts as to whether any plan could succeed. Coolidge expressed the pessimistic view that "until the country grows up to the roads and the people can be educated to see that their interest lies in the success and not in the ruin of Railroads, we must have a hard time. That . . . all railroads have been too greedy and grasping, does not alter the present condition of affairs." Dodge, ever sanguine, denied the rate wars were responsible for the fall in earnings. The problem, he argued, was simply that "in the last two years the strong lines added too much mileage in unproductive countries."

Traditionalists clung doggedly to the sentiment that the best solution was for Congress to restore the *status quo ante bellum* by legalizing pools. This inability to grasp the realities of changing times grated on men like Adams, Gould, and Hughitt. "The pool accomplishes nothing permanent," insisted Hughitt, "except to foster weak lines and to further the interests of the professional railway constructor." It legitimized new lines built on speculation by giving them a share of traffic and could never work unless every state first passed laws "rendering it difficult to build needless or parallel lines of railroad." The boldest remedy came from former Union Pacific government director E. P. Alexander, who seized on the crucial point in any new organization: the ability to enforce decisions. "The bankers have this power in their hands," he declared. They could force compliance by threatening to "throw out of all loans all securities of any road which either refuses to join the Association, or, having joined, refuses to abide arbitrations."

Adams shared these views but recognized their unpopularity among traditional railroad men, who were always reluctant to surrender power to anyone. Moreover, the bankers had as yet showed no signs of asserting themselves. "A railroad Bismarck is needed," he mused. "Will Pierpont Morgan develop the needed force?"

The first hint came on January 8, when the meetings resumed. Banker Oliver Peabody, Strong of the Atchison, and A. B. Stickney joined the talks, but no one from the Southern Pacific, Alton, or Illinois Central attended. As the discussion rambled on, attempts were made to call every plan up for a vote. A disapproving Adams reminded the others that everything depended on how what they did came before the public and urged again that the commissioners be involved in the process. Perkins, echoed by Frank Bond, growled that he would not attend a meeting with the commissioners in the room. Morgan, looking like anything but the new Bismarck, seemed intent only on pressing to a vote a plan offered by Bond. To Adams's dismay, sentiment shifted in that direction until Hughitt protested that the plan was merely another pool and therefore illegal. Adams jumped in to warn against ignoring "the prevailing sensitiveness of public opinion," a point Morgan seconded.

No more was heard of Bond's plan. The discussion drifted again, unable to find agreement on anything except that the final plan must conform to the Interstate act. While Stickney lectured his fellows on the subject, a smiling Oliver Peabody whispered to Adams that the only plan needed was one for enforcing general obedience to the law. The crux of the impasse was not a lack of ideas but a reluctance to do what must be done to crawl out of old ruts. Adams recognized this and suggested that all proposals be referred to a committee that would consult with the commissioners and report back the most feasible plan. This satisfied everyone's desire to get something accomplished. The group endorsed Cable's nomination of Adams, Strong, and Bond as members and agreed to meet again in two days. An elated Adams scheduled the committee's first session for that same afternoon.

Despite attempts at keeping the meetings secret, reporters swarmed the sidewalk outside Morgan's mansion, sniffing for rumors and badgering the participants for information as they departed. The New York *Herald*'s man got the story remarkably straight and pried from one banker the smug prediction that "The work is already done so far as the prevention of rate wars is concerned. You will hear of no more rate wars."

Although Adams thought Strong "had always evinced a jealousy of me," the committee worked together smoothly enough to produce a draft of their report in two hours. That evening Adams dined with Hughitt and enlisted his support of the plan. Earlier he had wired Thomas M. Cooley, the chairman of the ICC, to come over from Boston with his colleagues and join Adams's committee at a working dinner. Next day the committee wrapped up its report by five o'clock. Cooley had not yet arrived, but Adams found Commissioner W. R. Morrison at the Fifth Avenue Hotel and repeated his invitation for a joint dinner. Morrison rebuffed the overture. "Our country is just about half civilized," sniffed Adams afterward, "and the average public man belongs to the uncivilized portion. The idea of combining dinner with business was evidently beyond the mental grasp of Col. W. R. Morrison of Illinois."

Cooley, an erudite constitutional scholar, was deemed "half emerged from the primitive," but he, too, declined the dinner invitation. As a result the committee waited until nine-thirty that night to meet with Cooley, Morrison, and a third commissioner, Aldace F. Walker. The ICC men were at first startled by, then suspicious of, the new plan. Nevertheless, they listened closely and offered suggestions; Cooley labeled it a vast improvement over anything yet proposed. Beaming with pride as chief architect of the plan, Adams invited the commissioners to attend the meeting at Morgan's next morning. Cooley hesitated, then declined, explaining that he had nothing more to say about the plan. Despite this rebuff, Adams left the room elated. "The gun of hostile public opinion," he crowed, "was spiked!"

Next morning some new dignitaries swelled the ranks at Morgan's house in the form of the four Trunk-Line presidents and O. D. Ashley of the Wabash. Their presence alerted the press that something big was stirring. Adams submitted his report, which triggered another long and rambling debate. The strong language of the plan disturbed Perkins and George Roberts of the Pennsylvania, but after some haggling over details the general scheme was adopted. Hughitt moved that the presidents reconvene in Chicago to finalize the plan. Adams balked, then accepted a motion to adjourn until two that afternoon, when the presidents would meet again at the Windsor Hotel. He regretted the move at once, fearing "they had got away from me," but at that meeting the presidents adopted the entire scheme and agreed to meet in Chicago later that month to perfect the new organization.

"On the whole it was a good week's work," Adams gloated. Ahead lay the formidable task of breathing life into the new association. Adams was ready to assume a leadership role in that work. Modestly he compared his role with that of George Washington in bringing the Constitution to life. He would soon discover certain fatal flaws in that analogy.

But not at once. The new organization was tactfully called the Interstate Commerce Railway Association. As details of the scheme leaked out, some editors hailed it as the boldest innovation yet attempted. The New York *Sun* called it "the most sweeping reform that ever was instituted in a great commercial system. It is nothing short of a revolution in railroad methods." The staid *Chronicle* declared that " 'revolution' is a strong word, we are aware. But what else can the result be?" Stickney sounded a rare sour note by predicting that "the effect will be inconsequential. It deals too much in 'glittering generalities,' and does not, in my judgment, go to the root of the disease." Gould shared this opinion but kept his views private.

Everything depended on what happened in Chicago, where the presence of the bankers would not be felt so directly. Unfortunately, Adams had conflicting engagements and decided not to go to Chicago. Instead he sent Holcomb with orders to vote with Hughitt on every point. An alarmed Hughitt pleaded with Adams to reconsider. I REGARD YOUR PRESENCE [AS] INDISPENSABLE, he wired. I CANNOT PREDICT WHAT THE RESULTS WILL BE. Gould, still in mourning for his wife, who had recently died, also stayed home, and Perkins was in a snit over alleged rate cutting by the Rock Island.

When the meeting convened on January 24, everything went badly. Hughitt fell ill and yielded the chair to Strong, who grappled valiantly with the demands of roads that had not signed the New York agreement and refused to join without concessions. Adams's original plan was a modified version of the clearinghouse scheme. Strong watched helplessly as it was riddled with amendments until the final product amounted to little more than a rehash of existing agreements. A disappointed Hughitt lamely defended it as "not perfect" but containing "many wholesome provisions." His assurance did not appease Adams, whose only satisfaction came from the selection of the man he recommended, Aldace Walker, as the first ICRA commissioner.

Too late Adams realized his folly in not going to Chicago. His grand design had been whittled away to what he called "another case of impotence." The disappointment impressed him anew with the urgency of imposing in the Northwest the peace that eluded roads in the Southwest. "It will for years to come be a race for survival," he wrote grimly, "and those companies only will survive which do not waste themselves in competition. The Union Pacific must, therefore, avoid competition." This Darwinian imprint on his thinking would influence his course in the Oregon & Transcontinental fiasco as well as the quest for peace southwest of Chicago. As Hughitt said, the machinery of the new organization was far from perfect, but it was a start. "An individual must come to the front," Adams mused. "Am I not in this case the proper individual and would not my so doing redound immensely to the advantage of the Union Pacific?"

The presidents were to meet again in Chicago on February 19 to finalize the agreement. This time Adams attended, taking Darwin along to read, and quickly grew discouraged at what he found. The Burlington Northern and Illinois Central balked at joining, and other roads refused to sign unless every other road signed. Perkins could not shake his dark suspicion that Gould held some animus "against all decent people" and was scheming to "force honestly managed Roads into an agreement with him . . . which he knows they wont break & he will!" Roswell Miller of the St. Paul assailed the Burlington Northern as the prime culprit in rate cutting. While the recriminations flew, Adams and Hughitt pushed the others to go ahead with the organization rather than "slip helplessly back into anarchy." The response was hesitant; Miller would sign only if the Burlington Northern did, and half a dozen other roads attached similar conditions.

At this critical moment Miller jumped in with a new proposal. "The little strength still left over from our original New York plan," protested a shocked Adams, "was all dropped out of his impotent temporary arrangement." He countered with a motion placing all responsibility for failure on the St. Paul and Burlington Northern. Miller was infuriated, and so were other delegates, who rebuked Adams by voting to substitute Miller's plan. It was about time for lunch ("It always is 'lunch-time' at these meetings," Adams grumbled); a disgusted Adams decided to take the three o'clock train home, leaving his proxy with Hughitt. Before going he told Miller that he had no confidence in the new plan. On the way home he brooded over having "failed in a pinch." He supposed Miller was now in the saddle and would carry his plan. "As usual," he admitted later, "I got a wrong measurement of my man."

In Rochester Adams picked up a newspaper and was startled to learn that he had left the field too soon. A chastened Miller took his comments to heart and withdrew his substitute plan, opening the way for passage of the original proposal. The proviso requiring all roads to sign was dropped, all but four companies joined the new ICRA, and Walker was named commissioner. "The ship is in port," wrote Adams with muted joy. "It isn't much of a ship it is true, and those on board are a mutinous set." Everything depended on whether the ICRA could wield any clout with its members, and on that point Adams was unconvinced. "I propose to take care of the Union Pacific," he observed. "I am convinced there is going to be trouble."

* * *

The press sneered at the ICRA as the "Gentlemen's Agreement" because its enforcement still leaned heavily on the word of its members. It was an act of faith among men whose faith wavered habitually under duress. Even those who most wanted it to work watched events anxiously, ready to bolt at the first sign of trouble. There were procedural difficulties in setting up the machinery of the new organization. The regional associations did not go out of existence but merely used the ICRA as a sort of appellate court on matters of larger significance. As systems expanded, traffic men had trouble figuring out which lines ought to belong to which association. Their impulse was to create not fewer but more associations, which rendered the mosaic of competition even more intricate.

The agreement held firm through the spring despite a sharp drop in earnings on most western roads. In June, however, fresh clashes erupted in the Northwest and among the Kansas City lines. The Burlington Northern refused to join the ICRA or relent in its rate cutting, and the Alton grew so agitated over the fight for Kansas City traffic that it became the first road to serve notice of withdrawal from the ICRA. Although several companies were restless, Adams thought they would keep the association alive, because "they do not know what they will do if they disband." He blamed the trouble on two sources: the Burlington's refusal to absorb the Burlington Northern and control its rates, and the Atchison's decision to build its own line to Chicago instead of buying the Alton, which left the latter free to disturb rates.

Amid these tensions every road maneuvered for position, seeking ways to protect itself if a storm erupted. Gould and Huntington were both deep into plans to redirect the flow of eastbound traffic from the mid-continental routes to the tidewater ports on their roads. The indefatigable Dodge prodded Adams to put the Union Pacific on the same route by forming a syndicate to buy the bankrupt Katy. Adams brushed the suggestion aside, but it spurred his determination to plant the system solidly in the territories it needed to survive and prosper. Banker John S. McCook revived the notion of a rail trust modeled along the lines of Standard Oil, but few believed such a scheme could win public acceptance. Everywhere, the feeling prevailed that each road must take care of itself until the ICRA demonstrated its effectiveness or something better took its place.

The result was a curiously two-faced policy similar to that of nations in times of tension and uncertainty. Adams preached peace and prepared for war, pleaded for all sides to give the ICRA a chance to prove itself, while forging a system that would flourish if and when the ICRA folded. In this manner he and other presidents transformed their fears of the organization's failure into a self-fulfilling prophecy.

This reasoning drove Adams into the fight for the Oregon & Transcontinental and the alliance with Hill. Through these moves he hoped to ensure the presence of the Union Pacific in the country from Montana to Puget Sound. Acquisition of the Panhandle brought the company a giant step nearer the Gulf. At the same time Adams explored the possibility of a line into southern California from Utah. For years this route had intrigued promoters. Never mind that it traversed long stretches of forbidding desert; the farmers of southern California had demonstrated how wilderness could be transformed into acreage of bountiful productivity. Some Englishmen had built a small road from Nephi into the San Pete Valley in Utah but made no money from it. As early as 1886 Bishop Sharp informed Adams that the investors were discouraged and willing to sell or lease their road to someone.

A year later the owners offered the San Pete road to Adams, who showed little interest until an unknown syndicate began surveying possible lines from Salt Lake City to Los Angeles. Sharp and Potter both warned against allowing any rival to occupy the route ahead of the Union Pacific. With Adams's consent Sharp dispatched survey parties to find the best line from the Utah terminus to Barstow, California, on the Atchison. By early 1889 rumors were flying that either the Union Pacific or the Rio Grande Western would build to Los Angeles. J. S. Cameron, whose judgment Adams respected, examined the line and became a convert to its value as "a judicious investment." In May a new company, the Nevada Pacific, was chartered to build through that state if the project went forward.

In August 1889 Adams looked over the situation in Utah for himself and was impressed by its potential. Although he had his hands full with other projects, the fact that two competitors were inching toward the region disturbed him. Eventually he thought the Union Pacific would have to build from Milford to Barstow, but he was in no hurry because of the enormous cost. Nor did he wish to go through to Los Angeles. With great care he assured the Southern Pacific that he had no desire to repeat the folly of the Atchison by spending "some twenty or thirty million of dollars in duplicating the lines of the Southern Pacific already constructed." The key to the project lay in the coalfields of the Wasatch along the route. None of the California roads had decent coal supplies, and southern California paid fabulous prices for coal from Washington Territory. "Coal is the bed rock upon which that system has got to be built," he observed, "and until we find just where the bed rock is, and how far it extends, I should not advise doing anything more."

Chief Engineer Virgil Bogue argued that much of the country was "practically uninhabited" and that the road would never pay. Nevertheless, Cameron and Holcomb persuaded Adams to buy the San Pete road for later use. No sooner did Adams close the deal than he regretted it and, harassed by financial troubles, looked at once for the Rio Grande Western or some other line to take it off his hands. The route from Ogden to Los Angeles remained an idea whose time had not yet come. When the road was finally built, however, it followed the line surveyed in the 1880s.

Of all the moves Adams made to protect the Union Pacific system, none contradicted his support of the ICRA more directly than the traffic alliance with the Northwestern. The two companies not only joined forces but sought to add a third partner, the maverick Alton. It seemed a perfect fit. The Alton reached Kansas City, while the Northwestern was the only Iowa road without a line to that city. This would allow the Union Pacific to exchange traffic with the Northwestern at Omaha and the Alton at Kansas City; it would also eliminate the Alton as a disturber of rates. If, as rumor insisted, the Vanderbilts joined Adams's friends in buying the Alton outright, the result would be a combination of interests too powerful for any of the other Iowa roads to challenge.

The Iowa roads reacted with cautious restraint. The Rock Island and the St. Paul made a half-hearted attempt to invoke the provisions of the moribund Tripartite agreement. Adams expected little trouble from the St. Paul, which had close relations with the Northwestern, and Cable was uncharacteristically subdued in his response. Perkins professed to be hurt at being left out of the negotiations and sounded Adams on the possibility of a separate traffic agreement between the Burlington and the Union Pacific. "For once we have the call on the others," Adams chortled gleefully, "and Perkins walks the floor." But the advantage proved fleeting; protracted bargaining brought no agreement with either the Alton or the Burlington. Meanwhile the Iowa road presidents opened a new front by charging that the Northwestern traffic pact violated the provisions of the ICRA.

Their attack exposed the glaring contradiction in Adams's policy. He and Hughitt had been dominant figures in creating the organization that their new alliance threatened to tear apart. They had hoped wistfully to have it both ways, but no amount of wriggling could free them from the dilemma on which they were now impaled. For a year the ICRA had stumbled along, its machinery too weak and cumbersome to handle the load of disputes thrust upon it. The feeling of many railroad men had come full circle to the belief that the organization was ineffective and must be replaced by something stronger. Walker groped valiantly for a compromise solution, but the Iowa roads forced the issue stubbornly until the commissioner ruled in January 1890 that the alliance was indeed a violation and must be abrogated. Faced with a choice of dropping the agreement or leaving the ICRA, Adams and Hughitt did not even hesitate. In February their roads served notice of withdrawal.

The results were predictable. Gould doubted that the ICRA could survive without the Union Pacific and the Northwestern or that either would be welcome in a new organization "so long as they adhere to their present attitude." Already the Rock Island had signed a traffic agreement with Atchison. The Burlington Northern triggered another round of cuts in the Northwest, and rates softened in Kansas and Nebraska as well. Walker summoned a meeting of the presidents that accomplished nothing. Although the ICRA lingered on, the life had been squeezed from it. "Is it worth while for us to be represented at the meeting," Gould asked Silas Clark wryly, ". . . or shall we simply send flowers for the corpse?"

A few shortsighted officials hailed the collapse of the ICRA as a good thing. Charles Mellen, the general traffic manager, declared haughtily that the Union Pacific should get out of all the other associations as well to save the time and money wasted on them. This bold front soon wilted before the onslaught of reductions in every territory. As the situation worsened, Adams and Hughitt clung to each other like drowning sailors. From every side criticism was heaped on their alliance (along with the persistent cutting of the Burlington Northern) as the cause of the present troubles. Both had a strong sense of righteousness that blossomed into full flower under this withering attack. Hughitt loftily rejected any suggestion that the alliance might be "one of the causes for the existing rate disturbances."

Adams was no less defensive. In his exasperation he proposed meeting the cuts on Nebraska grain by slicing rates 50 percent, a threat so extreme it alarmed even Hughitt. He could do little to deflect criticism or advocate a new association so long as he insisted on maintaining the pact with the Northwestern. Gould, one of its most scathing critics, refused even to consider any proposal that recognized the validity of the alliance, and he was not alone. The rate wars continued to spread despite frantic efforts by the regional associations to arrange patchwork truces. In desperation Adams explored anew the possibility of buying the Alton, but that came to nothing. Anxious to take some positive action, he let Dodge lead him into a decision that seemed eminently reasonable. In fact, it would ultimately spawn a fresh round of conflict.

For some years Cable had been itching to get into Nebraska. In this desire he was joined by the St. Paul, the only Iowa road still without a line west of the Missouri River. Since 1886 both had sought some arrangement for reaching Omaha over the Union Pacific bridge, using as leverage the threat of building their own bridge. The Union Pacific stalled efforts to charter a new span, but by 1889 Adams was forced to reconsider his position. Cable wanted not only bridge rights but trackage into Lincoln, where some construction would enable the Rock Island to run trains to Colorado over a much shorter route. Perkins urged that the Rock Island be kept out of that volatile territory, but a new factor entered the picture. The Union Pacific and the Burlington were planning a large new union depot for Omaha, with yards extensive enough to handle all traffic reaching the city. It would be an expensive project to undertake and a financial load for years to come.

That fact struck Dodge as decisive. When Cable and the St. Paul threatened in March 1890 to build their own bridge, Dodge urged that concessions be made on the bridge and trackage rights. If competitors were going to invade the territory, why should the Union Pacific not get some income from their presence? And why should they not help carry the new depot? "It seems to me," he argued, "that $90,000 for trackage is a great thing for the Union Pacific, but a greater thing is getting them in on our grounds." Other officers had their doubts, but Adams came around to Dodge's point of view. On April 18 contracts with the Rock Island and the St. Paul were signed and approved by the executive committee four days later. Amid the rate wars and other troubles the deal went virtually unnoticed. Adams considered it a minor issue until events threw the agreements back in his face.

Through the spring the wars, intensified by a fierce struggle between Gould and Cable over passenger business, kept rates demoralized. Adams dragged himself to a presidents' meeting in Chicago and endured another round of "fumbling about over temporary expediencies and no getting at the root of the matter—indeed where is its root?" That was the question no one seemed able to answer. Although the volume of traffic remained heavy, it soon became clear that any gains from the Northwestern alliance were offset by the loss of business diverted to other roads. In July the lines to St. Louis and Kansas City arranged a truce restoring rates temporarily. Most roads welcomed this breathing space as the flow of traffic swamped them in what Adams called "a plethora of riches." When the ICC threw cold water on the settlement by reducing grain rates from the Missouri River to Chicago and St. Louis, the western roads banded together to defy the order.

Similar efforts were made to halt the fights over transcontinental business. The chief offender in these regions continued to be the Atchison, which slashed rates recklessly in a desperate effort to stem the road's financial hemorrhaging. During 1889 Strong was dumped in favor of Allen Manvel as president and George Magoun as chairman of the board. To the surprise of many, the new management pursued the same policy of expansion that had already brought the company to grief. In May 1890, while the wars raged, the Atchison acquired control of the Frisco, giving it a line into St. Louis.

By acquiring the Panhandle road, Adams extended the range of conflict from the Rockies to Texas. The situation in both Colorado and Texas was complicated and treacherous. While Mellen tried to arrange traffic agreements with the Southern Pacific and the Katy, C. F. Meek of the Panhandle closed one with the Rio Grande. Both Adams and Huntington were uneasy about the Rio Grande Western, which had broadened its track to standard gauge and was looking across the desert to the coast. The Atchison had moved into Denver and was rumored ready to grab the Rio Grande Western and enter Ogden. It was partly to forestall the Rio Grande Western that Adams decided to buy the San Pete road. This move brought the Rio Grande Western to the bargaining table for what amounted to a standoff. The Colorado Midland also excited alarm over its potential role in combinations of lines west of Denver.

In Texas a hostile legislature drove the leading roads to a unique form of cooperation. Disturbed by a threatened constitutional amendment to create a railroad commission, Adams sounded Gould on a joint pledge to build no new mileage in the state "until a different disposition from that now existing is manifested." Gould agreed at once and secured the assent of Huntington and H. K. Enos of the Katy as well. Their united front proved ineffectual; the amendment passed and the legislature created a commission the following spring. To halt rate cutting, Gould unveiled a much bolder plan. In September he persuaded the major roads south of Kansas City and west of the Missouri River to join him in forming a new association which, in the words of one impressed observer, possessed "powers as autocratic as those of the Czar." By placing full power over rates and traffic in the hands of a committee, the new association centralized authority in a way that the ICRA had failed to accomplish.

The new Southwestern Railroad & Steamship Association brought some semblance of order to one region, but rates elsewhere remained in shambles. A discouraged Mellen reported in September that "at no time since I have been connected with this company have freight rates been in so degenerated a condition as to-day. . . . Rates quoted to-day are so low that the Gulf line is of no avail being practically out of business." A truce curbed the worst fighting in Colorado and some of the bloodletting on transcontinental business, but no one expected peace to last. From Paris an ailing Dodge, who had gone abroad to take the cure, reported indignation among investors at the *"Honorable Gentlemen"* of the Atchison for "taking that property and cutting rates when all roads have more than they can haul." Even W. C. Van Horne of the Canadian Pacific was moved to denounce the hypocrisy of his American counterparts in unsparing language:

> Rates have for years been going from bad to worse, and in my opinion they will continue to do so in spite of "Gentlemen's Agreements," pledges of honor, and all that, until the Presidents show respect for their own offices and punish violations of their solemn agreements by something more severe than a wink.

By October 1890 Adams found himself under fire from all sides. A fresh controversy over rate divisions intensified the clash with the Iowa roads. The Union Pacific wanted a higher proportion of the rate on business to and from Chicago. After hard bargaining Mellen succeeded in persuading the Northwestern to allow the Union Pacific a seventy-five-cent division instead of sixty cents. Since the alliance between them did not permit the Union Pacific to grant better divisions to other lines, Mellen notified the Iowa roads that all traffic interchanged at Council Bluffs must be at the new rate as of November 1. The new division, he assured Adams, would fetch the company five hundred thousand dollars a year. It also brought war as the other roads retaliated with a boycott. For three weeks the test of wills dragged on before the boycott collapsed and everyone except the Burlington accepted the new divisions.

Although Mellen claimed a great victory, criticism of the Northwestern alliance grew in ferocity. Something more was needed to stop the wars that were becoming an act of self-immolation by all the roads. Even the cautious, discreet banker Henry Higginson was moved to warn Lane bluntly that "no matter what temporary shifts are made or temporary gains to you come, the result will be disastrous, & *that very soon too,* unless a satisfactory & full stop is put to the war of rates." Walker used even stronger language. In a letter to the presidents he urged the creation of a stronger organization to stop competition before the roads destroyed themselves. The ICRA, he added, "was a time of armed neutrality. Every line maintained its fighting force fully armed and equipped. A new treaty is now required, which should be based upon disarmament."

Most railroad men agreed; the problem, as always, was how to do it. The Gentlemen's Agreement had clearly failed; Adams snorted that a more realistic basis might be "honor among thieves." The best way, Walker suggested, was to relieve roads of all responsibility for establishing and maintaining rates. A central agency was needed to make rates and some sort of joint agency for maintaining them by eliminating all competition. Adams dismissed the latter notion as little more than a rehash of Albert Fink's Trunk Line pool, on which he and Fink had wasted years of fruitless labor. A surer but more radical way was consolidation of interests. Adams, Huntington, and others explored anew the possibility of creating the One Big Railroad Company in which all would hold shares. Although the idea was gaining support, it required too large a leap for many to swallow it.

By November there was widespread sentiment that the work of 1888 had to be done over again. New meetings had to be called and fresh proposals considered. Time was running out on the railroads; for Adams, although he was slow to realize it, time had already run out.

=== 31 ===

THE LEADER

Adams may have come into the Union Pacific as the man on horseback, but he spent most of his time playing the role of man on a tightrope. For six years he stepped gingerly through the perils of finance, expansion, the government debt, and a dozen other problems, seeking some delicate balance among them before he lost his own. The difficulties facing him would have crushed most men; possibly no one could have solved them. In the end, however, the fatal flaw that undid Adams lay not in the stars but in himself. The man on horseback did not know how to lead.

The problem was never lack of good intentions. Adams had entered office with the best motives and gone to work with vigor and purpose. He thought problems through and laid his plans carefully. No one doubted his integrity or willingness to innovate in an industry that shrank from change. His aim was nothing less than to transform the Union Pacific into a model of how the modern corporation should be run. None of it worked out the way he intended, in part because events defeated him. Intent on seizing the initiative, Adams was instead worn down by what he called "this everlasting rowing against wind and tide!" The best of men were taxed to hold the rudder firm against such forces, and Adams seldom considered himself the best of men.

In his peculiar purgative of self-pity and self-analysis, Adams placed the blame squarely on himself. Events had thwarted him, as had the inability of the Union Pacific to escape "the sin of its inception—the financiering of the Crédit Mobilier and the subsequent manipulations of Jay Gould." But even these might have been overcome if Adams had provided the leadership. "I did not develop high or great executive qualities," he confessed, "—a quick eye, a sure judgment and a constant will." He considered his ideas and methods sound, but he did not stick to them. "I lack combativeness," he mourned. "I get into a fight easily enough; but, being in it, I lack desperate courage. Neither am I alert and ready. I fail because I cannot make up my mind on the instant and my reserves are not at my command."

This blend of judgment and will was precisely what separated him from a man like Gould, who knew how to stand the hottest fire. In darker moments Adams was fond of saying that his subordinates failed him, that his tools broke in his hands. But he knew too that he had chosen those tools and had only himself to blame for their performance. No weakness did more to ruin him than his inability to judge men. He could not manage his troops because he could neither control nor understand them. It was a failure that extended to his own door. He lacked confidence in his lieutenants, but most of all he lacked confidence in himself.

* * *

In taking command of the Union Pacific, Adams spurred a transition that was already well underway. Every department had men who had been with the company since construction days. As in all companies, there existed complex strata of friction and intrigue among those anxious to improve their position or simply hold it against the winds of change. To these insecurities Adams added the pressure of a new philosophy of management that held traditional or "practical" railroad officers in contempt. In Adams's view the new era of management required a new breed of officer, "young men of a higher standard" with the education and breadth of vision to grasp changing conditions and respond to them. From the first, Adams set out to introduce such men, mostly young college graduates, into the lowest grades of service— "planting acorns," he liked to call it. His hope was that within a few years they would emerge as the road's chief officers.

Like most experiments, this one had mixed results. "I do not want any mistakes made in regard to these young men," Adams decreed. "I want only first class material sent out." Some of them did very well and earned promotions; others grew disillusioned and went home. Much depended on their expectations and on their ability to cope with the resentment shown by old hands toward eastern whippersnappers who posed a threat to their jobs, particularly in hard times when forces were reduced. Potter complained that "we are cutting off every clerk we can, and we cannot find places for any men unless we discharge others who have been with us for sometime." He had no use for eastern men anyway; his Burlington experience had convinced him that they "expected higher wages and better treatment than anybody else." A more sympathetic Holcomb admitted that some employees tended to "nag and annoy" young men known to have been sent out from Boston.

Some could not take the gaff or the crudeness of the West. Young Parker Choate was assigned to the Almy mine and expected "to be treated fairly and as a gentleman." He endured what he called "Mormonism, insult, ignorance and brute force as long as possible" before quitting in disgust. At Adams's request Hanna looked into the case and was satisfied that Choate had cut a poor figure, seldom rising before ten and devoting two hours or so a day to business. Others bred resentment by boasting that they were Boston's pets and sure to advance. Some favoritism was inevitable; the point was not to provide jobs for sons of friends but to run a "kindergarten" for future officers. Necessity forced the protégés to cluster in departments with friendly heads. It galled Adams that he could not easily place his young men where he needed them most, the operating department, because that amounted to throwing them to the wolves. The "practical" men, he sneered, "knew what this portended in the end and . . . set their faces like flint against the innovation. The poor, young fellows I sent out had a terrible time of it."

Nor could Adams wait for his acorns to ripen. The rapid growth of the system demanded more and better officers to handle its complexities. Every railroad faced this shortage of able men, which meant that no officer discharged from one company went long without another offer. Sometimes a change improved performance by eliminating personality clashes, but mere recycling could not increase the quantity or quality of officers. For Adams (and other presidents) this question was compounded by the problem of what to do with officers who had served the company long and well but could no longer meet the demands of their positions because of age or infirmity. In an era when pensions did not exist, no man surrendered his place unless forced to do so. It was a delicate, often poignant matter finding humane ways to ease out a loyal subordinate who had outlived his usefulness.

The Union Pacific had a large number of men who had grown up with the company and reached advanced age by the 1880s. Under the sensitive leadership of Judge Dillon, the law department handled this changing of the guard far better than most. The judge showed concern for everyone's welfare but his own; not until 1892 did he hesitantly ask for a raise in the ten thousand dollar salary he had received since becoming general solicitor in 1879. In Omaha the venerable Andrew Poppleton still presided, but his strength and eyesight were failing. Since 1884 his duties had been advisory, confined to pending litigation and supervising the lawyers scattered across the continent. As a source of information on the company's past, "Pop" was invaluable to Adams, but he was not a man to outstay his time. In January 1888 he surprised everyone by submitting his resignation, which was reluctantly accepted.

Only two lawyers could rival "Pop's" longevity of service to the Union Pacific. Sidney Bartlett had given legal advice to the board since its creation and continued to do so until his death in March 1889, three weeks after his ninetieth birthday. John P. Usher had served the Kansas Pacific almost as long and remained head of its legal department after the merger. By 1887 Adams considered Usher, then seventy, to be "somewhat in his decline" and arranged a reorganization that put the Kansas department under Poppleton's authority, shunted Usher into a consulting role, and replaced him with Archie L. Williams. The change mortified Usher, as it did so many men in like circumstance. "I cannot help but feel that I have been degraded and dishonored," he wrote Adams. "The whole thing looks to me like a charity."

Judge Dillon soothed Usher's feelings and persuaded him to accept the new arrangement. Later, when times grew hard, Williams graciously offered to forgo a salary increase rather "than have Judge Usher's cut off or diminished." He asked too that Usher "not be told that I interested myself in his behalf." Williams was anxious that Usher feel the company still appreciated him by continuing his pay voluntarily. "When a man, either through age or sickness, drops out of the ranks," he observed sorrowfully, "the surging world must go on and leave him, but this knowledge has never kept me from grieving at the sight." The request was granted but lasted only two months, until Usher's death in April 1889.

By 1889 a new generation of men presided over the legal department under the astute guidance of Judge Dillon, who was promoted from general solicitor to general counsel. The logical successor to Poppleton was John M. Thurston, an able, erudite lawyer whose only drawback in Boston's eyes was his political activity in Nebraska. Judge Dillon offered Thurston the post on condition that he renounce all political ambition, a stipulation Thurston accepted. After an initial scrape or two, Thurston honored his pledge and, together with Williams, gave the law department strong leadership through a turbulent decade. As the system grew, so did the amount of litigation; between 1888 and 1891 the lawyers handled 3,822 cases. The law department was almost alone in giving Adams satisfaction during those years.

A similar problem faced Adams in engineering, where the flinty Jake Blickensderfer resented hints that at seventy he was slowing down. During 1886 Adams resorted to the same tactic he had used with Usher. Young Virgil Bogue was plucked from the Northern Pacific and made chief engineer with Blickensderfer relegated to consulting engineer. The Dutchman accepted the change but objected to his salary being cut by a third. He appealed to his old friend Dodge, who induced Adams to let Blickensderfer hold his new position for two years at full salary. Adams thought it a mistake on Blickensderfer's part because after two years the obligation ceased, whereas "if he had accepted the retired pay which had been provided, he would probably have remained in our service as long as he lived. You know railroad companies cannot keep men in their employ after they have outlived their usefulness. We are not eleemosynary institutions; we are business concerns, and act on business principles. The old horse is turned out."

But not entirely. Two years later Blickensderfer found himself in the plight foreseen by Adams and offered forlornly to stay on as consultant for one hundred dollars a month. Once again Dodge interceded on his behalf with Adams, whose attitude toward old horses had softened. "We all have the kindest possible feeling toward Mr. Blickensderfer," he assured Dodge, "and

I should be very glad indeed to make his declining years more comfortable." The arrangement allowed the Dutchman to live at home in Missouri with his children while serving as consulting engineer.

In other departments the problem was not age but incompetence or intrigue, both of which perplexed Adams because everything came to him through others. The mechanical department had long been a source of dissatisfaction. Adams thought he had solved its troubles by replacing Hackney with Cushing early in 1889, but by the year's end he had reason to doubt Cushing's ability. At Holcomb's urging he gave Cushing more time to prove himself and soon regretted his leniency. The following spring presidential assistant L. S. Anderson, dispatched to Omaha to investigate the mechanical department, shocked Adams by reporting that Cushing was not only incompetent but possibly dishonest as well. To ingratiate himself with his men, Cushing had given in at once to their demand for a wage increase beyond what they had asked for. His generosity inspired men in the operating department to ask for comparable raises. Even worse, Anderson found evidence that Cushing was in collusion with certain contractors to supply parts of dubious value for the company's locomotives.

Adams was both disheartened and enraged by the revelations. "Whether the man was honest or not, I will not say," he stormed. "I am sure he was not competent." Cushing was sacked and replaced by Harvey Middleton, who impressed Adams as a man of education who "looks you straight in the eye and inspires confidence." The whole episode betrayed the weaknesses that would plague Adams again and again in personal matters: he had misjudged his man, heeded the wrong advice about him, and made the wrong choice. Amid the prolonged wrangling among subordinate officials this failing would haunt him repeatedly.

In all personnel questions, of course, Adams leaned heavily on the advice of his general manager. In fact he counted on the general manager to relieve him of all responsibility for Omaha affairs so that Boston could concentrate on questions of finance and policy. Personally Adams disliked being subjected to the petty squabbles of distant subordinates and loathed having to act as the court of appeal. Moreover, his stint in the military had left a deep imprint. Like most of his peers, Colonel Adams believed firmly in the chain of command. His job was to formulate the campaign, the grand design; the task of implementing it was delegated to his field officers, who had responsibility for seeing that the Union Pacific army was well organized and operated efficiently.

To succeed, however, this model required the right man as general manager. As in war, the wrong commanding general in the field invited disaster. The responsibility for choosing the general manager belonged to Adams, and it proved to be his Achilles' heel. To some extent he was the victim of bad luck, and he had to contend with the fact that there were more roads seeking good general managers than there were qualified or capable men to fill the post. But these factors account only in small part for the debacle of management that marred Adams's presidency. In the end he failed as a leader because of his repeated inability to put the right men in key positions. All his bright hopes and advanced ideas for a new era of railway management were shattered by his shortcomings in this critical area.

After becoming president in 1884 Adams wasted little time in deciding that Clark was not the man he wanted. Hugh Riddle's observation about the lack of good material within the company hit home at once. Unable to find a suitable replacement in the ranks, Adams plucked Samuel R. Callaway from the Grand Trunk line. Callaway was, he believed, a "safe man" and would do until Adams knew better what was required. Within a few months, however, tales of dissension began drifting eastward from Omaha. Callaway's handling of the labor crises disappointed Adams, as did the upward crawl of expenses. By late 1886 Adams was "boiling over with wrath and contempt for Callaway" and considered his appointment a disaster for which he alone was to blame. Thus began the familiar lament that "my tools have bent or broken in my hands!"

As his biographer noted, Adams's relationship with his chief operating lieutenant "began with elation at finding the right man, degenerated quickly into doubt, and ended in dismay and invective." Callaway became the first victim of this recurring cycle. Once Adams lost faith in a man, he felt betrayed and found nothing good to say about him. That the fault was his for selecting the man merely heightened his wrath and the venom of his denunciations. Never an easy man to work for, Adams tended to vent his frustrations by scourging his general manager with sharp, acid-tongued observations. He was a facile writer whose remarks were difficult to answer, and as the boss he could be rebuked only if one dared to risk the charge of insubordination or insolence. This advantage allowed him to demoralize even strong, well-meaning men. The result was antagonism that only exacerbated the problems at hand.

Quietly Adams scouted men from outside the company who might step in as vice president above Callaway. He sounded first R. S. Hayes of the Missouri Pacific, whose health was fragile, and Oakes of the Northern Pacific, who rejected the overtures. Meanwhile, the situation in Omaha went steadily downhill. Lane visited the officers there and reported that Callaway had "lost his head" and was "completely demoralized." A mood of uneasiness permeated the entire operation and could in Lane's opinion be relieved only by the appointment of a new vice president. But Adams had no one to appoint. In desperation he chose to undermine Callaway by making George M. Cumming, the land commissioner, assistant general manager. A lawyer by training, Cumming was as quixotic as he was ambitious. Imperious and waspish by nature, he saw himself being groomed to take Callaway's place and leaped at the chance. Adams nurtured that impression by letting Cumming know he would assume many of Callaway's responsibilities.

A few weeks later Cumming, who had no background in operations, startled Adams with a list of proposed changes in the Omaha organization. Worried that Cumming was moving too quickly, Adams agonized at once, "have I made another mistake in a man!" Whatever hope (if any) he had dangled before Cumming, Adams was still eager to find an experienced man for vice president. Elijah Smith suggested T. J. Potter of the Burlington, a choice vigorously seconded by Colgate Hoyt. Adams interviewed Potter and was impressed enough to offer him the job a few days later. On April 21, 1887, Potter accepted the position of first vice president and general manager. He exacted a steep price: a salary of thirty-five thousand dollars, a thirty-thousand-dollar bonus, and the power to make all appointments, subject to veto, in the West.

In Adams's eyes, Potter was another "promoted brakeman . . . subject to all a brakeman's limitations." But he was the best sort of practical railroad man, "quick, magnetic, a natural leader of men." He could make decisions and sometimes made them too hastily, but he had backbone and knew how to take hold of a situation. His instincts were sure even if he lacked what Adams called the ability to "recognize a philosophy in events." It seems never to have occurred to Adams that officers on the firing line seldom had the luxury of time to reflect on loftier themes. What Potter could do, as Adams soon learned, was stand up to his boss. Any man who cut his teeth under Perkins had to possess grit to survive.

A relieved Adams admitted that Potter's appointment "gets me out of a bad hole." However, it put both Callaway and Cumming in awkward positions. An ill, overwrought Callaway felt badly used and disdained the sop of "the barren title of manager without its power." Adams paid him a year's salary and sent him packing with obvious contempt, yet others regarded Callaway well enough to make him president of such major roads as the Lake Shore and the New York Central. For Cumming the change rudely shattered his dream of succession. "I presume that within the next two months," he sneered, "I shall know whether I can get on with our new master." Never a man comfortable as a subordinate to someone else, Cumming hung on until October before submitting his resignation.

"The road now has a man at the head of it and will trouble me no more," Adams noted gleefully two days after Potter took charge on May 14. Three weeks later he was already devising plans to make Potter president and himself chairman of the board sometime in the fall. Potter threw himself into the work with vigor and intelligence. Appalled by the "general disposition that exists to talk about and criticise the actions of superior officers," he vowed to end it with the terse remark that "I believe in loyalty all round." On a western swing Adams found Potter "mad all over at the extravagance, lax discipline and apparent inability to obey orders which I have so long been fretting over." This was precisely the response Adams hoped to see. "At last," he rejoiced, "there is a man in charge who feels as I do!"

With Adams's blessing, Potter set about putting the house in order. The newspapers spoke ominously of men "marked for decapitation," and Anderson unsettled Adams with a report that Potter was moving too fast in the wrong directions. Reluctantly Adams shelved his plans to leave the presidency and braced for another storm. Had Potter known how easily Adams's confidence vacillated, he might well have doubted his mandate. Adams wanted changes made, but once they were undertaken he invariably cringed and feared the worst. Although events soon restored his confidence, he revised his view of Potter downward to one who "knows his business, bold, energetic, great executive faculty, but not an organizer, autocratic and no developer of high-type men." No man could have pleased Adams in all these respects; Potter simply came closer than anyone else.

The demands on Potter were enough to exhaust a workhorse. Intent on putting his personal stamp on the operation, he found himself pulled in so many directions at once that he could seldom see any one project through to completion. His sense that the organization needed overhauling was correct, and every change would generate friction. Potter surveyed his six division superintendents and found three wanting, but where to get replacements? "With all the work I have had to do on the Union Pacific road," he told Adams, "it has been simply out of the question to make all the changes that ought to have been made." In drawing his rein over Omaha, he aroused the old fear that corruption might result if the auditor's office did not remain independent. Shrewdly Potter backed down somewhat and made his peace with that notorious curmudgeon Erastus Young.

The traffic department remained a sinkhole of problems even after its reorganization as the commercial department in 1884. General traffic manager Thomas L. Kimball, a grizzled survivor of the old regime, was an old friend of Clark and therefore distrusted by Adams. The general freight agent, J. A. Munroe, did not get along with Kimball, and neither man got along with the assistant general traffic manager, P. P. Shelby. As one of the new officers, Munroe antagonized people by parading his closeness to Adams. The shrewd, politic Kimball had the support of most Omaha business interests, whom he had always taken care to cultivate. His weakness, as Callaway observed, was a tendency to "ride too many horses, & please too many people."

While Callaway may have been right about Kimball, the real problem went beyond the traffic department. It involved the deep-rooted suspicion and tension between the old guard friendly to Clark and the new hands brought in by Adams to revamp the organization. The attempt to impose a new philosophy of management on men wedded to the traditional was itself enough to create serious friction. To this were added the jealousies and rivalries spawned by the arrival of ambitious young officers elbowing their way in front of older men who knew painfully well how little the new administration thought of them. Adams made no effort to conceal his disdain for the old guard or his conviction that Clark and his friends were bent on doing him any harm they could. If the leader could not rise above the petty clashes, how could he expect subordinates to do so?

Potter inherited this seething undertow of dissension and grappled valiantly with it. As a newcomer he made the most of his ability to draw the loyalty of both sides to himself. It was his way to impose a personal style of management, but in this case circumstances left him no choice. A forceful, vigorous, forthright executive, he commanded respect easily. No one doubted his ability or his knowledge of railroading. He had filled the vacuum of leadership exactly as Adams hoped he would do. Although Adams questioned some of Potter's actions, he clung to the belief that he had found the right man. Fate blasted that hope with cruel swiftness.

Adams suspected that Potter drank too much and later asserted that he "went from Denver to San Francisco on a fearful debauch, which alone was enough to demoralize an entire service by corrupting every young man in it." Whatever the truth of this charge, it soon became evident that Potter's crushing work load was wearing him down. On a visit to Omaha in January 1888, Lane noticed that Potter seemed "far from well." In fact Potter had caught a cold that soon developed into pneumonia. J. M. Eddy saw him and concluded he was "a very sick man, in fact in worse condition than *he* realized." The doctors sent Potter home to Burlington and then to New York for treatment. Anxious that he not be accused of "trying to get away from my contract," Potter assured Adams that he would be himself again after a short rest. A month later he was dead.

In Omaha Kimball arranged a special train for employees to attend the funeral in Burlington. The Boston office paid Potter the unique tribute of a memorial in the company's minutes and annual report. Well might they mourn, for his death occurred at the worst possible time. The vacuum of leadership in Omaha was more serious this time because the broad agenda of change initiated by Potter had been left undone or half done. A major transition in management had been halted in mid stride and dangled uncertainly with no one to guide it. Affairs in Omaha came to a standstill, paralyzed by grief and apprehension, but the jockeying for position had already begun. To make matters worse, a major strike had erupted against the Burlington and might spread at any moment to the Union Pacific. If that happened, a firm hand was desperately needed to cope with the upheaval.

Before leaving Omaha, Potter had assigned traffic and policy matters to Kimball and everything else to J. S. Cameron, whom he had brought to the road as an assistant. Cameron was able and energetic but a newcomer whose grasp of larger matters was as limited as his influence. This temporary arrangement had been verbal, giving neither Kimball nor Cameron any formal authority to take charge. Under the circumstances Adams saw no choice but to appoint Kimball acting general manager. He considered this purely a stopgap measure, although he knew it would fan the hopes of Kimball and his friends that it might be made permanent.

Adams was not alone in recognizing the threat posed by a vacuum in Omaha. The astute J. M. Eddy believed that Potter had done "a giant's work on the U. P." and had been "in truth the only Genl. Manager, the U. P. has ever had since it was operated." A few weeks before Potter's death Eddy warned Dodge that "The same shovel that undermined Clark and Calloway [sic], is digging away under Potter, *and he knows it also . . .* while he is in sight, things are in dress parade order, but when the 'cats away the mice will play' in other words a large healthy school room with the master absent, first frolic then fighting."

The same chilling suspicion haunted Adams. Here was yet another labyrinth leading him deeper into darkness. On a bleak February night, riding the train back to Boston from New York after stopping at Potter's bedside, he agonized over the dilemma that had engulfed him. "I don't know who to look to or which way to turn," he moaned. "Chaos is come again."

* * *

The turmoil of transition was not confined to Omaha. In the East, too, the ravages of age and illness were stripping the Union Pacific of men long associated with the company. David Dows, the financier who had a large investment in the Rock Island, had joined the board in 1877 as part of an arrangement with Gould. He remained a director until 1890 but ceased to be useful to Adams after 1887, when his health broke down. Ezra H. Baker, Jr., whose father had been one of the original Boston associates, died suddenly in June 1888. The aged Elisha Atkins held the vice presidency thirteen years before surrendering it to Potter. Despite a crippling stroke in November 1887, he stayed on the executive committee until his death a year later. His place was taken by his son, Edwin F. Atkins, whose emergence as a capable director heralded the arrival of a new generation of leadership. Of the old guard only Dillon, Dodge, Dexter, and Fred Ames remained.

The staff also suffered losses. Only a month after Potter's death, Henry McFarland, the longtime secretary-treasurer, was forced by ill health to resign. Adams used the occasion to revamp the organization by dividing McFarland's duties among several hands. Alexander Millar became secretary and James G. Harris treasurer, with Adams's assistant, L. S. Anderson, as assistant treasurer. Lane was promoted to second vice president. The key to the smooth running of the office remained the comptroller, Oliver Mink, but he, too, fell sick with a kidney ailment in May 1888. Gamely he promised to be back at his desk within days, but it was clear he was seriously ill. "Another Potter," cried Adams after visiting him, "all the best men!" Once again Judge Dillon intervened, this time to urge that Mink be given time off and some funds to improve his condition by traveling abroad.

To Mink's astonishment, that is precisely what Adams did. Having lost Potter, he determined not to lose Mink without a fight and packed him off on an extended vacation at the company's expense. A delighted Mink regained his strength at Saratoga, then sailed off to Europe with his wife to tour the watering holes. "I am acting, as well as I know how, the part of a robber baron," he joked from Interlaken, "plundering the Union Pacific right and left." Taking care to apprise Adams on the progress of Oliver's travels, Mink lingered in Europe over two months before returning to work in October with his health fully restored. In the end it proved one of the best investments the company ever made.

* * *

For months Adams brooded over the problem of Potter's replacement. Everyone had suggestions and advanced them freely. Dodge revived Hayes's name, Chief Justice Morrison R. Waite offered his son, and Kimball's legion of friends, including Congressman A. S. Paddock and General George Crook, pleaded his case. These appeals left Adams unmoved. His cold eye surveyed Kimball's performance and found "no quality of a strong, *executive* officer" but rather a "sly, procrastinating, make shift." He was content to leave Kimball in charge while he scoured the country in search of the right man.

No one offered Adams a more insightful analysis of the dilemma facing him than John M. Thurston, who understood that the Union Pacific "lies around loose all over this western country" and required "a strong hand upon the reins." Potter's loss was twofold. He had come to the road with a national reputation as a successful manager which, Thurston believed, "was more valuable to this company than was his conceded ability as a manager." It had restored the confidence of outsiders in the road's future at a critical time, a trend Thurston feared his death might reverse. Potter had erred, he thought, in trying to take the whole burden of management upon his own shoulders. Thurston doubted he would have succeeded had he lived, and he doubted even more whether any other man could accomplish it.

The solution, in Thurston's opinion, was "a system of management made up very largely upon the Department plan." A stronger infrastructure was needed to cope with the old tendency to shirk responsibility and "avoid action in matters of great moment or uncertainty and doubt by calling upon somebody above to decide." The departments should be strengthened and each one put in charge of a man capable of running it "without any desire to throw the burden of it upon anybody else." A strong general manager was needed to impose policy, resolve conflicts, and ensure harmony, but he must be willing to delegate authority and not try to do everything himself. This would improve performance and morale by giving men the hope of promotion for superior work. Thurston believed that Potter's radical changes had demoralized the service. He had brought in men from other roads with differing philosophies of management that did not always mix; as a result his death left "a very unsettled state of feeling in almost every direction."

For this reason Thurston thought it would be a calamity to bring in another outside man. "Successful managers," he argued, "have very largely grown up upon the system where they have reached the height of successful administration." Under the proposed system the best choice would be Kimball, who was favored by virtually all the employees and who for many years had been given large responsibilities without the authority to go with them. Aware of the axiom that traffic men seldom made good managers, Thurston conceded that Kimball might need a good operating lieutenant. One possibility was George W. Holdrege, the talented Burlington superintendent who was a Harvard graduate and also Kimball's son-in-law. Together they would in Thurston's view form "the strongest railroad combination possible."

To what extent Adams heeded this advice is unknown. No argument could induce him to accept Kimball, even in tandem with Holdrege. Through the long summer he combed the West in search of good men with disheartening results. None possessed a hint of vision or statesmanship or patience. "They were all uneducated, strong men,—energetic, rough and unscrupulous,—seeing what was immediately before them very clearly and nothing beyond." In short, they were all "practical" men who preached the gospel of experience. By his own reckoning, Adams was "at least ten years, and more probably twenty years in advance of the column." It seemed to him that every railroad system had outgrown its men, and all were in deep trouble for the want of leadership.

This reasoning led Adams to spurn some promising candidates. He ignored the application of Milton H. Smith, the hard-bitten vice president of the Louisville & Nashville and later its greatest president, probably because Smith had no experience in the West. At the urging of George Pullman he took a close look at E. T. Jeffery but decided against him; Jeffery went on to become president of the Rio Grande and the Rio Grande Western. Adams's distrust of Kimball ruled out Holdrege, one of the best operating men on the Burlington, a road renowned for its efficient management. The two men he did offer the job to, Oakes and Hayes, both declined it.

A chastened Cumming indicated his willingness to return to the company. Although not about to give him Potter's place, knowing full well how erratic Cumming could be, Adams still brought him back as general manager of the Grand Island. Then there was Charles S. Mellen of the Boston & Lowell, who would later lead the New York, New Haven & Hartford into ruin. Mellen had all the qualities of a star: brilliant, glittering, cold, and remote. Dillon wanted him as early as 1883 but left office before doing anything. When Mellen inquired about Potter's position, Adams hired him instead as purchasing agent for the reorganized supply department. Both Cumming and Mellen had potential and could be advanced rapidly if they performed well. Adams viewed them as a kind of insurance, the cost of which would soon stagger him.

Within his own ranks Adams found the cupboard bare except for his bright young men, none of whom were ready for high office, and W. H. Holcomb, who had been brought in by Potter to take charge of the Navigation Company. Tall, heavyset, affable, Holcomb had impressed Adams with his handling of a difficult situation in Oregon. He struck Adams as a typical Westerner: honest and forthright, lacking in vision or subtlety of intellect. Adams sized him up in April but did nothing until he scouted the outside candidates. When all of them fell short of his standards, the weary president felt hopelessly at sea. During one session with Kimball he found himself "disposing of matter after matter about which I felt I knew absolutely nothing." Then Kimball fell seriously ill in August, creating an utter vacuum of authority in Omaha. Reluctantly Adams made Mellen assistant traffic manager even though he had scant confidence in his judgment. "That man," he muttered, "goes off at half-cock with singular regularity!"

A month later J. A. Munroe, the general freight agent, broke down from overwork. "This practically completes the disorganization of our Commercial Department," groaned Adams. With Munroe gone indefinitely and Kimball laid up for months, he had only two of his young men, Baldwin and Tebbets, as reserves. "I want to see them go forward," he told Dodge, "but I do not like to eat my fruit green." Dodge canvassed the West for a replacement but could not find a suitable man. Adams was at his wit's end. He had spent months seeking just the right man only to have a decision forced on him. Grimly he hurried west, determined to stay until the house was put in order. The hard fact was that he had no one left except Holcomb. As late as October 3 he noted anxiously that "something decisive must be done, but not clear what." That same day he thrashed over a plan with Dodge.

Two days later he revealed the plan to Holcomb and Baldwin. "I saw by their faces that I had it," he chortled afterward, "and was once more top dog —it was a great relief!"

The plan was simple. Holcomb would be vice president with Kimball remaining as general manager; Mellen would serve as Kimball's assistant until Kimball recovered, after which he would become general traffic manager. Dickinson would continue as general superintendent, Munroe as general freight agent (when he recovered), and Tebbets as general passenger agent. Of those consulted, only Mellen urged that the plan be reconsidered, to which Adams responded with a succinct "bah!" Working briskly, counting the hours until he could flee Omaha, Adams put the new system into place and went home to get the board's approval. Afterward he gloated privately that "the company stands reorganized . . . on a new model, all mine."

Nothing betrayed Adams's insecurity more than this strangled cry of glee. How quickly he had rationalized disaster into triumph! In his desperate need to fill the vacuum that tormented him, he had in effect delivered the Omaha management into the hands of one man he did not know well and two others whose judgment he distrusted. Although one burned with resentment at being passed over and the other with ambition for further promotion, he expected them to work harmoniously together in a difficult situation. Blinded by his longing to rid himself of Omaha, he concocted a mixture ensuring that Omaha would haunt him like the worst of nightmares.

Like Potter before him, Holcomb took his mandate seriously. Within a month of his appointment he offered Adams a sweeping reorganization plan. Holcomb objected to the fact that all the chief operating officers were located at Omaha, making the road "top heavy" at that place. He also disliked having parallel operating and traffic organizations along the road because it left room for "too much friction and clashing between the departments." In its place Holcomb proposed a version of the division system used on the Northern Pacific. The position of general superintendent would be abolished in favor of two assistant general managers; one, situated at Green River, would control everything west of Cheyenne, the other everything east of Cheyenne. They would have charge of both operating and traffic matters, thereby curbing the rivalry between those departments.

A few days later Holcomb requested a wholesale overhaul of officers. Two changes were made at once. The crucial Wyoming division was given to Cumming, who had barely introduced himself to the Grand Island before handing it over to a promising newcomer, Edwin McNeill. On the Nebraska division, which had run down badly, the controversial Robert Blickensderfer was cashiered in favor of Charles F. Resseguie, another refugee from the Burlington who had handled the difficult Idaho division well. Holcomb had authority to make changes subject to Boston's approval, and he was politic enough to go no further without a nod from Adams. Dodge looked into the situation and endorsed Holcomb's plan, urging Adams to allow him "full play for everything and let him see what he can bring out for us."

Adams's response was typical. Having thrust a contradictory mandate on Holcomb, he found himself writhing in its coils. On one hand the company had been so unsettled by change in recent years that it urgently needed stability; on the other, Adams demanded improved performance, which required still more changes. He ached for a strong head at Omaha to relieve him of that burden, which meant giving Holcomb power to act, yet he cringed whenever that power was exercised. Unable to resolve this conflict within himself, he shunted its ambiguities onto Holcomb. As with Potter, he feared that Holcomb was "going too fast and stirring too many hornets' nests at once."

Holcomb was moving fast. Declaring his goal to be "raising the standard of morality, temperance, and truth on the Union Pacific system," he devised a second sweeping list of changes. For assistant general managers he wanted Mellen and Resseguie, who would shift jobs yet again. So would Cumming, who would take over Navigation. J. K. Choate, the superintendent in Denver, would go to Wyoming and young Baldwin to Denver. Munroe, who had in Holcomb's view lost his appetite for work, would be replaced along with several other officers. In defense of these requests Holcomb warned that, "A great many things are going wrong here and a great many expenses are being incurred that ought to be avoided." To turn the tide, it was essential to put the right men in the right positions. What was the right kind of man? Holcomb made no bones about his preferences:

> What this Company wants, Mr. Adams, is hard-working men who sacrifice everything and put away everything but an interest in their work, who come early and stay late, if necessary, and who are all the time faithfully plodding and trying to think of methods for improving their Departments. Men who spend all of their time, outside of office hours, at the club or in dissipation, either mild or strong, are not doing this. It is the men who have families dependent upon them for support and who give their time to their families when they can leave their official duties that we want.

Adams could hardly dispute these standards, but he fretted over the uproar that would follow so massive a shuffling. The first salvo came from Edward Dickinson, the general superintendent, who was to be dropped along with his office because, Holcomb asserted, "he is not competent for the position he holds." Dickinson was outraged. For nearly twenty years he had served the company faithfully. He had fought washouts, snow blockages, strikes, and train robbers, helped quell the riot at Rock Springs, and built the Cheyenne & Northern through bitter winter weather. Was this fit reward for his dedication? Dickinson appealed to Dodge, who was sympathetic but agreed privately that he was not the man to "stand up for discipline and get rid of this extra expense." Dodge replied evasively that loyalty to superiors was the first duty of every employee.

No man had been more loyal, Dickinson countered, though he was blunt and outspoken. He reminded Adams that he had "done some pretty rough and hard work for this Company" and outlined in detail his reasons why no changes should be made in the operating department. To this nine-page letter Adams, who moaned constantly that subordinates closed their ears when he told them truths, replied stiffly that if Dickinson held such views of Holcomb and his policy, he should not in justice remain with the company. A shocked Dickinson asked why he should be charged with disloyalty because he held dissenting views. In desperation he solicited the help of friends in Congress and one very important ally. Mark Hanna had admired Dickinson since the Rock Springs upheaval and did not hesitate to plead his case with Adams. He warned that past trouble in Omaha had more to do with Cumming and others than with Dickinson.

The beleaguered Adams could hardly ignore the argument of a man he respected as much as he did Hanna. He allowed Holcomb to put his new organization into effect but with Dickinson as an assistant general manager, to placate Hanna. Cumming was named as western assistant and Mellen the general traffic manager. Munroe recovered sufficiently to keep his post with Tebbets as his assistant. The arrangement gave Holcomb half a loaf, and an unpalatable one at that. He got cold comfort from Adams, who resumed his habit of flinging verbal barbs mercilessly. When Holcomb recommended a change in terminals, Adams observed snidely that "The ingenuity with which every succeeding man condemns in toto the work of his predecessor and insists that it shall all be undone and done over is most touching."

That spring fresh inklings of unrest in Omaha reached Adams along with reports of a decline in earnings. In June he began again to suspect Holcomb's judgment. Mellen fed this anxiety by turning up in Quincy with ominous tales about Omaha. A tour of the system in July left Adams troubled by what he saw, but two months later he returned and got exactly the opposite impression. A fuller understanding of conditions, he assured Dexter, convinced him that Holcomb's management "had been all that could have reasonably been hoped for." A new spirit pervaded the entire operation and was felt everywhere. "We have," he enthused, "a clean, courageous and intelligent local administration at last." Within months these words would come back to mock him.

By October 1889 Adams had finally gained control of Navigation and merged the Short Line with the Utah roads. These changes allowed him and Holcomb to complete the internal reorganization by promoting Kimball out of the way to third vice president and restructuring the road into four divisions, each headed by a general manager. Dickinson took charge of all lines in Kansas, Nebraska, and Colorado, and Cumming the mountain division (Wyoming, Utah, and Montana); C. J. Smith headed the Pacific division and McNeill the Grand Island. Mellen remained general traffic manager with Munroe as his assistant, but each division was given its own general freight and passenger agents. Adams embraced the new arrangement eagerly. "It has taken me over five long years to root out that old outfit," he chirped, "but it is done at last!" When problems arose, however, he was quick to refer to it as Holcomb's organization.

Other major roads saw merit in the system and also adopted it, but always the system depended on the men who ran it. If Adams and Holcomb thought the new arrangement would curb the bickering and intrigues, they were in for a rude awakening. Friction developed between Bogue and Cameron over their roles. T. M. Orr, a veteran officer displaced by the new order, questioned its worth and found himself charged with disloyalty to the company. After some wrangling he was offered a lesser post but left in a huff rather than accept a reduced salary. Cumming also balked. A nervous, intense man who admitted to being "on bad terms with a great many, if not all, of the Company's principal officers in the West," he took issue with Holcomb over his duties and managed to alienate one of his last supporters. Having, in Adams's words, made "an ass of himself" once before, Cumming did an encore by quitting again. This time he was not taken back.

By the year's end Adams felt an eerie sense of déjà vu: it was "poor, feeble Callaway" all over again in Omaha. Holcomb's solution for every problem was merely to shift men from one position to another until all grew dizzy from the shuffle. Perhaps what stung Adams most was the realization that he was guilty of the same game. "Overgrown children all," he raged, "myself included." Weary of the fight, longing for escape, he fled to Cuba on an extended vacation early in January and did not return until March 6. Once back in Boston, he found Holcomb on his doorstep bristling with tales of insubordination and intrigue. A conspiracy was underfoot, he insisted, among Mellen, Chambers H. McKibbin (the purchasing agent), Dickinson, and Choate to undermine his standing with Adams.

At first Adams dismissed these charges as more of Holcomb's whining, but his impatience was soon curbed by the intrusion of certain rude facts. In January the Union Pacific had absorbed the Panhandle road; within weeks an ailing Dodge found himself deluged with letters "complaining of everybody and generally from Union Pacific people." Appalled that any complaint should come to him without first going through channels, he admonished both Adams and Holcomb to insist on this procedure as "the only way in which the discipline and loyalty of your employees can be maintained." The problem, as Holcomb knew painfully well, was that Adams encouraged this talking out of school by his habit of discussing issues privately with other officers in person or by letter. In seeking information from all sources, Adams created channels of communication that bypassed Holcomb entirely and allowed subordinates to fill his ear with allegations and misinformation.

Having nurtured a grapevine of intrigue, Adams now saw its insidious effects. Omaha had become a hotbed of backbiting and conspiracy, with Holcomb helpless to control it. Mellen was the chief culprit, busily poisoning minds against Holcomb within the company or through the papers, his treachery abetted by McKibbin, the son of a general and one of the young men Adams had sent west. Nor was that all. The road's operation that winter had been a disaster. Heavy traffic, coupled with an acute shortage of motive power, triggered a crisis that overwhelmed the departments. Cushing, the man brought in by Holcomb to put the mechanical department in order, had utterly bungled the job. "Locomotives unfit for service could hardly get the trains over a track which was not safe," Adams noted bitterly. "There was hardly a pretense at a regular train service." A major reason, he concluded, was that the departments were too distracted by infighting and "company politics."

The result was a shocking climb in expenses that threatened Adams's entire financial program. A distraught Adams lay awake nights searching for a way to end the chaos in Omaha. "I find myself in a peck of trouble from the amount of clashing," he confessed to Dodge. The old general was equally outraged, especially when he learned that Mellen had gone after his man, C. F. Meek, the Gulf's manager. At first he admonished Meek to obey Mellen in all traffic matters; then he discovered that the attack on Meek sprang from deeper roots. Meek accused the same quartet of Mellen, McKibbin, Dickinson, and Choate of plotting his downfall because he was "loyal to superior officers." Dodge grasped the situation at once. "It is not Meek they are after," he warned Adams, "but Holcomb." In his disgust at the "wire pulling and the frivolous charges," he told Adams bluntly what must be done. "The whole trouble is that there is a determination to go over 'Holcomb' or any man who is at the head of our company and as you appreciate as fully as I do how an army should be run I hope you . . . will see that the army of the Union Pacific comes under discipline."

But the problem was not so simple. Mellen was to Adams a vintage New Englander, "active, quick witted, full of energy and ambition, hasty in judgment, indiscreet of speech," who could never "be contented while there is someone over him." He saw clearly that Mellen could not be trusted, that he would stop at nothing to claw his way to the top, yet he also considered him a superb traffic man and the most competent officer in Omaha. Adams knew he should dismiss Mellen for plunging Omaha into a "pandemonium of scandal and intrigue," but he could not bring himself to do it. Mellen was, he conceded grimly, "the one tool I have which always cuts."

Instead Adams blamed Holcomb for his "flabby incapacity and indecision in presence of the conspirators." A good commander would have quashed the revolt at its source; a weak one invited attack. Adams could not help feeling more in sympathy with the rebels than with Holcomb, if only because they had backbone. He conceded sorrowfully that Holcomb had become "another living monument to my inability to judge men correctly," but never did he admit the extent of his own role in undermining Holcomb's authority. Neither could he forgive Holcomb for thrusting the loathsome burden of Omaha back on his unwilling shoulders. That sin alone was enough to turn him against Holcomb forever.

In March McKibbin had written a letter so indiscreet in its criticism of Holcomb that Adams felt obliged to put him through "the worst kind of rolling mill." Then Choate journeyed to Boston to heap invectives on Holcomb and was soon followed by Mellen and McKibbin. Adams listened aghast at their charges of incompetence, his anger tempered by a suspicion that they were right. His position had become intolerable. However just their complaints, the conspirators had gone about it in such a way as to discredit themselves entirely. However great his contempt for Holcomb, Adams had no choice but to sustain his authority or the whole chain of command would fall to pieces. The only way to accomplish this was to confront the vipers in their lair, a prospect that oppressed him beyond words.

Taking along Fred Ames and Edwin Atkins to share his misery, Adams hurried west with clenched teeth, determined to unleash a "Boston cyclone" on Omaha. For four days the storm raged violently as Adams forced all sides to confront one another directly. One horror story followed another, the worst of them exposing McKibbin's dismal record of excess and deceit. For months the "boy," as Mellen called him, had been wallowing in dissipation, drinking heavily and spending money extravagantly, tyrannizing the men under him in every way possible, boasting constantly of his influence with Adams and displaying as proof a friendly letter from the president—one more bitter fruit of Adams's habit of carrying on private correspondence with his officers. All the while he flattered Adams with fawning letters until delusions of power led him into the reckless attack on Holcomb.

McKibbin had no defense. A furious Adams "wiped up the floor" with him so harshly that he resigned the next day. But the ugliness did not end there. Anderson was summoned west to investigate the supply department; his digging soon uncovered the wellspring for McKibbin's extravagance. Through contracts arranged by collusion or extortion, McKibbin had swindled the company out of large sums. Anderson estimated the loss on lumber alone at fifty thousand dollars and feared the final total might exceed $1 million. In one case McKibbin bought some fancy silk underwear and had the bill sent to a supplier, who paid it rather than lose the account. Eventually the company brought suit against McKibbin, but a more immediate problem presented itself in the form of McKibbin's close ties to Mellen.

From the first Mellen had been McKibbin's champion. The young man had been his assistant purchasing agent and actually ran the department when Mellen was promoted to traffic duties. Questions arose early about McKibbin's handling of certain accounts, but each time Mellen staunchly defended his "ability and honesty." When Holcomb proposed replacing McKibbin with his own man, Mellen was quick to intercede. McKibbin kept his place, received a raise, and was finally promoted to purchasing agent in October 1889. Once again questions arose over certain accounts. McKibbin deflected them by hurling charges of his own against the coal and hotel departments and the Navigation's supply department. The stakes now went beyond the friendship between Mellen and McKibbin. Early in Anderson's probe he found evidence that convinced him of Mellen's "complicity with McKibbin."

Aware that his career was on the line, Mellen fought savagely to detach himself from his disgraced protégé. With cold precision he parried each of Anderson's charges, retreating not an inch but demanding imperiously that every charge be investigated thoroughly to vindicate him. "You are wrong, wholly wrong, in your estimate of me," he told Adams haughtily, adding, "I have not deserved this at your hands." His steely resolve was more than a bluff. Ultimately Anderson absolved Mellen of any crime beyond a rash defense of his friend. Mellen's honesty had been salvaged, but his choice of so unworthy an ally again called his judgment into question.

"He ought to go," Adams told Dodge again, "but, in plain language, I cannot well spare him." Instead he waited to see what Holcomb would do, convinced that any man with backbone would fire Mellen himself. But how could he expect Holcomb to dismiss someone the president obviously favored? Holcomb might have thrown the gauntlet, insisted that Adams choose between himself and Mellen, but he did not. Taking his cue from Adams, he tried to make his peace with Mellen and even recommended a raise in salary for him. That, sneered Adams, was just what a weak man would do: "he temporised and sought to make the conspirators friendly to him at the expense of the company." From that moment his contempt for Holcomb knew no bounds.

Day after day, at the office or in the dreary little parlor of the Millard House, Adams tried to patch up the worst of the quarrels and restore order. Through it all he mulled over the question of "making a break for liberty" until at last, in a fit of exasperation, he told Ames and Atkins that he could bear it no longer and must resign. The outburst filled him with a mixture of shame and relief. Atkins looked at him in astonishment; Ames, who had heard the plea before, simply told Adams what he already knew. "There's no use talking about that now at any rate," he said sternly. "There's no one to put in your place, and we are in a bad situation. You have got to stay till we get out of it."

Nodding wearily, Adams finished up in Omaha and headed west to tour the system. All along the road the track looked bad, the stations slovenly, and the service subpar. At Butte, however, the sights improved and so did his mood. The reason was young Baldwin, whose intelligence and vigor sparkled in contrast to the gloom and incompetence at Omaha. The farther west he went, the more Adams was impressed anew with the sheer magnitude of the Union Pacific system. On a Sunday evening in Lewiston he climbed up the hills overlooking the town and gazed in awe at the junction of the Snake and the Clearwater rivers. Here was the gateway to the Pacific: to the west lay Portland and to the north Spokane. Destiny had not yet struck its magic there, but soon it would—Adams was certain of it. Once again ambition surged within him in spite of himself. How could he abandon a game of such grand stakes, whatever the personal cost?

And how could he leave in mid battle? The earnings for April had been bad, those for May disgraceful. Operating expenses had soared $1.6 million, or 22 percent, in four months, *exclusive of maintenance.* Holcomb seemed helpless to curb this appalling spiral or even account for it. Poring over the returns during his trip, Adams found a pattern. Potter had come in with a mandate to cut expenses, which he did rigorously. Before that policy could be reversed Potter died, leaving a vacuum in which maintenance was again neglected. When Holcomb arrived, a sharp drop in earnings again forced a policy of retrenchment. For three years, then, maintenance had suffered while tonnage and train mileage shot up dramatically. These factors, along with Cushing's incompetence, explained why the roadbed and power had gone to pieces. Moreover, the rate wars had compelled the Union Pacific to haul a huge tonnage "of low priced traffic in place of a large tonnage of high price traffic," and Adams saw no relief from this dilemma.

Grimly Adams recalled the observation made to Napoleon by one of his generals at Marengo: "Yes!—it is a battle lost; but it is only 4 o'cl and there is time to win another!" The army had to be reorganized and a stand made. The

Omaha showdown produced more than the firing of McKibbin. Cushing was drummed out along with Dickinson, who had narrowly escaped the ax before. Dickinson took his ouster hard, especially since Hanna had during the earlier fight secured him a position as manager of an Omaha stockyard company that Dickinson had declined on assurance that his place at Union Pacific was secure. As a parting shot Dickinson repeated his warning that the present organization was a disaster. "I came to the Union Pacific when a boy and have grown up with the road," he added mournfully. "To leave now is like leaving home the first time."

Adams showed little sympathy for Dickinson's plight, being absorbed in his own. His chief concern was what to do about Omaha. Dodge assured him that all trouble would vanish when the "mischief makers were brought face to face," but Adams knew better. Peace would reign only while he was on the line; once he returned to Boston, the fighting would resume. Who could he put in charge? He had already dismissed Holcomb as a "big, flabby chump" barely useful as a figurehead. Mellen could not be trusted with command; Adams had all he could do to reconcile him with Holcomb and Meek. Bringing in a new man was out of the question, if only because, Adams believed, no one could master the Union Pacific system in less than two years and he did not have the luxury of time. Young Baldwin seemed the best bet, but he was not yet ready and it would be cruel to throw him into the grinder too early. Who, then, was there?

The obvious answer was himself. He contemplated the possibility as he would a sentence to Devil's Island. Going west to stay was the one thing he had sworn never to do, yet he could find no way around it. Grudgingly a plan formed in his mind. Adams would assume command in Omaha, relegating Holcomb to his proper place as superintendent of operations. He would bring in Baldwin as his assistant, giving him a broad range of duties and absenting himself frequently so that Baldwin would "have to attend to almost every thing. Whatever is done will be done in my name, but by Baldwin, and to Baldwin everyone will be referred," until the young man was ready to "quietly step into his place." Lane would be groomed to take charge in Boston just as Baldwin would in Omaha.

Still Adams hesitated, searching first for some other way out while "slowly screwing up my courage for the sacrifice." On his return from Omaha he was convinced he would have to return almost at once, and he was right. The bickering and intrigue flared up anew, spurred by his "two edged tool," Mellen. Holcomb's plea that "I do not think any railroad official ever went through a more unpleasant experience than I have had during the past six months" left Adams unmoved. To his jaded eye he no longer had a vice president but a "muddle-headed, weak-hearted, flapping old hen." Aware that he could delay no longer, a dispirited Adams boarded train on July 23 for the long trip to the land where the problems, like the plains, seemed endless and unchanging.

THE TURNOVER

Adams had always been a man divided. The braggadocio of the man on horseback could not be sustained because it was a mere façade shielding an inner core riddled with insecurity and self-doubt. Introspection was a hair shirt he could never shed, making it difficult for him to escape his own reflection in everything he did. Adams lacked confidence in what he did because he lacked confidence in himself, and he lacked confidence in himself because he still did not know what he was or wanted to be. Like many men in that predicament, he inched toward a choice by discovering what he didn't want to be or could not be.

Part of him yearned to be an artist, a literary man. He felt most comfortable with that work, and it served him well as a refuge from the grind of business. During the Union Pacific years he nursed along a two-volume biography of Richard Henry Dana which was nearing completion in 1890. He considered his most pleasant memories of the past two decades as "the days and hours I devoted to literary work," an observation that smacked heavily of the grass-is-greener syndrome. The truth was that brother Henry, and even Brooks, were better writers (although Charles did not always think so), and certainly deeper thinkers. He could not escape their shadow as an artist or intellectual in the way he could as a businessman, and Charles was eager to leave his own stamp on his own field. The Union Pacific might have been that imprint, but he had failed wretchedly at it.

The more glaring that failure became and the more insurmountable the obstacles strewn in his path, the more Adams questioned whether he ought to be there at all. The doubts began early, only months after he took office.

"Why do I sacrifice so much to play this game?" he whined in February 1885. This theme repeated itself endlessly, swelling and softening with the pressure on him, until it developed a new variation two years later. "I ought to get out," he sang glumly. "The odds are too large and the object not large enough." When he headed west in June 1887, he took hope that it might be for the last time. It was not. He talked of resigning in December, and then the following October. "Am so anxious to get out of it," he wailed, "yet none of my work is done." To himself he insisted that he was not merely clinging to position and power, that at any moment he could "go out, or be put out, in a spirit of serene indifference."

Having guaranteed himself the worst of both worlds, Adams drifted on. By July 1889 he confessed to having "lost all interest" and journeyed west again with the fervent wish that it was the last time. The man on horseback had become the man at sea, allowing events to carry him where they would. He had not so much lost nerve as he had lost heart, a distinction appreciated more by philosophers than by generals. "Why not cut the knot?" he moaned in private agony, "why! oh why!" It was all so tedious and despicable, yet he could not bring himself simply to walk away. Instead he steeled himself to face once more the drab, dreary city on the plains he so hated, hoping yet again that it might be for the last time.

* * *

Nothing went according to plan in Omaha. Baldwin's wife was expecting a child, which delayed his arrival until September 1. Meanwhile, affairs on the Navigation had deteriorated so badly that Adams dismissed the general manager at once and replaced him with McNeill. He barked so roughly in Omaha that Holcomb felt obliged to offer his resignation, his pale blue eyes filled with hangdog hurt and incomprehension. After Adams returned home, Holcomb warned that prospects for the fall traffic looked discouraging. Three weeks later, as Adams churlishly predicted, Holcomb found himself swamped by a tonnage he could not even pretend to move.

A crisis erupted in Denver, an old trouble spot grown worse by its inability to move the crush of traffic clogging the yard. Denver was the most complicated yard in the system and the one most prone to labor strife. A switchmen's strike in December 1888 was averted by an agreement between Holcomb and Thomas Neasham of the employees' association which proved only a truce. The men continued to work fitfully and threatened constantly to strike. No superintendent seemed able to handle them; the weak got trampled on and the strong sparked antagonism. One yardmaster aroused such fierce resentment that in September 1890 the switchmen prepared to strike unless he was removed. Meek hesitated, unwilling to make any concession. Baldwin, just arrived in Omaha, was dispatched to help out and handled the crisis with impressive skill and tact. Although the old issues still smoldered, a strike was averted long enough for Baldwin to clean up the yard and put it in better shape to withstand the clash when it came.

The presence of Baldwin in Denver meant he could do nothing in Omaha, where he was urgently needed. The "mass of incompetence swathed in red tape" there seemed to Adams to grow worse daily. Overwhelmed with traffic and anxious to make the best possible showing, Holcomb pushed his trains relentlessly until "a carnival of accidents prevailed." Adams realized he should go west again but refused to budge until he had wrapped up both the Dana biography and his daughter's wedding. With Baldwin in Denver and Adams procrastinating, the vaunted plan to "go on deck" in Omaha never materialized. Even worse, Adams lost his most trusted advisor at this critical hour. For months Dodge had been hobbled by gout and the lingering effects of an old war wound. In August 1890 the general had a secret operation to treat the wound and was told to go abroad for rest. When he left in September, a despondent Adams bade him good-bye and added, "when,—six months hence—you come back, you will have to come back prepared to relieve me and take charge of this property. I have done all I can do for it."

Not until October 7 did Adams head west to "face disaster serenely, and get back my liberty," finding consolation only in the belief that this was surely the last time. At Chicago he ordered Mellen to take business only at established rates. He reached Omaha on a raw, cheerless day and went through his paces with Holcomb, Baldwin (just back from Denver), and other officials. At every stop the same litany pounded in his brain: "What mistakes I have been guilty of!" The ability of Baldwin, Harvey Middleton, and Jacob Brinkerhoff, the Kansas division superintendent, impressed him anew. He thought wistfully what a fine division superintendent Holcomb would make. If only he could get the right men in the right places!

Monuments to his failure surrounded him. The Denver fracas shredded the last of his enlightened views on labor. "Our employees are running the properties," Adams complained, "and it is difficult to find any one in our service who approaches an issue with them, except . . . with the feeling that he is whipped in advance. . . . The trouble is general and epidemic." He cringed at the dismal state of the road's power. New engines ordered in May had not yet arrived as promised, and some ordered earlier proved defective. "Our difficulty," he concluded, "is simply lack of motive power." He inspected the Denver yard thoroughly and was so appalled by its nightmare character that he authorized on his own the start of work on a new breaking-up yard. In Wyoming everything was overworked to the point of collapse. In the desperate attempt to move traffic, the line had run short of coal for its power and for the mines at Anaconda and elsewhere.

At every point Adams kept returning to the same source of trouble: "Flabby-guts!" and therefore himself. There had been, he confessed, "great incompetence in the management of the last year," and he willingly took full blame for allowing it to happen. Too late he realized that delaying his trip west had cost him a precious month to repair the damage, that the money lost in that time could not be recovered. He had the most difficult railroad in the country to manage and had permitted it to drift along with "no local executive head." The reasons were as clear to him as the solution was opaque. His old plan of taking charge in Omaha had been junked. "I cannot and will not make the necessary sacrifice," he told Atkins bluntly. "For me to pass from half to two-thirds of the coming winter at Omaha . . . would make life to me simply unbearable. I would rather by far give the whole thing up, break down, and go to Europe in order to get out of the way."

Instead he rigged a makeshift arrangement with Baldwin as Holcomb's assistant, acting on orders from the president. Holcomb saw through the plan and protested mournfully that it would strip him of all pretense of authority and result in chaos. Adams ignored his funereal expression and climbed eagerly aboard his car on October 30 to glimpse his "favorite view of Omaha," receding in the gloom behind him. For all his mistakes and his sense of impending doom, he still felt there was a fighting chance. The road would pull him out of trouble if he could skate through his financial woes. For days he struggled to reconcile the contradictions burning inside him. Nothing better illustrates the muddled state of his feelings than the discovery on the trip home that "the work at the West invigorates me and braces me up—I like it —while that at the East is simply loathsome to me."

* * *

The money hunt was always a major duty of the executive office. Boston depended on remittances from Omaha to pay its bills, and when Omaha did not deliver, it was necessary to borrow. Loans were procured from banks or insurance companies in New York and Boston, using treasury securities as collateral. Since borrowing put the company at the mercy of the money market, it preferred time loans (subject to repayment in a specified period of time, often four months) to demand loans (subject to payment at the call of the lender). When money was easy, the company could shop for the best terms; in a crunch, however, borrowers took what they could get at the going rate. For that reason it helped to have close ties with institutions that could be counted on in emergencies. "We must have some bank that can be depended on for helping us whenever an adverse money market prevails," Adams declared. "This is an absolute necessity of our financial existence." A bank willing to play this role got the company account; when one failed Adams in a pinch, he was quick to shift funds elsewhere.

Where Omaha provided cash flow, bond sales raised the proceeds to pay for expansion, construction, equipment, and special projects like the Missouri River bridge. Apart from its own stockholders, the Union Pacific peddled its bonds to investment bankers in Boston, New York, and overseas. Lane's trip to London in the summer of 1886 to sell bonds had met with scant success. Two foreign houses showed a keen interest in Union Pacific securities: Baring

Brothers (working through their American agent, Kidder, Peabody) and Blake, Boissevain, the London partnership of a Dutch firm, Adolph Boissevain & Company. At home Adams used Lee, Higginson or Kidder, Peabody whenever possible, because he preferred Boston to New York banks and Henry Higginson was an old school chum. But the bonds always went to the buyer offering the best price.

Since timing was crucial in the sale of bonds, it was desirable to wait for conditions that would fetch a good price. Until the bonds were sold, however, the expenditures covered by them had to be carried as floating debt and handled through time or demand loans. A large floating debt left the company vulnerable to the vagaries of the money market. This was the situation Adams had inherited in 1884, and it had taken him two years to pay off a floating debt in excess of $6 million. Never did the financial sun shine brighter for Adams than in the summer of 1886, when the debt was gone and cash overflowed the treasury. Six months later the bears were hammering Union Pacific and the returns from Omaha frightened Adams terribly. By fall 1887 Adams was scrounging desperately for cash after the Merchants Bank called some notes and the road was again immersed "in a mass of debt from which I have got to struggle out—somehow."

Expansion was the source of debt, and not just for the Union Pacific. As roads evolved into systems, new bond issues poured onto the market until the competition for buyers grew as savage as that for traffic. The glut drove bond prices down and forced companies to carry their floating debt longer than they wished. Early in 1888 Adams dreamed fondly of resuming dividends in the fall, but by October the plan was quietly shelved. Fred Ames made it clear he did not even want to buy new equipment without first selling bonds, insisting that he would "rather go without the equipment than provide the funds for it by a floating debt." When Baring Brothers declined to take any because they were loaded down with Atchison bonds, Henry Higginson agreed to take some branch bonds at premium prices. Adams did not begrudge his profit. He favored "letting some of these small things get out at figures which will enable the bankers to make some money. Then they will take hold of larger things with some degree of avidity."

Or would they? A unique factor for the Union Pacific was its government debt. Passage of a bill would strengthen all its securities enormously; delay left a question mark hanging over them. The payment of a dividend might help, but that idea was again abandoned as unwise in February 1889. Six months later Dodge closed the momentous deal with Villard for purchase of the Navigation stock. To pay for it, the company sold $4.5 million in short-term notes to Lee, Higginson, which it intended to redeem by a sale of new Short Line collateral trust bonds. By October the once vanished floating debt had soared to $11 million, but Adams did not worry as long as earnings were high. "With a railroad," he observed, "the monthly traffic returns are all in all!" He was counting on $10 million in obligations due the company by May

1890 and also had $16 million in new bonds, which he was in no hurry to peddle except on the best terms. When Lee, Higginson, and Kuhn, Loeb offered to take some of them, Adams let it be known that he was "not anxious to sell these bonds at this time."

Shortly afterward Adams left for his vacation in Cuba. When he returned in March 1890, the world seemed to have exploded in his face. Omaha was in turmoil, expenses had shot up, the money market had tightened, and unpleasant rumors about the company were adrift in Wall Street. Some said Gould was unhappy with both the policy and the management of the Union Pacific, others that the Vanderbilts were about to buy control. At the election in April Hughitt replaced the late David Dows on the board, but no other sign of Vanderbilt presence turned up. For himself, Adams confessed to being "more and more indolent in regard to work." Tired of the game and anxious to avoid anything resembling a fight, he chose a dangerous season to lapse into inertia.

Although money was plentiful as late as May 1890, Lane urged that the Short Line bonds be sold at once because he did not like the drift of things in Omaha. But it was already too late. The rising tidal wave of expenses depressed the price of all Union Pacific securities, and the market was saturated with bonds. The bankers who had wooed Adams earlier now disdained any new offering. Morgan was busy settling the estate of his late father, and Jacob Schiff of Kuhn, Loeb would do nothing until he had gone abroad to investigate the market there. No other house was large enough to handle a $12-million issue. A reluctant Henry Higginson put together a syndicate to take some of the bonds at 91, reminding Lane that last year's bonds had not yet been digested, because the company had overpriced them. It was an ominous time for floating debts. "I do not like to see you with so much paper," Higginson stressed, "and you do not like it any better than I."

Adams thought the bonds should go for at least 94. All along he had held out for top dollar, but the March returns frightened him as well. Aware that Omaha would be devouring money all summer, he accepted a lower price to trim the floating debt. Higginson took $2.5 million worth at 91 with an option for $3 million more, all at 91. Before they could be sold, the April returns showed a drop of $660,000 in earnings. "Great Scott!" cried Adams, who also learned that the plan for financing the Puget Sound road through an offering to the stockholders had collapsed. The only recourse left was an issue of bonds, but how to market them at the same time Higginson was peddling the Short Lines? Whatever hopes Adams had for the bond market were soon crushed. The company invited bids on some Navigation fives and got only one, at an absurdly low price.

The June returns were bad, those for July "very bad—worse than I had thought possible." Adams's worst nightmare had come true: he was saddled with poor earnings, a huge floating debt, and a tight money market. That autumn the money hunt began in earnest, spurred by due notes that could not be renewed. On September 30 Adams saw his daughter married; early the next morning he snapped awake in a panic, convinced that he was "caught in the grip of a great catastrophe." The sleepless nights came more often as the financial squeeze tightened. Stocks were dropping, money was scarce and expensive, and the overseas market was depressed.

At critical times the company relied on sterling loans, usually from Baring Brothers, to get along until the money market eased. Before heading west in early October, Adams arranged with Oliver Peabody for a sterling loan of eight hundred thousand pounds to relieve immediate needs. While Adams was gone, however, the Barings vetoed the loan for reasons that would soon become apparent. Hurriedly Lane and Fred Ames arranged a sterling loan with Drexel, Morgan for half the amount, but their relief was cut short by a new and ominous development. Amid the general fall of the stock market, someone was pounding Union Pacific. Bond prices too were knocked down, impairing their value as collateral. Poor earnings, coupled with the boycott of the Iowa lines against Union Pacific, helped the bear campaign. In January 1890 the stock had stood at 68; on October 28 it touched a low of 45 before rallying slightly.

Banker R. Suydam Grant and others urged Adams to issue a public statement boosting the road's prospects. Adams deemed matters critical enough to overcome his distaste for that sort of puffery, but it did little good. The shrinkage grew worse in November as several prominent stocks hit their lowest price in ten years despite the lack of any major failure or disturbance. As the financial gale howled louder, rumors swept Wall Street that Gould was so incensed at Adams's policies, he was buying control of Union Pacific for the purpose of throwing him out. These stories distressed Adams even though he did not believe them. For months he had puzzled over what Gould was up to. In April he warned Dodge that Gould was after the Union Pacific.

But why? There had been trouble over the Central Branch, which had been leased to Gould's Missouri Pacific since 1885. In recent years earnings had shriveled because of drought, crop failures, and new mileage built by rival lines. The Central Branch was little more than a derelict, yet Adams found himself squabbling with Gould over terms of the lease and a trackage agreement. The dispute was exasperating but hardly the stuff to trigger a war, and in October Gould agreed to arbitrate nearly all the issues in question.

Adams knew Gould was also unhappy over the Northwestern pact, but he was hardly alone in that feeling. Grant told Adams that railroad officials were "publicly condemning" the agreement. He thought the stock was being attacked by "men who talk with Gould and follow his leadership." This disturbed Adams enough to warn Hughitt of a "very formidable combination against the Union Pacific on account of its alliance with the Northwestern road." On November 10 he urged Hughitt to come east for some "lengthy sittings" as soon as possible, but Hughitt could not get there before the eighteenth. By then the situation had changed drastically.

The press attack grew uglier, charging mismanagement and insolvency. Gould was quoted as saying the Union Pacific was run by "Harvard graduates who have big heads and small experience." Then, on November 12, reports swirled that he had gained control of the company. Gould denied all the rumors, but the damage was done. Mellen, at a traffic meeting in Chicago, complained that "The situation here is wretched" because of the Gould rumors. A shaken Adams issued a denial and wired Mellen to "Keep perfectly firm, make no concessions, and don't get rattled." Atkins went to visit Gould in New York and found him "gentle and persuasive" as usual. While denying the remarks attributed to him by the papers, Gould admitted he had bought some stock and did not like what the Union Pacific management was doing. That same day a brokerage closely associated with Villard suspended, sending the market into a nosedive. The break gave Adams a double dose of anxiety, for both Union Pacific and his own finances were in deep water. Aware that the company could not make it through without help, he and Fred Ames decided to go to New York in search of assistance.

An urgent appeal went out for Dodge to come home, but the old general could not possibly return in time. The Union Pacific needed money fast; if Adams could not find someone to provide it, he must let Gould do it. "The whole pack, headed by Gould, are now at work to pull me down," he told Grant. Survival depended on what help the Northwestern, or more precisely the Vanderbilts, could render. On Saturday, November 15, Wall Street was shocked by news that Baring Brothers had failed, the victim of unwise investments in the Argentine. At last Adams understood why his sterling loans had fallen through. On Sunday evening Adams and Ames started their bleak mission to New York, conscious that the Baring failure left the Northwestern as their last hope.

Adams spent most of Monday at the Knickerbocker Club writing letters to go out with copies of his Dana biography, while Ames went downtown to see Morgan and Gould. He got no comfort from either. Gould revealed that he wanted control of Union Pacific as part of "some enormous, vague scheme he is meditating of a railroad combination which is to solve the problem, do away with competition, make everyone rich and, at one stroke, reduce chaos to order." Or so a sneering Adams described it. To realize that goal, Gould was willing to assume the load if Adams could no longer carry it. When Hughitt arrived next evening, Adams told him bluntly that it was "a case of aid or a receivership." Hughitt was sympathetic but offered little encouragement. The Vanderbilts, he sighed, were neither very enterprising nor inclined to enter new ventures. That night Adams went to bed "feeling that the Jaybird had me."

On Wednesday Adams read and wrote more letters until five in the afternoon, when Hughitt appeared with the expected news: the Vanderbilts would do nothing. Their policy was "fixed and limited to Chicago,—they would not go west of it." His last hope shattered, Adams prepared to surrender his sword to Gould. Within days he would learn that the little man's vision was no idle fantasy. For half a dozen years Gould had been out of the market, confining himself to developing the Missouri Pacific system. Then, in a lightning campaign worthy of his best days on the Street, he not only captured Union Pacific but also bought a large block of Atchison, secured enough Richmond Terminal stock to give him four seats on its board, and regained control of Pacific Mail. Wild rumors ricocheted around Wall Street that he, Huntington, and the Rockefellers planned some gigantic combination of railroads.

The full force of this whirlwind had not yet hit on Thursday morning, November 20, when Adams and Ames rode downtown to Gould's office in the Western Union Building. Finding him out, they made an appointment and went over to the Union Pacific office, where Adams saw James J. Hill about the Puget Sound road. For Adams the overriding feeling was one of great relief that "this was the last time I was ever to set foot in those hated localities" where he had "always been, and always felt myself, wholly out of place." Ames felt wretched for quite another reason. On one hand his family had long been close to the Adamses; on the other he had been Gould's business associate for two decades. He knew the humiliation Adams felt and longed to spare him this defeat, but he could not. The hard fact was that all of them, including Adams, had large sums invested in the Union Pacific, and Gould alone offered a chance to avoid huge losses.

At noon they found Gould waiting for them, looking, to Adams's jaded eye, "quiet, small, furtive, inscrutable." He greeted them politely and kept the small talk as pleasant as possible. When Adams mentioned the press attacks, Gould interrupted to label them "outrageous" and remind Adams that he had denied every one of them. Nevertheless, Adams added, the result was that his position and credit had been undermined to the point where he could no longer carry the burden. He sat erect, his patrician features stern, burning with humiliation, intent on playing this final scene with dignity. Gould was kind but diffident, anxious to spare Adams embarrassment but unsure of how to do it except through tactful silence. In his narcissism Adams missed this effort to spare his brittle ego by letting him down as gently as possible. He saw only the glaring contrast between himself and the worn, rumpled figure who seemed little more than an intellect housed in an eggshell of a body.

If he could not carry the load, Adams persisted, then Gould must do it. Gould nodded and asked how much the company owed. Getting a figure from Ames, he outlined a plan he thought might work. Adams agreed to call a meeting for the following Wednesday and stood up, leaving Ames to finish the details. Gould showed him to the door, where, as they shook hands, Adams found satisfaction in the manner of his exit. Gould seemed to him "smaller, meaner, more haggard and lined in the face, and more shrivelled up and ashamed of himself than usual;—his clothes seemed too big for him, and his eyes did not seek mine, but were fixed on the upper buttons of my waistcoat. I felt as if in the hour of my defeat I was over-awing him,—and as if he felt so, too."

To the last Adams displayed a pathetic inability to read men or events. In his self-absorption it never occurred to him that he was peering into the face of a dying man. He looked but did not see; his gaze was firm but blinded by concern over what kind of figure he cut in this final scene. Whatever consolation it afforded him could not erase the stinging ironies of his record as president. Adams had inherited a large floating debt from Gould and left behind an even larger one for Gould. The road's finances had been strained by expansion when he arrived and were still strained by expansion. The market for its securities had been weak then and was weak now. He had sworn to resolve the government debt and departed with it more unresolved than ever. He found the road undermaintained and left it undermaintained. He took an organization demoralized by bickering and corruption and transformed it into one demoralized by bickering and corruption. He had denounced the company for its lack of leadership and crept away in disgrace because he had failed to provide leadership.

Much had changed on the Union Pacific in six years, yet in all these vital areas little had changed. The man on horseback had been routed from the field of battle he longed most to conquer. "Gould, Sage and the pirate band were scrambling on deck at 10," he wrote morosely of the Wednesday board meeting. Gould, Sage, Henry B. Hyde of Equitable Life, and banker Alexander E. Orr were elected directors. Adams resigned as president and was replaced by none other than the venerable Dillon, an irony too fine to have escaped Adams's notice. By a singular coincidence his biography of Dana was published that very same day. The transition from businessman to literary man seemed too neat, and it was. For nearly two years Adams was to drown his journal in a flood of *mea culpas*. The pain of his failure ran deep and was not easily exorcised. He would always blame "Flabby-guts" for his downfall and Gould for exacting revenge against him. At the same time he recognized with galling clarity that the man truly responsible for his undoing stared back at him daily from his mirror.

* * *

The burning question was why Gould had recaptured the Union Pacific. His own explanation was as disarming as it was ingenuous. "There is nothing strange or mysterious about it," he smiled. "I knew it very intimately when it was a child, and I have merely returned to my first love."

As always with Gould, there was more to the story. Like other systems, his own Missouri Pacific suffered heavily from the chaotic forces battering the industry. The recent behavior of the Union Pacific disturbed Gould for several reasons. Its presence in the Northwest aggravated the rate wars there. Its control of the Panhandle threatened Gould's own plans for a line to the Gulf and posed the danger of an alliance with Huntington. The Northwestern pact had destroyed the ICRA and smashed all hope for rate stability. The agreement with the Rock Island and the St. Paul invited new competitors west of the river and allowed a hated rival of the Missouri Pacific, the Rock Island, to reach Colorado. In Gould's eyes, Adams's policy had nurtured conflict everywhere at a time when harmony was urgently needed. Somehow it had to be reversed or at least neutralized.

Then there was Pacific Mail, which still received a subsidy from the railroads because, as Kimball observed, "Every break we have had with that Company has cost the railways more in loss of revenue each quarter than we have paid it in a year." After leaving the Union Pacific, Gould had retained his interest in Pacific Mail, using it as a club to wield against rail competitors (especially Huntington) on transcontinental rates. In October 1887 Gould had taken control of the steamship company and installed his son George as president. For two years George worked to build up Pacific Mail's business. In 1890 he attempted to open a steamer service out of Tacoma in connection with the Northern Pacific. This move offended the Southern Pacific, Union Pacific, Great Northern, and Canadian Pacific, all of which opposed any new line that benefited the Northern Pacific at their expense.

In May 1890 Huntington helped Senator Calvin S. Brice and General Samuel Thomas gain control of Pacific Mail and drop the Goulds from its board. Adams was invited to join the fight but had no stomach for another Wall Street battle. The turnover in Pacific Mail coincided with Adams's contract for use of the Omaha bridge and left Gould no indirect way to exert pressure on transcontinental rates. He had lost a valuable weapon at a time when he most needed it. A few weeks earlier Union Pacific had absorbed the Panhandle line. Together these blows alerted Gould to the danger of an alliance between Huntington and Adams, which would pit the Union Pacific, Central Pacific, Southern Pacific, Panhandle, and Pacific Mail against him. In November the Rio Grande and the Colorado Midland opened their new line between Denver and Ogden, thereby enabling the Burlington and other Iowa roads to reach the coast independent of the Union Pacific.

After months of brooding over the rate debacle, Gould had long since concluded that the prosperity of his own system required a genuine and lasting agreement among the western lines. He had spent two years trying to play the apostle of peace only to have his plans rejected as too radical and because others distrusted anything that came from him. Yet he could not abandon the effort; the stakes were too high, and the old game was played out. One thing was clear: any consolidation of interests improved the chances for peace by reducing the number of parties to an agreement. For that reason he smiled on the Atchison's purchase of the Frisco. In November 1890 Gould struck with devastating swiftness to achieve the same result on a much grander scale. His attack was bold, brilliant, and wholly unexpected.

Seizing control of Union Pacific and Pacific Mail enabled him to bring those companies into harmony with his own views. If others balked at peace,

Gould could also use them to wreak havoc with transcontinental rates. Where others believed they enhanced his capacity for mischief, he regarded them as deterrents to mischief by others. Buying a large block of Atchison gave him leverage for bringing that road into a general agreement. One paper surmised that Gould wanted "interests in the principal Western roads large enough to enable him to absolutely command the situation." At the very least he wanted influence enough to compel lasting peace among those roads. The new Southwestern Association marked a step in that direction, and Gould was already at work with Huntington and Manvel on a more ambitious plan. To emphasize its importance, he unveiled its details at the very board meeting called to transfer power within the Union Pacific.

The proposed association would embrace all lines west of Chicago and St. Louis. It would be empowered to make through rates, manage competitive business, operate joint agencies for procuring traffic, and determine routing over member roads. Guarantees would be devised to prevent rebates or rate cutting. A board of arbitration would resolve disputes. The commissioner and his assistants would be elected by a two-thirds vote of the presidents. The most novel provision, one long favored by Gould, forbade members from building new lines "that might compete in the territory or with the business of another member" without the latter's consent.

Gould circulated the plan among other presidents and obtained signatures of approval from Huntington, Miller, Manvel, George Coppell of the Rio Grande, and Ashley of the Wabash. Already he had asked Morgan to summon another conference at which the plan might be considered. Gould knew the scheme would not be easy to sell. "I hardly look for permanent peace among the railroads until the millennium," he told one reporter wryly, "but if peace were secured for only a year that would be a great deal." The newspapers mangled the plan from the start; one called it "Gould's clearing house scheme," another the "same as the old trunkline pool." Perkins rejected it as "two years ago repeating itself" and sneered that "Gould, Huntington & Magoun are not the best leaders." Forbes disagreed. "Gould has not shown his usual good sense in making himself so prominent in this," he admitted, "but on the other hand . . . an agreement thro the agency of Gould seems better than drifting along at lower rates than we ought to get. In short it is better perhaps to assent to Goulds proposal than to continue the present state of things."

On the morning of December 15 the presidents reassembled at Morgan's home. The attendance was impressive: Gould, Dillon, Sage, Huntington, Hughitt, Perkins, Cable, Miller, Manvel, Ashley, Stuyvesant Fish of the Illinois Central, Stickney, Coppell, Palmer of the Rio Grande Western, Hill, Oakes, Aldace Walker, a sprinkling of directors from various roads, and the corps of bankers. Gould led off by presenting his plan and was dismayed to find little support for it despite the signatures obtained earlier. Again he had overestimated the presidents' willingness to reach beyond their fears. They shrank from any reform that threatened real change to the way they had always done things and instead took refuge in palliatives.

The discussion rambled aimlessly until Morgan put forth a plan agreed upon early by the Vanderbilt and Pennsylvania interests. It was, he noted, "simple but comprehensive, and . . . effective." With obvious relief the presidents poked and prodded at the plan; after some amendments all approved it except Stickney, who abstained. The new Western Traffic Association looked suspiciously like the old ICRA. It would be managed by an advisory board of the president and one director from each company, which was empowered to "establish and maintain uniform rates" and oversee all outside agencies securing traffic at competitive points. Established rates were binding on all members unless changed by a four-fifths vote of the board; any officer quoting a rate below the official tariff was to be discharged at once. Arbitrators and commissioners would be appointed and by-laws adopted as needed. The Alton, the Katy, and the Fort Scott would be invited to join. Miller was delegated to call the first meeting of the advisory board once the directors of each company ratified the plan.

Since reporters were barred from the meeting, they could only guess at what had happened. Many followed the lead of the *Herald* in labeling it a "GIGANTIC TRUST" wrought by Gould. Stickney tried to set the reporters straight, but few listened. The *Times* observed shrewdly that the new scheme was "merely the reconstruction of the former Morgan Association," a point also made by the outspoken Stickney. "Two years ago you formulated something similar and it was a failure," he chided his fellow presidents. "Railroad men are not built in such a way that they will abide by this contract."

No one was more disappointed than Gould. The Morgan plan stripped away his two pet provisions, the joint agency and the ban on construction into rival territories. Without these he did not see how any plan could be effective, but he swallowed his doubts and gamely talked up the prospects of the new organization. Several presidents wanted the first meeting of the new advisory board held in Chicago, but Gould, recalling the fiasco of two years earlier, insisted the session be in New York, "where the influence of stockholders and bondholders will be more plainly felt." If held in Chicago, he warned Morgan, "the public will say it is simply the old farce which killed the former Presidents' agreement." On this issue at least Gould got his way; the meeting took place in New York. In January, despite some haggling over details and a threat by Hill to walk out, the new WTA was organized with Walker as its commissioner.

It was small consolation. Gould saw full well that the presidents shared his sense of alarm but not his vision of what was required to avert disaster. They preferred to cling desperately to the familiar in hopes of riding out the storm. Events would demonstrate the folly of that choice. The financial squalls of recent years were but prelude to a coming storm of immense fury. If the western roads would not huddle together for mutual protection, Gould had no choice but to lead his own to shelter. The Union Pacific was by far the most vulnerable, its appetite for money already insatiable.

* * *

The clouds of gloom hanging over Wall Street parted only briefly at the lightning bolts of Gould's purchases before closing again. As money grew tighter, Adams was moved to compare the worsening crisis with those of 1857 and 1873. The chances of carrying a floating debt of $11.5 million looked slim in so squeezed a market, especially when the Union Pacific statement for October showed another decline of five hundred thousand dollars. Rumors of receivership swirled despite repeated denials, as did reports that the Boston directors had sold out their interest in the road. Dillon instructed Holcomb to cut expenses wherever possible. "We are so short of money here," he stressed, "that it is necessary for you to postpone the payment of every bill possible, including taxes." By early December Adams, who was himself over extended, feared that Gould was "not going to carry the U. P. through."

He was wrong again. Dillon persuaded some New York banks to extend notes falling due and urged the Boston directors to "put the shoulder to the wheel and help and assist me in every way possible." Pacific Express was induced to pay its January dividend to Union Pacific a month early. Gould then advanced enough cash to meet obligations until the first of the year, when the money hunt would resume with a vengeance. Still Adams was not convinced. "I have no confidence in [Gould] or his management," he told Dodge frankly. "I do not believe the Union Pacific is in position to stand it for one year. Certainly his course in placing Mr. Dillon at the head of the concern confounds everyone. My own fear is that he will put S. H. H. Clark there. Should he do that, it would simply mean the undoing of whatever I may have accomplished."

A few days later Dillon appointed Clark general manager. Holcomb bailed desperately to keep his job, going so far as to propose a change in organization that reversed his plan of two years earlier. When this suggestion was ignored, he meekly accepted the post of Clark's assistant. Since Clark was also chief operating officer for the Missouri Pacific, he had command of two major systems at once. For a brief time this peculiar arrangement foreshadowed the merger that would unite these same systems a century later. Dillon gave Clark the expected mandate. "You are authorized to use the pruning knife . . . I am afraid we have given you a big contract."

Whatever motive or ambition burned within the breast of Silas Clark remained a mystery even to those who knew him well. So quiet was he of manner, so unrevealing of self, that no one glimpsed what lay beneath that stolid surface. Clark was a man of few words and fewer explanations, whose notion of railroading was traditional to the point of archaic. Fate having restored him to the position from which he had been cashiered, it is hard to believe that revenge or at least vindication was not a driving force in what he did. Gould and Dillon gave him a free hand because they had no choice; the financial crisis and other problems absorbed their energies. The road was in shambles and needed a strong hand at the helm. Clark was the only operating man they trusted implicitly to handle so large a job.

Dillon was a tired old man driving himself too hard to save the road he had helped build, refusing even to take a salary as president for his fifteen-hour days. Gould shared this loyalty toward the Union Pacific, but at fifty-four he was a dying man. Apart from his old frailties, Gould had suffered from tuberculosis for more than a year. No one knew of the disease, not even his own family. Through a remarkable display of will he kept his secret so well that the outside world learned of it only from his death certificate. But it meant that Gould required long trips to the dry climate of the Southwest, which he masked as inspection tours, and it limited the amount of work he could do at a stretch. Increasingly Gould came to depend on his son George, who was being groomed as his successor.

Given his mandate, Clark lost no time in realizing the worst of Adams's fears. After a week in Omaha he found nothing of value in the changes Adams had made or the men he had hired. The officers were demoralized and the men on the verge of striking, which Clark averted by making small but crucial concessions. Operations were in shambles and the rolling stock, especially the locomotives, "much below standard." Friends informed Clark that most of the officers in the operating department were interested in speculations along the line of the road. "You will be astonished as these matters develop," he told Dillon, adding that the road was, in his opinion, "overweighted with too many officials, drawing high salaries, all of which officials must necessarily have a retinue of clerks, etc., thereby creating unnecessary expenses." On the Oregon Short Line, a confidant reported, "no one seems to be taking any interest in the welfare of the property; every man for himself, first and last." Everywhere Clark found the company tied up in vicious and inexplicable contracts. "This great property which six years ago was entirely free and independent," he asserted, "is now bound hand and foot."

On these allegations Clark provided few details, not wishing to burden men as busy as Gould and Dillon. Many of his points were indisputable. As Adams well knew, the demoralization of men and deterioration of equipment were rampant for reasons Clark did not bother to examine. Both salaries and staff size had risen steadily under Adams, especially in recent years. Clark did not care why this had happened; his only concern was to reverse the trend by undoing most of what Adams had done and "endeavoring to operate the line upon the old principals [sic]." In effect Clark proposed to put the Union Pacific through a time warp by throwing out the changes in organization since 1884 and slicing the staff back to something near what it had been in the old days. Officers with large salaries would accept reductions or be replaced by men at lower figures. "Really, unless I can proceed to lop off these high salaried men," Clark argued, "there will be little use in trying to make a success in reduction of office expenses."

Clark wielded his ax ruthlessly. Most of his targets were the men held in highest regard by Adams. Bogue and Cameron were summarily dismissed in favor of a man who received a quarter of their combined salaries. The small sum paid old Jake Blickensderfer as consulting engineer was cut off. Harvey Middleton, the master mechanic, was also let go, as was Tebbets. C. F. Meek, who had aspired to the job of general manager, left to pursue a venture outside of railroading, and Baldwin soon followed. Mellen joined the procession after his salary was sliced 20 percent. Two superintendents, including Resseguie, were dumped; one of their replacements was an ambitious man named E. E. Calvin, who would ultimately rise to the presidency. The hapless Holcomb had his pay cut, then was charged with having a personal interest in an elevator contract on the road. Although Holcomb offered a persuasive explanation, Clark closed his ears and sent him packing.

The purge quickly drew criticism. Asked by Dodge to reconsider Bogue's firing, Clark relented only by allowing Bogue to remain in charge of the Puget Sound construction. Nor did he offer much explanation for the move. "I felt from what I saw of matters here," he said in his laconic way, "that I did not care to have him longer." Fred Ames was livid over the dismissal of Middleton. Never before, he stormed, had such a change been made without the consent of the president and executive committee. More important, Ames was convinced a change in that position could not be made "without costing the company at least a million of dollars." To this complaint Clark replied simply, "Have nothing whatever against Mr. Middleton; but when I learned he had never been through the Omaha shops; has never been through Pocatello shops, concluded he was not the character of man the Union Pacific needed, and thought it best to replace him with some one who knew our methods of transacting business."

And who knew those methods better than old hands? As his assistant, Clark brought back Edward Dickinson, who had the satisfaction of taking Holcomb's place. Jacob Brinkerhoff was put back on the Kansas division, and the Nebraska division was restored to Robert Blickensderfer, who lasted only a year on the job. It was not sentiment that ruled Clark but economy and familiarity. Like many old-timers, Kimball hailed the return of Dillon and Clark with open arms, but his joy soon faded when Clark, noting correctly that the third vice president drew ten thousand dollars a year and did nothing to earn it, stripped away his title and a large chunk of his pay. The salaries of most officers were cut, and Clark took to the warpath against a host of what he deemed extravagances, including excessive use of private cars by officers. The company in its present condition, he insisted, could not "afford a single superfluous man or salary; nor can I as a loyal officer see anyone here who I feel does not absolutely earn his wages."

These were not idle words to Clark. When the executive committee fixed

Holcomb's salary at what he deemed too high a figure, Clark asked to be relieved at once. He expected his superiors to sustain his every act while holding him accountable for results. "Discipline and economy are two things the road absolutely requires," he told Dillon, and the Holcomb action destroyed both. "It forces a man upon me whether I want him or not, and fixes a salary which in my judgment is exorbitant for the service to be rendered." The committee's action was overruled, and two months later Holcomb was gone. "As for your being sustained, you need have no fear," Dillon assured him. The board expected him to "keep the pruning knife at work until every decayed limb is cut off." If Clark still harbored doubts, Dillon took pains to remove them. "I rise or fall," he said earnestly, "with you in your management of the Union Pacific."

There was a savage irony in this transaction. In taking this stand to protect his authority, Clark showed the grit that Adams found so woefully lacking in Holcomb. But he had done it to reverse everything Adams had tried to accomplish for the Union Pacific. Unlike Adams, who agonized over every decision, Clark was confident his policy would bring quick results. Adams, of course, thought he knew exactly what those results would be. "The thing is going to pieces," he noted ruefully, "and the class of men he is putting in are so grossly and atrociously incompetent that a disaster cannot be long averted. He is simply running the property out."

* * *

When Gould took charge of Union Pacific, it was widely assumed that his first target would be the Northwestern alliance. In his usual fashion he surprised everyone by attacking instead the bridge contract with the Rock Island and the St. Paul, perhaps because this arrangement posed a graver threat to his own Missouri Pacific. Gould had long been at war with Cable, whom Dodge once called "the most active and most agressive [sic] man west of Chicago." The situation was a tricky one. Although the agreement had been made in the spring of 1890, trains were not due to start running until late December. Allowing any Rock Island or St. Paul trains to cross the bridge would in effect admit the validity of the contract, which meant that any action had to be taken at once. However, challenging the contract promised a fight not only with the two Iowa roads but also with Omaha, because use of the bridge was part of the contract with the city under which the new union depot was being constructed.

Shortly after arriving in Omaha, Clark alerted Dillon to the need for an immediate decision on the contract, which he called "a most vicious one" for the Union Pacific. He was instructed to delay the arrangements for commencing service across the bridge, which brought vehement protests from Cable. Gould asked Judge Dillon for a legal opinion on the validity of the contract and was told on December 23 it might be *ultra vires* even though the judge must have assured Adams earlier that it lay within the company's power.

Next day Gould informed Fred Ames that in his opinion the contract "would prove very disastrous to the Union Pacific." In reply Ames recalled that the contract had been made "almost entirely, I think, on the influence and judgment of Messrs. Holcomb, Cameron and others at Omaha." Personally he doubted its wisdom but had yielded to the judgment of those on the spot; now he thought it would be "poor policy" to renege unless solid legal grounds existed to dispute the contract.

The mystery deepened when Holcomb denied advocating the leases. "Who, then," persisted Gould, "could have been the party to recommend them?" Thurston thought that Cameron had been the guiding hand. Dillon, too, condemned the leases, but a search of the files revealed that both he and Holcomb had originally favored them. Only Dodge was forthright in admitting that he had urged the leases on the company and still believed in them. There was no difficulty in finding who opposed the agreements. "How any sane railway man in charge of the Union Pacific could assent to contracts of this character is beyond my comprehension," Clark told Dillon bluntly. Although Ames pressed his belief that a controversy would cause more harm than good, Gould had made up his mind. Judge Dillon offered an opinion that the company could not legally lease any part of its line or give certain roads preferential terms (what then of the Northwestern pact?) and even dredged up the tired argument that the Tripartite contract was still in force. On that basis Clark notified the Rock Island and the St. Paul that their trains would not be permitted to cross the bridge.

The timing of this challenge was delicate, coming amid the meetings to create the new Western Traffic Association. Some predicted the fight would doom the new organization. Gould assured Miller that the Union Pacific would treat all connecting roads with "perfect fairness" and sent Clark to work out some compromise agreement on the basis of "abandoning the right to use our terminals for competing line west of Omaha." Caught by surprise, Miller rebuffed all overtures for revised terms. "The contract is legally binding," he retorted, "and I don't see how the Union Pacific can set it aside." Miller and Cable each applied for a court order to compel the Union Pacific to accept his trains. Clark welcomed the fight, arguing that the best course was "never acknowledge the Milwaukee-Rock Island contract, or allow these companies to use our bridge and terminals under such contract." Judge Dillon suggested resisting the agreements on the grounds that they were "improvidently made and are harsh and oppressive."

Fred Ames and the other Boston directors, already upset by the firing of Middleton, were deeply disturbed. Like Dodge, they believed true policy was to accommodate other roads in Omaha and thereby defray terminal costs; Gould opposed allowing any rival through line into a major terminal point, especially when it gave that line a shorter route to Colorado. Moreover, the attempt to repudiate the contract, complained Ames, had "absolutely ruined the credit of the Union Pacific in Boston" and confirmed the worst fears of those apprehensive about Gould's return to the management. But several days later Ames grudgingly threw his support to Gould as the executive committee unanimously endorsed a vote to resist the contracts. "The more the extraordinary character of those contracts was examined," Gould reported to Clark, "the worse they appeared."

Gould understood that the legal fight would drag on for months, during which time no trains would run under the contracts. The decision was not handed down until late July, when the court ruled that the contract had been properly drawn and was not *ultra vires.* The Union Pacific promptly appealed and lost again, but Gould used the interlude to divide his two antagonists. In recent months the Rock Island and the St. Paul had shifted westbound business from the Union Pacific to the Burlington. Gould considered Miller more reasonable than Cable and also knew that Morgan dominated the St. Paul. Accordingly, he persuaded Miller that "it was for our interest to take them in bed with us." By November 1891 the St. Paul was working exclusively with the Union Pacific and Gould instructed Clark to work out an agreement "in such a way as not to let the R. I. get any advantage from it."

Although these issues created rifts between the Boston and the New York directors, neither side could afford the luxury of a prolonged feud. Their energies were engaged in a common struggle to keep the Union Pacific afloat in a sea of debt which by 1891 threatened to drown them all.

THE COLLAPSE

Lane tried to follow Adams out the door but was persuaded to remain by Dillon, who considered his services "absolutely necessary." One talent in particular, that of raising money, was desperately needed as 1891 opened. The company required $622,000 to meet due obligations. A large portion of this came from Gould, who had already loaned the Union Pacific more than $500,000. As the money market eased, Lane was instructed to find time loans to take up maturing sterling loans. In February Gould and Dillon fled south on a six-week tour of the Richmond Terminal system, the one exhausted from illness and the other from trying to maintain a pace his age would no longer permit. Before leaving, Dillon assured Clark that together they would "bring the old Union Pacific up to where it belongs."

Their respite was brief. Fears that the company would not meet its payments on the Navigation lease in March sent Navigation stock tumbling, which impaired its value as collateral. Banker Adolph Boissevain inquired apologetically about new rumors of receivership, touching off another frantic search for loans and collateral. Unable to find time loans, the company reluctantly renewed the sterling loans with Morgan. Gould was finding it more difficult to get off the treadmill of short-term notes than he had anticipated. Hopefully he floated the idea of a blanket mortgage as a trial balloon and got a chilly response; one critic predicted it would hasten the disintegration of the Union Pacific system. Obliged to leave on another rail tour in April, Gould used the time to perfect a new plan for a $25-million collateral trust mortgage. "I don't know a better security," he declared when the plan was unveiled at the annual meeting in April.

Although the *Chronicle* gave the Union Pacific a cautious approval, the market was unimpressed and the issue flopped. The scramble began anew to meet the July interest in the teeth of news that May earnings were $750,000 gross and $300,000 net below the previous year's dismal record. The *Times* alleged that the Union Pacific was all but bankrupt. Gould had now advanced the company more than $660,000, some of it without collateral or notes. When the money hunt for July fell short, he put up another $650,000 and arranged a loan of $100,000 from one of his other companies, Manhattan Elevated. The Boston directors agreed to take part of a new loan, then balked when Sage and Henry Hyde delayed taking their portion. Despite this fresh tension between Boston and New York, the company staggered through its July payments.

A relieved Dillon, home from a tour of the road, reminisced with a reporter over his long connection with the Union Pacific and remarked that he had not only supervised its construction but personally driven its first and last spikes. Tired old men were permitted lapses of memory, but critics were not so forgiving of their performance as executive officers. Adams, hardly a neutral observer, was appalled by the new management's policy and wondered how long it could last. "If it will only hold out six months more!" he prayed for the sake of his own finances, but he doubted even Gould's ability to pull off that miracle. When the crash came, would Gould's body be found under the debris? Adams thought not. Gould was "an infernal scoundrel—a moral monstrosity,—but he is astonishingly quick!"

That quickness was soon tested again. An exhausted Gould took to the rails once more, reviving his strength with a lengthy tour over the Union Pacific system. Lane submitted his resignation and prepared to sail for Europe in August. A shrinkage of values in the market during July led to some calls for more collateral, but no one was alarmed by the fall. On Friday, July 31, Gould and Hyde were both out West. Fred Ames had gone to Europe, Dillon to his home in Litchfield, Connecticut, and George Gould to his lodge in the Catskills. Without warning a rash of calls on loans hit the New York office. Dillon got word of the trouble and alerted both Goulds. With Jay unavailable, George agreed to provide $100,000 to see the company through the weekend. That week, however, the rush of calls swelled into an avalanche. While the treasurer, James Harris, scrounged everywhere for funds, rumors spread that the Union Pacific would default on its loans and tumble into receivership. Someone was raiding the stock; heavy trading battered it down to 35⅞, its lowest figure since the dark days of June 1884.

Atkins hurried over from Boston and found Dillon wilting from the strain and the summer heat. At once he wired Gould that Dillon was so nervous he might break down unless relieved of the pressure, and that $1.5 million of new money was needed to ease the crisis. George sent a similar message. Gould answered that his own health was too fragile to carry the load and suggested a receiver. This reply was surely bait to test the resolve of the jittery

Bostonians to stand fast. Dexter arrived in New York and agreed with Atkins that they could not "safely furnish money." They informed Gould that "Unanimous opinion of every director that Receivership should be avoided if possible. . . . Can you not encourage and assist."

Gould found himself caught in a dilemma he could not reveal. His leadership was urgently needed in New York. He could not exert it from afar, yet his illness did not permit him to return and he could not explain why without revealing his secret. Instead he submitted a plan designed not merely to stave off receivership but also to free the company from the shackles of demand loans that kept everyone scurrying frantically for cash. Having failed to achieve this with the new collateral trust bonds, he proposed asking the creditors directly to exchange their demand notes for time loans of two or three years. In return the Union Pacific would deposit with each creditor some securities as collateral and pay a premium. Any creditors refusing the offer would be paid off with funds provided by a syndicate of the road's friends. Gould suggested that J. P. Morgan be asked to put the plan together. He also urged Dillon to "let the younger Directors do the work" and added, "I am more impressed with the future of the Union Pacific the more I see of it."

The news was just the tonic Dillon needed. "I was half sick, tired and discouraged about Union Pacific until your last suggestion came," he wrote Gould. "We feel in New York that that can be carried through if all work with a will." Sage liked the plan, Dodge promised to take half a million in the syndicate, Dillon himself the same, and Ames would surely do his part. Dillon feared the worst if the road went into receivership and admitted "it would break my heart to see it wrested from us . . . shall we lay down and see the Union Pacific taken from us? I say 'No' and hope you say the same." To Clark he said, "It would be terrible to let go that which we have fostered so long." George advised the old man gently to go home and rest for a few days, and Lane, one foot on the gangplank, agreed to stay on until the crisis passed. Gould and others provided enough cash to stave off immediate calls. By Friday, August 7, things had quieted.

News of the plan boosted the stock to 39, but within a week it sank to 32 as snags developed. The money was slow in coming forth, a few restless banks made new calls, and large blocks of Union Pacific were dumped on the market. Everyone, including Morgan, seemed to be out of town at this critical time, and rumor insinuated that Morgan denied being part of any syndicate. One observer asked pointedly who was in charge of Union Pacific. Gould and Ames were away, Dillon was "about 80 years old and does little," Clark had charge only of operations and Lane of loans, and no other director played a major role. "There is no real head to the property," the observer concluded, "and for the lack of this essential the whole thing is going to pieces."

From Idaho Gould authorized George to subscribe for $2 million in the new plan, but Sage and some others hesitated. A distraught Dillon begged them to respond and refused to leave his post despite having lost twenty pounds from anxiety. "All New York looks upon you as the great barometer in Union Pacific," he implored Gould. "I know you are. You will have to give some further encouragement than you have to stimulate the parties." Gould sent George to confer with Morgan, who finally agreed to fill the leadership vacuum along with Alexander E. Orr, who had come onto the board with Gould. The banking partner of the late David Dows and holder of his interest in the Union Pacific and the Rock Island, Orr wielded considerable influence in financial circles. On August 18 the board was told the floating debt exceeded $20 million. With little debate it passed a revised version of Gould's plan and appointed a committee headed by Morgan to represent both the company and its creditors. Under the plan creditors were offered three-year, 6-percent notes secured by nearly $42 million market value of collateral deposited with Drexel, Morgan.

"Again Mr. J. P. Morgan steps in to avert a disaster which hung over Wall Street," averred the *Chronicle.* When Gould was slow to lend his signature to the agreement, the press concocted tales of a feud between him and Morgan. While these fantasies made the rounds, the company struggled to make ends meet until the creditors' agreement went into effect. "If I can once more get the control of the cash into my own hands, I will keep things straight," promised the harassed treasurer, James Harris, "but for the last three days it has been run on the town meeting plan,—one instructs me this way, and another that way, and among them all I am between the devil and the deep blue sea."

The executive committee formally executed the agreement on September 4, a few days before Gould's return. The securing of assents from creditors was not helped by gloomy news from Mink, who reported that the system ran a deficit of nearly $1.2 million for the first seven months of 1891. The receivership rumors revived and were fanned by explosive new accounts of a clash between Morgan and Gould over who was in charge of the Union Pacific. Gould was said to have "sulked and practically retarded the scheme" until Morgan gave him a dressing down and threatened to run him out of both the Union Pacific and Wall Street unless he cooperated. This blather provided more entertainment than insight, although a snag had developed. Gould, besides pledging $2 million to the new agreement, had also endorsed another $2 million in sterling loans held by Drexel, Morgan and wished this dual liability clarified before signing. By late September this difficulty was resolved and the plan was declared operative.

The success of the new agreement relieved the pressure and gave the company breathing room. Lane finally took his leave on September 30, but Dillon was slow to recover. The ordeal had greatly taxed the old warrior's stamina, and it soon became evident that his loss of weight was caused by something more than anxiety. Gould, too, was worn out and got no respite, for he was also embroiled in a bitter controversy over his decision to stop dividends on the Missouri Pacific. Clearly the older generation was wearing out, dropping in harness from overwork. That fact was underscored in December when the venerable Bishop John Sharp died, severing a tie with the road that traced back to its construction days. It disturbed more than one observer that the old order was passing with no sign of a new order in sight.

*　*　*

By 1890 western railroads had come full circle. War had bred expansion, expansion bred more wars, and now the cost of war put an end to expansion. Except for Hill, who was driving relentlessly toward Puget Sound, no other transcontinental lines were built as the major roads turned to constructing branch mileage. On the Union Pacific even branch construction ground to an abrupt halt, another casualty of the financial crunch.

The old goad to lay track before a rival road got there first was finally losing some of its bite. During the fall of 1891 Clark urged an extension to Tintic, Utah, before the Rio Grande Western preempted the region and built across Nevada. The company had no money to undertake even the sixty miles Clark wanted, and its directors showed no interest in putting up their own funds for a project through desert promising in its mineral deposits but barren of people or other resources. Despite a plea from John Sharp only days before his death, the idea was dropped.

By far the largest ongoing project was the Portland & Puget Sound, undertaken in partnership with the Great Northern. Almost everything had gone wrong, ranging from disputed surveys of the route to botched estimates on both the line and the Vancouver bridge. When Dillon took office, the Puget Sound was a white elephant swallowing money faster than the Short Line could provide it. He and Hill agreed to stop work on the project at once but found it difficult to get out cleanly. The contractors were caught short and begged for funds to pay off their men. So abruptly were men discharged in Portland that city authorities had to help feed and house them. The settlement of these claims was marred by suspicions of overcharges and took months to resolve.

A dispute also erupted between Hill and Dillon over their obligations under the joint contract. The bickering dragged on until spring, when an attempt was made to revive the work. Bogue took charge of the project after being relieved as chief engineer, but his and Dodge's enthusiasm could not surmount the worsening financial crisis. In August Hill and Dillon came to terms and the project was finally abandoned. There was talk of seeking trackage rights to Tacoma from the Northern Pacific and of reaching the coast by extending to Astoria, but no rail was laid and the prize of Tacoma remained elusive. In the race to dominate the Northwest, the Union Pacific dropped behind the Great Northern and the Northern Pacific.

Serious strains within the Union Pacific system had also begun to surface. The reorganized Grand Island had never run smoothly. Adams clashed repeatedly with James Benedict over the road's financial structure and operation. Two issues especially infuriated Benedict: the transfer of Grand Island accounts to Omaha, and the Union Pacific's handling of the branch's rolling stock. "What I object to specially," he snapped, "is being run by any accountant." He also accused the Union Pacific of keeping Grand Island cars for its own traffic during the busy season when the branch desperately needed them. The change of management brought no change in Benedict's complaints. The real issue, he insisted, was that the Union Pacific had simply ignored the provision in the 1885 agreement that the Grand Island be run as an independent line and instead sacrificed the Grand Island's interests to improve the showing of the main line.

Dillon feared the complaint might be just but took umbrage that Benedict did not approach him directly with it. Mink advised against any compromise on the grounds that it might carry "an implied admission of mismanagement"; like any good accountant he opposed a truly independent management because it would increase expenses. When it was suggested that the Grand Island's president be allowed to appoint his own general manager, Fred Ames bristled at once. The Union Pacific, he said stiffly, could not guarantee the large sums required under the agreement unless it controlled the road's manager. A settlement in January 1891 removed the immediate sources of friction but left the basic issues unresolved.

A far more important branch, the Panhandle, also complained bitterly that its interests were being sacrificed to the parent road. Despite vigorous efforts by Dodge, the Union Pacific had not properly digested the Gulf line. Constant friction on a host of issues forced Dodge into a hopeless conflict of loyalties between the two roads in which he was most involved personally and financially. Moreover, he had staked his reputation on the merger and had to answer for it to skeptics like John Evans, who distrusted the Union Pacific and suspected Dodge of being in league with its masters. Whenever trouble arose, the general found himself in the middle and obliged to mediate between the contending factions. It was not a role Dodge relished.

The problems had begun long before Adams left office. Meek clashed with Mellen, and Dodge protested bitterly that a new traffic man in Denver was "discharging a good many of our best men." Both of them disliked hauling ninety cars of company coal a day from Trinidad to Denver for use by the Union Pacific at the absurd rate of a half cent per ton-mile. Like the Grand Island, the Gulf line blamed the parent road for its perpetual shortage of cars. One mine north of Denver had contracted for sixty coal cars a day and was lucky to get six a day. The slump in earnings during 1890 sharpened every difference with an edge of recrimination. Adams had tried to resolve these disputes but had been too overwhelmed by his own woes to accomplish much.

The turnover reunited Dodge with men he had long known and trusted, but times were hard and the thread of their interests even more tangled than his own. Meek's departure upset him, as did Mellen's practice of routing traffic away from the Gulf line. In his usual blunt fashion Dodge showered both Dillon and Clark with advice on traffic policy, most of it opposing Mellen's course. Morgan Jones, who was in charge of the Gulf line, warned Dodge that the Union Pacific was shortchanging its subsidiary on equipment and then charging it large sums for leased cars. A continued fall in earnings reinforced the suspicion that the Union Pacific was weighting traffic and differentials in its own favor at the expense of the Panhandle. Dodge began to wonder about Clark's dual role as head of both Union Pacific and Missouri Pacific. Was the Union Pacific being run in its own interest or for that of the Gould lines, and how did that affect the Gulf line?

A western tour in November 1891 did little to improve relations. Clark and Atkins showed little enthusiasm for the Gulf road's prospects. Mink, who liked much of what he saw elsewhere, was not impressed "with the strength of this Gulf system." Dodge sounded Fred Ames on his views and learned that opinion within the Union Pacific was sharply divided over the worth of the Gulf line. Undaunted, Dodge hammered away at his protest campaign. Mink observed sourly that the general was "creating a good deal of disturbance." But Mellen refused to budge, and Mink proclaimed that "the position of Mr. Clark and Mr. Mellen is unassailable." Still Dodge did not relent until the evidence he accumulated impressed Clark enough to reverse some of Mellen's actions in March 1892. A few days later Mellen left the Union Pacific.

Disputes also arose over the terms of the merger, which Dodge tried patiently to reconcile. As father of the consolidation he still believed fervently in the benefits it could bestow on both roads if handled intelligently, but he was caught between the devilish John Evans and the deep blue sea of Union Pacific's management. After the merger Dodge had insisted that Evans be kept on the board of the Gulf road, a concession that left Evans unmoved. The wily governor's position had changed little in two decades: he wanted a Denver-based system that catered to the needs of the Rocky Mountain region rather than the interests of a distant master. He did not trust the Union Pacific or Dodge, whom he suspected of being in league with Gould and Dillon. Although both Evans and Dodge had large stakes in the merged system and were crucial to its success, there was remarkably little contact between them. Pride and mutual suspicion kept them apart at a time when circumstances urgently required their cooperation.

While Dodge toiled to make the merger work, Evans tugged quietly in the opposite direction. As early as July 1891 he was exploring legal tactics to break the traffic contract between the two roads. That year net earnings on the Gulf road slumped 19 percent, leaving it about $465,000 short of the amount needed to pay interest, taxes, and betterments. Gould assumed the Union Pacific was obliged to guarantee only the Gulf line's interest; to his chagrin he learned that the traffic contract required payment of the entire sum needed for these items. Grudgingly the Union Pacific advanced the funds, but Evans was not impressed. At the stockholders' meeting in April

1892 he vented his displeasure by introducing a list of complaints and some resolutions to correct them. His proposals were voted down but the point was made. Surprised by Evans's move, Dodge was preparing for another lengthy sojourn in Europe and could do little about it. A committee appointed by the Union Pacific investigated the complaints and predictably found them "utterly without foundation in fact."

This whitewash left matters ominously unsettled. In his last days before sailing, Dodge alerted Morgan Jones to the friction between the roads. To get rid of it, he added, "they would like to have all the companies under one head,—that is the President of the Union Pacific. It is a mistake." Still he clung to the belief that "another year will get us squarely on our feet if they give us the business to which we are entitled and treat us right." He could not have picked a worse time to ask for another year.

* * *

Through the first uneasy months of its existence the Western Traffic Association ran more smoothly than the presidents had dared hope. It helped that 1891 produced bountiful crops of wheat and corn, huge livestock shipments, and a heavy tonnage of coal and lumber. Buoyed by this immense volume of traffic, managers boldly increased rates in the war-torn Northwest and Southwest. Some roads even restored dividends they had reduced earlier. Despite this good fortune, few harbored illusions that the worst had passed. The national financial picture still looked bleak, and several key roads still had not joined the WTA. Hill remained a wild card in the Northwest, where he did not hesitate to cut rates. The Alton kept rates on Kansas City traffic in flux, and trouble among the transcontinental lines flared up periodically. Denver became a hotbed of intrigue as the systems reaching there schemed to get control of the other line to Ogden, the Rio Grande Western.

Skeptical observers still viewed the new organization as fragile and made much of Gould's failure to attend its quarterly meeting in April 1891. The Chicago meeting adjourned for lack of a quorum and agreed to reconvene a month later in New York. A miffed Perkins objected to changing the location to suit Gould. "The newspapers, especially the Chicago papers," he scowled, "try to give the impression all over the West that Gould runs all the railroads, and the roads themselves seem determined to do what they can to give a foundation for that belief." In fact Gould was absent on another of his inspection trips to restore his flagging strength. He returned in time for the May meeting to face charges that his own Missouri Pacific and its traffic manager, J. S. Leeds, had cut rates on sugar. When the board found Leeds guilty, Gould reluctantly obeyed the WTA's rules and fired Leeds. "I made the best fight I knew how," he told an unhappy Clark, "but when the unanimous vote was against me I felt it was my duty to acquiesce & thus save a general breaking up."

Contrary to rumors, Gould was anxious to keep the WTA alive and well.

No other president went so far as to sack a valuable man to comply with its regulations. In return the WTA board promised to consider one of Gould's pet plans, the joint agency, at its July meeting. Gould had long believed that one way to curb the underhanded practices of traffic officers was to abolish individual agencies in favor of joint agencies for soliciting business. He also shared Walker's view that the time was ripe to recruit disturbing roads into the WTA. Letters were sent to ten outside lines inviting them to join, but the response was disappointing. The Alton's president refused, saying he doubted any association would actually practice what it preached. Van Horne of the Canadian Pacific also declined, citing "practical difficulties" and the effort by WTA members to obtain hostile legislation from Congress as his reasons. The Soo Line, Katy, and other roads also stayed out.

Rates were again softening when the advisory board convened in July. The Alton bared its fangs by leaving the Western Passenger Association and cutting rates. Until some way was found to muzzle the renegade roads, many WTA members balked at the joint-agency plan. Ashley of the Wabash quelled a heated debate by moving to postpone consideration until October. "The joint agency is sure to come sooner or later," Walker assured reporters, "but it is unwise for five or six roads to establish a joint agency as long as there are other roads unwilling to join it." The *World* hailed this action as proof that Gould could not run the association. In October nothing was done on the plan or on a resolution proposed by Perkins. The Burlington complained that it was not being treated fairly by the WTA, a protest that was soon echoed by other lines.

The need for meaningful action was never greater, yet the presidents shrank from any novel proposal. Perhaps nothing they did would have made a difference; the point is that in the face of impending disaster they could not bring themselves even to try. Like cattle driven over a cliff by a storm, they marched blindly to their doom because it was all they knew how to do. A despondent Walker admitted he was disappointed "to find corporations accepting general principles abstractly while they obstruct in every way their application concretely." His job had become thoroughly disagreeable from the constant need "to find some affirmative sanction of authority under which members can be compelled to do what they ought to do gladly." Tired of nagging the presidents to see where their own best interests lay, Walker talked of resuming his law practice. Perkins tried to lift his spirits but conceded that "I do not think any board of directors can, even for ninety days, properly say they will be governed by what somebody says is fair."

Although Walker stayed at his post, his efforts to strengthen the WTA were frustrated. The January meeting confessed complete failure in the campaign to recruit outside lines. Dodge wanted the Gulf line out of the association, "because all of our competitive lines are out of it." Rate cutting began anew, secretly at first through rebates, and then more overtly. By the spring of 1892 a tug of war among competing roads threatened to tear the WTA apart. Gould, again a reluctant exile in the Southwest, learned from his son George that all the western associations were near collapse. "In that case," he noted grimly, "general demoralization is likely to ensue." At the May meeting the Burlington and the Rock Island asked that rates to Colorado and Utah be lowered to levels already created by rebates. A flood of exceptions on traffic rulings were sought as roads hurled accusations and denials at each other.

Embittered over a decision against the Burlington, Perkins was ready to leave the WTA. Everybody knew, he stormed, "that the whole affair is a delusion and a hollow mockery; and many of the members want to break it up, and are only waiting for a chance to say somebody else did it." The advisory board amounted to "nothing but a sort of public exhibition of railroad dirty linen" which did little more than alarm investors. Ever righteous, Perkins believed everyone else was cheating and taking advantage of the Burlington "because we keep the agreement, while others break it." It seems never to have occurred to him that other presidents felt precisely the same way or that this lack of trust was the fatal disease that made Walker so heartsick. As a remedy Perkins could offer only the stale prescription that had already bled the roads half to death: "There is only one way to meet the situation; and that is by open reductions of rates until all hands are sick of it, and will make a new agreement on a better basis."

Perkins did not attend the July meeting but sent it an ultimatum: unless his board's interpretation of a pivotal article in the WTA constitution was accepted, the Burlington would withdraw from the association. Aware that without the Burlington there would be no quorum, the advisory board adjourned without doing anything. Perkins construed this as failing to comply with his demand and served notice of withdrawal. The Southern Pacific and the Missouri Pacific followed suit, and the last meeting in October confirmed the WTA's demise. The Transcontinental Association had just crumbled, and the Trans-Missouri and the Western Passenger associations collapsed soon afterward. Walker talked hopefully of a new organization built around the joint-agency idea, but few listened. The associations were gone, and with them perished the last semblance of cooperation among roads to maintain rates.

Hill was again slashing rates in the Northwest, and the specter of renewed war loomed in every region. The Union Pacific found itself engulfed in clashes on every front over passenger business. When the Union Pacific refused to divide business at Ogden and Denver instead of Omaha, half a dozen other lines retaliated with the threat of another boycott. Through the long, dreary months of 1893 the passenger war raged along with the fight against Hill. Repeated attempts to negotiate peace or even a truce proved futile. The imprint of these wars on a later generation would drive them to end "ruinous competition" at all costs, but that lesson had yet to be learned in full. For now the message to officers of the Union Pacific was painfully clear. Good rates and good luck were needed to pull them through the financial crisis. The collapse of the associations blasted all hopes for good rates.

* * *

With Gould absent on a prolonged trip to the Southwest in the winter of 1892, the old question reared its head anew: who was in charge of Union Pacific? Dillon could no longer exert even a semblance of authority. His stomach trouble persisted until it became clear that the problem was not merely age or anxiety but disease, probably cancer. In March he was confined to his house and never returned to work; by early April he was too weak even to sign papers. Clark mourned the debility of this "great, grand, good man; one to whom I am greatly indebted" and hurried to New York, where a fight for control of the company was expected at the annual election. The foreign holders, led by Adolph Boissevain, demanded the ouster of Gould's faction, and their gathering of proxies made them confident enough to name their candidate for the presidency. No one expected the incumbent ticket to win, especially with Gould away and Dillon indisposed.

Adams joined the crowd of stockholders gleefully awaiting their chance to turn out Gould and Sage, but they reckoned without the diligence of young George Gould, who discovered that a London firm owning twenty-six thousand shares had first given their proxies to Boissevain, then transferred them to their American agents, the Wormser brothers. Since the Wormsers had long done business with Gould, George persuaded them to vote for his ticket. At the eleventh hour the Boston directors stood by Gould, terming the effort to displace him "a grave mistake." As a result Gould's ticket squeaked home by little over twenty-three thousand votes, provoking howls of protest that the London shares had been voted improperly. Gould was delighted at the victory, the more so because his son, the heir apparent, had managed it. "They had crowed so loud that they had a walk over," he wrote from distant El Paso. "We have now a year leeway to look over this property & can probably by [sic] the stock cheap as earnings I think are likely to be poor."

The victory was sweet but only emphasized the vacuum of leadership. Obviously Dillon could not continue as president, and no one on the board wanted the position. The only logical candidate was Clark, who gave the Bostonians pause, but even they conceded that there was no one else. His election marked a break in the tradition of having one of the eastern financial officers serve as president. Instead the directors created the position of chairman of the board and tendered it first to Dillon as an honor. At the same time the board passed resolutions in praise of his long service, but Dillon was too ill even to read them. On June 9 the old lion died, worn out in the end by the road to which he had devoted so much of his life. Of the old guard who had built the Union Pacific, Dodge alone remained.

Dillon's passing ushered in a period of instability that did nothing to make Clark's job easier. The New York office was closed. With Gould still in charge of finances, there was no need to elect a new chairman of the board. But no one yet realized how sick Gould was. Drawn and gaunt from fighting his disease, he returned east in the summer because he could no longer stay away, and undertook a limited work schedule. An improved showing in 1891 still had not convinced him that the Union Pacific would survive. In October he attended the last session of the WTA, where Palmer found him "more chirruppy than ever, and with a tone of injured innocence that was lovely to behold." It was in fact the last business meeting Gould would attend, a requiem not only for himself but for four years of hard work to promote unity. As the cold weather came on, he could not bring himself to head west again on the rail car that had become a prison for him. Week after week he postponed the trip until late November, when his disease entered the miliary, or terminal, phase. On December 2, 1892, he died at his home on Fifth Avenue at the age of fifty-six.

Suddenly Clark found himself alone at the top. The men on whom he had leaned for nearly two decades were gone, leaving only the Bostonians. Of the old guard only Fred Ames and Dexter remained, and they were not accustomed to playing dominant roles in the company. Edwin Atkins was a capable executive but, like Orr and Hyde, distracted by other business concerns. The Union Pacific's future rested on the frail shoulders of a man known to be prickly and subject to periodic physical breakdowns. Long before Gould's death, Clark's dual position with the Union Pacific and the Missouri Pacific had become a bone of contention; indeed it was a major complaint of the foreign holders who tried to seize control of the company. Clark insisted that he had in fact resigned from the Missouri Pacific, but in Gould's absence a quorum of the board could not be found to accept it.

Some thought Gould's death would rekindle the fight for control, but Boissevain sensed that a struggle would weaken the property disastrously. Instead he assured Lane of his confidence in Clark and desire for harmony within the management. A relieved board elected George Gould to replace his father and Sidney Dillon Ripley to his grandfather's place, making a total of five directors who had virtually inherited their seats. Boissevain declared that the company was "stronger than it has been at any previous time." But within two months Clark found himself embroiled in controversy. After Mellen's departure he told Fred Ames that a general traffic manager was not needed and asked that Munroe be promoted to general freight agent. Dodge did not object to that, but he was disturbed by the poor performance of the traffic department. "The general sentiment among all railroad men," he warned Clark, "is that the U. P. don't care much whether it gets business or not." The controversy delayed Munroe's appointment until October 1892. Then, four months later, Clark promoted Edward Dickinson to general manager.

When complaints over the choice arose, Clark reacted by threatening to quit. The pressure of his dual role had become intolerable to him. For weeks he brooded over what to do, saying nothing to close friends like Dodge even though they were together for much of the time. Finally, without telling anyone, he scribbled a note to Ames saying, "I have worried myself sick over the Union Pacific situation. I have decided to leave, and this is my resignation as President of the Company." Ames and the other directors were dumfounded. A shocked Dodge heard the news from a broker and promptly scolded Clark for his discourtesy. No one knew who to put in his place. Dodge wanted Ames to take the position, but Ames refused adamantly to accept the responsibility. Mink was suggested even though he was an accountant with no operating experience, as was J. H. Millard, an Omaha banker who was then a government director.

For all his personal and physical frailties, Clark was the man the Bostonians wanted. Since his plan was to devote himself to the Missouri Pacific, the key figure in settling the matter was George Gould, who was both head of that road and a director in Union Pacific. George had also been close to Clark since his boyhood. Anxious to maintain harmony between the systems, he persuaded Clark that everyone's interests could best be served by his remaining with the Union Pacific. After some soul-searching Clark withdrew his resignation and severed all ties with the Missouri Pacific. In April Mink was elevated to vice president and Alexander E. Orr assumed the position of chairman of the board, giving the company an old management team in a new lineup. Boissevain bestowed his blessing, and harmony prevailed at the annual election. In making his own peace with Clark, Dodge exhorted him to "settle down on the U. P., prepared to take care of it from now on; and let us all get our shoulders to the wheels, and lay our plans, and work to them, for the purpose of getting out from under the government debt."

* * *

Although Adams had finally abandoned all hope of settling the government debt, the issue did not go away. Never did the Union Pacific dare to look away from Washington, where new threats loomed and old ones rose from the dead at every session of Congress. The company lobby there had been trimmed down but not disbanded. Shellabarger & Wilson still handled all ICC business, and Ayres remained on the payroll. Dillon had found in 1891 that the salaries paid in Washington totaled $17,800 a year and were difficult to cut. In 1889 Adams had hired a man at $3,000 a year just to look after the company's interminable quarrel with the Post Office over mail pay. "This company has literally been robbed for a number of years on the distribution of the mail it was entitled to get," Thurston snapped, "which has been sent to other rival lines without rhyme or reason." Since the disputed payments amounted to more than $300,000, the lobbyist was retained after Gould regained control.

During the summer of 1892 an old issue flared up in new form when Congress attached an amendment to the army appropriations bill withholding payment for government transportation over all *branches* owned or operated by the Union Pacific. This proviso extended the dispute to lines on which no government bonds had been issued. Government director Rufus Bullock, whose political credentials included service as carpetbag governor of Georgia during Reconstruction, headed the campaign to quash the amendment. The bill had gone to committee, where the Senate delegation opposed and the House members favored the amendment. "There is a very *bitter* feeling in the House against Pacific Roads," Bullock reported, "& it has come to be a party question." After weeks of wrangling, both sides agreed to a revised version that excluded lines leased and operated but not owned by the Pacific roads. It was, Bullock sighed, the best he could get when tempers were short and the mood of Congress so sour.

The Democrats were behind the amendment, and that autumn the party squeaked back into power with the return of Grover Cleveland to the White House in 1893. The first government bonds were due to mature in 1895. Action on some form of settlement had become imperative, but the struggle would be uphill against a hostile administration. Public misconceptions about the government debt and the legend of Crédit Mobilier still persisted, and the return of Gould had aroused fresh resentment in some quarters. "Probably the best thing that the Government can do under the circumstances," grumbled the New York *World,* "will be to foreclose the mortgage and sell the road." Gould helped Huntington revive the bill extending the debt at low interest but got nowhere. His death a month after Cleveland's election cleared the air for another try.

Everyone assumed a settlement would be reached during Cleveland's term. The Senate bill desired by Huntington and Gould was endorsed by the commissioner of railroads with only minor amendments. Although the New York *Tribune* warned that "action cannot be much longer delayed," Congress showed little disposition to act. The Union Pacific insisted again that it could not pay the debt when it fell due, and only a few diehards seriously advocated the government's taking control of the road, yet a curious malaise held both sides inert. Mink assured Bullock that "nothing remains for us to do but await action on the part of the Government," which amounted to waiting for Godot. In February 1893 Ayres concluded that "with proper and well directed efforts" a funding bill could be passed at the first session of the new Congress. But no such effort was made.

When Congress called a special session in August, Ayres repeated his view that the time was ripe to get a bill passed. "You and I are thoroughly in accord in the view that this is the crucial period for the U. P.," he told Mink, "and we must win everything or imperil all." The votes were there, the House committee was sympathetic, and the Speaker favored speedy passage. Hopefully Ayres laid his plans while urging the company to bring its influence to bear in every quarter. But it was too late, for in every sense time had run out on the Union Pacific.

* * *

One by one the doorways to survival slammed shut on the Union Pacific. Failure to end the rate wars left the system hauling too much traffic at low rates, which in turn wore out its physical plant at an alarming rate. After twenty years of fighting, the War of the Government Debt dragged on with no solution in sight. In the public eye the road had become a prisoner of its own myths, most notably the legend of Crédit Mobilier. The generation of leadership decimated by age and death had not been replaced by one of comparable stature or ability. The financial crisis had been staved off but not solved, leaving the company vulnerable to any unexpected shifts in the market or the economy.

Through 1892 the Union Pacific's luck had held firm. The creditors' committee reduced the amount of collateral trust notes by selling some of the underlying securities, mostly to the foreign holders. By May 1893 only $11.5 million of the original $18.5 million in notes was still outstanding. Despite a bear attack on the stock that winter, the outlook seemed promising. But the economy was wobbly at best, and a financial crisis had been brewing for months. In May it struck with the fury of a hurricane. The market plummeted, rallied fitfully, then succumbed to panic in June. Before the storm passed, nearly five hundred banks and fifteen thousand commercial firms would fail. Gradually it became clear that the disturbance was no mere panic but the onset of the worst depression yet experienced by Americans.

The first inkling of trouble reached Mink in the earnings estimates for the first week of June. The decline was not only severe but spread across every division. BOTTOM DROPPED OUT OF WEST BOUND TRANSCONTINENTAL BUSINESS, Clark wired, with no relief in sight. The drop was so pervasive that Mink realized it was not due to rate reductions but to "the slack in business generally." Other roads showed the same dismal record. Mink thought the depression far too acute to last more than a few days, but he was wrong. Weeks passed with no improvement, forcing the company to consider such drastic steps as canceling orders for new equipment. Clark was in no condition to deal with the crisis. Still weak from an attack of the grippe that had prostrated him during the winter, he fled to the Pennsylvania mountains for relief late in June and did not return until September. During his absence the first rumors of impending receivership began to surface and were met with indignant denials.

"We evidently are to have a long siege on Ry earnings," noted Dodge, who considered it a golden opportunity to cut the cost of labor by as much as one third. He wanted the western roads to meet secretly on the question; meanwhile "the western papers should Begin to discuss it," he added, "and prepare the minds of the employees to meet and accept it. They will see its necessity as man after man is discharged and as rates continually go down." Clark agreed that the men would resist any attempt by Union Pacific alone to reduce wages. In April he had weathered a brief strike that threatened to tie up the entire road before the union backed down, and he did not figure them to be in any better mood to accept lower wages now. While management hesitated over what to do about wages, it ordered all salaries slashed on a scale ranging from 10 percent for those earning sixty to one hundred dollars per month to 20 percent for those over five hundred dollars. If nothing else, this measure served notice that draconian measures were needed to survive the crisis.

Rumors of receivership soared anew and would not die down despite repeated denials. As Union Pacific stock sank lower, Perkins eyed it longingly and sounded Hill on forming a syndicate to acquire a large block "with a view to making the property a paying one on a neutral basis." No one inside the Union Pacific was ready to surrender so easily. Mink was busily at work on a plan to pare expenses and promised it would be radical, but past reductions left little fat to cut. Every bill possible was staved off and orders for new equipment or other work stopped. Apart from the usual interest payments, an immediate crisis loomed in the form of the sinking-fund bonds issued amid another financial upheaval in 1873 and due to mature in September 1893. There remained outstanding about $5.2 million of these bonds, for which the trustee had only about $1.4 million for redemption. Hurriedly Atkins readied a plan to extend the remaining $3.8 million, using land contracts as part of the security.

Although the weird pattern of business made it impossible to predict earnings, Atkins took heart. "I have faith we shall pull through some how," he said hopefully. Ten days later a new and unexpected threat erupted. For months the wily John Evans had bided his time, waiting patiently for the moment to strike; the mounting woes of the Union Pacific provided the opening he sought. On August 12 he filed suit in Denver charging that the Union Pacific had not lived up to the traffic agreement and seeking a receiver for the Gulf line who was not an officer of the parent company. The move caught everyone by surprise. Judge Dillon, who was busy preparing a secret plan for receivership if the bond extension failed, hastily sent instructions for removing the Evans suit to federal court. This was done, but on September 15 Evans filed an amended complaint that was, Mink groused, "bigger than a family bible."

Although Judge Dillon was confident Evans could be thwarted, the fight promised to be a long and ugly one. Meanwhile the struggle for financial survival went on with no sign of improvement in earnings. "The interruptions to our traffic are so general," Mink noted in exasperation, "that it is difficult to offer a satisfactory explanation." The glut of silver, coupled with Cleveland's vow to repeal the Sherman Silver Purchase Act, virtually wiped out shipments of that ore, and grain was not moving because money was so tight. All traffic to mining localities had dropped off severely, and Mink expected the July statement to show a drop of about seven hundred thousand dollars in net earnings. Expenses had been pared to the bone, but some work could not be deferred. As Clark pointed out, on one project the extra costs arising from not doing the work exceeded the cost of the work itself.

On the evening of September 12 Fred Ames boarded the Fall River Line steamer for New York, a journey he had made countless times. Worn down from the summer's strain and unable to sleep, he retired to his cabin early. When he did not appear for breakfast, the captain entered his room and found Ames dead, the victim of apoplexy as both his mother and his sister had been. The news sent everyone connected with Union Pacific into shock. "It is a severe blow to all our interests," wrote a distraught Dodge, "and as you know a fearful one to me." Adams, who had always been close to Ames, mourned that "There is something gone out of my future." Those who made the gloomy pilgrimage to North Easton for the funeral agreed that a part of the Union Pacific's history was buried with Fred Ames. Although the time had long passed when the Ames family controlled the road, they had stayed with it even in lean times and were more identified with it than anyone else. Fred Ames had poured money into its securities even when, as an observer noted, "such a policy would not have been dictated by cold common sense."

Fred Ames could not save or even dominate the Union Pacific. Like so many other corporations, it had long since outgrown its founders and their descendants. But his presence was no less vital for being as much symbolic as real. Apart from its effect on the company's finances, Ames's death was a spiritual blow from which the Union Pacific could not recover. Except for Dodge, the giants of its past were all dead, the links to its history severed forever. The men who now ran the company were functionaries, diligent and dedicated, loyal to a fault, but quite another breed from the entrepreneurs who had built and expanded the road. Where others had risked everything on their visions, they were managers who inherited the results to perpetuate and improve if possible. In times of crisis they could command neither the influence nor the following to overcome great obstacles.

Certainly no one could save the Union Pacific from the depression fast falling across the country. Even hardened observers were stunned by the figures pouring in from the West. For the first half of 1893 the Union Pacific lost eight hundred thousand dollars in net revenue compared to the previous year; in July and August the amount soared to $2 million, and in September alone $1.5 million. For the entire year gross earnings would plummet nearly $8 million, or 17 percent. Even with reduced expenses the company faced a shortfall of $2.6 million in meeting its fixed charges. No one knew where to get that amount of money in the teeth of a depression. Other roads faced the same problem, and one overbuilt system after another succumbed to bankruptcy until more than a third of the railway mileage in America fell victim to receivership before the depression had run its course.

That plenty of company shared their misery was no consolation to the Union Pacific's officers. Their proud road had staved off disaster again and again through the years, but its luck had run out. Frantic efforts to scrounge cash could not even come close to the amount needed. In October the receivership rumors grew more insistent, the denials more subdued. The treasurer in Omaha reported unpaid vouchers running some three hundred thousand dollars above normal levels. One analyst called receivership "almost inevitable," and a frustrated director admitted he had "never known a time before this when Union Pacific's business so completely collapsed in all directions." A wave of selling orders hit Wall Street as the board met to search for a way out.

There was none. On October 12 a worried Adolph Boissevain, seeking inside information from Mink, suggested that receivership might be helpful in the long run. The next day he was stunned to learn that friends of the board had already applied in Omaha and the court had appointed Clark and Mink as receivers. E. Ellery Anderson, then a government director, was also named receiver on behalf of the government. The functionaries had become caretakers. The receivers and the board alike resolved to operate the road "as one system so long as the said receivership may continue." That would not be easy in the face of the Evans suit, which gained momentum from the bankruptcy. In Omaha the mood was somber and anxious as the men waited for another ax of retrenchment to fall. Old-timers shook their heads in disbelief, recalling the depressions and scrapes of earlier times. The Ames brothers would never have let such a thing happen, they muttered bitterly, nor would Gould and Dillon. Times had changed, and not for the better.

There was blame enough to parcel out in every direction, but it was an exercise in futility. A great road had gone down, and no one yet knew how long it would take to bring it back. The first period in the company's history had drawn to an inglorious close. Every American knew a little something about the saga of its past; the unanswered question now was whether or not the Union Pacific had a future.

A victim of the relocated line was the Ames Monument, which was planted at the road's highest point on Sherman Hill so that travelers coming in both directions could glimpse it. Now it sits alone and forlorn, not gone but forgotten. The man at its base suggests the size of the monument.

A Note on Sources

This history of the Union Pacific Railroad is based on a wide range of primary source materials. The massive amount of documentation, coupled with the length of the book itself, made it impractical to include the footnotes with the text. The reader may obtain a copy of all the notes in pamphlet form free of charge by writing to the following address:

History Footnotes
Union Pacific Museum
1416 Dodge Street
Omaha, NE 68179

The following list contains the basic manuscript collections used in the writing of this volume:

Burlington Archives, Newberry Library, Chicago, Illinois.
Brigham Young papers, LDS Church Library, Salt Lake City, Utah.
Charles E. Ames papers, Baker Library, Harvard Graduate School of Business Administration, Boston.
Charles Francis Adams, Jr. papers, Massachusetts Historical Society, Boston.
William E. Chandler papers, Library of Congress.
Casement papers, American Heritage Center, University of Wyoming, Laramie.
Collis P. Huntington papers, microfilm edition, University of Iowa library, Iowa City.
Cornelius S. Bushnell papers, Union Pacific Collection, Nebraska State Museum and Archives, Lincoln.
Autobiography of Grenville M. Dodge, Dodge papers, Iowa State Department of Archives and History, Des Moines.
Grenville M. Dodge papers, Iowa State Department of Archives and History, Des Moines.
Grenville M. Dodge papers, Western Historical Collection, Denver Public Library, Denver.
Dodge Record, Iowa State Department of Archives and History, Des Moines.
Denver & Rio Grande Western Archives, Colorado State Museum, Denver.
Jay Gould papers, Library of Congress.
Garrett family papers, Library of Congress.
Rowland G. Hazard papers, Rhode Island Historical Society, Providence.

Henry S. McComb papers, Eleutherian Mills Historical Library, Wilmington, Del.

Henry Villard papers, Baker Library, Harvard Graduate School of Business Administration, Boston.

John Evans papers, Colorado State Museum, Denver.

James F. Joy papers, Burton Historical Collection, Detroit Public Library.

Jay Gould letters and letterbooks in possession of Kingdon Gould, Jr.

Jay Gould papers at Lyndhurst, the former Gould mansion in Tarrytown, N.Y., now owned by the National Trust for Historic Preservation.

James J. Hill papers, J. J. Hill Reference Library, St. Paul, Minnesota.

Materials in library of Church of Jesus Christ of Latter-day Saints, Salt Lake City, Utah.

Levi O. Leonard Collection, University of Iowa Library, Iowa City, Iowa.

Huntington, Crocker, Stanford, and Colton letters, Mariners Museum, Newport News, Virginia.

Archives of Missouri Pacific Railroad Company, St. Louis, Missouri.

Oliver Ames papers, Arnold B. Tofias Industrial Archives, Stonehill College library, North Easton, Massachusetts.

Oregon Railway & Navigation Company records, Oregon Historical Society, Portland.

United States Pacific Railway Commission (9 vols.), 1887.

Texas & Pacific Historical Records, archives of Missouri Pacific Railroad Company, St. Louis.

Union Pacific Railroad Company Collection, Nebraska State Museum and Archives, Lincoln.

Records of Union Pacific Railroad Company still in possession of Union Pacific System, Omaha.

Selected Bibliography

Adams, Charles Francis Jr. *Railroads: Their Origin and Problems* (New York, 1878).

Ames, Charles Edgar. *Pioneering the Union Pacific* (New York, 1969).

Athearn, Robert G. *The Denver and Rio Grande Western Railroad* (Lincoln, Neb., 1977).

———. *Union Pacific Country* (New York, 1971).

Bryant, Keith L. Jr. *History of the Atchison, Topeka and Santa Fe Railway* (New York, 1974).

Chandler, Alfred D. Jr. *The Visible Hand: The Managerial Revolution in American Business* (Cambridge, Mass., 1977).

Cochran, Thomas C. *Railroad Leaders* (Cambridge, Mass., 1953).

Combs, Barry B. *Westward to Promontory* (Palo Alto, Calif., 1969).

Crawford, J. B. *The Crédit Mobilier of America* (Boston, 1880).

Davis, John P. *The Union Pacific Railway* (Chicago, 1894).

Dick, Everett. *Conquering the Great American Desert* (Lincoln, Neb., 1975).

Fogel, Robert W. *The Union Pacific Railroad: A Case Study in Premature Enterprise* (Baltimore, 1960).

Galloway, John D. *The First Transcontinental Railroad* (New York, 1950).

Gould, Lewis L. *Wyoming: A Political History, 1868–1896* (New Haven, Conn., 1968).

Griswold, Wesley S. *A Work of Giants: Building the First Transcontinental Railroad* (New York, 1962).

Grodinsky, Julius. *The Iowa Pool* (Chicago, 1950).

———. *Jay Gould: His Business Career 1867–1892* (Philadelphia, 1957).

———. *Transcontinental Railway Strategy 1869–1893* (Philadelphia, 1962).

Haney, Lewis H. *A Congressional History of Railways in the United States* (Madison, Wisc., 1908–10), 2 vols.

Hayes, William E. *Iron Road to Empire* (Chicago, 1953).

Hazard, Rowland. *The Crédit Mobilier of America* (Providence, R.I., 1881).

Hedges, James B. *Henry Villard and the Railways of the Pacific Northwest* (New Haven, Conn., 1930).

Hirshson, Stanley P. *Grenville M. Dodge: Soldier, Politician, Railroad Pioneer* (Bloomington, Ind., 1967).

Hoogenboom, Ari and Olive. *A History of the ICC: From Panacea to Palliative* (New York, 1976).

Johnson, Arthur M. and Barry E. Supple. *Boston Capitalists and Western Railroads* (Cambridge, Mass., 1967).

Kirkland, Edward C. *Charles Francis Adams, Jr., 1835–1915: The Patrician at Bay* (Cambridge, Mass., 1965).

Klein, Maury. *The Life and Legend of Jay Gould* (Baltimore, 1986).

Larson, John Lauritz. *Bonds of Enterprise: John Murray Forbes and Western Development in America's Railway Age* (Cambridge, Mass., 1984).

Larson, T. A. *History of Wyoming* (Lincoln, Neb., 1965).

Lass, William E. *From the Missouri to the Great Salt Lake, 1868–1896* (Lincoln, Neb., 1972).

Lavender, David. *The Great Persuader* (New York, 1970).

Lewis, Oscar. *The Big Four* (New York, 1938).

Licht, Walter. *Working for the Railroad* (Princeton, N.J., 1983).

Malone, Michael P. *The Battle for Butte: Mining and Politics on the Northern Frontier, 1864–1906* (Seattle, 1981).

Malone, Michael P. and Roeder, Richard B. *Montana: A History of Two Centuries* (Seattle, 1976).

Martin, Albro. *James J. Hill and the Opening of the Northwest* (New York, 1976).

Miller, George H. *Railroads and the Granger Laws* (Madison, Wisc., 1971).

Miner, H. Craig. *The St. Louis–San Francisco Transcontinental Railroad* (Lawrence, Kans., 1972).

Olson, James C. *History of Nebraska* (Lincoln, Neb., 1955).

Overton, Richard C. *Burlington Route* (New York, 1965).

———. *Gulf to Rockies* (Austin, Texas, 1953).

Perkins, J. R. *Trails, Rails and War: The Life of General G. M. Dodge* (Indianapolis, Ind., 1929).

Poor, Henry V. *Manual of the Railroads of the United States* (New York, 1867–1894).

Riegel, Robert E. *The Story of the Western Railroads* (New York, 1926).

Richardson, Leon Burr. *William E. Chandler, Republican* (New York, 1940).

Sabin, Edwin L. *Building the Pacific Railway* (Balboa Island, Calif., 1919).

Stover, John F. *American Railroads* (Chicago, 1961).

Trottman, Nelson M. *History of the Union Pacific: A Financial and Economic Survey* (New York, 1923).

Villard, Henry. *Memoirs* (Boston, 1904), 2 vols.

Wall, Joseph Frazier. *Andrew Carnegie* (New York, 1970).

White, Henry Kirke. *History of the Union Pacific Railway* (Chicago, 1895).

INDEX

NOTE: page numbers in *italics* refer to illustrations

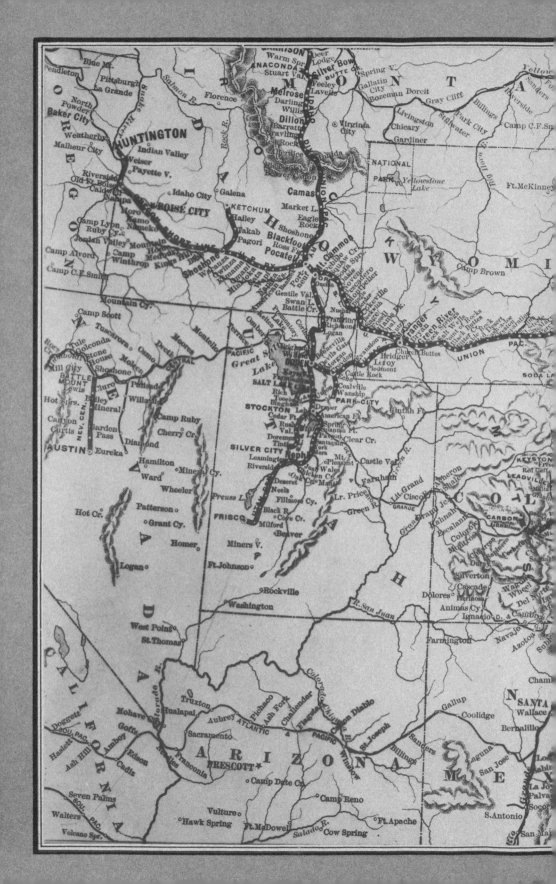